# Communication Law in America

*Paul Siegel*

*Gallaudet University*

**Allyn and Bacon**

*Boston* ■ *London* ■ *Toronto* ■ *Sydney* ■ *Tokyo* ■ *Singapore*

*Series Editor:* Molly Taylor
*Editor-in-Chief, Social Sciences:* Karen Hanson
*Editorial Assistant:* Michael Kish
*Editorial-Production Service:* Omegatype Typography, Inc.
*Composition and Prepress Buyer:* Linda Cox
*Manufacturing Buyer:* Julie McNeill
*Cover Administrator:* Linda Knowles
*Electronic Composition:* Omegatype Typography, Inc.

Copyright © 2002 by Allyn & Bacon
A Pearson Education Company
75 Arlington Street
Boston, MA 02116

Internet: www.ablongman.com

Between the time Website information is gathered and then published, it is not unusual for some sites to have closed. Also, the transcription of URLs can result in unintended typographical errors. The publisher would appreciate notification where these occur so that they may be corrected in subsequent editions. Thank you.

Many of the designations used by manufacturers and sellers to distinguish their products are claimed as trademarks. Where those designations appear in this book, and Allyn and Bacon was aware of a trademark claim, the designations have been printed with an initial capital. Designations within quotation marks represent hypothetical products.

**Library of Congress Cataloging-in-Publication Data**

Siegel, Paul
    Communication law in America / Paul Siegel.
      p.  cm.
    Includes index.
    ISBN 0-205-28987-8 (alk. paper)
    1. Mass media—Law and legislation—United States.  2. Press law—United States.  3. Freedom of speech—United States.  I. Title.

KF2750 .S53  2002
343.7309'9—dc21

                        2001022105

Printed in the United States of America

10  9  8  7  6  5  4  3  2  1      06  05  04  03  02  01

# For Ernest Siegel (1922–1997)

*Dad, you did not live long enough to see this hit the proverbial newsstands,*
*but you surely did badger me often enough to make sure I got it done.*
*For that, and for millions of other kindnesses, I thank you.*

# Contents

## 1 Introducing the American Legal System    1

## 2 The Development of Freedom of Speech    35

# 6 Copyright and Trademark     197

# 7   Access to Information     238

# 11    Sexually Oriented Speech    389

# 13 Communication Law and the Internet    481

# Preface

Embarking on a project such as *Communication Law in America* is an exercise in both humility and *chutzpah*. For any fledgling textbook author to take to pen (there's an expression that will soon disappear from the lexicon!) is necessarily to suggest that he or she has something to say, something not already being said by the many other competing textbooks already on the market. That takes nerve.

The humility sinks in soon enough. One of the reviewers of the original prospectus for this book must have been stifling a laugh when, in response to my naive assumption that the chapters would flow easily and swiftly from the lecture notes I had accumulated over twenty years of teaching media law classes, gently suggested that "the author would be wise to rethink this." The reviewer was right, of course. There is a tremendous difference between teaching from an established text and writing one's own. The text writer must realize at the outset that he is not a sage, but a student. There is nothing like writing a textbook to force the teacher/author to develop a far deeper and broader body of knowledge than needed before. Especially in a fast-changing subject matter such as communication law—who would have dreamed a few years ago that books such as these would devote a chapter to something called "cyberspace"?—keeping up with new developments is truly a challenge.

Although my name alone appears on the book's cover, many individuals' help was invaluable. I wish to thank the many cartoon artists who allowed me to reprint their work in these pages, usually at a small fraction of their usual fees. Although their individual syndicates are also deserving of gratitude and are acknowledged throughout the book, here I would like to thank the artists themselves. They include political cartoonists Herb Block of the *Washington Post,* Jim Borgman of the *Cincinnati Enquirer,* Tom Englehardt of the *Saint Louis Post-Dispatch,* and Jim Margulies of the *Bergen Record;* Sidney Harris, four of whose panels ribbing the legal profession appear in these pages; as well as Tom Armstrong (*Marvin*); Johnny Hart and Brant Parker (*The Wizard of Id*); Bill Hinds and Jeff Millar (*Tank McNamara*); Hank Ketcham (*Dennis the Menace*); John McPherson (*Close to Home*); Wiley Miller (*Non Sequitur*); Russell Myers (*BroomHilda*); Tom Thaves (*Frank and Ernest*); Gary Trudeau (*Doonesbury*); and Mike Twohy (*That's Life*). Thanks are due also to LFP, Incorporated, for permitting me to reprint the famous "Jerry Falwell's First Time" parody ad and to George Carlin for allowing the use here of detailed excerpts from his at least equally famous "Filthy Words" monologue.

Thanks also to Jeffrey Fister and Eileen Dugan of *West End Word;* attorney "R.M.J." from Missouri; photographer Annie Leibovitz and Paramount Studios;

*Reader's Digest* and *Conservative Digest*'s Larry Abraham and Scott Stanley; Tom Lehrer (I'm a big fan, Tom!); People for the Ethical Treatment of Animals; and Steven Spielberg's Dreamworks, Universal Studios, and Helen Harris of RP, International for permitting us to reprint portions of the video description scripts from the films *E.T.* and *Titanic*.

Numerous individuals helped with the research for the book, sometimes pointing me in the right direction, sometimes uncovering artifacts to which they had more handy access, and sometimes, I admit, doing my homework for me. Among these are Pat Petit of the Catholic University Law School; Bruce Lockard of the Second Circuit Court of Appeals; Stuart Sigman of Emerson College; Roger Mellen of George Mason University; Lawrence Rosenfeld of the University of North Carolina; John Vivian of Minnesota State University–Winona; Alex Tang of the Federal Trade Commission; Art Spitzer, legal director of the ACLU of the National Capital Area; Kris and Paul Oehlke; Jeff Lofton; Joshua Singer; and Lee Templeman.

Karon Bowers, my editor at Allyn and Bacon, demonstrated extraordinary patience throughout the project. Thanks to you, too, Ron Goldfarb, my lawyer and agent, for encouraging me in the beginning stages of the writing and for shopping the manuscript around with your winning smile and charming manner.

Paula E. Tucker, one of my colleagues at Gallaudet University, did me the great favor of working with my inferior camera and highly nontelegenic mug to produce the photo of me reproduced in this book.

I am indebted to Gallaudet University, and specifically to Rosemary Weller, Bill Moses, and Roz Rosen, for permitting me to take a full-year sabbatical in furtherance of this project; also to my media law students at American University and George Mason University for critiquing prepublication, homemade CD-ROM versions of the book in their classes with me. Sunil Tellis, a talented young man I met through our affiliations with George Mason University, produced the Power-Point slide presentation associated with this book.

Many thanks are also due my numerous colleagues in various professional associations' communication law and free speech interest groups. A special measure of gratitude is due Frank Haiman, professor emeritus of communication studies at Northwestern University, for first stimulating my interest in this exciting and mind-boggling subject.

The numerous reviewers who helped to shape the manuscript over the past two years deserve special credit. Among them were Carrie Anna Criado, Southern Methodist University; Thomas V. Dickson, Southwest Missouri State University; Wallace B. Eberhard, University of Georgia; Steven Helle, University of Illinois; Dale Herbeck, Boston College; Robert Jensen, University of Texas; J. R. Rush, Brigham Young University; and Jeffery A. Smith, University of Iowa. They provided a wealth of insights and suggestions and corrected more errors along the way than I would like to admit. As to any errors that remain, well, I am sure we can find a way to blame them on Bill Gates, aren't you?

# About the Author

Paul Siegel is professor and formerly chairperson of communication studies at Gallaudet University in Washington, D.C., the world's only comprehensive university designed specifically for deaf and hard-of-hearing students. As an adjunct, he teaches journalism law classes at George Mason University and American University.

He has also taught at Illinois State University, St. Cloud State University, Catholic University, the University of Missouri–Kansas City, and Tulane University. He has published dozens of essays in journals of communication, sociology, and anthropology, as well as in law reviews and book chapters. Sample titles include "Second-Hand Prejudice, Racial Analogies and Shared Showers: Why 'Don't Ask, Don't Tell' Won't Sell," (*Notre Dame Journal of Law, Ethics and Public Policy*); "Smart Shopping as Patriotism: Avoidance, Denial and Advertising" (*Communications and the Law*); and "Privacy: Control over Stimulus Input, Stimulus Output, and Self-Regarding Conduct" (*Buffalo Law Review*). A long-time associate editor of the *Free Speech Yearbook,* Siegel also edited a collection of readings on the Clarence Thomas hearings (*Outsiders Looking In,* published by Hampton Press).

Siegel's bachelor's degree in speech and psychology was awarded by the University of New Mexico. He earned a master's degree in interpersonal communications from the University of Wisconsin; his doctoral degree in communication studies is from Northwestern University.

#  Recent Developments in Communication Law

As this book is going to press in late May 2001, several weeks remain before the end of the Supreme Court's 2000–2001 term. Yet to be handed down is the most closely watched First Amendment case of the season, the *Tasini* case (discussed in Chapter 13) involving freelance writers and such digital databases as NEXIS. Allyn and Bacon and I are committed to providing seasonal updates for this book on the publisher's Web site. The *Tasini* case will surely be the subject of the first such update.

Three late-breaking decisions handed down since the main portion of this text was typeset—one from the U. S. Supreme Court, two federal appellate cases, both of which overturned lower court decisions—are worthy of note. The Supreme Court decision is *Bartnicki v. Vopper*,[1] which affirmed the appellate decision of the same name discussed in Chapter 5. At issue was whether a radio station that had broadcast telephone conversations recorded in violation of the federal wiretapping law could be liable for damages. In a 6–3 decision, the Court ruled that the relevant statute could not be constitutionally applied to the media, at least not when the media defendant had no role in the illegal taping, and the conversations included information on matters of public interest.

The second decision reviewed here is *Suntrust Bank v. Houghton Mifflin Company*,[2] through which holders of the copyright to *Gone With the Wind* obtained an injunction preventing publication of a novel called *The Wind Done Gone*. The latter book's author described it as a parody of Margaret Mitchell's famous work, arguing that her own work amounted to a retelling of the Reconstruction era, focusing on the lives of the plantation slaves rather than on Scarlett O'Hara and Rhett Butler. Judge Charles A. Pannell concluded, however, that *The Wind Done Gone* was, at its core, an unauthorized sequel to *Gone With the Wind*. Fifteen of the characters from *Gone With The Wind* show up in the newer work, which incorporates "their physical attributes, mannerisms, and the distinct features that Ms. Mitchell used to describe them, as well as their complex relationships with each other." Applying the four Fair Use questions outlined in Chapter 6, Judge Pannell found that *The Wind Done Gone* had copied far more from the more famous novel than would

---

[1] 121 S. Ct. ____ (2001).

[2] 2001 U.S. Dist. LEXIS 5036 (N.D. Ga. 2001).

have been necessary if its author's true motive was to produce a parody. Judge Pannell's decision has been roundly criticized in the popular press; some of the more vociferous commentaries have had strong racial overtones, suggesting that the decision amounted to a silencing of African-American perspectives on a literary and cultural icon.

On May 25, 2001, less than an hour after hearing oral arguments, a three-judge panel of the Eleventh Circuit Court of Appeals lifted the lower court's injunction, describing it as "an extraordinary and drastic remedy" and an "unlawful prior restraint."[3] As we go to press, the drama is still unfolding, with Houghton Mifflin intending to rush *The Wind Done Gone* into press within a few weeks, and the plaintiff's attorneys seeking an expedited appeal to the court for a rehearing *en banc*.

Completing our trio of late-breaking cases is an appellate decision overturning a damage award in excess of $100 million against a prolife group for having posted to the Internet the names, addresses, and photos of physicians who perform abortions, along with a promised reward for anyone who succeeds, within the bounds of law, at stopping the doctors from doing any more such procedures.[4] The group's Web presence was called the "Nuremberg Files" site, in that the writers looked towards a future America sufficiently enlightened about the evils of abortion so as to commence war crimes prosecutions against the named physicians similar to the trials of Nazi architects following World War II. Although the jury award was issued back in 1999, there is no earlier mention of it in this text book, precisely because I saw it as an aberration destined to be overturned on appeal.

Writing for the appellate panel, Judge Alex Kosinski allowed that the dissemination of the doctors' identities might make violence against them more likely; the imparting of this information in the context of a heated political debate about abortion, he added, is nonetheless protected speech. There was nothing in the messages to suggest that the defendant group itself intended to do the doctors any harm, nor that the sending of the messages would lead to the kind of "imminent lawless action" demanded by the *Brandenburg* test (discussed at length in Chapter 2) to be proscribable. Kosinski noted too that the Web site included such nonverbal cues as crossing out the pictures of doctors who had been murdered by anti-abortion activists. Even taken at its worst, however, such speech is protected; there is a difference between inciting or threatening future violence, and expressing pleasure at past violence.

One final artifact that has recently crossed my desk is worthy of mention here. In the discussion of zoning laws applied to adult-oriented businesses in Chapter 11, we see that regulations placed upon such businesses—which may have never been prosecuted for actually selling *obscene* materials—are generally upheld if aimed at such "secondary effects" as an increase in overall crime or a decrease in property values. A recent addition to the scholarly literature offers a

---

[3] "'Wind Done Gone' Wins on Appeal," *Washington Post,* 26 May 2001, p. C1.

[4] *Planned Parenthood of the Columbia/Williamette, Inc. v. American Coalition of Life Activists,* 244 F.3d 1007 (9th Cir. 2001).

scathing review of the kinds of evidence used by courts to establish a nexus between such effects and the proliferation of adult-oriented bookstores.[5] The authors uncovered the original data from the most frequently cited studies used over and over again by courts nationwide. After comparing that data and the research designs underlying them to accepted practices in the social sciences, the authors concluded that the scientific validity of the claims is questionable, and the methods used were "often fatally flawed." A more detailed discussion of the article will surely be a feature of this book's next edition.

---

[5]Bryant Paul, Daniel Linz, and Bradley J. Shaffer, "Government Regulation of 'Adult' Businesses Through Zoning and Anti-Nudity Ordinances: Debunking the Legal Myth of Negative Secondary Effects," 6 *Communication Law and Policy* 355 (2001).

# *Introducing the American Legal System*

Americans are fascinated with the law. Cop shows and lawyer shows have been popular prime-time television offerings for decades. Court cases, sometimes because they involve celebrities and sometimes because the facts are bizarre or especially disturbing, receive intense media attention. We enjoy pontificating with classmates and coworkers about such legal disputes. Who among us has not engaged in conversations about the O. J. Simpson trials, Paula Jones's suit against President Bill Clinton, or the prolonged investigation of the JonBenet Ramsey, "child beauty queen" murder?

The news media are not at all reluctant to satisfy our hunger for stories about legal conflicts. In the three-week period immediately following the famous white Bronco chase scene, ABC's *Nightline* devoted twelve of fifteen programs to the O. J. Simpson saga. Just as *Nightline* itself was born of our fascination with a specific, slowly unfolding story—the holding of U.S. hostages in Iran—so, too, the Simpson case spawned CNN's *Burden of Proof,* one of that cable television network's most popular programs.

## Why Are You Here?

If you are reading this book, you are probably enrolled in an upper-level college course called, perhaps, Mass Media Law, Journalism Law, or Freedom of the Press. Perhaps you are taking this class as part of a sequence of course work toward a major in a department or school of journalism. If so, and if your program is an accredited one, your course is a requirement for graduation. Why, though, should you be required to take such a course, you might ask, if you want to be a journalist (or other media professional), not a lawyer?

One reason media professionals should have a strong background in communication law is that legal questions arise every day in the workplace, and relatively few media organizations have in-house legal counsel to answer questions on a moment's notice. The course you are taking now will offer you the facts you need and the tools to research new facts so as to avoid or minimize legal liability. Media professionals should also be familiar with communication law because the history of journalism in the United States is inextricably intertwined with its legal history. Please recall this admonition if you find yourself rebelling at having to learn a host of court cases and judicial doctrines that seem at first blush to have very little to do with your own day-to-day functioning. Much of the case law discussed here involves radical political street corner speakers, not modern-day journalists; the ways in which U.S. courts have treated their legal claims have strong implications for how the media's rights are protected today.

Another reason for students in any major to learn about communication law is to develop a better understanding of their own society. We can learn a great deal about ourselves by seeing how others see us. Citizens of many other countries, including most of the more enlightened Western democracies around the world, consider the United States to be almost fetishistically attached to freedom of the press. Why is it, they wonder, that freedom of the press and freedom of speech almost inevitably win out in U.S. courts when they compete against other important interests? In the United States, for example, when a newsworthy trial is taking place, the general rule is to allow the media to report as much as possible to the public as quickly as possible. In Canada, it is taken for granted that the public will not be ill-served if it has to wait until the end of the trial to read all the gory details. So, which is more important, freedom of the press or the right to a fair trial? There is no easy answer, but we will come to understand ourselves better as Americans if we become familiar with our own society's history of dealing with such conflicts.

Yet one more reason for becoming familiar with the precepts of communication law is that the U.S. political system works best if citizens participate actively in decision making. Your participation need not take the form of running for office, but your vote and your ability to persuade others to your viewpoint through interpersonal communication are both more meaningful if you take the time to educate yourself about the important issues of the day. In other words, our representative democracy works to the extent that we all take responsibility for using our freedom of speech (and the corollary freedoms to listen and to learn) forcefully and frequently. In doing so, it surely helps to know the full gamut of our legal rights as well as the limitations on those rights.

## Sources of Communication Law

If you were to try to explain the U.S. system of law to a foreign friend, you would probably begin by pointing out that our federal government has three branches with complementary functions and that state and local governments also have a role to play. Communication law is really no different from any other kind of law in this regard. There are several different sources of law. The main ones are **constitu-**

---

*Note:* Throughout this book, the first mention of any concept defined in the Glossary appears in **boldface** type.

tions, statutes, executive orders, decisions by **administrative agencies,** and the **common law.** Let us take a look at each source.

### Constitutions as Sources of Communication Law

One source of communication law is constitutions. Notice the use of the plural here. Every state of the union has its own constitution. So although we start our discussion here with a summary of important features of the *federal* constitution, we say more about state constitutions later.

***The First Amendment.*** To be sure, the section of the United States Constitution of most relevance to the act of communication is the First Amendment of the Bill of Rights. Here is the wording of that provision, which was adopted on 15 December 1791:

# The First Amendment

Congress shall make no law respecting an establishment of religion, or prohibiting the free exercise thereof; or abridging the freedom of speech, or of the press; or the right of the people peaceably to assemble, and to petition the Government for a redress of grievances.

The first thing apparent from the text is that the amendment is not talking to *us,* but rather to our elected representatives. It does not tell us what we have or do not have a right to do. It is in the form of a list of admonitions to Congress, warning that *its* right to pass certain kinds of laws is restricted. James Madison originally proposed very different wording, that "the people shall not be deprived or abridged of their right to speak, write or to publish their sentiments."

Although the First Amendment's reference to Congress has always been taken to refer to the entire federal government, individual states and localities were free to regulate the speech of their own citizens without running afoul of the First Amendment, at least until a Supreme Court ruling handed down more than 130 years after ratification of the Bill of Rights.[1] That decision is discussed in Chapter 2.

It is also worth emphasizing that even today the First Amendment's prohibitions apply only to *governmental* entities. When private individuals or companies prohibit us from engaging in some kinds of speech—perhaps our parents demand that we not talk about religious differences with them or our employer (unless our employer *is* the government) asks that we not talk about politics with our coworkers—they are not in violation of the First Amendment.

Strange though it may seem, it is not always easy to discern whether an organization is part of government or is purely private. Is your campus newspaper a

---

[1] *Gitlow v. New York,* 268 U.S. 652 (1925).

private entity, like the *New York Times*? Or, to the extent that it receives government funding in the form of earmarked monies from mandatory student fees, is it an agent of the state? The answer to this question may determine if an outside group has a right to advertise in the paper.[2]

In 1995, the Supreme Court was called upon to determine whether Amtrak had violated an artist's First Amendment rights when it refused him permission to rent a billboard in New York's Pennsylvania Station for the purpose of displaying one of his works.[3] The main issue the Court had to address was whether or not Amtrak qualified as a governmental agent, whether it was definitionally capable of violating anyone's First Amendment rights. The Court determined that even though the congressional act creating Amtrak explicitly set it up as a private corporation, the corporation's purpose was to provide a governmental function and the directors would be ultimately accountable to the government. As such, Amtrak's behavior could possibly be a First Amendment violation. As it turns out, the artist in this case won the battle but lost the war. The Supreme Court sent the case back to a lower court to determine if Amtrak's policy of permitting billboard displays only for purely commercial rather than for political messages was permissible under the First Amendment. The lower court concluded that the policy was a sound one and that the artist thus did not have a First Amendment right to display his particular message.[4]

More recently, the Supreme Court held that a nonprofit association regulating interscholastic sports in both public and private schools must be considered a governmental entity for the purposes of First Amendment challenges to its authority. The Court emphasized that the vast majority of the association's members were public schools, and that the association's employees, although not technically government workers, nonetheless participated in the state's retirement system.[5]

Think again about the wording of the First Amendment. It contains five specific admonitions, five clauses. The first two—the **Establishment Clause** and the **Free Exercise Clause**—are often referred to together as the "religion clauses." The Establishment Clause is most frequently described as freedom *from* religious indoctrination. It is under the Establishment Clause that the Supreme Court removed institutionalized prayer from the public schools. The Free Exercise Clause gives us the freedom *to* practice our religions to the extent that such practice does not interfere with a compelling governmental interest. You will not be permitted to engage in human sacrifice or in child molestation, for example, even if your sincere religious convictions tell you these are necessary practices.

One might think that the religion clauses have no relevance to the professional communicator, but such a conclusion would be both hasty and wrong. Al-

---

[2]*Mississippi Gay Alliance v. Goudelock,* 536 F.2d 1073 (5th Cir. 1976).

[3]*Lebron v. National Railroad Passenger Corporation,* 513 U.S. 374 (1995).

[4]*Lebron v. National Railroad Passenger Corporation,* 69 F.3d 650 (2d Cir. 1995).

[5]*Brentwood Academy v. Tennessee Secondary School Athletic Association,* 121 S. Ct. 924 (2001).

though journalism law cases rarely invoke these parts of the First Amendment, one of the most important Supreme Court cases of the 1990s, which concerned the rights of newspaper editors, involved both of the religion clauses.[6] By a 5–4 vote, the Court ruled that the University of Virginia could not refuse to help fund a Christian student group's cost of publishing its newspaper, called *Wide Awake.* There was tremendous difference of opinion among the justices concerning not only which part of the First Amendment should prevail, but also about whether the newspaper was religious enough to even trigger the Establishment Clause. So complex are the Court's recent religion clause cases that the Virginia decision turned at least in part on the monies going directly to the printer with whom the religious group had contracted rather than directly to the group itself.

Let us skip ahead for a moment to the First Amendment's last clause, the one that gives us the right to "peacefully assemble" and to "petition the government for redress of grievances." The **Petition Clause** has been interpreted by courts as giving permission to hold street demonstrations, sit-ins, and the like. Again we might be tempted to conclude—wrongly—that it is of little relevance to journalists. In the early 1980s, Robert McDonald wrote a letter to President Reagan and to numerous other government officials asking that the pending appointment of David Smith as a U.S. attorney for North Carolina be rescinded. The letter accused Smith of violating the civil rights of many individuals while he was a state court judge, of "fraud," and of numerous "violations of professional ethics." When Smith learned of the letter, he sued McDonald for **defamation,** and Smith's novel defense—unsuccessful in this case—was that the Petition Clause should be read so as to give him absolute immunity from the lawsuit. After all, what purer example could we find of exercising one's Petition Clause rights than writing to one's president, imploring him to take a particular action?[7]

More recently, the most carefully scrutinized decision of the Supreme Court's 1995–1996 term was a case from Colorado that, although not actually argued on Petition Clause grounds, centered on a state constitutional provision that would surely have had the effect of limiting the ability of one group of Coloradans to petition their elected representatives for redress of grievances.[8] The Court struck down Colorado's Amendment Two, a provision that would have had the effect of removing from the books any local civil rights statutes aimed at protecting the interests of lesbians and gay men and would have prevented any new such laws from ever being passed. Only by passing another state constitutional amendment could gays achieve protection against employment and housing discrimination. As such, city council members and state representatives would be able to listen to gays' "petitions," but would not be able to act on them.

---

[6]*Rosenberger v. University of Virginia,* 515 U.S. 819 (1995).

[7]*McDonald v. Smith,* 472 U.S. 479 (1985).

[8]*Romer v. Evans,* 517 U.S. 620 (1996).

Petition Clause claims may become more frequent in future years because of a phenomenon called the **SLAPP suit.** The acronym stands for strategic lawsuit against public participation, a kind of libel suit aimed at preventing citizen activists from speaking out against businesses and even against government officials. Many social critics argue that these suits are inconsistent with the spirit of the Petition Clause in that they often result from citizens' comments at public hearings, the kind of forums that are specifically designed to have elected officials listen to grievances.

Not much time is spent here explicating the **Free Speech Clause** and the **Free Press Clause,** because they are the focus of almost this entire book. When courts are asked to determine whether a specific governmental action is in violation of the First Amendment rights of media professionals, it is virtually always these two clauses that are at issue. One point does deserve special attention—that we are talking about two clauses rather than one. Does freedom of speech not include both oral and written communication? How can we explain this apparent redundancy in the Bill of Rights? Whatever may have been on the minds of our Founding Fathers, one school of thought today suggests that freedom of the *press* refers to the professional journalist.

Certainly members of the working press, with credentials, are able to go places and do things that other people cannot. Police will often permit only emergency personnel and reporters near the scenes of accidents. There is a separate section of desirable seats for members of the working press to watch the Supreme Court conduct oral arguments, whereas ordinary visitors must typically wait in line outdoors for many hours for one of the few seats available to the public. In most states, members of the working press are given some form of statutory immunity from having to testify about their news sources. The name we give to such statutes—**reporter shield laws**—is a clear indication that here too we have an example of freedom of the press meaning something different from and more than freedom of speech.

Former Supreme Court Justice Potter Stewart thought it very appropriate that media professionals be given more First Amendment rights than the rest of us. He argued this position forcefully in an address at the Yale Law School, later reprinted as a law review article. The title of the lecture and article consists of four words taken from the text of the First Amendment itself: *or of the press.* Stewart says that "the publishing business is, in short, the only organized private business that is given explicit constitutional protection."[9] Whether or not the working press should enjoy First Amendment protections above and beyond those of ordinary citizens is a continuing focus of debate among legal scholars. It is clear, however, that from time to time the Supreme Court has singled out the media for a special measure of freedom, as seen throughout this book.

---

[9]Potter Stewart, "Or of the Press," 26 *Hastings Law Journal* 631, 633 (1975).

# Things to Remember

**THE FIVE CLAUSES OF THE FIRST AMENDMENT**

■ Establishment Clause: Freedom *from* religious indoctrination
■ Free Exercise Clause: Freedom *to* practice religion
■ Free Speech Clause: Freedom of expression for us all
■ Free Press Clause: Freedom for the press as an institution
■ Petition Clause: Freedom to complain to government officials

***Other Sources of Communication Law in the Federal Constitution.*** The First Amendment is not the only part of the Bill of Rights of relevance to communication law. Consider the Fourth Amendment's protection against "unreasonable searches and seizures." Because of this amendment, law enforcement officials generally may not detain us, frisk us, or rummage through our personal effects without first obtaining a **search warrant.** To get a search warrant, an officer must persuade a judge that there is **probable cause** to believe that important and clearly definable evidence will be uncovered by the search. Frequently, law enforcement officials, persuaded that the offices of a newspaper or television station are harboring evidence crucial to a criminal investigation, will search the premises of these media outlets. As we see in Chapter 9, the Supreme Court has said that the media have no special immunity from such searches.[10] We also see that media outrage over that decision led Congress to pass a major piece of legislation that statutorily provides the press with protections that the Court refused to read into the Bill of Rights.[11] The Fourth Amendment is of relevance to communications professionals for yet another reason. As we see in Chapter 5, there have been times when media have cooperated so closely with law enforcement officials—accompanying them on raids, for example—that the reporters themselves may later be sued for violating the target's Fourth Amendment privacy rights. In 1999, the Supreme Court ruled that police may be in violation of the Fourth Amendment for bringing reporters along as they arrest a suspect or search a suspect's home.[12]

The Fifth and Fourteenth Amendments are also very much of relevance. The Fifth Amendment is probably best known for its protection against self-incrimination, thus the countless times we hear courtroom witnesses, real and

---

[10]*Zurcher v. Stanford Daily,* 436 U.S. 547 (1978).

[11]*Privacy Protection Act of 1980,* 42 U.S.C. sec. 2000aa (1997).

[12]*Wilson v. Layne,* 526 U.S. 603 (1999).

fictional, "plead the Fifth." This amendment also tells the federal government (the Fourteenth Amendment has parallel wording applicable to the states) that it may not deprive persons of "life, liberty, or property without due process of law." It is this last provision that is most often of relevance to public communicators, because one aspect of **due process** that courts have demanded over the years is for laws and regulations to be worded precisely enough so that we know *how* to obey them. We expect that traffic regulations will spell out how many feet from a fire hydrant we must park our cars rather than admonish us in vague terms "not to park too close." Similarly vague would be regulations prohibiting prisoners from mailing any correspondence that "unduly complains, magnifies grievances, or expresses inflammatory views or beliefs."[13] What is an "inflammatory" belief? When has one "magnified" a grievance rather than merely described it?

So important is a working knowledge of the Sixth Amendment for the professional communicator that this book devotes Chapter 8 to the subject. The Sixth Amendment ensures criminal suspects the right to a speedy and public trial by an impartial jury. There has likely always been a good deal of tension between First and Sixth Amendment guarantees. What kinds of pretrial reportage might make it difficult to empanel an impartial jury? Once a trial has begun, may the trial judge impose restrictions on the press so that jurors do not learn in their living rooms things that would be inadmissible as evidence in the courtroom? The Supreme Court and lower courts have struggled with these kinds of questions for decades.

The Fourteenth Amendment, passed shortly after the end of the Civil War, is important to professional communicators for at least two reasons. First, that same due process language has been treated by the Supreme Court as a kind of funnel through which many provisions of the Bill of Rights—including freedom of speech and freedom of the press—have been applied to the states. This process is known as the **doctrine of incorporation,** and we say more about it in the next chapter. The Fourteenth Amendment also tells the states that they may not deny any person "the equal protection of its laws." This **Equal Protection Clause** has been the main weapon by which the media have had invalidated statutes that single out media industries for special taxation or other obligations or that seem to discriminate among mass media.[14]

The Bill of Rights and later amendments are not the only federal constitutional provisions of relevance to the act of communication. Article I, Section 8, of the Constitution enumerates specific powers granted to Congress by the nation's Founders. Here Congress is told that it may pass laws "to promote the progress of...useful arts, by securing for limited times to authors...the exclusive right to their respective writing and discoveries." This section is the basis for U.S. **copyright** law, the subject of Chapter 6.

---

[13]*Martinez v. Procunier,* 354 F. Supp. 1092 (N. D. Cal. 1973), *aff'd,* 416 U.S. 396 (1974).

[14]*Arkansas Writers' Project, Inc. v. Ragland,* 481 U.S. 221 (1987).

# Things to Remember

**THE U.S. CONSTITUTION AND COMMUNICATIONS LAW:
BEYOND THE FIRST AMENDMENT**

- Fourth Amendment:
  - Search of newsrooms
  - Press has no constitutional right to avoid a legitimate search
- Fifth Amendment:
  - Due process of law applied to federal government
  - Void for vagueness doctrine
- Sixth Amendment:
  - Right to a speedy, public, and fair trial
  - Can conflict with press freedom
- Fourteenth Amendment:
  - Due process applied to the states
  - Equal protection of laws
- Article I, Section 8:
  - Authorizes copyright laws

*State Constitutions and Communication Law.* We must look not only to the federal constitution but also to the various state constitutions as sources of communications law. Most state constitutional provisions concerning communication are co-extensive with the First Amendment, granting no greater and no fewer rights than are given in the federal constitution. Some states, however, have decided that their citizens will enjoy a larger measure of freedom of expression than will other Americans. Typically, the relevant section of these states' constitutions affirmatively give their citizens the right to "freely speak, write, and publish." Notice that such wording is far more sweeping than the First Amendment, which tells Congress only that *it* may not abridge free speech. If citizens are told explicitly that they have a right to free speech, such a right would seem to prohibit even private individuals and corporations from abridging such a right. There need be no proof of "state action" to have an alleged infringement on freedom of speech taken seriously in a court of law.

State constitutional provisions often differ from the wording of the First Amendment in an opposite direction as well. Whereas the federal provision is worded quite absolutely—"Congress shall make *no* law"—many state provisions put citizens on notice that they will be "responsible for any abuse" of their freedom of speech. Then too, whereas the federal constitution is silent with respect to the kinds of such abuses that might lead one individual to sue another, some state constitutions explicitly give citizens a right to sue for **libel** and/or invasion of privacy. Texans, for example, are assured in Article 1, section 13, of their constitution that the state's courts are open to them to press claims stemming from injuries done to their "lands, goods, person *or reputation*" (emphasis added).

By far the most frequently recurring question related to state constitutional free speech provisions has been whether one has a right to engage in political dialogue with and hand out leaflets to shoppers in privately owned malls. The U.S. Supreme Court has made clear that there is no federal constitutional right to speak out on issues of one's choosing when at a mall. Yet, in that very same decision, the Court made equally clear that the states may conclude that their own constitutions grant such a right.[15] In the years since the *Pruneyard* decision, several other states have addressed the same issue, with mixed results. States that have found in their constitutions at least a limited right to engage in expressive activity on the grounds of privately owned shopping centers include Colorado, Massachusetts, New Jersey, Oregon, and Washington.[16] States that have instead found that their own constitutional provisions go no further than the protections granted in the First Amendment with respect to shopping mall speech include Connecticut, Iowa, Michigan, Montana, New York, North Carolina, Ohio, Pennsylvania, South Carolina, and Wisconsin.[17]

## Statutes as Sources of Communication Law

The U.S. Constitution takes up only a few dozen pages of text. By bulk, and probably also in terms of impact on our daily lives, we are far more affected by the laws passed every year by Congress, state legislatures, city councils, and numerous other local legislative bodies nationwide. States pass **obscenity** laws, Congress creates the **Freedom of Information Act,** and perhaps your municipality has a local ordinance governing the size and aesthetics of billboard advertising. In each of these instances, the enactment of the law might not be the last word on any particular issue because laws are often challenged in court by affected parties who will claim that the laws are a violation of one or another state or federal constitutional provision. This process of **judicial review** resulted, to cite just one example, in the striking down by the Supreme Court of the Communications Decency Act

---

[15]*Pruneyard Shopping Center v. Robins,* 447 U.S. 74 (1980).

[16]*Bock v. Westminister Mall,* 819 P.2d 55 (1991); *Batchelder v. Allied Stores International,* 445 N.E.2d 590 (1983); *State v. Schmid,* 423 A.2d 615 (1980); *Fred Meyer, Inc. v. Casey,* 67 F.3d 1412 (9th Cir. 1995) (right limited to gathering signatures for specific citizen referenda); *Alderwood Association v. Washington Environmental Council,* 635 P.2d 108 (1981).

[17]*Cologne v. Westfarms Association,* 469 A.2d 1204 (1984); *State v. Lacey,* 465 N.W.2d 537 (1991); *Woodland v. Michigan Citizens Lobby,* 378 N.W.2d 337 (1985); *City of Billings v. Laedeke,* 805 P.2d 1348 (1991); *SHAD Alliance v. Smith Haven Mall,* 488 N.E.2d 1211 (1985); *State v. Felmet,* 273 S.E.2d 708 (1981); *Eastwood Mall v. Slanco,* 626 N.E.2d 59 (1994); *Valenti v. Pennsylvania Democratic State Committee,* 844 F. Supp. 1015 (1994); *Charleston Joint Venture v. McPherson,* 417 S.E.2d 544 (1992); *Jacobs v. Major,* 407 N.W.2d 832 (1987).

through which Congress had attempted to prevent the posting of **indecent** messages likely to be seen by minors on the **Internet.**[18]

Even if litigants do not seek to have a law declared unconstitutional, they will sometimes feel the need to ask a court to clarify a law's meaning. We call this process **statutory construction.** One notable example is comedienne Carol Burnett's libel suit against the *National Enquirer,* which had published an article alleging that Burnett behaved very strangely, as if intoxicated, in a fancy restaurant. In that California libel law is slightly different for newspapers and for magazines, the court first needed to determine exactly what *is* a newspaper and how it differs from a magazine. Having done so, the court could then conclude that the *National Enquirer* is more of a magazine than a newspaper and could apply the appropriate state law.[19] Sometimes the courts are thrust in the role of grammarians as they try to make sense of laws worded so poorly that, if taken literally, they cannot possibly be constitutional. This situation happened in *United States v. X-citement Video,*[20] a Supreme Court case stemming from the defendant's having sold to an undercover police officer some videotapes of then-underage porn star Traci Lords. The case involved the federal Protection of Children Against Sexual Exploitation Act and includes a lengthy analysis by the Court of the placement of the word *knowingly* in a key sentence.

### Executive Orders as Sources of Communication Law

As a general principle, the separation of powers that defines our form of government provides that Congress makes the laws, the president carries out the laws, and the judiciary interprets and determines the constitutionality of the laws. In reality, however, the president—or, at other levels of government, governors and mayors—can also make law. The president does so by appointing officials to the various regulatory agencies, negotiating treaties and trade agreements, and issuing executive orders. Then, too, the president has an enormous long-term effect on the law through the process of nominating persons for lifetime appointments as federal judges.

Professional journalists are keenly aware that the executive branch affects the overall atmosphere in which they conduct their jobs. Public access to governmental information is usually considered one facet of communication law. Indeed, this book devotes a whole chapter to the issue. Such seemingly mundane matters as how often the president holds press conferences, how many employees are hired by each federal agency to expedite Freedom of Information Act requests, and what kind of guidance agency heads are given about how liberally or sparingly to exercise the power to "classify" government documents are thus all parts of communication law.

---

[18] *Reno v. American Civil Liberties Union,* 521 U.S. 844 (1997).

[19] *Burnett v. National Enquirer,* 144 Cal. App. 3d 991 (1983).

[20] 513 U.S. 64 (1994).

### Administrative Agencies and Communication Law

It was already mentioned that Article I of the U.S. Constitution enumerates the powers granted to Congress. These powers range broadly, from building roads to establishing procedures for immigration and naturalization to printing money, and to maintaining the armed forces. They are also as broad in scope as regulating commerce among the states. The few hundred members of Congress could not possibly perform all the many functions required of them without creating a sizable federal bureaucracy. So it is that Washington, D.C., is a veritable alphabet soup of hundreds of regulatory agencies and departments. Several of these agencies have responsibilities of direct relevance for the professional communicator.

Clearly, the most important agency, especially if you plan a career in TV, radio, satellite communications, or cyberspace, is the **Federal Communications Commission** (FCC). Chapter 12, where we examine those laws and regulations that apply exclusively to such electronic media as broadcasting and cable, also includes a detailed description of this agency's history and powers. Another agency whose rulings are relevant to communication law is the **Federal Trade Commission** (FTC), one of whose powers is to set forth rules and mediate disputes so as to protect consumers from deceptive advertising. The **Food and Drug Administration** (FDA) also has a voice in the regulation of advertising for and labeling of—you guessed it—food and drugs. In the late 1990s, for example, tobacco companies became very concerned about the implications of a move to allow the FDA to classify cigarettes, because of their nicotine content, as "drug delivery systems." In 2000, however, the Supreme Court held that Congress never intended to give the FDA regulatory authority over cigarettes, including what, if any, kinds of advertising should be allowed for tobacco products.[21]

The **Federal Elections Commission** (FEC) also has jurisdiction over issues of relevance to professional communicators because federal legislation sets limits on certain kinds of candidate fundraising and candidate expenditures. The vast majority of funds raised in national campaigns is used to buy advertising time on TV and radio, so the FEC's powers are of special relevance to media advertising salespersons and political campaign consultants.

Although these federal agencies are likely the most important sources of communications law, media professionals will discover that dozens of other agencies also have some power over the way in which they conduct their business. To cite just one example, in the mid-1980s the **Securities and Exchange Commission** (SEC) argued that it had the right to prevent anyone whose credentials as an investment advisor had been revoked by the Commission (typically, because of criminal wrongdoing) from offering formal investment advice, even in a newsletter advice column. The Supreme Court determined that Congress never intended for the Commission to have this particular power.[22]

---

[21]*FDA v. Brown & Williamson Corporation,* 529 U.S. 120 (2000).

[22]*Lowe v. SEC,* 472 U.S. 181 (1985).

# Things to Remember

## COMMUNICATION LAW: BEYOND THE U.S. CONSTITUTION

- State constitutions are a source of communication law.
  - Some states simply mimic the wording of the First Amendment.
  - Other states affirmatively enumerate citizens' communication rights.
  - Often, states give more rights than the First Amendment does.
- Statutes are a source of communication law.
  - Legislative bodies at all levels of government may pass laws or regulations.
  - Courts sometimes must decide if they are constitutional (judicial review).
  - Courts also may tell us what a law really means (statutory construction).
- Executive orders are sources of communication law.
  - The president often has "wiggle room" in the enforcement of laws.
  - Presidents also affect law through appointments and through international negotiations.
- Some of the many federal agencies that have an effect on communication law are the FCC, FTC, FDA, and FEC.

### Common Law and the Law of Equity

Anyone who has watched police and lawyer programs on prime-time television knows the scene well. An attorney is making a motion to the court, asking the judge to take a particular action. The opposing attorney objects. The judge appears thoughtful, glances in the direction of the first lawyer, and asks, "Can you cite any relevant **precedents**?"

The judge in this scenario is seeking guidance from common law, sometimes called judge-made law. Common law really means to argue based on tradition and custom, ideally backed up with one or more prior court decisions on the same or a similar point. The U.S. legal system depends for its consistency on a large body of common law so that litigants can make some reasonable predictions about how courts will rule on specific issues today based on how they have ruled in the past.

Common law is not a uniquely American invention. Indeed, we imported the idea of lawmaking by precedent from English common law dating back many centuries before any British colonists set foot in the New World. Another, less visible tradition that the United States borrowed from England is the right of litigants to seek a judicial remedy in **courts of equity** in situations where the common-law traditions cannot help. A detailed history of the relationship between the development of common law and the law of equity is beyond the scope of this book, in part because only four states—Arkansas, Delaware, Mississippi, and Tennessee— continue to maintain separate courts of equity. Still, it is important to realize that one impetus for the development of equity was a perceived dichotomy in English legal tradition between rights and remedies. Plaintiffs may have been able to establish to a court's satisfaction that they had been wronged, but no remedy existed in the law to make the plaintiff whole again.[23] The development of such remedies as **subpoenas** (compelling someone to appear before a court at a later date and to produce papers or otherwise give testimony in reply to specific judicial inquiries) and **injunctions** (ordering that a planned action not be taken, lest a litigant be irreparably wronged) was an outgrowth of the courts of equity. Whenever the phrase "common law" is used throughout the remainder of this text, reference will be made implicitly as well to the law of equity.

The common law should not be thought of as a judicial straitjacket, with no opportunity for evolution. The law does in fact change over time, in part because customs and traditions change. When faced with an arguably relevant precedent, a court always has several options available to it. The first option and the most likely one is to accept and follow the precedent. The Latin phrase ***stare decisis,*** or "let the decision stand," is often used as a catchphrase to refer to the practice of following precedent.

At the other extreme, a court may decide that the time has come to **overturn** a precedent, to admit forthrightly (at least sometimes it is done forthrightly) that the original decision was wrong. Occasionally a Supreme Court precedent in the field of communication law has been overturned by a later Court. For example, the Supreme Court had held for many years that motion pictures were not deserving of constitutional protection.[24] "The exhibition of moving pictures is a business, pure and simple, originated and conducted for profit like other spectacles," the Court said back in 1915, "and not to be regarded as part of the press of the country or as organs of public opinion within the meaning of freedom of speech." Not until the 1950s did the Supreme Court explicitly overrule its earlier decision, finding that motion pictures had become "a significant medium for the communication of ideas."[25]

The Supreme Court also took several decades to change its mind about the place of advertising in the U.S. system of free expression. In a 1942 case, the Court held that advertising is completely outside the First Amendment's protection.[26] More than thirty years later, the Court changed its mind, holding for the first time that purely commercial advertising whose message is simply that person A offers to sell something to person B for a specified price is protected speech.[27] The development of the Court's commercial speech doctrine is so important that it is a large part of the focus of Chapter 10.

---

[23]Morton Gitelman, "The Separation of Law and Equity and the Arkansas Chancery Courts: Historical Anomalies and Political Realities," 17 *University of Arkansas at Little Rock Law Journal* 215 (1995).

[24]*Mutual Film Corporation v. Industrial Commission of Ohio,* 236 U.S. 230 (1915).

[25]*Burstyn, Inc. v. Wilson,* 43 U.S. 495 (1952).

[26]*Valentine v. Chrestensen,* 316 U.S. 52 (1942).

[27]*Virginia State Board of Pharmacy v. Virginia Citizens Consumer Council,* 425 U.S. 748 (1976).

On rare occasions, the Court has changed its mind without waiting for so many years to pass. Probably the best example is *West Virginia State Board of Education v. Barnette,*[28] in which the Court ruled unconstitutional the practice of requiring that public school students recite the Pledge of Allegiance to the flag. The Court had made a directly contrary ruling a mere three years earlier.[29]

Most of the time, courts follow precedents. Sometimes, especially after many years have passed since a precedent has been handed down, judges feel free to overturn the precedent, to change their minds. In between these two opposite actions are two other options for dealing with a precedent. Often, one or the other is employed en route to an eventual overturning.

The first of the two options is to **distinguish** the precedent, and the word means much the same in this context as it does in everyday conversation. When judges distinguish an earlier decision, they are really saying that the case is not a precedent worthy of following at all, *given the facts of the controversy now before them.* This last phrase is the key. The facts of the two cases are different. In communication law, the opportunities for building arguments in favor of distinguishing a precedent are many and varied. The earlier case might deal with a movie that has been found to meet the current definition of obscenity, whereas the case we are looking at today might involve a film that has some sexy scenes in it yet could not be considered so hardcore as to be obscene. The earlier decision might have been a libel case in which the plaintiff was a famous person, what the courts have come to call a **public figure.** If the case we are looking at today involves a libel plaintiff who is not at all famous, many features of libel law that were applied in the earlier case will be inapplicable. The earlier case might have involved political advertising on television, whereas the current case involves political advertising in a newspaper. As it turns out, the law governing the same content on the two media is very different. The two situations again can thus be distinguished.

The fourth and last option is to **modify** the earlier precedent. Knowing the dictionary definition of *modify* is not going to be much help here. In the law, to modify a precedent is to follow, in a very general way, the rule that seems to explain the earlier case but to at the same time show a recognition that something "out there, in the *real* world," has changed. Perhaps an example or two will clarify. In libel law, one of the things that plaintiffs must prove is that an utterance or publication was truly defamatory, that it damaged their reputation. Traditionally, we assumed that to accuse a woman of having had sexual relations before marriage would be defamatory. Suppose, however, that you live in a state where courts have held that societal customs and values have changed and that accusing an unmarried woman of not being chaste need not be defamatory. The general rule—libel demands a finding of defamation—still holds and we are still following it in

---

[28]319 U.S. 624 (1943).

[29]*Minersville School District v. Gobitis,* 310 U.S. 586 (1940).

principle, but the world has changed to the point where that which used to be thought of as defamatory might no longer be considered so.

The Supreme Court's changing thinking about TV in courtrooms provides another example of modifying a precedent. In the 1960s, the Court overturned the swindling conviction of one of President Johnson's Texas friends because the TV cameras permitted at his trial created a zoolike atmosphere.[30] Less than twenty years later, the Court upheld the **conspiracy** convictions of some Florida police officers who had argued unsuccessfully that TV at their trial was a violation of their constitutional rights.[31] How can we explain the two differing results, when the Court did not actually overturn the earlier case? Something "out there," in the real world, had changed. Television technology had grown more sophisticated and far less intrusive to the point where the technology now could be introduced into the courtroom without disrupting the proceedings.

Having now reviewed the four options open to a court that is presented with a precedent for consideration, it should be emphasized that it is not always perfectly clear which option the court has exercised. Recall that we treated the question of whether films are protected by the First Amendment as an example of the Supreme Court's having overruled itself after a few decades had passed. That same constitutional history, however, could be seen as an example of modifying the earlier precedent. It could be argued that, in the early days of motion pictures, films had no message to impart, no story to tell; they were merely toys. We flocked to the movie theaters because we were fascinated with the optical illusion itself. We were enthralled by the very sense of seeing movement. Perhaps, then, it would make no more sense to say that films are protected "expression" than to say that a telescope is protected expression. For the Court many years after that decision to recognize that motion pictures *now* were being used to tell stories, to delight but also to inspire and educate, would be more an example of modifying than of overruling. That which would have changed would not be the minds of the justices, but motion pictures' place in society.

Another reason it is not always clear which strategy a court has used is that there is a strong tendency in the law toward a kind of inertia, away from the outright overturning of precedents. As one commentator put it, "Most of what seems essentially false in judges' opinions [is] the repeated insistence that they are not changing the law at all when they obviously are."[32] It is worth noting too that in only six of the almost two hundred times the Supreme Court has overturned its prior rulings has it explicitly admitted that the earlier decision had been a mistake.[33]

---

[30]*Estes v. Texas,* 381 U.S. 532 (1965).

[31]*Chandler v. Florida,* 449 U.S. 560 (1981).

[32]M. Shapiro, "Incremental Decision Making," in *Courts, Law, and Judicial Processes,* ed. S. Ulmer, (New York: Free Press, 1981), 316.

[33]Philip P. Frickey, "*Stare Decisis* in Constitutional Cases: Reconsidering *National League of Cities,*" 2 *Constitutional Commentary* 123, 128 n.21 (1985).

# Things to Remember

**COMMON-LAW PRECEDENTS**

■ The common law, or "judge-made law," is the body of precedents that can inform a current controversy.
■ When presented with a precedent, a court may do one of four things:
  • Follow it (the principle of *stare decisis*).
  • Distinguish it.
  • Modify it.
  • Overturn it.

## An Overview of the American Judiciary

Now that we know what courts may do with common-law precedents, we need to develop an understanding of how the judiciary is structured in this country. In other words, what does it mean to "go to court"?

We should first realize that there is not one judicial system in the United States, but rather a federal system, a system for each of the states, and one for the District of Columbia. There are fifty-two systems in all, without even counting the courts governing such places as Puerto Rico or the Virgin Islands. It is important to keep that in mind throughout this book because we will often be able to offer only generalizations rather than definitive answers about the status of a particular legal doctrine. The law varies from state to state and from one region of the federal judiciary to another.

### A Three-Tiered Hierarchy

The structure of the judiciary itself need not be a source of complete bewilderment. Indeed, the hierarchy of courts in the states is almost without exception modeled after the federal system. There are three layers. At the bottom are the **trial courts.** In the federal system, these are called **federal district courts.** The names of the trial courts vary greatly from state to state, but are most frequently called **superior courts.**

Litigants who are unhappy with the trial court result have the option of bringing an appeal to the next layer of the judiciary. In the federal system, and in that of most states, these courts are called, intuitively enough, **appellate courts.** In the federal system, these appellate courts govern a specific region of the country, called a **federal circuit.** There are thirteen such circuits. Eleven of them are given numbers. The jurisdiction of each of these appellate courts is as follows:

**First:** Maine, Massachusetts, New Hampshire, Rhode Island, Puerto Rico
**Second:** Connecticut, New York, Vermont

**Third:** Delaware, New Jersey, Pennsylvania (also the Virgin Islands)

**Fourth:** Maryland, North Carolina, South Carolina, Virginia, West Virginia

**Fifth:** Texas, Mississippi, Louisiana

**Sixth:** Kentucky, Michigan, Ohio, Tennessee

**Seventh:** Illinois, Indiana, Wisconsin

**Eighth:** Arkansas, Iowa, Minnesota, Missouri, Nebraska, North Dakota, South Dakota

**Ninth:** Alaska, Arizona, California, Hawaii, Idaho, Montana, Nevada, Oregon, Washington (also Guam and Northern Mariana Islands)

**Tenth:** Colorado, Kansas, New Mexico, Oklahoma, Utah, Wyoming

**Eleventh:** Alabama, Florida, Georgia (also the Panama Canal Zone)

There is also an appellate court for the District of Columbia. That particular court has jurisdiction over most appeals from decisions of the FCC and other federal agencies. If you work in the electronic media or cable television industries, this one court may thus be the most important one governing your professional life. The thirteenth federal appellate court is the one for the Federal Circuit, a special court created by Congress in 1982 to handle specialized appeals such as in patent and trademark cases.

Litigants who are not satisfied with an appellate ruling can sometimes take their grievance one step higher. The pinnacle of the judiciary in both the federal and state systems is also an appellate court, but it goes by a special name. We have already made many references to the United States Supreme Court. The highest court in most states is also referred to as a supreme court, although there are some exceptions. New York's highest court, for example, is its Court of Appeals.

Although we often hear aggrieved parties vow that they will take their cases "all the way to the Supreme Court, if necessary," in fact this is romantic fancy because the justices of the Supreme Court have tremendous latitude about which of the thousands of appeals filed there will ever be heard. In recent years, the justices have chosen to hear only a hundred or fewer cases on average annually. Many state supreme courts have similar discretion to determine which cases they will hear. As such, often litigants are realistically limited to having their grievances heard in two, rather than three, rungs of the judicial system.

## The Scope of a Precedent

Thus far, we have used the word *precedent* to refer to an earlier court decision that might lead a court today to rule similarly. Not all precedents are equal, however. A precedent in a state court in Wisconsin, for example, even if decided by that state's highest court, has no *binding* precedential value on a state judge in California. The California court might be persuaded by the logic of the Wisconsin court's arguments, but it is not required to follow the precedent. If a judge hears a case that raises issues that have never been raised before in his or her jurisdiction, the controversy is often referred to as one of **first impression.** If you have ever seen the film *Whose Life Is It Anyway?* you may recall the scene where a trial judge comes to the hospital to decide whether Richard Dreyfuss's paraplegic character has a right to die. In this judge's jurisdiction, the issue was depicted as a case of first impression, although the judge was aware of precedents from other states.

You as a judge are bound by precedents only by higher courts in the same area, or **jurisdiction,** as your own. If you are a state trial court judge, you are bound by relevant decisions of the U.S. Supreme Court, by your state's supreme court, as well as by any appellate rulings from courts in the same appellate division (geographic region of the state) as your own. If you are a federal trial judge, you are bound by U.S. Supreme Court decisions as well as by federal appellate decisions that come from the same circuit in which you find yourself. Until the U.S. Supreme Court gives guidance with a definitive ruling, conflicting decisions among the circuits often seem to be the rule rather than the exception. We see frequent examples of this phenomenon throughout this book.

The U.S. Supreme Court is the ultimate arbiter of what the U.S. Constitution means. It must be emphasized, however, that the Court has no authority whatsoever to interpret state constitutions; that is the province of the individual state supreme courts. Perhaps the best example of this principle in practice in recent years is the question of whether state sodomy laws—laws that make certain consensual sexual practices illegal and that are often enforced disproportionately against homosexuals—are constitutional. The U.S. Supreme Court, in 1986, ruled 5–4 that the existence of such laws is not a violation of any federal constitutional principle.[34] Since that date, however, numerous state appellate courts have ruled in consensual sodomy cases and at least in three instances have found these laws in violation of their own state constitutions' privacy provisions.[35] Such decisions cannot be appealed to the U.S. Supreme Court.

### The Current U.S. Supreme Court

The members of the U.S. Supreme Court from its 1996–1997 term, pictured on page 20, were last officially photographed when the most recently appointed justice was added to the court. A new official photo of the justices will be taken when one or more justices retires and is replaced—a highly likely set of events, by most accounts, with the election of George W. Bush. Figure 1.1 gives information on each justice, including the date of appointment and the name of the president who made the appointment. Note that seven of the nine justices were appointed by Republican presidents. U.S. Supreme Court justices are appointed, with the

---

[34]*Bowers v. Hardwick,* 478 U.S. 186 (1986).

[35]*Powell v. State,* 510 S.E.2d 18 (Ga. 1998); *Commonwealth v. Wasson,* 842 S.W.2d 487 (Ky. 1992); *State v. Morales,* 826 S.W.2d 201 (Tex. 1992).

Seated [from L to R]: Associate Justices Antonin Scalia and John Paul Stevens, Chief Justice William Rehnquist, Associate Justices Sandra Day O'Connor and Anthony Kennedy. Standing [from L to R]: Associate Justices Ruth Bader Ginsburg, David Souter, Clarence Thomas, and Stephen Breyer.

*Photo by Richard Strauss, Smithsonian Institution; Collection of the U.S. Supreme Court*

"advice and consent" of the Senate, to lifetime terms, as are all federal judges. The Senate confirmation process can be rather stormy, as evidenced in recent years by the media spectacles surrounding Senate Judiciary Committee hearings on the candidacies of Judges Robert Bork (rejected) and Clarence Thomas (ultimately prevailing by a slim 52–48 vote in the full Senate).

Certainly, volumes could be written about each justice's legal philosophy and more specifically each's tendency to interpret the First Amendment either liberally or stingily. Such an undertaking will not be attempted here. Two necessarily over-simplified points will have to suffice for now. First, those jurists who enjoy well-deserved reputations as political conservatives may nonetheless believe in rather broad interpretation of at least some First Amendment principles. Justice Antonin Scalia is probably the best example of this phenomenon on the current Court. Second, it is very misleading to label a justice as a First Amendment progressive or a First Amendment conservative without giving a bit of context. In the 1970s, for example, Justice John Paul Stevens wrote an opinion for the Court holding that a radio station had no First Amendment right to broadcast one of comedian George Carlin's "dirty words" monologues. Although such an opinion would seem to qualify Justice Stevens for the conservative label, today he is viewed as perhaps the justice most supportive of First Amendment rights.

### Going to Court: Civil or Criminal

Conflicts resulting in a trip to the courtroom are generally of two types, **civil** and **criminal.** The name of the proceeding is usually an indication of which category

Figure 1.1   *The Justices of the U.S. Supreme Court*

|  | **Born** | **Appointment** | **Past Lives** |
|---|---|---|---|
| William Rehnquist | 1 October 1924 | 1972/Nixon* | Assistant U.S. Attorney General<br>Private practice<br>State prosecutor |
| John Paul Stevens | 20 April 1920 | 1975/Ford | Federal appellate judge<br>Private practice |
| Sandra Day O'Connor | 26 March 1930 | 1981/Reagan | Assistant Attorney General, Arizona<br>Arizona state senator (majority leader)<br>State judge (trial and appellate) |
| Antonin Scalia | 11 March 1936 | 1986/Reagan | Assistant U.S. Attorney General<br>Law professor (University of Chicago)<br>Federal appellate judge |
| Anthony Kennedy | 23 July 1936 | 1988/Reagan | Federal appellate judge<br>Law professor (University of the Pacific) |
| David Souter | 17 September 1939 | 1990/Bush | State superior court justice, New Hampshire<br>New Hampshire Attorney General |
| Clarence Thomas | 23 June 1946 | 1991/Bush | Director, Civil Rights, U.S. Department of Education<br>Head, Equal Employment Opportunity Commission<br>Federal appellate judge |
| Ruth Bader Ginsburg | 15 March 1933 | 1993/Clinton | Law professor (Rutgers University & Columbia University)<br>Director, Women's Rights Project, ACLU<br>Federal appellate judge |
| Stephen Breyer | 15 August 1938 | 1994/Clinton | Law professor (Harvard)<br>Chief counsel, U.S. Senate Judiciary Committee<br>Federal appellate judge |

*Elevated to Chief Justice in 1986 by President Reagan.*

we have before us. Civil cases are given names of the form *A v. B* (e.g., *Smith v. Jones*), where person A is the **plaintiff** who is suing person B, the **defendant.** In criminal proceedings, the "plaintiff" becomes the government, which is said to **prosecute** the case against the defendant. Thus, we may have names such as *United States v. Dennis* or *Georgia v. Stanley.*

In civil disputes, the case begins with the plaintiff filing in court a **complaint,** which enumerates the specific allegations of misconduct against the defendant. The defendant then has an opportunity to file a response to the complaint, referred to as the **answer.**

The process of **discovery** then takes place, and it can be both lengthy and costly. The label makes sense because this step is when each side of the dispute discovers the nature of the other's case. Lawyers for one side will question the other's witnesses, and transcripts of such pretrial **depositions** are made that can be used later at trial to ensure that witnesses' stories remain consistent.

Typically, a flurry of legal paper filings will then ensue. Some filings might seek to avoid a trial by having the court grant **summary judgment** to one side or the other (more frequently to the defense). Such an order would be appropriate if the judge believes that those facts on which both the plaintiff and defendant agree establish a scenario whereby one and only one legal answer is possible. Keep in mind that mass media defendants are often very unpopular with juries. As such, motions for summary judgment are very important to professional communicators.

Often, too, motions are made that are aimed at setting the ground rules should a trial be necessary. In a sexual abuse case involving juveniles, for example, will testimony from alleged victims be accepted on videotape? As we see in Chapter 4, one of the most important pretrial issues to have settled in libel disputes is whether the plaintiff is a public figure or an ordinary private citizen. The answer to that one question often determines the ultimate winner and loser of the case.

If you have ever been called for jury duty, you may have noted that legal disputes are often settled at the last minute, even on the day a trial is scheduled to begin. Indeed, a very tiny percent of court cases, civil or criminal, ever actually comes to trial. Sometimes these pretrial settlements (in criminal law, they usually involve **plea bargaining** to a lesser charge) occur at the very last minute, after the careful questioning of potential jurors (called the **voir dire** hearing) has been completed and both sides see the jury that will actually hear the case.

Criminal cases involve some unique features with which communication professionals should have at least some familiarity. Typically, the prosecution of the case begins with the arrest of the suspect. The **arraignment,** at which a judge formally reads to the suspect the charges against him or her and at which the suspect may make an initial **plea,** follows soon after. Should the defendant plead guilty, sentencing may take place immediately or soon after additional facts about any mitigating or aggravating circumstances surrounding the offense are brought to the judge's attention in the form of a **presentencing report.**

If the defendant pleads not guilty, there is usually at least one more major step in the process prior to a trial itself. In some settings, this step is the **preliminary hearing.** In other jurisdictions, and in federal prosecutions, it is the seeking of an **indictment** by a **grand jury.** In either case, the purpose of this pretrial step is to ensure that the state does in fact have enough evidence to justify "holding the defendant over," that the taxpayers' money will not be wasted by going to trial. Although grand juries and "real" juries (usually called **petit juries**) are typically drawn from the same jury pools (e.g., from voter registration lists), there are two important differences between the two. First, whereas that which petit jurors hear are full-blown criminal trials, traditionally open to the press and public, the evidence presented to a grand jury by a district attorney is traditionally kept secret. Second, the burden of proof demanded by petit jurors is that the state establish its case "beyond a reasonable doubt," whereas grand jurors, to indict a suspect, need only find that there is "probable cause" to believe that the defendant is guilty.

Not all trials are jury trials, of course. The rules governing when litigants in a civil case have a right to a jury trial vary among jurisdictions. Sometimes it may be wise for one or the other party in a lawsuit to forgo that right. It is commonly believed, for example, that libel plaintiffs prefer jury trials, whereas media defendants in such trials prefer a trial by a judge. Juries are more likely to be swayed by the emotionalism and immediacy of seeing a wronged plaintiff, or so the reasoning goes, whereas they might not be swayed by the more abstract philosophies in support of freedom of the press, especially if the press in the case before them got its facts wrong and hurt someone in their community.[36]

---

[36]Rodney A. Smolla, *Suing the Press: Libel, the Media, and Power* (New York: Oxford University Press, 1986), 194–195.

 # Things to Remember

---

### THE BASIC STRUCTURE OF THE LEGAL SYSTEM

- The federal judiciary has three levels—district courts, circuit courts of appeal, and the U.S. Supreme Court—and most states mirror this system.
- The U.S. Supreme Court, as well as many other state supreme courts, is not required to accept any invitation to hear an appeal from lower courts.
- Lower court judges are legally *bound* to follow precedents only from superior courts in their own jurisdictions.
- Courts hear both civil cases (in which an individual plaintiff sues a defendant) and criminal prosecutions by the state.
- Prior to the convening of an actual trial, much discovery takes place, and there may also be motions to avoid a trial by seeking summary judgment.

**The Appeals Process**

Whichever side wins at the trial level in a civil dispute, and if a criminal prosecution results in a conviction, an appeal may be the next step. There are many differences between trials and appellate hearings. Trials typically take much longer than appellate hearings. Only trials can have jurors and witnesses. Appellate hearings are much less populous affairs; typically, one attorney for each side makes **oral arguments** in front of the court for a half hour or so, arguments that can be interrupted at any time by questions from the bench. The oral argument usually takes place weeks or months after lengthy position papers called **briefs** have been filed in court by each side. Sometimes, too, parties beyond those immediately involved in the dispute file a brief. In a media law case, for example, organizations such as the American Society of Newspaper Editors or the National Association of Broadcasters may ask to have their thoughts on the controversy entertained by the court. The papers filed by such associations are called **amicus briefs,** "amicus" being Latin for "friend." Sometimes you may encounter the phrase **amicus curiae** ("friend of the Court") to describe a group filing an amicus brief.

Although only trial courts have witnesses and jurors, in one sense the appellate courtroom is more crowded. Trial courts generally are presided over by one judge, whereas at the appellate level a panel of judges is involved. In federal procedure, the appellate panels consist of three randomly assigned judges from that circuit (see Figure 1.2). An **en banc** ruling by all the judges of a circuit (usually a dozen or more)

 Figure 1.2

"WHAT I REALLY MISS IS NOT HAVING MY OWN GAVEL, AND NOT BEING ABLE TO SHOUT, 'ORDER IN THE COURT!'"

The speaker seems to be lamenting his having been promoted recently from trial judge to appellate judge. Appellate judges do not run their own courtrooms, nor do they generally get to call for "order in the court," because appellate proceedings do not include jurors or witnesses, only attorneys.

*Copyright © 1993 Sidney Harris. Reprinted with permission.*

may be sought as an intermediate level of appeal after an unsuccessful hearing in front of a three-judge panel and before petitioning the U.S. Supreme Court.

Another key difference between trial and appellate proceedings is the kinds of issues addressed by the courts. Trial courts entertain questions both of **fact** and **law,** whereas appellate courts generally deal only with questions of law. One major exception to this general principle is the **clearly erroneous rule** of Federal Civil Procedure. This rule permits a federal appellate court to look at the facts of the case independently if the court first determines that the trial judge made a clearly erroneous finding of fact. The rule is not often invoked. It is viewed as strong medicine, in part because leveling such an accusation against a lower court judge is rather insulting and because the invoking of the rule is itself ultimately reviewable by a yet higher court.

Questions of fact ask, What happened? In a homicide case, for example, we would ask if this criminal suspect emptied a revolver into the deceased and if the victim died from the wounds thus inflicted or from some other cause. Whether the answers to those and other facts demand a finding of first-degree or second-degree homicide, or involuntary manslaughter, however, is a question of law. In an obscenity prosecution, issues such as what kind of sexual acts are engaged in and with what frequency by the on-screen talent are questions of fact. Whether the film as a whole satisfies a statute's definition of obscenity and whether that definition in turn satisfies the requirements set forth by relevant Supreme Court rulings are questions of law.

This distinction can be very important to mass media defendants. Journalists frequently find that they are not very popular with most Americans and therefore with most American jurors. If an adverse trial court ruling stems in part from findings of law, the judgment is more easily appealable, and appellate judges have often shown themselves far more sympathetic to First Amendment arguments than were the jurors down below.

***Decisions and Opinions.***   Because appellate courts have several judges hearing a dispute, the permutations of votes for one side or the other and the reasoning behind each such vote become more complicated than in a single-judge trial. A whole nomenclature has developed to describe such matters. Let us use the nine justices of the U.S. Supreme Court as the model in this discussion. We begin by emphasizing the rather intuitive distinction between a **decision** and an **opinion.** A decision tells us who wins the case, whereas an opinion tells us why. In the extreme, we might have a unanimous decision with nine separate opinions. Such a situation would tell us who prevailed, but would probably give lower courts little if any guidance as to what the decision really means and how to apply it to slightly different facts in the future.

First, let us consider the **majority opinion.** (When you read actual Supreme Court cases, you will not find majority opinions referred to as such. Rather, you will typically find phrasing such as, "Justice Green delivered the opinion for the Court, in which Justices Brown, White, Blue, and Orange joined.") U.S. Supreme

Court majority opinions must command at least five votes, presuming that all nine members have participated in a case. For any number of reasons, however, fewer than nine may vote in any given case. Sometimes justices feel the need to **recuse** themselves—that is, to purposely decide not to participate in a case—for ethical reasons. Maybe one justice's daughter is a student at a university that is party to a case, or perhaps another owns stock in a corporation that is one of the litigants. If only seven justices participate in a case, four votes are all that are needed to produce a majority decision.

Majority opinions tend to have a certain structure. They will often begin by reciting the facts of the case, such as who did what to whom, who brought suit and why, and what the lower courts ruled. Typically, at or near the very end of the opinion we will learn the Court's **holding**—what the case stands for and what specific guidance the justices intend lower courts to take from their decision. The holdings of some landmark decisions are well known to most Americans, such as the *Gideon*[37] holding that indigent criminal suspects must be provided with free legal counsel or the *Miranda*[38] holding that information learned from suspects in police interrogations shall be inadmissible if the accused is not advised of certain of his or her constitutional rights prior to questioning. Much of what appears in majority opinions between the recitation of the facts and the setting forth of the holding is called **dicta.** Some of the dicta may consist of reasoning in support of the Court's ultimate conclusion. Then, too, dicta often include predictable, almost formulaic repetitions of boilerplate paragraphs from previous cases. Virtually any case involving student newspapers, for example, no matter which side actually prevails, will include a famous dictum from the Vietnam War era *Tinker* case to the effect that students do not "shed their constitutional rights to freedom of speech or expression at the schoolhouse gate."[39]

Dicta carry much less precedential value than the actual holding of a case for at least two reasons. First, in our constitutional system of separation of powers, courts are empowered to decide immediate controversies set before them, not to create law in the abstract. Because dicta by their very nature often reach far beyond the immediate conflict being adjudicated, giving them too much weight would have the long-term effect of making the judiciary into a minilegislature. Second, only the holding of a case tells the parties involved exactly why the one side has won, and only the holding is supposed to tell lower courts exactly what lesson to learn from the case at hand. As such, judges do not have any immediate incentive to consider their dicta as carefully as they do their holdings, and the imprecision likely to result from this lack of incentive will be ultimately destructive. The two reasons for discounting dicta, then, concern issues of legitimacy and accuracy.[40]

[37]*Gideon v. Wainwright,* 372 U.S. 335 (1963).

[38]*Miranda v. Arizona,* 384 U.S. 436 (1966).

[39]*Tinker v. Des Moines Independent Community School District,* 393 U.S. 503, 506 (1969).

[40]Michael C. Dorf, "Dicta and Article III," 142 *University of Pennsylvania Law Review* 1997 (1994).

A very special situation arises when the Supreme Court has only eight members sitting and produces a 4–4 tie vote. The lower court decision is affirmed, but that affirmance does not carry any binding precedential weight beyond the jurisdiction of the lower court. The Supreme Court's tie vote does not produce the "law of the land." Thus, if a case is appealed from the Supreme Court of Wisconsin, resulting in such a 4–4 tie, the legal doctrine established by the lower court will be binding only in Wisconsin. In essence, the result is as if the case had never been heard by the U.S. Supreme Court. Typically, no opinion is written when a case produces a 4–4 tie.

From the vantage point of lower court judges looking to the U.S. Supreme Court for guidance, an especially troublesome result occurs when a clear majority decision is announced, but not enough justices can agree on the rationale behind the decision to produce a majority opinion. The opinion that commands the most votes—it might be three, it might be four—is referred to as a **plurality opinion.** The reasoning offered in such an opinion will not carry any precedential value, although it can offer some insights as to how the Court might react to slightly different situations in the future.

Assuming that a case does produce a clear majority opinion, some justices who voted with the winning side and who even signed on to the majority opinion may still feel the need to write a separate **concurring opinion** to indicate how their own views of the case may differ a bit from that espoused by the majority. Then, too, a justice might "concur in the decision only," which means that the

# Things to Remember

## APPELLATE PROCEDURES, DECISIONS, AND OPINIONS

- The losing party in a trial may bring an appeal to a higher court.
- Both parties will then file written briefs, followed by oral arguments before a panel of judges.
- Other parties may express their views through the use of amicus briefs.
- Losing parties in a federal appellate court can petition the entire court to hear the case again en banc, prior to contemplating a U.S. Supreme Court appeal.
- Generally, appellate courts may only address questions of law, whereas trial courts look also at questions of fact.
- Decisions tell who wins a case; opinions tell why.
- The actual holding of a decision is its true precedential value; often, the bulk of the text in an opinion consists of dicta, which have very limited precedential value.
- Depending on how many judges join in an opinion and which way they vote, the opinion may be referred to as majority, plurality, concurring, or dissenting.

justice will vote with the majority but want to emphasize that he or she wholly rejects the majority's reasoning. Concurring opinions are often written by the justice who provided the "swing vote" in a 5–4 decision. Justice Lewis Powell was famous for writing such opinions, and we come across some of them in this book. As you may well imagine, the tone of such opinions frequently suggests that "I will go this far, *but no farther.*"

The chance to write opinions is not restricted to those who vote on the winning side, of course. Those justices whose votes place them in the minority will produce at least one **dissenting opinion.** Sometimes the reasoning espoused by a dissenting justice today becomes majority opinion tomorrow.

Two final categories of opinions you may encounter are the ***per curiam* opinion** and the **memorandum order.** *Per curiam* means "by the Court," and a per curiam opinion is a majority opinion that is not signed by any particular justice. A memorandum order is a court decision that is not accompanied by an opinion. We learn who won, but little if anything else.

## Where to Find the Cases

There are at least two reasons you will want to learn how to find the full text of court opinions on your own rather than depending entirely upon a book such as this one to summarize the leading cases. The first reason is that your instructor might require you to do some original research rather than simply take exams on the material in this book. The second reason has a more long-term payoff. This book is already out of date. So rapid are changes in the law that any legal textbook, even assuming the speediest of production schedules, is several months out of date the moment it arrives at your bookstore. Your instructor will be able to provide updates, pointing out, for example, court cases cited here that may have been overturned on appeal while we went to press. Your time with your instructor is limited, however, and it is thus a good idea to develop the ability to do your own updating as a media professional.

In the best of all possible worlds, you are taking this class at an institution that has a law school, that permits students campuswide to use the law library, and that boasts convenient access to computer-assisted legal resources such as the Westlaw or LEXIS databases. Even if you do not have a law school on campus, your library probably maintains at least the kind of legal collection that will allow you to research court cases. If you are on a campus without such a collection, you might find it necessary to visit a neighboring campus or the library at your county courthouse.

***Finding U.S. Supreme Court Cases.*** Let us suppose you are listening to the radio one morning in the car on the way to school, and you hear that the Supreme Court just handed down an important decision. (The decisions are usually released to the press at 10 A.M. Eastern time.) Where are some of the different places you might be able to find it? If you have access to computer-assisted research, you will likely be able to find the full text of the opinion online within a few hours. In LEXIS, Supreme Court decisions are most conveniently found in the "US" file within the GENFED library. Numerous Internet Web sites also boast Supreme Court and other court decisions. Several helpful Web sites for legal research are highlighted later in this chapter.

What if you do not have convenient online access? If the case is truly a landmark decision, you may find very detailed excerpts of it published the next morning in such national newspapers as the *New York Times* and the *Washington Post.* Within a week or so, the full text will also be available in libraries around the country in a publication called *United States Law Week* (abbreviated U.S.L.W.). The more traditional places to find the full text of U.S. Supreme Court opinions are in a series called the *Supreme Court Reporter* (abbreviated S. Ct.) and another called *United States Reports* (abbreviated U.S.). Yet another source owned by many academic libraries is the *United States Supreme Court Reports, Lawyers' Edition* (abbreviated L. Ed. or, for more recent cases, L. Ed. 2d), published by LEXIS.

***Finding Other Court Decisions.*** Federal district court opinions, when they are published at all, appear most conveniently in a series from the St. Paul, Minnesota–based West Publishing Company, called *Federal Supplement* (or F. Supp.). As of 1998, the volume numbering system began anew (rather than climb higher than 999), and so the most recent federal district cases are found in the *Federal Supplement,* second edition (abbreviated F. Supp. 2d). Federal appellate decisions are found in another West publication called the *Federal Reporter* (abbreviated simply as F.). In 1924, after publishing volume number 300, the *Federal Reporter* began numbering anew, and from that date until 1993, cases were thus found in the *Federal Reporter,* second edition (F.2d). Volume 999 of the second edition was published in 1993; thus, the most recent federal appellate decisions appear in the *Federal Reporter,* third edition (F.3d).

Each state's judiciary publishes its own case reports. Thus, we may see references, for example, to the *Wisconsin Reporter* or the *New York Supplement.* Academic libraries at most colleges without law schools do not bother to subscribe to each and every state's reporters. Rather, they tend to subscribe to yet another West series of publications. West's regional reporters conveniently break down the states into seven separate areas: the Atlantic (A.), the Pacific (P.), the Northeastern (N.E.), the Northwestern (N.W.), the Southern (So.), the Southeastern (S.E.), and the South-western (S.W.). Two important caveats are in order. First, do not always look for logic, geographic or otherwise, in the assignment of a state to a region. Illinois decisions are found in the Northeastern Reporter, Michigan's in the Northwestern Reporter. Second, because a case appears in one West regional reporter and not another is not at all relevant to the precedential value of a case. In other words, do not confuse a federal appellate decision's *circuit* (very important to know when determining the case's precedential scope) and a state decision's West Publishing region.

Here are the states that each of West's regional reporters covers:

**Atlantic:** Connecticut, Delaware, the District of Columbia, Maine, Maryland, New Hampshire, New Jersey, Pennsylvania, Rhode Island, Vermont

**Northeastern:** Illinois, Indiana, Massachusetts, New York, Ohio

**Northwestern:** Iowa, Michigan, Minnesota, Nebraska, North Dakota, South Dakota, Wisconsin

**Pacific:** Alaska, Arizona, California, Colorado, Hawaii, Idaho, Kansas, Montana, Nevada, New Mexico, Oklahoma, Oregon, Utah, Washington, Wyoming

**Southeastern:** Georgia, North Carolina, South Carolina, Virginia, West Virginia

**Southern:** Alabama, Florida, Louisiana, Mississippi

**Southwestern:** Arkansas, Kentucky, Missouri, Tennessee, Texas

Just as was the case with the reporting of federal appellate cases, when the volume number of a regional reporter gets very high, West will start numbering again in a new series. Some of the regionals are in their second editions, some in their third.

*Legal Citations.*    If you have been glancing at the footnotes in this chapter, you already have been exposed to the way in which court decisions are cited. The general format is always the same. First, we have the name of the case. Generically, the name is *A v. B.* At the trial level, this name means that A is the plaintiff and B is the defendant. If this case had reached the appellate level, A is the **appellant** (the unsuccessful litigant at the level below) and B is the **respondent** (i.e., B won below).

The next part of the citation is the volume number, followed by the name of the reporter and the page number where the case's text begins. Finally, in parentheses, is the date when the court decided the case. If the context would not otherwise already have indicated it, this date may be preceded by an abbreviation telling which court made the decision. With federal appellate decisions, this notation is typically the number of the federal circuit. With federal district decisions, it will be the name of the district court (every state has at least one federal district, and some may have an "eastern" and a "western" or a "northern" and a "southern" district). Because citations for the West regional reporters do not tell which state court issued a particular ruling—any of thirteen states' courts may have written a decision that ends up in the *Pacific Reporter*—we often find a reference to the specific court here, too.

One additional complication needs mentioning. When a legal dispute has been through more than one layer of adjudication, we sometimes find it helpful to give its entire judicial "pedigree" in its citation. The most frequent additions to the citation thus indicate whether a lower court ruling had been affirmed (typically abbreviated *aff'd*) or reversed (*rev'd*) on appeal.

Let us look at an example or two.

*Harper & Row v. Nation Enterprises,* 557 F. Supp. 1067 (S.D.N.Y. 1983), *rev'd,* 723 F.2d 195 (2d Cir. 1983), *rev'd,* 471 U.S. 539 (1985).

This example is a full citation to a real court case that we discuss in Chapter 6 when we talk about copyright. For now, what can we learn about the case's history from its citation?

- The litigants are publisher Harper and Row and Nation Enterprises, the company that publishes *The Nation* magazine.
- The federal district court for the Southern District of New York heard the case and issued its decision in 1983. The district court decision can be found beginning on page 1067 of volume 557 of the *Federal Supplement.* Who won? We can infer, even without reading the trial-level opinion, that Harper and Row won. How do we know? We know because at the Supreme Court level, Harper and Row is the appellant (the *A* in *A v. B*), which means that *The Nation* won at the appellate level. Because the appellate court reversed the trial court, we also know that the federal district court ruled for Harper and Row.
- The federal appellate court for the Second Circuit's opinion, handed down later in 1983, can be found beginning on page 195 of volume 723 of the *Federal Reporter,* second edition.
- The U.S. Supreme Court took the appeal and reversed the federal appellate court. Thus, Harper and Row, the original plaintiff, ultimately prevailed. The Court decision, handed down in 1985, can be found beginning on page 539 of *United States Reports.*

Let us look at another example, the citation for the *Pruneyard* case (discussed earlier in this chapter), which involved the California state constitution's provisions for activists who wished to leaflet patrons of a privately owned shopping mall.

*Pruneyard Shopping Center v. Robins,* 592 P.2d 341 (Sup. Ct. Cal. 1979), *aff'd,* 447 U.S. 74 (1980).

From this case's citation, we learn the following:

- The California Supreme Court ruled (in favor of Robins and the other leafleteers). The court's opinion can be found beginning on page 341 of volume 592 of the *Pacific Reporter,* second edition.

- The U.S. Supreme Court decision affirming the lower court judgment can be found beginning on page 74 in volume 447 of *United States Reports.*

The case did not begin in the California Supreme Court, of course, but the original trial court decision is, as is so often the case, unpublished.

### Some Additional Legal Research Tools

In these few pages, we cannot possibly cover everything you need to know about conducting legal research. Law students take full courses on the subject. Nonetheless, it is helpful to know how to find the text of laws themselves and how to find information about general principles of law even when you do not have a particular court case in mind.

You already know that you can obtain the full text of court cases from either official government publications or from the West Publishing Company. The same is true of the texts of federal laws. Congress publishes an official version, called *United States Code* (abbreviated U.S.C.). For several reasons, however, most researchers prefer to use privately published versions of the code, either West's *United States Code Annotated* (abbreviated U.S.C.A.) or LEXIS Law Publishing's *United States Code Service* (abbreviated U.S.C.S.). These sources include not only the text of a law, but also convenient references to other related statutes and court decisions that have interpreted it or may have even struck down portions of it as unconstitutional. Each state publishes its own laws as well, and in each state at least one privately published, annotated version of the law is also available.

Suppose you find yourself in a law library with a general research question in mind rather than the name of a specific court case or citation to a particular statute. Although maneuvering through a legal collection can be quite daunting, there exist standard reference works in the law that are not really more difficult to use than ordinary encyclopedias. The *American Law Reports* (ALR) series, for example, is a reference work consisting of appellate court cases that the editors believe to have established an important principle of law. The ALR series is indexed topically and includes references to related court cases and to critical commentaries. *Corpus Juris Secundum,* published by West, is a helpful resource that boasts over a hundred volumes and a comprehensive index of legal subjects, including many of direct relevance to communication law. Another frequently consulted source is *American Jurisprudence,* second edition, once published by Lawyers Cooperative Publishing, but since taken over by West. Several states have their own encyclopedias as well, such as *Massachusetts Jurisprudence* and *Illinois Law and Practice.*

Law review articles, another research tool, are also helpful. Virtually every major law school in this country and throughout the world publishes at least one scholarly journal, called a law review. Most law reviews are designed to be of interest to a general legal audience, such as the *Harvard Law Review* or the *Yale Law Journal.* There are, however, a number of legal periodicals—some published by law schools, some by nonprofit associations—that specialize in communication law. Among them are *CommLaw Conspectus, Communication and the Law, Communication Law and Policy,* the *Federal Communication Bar Journal,* the *Free Speech Yearbook, Hastings Communication and Entertainment Law Journal,* the *Journal of Art and Entertainment Law, Loyola of Los Angeles Entertainment Law Review, Media Law and Policy, Michigan Telecommunications and Technology Law Review,* and *UCLA Entertainment Law Review.*

Just as the *Readers' Guide to Periodical Literature* is a handy guide to general circulation magazines, there are a few indexes to the major and even the more obscure law journals. By far, the most often consulted such resource is the *Index to Legal Periodicals.* You can also search through law review articles online, as in LEXIS's LAWREV library.

The various *Shepherd's Citations* series can help you to make sure that a case you have read is still "good law," that it has not been overturned by a higher court. Your librarian or your instructor will be able to show you how to use this valuable reference. The online version of *Shepherd's* is especially valuable in that the user is forewarned that a given court case has received "negative references" and may have been overturned by later decisions.

Finally, there has been an explosion of freely available Web sites for doing legal research. Some are managed by individual colleges or universities, others by private companies and nonprofit organizations. Many such sites pop up every year, and so no listing of them can possibly be complete or up to date. One especially helpful Web site for students of communication law, maintained by Professor Dale Herbeck of Boston College, provides in one handy place the full text of dozens of landmark U.S. Supreme Court communication law decisions. The URL for Herbeck's Web site is www.bc.edu/bc_org/avp/cas/comm/free_speech/decisions.html. You may also find some of the following sites helpful.

- **American Law Resources On-Line** <www.lawsource.com/also> This Web site provides federal and state cases and statutes as well as Canadian and Mexican sources.

- **Center for Information Law and Policy** <www.law.vill.edu> Jointly operated by Villanova University and the Illinois Institute of Technology, this Web site includes handy links to federal, state, and international legal materials.

- **CourtTV** <www.courttv.com> This cable network's Web site is a great source of background information, especially concerning high-profile cases.

- **FindLaw** <www.findlaw.com> This company's Web site includes federal and state cases, law reviews, and information about law schools.

- **Internet Legal Research Guide** <www.ilrg.com> This Web site is most useful as an index to other legal sites; it lists thousands of them worldwide.

- **Thomas** <http://thomas.loc.gov> This Web site, the Library of Congress's own server, is a great source of information on bills and legislative histories.

# Things to Remember

### FINDING THE CASES

- U.S. Supreme Court decisions can be found in many places:
  - *United States Reports* (abbreviated U.S.).
  - *Supreme Court Reporter* (S. Ct.).
  - *United States Law Week* (U.S.L.W.).
- Federal appellate decisions are most easily found in the *Federal Reporter* (F., F.2d, or F.3d).
- Federal district court decisions are found in the *Federal Supplement* (F. Supp. or F. Supp. 2d).
- State decisions can be found in official state reporters or, more frequently, in academic libraries, in West Publishing Company's "regional reporters" (Atlantic, Pacific, Northeastern, Northwestern, Southern, Southeastern, and Southwestern).
- Legal citations are generally in the form of volume number, name of reporter, page number, court, and date decided, as in 878 S.W.2d 577 (Tex. 1994).
- The text of federal and state statutes follows a similar citation format.
- Law libraries also boast several topically organized encyclopedias and indexes that can help in doing research.
- Many World Wide Web sites can also be helpful to students of communication law.

## Chapter Summary

That which we call communications law actually comes from many sources, including the federal and state constitutions, statutes, actions by regulatory agencies, executive orders, and the common law.

With respect to the U.S. Constitution, the First Amendment, especially its Free Speech Clause and Free Press Clause, is of most importance to media professionals. Several other provisions of the Constitution have implications for the practice of journalism. Some state constitutions give more rights to free speech than the First Amendment does.

The common-law tradition of establishing and adjusting precedents is an important part of our jurisprudence. Courts may follow, modify, distinguish, or overturn an earlier case. Judges' decisions tell who wins a case; their opinions tell why they reached this result. Opinions may be majority, plurality, concurring, or dissenting. The federal judiciary as well as most state systems are in three layers, a trial level and two appellate levels. Trial courts deal with questions of law and fact, whereas appellate courts are generally restricted to matters of law.

chapter

# *The Development of Freedom of Speech*

Granting freedom of speech to others is a courageously unnatural act. Rulers who are at all insecure about the power they wield look upon free speech as a dangerous weapon indeed. Freedom of expression enables dissenters to organize, validate their grievances, and even foment revolutions. It is no surprise that the advent of each communication technology through the ages has been joined by efforts on the part of governments to diminish the new medium's potential for wider dissemination of information. This has been true of the development and increasing portability of writing, the printing press, motion pictures, and, more recently, the Internet.

Americans often presume that freedom of speech began with our own colonial experience or was imported to the United States after having begun in England. In fact, an appreciation for freedom of expression can be traced to ancient Greece and to the Confucian era in China, indeed perhaps even to preliterate societies.[1] A lengthy discourse on freedom of speech through the ages is beyond the scope of this book. Some familiarity with the concept as it was understood during the colonial period and the British experience that so influenced the Founders is, however, essential to understanding the various legal doctrines presented in subsequent chapters.

## Speech as *the* American Freedom?

An often repeated story tells of nineteenth-century statesman Daniel Webster who, when asked which of the many freedoms enjoyed by Americans is most important, unhesitatingly replied that it must be freedom of speech. If stripped of all other freedoms, his reasoning went, this freedom is the one he could use to win each of the others back. Along these lines, it is worth remembering also that when FDR delivered his famous "four freedoms" speech to the Congress in 1941, the

---

[1]Douglas Fraleigh and Joseph Tuman, *Freedom of Speech in the Marketplace of Ideas* (New York: St. Martin's), 1997, chap. 2.

first of the "essential human freedoms" he felt all world citizens should be granted was freedom of speech.

Perhaps we should not carry this romance with free speech too far. The Founding Fathers have often had attributed to them the belief that freedom of speech was surely the most important of all the principles articulated in the Bill of Rights; after all, they did put it in the *First* Amendment. The facts get in the way of this assertion, however. That which we now call the First Amendment was actually submitted as amendment number three in the Bill of Rights. The first two amendments—one dealing with apportionment of seats in the House of Representatives and the other prohibiting members of Congress from granting themselves a raise in salary that would take effect before the next election—failed to win approval. Even if the "firstness" of the First Amendment is a historic accident rather than a symbol of the Founders' priorities, the wording of that constitutional provision seems to suggest that issues of freedom of speech and press were indeed very special to the document's drafters. The First Amendment is written as an absolute promise that Congress shall make *no* law abridging the freedoms enumerated within. Unlike the wording of many other nations' analogous guarantees and those in many state constitutions, there is no requirement that citizens behave "responsibly" to enjoy these rights. Think, too, of some of the other guarantees provided in the Bill of Rights. In the Fourth Amendment, for example, we learn that we are free only from "unreasonable" searches and seizures. The Fifth Amendment warns that our property, our liberty, and even our life can be taken away from us as long as the government follows an unarticulated set of rules that together constitute "due process." The Eighth Amendment does not, of course, protect us from any and all kinds of punishment, but only from the "cruel and unusual" ones; that same amendment also tells us that if we are suspected of a crime, we may be required to pay any amount of bail short of "excessive" should we wish to avoid staying in jail until our trial date.

A claimed reverence for freedom of speech does seem to be one of the most defining characteristics of our nation, even as compared with other Western style democracies. (I say "claimed" reverence because Americans are also, paradoxically, notoriously disconnected from this freedom; the majority of citizens do not bother to vote, and far fewer get actively involved in the political process.) In the United States, for example, the existence of a Freedom of Information Act makes it more difficult for the government to withhold information from its citizens than is the case in Great Britain, which has an Official Secrets Act. For better or worse, the United States is very unusual in the degree to which it tolerates hate speech. Whereas some nations (such as India) have followed the American model of libel law that makes it very difficult for government officials to sue for defamation, both Canada and England have rejected it. The Canadian Supreme Court has embraced a theory, resoundingly rejected by the U.S. judiciary, of sexually oriented speech as a civil rights violation.

If participation in a system of freedom of expression is so much a part of what it means to be American, it behooves us to know something about the origins of that freedom. The discussion of that history is broken down into two time periods. The first covers the period from Europeans' arrival in the Americas up through World War I. Then the story is carried forward from that era—when the Supreme Court first began to give some guidance as to the meaning of the First Amendment—to the present.

## Freedom of Speech from the Colonial Period through World War I

Ask any school child in the U.S. why groups of British, Spanish, and other nationalities made the arduous journey across the Atlantic in the 1500s and beyond, and you will hear a tale of courageous and oppressed minorities seeking political and religious freedom. Certainly there is more than a kernel of truth to this assessment, although more mundane commercial interests also played a large part. Still, most of the individual groups of settlers were rather homogeneous, especially in terms of their religious preferences. Thus, it is not surprising that many of these groups, once settled in what were to become the Americas, established communities every bit as inhospitable to those with differing views as were the regimes they fled.

The Puritans who settled the Massachusetts Bay Colony were not especially noted for tolerance of diverse views. Banishments, excommunication, public whippings, and mutilations were common punishments for speaking out against the faith or against the colonies' government. Similarly harsh sanctions were often imposed in Connecticut and throughout New England. Governor Dale's Code governing Virginia as of 1610, for example, established the death penalty for anyone who spoke out against the tenets of Christian faith. Even the most tolerant of the colonies seem rather intolerant by today's standards in that freedom of religious expression was generally granted only to professed Christians.

Concerning the early colonists' respect for the working press, consider that the very first newspaper in the New World, Benjamin Harris's *Publick Occurrences Both Foreign and Domestic,* was shut down in Massachusetts after its very first issue was printed. When James Franklin's *New England Courant* published an article critical of the colony's government, he was promptly jailed (during which time his younger brother Benjamin took over the paper).

To be fair, there is some evidence of increasing tolerance for dissenting views during the colonial period. Even as early as the 1600s, there was a trend toward treating those judged guilty of seditious libel (i.e., criticizing the government) more and more leniently. Such punishments as physical violence (ear cropping, breaking arms and legs, tongue boring, and whipping) and public humiliation (use of the pillory or the stocks, or simply forcing the accused to recant publicly and beg for forgiveness) gave way over time to such sanctions as fines or the required posting of a bond that would be forfeitable only in the event of further transgressions.[2]

---

[2]Larry D. Eldridge, *A Distant Heritage: The Growth of Free Speech in Early America* (New York: New York University Press, 1994).

Probably the most dramatic example of how strongly at least some of the colonists felt towards freedom of the press was the seditious libel prosecution in the 1730s of *New York Weekly Journal* publisher John Peter Zenger, who had been imprisoned for several months prior to his trial for publishing statements highly critical of the colony's governor, William Crosby. During this era, truth was not an accepted defense to the charge of sedition. Indeed, the logic of the day suggested that, because the purpose of such laws was to avoid inflaming the passions of the people against the King and his governors, truthful criticisms would be all the more dangerous.

Andrew Hamilton, who made the closing arguments on behalf of Zenger, openly invited the jury to ignore the letter of the law and to find on behalf of Zenger precisely because he had not printed any substantial untruths. The jury did indeed acquit Zenger, to the delight of those assembled in the courtroom.

The Founders would not have been able to muster the necessary votes to ensure the Constitution's adoption had they not assured their constituents that a Bill of Rights would be added. The drafting of the First Amendment was characterized by much difference of opinion concerning whether the individual states should be enjoined from abridging citizens' freedom of expression or whether the proscription would apply only to the newly formed federal government. The latter view prevailed; thus, the Amendment was phrased in terms of what *Congress* shall not do. Historians of the period point out also that it is not entirely clear what "freedom of speech" and "freedom of the press" meant to the drafters. Were citizens being promised freedom from any and all postpublication sanctions for communicative acts, or were they merely being assured that they would not be subject to **prior restraint,** to prepublication censorship? A later section of this chapter explores the issue of prior restraint in more detail.

Despite the First Amendment's strong wording, it took a rather short amount of time for the new Congress to enact laws that abridged freedom of speech. France and England were at war, and fears ran high that the United States would be drawn into the conflict. Congress passed and President Adams signed the **Alien and Sedition Acts.** Collectively, these Acts gave the government increased powers to detain and deport noncitizens and criminalized the dissemination of some kinds of criticisms of that government. The following are excerpts from the Sedition Act.

# The Sedition Act of 1798

If any persons shall unlawfully combine or conspire together, with intent to oppose any measure or measures of the government of the United States, and if any person or persons shall counsel, advise or attempt to procure any insurrection, riot, unlawful assembly, or combination, he or she shall be deemed guilty of a high misdemeanor.

If any person shall write, print, utter, or shall cause or procure to be written, printed, uttered, or published any false, scandalous and malicious writing or writings against the government of the United States, or either house of the Congress, or the President, with intent to defame or to bring them…into contempt or disrepute, or to excite against them the hatred of the good people of the United States, or to stir up sedition within the United States for opposing or resisting any law of the United States, or any act of the President of the United States, then such person shall be punished.

Persons convicted under the Sedition Act could be fined heavily and imprisoned for up to five years. There were over a dozen prosecutions under the law, several directed against editors of the leading opposition newspapers of the day. Two lessons can be culled from the Sedition Act. First, the Act compels us to remember that the same Founders who had voted for the Bill of Rights also convinced themselves of the need to stifle political speech. Second, the Act was a strategic failure in that those jailed for violating it became folk heroes; moreover, the demise of the Federalists resulted in large part from popular animosity toward that party's support of the Act.

The period between 1801 (when the Sedition Act expired) and 1917 (when Congress passed the Espionage Act, discussed below) is characterized by a lack of major developments in First Amendment jurisprudence (even though the Supreme Court handed down dozens of decisions affecting the act of communication). Certainly there was much censorship in the Civil War era, especially directed against those speaking out against slavery. Then, too, the latter portion of the nineteenth century required the courts to deal repeatedly with the issue of obscenity in response to Congressional actions that, among other things, prohibited the use of the mails to send sexually oriented matter. By and large, at least with respect to

 # Things to Remember

### THE COLONIAL EXPERIENCE FORWARD

- The early colonial experience included much political and religious intolerance.
- The Zenger jury concluded that true speech should not be punished.
- The Founders chose not to apply the First Amendment to the individual states.
- For at least some of the Founders, freedom of speech and freedom of the press probably only meant freedom from prior restraint.
- That the First Amendment *is* first in the Bill of Rights is merely a coincidence.
- Despite the First Amendment, Congress quickly enacted the Sedition Act.

definitive Supreme Court interpretations of the First Amendment, these "forgotten years"[3] were not a time of much doctrinal advance and also not the focus of much scholarship. Therefore, a discussion of the Court's First Amendment doctrine as it developed in the World War I era and beyond is appropriate.

## Freedom of Speech Doctrine Emerges

In March 1993, a brutal triple murder was committed in Silver Spring, Maryland, a suburb of Washington, D.C. James Perry killed Mildred Horn, her eight-year-old quadriplegic son Trevor, and Trevor's nurse, Janice Saunders, by shooting Mildred Horn and Saunders through the eyes and by strangling the boy. Perry acted as a contract killer hired by Ms. Horn's ex-husband. After Perry was successfully prosecuted, the victims' families brought suit in federal court against the publisher of a book called *Hit Man* that Perry apparently consulted in planning his crime. A three-judge panel of the Court of Appeals for the Fourth Circuit held against the publisher in late 1997, finding that the book was little more than a blueprint for homicide that inarguably aided and abetted Perry in the commission of his heinous offenses.[4]

Is such a ruling consistent with the First Amendment? What of a "copycat" terrorist who hones his or her craft by taking careful notes from detailed journalistic explanations as to how pipe bombs are constructed (after the Centennial Olympic Park bombing in Atlanta) or how fertilizer can be used as a powerfully destructive explosive (as in the Oklahoma City case)? Might victims' families be permitted to win damages from the likes of CNN? Consider also that many talented mystery writers include in their stories much factual information that can similarly aid in the commission of future crimes.

The process of seeking answers to these questions is complicated and requires that we develop an understanding of the Supreme Court's doctrine concerning when speech that might incite others to commit crimes can itself be criminalized. This doctrine began to emerge in the World War I era and continued through the McCarthy period and beyond. It is not an exaggeration to say that the Court used the cases we discuss here to explain what the First Amendment means.

In the pages that follow you will learn much about antiwar activists, anarchists, and political dissidents of many persuasions. These early cases did not

---

[3]David M. Rabban, "The First Amendment in Its Forgotten Years," 90 *Yale Law Journal* 514 (1981).

[4]*Rice v. Paladin Enterprises,* 128 F.3d 233 (4th Cir. 1997). The Supreme Court, in April 1998, refused to hear the appeal, thus setting the stage for a possible trial in the case. In May 1999, however, the parties entered an out-of-court settlement involving a multimillion dollar payment to the plaintiffs and the turning over to them of all the publisher's remaining copies of *Hit Man*.

typically involve the mass media. Much of the doctrine that emerged from these cases, however, has laid the foundation for contemporary applications of the First Amendment in a wide variety of circumstances, from regulation of advertising to broadcast station licensing.

## The Clear and Present Danger Test: *Schenck v. United States*

The United States had entered into the "war to end all wars," which would later be known as World War I. Almost without exception, even the freest of nations curtail the amount of liberty enjoyed by their citizens the moment war is declared. The United States in 1917 certainly manifested this tendency when Congress passed the Espionage Act (amended in 1918). Not surprisingly, the Act forbade any attempt to cause insubordination among the military or in any way to obstruct the draft. It also criminalized any speech or writing deemed "disloyal, profane, scurrilous, or abusive" of "the form of government of the United States…or the flag." The penalty for violating the law could be as severe as twenty years' imprisonment.

Charles Schenck, the general secretary of the Socialist Party, was convicted under the Espionage Act for sending leaflets to young men who had been called and accepted for military service, imploring them to resist the draft and to recognize that draftees are little more than slaves. Writing for a unanimous Supreme Court, Justice Holmes upheld Schenck's conviction. The only acceptable justification for suppressing political speech, Justice Holmes concluded, is if the speaker's words "are used in such circumstances and are of such a nature as to create a clear and present danger that they will bring about the substantive evils that Congress has a right to prevent."[5] Holmes' opinion in *Schenck*—also remembered for having added to the lexicon the admonition that freedom of speech, although important, does not protect us from "falsely shouting fire in a crowded theatre"—was the birth of the "clear and present danger" test for measuring the scope of First Amendment freedoms. Although the test's first appearance is in the context of an opinion *upholding* a criminal conviction for engaging in dissident speech, in later years the test evolved so as to emphasize that the state's power to punish such speech is very limited. The Supreme Court has cited *Schenck*'s famous phrase dozens of times in adjudicating First Amendment issues ranging from leased access channels on cable TV systems and FCC broadcast indecency standards to regulation of advertising and campaign finance reform.

## The Marketplace of Ideas: *Abrams v. United States*

A few months after *Schenck,* the Supreme Court upheld another Espionage Act conviction. In this instance, however, Justice Holmes (joined by Justice Brandeis) dissented and in so doing gave birth to a metaphor more influential than any other

---

[5]*Schenck v. United States,* 249 U.S. 47 (1919).

in the history of First Amendment jurisprudence. At issue again were antiwar leaflets, this time printed by Jacob Abrams and four other Russian nationals living in the U.S. and distributed by such means as dropping them out of an office building window. Writing for a seven-person majority, Justice Clarke found that the intent of the offending literature was "to persuade the persons to whom it was addressed to turn a deaf ear to patriotic appeals in behalf of the Government of the United States, and to cease to render it assistance in the prosecution of the war."[6]

Justices Holmes and Brandeis expressed dismay for the defendants being sentenced to twenty years in jail "for the publishing of two leaflets that [they] have as much right to publish as the government has to publish the Constitution of the United States now vainly invoked by them." For them, the defendants' intent was to express support for the Russian Revolution, not to hinder the U.S. war effort. The government's prosecution, the dissenters argued, did not seem aimed at the ends sought by the defendants, but rather at their political ideology itself. They argued that such government actions, designed to "sweep away all opposition," ignore the "theory of our Constitution" that "the best test of truth is the power of [a] thought to get itself accepted in the competition of the market."[7]

The "marketplace of ideas" metaphor has served as a rationale for dozens of Supreme Court and hundreds of lower court decisions. As expressed by Justice Holmes, it seems to be an instrumental value, one whose good comes from its likelihood to help the truth emerge. It can also be viewed as a good in and of itself. It has often seemed to be, for example, a principle the FCC has claimed to embrace over the years, that a multitude of voices speaking over broadcast and cable channels is a desirable thing.

### Not Only Congress, but the States, Too: *Gitlow v. New York*

The First Amendment, it will be recalled, tells only the *federal* government (indeed, only Congress) that it may not abridge freedom of speech and freedom of the press. This decision was a conscious one on the part of the drafters, who considered and rejected an alternate phrasing that would have restricted the power of each individual state government as well. In 1925, 134 years after the formal adoption of the Bill of Rights, the Supreme Court somewhat unceremoniously held that the First Amendment bars the states, too, from abridging Americans' freedom of expression. Justice Sanford accomplished this change in one sentence. "For present purposes we may and do assume," he said, "that freedom of speech and of the press—which are protected by the First Amendment from abridgment by Congress—are among the fundamental personal rights and 'liberties' protected by the due process clause of the Fourteenth Amendment from impairment by the States."[8]

---

[6]*Abrams v. United States,* 250 U.S. 616 (1919).

[7]*Abrams v. United States,* 250 U.S. 620–1, 629–30 (1919).

[8]*Gitlow v. New York,* 268 U.S. 652 (1925).

The context was the Supreme Court's upholding Benjamin Gitlow's conviction, under New York State's Criminal Anarchy statute, for having written a "Left-Wing Manifesto" seeming to advocate the government's overthrow, by violent means if necessary. The majority opinion also posits a distinction between "abstract doctrine" or "academic discussion," which would presumably be protected by the First Amendment, and "language advocating, advising, or teaching the overthrow of organized government by unlawful means," which the New York law appropriately prohibited. The distinction was one that Justices Holmes and Brandeis found unacceptable. Gitlow was not trying to "induce an uprising against government at once"; at most he sought such action "at some indefinite time in the future." The dissenters thus emphasized that a "clear and present danger" must in fact be *present*.

## The "More Speech" Prescription: *Whitney v. California*

Two years after the *Gitlow* decision made clear that the First Amendment applied not only to federal but also state infringements on free speech, another criminal syndicalism prosecution, this time from the other coast, was before the Supreme Court.[9] Anita Whitney, who coincidentally was the niece of former Supreme Court Justice Stephen Field, had been an active member of the Communist Labor Party in California. The immediate impetus for her prosecution seems to have been her attendance at the Party's organizing convention where, although she herself argued for a more moderate stance, the gathered delegates voted their full allegiance to the goal of an international workers' revolution.

The Supreme Court unanimously upheld Whitney's conviction under the state law, in large part owing to her attorneys' having failed to raise timely the federal constitutional issue that might have led to her vindication: whether her participation at the Party convention constituted a "clear and present danger" to the state. Thus, even Justice Brandeis's stirring words from the case were part of a concurring rather than dissenting opinion:

> No danger flowing from speech can be deemed clear and present unless the incidence of the evil apprehended is so imminent that it may befall before there is opportunity for full discussion. If there be time to expose through discussion the falsehood and fallacies, to avert the evil by the processes of education, *the remedy to be applied is more speech, not enforced silence.* (emphasis added)

The emphasized phrase carries enormous implications for First Amendment jurisprudence. Rather than prohibiting political, religious, or similar charitable groups from soliciting donations in airports, the "more speech, not enforced silence" prescription argues instead for the use of prominently placed signs and

---

[9]*Whitney v. California,* 274 U.S. 357 (1927).

frequently made announcements to the effect that the solicitors are acting on their own behalf only, not with the approval of the airport's governing authority. Such additional speech might even caution the public to donate only to reputable organizations, to say "no" if in doubt. The *Whitney* rationale also seems to argue for permitting advertisers to use clever graphics and production techniques so as to make their print ads look almost like news articles and their infomercials resemble television interview programs, just as long as some additional speech explicitly alerting consumers that they are in fact advertisements is required. That same rationale suggests that attorneys who advertise that they will take cases on a contingency fee basis—that clients "pay us nothing unless we win"—make clear somewhere in their ads details of the promise. Does it apply only to the lawyers' own fees, or also to reimbursement of out-of-pocket expenses such as court filing fees? In fact, courts and regulating agencies have used the *Whitney* rationale in all these kinds of situations and more.

## The Smith Act Cases

The Cold War intensified in the late 1940s and throughout the 1950s. The atrocities that accompanied Joseph Stalin's reign began to come to light. Winston Churchill's famous "Iron Curtain" speech warned the free world that communism could be every bit as threatening as was fascism. So it was that a statute passed by Congress in 1940 out of fear that radical right-wing politics could destroy the American way of life was now applied to the political left. The Alien Registration Act, popularly known as the Smith Act, criminalized advocacy of the government's overthrow as well as knowingly becoming part of a group whose members embraced such a goal. Eugene Dennis, the secretary general of the American Communist Party, along with several other Party officials, was prosecuted under this Act. In upholding their convictions, Chief Justice Vinson wrote that the Smith Act was constitutional because it "is directed at advocacy, not discussion," that the clear and present danger test "cannot mean that before the Government may act, it must wait until the *putsch* is about to be executed, the plans have been laid and the signal is awaited." Rather, Vinson adopted the interpretation suggested by a lower court: "In each case [courts must decide] whether the gravity of the evil, discounted by its improbability, justifies such invasion of free speech as is necessary to avoid the danger."[10] There is always some competing interest to be balanced against free speech claims, Vinson was telling us, and one can hardly imagine a more serious counterweight than the fear that the government might be violently overthrown. Over the years, courts have used this test to determine whether the First Amendment was violated by such things as a judge's gag rule,[11] a state uni-

---

[10]*Dennis v. United States,* 341 U.S. 494 (1951).

[11]*Nebraska Press Association v. Stuart,* 427 U.S. 539 (1976).

versity's refusal to recognize its campus gay student organization,[12] and a public school district's regulation of male students' hair length.[13]

Whereas *Dennis* turned on the distinction between "advocacy" of revolution and mere "discussion" of revolution, six years later the Court shifted the line a bit, holding that advocacy of abstract doctrine would be permissible, but not advocacy of action. The occasion was the justices' reviewing the Smith Act convictions of fourteen leftists from California.[14] The government's case against the accused consisted primarily of pointing to their having assumed leadership positions within the Communist Party and their having written some articles in *The Daily Worker,* the Party's newspaper. This time, however, the Court overturned the convictions. Justice Harlan's opinion criticized the lower court for having assumed that "advocacy, irrespective of its tendency to generate action, is punishable." Such an interpretation of the Act is far too broad, Harlan concluded. Instead, the crucial distinction should be that "those to whom the advocacy is addressed must be urged to do something, now or in the future, rather than merely to believe in something."

The *Yates* doctrine was quite an advance over previous doctrine in terms of the amount of political speech it protected. The Court, however, had not yet completed its rewriting of the clear and present danger test. That task would have to wait another dozen years.

## The *Brandenburg* Test: Imminent Lawless Action

At a Ku Klux Klan rally on a farm in Hamilton County, Ohio, Klan leader Clarence Brandenburg told his handful of supporters that "we're not a revengent organization, but if our President, our Congress, our Supreme Court, continues to suppress the white, Caucasian race, it's possible that there might have to be some revengeance taken." Participants were also overheard to offer such prescriptions for society's ills as "burying the Niggers" and "sending the Jews back to Israel." Brandenburg was convicted of violating Ohio's Criminal Syndicalism statute. The Supreme Court's unanimous decision overturning that conviction established the test that to this day still determines when political speech is protected by the First Amendment. The test, appearing in a short *per curiam* opinion, says that "the constitutional guarantees of free speech and free press do not permit a State to forbid or proscribe advocacy of the use of force or of law violation except where such advocacy is directed to inciting or producing imminent lawless action and is likely to incite or produce such action."[15]

---

[12]*Gay Lib v. University of Missouri,* 558 F.2d 848 (8th Cir. 1977).

[13]*Sherling v. Townley,* 464 F.2d 587 (5th Cir. 1972).

[14]*Yates v. United States,* 354 U.S. 298 (1957).

[15]*Brandenburg v. Ohio,* 395 U.S. 444, 447 (1969).

Notice that the test has elements of both content and context. As to content, the Court emphasizes that only very specific kinds of advocacy may be prohibited. The "imminence" requirement is a forceful restatement of the earlier "clear and *present*" danger test. We know from later decisions that the Court takes the imminence requirement very seriously. In 1973, for example, a unanimous Court overturned a Vietnam War protester's incitement conviction in large part because he told his cohorts, in response to the police having set up barricades, that they would all "take the fucking street *later.*" The Court's interpretation of this sentence was that "at best the statement could be taken as counsel for present moderation" and that "at worst it amounted to nothing more than advocacy of illegal action *at some indefinite future time.*"[16]

The *Brandenburg* test's contextual elements are apparent from the demand that words must be *likely to* result in the speaker's desired lawbreaking. Speakers must be addressing an audience sufficiently sympathetic to their cause and sufficiently aroused to action that imminent illegality is, in fact, a likely outcome of their advocacy. This requirement leads us back to the *Hit Man* case introduced earlier in this chapter. The decision by the Sixth Circuit appellate panel is quite an anomaly, the first time a mass-distributed book has ever been held to constitute "incitement" under the *Brandenburg* test. More typically, courts find that authors of printed texts, removed from their eventual readers by both time and space, are incapable of producing *imminent* lawless action.[17]

On rare occasions, however, print media have been held liable because of the actions taken by readers. The leading case is an Eleventh Circuit decision involving an ad placed in *Soldier of Fortune* magazine by the aptly named Michael Savage, offering himself as a "gun for hire," a "professional mercenary" willing to consider "all jobs." Atlanta resident Bruce Gastwirth contacted Savage for help in murdering his business partner, which resulted soon thereafter in the contract killing of Richard Braun and the wounding of his son. By a 2–1 vote, the appellate court upheld a multimillion dollar damages award on the grounds that the magazine had created a "clearly identifiable, unreasonable risk of harm to the public."[18] The majority distinguished the facts of the case from an earlier ruling also involving a personal ad placed in the same magazine that had similarly resulted in a contract killing. The ad in the earlier case was more ambiguously worded, offering the services of a group of "ex-Marines" willing to engage in "high risk assignments."[19]

---

[16]*Hess v. Indiana,* 414 U.S. 105, 108 (1973) (emphasis added).

[17]*Davidson v. Time Warner, Inc.,* 1997 U.S. Dist. LEXIS 21559, 25 *Media Law Rptr.* 1705 (S.D. Tex. 1997); *Herceg v. Hustler Magazine,* 814 F.2d 1020 (5th Cir. 1987); *Olivia N. v. NBC,* 178 Cal. Rptr. 888 (Ct. App. 1981); *McCollum v. CBS, Inc.,* 249 Cal. Rptr. 187 (Ct. App. 1988); *Watters v. TSR, Inc.,* 715 F. Supp. 819 (W.D. Ky. 1989).

[18]*Braun v. Soldier of Fortune* Magazine, 968 F.2d 1110 (11th Cir. 1992).

[19]*Eimann v. Soldier of Fortune Magazine,* 880 F.2d 830 (5th Cir. 1989).

Things to Remember

---

**EVOLUTION OF FIRST AMENDMENT DOCTRINE**

- The Court's First Amendment doctrine emerged from cases involving incitement to illegal action.
- The following cases involved the Espionage Act, the later Smith Act, or various state criminal syndicalism laws.
  - *Schenck v. United States:*
    Birth of the clear and present danger test.
    Falsely shouting fire in a crowded theater metaphor.
  - *Abrams v. United States:*
    Marketplace of ideas.
  - *Gitlow v. New York:*
    First Amendment now applies to the states, too.
    Holmes's dissent says that "every idea is an incitement."
  - *Whitney v. California:*
    Proper remedy to bad speech is more speech, not enforced silence.
  - *Dennis v. United States:*
    "The gravity of the evil discounted by its improbability."
    Actual advocacy versus "mere discussion."
  - *Yates v. United States:*
    Advocacy of action versus advocacy of abstract doctrine.
  - *Brandenburg v. Ohio:*
    Advocacy of "imminent lawless action."
    Must also be "likely to produce such action."

---

## Theories of First Amendment Adjudication

As we have seen, the Supreme Court's First Amendment jurisprudence began in earnest in the World War I era. The cases that produced this body of case law, culminating in the *Brandenburg* test, generally have involved criminal defendants whose words were uttered so as to incite presumably sympathetic listeners to engage in conduct that itself would likely be illegal. Such a scenario describes only one of many conflicts raising First Amendment issues. Most of the kinds of speech that define the scope of the chapters in this book—such as libel, invasion of privacy, covering the courts, and copyright and trademark infringements—do not involve speakers trying to incite others to take specific actions. It is no surprise, then, that there have been many different approaches to First Amendment litigation over the years. Indeed, neither the Supreme Court nor the many philosophers, political scientists, communication scholars, and law professors who have written lengthy essays on the topic have reached consensus as to what freedom of speech should include or when free speech claims should prevail over competing interests. In this section, several of the competing theories of First Amendment adjudication are presented.

### Free Speech as the Absence of Prior Restraint?

Dating back at least to the sixteenth century, the preferred method of controlling the press in England had been to prevent offensive tracts from ever being published (rather than punishing the authors or the publishers after the fact). Either the Crown, the Church, or both controlled the printed word by such means as licensing only a tiny group of publishing companies and requiring printers to post sizable monetary bonds that would be forfeited if their houses were ever to publish offensive materials.

The prevailing wisdom around the time of the American Revolution was that freedom of the press referred only to the absence of such prior restraints on the act of communication. One of the Founders' contemporaries was the British jurist William Blackstone. James Madison, Thomas Jefferson, John Adams, and the others were quite familiar with Blackstone's *Commentaries on the Law of England,* published in 1769, which argued that the "liberty of speech...consists in laying no previous restraints upon publications, and not in freedom from censure for criminal matter when published."

As Steven Helle of the University of Illinois points out, one can argue both ends against the middle in a futile attempt to determine exactly what the Founders themselves meant by "freedom of speech" and "freedom of the press." To be sure, Blackstone's definition of communication law was the prevailing one at the time. Had the Framers adopted that definition as their own, or does their very act of crafting the First Amendment mean that they intended something more? Why enumerate protections for conduct already presumed to be protected? Then, too, scholars have come down on both sides of the issue as to what should be made of Congress's having passed the Alien and Sedition Acts so soon after approving the First Amendment. Does the enactment of those oppressive laws count as evidence that the Framers saw such after-the-fact punishments as consistent with the First Amendment, thus suggesting that the latter only protected against prior restraints? Then again, if the common wisdom was that the First Amendment protected only against prior restraints on communication, why the need for a law granting the government the "right" to prosecute seditious libels. Should not such a right be presumed?[20]

Whatever the Framers may have meant by "freedom of the press," the more modern view, embraced by the U.S. Supreme Court at least since the 1930s, is that the First Amendment protects against more than prior restraints, but that prior

---

[20]Steven Helle, "Prior Restraint," in *Communication and the Law,* ed. W. Wat Hopkins (Northport, Ala: Vision Press, 2000), 52–53.

restraints are so especially odious that they carry with them "a heavy presumption against [their own] constitutional validity."[21] Writing in 1955, Thomas Emerson, a Yale law professor, offered the following rationales for treating prior restraints with a special measure of skepticism:[22]

- Whereas after-the-fact ("*post facto*") punishments are narrowly targeted at individual publications, prior restraints affect *all* publications.
- Even if a publisher is eventually punished for his or her writings, at least those writings will have entered the "marketplace of ideas"; prior restraints, on the other hand, deprive the citizenry of the ideas.
- Timing is sometimes very important to a publisher, but prior restraints place in the government's hands the power to decide not only if, but also *when,* a work will reach the public.
- As the adage "It is easier to beg forgiveness than request permission" suggests, the very existence of a mechanism for imposing prior restraints virtually ensures that censorship will be imposed, whereas the expense and inconvenience of forcing a publisher to face trial may make it less likely that after-the-fact punishments will be imposed.

The Supreme Court's modern prior restraint doctrine is usually traced to a 1931 decision, *Near v. Minnesota*.[23] Jay Near, publisher of the controversial *Saturday Press,* was prosecuted as a "public nuisance" for having published "malicious, scandalous, and defamatory articles" about the mayor of Minneapolis and other public officials as well as the "Jewish race" in general. The case was one of prior restraint because the punishment meted out was an injunction that had the effect of closing down the newspaper. In holding the injunction unconstitutional, the Court allowed that freedom from prior restraints is not "absolutely unlimited," but it also made clear that such governmental censorship would be upheld "only in exceptional cases."

Perhaps the most famous case of prior restraint ever to be decided by the Supreme Court involved the Pentagon Papers, classified government documents leaked to the *Washington Post* and the *New York Times* that showed some of the ways the government misled us about its participation in the Vietnam War.[24] After two conflicting federal appellate decisions were handed down—one enjoining the *New York Times* from publishing the papers, the other refusing to enjoin the *Post*—the Supreme Court granted expedited review and produced a somewhat confusing

---

[21]*Bantam Books v. Sullivan,* 372 U.S. 58, 70 (1963).

[22]Thomas Emerson, "The Doctrine of Prior Restraint," 20 *Law and Contemporary Problems* 648 (1955).

[23]283 U.S. 697 (1931).

[24]*New York Times v. United States,* 403 U.S. 713 (1971).

6–3 decision rejecting the government's claim that publication of the papers posed a serious threat to the national security.

The majority's official pronouncement in the case was a surprisingly brief *per curiam* opinion, the thrust of which was that the government had not met the "heavy burden" of proof necessary to sustain a prior restraint on speech. The opinion does not, however, indicate exactly what the burden of proof should be or why in this case the government had failed to meet it.

Readers would have to make careful analyses of the nine separate signed opinions by the justices to make sense of the Pentagon Papers case. Two of the justices in the majority (Black and Douglas) espoused a rather absolutist view of the matter, suggesting that the government might never be able to justify a prior restraint on speech.

Each of the other justices in the Pentagon Papers majority allowed that there might be circumstances in which prior restraints are permissible. Justice Stewart offered a description of the government's burden of proof that has been cited dozens of times since by lower courts. Prior restraints, Stewart suggested, should be permitted only when the state can demonstrate that publication will cause "direct, immediate, and irreparable damage."

In the late 1970s, the government had occasion to argue that such serious harm would result if the *Progressive* magazine were permitted to publish an article about the hydrogen bomb. The thesis of the article was that Americans were being lulled into a false sense of security about the unlikelihood of nuclear disaster. The article's author, whose training in the hard sciences was limited to a bachelor's degree, was able to piece together from readily available public documents a blueprint for constructing a working nuclear device. Federal District Judge Robert Warren issued a restraining order against the magazine.[25] Although he admitted that "cherished First Amendment rights" were at stake, he feared that ruling for the magazine "could pave the way for thermonuclear annihilation for us all." The magazine appealed Judge Warren's ruling to the Seventh Circuit Court of Appeals in Chicago, which held oral arguments on the case in September 1979. The judges' decision was never learned, however; while the case was pending, a handful of newspapers in other venues published essays highly similar to the one at issue in the case. The government promptly dropped its case against the *Progressive,* which went to press with its hydrogen bomb piece in November, seven months later than it had planned.

In 1990, the Supreme Court refused to hear a prior restraint controversy involving Panamanian dictator Manuel Noriega, who had been seized by U.S. authorities and jailed in Miami on drug trafficking charges. CNN had somehow obtained copies of tape-recorded conversations between Noriega and his attorneys. Noriega obtained an injunction, prohibiting the cable network from airing the tapes and demanding that they be turned over to U.S. District Judge William

---

[25]*United States v. The Progressive,* 467 F. Supp. 990 (W.D. Wis. 1979).

Hoeveler for review.[26] The case was complicated by CNN's having disobeyed the judge's order. The network aired some tapes, and withheld all the tapes from Hoeveler for ten days.

Although it is clear that the government takes on a heavy burden of proof when it imposes a prior restraint, it is not always clear what kinds of governmental actions count as prior restraints. For example, government employees may be required to sign documents promising never to reveal certain information they learn on the job, or they may have any proposed publications cleared through their employers. The most celebrated cases involving such prepublication clearance agreements have involved employees of the Central Intelligence Agency. The courts have upheld the use of such agreements and have avoided the First Amendment issues involved by treating the disputes as straightforward "breach of contract" claims.[27] Also, as we see in Chapter 11's discussion of obscenity law, the Supreme Court has upheld the government's confiscation of a convicted pornographer's entire inventory.[28] While this would seem to be a classic prior restraint akin to that suffered by Minnesota publisher Jay Near—publish a few offensive things and you will not be permitted to publish at all in the future—the Court held that it was not a restraint on speech. All the government had done was to seize the defendant's property; it had not actually enjoined him from selling sexually oriented films and magazines in the future.

Finally, it is important to note that the Supreme Court, in a 1988 decision, made clear that the government's burden is greatly diminished when it imposes a prior restraint on a newspaper published by public high school students.[29] The case involved *Spectrum,* the student newspaper from Hazelwood East High School in a St. Louis, Missouri suburb. When the school administration killed a couple of stories— one on student pregnancy, the other on coping with divorce—the student-editor sued the school. In a 5–3 ruling, the Court held that public schools may exercise editorial control over student publications that "may fairly be characterized as part of the school curriculum,…so long as their actions are reasonably related to legitimate pedagogical concerns." In 1999, a three-judge panel of the Sixth Circuit Court of Appeals caused quite a stir when it applied the *Hazelwood* reasoning to the university setting, upholding the actions of a Kentucky State University administrator who confiscated all copies of the school's yearbook for such infractions as failing to use the school's traditional official gold and green colors on the cover. In a later *en banc* ruling, however, the same court overturned itself, making clear that the *Hazelwood* decision's precedential value should be limited to the secondary school setting.[30]

---

[26]*United States v. Noriega,* 752 F. Supp. 1045 (S.D. Fla. 1990).

[27]*United States v. Marchetti,* 466 F.2d 1309 (4th Cir. 1972); *Knopf v. Colby,* 509 F.2d 1362 (4th Cir. 1975); *United States v. Snepp,* 444 U.S. 507 (1980).

[28]*Alexander v. United States,* 509 U.S. 544 (1993).

[29]*Hazelwood v. Kuhlmeier,* 484 U.S. 260 (1988).

[30]*Kincaid v. Gibson,* 191 F.3d 719 (6th Cir. 1999).

## First Amendment Absolutism

Recall the first five words of the First Amendment: "Congress shall make no law," it tells us, before enumerating the kinds of rights (including freedom of speech and freedom of the press) that the government may not abridge. The wording is absolute. It is not surprising, then, that some jurists and scholars have been known as First Amendment absolutists. Supreme Court Justice Hugo Black is probably most often associated with absolutist theory. When the Founders drafted the First Amendment, Black said, "they knew what they were talking about." They consciously intended to prevent the government from telling its citizens "what they should believe or say or publish." That the First Amendment says "no law" is appropriate, he added, and "that is what I believe it means."[31]

First Amendment absolutism has obvious problems. There are numerous things one can do via speech that almost any reasonable person would agree should be illegal (see Figure 2.1). Committing perjury is one example. So, too, is bribery, as is threatening to kill another human being. One way around this problem is to decide, somewhat artificially, that certain kinds of utterances simply will not *count* as speech. This strategy has been embraced by the Supreme Court, for example, with obscenity. Obscene messages have been declared outside the bounds of First Amendment protection, period.

---

[31]Edmund Cahn, "Justice Black and First Amendment 'Absolutes': A Public Interview," 37 N.Y.U.L. REV. 549, 554 (1962).

 Figure 2.1

### Frank and Ernest

True First Amendment absolutism would seem to demand that the judge in this cartoon accept the accused's defense.

*Copyright © 1997 Thaves. Reprinted with permission.*

Another way to reconcile absolutism with practicality is to decide that the drafters of the Bill of Rights themselves had a relatively limited class of speech in mind when they used the phrase "freedom of speech." First Amendment theorist Alexander Meiklejohn is probably the best-known advocate of this approach. For Meiklejohn, "freedom of speech" refers only to political speech, speech on the kinds of matters upon which the electorate may be called to vote.[32] (In later writings, Meiklejohn softened his stance somewhat so as to include within his definition of "the political" such matters as the arts, education, and the sciences.)[33] Meiklejohnian theory posits that political speech is absolutely protected by the First Amendment, whereas other, lesser kinds of speech (advertising, for example) will find some protection in the Fifth Amendment. Engaging in such speech is seen as one of the liberties that the government may not take away without due process of law.

In recent years, Supreme Court Justice Anthony Kennedy has espoused a new kind of absolutism, what might be called "absolutism with exceptions." He argued that the First Amendment means what it says except for those categories of speech that the Court has long held fall outside the amendment's protection. Justice Kennedy most clearly articulated his theory in a case that found the Court invalidating New York State's "Son of Sam" law, which prohibited criminals from making money by writing about their wrongdoing. Laws such as this one, Justice Kennedy argued, amount to "raw censorship." For him, First Amendment adjudication should consist initially of asking whether the speech taken aim at by a particular law falls into the categorical exceptions to constitutional protection, such as knowing libels, obscenity, child pornography, and incitement to illegal action. If the speech does not fit into any of these categories, it enjoys absolute First Amendment protection.[34]

It is clear, then, that the "no" in "Congress shall make no law" is not to be taken literally. The legislative branch of government at all levels imposes a wide array of laws and regulations that may affect the act of communication. Figure 2.2 provides a necessarily simplified model of how the contemporary Supreme Court goes about determining if a specific law is constitutional.

## Access Theory

Tulane University law student Donna Bird asked the *Times-Picayune* in New Orleans to publish an announcement of her "commitment ceremony" to Ms. Leslie

---

[32]Alexander Meiklejohn, *Free Speech and Its Relation to Self-Government* (New York: Harper and Row, 1948).

[33]Alexander Meiklejohn, "The First Amendment Is an Absolute," 1961 *Supreme Court Review* 245, 255–257.

[34]*Simon & Schuster, Inc. v. Members of the New York State Crime Victims Board,* 502 U.S. 105, 128 (1991) (Kennedy, J., concurring).

Figure 2.2    *A Model of First Amendment Adjudication*

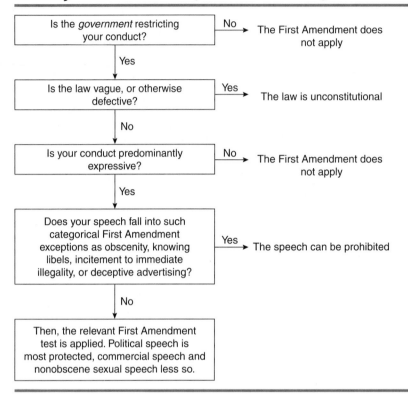

Nehring, a pediatric critical care nurse. The newspaper refused,[35] as have most but not all mainstream media outlets that have considered whether to open up their marriages and engagements pages to same-sex couples. This controversy has been repeated in numerous locales around the country in recent years, and it raises some interesting questions. Is accepting such announcements from gay males and lesbians more morally defensible than refusing them? Does it make good business sense? More directly relevant to the purview of this book, should Bird be able to force the paper to accept her announcement? (She did, in fact, seek the help of her local human relations commission, hoping it would find the newspaper to be in violation of local civil rights laws.)

Although the issue of gay commitment ceremony announcements is relatively new, the more general question as to whether the media may ever be forced to turn over column inches or broadcast airtime to outsiders has been debated for many decades. Best known among those who have argued for such compelled

---

[35]Susan Finch, "Lesbians Allege TP Bias in Commitment Policy," *Times-Picayune,* 7 Feb. 1995, p. B1.

access is Professor Jerome Barron of the George Washington University Law School. In 1967, Barron published a seminal article in the *Harvard Law Review*[36] that he later expanded into a book.[37] Barron bemoaned the concentration of media ownership, which he described as an "economic revolution" placing "with fewer and fewer persons the power to decide whatever larger and larger number shall see, hear, and read."

Access theorists have enjoyed only mixed success in the United States, depending on the specific medium involved. The print media are generally free from intrusions into their editorial discretion. Television and radio fare much differently. Section 315 of the Federal Communications Act, for example, provides a complicated array of rules and exceptions telling station managers that candidates for political office must be granted equal access to their airwaves. Then, too, in the late 1990s and in the 2000 presidential campaigns, several proposals for campaign finance reform were predicated in part on the possibility of requiring broadcast stations to donate a certain number of hours of free airtime to candidates so as to alleviate the candidates' need to hustle for donor dollars. The cable television industry is also subject to some kinds of compelled access. In many locales, the city's contract with the cable franchise requires that a small number of stations be set aside for "community access," generally made available on a first-come, first-served basis to any community groups wishing to produce programming.

Although Barron was concerned primarily with the rights of the public to use the airwaves and the print media, another access issue is the relationship among reporters, editors, and publishers. Social critic A. J. Liebling reminds us that "freedom of the press is guaranteed only to those who own one," a lesson that media employees often learn the hard way. Former *New Republic* magazine editor Michael Kelly, for example, is generally presumed to have lost that job because he wrote one too many criticisms of Vice President Al Gore, a close friend of publisher Martin Peretz.[38] Or consider the plight of reporter Marsden Epworth, who was fired from the Torrington, Connecticut, *Register Citizen* for having mentioned, in an article generally touting the paper's new Sunday edition, that many subscribers were upset by distribution problems that found them "waiting in vain for their historic first edition." Publisher Geoffrey L. Moser let it be known that his staff was not permitted to "write anything that embarrasses the Journal Register Company."[39] In the absence of a clear employment contract to the contrary, reporters and editors, like most employees in the United States, serve at the pleasure of their bosses and can be fired at any time for any reason not otherwise in violation of law.

---

[36]Jerome Barron, "Access to the Press: A New First Amendment Right," 80 *Harvard Law Review* 1641 (1967).

[37]Jerome Barron, *Freedom of Press for Whom? The Right of Access to Mass Media* (Bloomington: Indiana University Press, 1973).

[38]Paul D. Colford, "Conservative Journals Are Yukking It Up," *Los Angeles Times,* 5 Feb. 1998, p. 5.

[39]"Darts and Laurels," *Columbia Journalism Review,* May 1994, p. 23.

That their firing transgression may have been to communicate with the public is generally deemed irrelevant.

## Balancing Theories

The moment we reject absolutist positions we are necessarily in the business of balancing of some kind. Courts engage in **ad hoc balancing** when they ask, "In this particular case, which is more important, freedom of speech or the competing interest?" One party's free speech claims will then be weighed against whatever interests form the opposing side's case. The competing interest might be to protect a plaintiff's reputation, as in libel cases. It could be to preserve the peace, as in incitement prosecutions. A state may have an antiobscenity law through which it seeks to preserve a certain moral climate. As Justice Harlan put it in a McCarthy era case, First Amendment jurisprudence "always involves a balancing by the courts of the competing private and public interests at stake in the particular circumstances shown."[40]

In recent years, probably the best-known advocate of pure and simple balancing has been Duke University Professor Stanley Fish. In his provocatively titled 1994 book, *There's No Such Thing As Free Speech, and It's a Good Thing, Too,* Fish seeks to debunk what he sees as unnecessarily fancy and somewhat intellectually dishonest theories of the First Amendment. Courts engage in balancing, he writes, and we should not be upset by this revelation. "When a court invalidates legislation because it infringes on protected speech," Fish says, "it is not because the speech in question is without consequences but because the consequences have been discounted in relation to a good that is judged to outweigh them."[41]

One thing about real-world First Amendment adjudication is missing from the ad hoc balancing model: courts cheat a bit in favor of the litigants raising First Amendment claims. So important is freedom of speech in the calculus of rights Americans enjoy that courts purposely tip the scales. Judges do not simply ask, "Which interest is more important in this particular case?" Rather, they ask, "Does the antispeech litigant have a strong enough case to overcome the presumption in favor of free speech?"

This kind of inquiry is often referred to as **preferred position balancing.** The Supreme Court has used the admittedly vague phrase "preferred position" to describe freedom of speech in over a dozen decisions since the 1940s. In a concurring opinion from a 1949 decision, Justice Frankfurter dismissed it as a "mischievous phrase" that "radiates a constitutional doctrine without avowing it.... that any law touching communication is infected with presumptive invalidity."[42] Mischie-

---

[40]*Barenblatt v. United States,* 360 U.S. 109, 126 (1959).

[41]Stanley Fish, *There's No Such Thing As Free Speech, and It's a Good Thing, Too* (New York: Oxford University Press, 1994), 106.

[42]*Kovacs v. Cooper,* 336 U.S. 77, 89–90 (1949) (Frankfurter, J., concurring).

**Things to Remember**

### SOME APPROACHES TO FIRST AMENDMENT ADJUDICATION

- Prior restraint doctrine:
  - In colonial times, freedom of the press likely meant only freedom from prepublication censorship.
  - Although the First Amendment also applies to after-the-fact punishments, prior restraints are still viewed by the Supreme Court as especially odious.
- Absolutist theory:
  - The "no" in "Congress shall pass *no* law..." is emphasized.
  - Alexander Meiklejohn said that only political speech is absolutely protected.
  - Justice Kennedy embraces "absolutism with exceptions."
- Access theory:
  - Freedom of the press should not be just for those who own one.
  - Courts have generally rejected it for print, accepted it somewhat for broadcast.
- Ad hoc balancing:
  - "Which is more important in this case, free speech or the competing interest?"
  - Stanley Fish of Duke University has revitalized interest in this approach.
- Preferred position balancing:
  - This frequently used approach consists of balancing with a dishonest scale, assuming that free speech will win.

vous or not, the phrase does seem to mean something very much like what Frankfurter feared it had come to mean. When asked to determine the constitutionality of laws or regulations seeming to abridge a fundamental right such as freedom of speech (freedom of the press and freedom of religion are treated similarly), courts employ the highest level of scrutiny. Using this "strict scrutiny," courts demand that the state will have a "compelling interest" to infringe on the right to communicate. Preferred position balancing is the theory of First Amendment adjudication most often employed by the modern Supreme Court (even though it does not use the phrase as often these days as in decades passed). This reality leads to a question that is as easy to articulate as it is difficult to answer: *Why* is free speech so important as to occupy a preferred position?

## The Value of Freedom of Expression

In the same concurring opinion from *Whitney v. California* that gave us the famous "more speech, not enforced silence" prescription, Justice Brandeis also provides an elegantly worded list of functions served by freedom of speech. "Those who won our independence," he wrote, believed that "freedom to think as you will and to speak as you think are means indispensable to the discovery and spread of political truth." He further contended that engaging in public discussion on the issues of the day is a "political duty" that should be recognized as a "fundamental principle of the American government." The opinion suggests too that law and order "cannot be secured merely through fear of punishment," that "it is hazardous to discourage thought, hope and imagination," because "fear breeds repression" and "repression breeds hate," the kind of hate that "menaces stable government."[43]

Freedom of speech, then, is important because it helps us find the truth; it is essential to our role as self-governors in a democracy and it provides a kind of "safety valve" against possibly violent turmoil. Yale University Law Professor Thomas Emerson incorporated these three functions into his own theory of free speech and suggested also that free speech serves a more individual "self-fulfillment" function.[44]

### The Truth-Seeking Function of Free Speech

Imagine for a moment that you are a member of a self-sustaining and very homogeneous people—descendants of the *Gilligan's Island* crew, perhaps—who have been cut off from the outside world for many centuries. Such a society will tend to develop very strongly held, rather inflexible views of the world. For such a people, the phrase "we do it this way because…well, we have *always* done it this way" is not a laughable cliché, but rather a matter-of-fact statement of allegiance to unquestioned wisdom.

Now suppose that, one day, a ship from another land is seen approaching. Your people may very well convene something akin to a town meeting so that you can decide whether to welcome the visitors or hide all traces of your presence from them in the hope that they will go away. The former option would be a courageous one indeed, opening yourselves to interactions with strangers whose ways may be very different from your own.

Nineteenth-century philosopher John Stuart Mill did not depend on such an intercultural fantasy in setting forth his influential free speech theory, but the narrative does provide a convenient lens through which to examine his elegant defense of viewpoint diversity. Mill's famous 1859 essay, *On Liberty,* asks us to consider whether we would be open to a new idea or whether we would feel an urge to censor it. We cannot ignore the possibility that the new idea is more correct than our handed-down wisdom. For would-be censors "to refuse a hearing to an opinion because they are sure that it is false is to assume that their certainty is the same thing as absolute certainty."

Suppose, however, that we were magically able to view the "Gilligan-ders'" dilemma from an omniscient vantage point, and that the homogeneous people's

---

[43]274 U.S. 357, 375 (1927) (Brandeis, J., concurring).

[44]Thomas I. Emerson, *The System of Freedom of Expression* (New York: Random House, 1970).

long-held truths were inarguably, unquestionably true. What benefit could possibly result from opening the door to the visitors' falsehoods? Mill answers that we will gain a "clearer perception and livelier impression" of our own truths, by their "collision with error"; failure to engage opposing views, Mill warns, will ensure that our own beliefs "will be held as a dead dogma, not a living truth, apt to give way before the slightest semblance of an argument. Truth thus held is but superstition."

In the real world, of course, we do not have the omniscience to know whose ideas are correct in advance of a full debate. Indeed, in most important clashes of ideas, the "truth" such as it is tends to be somewhere between the extremes. Yet we cannot often afford the luxury of waiting until all the facts are in. The modern world is characterized by the need to make decisions and take action on the basis of incomplete and often contradictory information. Professor Benjamin DuVal tells us that we derive our moral authority to make decisions and take actions by making, ironically enough, a "pact with the devil." The devil gives us permission to function, to act, only if we promise in return that we will not censor new ideas, that we will always keep ourselves open to the possibility that new facts will require that we alter our course of behavior.[45]

## The Self-Governing Function of Free Speech

First Amendment scholar Alexander Meiklejohn's theory of freedom of expression emphasizes Americans' role as "self-governors." We vote on important matters of the day, or at least choose among candidates in large part on what they promise to do about those same issues. For Meiklejohn, just as the Speech and Debate Clause in Article I of the Constitution gives our elected federal representatives an absolute right to free speech in carrying out their duties, so too should the First Amendment be interpreted so as to give all Americans an absolute right to speak out about political issues.

In Meiklejohnian theory, political speech is the core of the system of free expression, protected absolutely by the First Amendment, whereas more private speech enjoys the far lesser degree of protection offered by the Fifth Amendment's due process clause. When Oprah Winfrey uses her program to discuss the safety of federal meat inspection programs, according to Meiklejohn she and her guests enjoy absolute freedom from liability. If instead she devotes an hour to a movie star's personal bout with marital infidelity, the First Amendment might not be implicated at all.

Although the Supreme Court rejects Meiklejohn's argument that speech we do not need in our role of self-governors lacks First Amendment protection, it has on many occasions made clear that political speech is the most important kind. In 1995, for example, the Court overturned an Ohio law that required all printed

---

[45]Benjamin DuVal, "Free Communication of Ideas and the Quest for Truth: Toward a Teleological Approach to First Amendment Adjudication," 41 *George Washington Law Review* 161 (1972).

campaign literature to include the name and address of the leaflet's author. The law's downfall was obvious early on in that the Court's opinion expressed amazement that the state had singled out "core political speech,…publications containing speech designed to influence the voters in an election," for regulation.[46] A few years earlier, the Court similarly invalidated a District of Columbia ordinance that prohibited the display within 500 feet of any foreign embassy a sign bearing a message critical of that embassy's government. The law had to be struck down, the Court held, in that it so obviously trampled on "classically protected" political speech.[47]

## The Checking Function of Free Speech

In the United States, the press is often referred to as the Fourth Estate, a way of emphasizing that we depend on a free press to keep us informed about the performance of the three branches of government, legislative, executive, and judicial. Much of what we think of as hard news involves the press looking over the shoulders of government bureaucrats and reporting their successes and failures. The ABC News regular feature "Your Money," which looks at a specific government program and suggests to viewers whether or not they are getting a good return on their tax dollars, is a clear example of this watchdog function.

A 1977 article by Vincent Blasi argued that empowering the press to keep a watchful eye on the government is the main reason for valuing freedom of speech. He calls it the checking function. Abuses by the government are "an especially serious evil," Blasi argued, more so than abuses by large corporations or other powerful agents. Government, after all, is unique in its "capacity to employ legitimized violence"; we give the police, not the CEOs, the right to use guns against us.[48] From Blasi's perspective, then, TV stations that showed us again and again the videotape of the Rodney King beating were engaged in the checking function. Reporting on whether or not Microsoft is engaged in monopolistic practices in restraint of trade is not part of the checking function, unless the story's focus is the Department of Justice decision to prosecute the company.

## The Safety Valve Function of Free Speech

If we suppress a viewpoint that we despise, does it go away? Or do its proponents go underground and their discontent fester until it is all the more likely to be

---

[46]*McIntyre v. Ohio Elections Commission,* 514 U.S. 334 (1995).

[47]*Boos v. Barry,* 485 U.S. 312 (1988).

[48]Vincent Blasi, "The Checking Value in First Amendment Theory," *American Bar Foundation Research Journal* 521, 538, (1977).

manifested in violence? The safety valve function of free speech stems from the latter hypothesis. As Emerson explains, freedom of speech "promotes greater cohesion in a society because people are more ready to accept decisions that go against them if they have a part in the decision-making process."[49] Unsuccessful advocates of change are less likely to foment violent revolution if they are at least allowed to advocate.

More recently, President Lee Bollinger of the University of Michigan has argued that we benefit, for at least two reasons, from seeing the depth of dissatisfaction and dissent felt by those who feel driven to engage in extremist speech. First, some of their grievances may be real—inadequate educational or employment opportunities, for example—and only by hearing them can we make public policy decisions to address them. Then, too, it is "preferable to have these potentially disruptive individuals and groups operating in public rather than in private, where the unwanted weeds of frustration and revolt may grow more rapidly from inattention and where the falsehoods being propagated may less easily be exposed for their error." A system of freedom of expression thus acts as a "social thermometer for registering the presence of disease within the body politic and the best opportunity of administering a speedy cure."[50]

## The Self-Fulfillment Function of Free Speech

Virtually anytime the media report on a survey about "things that frighten most Americans," being called on to deliver a speech in public ranks at or near the top. This finding obscures another reality about self-expression that may seem a contradiction yet is no less true: It feels good to express yourself.

If you have ever lived for an extended period of time in a foreign country whose language you spoke well enough to get by but not fluently, you know firsthand the truth of this simple statement. When challenged to speak in that foreign language, you will be able to get your basic daily needs met and you will be able to express in a combination of verbal and nonverbal ways that you are a likable individual, but you will probably sorely miss the chance to share in the nuances supplied by very specific word choice and inflection, the effortless expression of your core individuality.

This example is offered only to give you a way of gauging how much self-fulfillment you derive from communicating with others. Most barriers to free speech imposed by governments, of course, are not addressed to which language you will be permitted to speak. (Controversies surrounding bilingual education and "English only" proposals are notable exceptions.) The more general question posed by the self-fulfillment function of free speech is, What would you miss most if you

---

[49]Emerson, *The System of Freedom of Expression,* 7.

[50]Lee Bollinger, *The Tolerant Society* (New York: Oxford University Press, 1986), 55.

were not permitted the freedom of speech? C. Edwin Baker, who was a student of Emerson's at Yale, later went on to create his own freedom of speech theory that emphasizes the self-fulfillment function of expression above all others. His theory leads to some intriguing propositions, such as defining advertising and other commercial speech as generally outside the protection of the First Amendment in that speakers sending such messages are motivated by potential profits rather than by a desire for individual self-fulfillment. Baker argues further that even that which we think of as political speech might be more appropriately viewed as highly personal expressions of self. Consider the plight of the war protestor at a rally, chanting "Stop this war now" or some similar slogan. Rarely do such speakers have any serious expectation that their singular act of political speech will affect the government's war policy or indeed even be heard by those in charge of prosecuting the war effort. Why do it then? The answer in part, at least, is because engaging in such speech serves to define oneself to others, *as well as to oneself,* as a person in opposition.[51]

## The Societal Self-Definition Function of Free Speech

These then are the traditionally accepted functions of freedom of speech: a quest for truth, helping us in our role as self-governors, the "safety valve," and the furtherance of individual self-fulfillment. Some writers have provided eloquent critiques of these functions and have found them deficient. In this section, we look at two such writers, Lee Bollinger of the University of Michigan and Ruth McGaffey of the University of Wisconsin. Both Bollinger and McGaffey argue that the best way of explaining the uniquely American system of free expression is that the system itself serves to define what it means to be an American. This explanation will make more sense if we look at another similarity between the two theorists. Both authors derive much of their analysis from a 1970s incident involving the village of Skokie, Illinois. Frank Collin and his small group of neo-Nazis, after initially being denied a parade permit in Chicago, began to search for alternative local venues and settled on Skokie, a northwest suburb with a large Jewish population and an unusually large number of Holocaust survivors. The village responded by passing a series of laws designed to prevent Collin's proposed march, laws which were eventually found unconstitutional by a federal appellate court.[52]

McGaffey attended the Nazi group's demonstration that eventually did take place in Chicago's Marquette Park and that attracted a large group of counter demonstrators. McGaffey describes the screaming for blood on both sides. "This was not a football game, and the opposing yells were not those of friendly rivalry. The hatred was so thick you could feel it." The radio reported the next day that a body had been fished out of a lagoon in the park.

---

[51]C. Edwin Baker, *Human Liberty and Freedom of Speech* (New York: Oxford University Press, 1989), 53.

[52]*Collin v. Smith,* 578 F.2d 1197 (7th Cir. 1978).

McGaffey's experience at the Marquette Park rally could not help but compel her to question Americans' assumptions about the value of free speech. Free speech's "truth-seeking" value notwithstanding, surely it should be possible to fashion laws that guarantee freedom of expression "without allowing every repulsive creep to tie up the police force of a huge city whenever he wants his ego inflated." As to the safety valve function of free speech, McGaffey wonders whether "letting off that kind of steam prevents trouble or contributes to orderly change." Not surprisingly, she also finds herself unenthusiastic about the call to protect Collin's need for "self-fulfillment" through hate mongering. Yet McGaffey emerges from Chicago with a vital and new reason for protecting freedom of speech. We need to see that there are people "who will burn crosses or beat up Blacks or break windows in synagogues when their own little worlds are threatened." We need to permit such persons to engage in free speech, not for their benefit, but so that observers can "realize what a lousy bunch of people we are" and that "we must be a pretty strong country in order to have survived with so many lousy people."[53]

The argument may seem a bit circular: we should value free speech because it permits us to observe firsthand how tolerant of extremists we can be. Yet there is something about this "self-definition" rationale that seems to ring true, as Bollinger also finds. Bollinger calls his book outlining his own theory *The Tolerant Society* as if to emphasize that Americans enjoy seeing themselves as a tolerant people. He reminds us that the United States is virtually unique among free societies in its high degree of legal tolerance for ideas we hate. This tolerance does not mean we shy away from judgment; we do not, for example, equate the neo-Nazi movement with the Civil Rights movement. We feel strongly as a people, however, that we should use means *short of legal suppression* to express our disdain for race-baiters and other extremists. We can shun them. If they hold public office, we can demand their immediate resignation. We should not fall into the trap, though, of making their speech unlawful.[54]

Our system of freedom of expression serves to define ourselves as a people, and we take pride in this aspect of our collective self-concept. Bollinger finds some support for this proposition in portions of the federal appellate decision granting Frank Collin and his followers the right to march in Skokie. Consider this little zinger the court sent Collin's way: "it is, after all, in part the fact that our constitutional system protects minorities unpopular at a particular time or place from governmental harassment and intimidation, that distinguishes life in this country from life under the Third Reich."[55] Implicit in the court's language is an admonition to all Americans: *Celebrate,* do not lament, the high degree of tolerance for extremists demanded by the First Amendment.

---

[53]Ruth McGaffey, "Free Speech in Marquette Park: A Realistic Look at the Marketplace of Ideas," *Free Speech Yearbook* 1, 8–9, (1978).

[54]Bollinger, *The Tolerant Society,* 12–14.

[55]578 F.2d at 1201.

# Things to Remember

**FUNCTIONS OF FREE SPEECH**

- The truth-seeking function:
  - John Stuart Mill emphasized the need to hear even false ideas so as to remind us why the true ideas are true.
  - Benjamin DuVal's pact with the devil allows us to make decisions only if we promise to remain open to new ideas.
- The self-governing function:
  - Alexander Meiklejohn is most closely associated with the self-governing stance.
  - Political speech is an absolute First Amendment freedom.
  - Nonpolitical speech is a Fifth Amendment liberty.
- The checking function:
  - The free press is essential in a democracy as a Fourth Estate, the check on the other three branches of government.
- The safety valve function:
  - Political dissidents must be permitted to "blow off steam."
  - Peaceful evolution helps avoid violent revolution.
- The self-fulfillment function:
  - Expressing ourselves feels good.
  - C. Edwin Baker's theory is based on the self-fulfillment function.
- The societal self-definition function:
  - Bollinger says that Americans like to think of themselves as a tolerant people.
  - McGaffey points to the need to see how "lousy" and intolerant we can be too.

## Is Freedom of Expression Overrated?

All the First Amendment theories examined so far have in common an underlying assumption that free speech is a good thing. The theories differ only in terms of the answer they offer to the question of why it is a good thing. Many theorists, however, argue that freedom of expression is placed on too high a pedestal in the United States, that it is allowed to ride roughshod over more important rights and interests. In this section, the thoughts of some Marxist, feminist, and critical race theorists who agree that freedom of speech as we typically understand it in this country is indeed overrated are examined.

Karl Marx said that religion is "the opiate of the people." An emphasis on the afterlife, he suggested, is conveniently consistent with the need on the part of those in power to keep the masses contented with their small share of material resources in *this* life. Writing several generations later, a group of Marxists argued similarly that freedom of speech is an opiate, or at least a distraction. Chief among these writers was Herbert Marcuse, who pointed out that having the right to speak out against injustice is quite different from having any real power to change what he perceived as a fundamentally unjust system of allocating wealth.[56] For Marcuse and his followers, "free speech operates freely only because society realizes that free speech is devoid of any real power of change."[57]

One need not be a Marxist, of course, to level that same criticism against American journalism, especially TV news. That the main purpose of the news is not to inform but rather to entertain just enough so that viewers pay attention to the commercials is the thesis of Neil Postman's well-received book, *Amusing Ourselves to Death.* Postman, a communications professor at New York University, describes what he calls the "Now, this…" grammar of TV news. The phrase alerts us that the TV news item we have just seen "has no relevance to what one is about to see." It is the newscaster's way of saying "that you have thought long enough on the previous matter (approximately forty-five seconds), that you must not be morbidly preoccupied with it…and that you must now give your attention to another fragment of news or a commercial."[58]

Whereas Postman warns that the media discourage us from paying too close attention to the issues of the day, pioneering mass media theorists Paul Lasarsfeld and Robert Merton have argued that we may be guilty of paying such close attention to the information with which the media bombard us that we get lulled into political inactivity. We come to confuse *knowing* about social problems with *doing* something about them. They call this confusion the *narcotizing* dysfunction of media.[59]

To the extent that American media exist primarily to sell viewers' and readers' attentive eyeballs to advertisers, we expect to find a tendency to avoid airing any political views that disturb consumers too much, that make us tune out. Such a criticism is reminiscent of Dorothy Parker's famously stinging remark about an actress of her day whose performance "ran the gamut of emotions from 'A' to 'B.'" We rarely encounter truly radical political points of view in American media, many contemporary social critics argue. From this perspective, the spokespersons "from the left" and "from the right" that CNN so proudly pits against each other in its *Crossfire* program would be more accurately described as *a bit* left of center versus *a bit* right of center.

---

[56]Herbert Marcuse, "Repressive Tolerance," in *A Critique of Pure Tolerance,* eds. Robert Paul Wolff, Barrington Moore Jr., and Herbert Marcuse (Boston: Beacon Press, 1965), 81–123.

[57]Joyce Flory, "Implications of Marcuse's Theory of Freedom for Freedom of Speech," in *Perspectives on Freedom of Speech,* eds. Thomas L. Tedford, John J. Makay, and David L. Jamison (Carbondale: Southern Illinois Press, 1987), 79.

[58]Neil Postman, *Amusing Ourselves to Death: Public Discourse in the Age of Show Business* (New York: Penguin Books, 1985), 99–100.

[59]Paul F. Lasarsfeld and Robert K. Merton, "Mass Communication, Popular Taste, and Organized Social Action," in *The Communication of Ideas,* ed. Lymon Bryson (New York: Harper, 1948), 95–118.

If the marketplace of ideas offers only a very limited spectrum of viewpoints, one possible result could be what sociologist Elizabeth Noelle-Neumann has described as the "spiral of silence." Consumers of news who themselves favor political views more on the fringes than one typically sees described in the media will become cowered over time, afraid to share their views with others for fear of being branded a radical. The media will thus be less and less likely over time to be able to identify and feature responsible spokespersons for any but the most mainstream of perspectives.[60] It is perhaps worth noting that Noelle-Neumann was writing from anything but a Marxist perspective. Indeed, in her younger years she was apparently very active in the German Nazi Party.[61]

In recent years, much scholarship has been written by feminists who, in the course of questioning the most basic assumptions of U.S. society, understandably have much to say about whether deference to First Amendment rights is always in women's best interest. These theorists say that the purpose of their scholarship is to ask "the woman question," sometimes phrased as, "What would the law be like if women had been considered by the drafters?"[62] Feminist theory has been applied to dozens of distinct areas of law, from bankruptcy to health care regulation.[63] Perhaps most relevant for the study of communication law are those feminists who have argued that we need to rethink our attitudes toward the use of pornographic images of women. By far the best known writers in this area have been Andrea Dworkin[64] and Catherine MacKinnon.[65] We examine their antipornography arguments in Chapter 11, which deals with obscenity and other sexually oriented speech.

Feminists are not the only representatives of historically oppressed groups to question what they perceive as the U.S. legal system's tendency to value free speech interests above concerns about inequality. Such critical race theorists as Mari Mat-

---

[60]Elisabeth Noelle-Neumann, *The Spiral of Silence* (Chicago: University of Chicago Press, 1984).

[61]Christopher Simpson, "Elisabeth Noelle Neumann's 'Spiral of Silence' and the Historical Context of Communication Theory," 43 *Journal of Communication,* no. 3 (Summer), 149–73 (1996).

[62]Janet E. Ainsworth, "In a Different Register: The Pragmatics of Powerlessness in Police Interrogation," 103 *Yale Law Journal* 259, 262 (1993).

[63]Lydia A. Clougherty, "Feminist Legal Methods and the First Amendment Defense to Sexual Harassment Liability," 75 *Nebraska Law Review* 1, 4 (1996).

[64]Andrea Dworkin, "Against the Male Flood: Censorship, Pornography, and Equality," 8 *Harvard Women's Law Journal* 1 (1985); Andrea Dworkin, *Pornography: Men Possessing Women* (New York: Plume, 1989).

[65]Catherine MacKinnon, *Feminism Unmodified* (Cambridge: Harvard University Press, 1987); Catherine MacKinnon, *Only Words* (Cambridge: Harvard University Press, 1993); Catherine MacKinnon, *Towards a Feminist Theory of the State* (Cambridge: Harvard University Press, 1989); Catharine MacKinnon, "Pornography, Civil Rights, and Speech," 20 *Harvard Civil Rights—Civil Liberties Law Review* 1 (1985).

**Things to Remember**

---

**SOME CRITICISMS OF THE U.S. STYLE OF FREE SPEECH**

- Free speech as an "opiate":
  - The right to complain is not as important as the power to change things.
  - We confuse knowing about problems with doing something about them.
  - Political dialogue in the United States is merely a commodity to attract eyeballs to ads.
  - The media cannot afford to offend us, so the marketplace of ideas is very narrow.
- Feminists and critical race theorists express concern:
  - We need to pay attention to the aggrieved person's narratives.
  - Free speech is not necessarily more important than equality.

---

suda[66] and Richard Delgado[67] argue in their writings that the courts should not automatically assume that the First Amendment prohibits minority group members from bringing civil actions against persons who use racial epithets against them. These writers emphasize that whites and people of color live in two very different perceptual worlds. When confronted by the same stories of hate speech incidents, people of color react with alarm, hurt feelings, and a desire for redress, whereas most whites seek to dismiss such occurrences as "isolated pranks." The whole process of telling and listening to stories is crucial for critical race theorists, who argue in favor of a new, "outsider jurisprudence" that will be more sympathetic to historically powerless groups.

## Some Transcendent First Amendment Doctrines

The remainder of this book's chapters are organized around either message content issues (libel, invasion of privacy, advertising) or issues unique to specific communications media (broadcast and cable or the Internet). Other important communication law issues transcend these categories. We deal here with four of them: the right to hear, the right not to speak, the issue of symbolic conduct, and the kinds of content-neutral governmental policies often referred to as time, place, and manner regulations.

---

[66]Mari Matsuda, "Legal Storytelling: Public Response to Racist Speech: Considering the Victim's Story," 87 *Michigan Law Review* 2320 (1989).

[67]Richard Delgado, "Words That Wound: A Tort Action for Racial Insults, Epithets, and Name-Calling," 17 *Harvard Civil Rights—Civil Liberties Law Review* 133 (1982).

## A Right to Hear (and Read)

The First Amendment tells us that Congress shall not abridge the freedom to speak. Over the years, the judiciary has come to recognize that freedom of speech would be incomplete were it not to entail also a right to hear (or read). The Supreme Court has emphasized in more than a dozen of its free speech cases that the First Amendment protects the act of communication and that this act involves not only senders of messages, but receivers as well. As we see in later chapters focusing on obscenity and advertising, the right to hear is an integral part of the law governing those kinds of speech. Thus, for example, the Court has said that although selling or distributing obscene works can be criminalized, one may own and read in the privacy of one's own home virtually any sexually oriented materials that do not include lewd depictions of children.[68] Then, too, in the Court's 1976 decision first holding that purely commercial advertising is protected by the First Amendment, that protection was based primarily on the consumers' interest in obtaining comparative pricing information.[69]

The Court first made reference to a "right to hear" in the course of overturning a contempt of court judgment against United Automobile Workers President R. J. Thomas, who had delivered a speech, in defiance of a court order, to a group of Houston workers. Writing for a 5–4 majority, Justice Rutledge found that both Thomas's right to speak and "the rights of the workers to hear what he had to say" were at issue.[70] The right to hear formed the basis of the Court's 1969 decision upholding the constitutionality of the "fairness doctrine" applied by the FCC to the broadcast media. That doctrine—which required that broadcast licensees not shy away from covering controversial issues and that such issues be covered in a balanced way—is no longer enforced. Nonetheless, the philosophy embraced by the Court at the time, that it is "the right of the viewers and listeners, not the right of the broadcasters, which is paramount," remains to this day one of the judiciary's most dramatic endorsements of a right to hear.[71]

The rights of PBS's viewers to hear carried the day in *FCC v. League of Women Voters of California,* which invalidated a portion of the Public Broadcasting Act of 1967 that prohibited PBS and NPR stations to editorialize on issues of the day. Editorializing, the Court held, can be an important means "of satisfying the public's interest in receiving a wide variety of ideas and views."[72] More recently, the Court invalidated a federal statute that prohibited virtually all government workers above a certain salary scale to make any money "moonlighting" as writers or lecturers, even on matters wholly unrelated to their official job duties. The regula-

---

[68]*Stanley v. Georgia,* 394 U.S. 557 (1969).

[69]*Virginia State Board of Pharmacy v. Virginia Citizens Consumer Council,* 425 U.S. 748 (1976).

[70]*Thomas v. Collins,* 323 U.S. 516, 534 (1945).

[71]*Red Lion Broadcasting v. FCC,* 395 U.S. 367, 390 (1969).

[72]468 U.S. 364, 382 (1984).

tion, Justice Stevens found, imposed "a significant burden on the public's right to read and hear what the employees would otherwise have written and said."[73]

## A Right *Not* to Speak

Anyone who has ever seen a real or fictional character on a TV show "take the Fifth" knows that the Bill of Rights boasts at least one protection against being forced to speak. The Fifth Amendment's provision is a very limited one, however, applying only to criminal suspects and others in danger of prosecution. The Supreme Court has also found a more generalized right not to speak in the First Amendment. In the beginnings of the modern civil rights movement, some southern states felt threatened by the emergence of such groups as the NAACP and employed a number of tactics to stifle their growth. One such tactic was compelling the groups to disclose their membership lists. In a 1957 decision, the Supreme Court blocked such forced disclosure, ruling in essence that such organizations have a right not to speak, at least when doing so would likely bring violent reprisals on their supporters.[74]

In the 1988 presidential race, George Bush criticized Michael Dukakis for having vetoed legislation that would have required Massachusetts public school teachers to lead their students in a daily Pledge of Allegiance to the flag. Dukakis defended his veto on the grounds that the law seemed inconsistent with a U.S. Supreme Court decision from the 1940s holding that public school students could not be forced to utter the Pledge. Most interesting about the case for communication law is that the plaintiffs, a group of Jehovah's Witnesses, argued that the compelled speech was a violation of their right to practice their religion, a Free Exercise Clause issue. Justice Jackson's opinion for the Court, however, was based on the far broader "right not to speak" implicit in the Free Speech Clause. If the First Amendment allows us to speak our mind, surely it must also mean that the government may not compel us to "utter what is not in [our mind]," he wrote at the time.[75]

The right not to speak was emphasized even more forcefully in a later case involving another Jehovah's Witness, New Hampshire resident George Maynard, who strongly disagreed with the state motto ("Live Free or Die") and therefore covered up the words on his automobile license plate. In ruling for Maynard, the Supreme Court held explicitly that the First Amendment provides for "both the right to speak freely and the right to refrain from speaking at all."[76]

Note that the Jehovah's Witnesses in *Barnette* and in *Wooley* invoked the First Amendment as a shield from having to utter someone else's message: the Pledge of

---

[73]*United States v. National Treasury Employees Union,* 513 U.S. 454, 470 (1995).

[74]*NAACP v. Alabama,* 357 U.S. 449 (1957).

[75]*West Virginia Board of Education v. Barnette,* 319 U.S. 624 (1943).

[76]*Wooley v. Maynard,* 430 U.S. 705 (1977).

Allegiance in the one case and the state's motto in the other. The right not to speak can also provide protection from being forced to express our own ideas. Although most of the witnesses who refused to testify in the 1950s before the House Committee on Un-American Activities invoked the Fifth Amendment right against self-incrimination, at least a few based their silence instead on the First Amendment right not to speak. Even though these litigants ultimately lost, the Supreme Court at least allowed that a First Amendment right of silence exists.[77]

The Supreme Court's most recent "right not to speak" case involved the controversial issue of term limits. Voters in the state of Missouri amended their state constitution so as to require that future ballots include a reference indicating which candidates had "DECLINED TO PLEDGE TO SUPPORT TERM LIMITS." The Supreme Court overturned the provision as a violation of the First Amendment (among other federal constitutional provisions). Missouri was guilty not only of compelling candidates to speak out on an issue they might otherwise choose to avoid—the state was planning to punish candidates who did not take the preferred stance on that issue.[78]

Litigants have sometimes argued, with mixed results, that their First Amendment rights are violated when they are forced to support financially the speech of others whose views they find offensive. Teachers might be forced to join a union,[79] or lawyers a bar association;[80] their fees must be used for purposes directly germane to that membership, however, not for advocacy of political causes or candidates. Public universities, though, may use mandatory student activity fees to fund extracurricular student organizations—no matter how "offensive"—as long as funding is not a function of the groups' political viewpoint.[81]

Mass media litigants have benefited from a First Amendment right not to speak (or print). When the state of Florida tried to force the *Miami Herald* to publish a reply written by a candidate for office who had been criticized in the paper's editorial pages, the Supreme Court invalidated the statute that served as the state's basis for the request. The First Amendment prevents the government from compelling editors "to publish that which reason tells them should not be published," Chief Justice Burger wrote for the Court.[82]

## Symbolic Conduct

The "speech" protected by the First Amendment need not involve vocal cords. Human beings engage in many kinds of behaviors designed to send messages:

---

[77]*Barenblatt v. United States,* 360 U.S. 109 (1959); *Wilkinson v. United States,* 365 U.S. 399 (1961).

[78]*Cook v. Gralike,* 531 U.S. 510 (2001).

[79]*Abood v. Detroit Board of Education,* 431 U.S. 209 (1977).

[80]*Keller v. State Bar of California,* 496 U.S. 1 (1990).

[81]*Board of Regents of the University of Wisconsin v. Southworth,* 529 U.S. 217 (2000).

[82]*Miami Herald v. Tornillo,* 418 U.S. 241, 256 (1974).

marching, dancing, and sitting as well as flag waving *and* flag burning. Over the years the courts have determined that, depending on the context, all these behaviors and more are within the First Amendment's protection. Justice Jackson, in the case invalidating West Virginia's compulsory public school flag salute, wrote that "symbolism is a primitive but effective way of communicating ideas, a short cut from mind to mind."

None of this discussion is to suggest that all forms of symbolic conduct in all contexts will be granted First Amendment protection. This lesson was learned all too clearly by Vietnam War protestor David Paul O'Brien, who was found in violation of a federal law that forbade the knowing destruction of one's draft card. Upholding his conviction, the Supreme Court set forth a list of criteria still often used to determine when laws or regulations affecting symbolic conduct are compatible with the First Amendment. The *O'Brien* test demands that any such regulations "further an important and substantial government interest," that the state's interest "is unrelated to the suppression of free expression," and that "the incidental restriction on alleged First Amendment freedoms is no greater than is essential to the furtherance of that interest."[83] The federal statute under which O'Brien was prosecuted was deemed an expression of several legitimate state's interests that were themselves unrelated to the defendant's message, such as ensuring the effective functioning of the Selective Service System.

A few years after *O'Brien,* the Supreme Court offered some further guidance as to the place of symbolic conduct within the system of freedom of expression. In response to the U.S. military's bombing of Cambodia and the killings at Kent State University, college student Harold Spence hung an upside-down American flag with a peace symbol affixed to it from his Seattle, Washington, apartment window. The Supreme Court ruled that Spence's action was protected symbolic conduct in that he had an "intent to convey a particularized message" and because "in the surrounding circumstances the likelihood was great that the message would be understood by those who viewed it."[84] The *Spence* test, which focuses on the speaker's communicational intent and on whether the message will indeed be perceived, is not incompatible with the *O'Brien* test. Indeed, the *Spence* Court indicates that the *O'Brien* test demanded the overturning of Spence's conviction. His prosecution (interestingly, for displaying a flag improperly rather than for "desecrating" the flag) resulted from the state's displeasure with his intended message and was thus not "unrelated to the suppression of free expression."

The *O'Brien* test has been employed by the Court to adjudicate zoning regulations affecting "adult" movie theaters,[85] and even an outright ban of nightclubs

---

[83]*United States v. O'Brien,* 391 U.S. 367, 376 (1968).

[84]*Spence v. Washington,* 418 U.S. 405, 410–11 (1974).

[85]*Young v. American Mini-Theatres,* 427 U.S. 50 (1976).

featuring nude dancing.[86] States have more freedom to regulate otherwise protected First Amendment activity, the Court reasoned, if the regulations are unrelated to the expression itself, but rather are aimed at the "secondary effects" of the expression (such as increases in prostitution and other crime).

### "You Can't Do That *Here!*" Time, Place, and Manner Restrictions

The *O'Brien* test, we have seen, asks us to consider whether a governmental regulation is aimed at the expressive components of conduct. We thus must recognize that a whole host of laws or regulations that may have the effect of stifling speech are not *designed* to keep any particular message from being heard. Suppose, for example, that you answer your door to a police officer advising you that your neighbors would appreciate it if you and your party guests make a bit less noise. The content of the message or messages being exchanged among your friends is not at issue in such a situation. The legal intervention stems instead from the *time* (late at night, perhaps, when neighbors are trying to sleep), *place* (a residential, as opposed to purely commercial, area of town), or *manner* (the decibel level itself) of the communication.

Although the Supreme Court has never ruled on a "noisy party complaint" case, it has upheld the notion that content-neutral limitations on a message's loudness or inappropriate choice of venue are permissible. In 1972, in his majority opinion upholding the conviction of a group of civil rights demonstrators for staging a potentially disruptive protest too close to a public school, Justice Marshall indicated why time, place, and manner restrictions were not only permissible, but necessary. After all, "two parades cannot march on the same street simultaneously." Moreover, although "a silent vigil may not unduly interfere with a public library, making a speech in the reading room almost certainly would.... The crucial question is whether the manner of expression is basically incompatible with the normal activity of a particular place at a particular time."[87]

Over the years, the Supreme Court has created a three-part test to determine the constitutionality of time, place, and manner restrictions on speech. First, the regulation must be content neutral. It must not be motivated by governmental displeasure at the specific message being sent. An ordinance forbidding the use of overly loud sound trucks, for example, passes this test in that it does not matter what is said as long as it is not said at a deafening volume.[88] So, too, a New York City regulation governing the loudness of amplified concerts in Central Park was upheld. After all, it did not prescribe one decibel level for rap music and another for the *1812* Overture.[89]

---

[86]*City of Erie v. Pap's A. M. TDBA "Kandyland",* 529 U.S. 277 (2000).

[87]*Grayned v. City of Rockford, Illinois,* 408 U.S. 104, 115–16 (1972).

[88]*Kovacs v. Cooper,* 336 U.S. 558 (1948).

[89]*Ward v. Rock Against Racism,* 491 U.S. 781 (1989).

The second part of the test requires that the regulation be narrowly tailored to further an important government interest. In 1939, the Supreme Court struck down as unconstitutional laws in a handful of cities that, in the interests of preventing littering, prohibited all distribution of printed literature on street corners. The Court ruled that if these cities wanted to decrease littering, they should have more directly punished "those who actually throw papers on the streets," not persons engaged in otherwise protected First Amendment activity.[90]

Finally, restrictions on the time, place, and manner of communication must permit ample alternative means for speakers to transmit their messages. Thus, much to the dismay of a homeless persons' advocacy group organizing a political demonstration over several days in Lafayette Park (a small, grassy area across the street from the White House), the Supreme Court upheld the constitutionality of a U.S. Park Service regulation prohibiting sleeping overnight in the park. The regulation did not prevent the demonstrators from communicating the plight of the homeless, Justice White concluded. Indeed, as long as the participants were willing to take turns, they could even collectively maintain a twenty-four hour presence in the park.[91] Or consider Justice Marshall's reasoning in a decision invalidating a New Jersey municipality's law against the posting of "For Sale" signs on residential lawns. The law, which was aimed at curbing the practice of panic selling stemming from racial fears, was admittedly not content neutral in that it proscribed one specific message. Marshall went out of his way to point out that the law also could not pass the "ample alternative means of communication" requirement in

---

[90]*Schneider v. State,* 308 U.S. 147 (1939).

[91]*Clark v. Community for Creative Non-Violence,* 468 U.S. 288 (1984).

 # Things to Remember

**SOME ADDITIONAL FIRST AMENDMENT DOCTRINES**

- The First Amendment includes a right to hear.
- It also includes a right not to speak.
- Free speech includes some kinds of symbolic conduct.
- The *O'Brien* test determines constitutionality of regulations aimed at symbolic conduct.
  - The regulation must further an important interest.
  - That interest must not be simply to stifle a specific message.
  - The regulation must be narrowly drawn.
- Time, place, and manner restrictions are not subject to strict scrutiny.
  - The regulations must be content neutral.
  - They must be narrowly tailored.
  - They must permit sufficient alternative media of communication.

that the signs reach a specific audience—the casual buyer, not necessarily looking to buy a home and thus not in the habit of reading the classified pages or consulting realtors—not easily reached via any other medium.[92]

## Regulating the Business of Communication

Not all legal interventions affecting communication industries should necessarily be considered communication law. If a local police chief, upset at the coverage given him by the town's "alternative" free weekly, effectively shuts down the paper by barging into the newsroom and confiscating the publisher's computer, we would have a clear (and clearly unconstitutional) example of "media law" at work. If that same publisher, however, is a divorced father who is tens of thousands of dollars behind in his child support payments, the confiscation of that same computer through a judgment obtained by the Division of Family Services would not be at all relevant to the study of communication law.

Media industries are governed by much the same legal environment affecting other businesses. They must pay their workers at least the minimum wage. They must provide safe and nonharassing working conditions. They must contribute their legally mandated share of employees' Social Security payments.

In this final section of the chapter, three areas of the law that are applied to media industries just as to other industries are examined. When applied to the media, however, they have a special impact on the act of communication, either by determining who may speak or what may be said. The three topics to be addressed are antitrust, taxation, and workplace laws.

### Antitrust Laws

The Sherman Act of 1890[93]and the Clayton Act of 1914[94] give the Department of Justice license to bring both civil and criminal proceedings against businesses that function "in restraint of trade." Media outlets have often behaved in an anticompetitive manner, and sometimes this behavior has prompted the government to pursue them for antitrust violations. In 1951, the Supreme Court held that the *Lorain Journal* in Ohio was in violation of antitrust laws when it refused to accept advertising from businesses that had also advertised in competing local media.[95]

Several anticompetitive practices on the part of the *Kansas City Star*'s publisher attracted the government's attention a few years later. The company owned both the morning and afternoon daily papers (the *Times* and the *Star,* respectively)

---

[92]*Linmark Associates v. Township of Willingboro,* 431 U.S. 85, 93 (1977).

[93]15 U.S.C. sec. 1, 2 (1994).

[94]15 U.S.C. sec. 18–9 (1994).

[95]*Lorain Journal Company v. United States,* 342 U.S. 143 (1951).

and the *Sunday Star* as well as a radio station and a TV station. As was the case with the earlier *Lorain Journal* case, here, too, the company's agents made clear to some local businesses that if they advertised in competing publications, their ads might not be welcome again in the *Star*'s papers. Also, advertisers wishing to patronize one of the *Star* newspapers were instead required to place ads in all three. Subscribers were similarly forced into a "take all three or get none" deal. Perhaps most troubling to the court was that the traditionally respected wall between the advertising and editorial functions of the newspaper had apparently come down, in a distinctively anticompetitive manner. It seems that a major league baseball player was a partner in a local florist shop. He was told that if he failed to convince his partners to cease advertising the shop in a competing newspaper, coverage in the *Star* of his baseball career would diminish or disappear.

Writing for a panel of three judges on the Eighth Circuit Court of Appeals, Judge Vogel thought it ironic that the *Star* would try to shield itself from this Sherman Act prosecution by invoking the First Amendment. "Publishers of newspapers," he reminded the defendants, "must answer for their actions in the same manner as anyone else.... Freedom to print does not mean freedom to destroy."[96]

Newspapers have not been the only media industries to become antitrust defendants over the years. The structure of the motion picture industry was shaped in large part by a 1948 Supreme Court decision holding that **block-booking** (whereby theater owners were forced by movie studios to exhibit their less desirable "B" movies along with the more popular films likely to produce a profit) was a violation of the Sherman Act.[97] Major Hollywood studios at the time also owned huge chains of theaters, an arrangement that produced its own host of anticompetitive practices. Independent theater owners naturally found it hard to get access to the best pictures, which the studios preferred to keep for their own screens. The government successfully pressured the studios to sell off their movie theatres in the late 1940s.

Perhaps the most dramatic litigation in recent years alleging anticompetitive practices on the part of a communications industry has been the Department of Justice's allegations against the Microsoft Corporation. The government alleged—and Judge Thomas Penfield Jackson agreed—that Microsoft used its virtual monopoly in personal computer operating systems (Windows) to create an unfair advantage in marketing its own Internet browser (Internet Explorer). Microsoft argued that its browser is an integral part of its operating system and that to force it to remove the Explorer would be akin to forcing a cookie manufacturer to take the chocolate chips out of its cookies so as to protect the market share of companies that wished to sell consumers chocolate chips separately. Judge Jackson ordered

---

[96] *United States v. Kansas City Star,* 240 F.2d 643, 666 (8th Cir. 1957).

[97] *United States v. Paramount Pictures,* 334 U.S. 131 (1948); see also *United States v. Loew's, Incorporated,* 371 U.S. 38 (1962) (movie studios' "block-booking" of films to TV stations held a violation of antitrust laws).

Microsoft to be split into two companies.[98] In February 2001, the D.C. Circuit Court of Appeals heard the software giant's appeal. As we were going to press, most observers doubted that the break-up order would be upheld.

Antitrust laws can be triggered not only by a company's engaging in specific anticompetitive practices, but also by one or a small group of companies simply growing so big that a monopoly or quasi-monopoly results. Such monopolies can happen with media outlets just as they can among car manufacturers or soft drink producers. The federal government has often brought actions against media companies that have achieved too large a size of market share. For example, in the 1960s, the *Los Angeles Times* was forced to divest itself of newspapers it had recently purchased in neighboring San Bernardino County.[99] The government has also had to approve the many mergers that resulted from the Telecommunications Act of 1996, discussed in more detail in Chapter 12.

In 1970, Congress adopted the **Newspaper Preservation Act,** which permitted competing newspapers in the same town to function under a **joint operating agreement** (JOA), whereby the advertising, circulation, and printing portions of the two papers would be joined but each would maintain separate editorial functions. These exceptions to the usual behaviors one would expect under existing antitrust law were to be permitted only if at least one of the two newspapers was otherwise in danger of failing. The Act was thus the federal government's way of expressing the value of having more than one major newspaper in a community. In the late 1970s, there were functioning JOAs in twenty-eight cities nationwide, but that number diminished more than 50 percent by the end of the century, with most of the remaining agreements likely also to die out soon. Very few cities still have more than one newspaper, and even in those cities, one paper is usually so clearly the marketplace leader that it has "little incentive...to agree to peaceful coexistence."[100]

## Taxation

Although the press may be taxed in the same way as any industry,[101] taxes that discriminatorily target media outlets may be found unconstitutional. This principle was established clearly in a 1936 case from Louisiana, whose legislature had enacted a tax on the advertising revenues from newspapers with circulations of more than 20,000 subscribers. The tax seemed designed cleverly to burden, even

---

[98]*United States v. Microsoft Corporation,* 97 F. Supp. 2d 59 (D.C. 2000).

[99]*United States v. Times-Mirror Corporation,* 274 F. Supp. 606 (C.D. Cal. 1967), *aff'd,* 390 U.S. 712, *reh'g denied,* 391 U.S. 971 (1968).

[100]Paul Farhi, "The Death of the JOA," *American Journalism Review,* Sept. 1999, pp. 48–52.

[101]*Arizona Publishing Company v. O'Neil,* 304 U.S. 543 (1938); *City of Corona v. Corona Daily Independent,* 252 P.2d 56 (Cal. Ct. App. 1953).

silence, critics of Senator Huey Long, who was most vociferously challenged by editors of the state's largest newspapers. In his majority opinion striking down the law, Justice Sutherland described the tax as "a deliberate and calculated device…to limit the circulation of information to which the public is entitled."[102]

Even in the absence of as colorful a figure as Huey Long, the Supreme Court reached a similar result in 1983 when it struck down a Minnesota tax on paper and ink that, by exempting the first $100,000 of use, effectively targeted the tax so narrowly that one newspaper paid almost two-thirds of it. Even if the legislature had no personal animus against the Minneapolis Star and Tribune Company, Justice O'Connor ruled, singling out only a few media companies for taxation presents too strong "a potential for abuse."[103]

The state of Arkansas was also held in violation of the First Amendment when it enacted a tax that at first blush would seem to be constitutional, because it was aimed at "tangible personal property" generally. The constitutional infirmity was in the tax's application to some magazines but its exemption for locally published "religious," "professional," and "trade and sports journals." Taxes may not discriminate on the basis of a publication's content, the Court ruled.[104] Similarly, Texas was not permitted to exempt only *religious* periodicals from a general sales tax. The Court's decision here rested upon the First Amendment's Establishment Clause.[105] The same constitutional provision was used in 1999 by the Pennsylvania Supreme Court to strike down a sales tax exemption for Bibles and other religious publications.[106]

Taxes that apply to some but not all media industries are not necessarily in violation of the Constitution, however. In 1991, for example, the Supreme Court upheld an Arkansas sales tax levied against cable television companies but not magazines, newspapers, or even home satellite systems. Justice O'Connor's majority opinion indicated that "differential taxation of speakers, even members of the press, does not implicate the First Amendment unless the tax is directed at, or presents the danger of, suppressing particular ideas."[107] Whether a sales tax may constitutionally be applied to magazines while exempting newspapers is still an open question, however. Courts have come down on both sides of this issue.[108]

---

[102]*Grosjean v. American Press Company,* 297 U.S. 233, 250 (1936).

[103]*Minneapolis Star v. Minnesota Commissioner of Revenue,* 460 U.S. 575 (1983).

[104]*Arkansas Writers' Project v. Ragland,* 481 U.S. 221 (1987).

[105]*Texas Monthly v. Bullock,* 489 U.S. 1 (1989).

[106]*Haller v. Commonwealth,* 728 A.2d 351 (Pa. Sup. Ct. 1999).

[107]*Leathers v. Medlock,* 499 U.S. 439 (1991).

[108]*Southern Living v. Celauro,* 789 S.W.2d 251 (Tenn. 1990) (striking down the differential taxation of magazines and newspapers); *Hearst Corporation v. Iowa Department of Revenue & Finance,* 461 N.W.2d 295 (Iowa 1990) (upholding such differential treatment).

## Workplace Law

Just as taxes that are applied to industry generally may be applied to media outlets, so also must media industries obey relevant federal, state, and local labor laws in their relationships with their employees. Interesting questions often arise, however, when courts try to determine how to apply this body of law to professional communicators. In this section, two areas of labor law that have attracted much judicial attention, the Fair Labor Standards Act and the National Labor Relations Act, are explored.

One of the key provisions of the Fair Labor Standards Act (FLSA) of 1938 is that employees not exempted from its scope must be paid overtime wages for work in excess of forty hours weekly. Certain categories of professional employees are exempt from the Act—thus the references to "exempt" and "nonexempt" employees in human resources offices nationwide—and courts have often been called on to determine when media employees should be considered such professionals. This body of case law often forces media litigants to make arguments contrary to their customary economic bargaining positions. Management must claim that employees' work is distinct and creative (and thus not qualifying for overtime pay), whereas workers counter that their output is routine and uninspired.[109]

Ever since the 1940s, the Secretary of Labor, who has initial responsibility for enforcement of the FLSA, has maintained that only a very small number of working journalists are "professionals" exempt from the Act's overtime pay provisions. Only "editorial writers, columnists, critics, and 'top-flight' writers of analytical and interpretative articles" should be considered exempt, the Department of Labor argues. Although it is fair to say that the vast majority of reporters are valued for their "intelligence, diligence, and accuracy," only these categories of employees are called on as their "primary duty" to produce work requiring "invention, imagination, or talent," work that is "original and creative in character." The Department of Labor also emphasizes that reporters, unlike such professionals as doctors and lawyers, do not have to master a prescribed body of knowledge to function in their careers; they need not have journalism degrees and often do not have college degrees at all. Courts have generally accepted the Department of Labor's interpretation of the FLSA's applicability to the newsroom.[110] The one exceptional case involved *Washington Post* writers who were considered professionals exempt from the FLSA's overtime wages provisions. In that case, the court emphasized that *Post* reporters are very highly paid national leaders in the field of journalism, often called on to teach at universities, to write books, and to serve as guests on talk show and public affairs programs. Moreover, these reporters functioned in a professionally collegial atmosphere that would be envied by their counterparts at other papers. They were

[109]*Reich v. Newspapers of New England*, 44 F.3d 1060, 1075 n.12 (1st Cir. 1995); see also *Freeman v. National Broadcasting Company*, 846 F. Supp. 1109, 1123 (S.D.N.Y. 1993).

[110]*Dalheim v. KDFW-TV*, 706 F. Supp. 493 (N.D. Tex. 1988), *aff'd*, 918 F.2d 1220 (5th Cir. 1990); *Freeman v. National Broadcasting Company*, 846 F. Supp. 1109 (S.D.N.Y. 1993); *Reich v. Newspapers of New England*, 44 F.3d 1060 (1st Cir. 1995); *Reich v. Gateway Press*, 13 F.3d 685 (3d Cir. 1994).

encouraged to generate their own story ideas and to decide not only how to pursue stories, but also when it might be wisest to "kill" a story.[111]

The National Labor Relations Act also has an impact on how media outlets are regulated as businesses. The Act provides most employees with the right to organize, to form unions, to collectively bargain, and to engage in all these activities without fear of retribution from their employers. What happens if the employer is a newspaper, however, and the alleged retribution takes the form of reassigning a reporter to new duties? Such was the case when Mitchell Stoddard, a columnist for the *Passaic Daily News* in New Jersey, had been active in a union organizing drive and later learned that his employer no longer planned to run his weekly column. The National Labor Relations Board (NLRB) ordered the newspaper to restore the status quo, to continue to run Stoddard's column. The newspaper appealed, arguing that the NLRB's chosen remedy was a violation of its right to determine what will and will not run in its pages, the "right not to speak" corollary First Amendment right discussed earlier in this chapter. The D.C. Circuit Court of Appeals recognized that the NLRB's goals were legitimate: to ensure both that the company not be allowed to retaliate against Stoddard and that "meaningful remedies for [future] victims of unlawful discrimination" be in place. Here, however, the Board went too far in that it injected itself "into the editorial decision-making process." The court remanded the case back to the NLRB, suggesting that an order "direct[ing] the Company to not discriminate against Stoddard on the basis of his union activity" might be a more appropriate remedy. On remand, the NLRB ordered the paper to restore Stoddard's "column-writing duties" but did not compel the newspaper to actually publish whatever columns he writes, just as long as that decision flows from considerations other than his union activities.[112]

The strained judicial compromise reached in *Passaic Daily News* underscores the more general proposition that deference to publishers' free press rights necessarily means that media company employees may have fewer free speech rights than workers in other industries.[113] Thus, for example, the state of Washington's Fair Campaign Practices Act, which protects employees from retaliation for their off-the-job political activities, was held inapplicable to a newspaper reporter who had been dismissed by the Tacoma *Morning News Tribune* for having participated in a prochoice abortion rally and for ignoring management's request that she refrain from any high-profile political activities. The newspaper's need to protect its reputation for objectivity in reporting the news must prevail over the reporter's interests, the court held.[114]

---

[111]*Sherwood v. Washington Post*, 677 F. Supp. 9 (D.D.C. 1988), *rev'd and remanded on other grounds,* 871 F.2d 1144 (D.C. Cir. 1989).

[112]*Passaic Daily News v. National Labor Relations Board*, 736 F.2d 1543 (D.C. Cir. 1984).

[113]Louis Day, "The Journalist as Citizen Activist: The Ethical Limits of Free Speech," 4 *Communication Law and Policy* 1 (1999).

[114]*Nelson v. McClatchy Newspapers, Inc.*, 936 P.2d 1123 (Wash. Sup. Ct. 1997).

# Things to Remember

### REGULATING MEDIA AS A BUSINESS

- Federal antitrust laws have been used against:
  - Newspapers that refuse to accept advertising from businesses already advertising in competing media.
  - Movie studios that demand theater owners to accept less known "B" movies if they want to show the true blockbusters.
  - Movie studios that owned too many movie theaters.
  - Any media company that has grown so huge and commands such a large market share that it threatens to stifle competition.
- The Newspaper Preservation Act sometimes permits otherwise competing newspapers to form JOAs to share noneditorial costs.
- The media may be subject to the same kinds of taxes as any other business, but taxes that single out the media or that discriminate among media outlets might be found unconstitutional.
- Taxes that exempt only *religious* media are especially likely to be found unconstitutional.
- Most media employees are considered "nonexempt" and thus eligible for such worker benefits as overtime pay.
- Journalists can generally be prevented by their employers from engaging in overt political activity.

## Chapter Summary

Although freedom of speech can be traced back to the ancients, the American experience results primarily from the British common law. Early colonial experience was characterized by much intolerance of dissent, and the Alien and Sedition Acts followed swiftly upon the formation of the new nation.

The Supreme Court had very little to say about the First Amendment's meaning until the World War I era when, in a long series of cases continuing through the 1960s, the Court dealt with the issue of incitement to overthrowing of the govern-

ment or of other violent action. The current test for such speech is found in *Brandenburg v. Ohio,* a 1969 decision.

Over the years, many competing First Amendment theories have been proposed, including absolutist theory, access theory, and various balancing approaches. Generally, the modern judiciary engages in preferred position balancing.

Theorists have also identified many functions served by freedom of speech, including seeking truth, enabling us to be better self-governors, checking on government abuse, providing for individual fulfillment and for a societal safety valve, and simply helping us see ourselves as a tolerant people.

Other theorists, including Marxists, feminists, and critical race theorists, have questioned the place of freedom of speech in the hierarchy of values.

The First Amendment has been interpreted so as to include a right to hear, a right not to speak, and a right to engage in symbolic conduct.

Government restrictions on speech that are not aimed at the actual content of the message do not require as exacting scrutiny as purer forms of censorship.

chapter

# *Defamation: Common–Law Elements*

The ritual has been played out in countless movies. One person, angered at another's having maligned his good name, slaps the offender with his glove and demands the "honor" of a duel. The centuries-old common law of libel developed at least in part as a "substitute for dueling, as a deterrent to murder."[1] By no means does this suggest that an individual accused of libel in court rather than on the dueling field would always emerge unscathed. Consider the sentence for **criminal libel** imposed on barrister William Prynne in the 1600s by England's notorious **Star Chamber.** Prynne was disbarred and deprived of his university degrees, fined $5,000 pounds, imprisoned "perpetually," and made to "stand twice in the pillory, and to have one ear cut off each time."[2]

Libel law is designed, of course, to protect a person's reputation from blemish. In Shakespeare's *Othello,* the treacherous Iago famously reminds us that an ordinary thief, one who "steals my purse … steals trash," but that a defamer, someone who "flinches from me my good name … makes me poor indeed."

More routine though less poetic definitions of libel are readily available in standard legal publications. *Black's Law Dictionary* defines libel as "an intentional false communication…that injures another's reputation or good name." The *Restatement of Torts* reports that messages are libelous if they "tend so to harm the reputation of another as to lower him in the estimation of the community or to deter third persons from associating or dealing with him."

Libel plaintiffs range from the most powerful persons in society to the lowest of the low, a truism plainly exemplified by two libel cases that were much in the news in the late 1990s. It was in August of 1997 that Sidney Blumenthal, one of President Clinton's senior staff members, filed a $30 million libel suit against the keeper of a World Wide Web site who had bluntly asserted via the Internet that

---

[1]Irving Brant, *The Bill of Rights: Its Origin and Meaning* (Indianapolis: Bobbs-Merril, 1965), 502.

[2]*Faretta v. California*, 422 U.S. 806, 823 (1975).

Blumenthal had a history of physically abusing his wife.[3] The month prior, a California jury ruled in a libel case that had been filed against actor Carroll O'Connor by the man convicted of having sold cocaine to O'Connor's deceased son. Perhaps Harry Perzigian's suit could be seen as his way of saying that it is one thing to have it known that one derives income from purveying illicit substances, but quite another to be labeled "a partner in murder."[4]

Media professionals are more likely to get into legal trouble over alleged libels than over any other issue that this book addresses. The costs can be staggering. Jury awards in the millions of dollars are no longer especially newsworthy events. Even if the media defendant ultimately prevails, as typically happens at least on the appellate level, the legal fees involved and the enormous amount of time taken from writing new stories so as to defend old ones would alone constitute ample reason to avoid publishing defamatory materials.

For most of the country's history, that the press could be sued and even criminally prosecuted for libel never seemed to raise any constitutional objections. The First Amendment, it will be recalled, tells *Congress* that it cannot abridge freedom of speech and of the press. Defamation had always been handled at the state level. Moreover, that the Founders clearly knew of the existence of libel laws and mentioned not one word about them in the text of the Constitution seems to suggest that they saw no philosophic conflict between the system of freedom of expression they intended to create and the continuing use of laws against defamation. In this chapter, we examine the traditional, common-law definition of libel as it has evolved in the states. In 1964, the U.S. Supreme Court intervened, ruling that the First Amendment does impose significant restrictions on libel law.[5] So dramatic have been the changes in libel since that seminal ruling that we devote Chapter 4 to an examination of the Supreme Court's libel doctrine as it has developed in the past few decades.

## Elements of a Libel Suit

Defamation can be defined as false statements of fact disseminated about a person that result in damage to that person's reputation. Traditionally, the law recognized separate actions for libel (written defamations) and **slander** (spoken defamations). In the several centuries after the invention of the printing press but before the discovery of radio, this separation was logical for at least two reasons. First, the

---

[3]*Blumenthal v. Drudge,* 992 F. Supp. 44 (D.C. Dist. 1998). The case was settled out of court in May 2001.

[4]Ann W. O'Neill and Joe Mozingo, "O'Connor Cleared of Defamation," *Los Angeles Times,* 26 July 1997, p. A1.

[5]*New York Times v. Sullivan,* 376 U.S. 254 (1964).

unamplified spoken word could damage a person's reputation in the minds of only those who were physically present to hear the speech. Unless the speaker had access to a physical setting with extraordinary acoustics, the audience would probably be a few hundred people at most. Then, too, the spoken word has a more ephemeral quality than the written word. The expression "here today, gone tomorrow" actually exaggerates the life of the spoken word, which is more accurately described as gone in the *moment* after it is uttered. The written word, by contrast, has a life that transcends space and time. Recipients of the message can show it to others, and they can discuss it and amplify its effects. Libels could reach a larger audience, and do much more lasting reputational harm, than slanders.

The advent of the electronic mass media muddied the waters to the point where today the distinction between libel and slander has all but disappeared in law. Even the least viewed programs on national network television, after all, reach an audience many times the size of the circulation figures for the country's most popular magazines and newspapers. Moreover, the widespread use of tape recorders and VCRs ensures that the spoken word now can have a shelf life as long as any written message. Thus, it has become more and more difficult to justify two separate systems of defamation law based on the communication channel used by the libel defendant. Although some states still make some parts of a libel suit easier to prove against a "libeler" than a "slanderer," such differences are few. Therefore, this book follows the lead of most courts and commentators by using the word *libel* to refer to both written and spoken defamatory utterances.

One caveat should be added. As shown in Chapter 4, some aspects of the Supreme Court's libel doctrine developed since 1964 make it more difficult for libel plaintiffs to win their suits against representatives of the institutionalized mass media than against ordinary citizens. This distinction seems to be based on the channel of communication used to disseminate a libel that operates in the opposite direction from the traditional distinction between libel and slander. After all, mass mediated libels, precisely because they reach a large audience, are more likely to do reputational harm than are libels disseminated by ordinary citizens who do not have access to the media. The Court's logic, when it has been expressed, seems to be in keeping with Justice Stewart's own reasoning as discussed in Chapter 1. The media are especially deserving of First Amendment protection because they serve as our eyes and ears, because most of us are wholly dependent on mass media for information about the issues of the day.

Generally speaking, libel plaintiffs must prove four elements[6] to prevail. They must establish defamation, of course, but also **publication, identification,** and

---

[6]Some writers include **falsity** as a fifth element. This book does not do so in that the common law traditionally placed the burden of proof instead on the defendant to establish the truth of the defamatory statements. Moreover, in some states, even today, truth is not an absolute defense to a libel action. Although the Supreme Court has had some things to say about this issue, it has not gone so far as to wholly reverse the common-law tradition. This point will be expanded on when we discuss the Court's ruling in *Philadelphia Newspapers, Inc. v. Hepps* in Chapter 4.

**fault.** The discussion of the first three of these elements takes up the rest of this chapter. In that the Supreme Court's libel doctrine, which has been evolving since the 1960s, has focused almost entirely on the issue of fault, the discussion of that fourth element is necessarily rather lengthy and complex. Chapter 4 examines the Supreme Court's 1964 intervention into libel law and later cases that have fine-tuned and generally expanded the First Amendment protections provided in that case.

## Defamation

Defamatory utterances are those that, if believed, will make a listener think less highly of the persons described, avoid their company in social situations, or avoid seeking out their services in business relationships. The following discussion of this first element examines several key questions courts address as libel plaintiffs try to build their cases. First, we consider whether the defamatory meaning is explicit and obvious, or whether readers would need additional information to understand the insult. Then we focus on the audience, as we try to ascertain *in whose minds* the complainant has been damaged. Next, with respect to the message itself, we will see that courts have sometimes excused arguably libelous statements as "rhetorical hyperbole." The focus then shifts to the relationship between the defamation element and the kinds and amounts of damages successful plaintiffs may be awarded. Finally, we will examine how corporations, and even products, can be libeled.

***Libel Per Se and Libel Per Quod.*** Traditionally, the common law of libel has recognized two categories of defamatory statements. Although Supreme Court intervention into libel law has made the distinctions less important to litigants than was once the case, the categories still help to understand the overall concept of defamation. The first category of defamations are **libel per se,** allegations that would obviously, with no further embellishment by the speaker or special knowledge on the part of the listener, damage the reputation of the persons described. The kinds of defamations generally recognized as libel per se have included allegations of criminal wrongdoing, of gross incompetence in one's chosen career, of such serious moral failings as being a chronic liar, or of having a loathsome and contagious disease. To accuse a woman of sexual misconduct has also been viewed as libelous per se.[7] The second broad category of defamations is **libel per quod,** those that seem innocent enough on their face, but when added to specific facts presumably already known by readers would be injurious

---

[7]U.S. courts even in recent years have taken female libel plaintiffs' claims far more seriously when the defamatory statements concerned their sexual "virtue" rather than, say, their professional competence. Diane L. Borden, "Patterns of Harm: An Analysis of Gender and Defamation," 1 *Communication Law and Policy* 105, 133–134 (1997).

to reputation. Suppose that a campus paper were to write that "Professor Jones was seen gardening in her backyard yesterday and appeared to be vigorous, energetic, and healthy." These would hardly seem to be defamatory statements, but what if Jones had recently filed for disability benefits? Knowledgeable readers might correctly surmise that the reporter had intended to suggest that Jones was engaged in fraud.

That readers may have some special knowledge above and beyond the recitation in a defamatory article does not necessarily place the defamations in the libel per quod category. The special knowledge must be about the individual described in the article rather than about the world in general. An often cited and rather bizarre case from the 1920s in New York State makes this point well.[8] Ms. Florence Ben-Oliel was a sought-after expert on Middle Eastern cultures. When she discovered that a newspaper had not only published an article in her field that was falsely attributed to her,[9] but also that the article included several bits of misinformation about Palestinian customs relating to marriage and divorce, she brought

---

[8]*Ben-Oliel v. Press Publishing Company,* 167 N. E. 432 (1929).

[9]This kind of transgression alone could open up a publisher to a claim of misappropriation, a topic discussed in Chapter 5.

 # Things to Remember

**TRADITIONAL LIBEL PER SE CATEGORIES**

*Criminal Activity*
  "Jones is an embezzler."
  "Smith is an organized crime lynchpin."

*Professional Incompetence*
  "Siegel has left more sponges inside his patients than most households go through in a year."

*Serious Character Flaws*
  "We would have loved to interview Chambers for this article, but he is such a chronic liar it hardly seemed worth the effort."

*Having a "Loathsome, Contagious" Disease*
  "Apparently the reason the star has not shown up on the set for the last two days is that he is dealing with his recent AIDS diagnosis."

*Lack of Chastity Attributed to an Unmarried Woman*
  "Accounts of their wedding in the society pages that described the bride as 'blushing' and 'virginal' were, at best, half-truths."

suit for libel. The court determined that the factual errors in the article constituted libel per se in that they collectively served to label Ben-Oliel an "ignorant imposter" just as effectively as if the editors had used that epithet to refer to her directly. "One may say of a physician that he is an ignorant quack," the court said, "or he may print a statement [falsely attributed to] the physician regarding some operation performed by him or some treatment of a disease which shows him to the profession to be an ignoramus and a bungler. Both of these publications would be libelous [per se]."[10]

***Who Has to Believe?***   The *Ben-Oliel* case offers another lesson about proving the element of defamation in a libel suit. For a report to be found defamatory does not require that the vast majority of readers did in fact hold the libeled party in lower esteem after seeing the charges. So specialized was Ben-Oliel's field of expertise that only a tiny portion of the newspaper's readership would have sufficient knowledge of it to recognize the errors that had been falsely attributed to her. This number is sufficient to find defamation, however, in that courts will gauge the negative effects of the libels on any right-minded individuals who together constitute a community of relevance to the plaintiff.

Adjudication becomes quite complicated if a plaintiff's "community" is an identifiable group with values far different from those of the society at large. Would it be defamatory for the press to report that world-famous safecracker "Frankie the Fingers" has "lost his touch"? Certainly such an allegation, if believed, would make professional criminals less likely to seek out Frankie's services. The charge would also seem to fit into the traditional libel per se category of attributing "professional incompetence" to the person described. More generally, Professor Lyrissa Lidsky of the University of Florida points out that in some neighborhoods and in some social circles, being accused of having "cooperated with the police" might diminish one's reputation greatly.[11] The courts' general reply to these insights is that libel law is not concerned with how esteemed one is in the eyes of criminals, but rather with an utterance's effect on one's reputation among a community of listeners that is both substantial and respectable.

Sometimes a potential libel plaintiff's reputation in the mainstream community, long before publication of allegedly defamatory remarks, is so irredeemable that a few more insults could not hurt. Such **libel-proof plaintiffs,** as they are known in the law, are generally not able to prevail in defamation cases. This reasoning may have been what prompted the jury in the libel suit pressed by known drug pusher Harry Perzigian to find for the defendant, actor Carroll O'Connor.

---

[10]167 N. E. at 433–34.

[11]Lyrissa Barnett Lidsky, "Defamation, Reputation and the Myth of Community," 71 *Washington Law Review* 1, 8 (1996).

Defendant Carroll O'Connor on the witness stand in *Perzigian v. O'Connor.*

*Copyright © 1997 Court TV. Reprinted with permission.*

Another complication in adjudicating the defamation element of libel is that community standards are not static. To falsely assert that a person is Black would surely not be considered defamatory today, but just as surely that assertion *was* considered defamatory in the first half of the twentieth century. There are a number of libel cases on the books involving allegations of homosexuality. Whether such a charge would be held libelous today is not entirely clear. Although sodomy laws directed specifically at gays remain on the books only in a minority of the states, some courts have distinguished allegations that someone "is gay" from specific allegations of criminal sexual conduct, the logic seeming to be that one might self-identify as gay without ever acting on one's desires.[12] When a tabloid

---

[12]*Stein v. Trager,* 232 N.Y.S.2d 362 (Sup. Ct., Erie County, 1962).

 # Things to Remember

### THE DEFAMATION ELEMENT AND THE AUDIENCE

- To be actionable, a libelous statement must be believed by a significant number of reasonable persons.
- That people who are themselves unsavory characters think less of you will not constitute your being libeled.
- Some libel plaintiffs are themselves already held in such low esteem that they are deemed "libel-proof."
- Society's concept of what kinds of charges are libelous changes over time.

newspaper published a story suggesting that Tom Selleck is gay, the actor sued for libel, but settled out of court. Interestingly, Selleck later played the openly gay TV reporter who helps teacher Kevin Kline come to terms with his own homosexuality in the 1997 film *In and Out*.

***What Does It All Mean?*** Sometimes language can be ambiguous, subject to multiple interpretations. The Supreme Court was asked if it was libelous for the *Greenbelt News Review* in Maryland to suggest that local real estate developer C. S. Bresler was in the process of "blackmailing" the city (a phrase used by several participants at Greenbelt City Council meetings).[13] The developer had been engaged in negotiations with the city council to obtain certain zoning variances that would allow the construction of high-density housing on land owned by him. At the same time, the city was attempting to acquire another tract of his land for the construction of a new high school. Bresler made clear his intention to force the city to engage in extensive litigation concerning compensation for the school site should the zoning waivers he sought be denied.

Although the word *blackmail* could certainly refer to the criminal act of extortion, the Court held that the most natural interpretation of the paper's use of the word was more benign. "Even the most careless reader," Justice Stewart wrote for the majority, would recognize that the epithet was used only so as to suggest that "Bresler's negotiating position [was] extremely unreasonable."

A bitter exchange between representatives of the Church of Scientology and of the Eli Lilly drug company resulted in a libel decision that also raised the question of whether exaggeration or hyperbole can be deemed defamatory.[14] The church had taken out a series of full page ads in *USA Today* expressing concern about the overuse of tranquilizers and antidepressants, singling out the Lilly company for its role in promoting the use of Prozac. Lilly Vice President Mitchell Daniels sought and obtained a meeting with the newspaper's editorial board. The newspaper published an account of that meeting, attributing to Daniels the assertions that the Church of Scientology "is no church," but rather "a commercial enterprise…organized for only one purpose, which is to make money." After the church sued for libel, the federal district court granted summary judgment to Daniels on the grounds that the quoted allegations, as a matter of law, could not be found defamatory. The district court opinion is unpublished, so the court's precise reasoning must be inferred from the appellate court's references to the adjudication below. It is most likely that the district court found such phrases "for only *one* purpose" to be mere hyperbole, not to be taken literally. The appellate court affirmed, although on other grounds.

---

[13]*Greenbelt Cooperative Publishing Association v. Bresler,* 398 U.S. 6 (1970).

[14]*Church of Scientology International v. Mitchell Daniels,* 992 F. 2d 1329 (4th Cir. 1993).

A similarly vitriolic exchange, this time conducted on the editorial page of a small Columbia, South Carolina, newspaper on the controversial issue of the causes of homosexuality, is also instructive.[15] An op-ed piece written by Marie-Therese Assa'ad Faltas, a University of South Carolina Medical School resident, took aim at research suggesting that sexual orientation has strong genetic or hormonal components rather than constituting a personal choice. The newspaper later published a handful of letters it received critical of the Faltas op-ed. One of those letters, written by a Chris Riley, accused Faltas of having used "spurious and twisted logic" and of using her professional status "as an opportunity to present lies as truth." A federal district court in South Carolina dismissed Faltas's libel suit, having concluded that Riley's words were not capable of establishing the element of defamation. "A reasonable reader," Judge Joseph Anderson wrote, "would presume the letter is an impassioned response to the positions taken by Dr. Faltas in her article, and nothing more." He added that homosexuality is a controversial subject upon which experts often disagree "in less than collegial tones."

The issue of rhetorical hyperbole is really a special instance of the more general maxim that courts will determine whether an utterance is capable of a defamatory reading by looking at the overall context and the most natural, plausible meaning of the words. Two aspects of the overall context of special concern to print media professionals are headlines and **jump cuts.** Some courts have found that a carelessly worded headline can itself be found defamatory even if the article it introduces contains no actionable statements.

The West Virginia Supreme Court upheld a libel judgment against the *Charleston Daily Mail,* which had published, just prior to a gubernatorial election, a series of articles critical of candidate James Sprouse's real estate dealings. The court indicated that the jury could legitimately have found defamatory content in the headlines alone in that they included phrases—for example, "Land Grab" and "Realty Bonanza"—that seemed more pejorative than the facts outlined in the articles themselves justified.[16] A similar result is found in a New York appellate court ruling stemming from state senator Richard Schermerhorn's libel action against a reporter for the *Times Herald Record.* The senator's proposal for an urban renewal project in the town of Newburgh had created a good deal of controversy, especially among those minority residents of the area who felt that their neighborhoods would be most likely to experience disruption. The headline of an article appearing in the *Herald Record* attributed to the senator the belief that the governing board that would be appointed to oversee the proposed urban renewal project "could do without Blacks." Apparently the senator had said no such thing, and the article itself did not claim that he had. The headline was deemed sufficient to find the element of defamation.[17]

---

[15]*Marie-Therese Assa'ad Faltas v. The State Newspaper,* 928 F. Supp. 637 (S.C. 1996), *aff' without opinion,* 155 F. 3d 557 (4th Cir. 1998).

[16]*Sprouse v. Clay,* 211 S.E. 2d 674 (1975).

[17]*Schermerhorn v. Rosenberg,* 426 N.Y.S.2d 274 (2d App. Div. N.Y. 1980).

Whether potentially libelous words in headlines or in the initial sentences of an article will be found defamatory sometimes is a function of how much energy readers must expend before encountering the clarifying facts. Defendants are more likely to prevail if the exculpatory facts appear early on, ideally on the same page where the article began. If readers must pore over paragraph after paragraph, and especially if they must follow one or more jump cuts to other pages inside the newspaper, courts may not be so lenient. This lesson was learned in a case stemming from an article that appeared in the *Seattle Post Intelligencer.* Here is the headline and beginning words of that article:

# The High Cost of a Divorce

Five years ago, Barbara Evans hired a lawyer to represent her in a divorce action.…
 Today the lawyer owns the home, worth between $55,000 and $65,000, which Mrs. Evans received as part of the 1966 divorce settlement.

If you read these words, how would you interpret them? Might you presume that the attorney had swindled or at least grossly overcharged Evans? The federal appellate court thought so and expressed concern that readers would not learn until toward the very end of the article that Evans had been charged only $3,000 by her attorney and that she lost her house because of a complicated set of events involving second, third, and even fourth mortgages set in motion by the failure of her ex-husband to meet the financial obligations placed on him by the divorce court. The attorney had done no wrong, but one would have to read the article's additional fifty or so paragraphs and flip pages three times before realizing how misleading the opening had been. Granting summary judgment to the newspaper, as the lower court had done, was deemed inappropriate. "What a newspaper regards as newsworthy usually makes its appearance in the headline and lead paragraphs," the appellate court wrote. "This is what is intended to compel the reader's attention."[18]

A similar result was reached more recently in Brian "Kato" Kaelin's lawsuit against the publisher of the *National Examiner* tabloid. The week after O. J. Simpson was acquitted in the homicides of Nicole Brown Simpson and Ron Goldman, the paper ran a large headline proclaiming that the "COPS THINK KATO DID IT!" In overturning a lower court decision granting summary judgment to the defendant publishers, the Court of Appeals for the Ninth Circuit emphasized that readers would not learn until turning to the article itself, on page 17, that at worst Kaelin might be suspected of not telling all that he knows and thus of having derailed the prosecution's case. He was not a suspect in the homicides themselves. The

---

[18]*McNair v. The Hearst Corporation,* 494 F.2d 1309, 1311 (9th Cir. 1974).

## Things to Remember

### DEFAMATION AND MEANING

- Highly inflammatory remarks that fall into the category of rhetorical hyperbole are generally not actionable as libels.
- A misleading newspaper headline can be libelous even if nothing in the article itself is libelous.
- A clarifying or disclaiming statement that does not appear until very late in an article, especially if the placement requires the reader to flip through one or more pages to find it, might not save a publisher from liability for earlier sections of the article.

amount of effort readers would need to expend to learn the true meaning of the headline was extraordinary, the court said, because the tabloid's layout "is unlike a conventional headline that immediately precedes a newspaper story."[19]

***Defaming People, Corporations, and Products.*** Most of the libel cases used as examples so far have involved individual plaintiffs. Another commonality among the plaintiffs is that they were living when they brought suit. Libel suits cannot be brought on behalf of deceased individuals; the logic is that when you are dead, you really do not care very much about what others think of you. Libel suits commenced by a living plaintiff who dies while the litigation is pending, however, can be pursued by the deceased's heirs or estate. Then, too, libelous statements are sometimes painted with such a broad brush that they affect the reputations of persons closely associated with the individual specifically mentioned. For example, if you suggest in an obituary that a particular individual was a member in good standing of an international network of swingers and spouse swappers, the deceased's widow might choose to sue you for having thus libeled *her* by implication.

Individuals are not the only potential libel plaintiffs. The case cited above involving the Church of Scientology demonstrates that corporations can and often do sue for libel. So, too, do nonprofit associations and labor unions. To falsely claim that an organization has engaged in fraudulent or deceptive practices can be, as one would expect, just as libelous as to make the same charges against an individual. Corporations may also sue for libel if a story falsely alleges that the company is on the brink of financial disaster. Such a story prompted a legal dispute that got to the Supreme Court in 1985, when a credit reporting agency, in a newsletter with limited circulation, mistakenly reported that a construction company in

---

[19]*Kaelin v. Globe Communications Corporation,* 162 F.3d 1036 (9th Cir. 1998).

Vermont had filed for bankruptcy. It seems that a teenager hired as a "stringer" for the Dun & Bradstreet agency misinterpreted a document showing that a former employee of Greenmoss Builders had filed for *personal* bankruptcy.[20]

Sometimes corporations will sue because of negative comments made about their products or services themselves. In such situations—where there is not even a hint in the allegedly libelous report that the company itself has engaged in dishonesty, only that the product is an inferior one—the cause of action is called **trade libel** or **product disparagement.** It is important to understand the difference between defaming the company and disparaging the product. If, through overreliance on misinformed sources or through other shoddy reporting, you publish an article alleging that a certain model of automobile is unsafe, you might open yourself up to a trade libel suit. If the same article alleges that the car's manufacturers likely knew that the car was a road hazard, but rushed to bring it to market anyway, the company would be able also to sue for ordinary libel.

A phenomenon that has received much media attention is the enactment in several states of "veggie libel" laws. These statutes, passed in the 1990s by more than a dozen states, permit producers of perishable food products to sue anyone who makes false statements about their products that result in a loss of revenue. The impetus for the laws was industry frustration at an unsuccessful lawsuit against the producers of the CBS program *60 Minutes,* which in 1989 broadcast a story warning viewers that the residue from a pesticide called Alar could make apples carcinogenic.[21] The story had been based largely on studies done with laboratory animals; no epidemiological reports were available on humans. The federal courts found that this limitation in the available scientific data was insufficient for any reasonable jury to find that *60 Minutes'* conclusions were false. In 1997, a cattle feed operator in Amarillo, Texas, used that state's veggie libel law to bring an ultimately unsuccessful suit against Oprah Winfrey, claiming that her TV talk show's discussion of "mad cow disease" resulted in plummeting beef sales and a personal loss of millions of dollars. The "veggie libel" aspect of the law was removed from jury consideration in that the trial judge determined that the Texas statute was applicable only to "perishable food products," not to cattle.[22] These kinds of statutes have already received a fair amount of critical commentary in legal academic circles, and the consensus seems to be that most of them will, if challenged, be struck down as unconstitutional infringements on freedom of speech.[23]

---

[20]*Dun & Bradstreet v. Greenmoss Builders,* 472 U.S. 749 (1985).

[21]*Auvil v. CBS "60 Minutes,"* 800 F. Supp. 928 (E.D. Wash, 1992), *aff'd,* 67 F.3d 816 (9th Cir. 1995).

[22]*Texas Beef Group v. Winfrey,* 11 F. Supp. 2d 858 (N.D. Tex. 1998), aff'd, 212 F. 3d 597(5th Cir. 2000).

[23]See, for example, David J. Bederman, Scott M. Christensen, and Scott Dean Quesenberry, "Of Banana Bills and Veggie Hate Crimes: The Constitutionality of Agricultural Disparagement Statutes," 34 *Harvard Journal on Legislation* 135 (1997).

Figure 3.1

*"YOU SAY THAT OPRAH MAY HAVE HURT YOUR REPUTATION BUT POSSIBLY SAVED YOUR LIFE"*

*I'M NOT MAD AT ANYBODY*

Although the "veggie libel" suit against Oprah Winfrey for expressing fear about getting mad cow disease was dismissed, some other states' statutes may be upheld.

*Copyright © 1998 by Herblock in* The Washington Post. *Reprinted with permission.*

 # Things to Remember

### DEFAMATION AND THE PLAINTIFF

- Libel actions generally cannot be brought on behalf of deceased individuals.
- Corporations can sue for libelous remarks suggesting that their officers or employees have engaged in fraudulent or other reprehensible activities.
- Corporations can sue for trade libel or product disparagement when the offensive criticisms concern the product line itself, rather than its manufacturers.
- In the 1990s, more than a dozen states passed "veggie libel" laws, specifically targeting speech suggesting that perishable food products are unsafe.

**How Much Does It Hurt?**    When people bring civil suits against each other, the end result they seek is usually the awarding of money damages. How much money plaintiffs are awarded is, at least in part, a function of in what ways and how badly they were hurt. As such, in libel law the matter of damages is almost inextricable from the element of defamation.

Generally speaking, the law recognizes two broad categories of damages, compensatory and punitive. **Punitive damages** are designed to punish the defendants for outrageous behavior as well as to make an example of them that may deter others. Juries may not reach the issue of punitive damages unless some form of compensatory damages are also granted. The logic here is straightforward enough: no matter how egregious the press's behavior, they should not be punished unless they did some harm by that behavior. As we see in the next chapter, the U.S. Supreme Court's intervention into the law of libel in recent decades has put additional limits on the kinds of situations that permit the awarding of punitive damages.[24]

**Compensatory damages** fall into three subcategories. **Presumed damages** are much what the name implies. Common-law practice is for juries to grant presumed damages without demanding that the plaintiffs demonstrate how, specifically, they were harmed. In libel law, presumed damages tended to be sought in cases involving the libel per se categories of defamations discussed earlier. Libel per se plaintiffs did not have to prove how or why the words written about them damaged their reputation in that some categories of accusations, if believed, could be presumed to lower one's standing in a community. Presumed damages would logically go hand in hand in that they similarly did not demand a showing of any specific kind of harm.

The other two subcategories of compensatory damages have names that may seem counterintuitive. **Actual damages** can be distinguished from presumed damages in that the plaintiff must at least make some showing of harm. The harm, however, can be a rather intangible one. Defamation actions are quite different in this way from, say, medical malpractice suits. In the latter kind of case, we expect to see the crutches, the neck braces, the prognoses of expert witnesses. To win actual damages, the *Gertz* Court said, libel plaintiffs need only show that they have suffered "impairment of reputation and standing in the community, personal humiliation, [or] mental anguish and suffering."

---

[24]*Gertz v. Welch Inc.,* 418 U.S. 323, 348 (1974).

 # Things to Remember

**DAMAGES**

- Punitive damages:
  - Designed to punish the defamer and to deter others
- Compensatory damages:
  - Presumed: no proof of harm needed
  - Actual: some proof of harm needed, but it does not need to be very tangible
  - Special: highly specific and measurable proof of harm required

So, do not get confused. Actual damages do not require that plaintiffs demonstrate anything in the way of measurable, tangible harm. If a plaintiff is able to pinpoint actual dollar amounts of loss resulting from libel, such as being terminated because an employer believed the lies or being thrown out by a landlord, we move into the realm of what are called **special damages.** References to special damages are most frequently seen in trade libel cases, as a company tries to establish the specific amount of market share forfeited as a result of remarks disparaging of their products.

## Publication

The word *publication* is an unfortunate one as applied to libel law. It is misleading in two ways. First, it seems to suggest, erroneously, that only the mass media can possibly libel anyone, because we tend to think of "publishing" as something only media industries do. A related and equally erroneous implication of the word is that defamatory comments must reach a mass audience before they can be actionable.

In libel law, however, publication has a very narrow and special meaning. It means that the speaker or writer has shared the allegedly defamatory comments about another person with at least one third party. (Of course, because the *defamation* element requires that many people actually believe the untruths, we assume here that the one person you tell in turn spreads the word to others.) If you complain directly to your teacher that you think he is having an affair with a classmate, that would be one-to-one communication, with no publication; if you share this same conjecture with your teacher's spouse or the dean, the element of publication will have been established.

Legal doctrines that have evolved over centuries usually pick up a few exceptions along the way, and so it is with the concept of publication. There are times when person A saying something nasty to person B *about* person B can be sufficient to establish publication. Such is the case if the defamation is offered in a context where it is all but unavoidable that the recipient will himself have to share it with at least one third party. Such instances are collectively referred to in libel law as **self-publication.** For example, writing an insulting letter to a blind person could constitute publication in that the person will likely have to seek out a sighted individual to read the letter aloud. The same would be true of a letter written to and about a preliterate child. A more recent phenomenon is for courts to hold that an employer's letter of termination to an employee can be sufficient to find publication in that the fired employee will feel compelled to share the reasons for termination during interviews with potential future employers.[25]

It is important that we not confuse the elements of defamation and publication. Whereas the latter requires that only one third party hear or read the libelous remarks, the former requires that the remarks were capable of lowering the defamed person's status with an undefined but fairly sizable number of potential recipients of the message.

---

[25]Markita D. Cooper, "Between a Rock and a Hard Case: Time for a New Doctrine of Compelled Self-Publication," 72 *Notre Dame Law Review* 373 (1997).

Figure 3.2

NON SEQUITUR by WILEY

Although many of us enjoy devouring stories based on gossip and rumors, the media cannot avoid liability for defamation by claiming to have reported truthfully that "there is a rumor floating about."

*Copyright © 1997, Washington Post Writers Group. Reprinted with permission.*

The element of publication becomes more complicated, and also becomes of special relevance to media professionals, when we recognize that a **republication** of a libel can be just as actionable as the original act of libel. Your printing or broadcasting that "Smith said Jones is a child molester" can create as much liability for you as had been created for Smith. A newspaper can be sued for publishing a defamatory letter to the editor or a defamatory advertisement.

Do you remember Richard Jewell, the Olympic Park hero who soon became a bombing suspect (or so it seemed)? The *Atlanta Journal-Constitution*'s coverage had described Jewell as fitting "the profile of the lone bomber...a frustrated white man who is a former police officer, member of the military or police 'wannabe' who seeks to become a hero."[26] Should his libel suit against the paper ever go to trial (Jewell settled out of court with both NBC and CNN), a claim to the effect that "we only printed what others were saying" will not constitute an adequate defense.

The Atlanta papers might prevail if they could prove that all of the defamatory information came from official pronouncements made by the FBI or other law enforcement agencies. At the other extreme, the defense would collapse if the libels were based on nothing more than "rumors floating about" the Olympic Park area (see Figure 3.2).

In several circumstances, the act of repeating another's libelous utterance, although technically satisfying the requirements of the publication element, will

---

[26]John M. Touhy and Jeffrey W. Sarles, "Defamation Law," *National Law Journal,* 8 Sept. 1997, p. B6.

nonetheless be deemed protected speech. In some jurisdictions, newspapers that publish stories from reputable wire services will escape liability.[27] This wire services defense, dating from the 1930s,[28] is actually a special instance of a more general rule to the effect that if the media outlet had legitimate cause to believe in the reliability of the original source, the dissemination of that source's words should not be actionable. "The rationale behind the defense," a Michigan court recently wrote, "is that no local news organization could assume the burden of verifying every news item reported to it by established news-gathering agencies and continue to satisfy the demands of modern society for up-to-the-minute global information."[29]

Not everyone involved in the process of spreading a defamatory message to a larger audience is necessarily liable for damages. There is a long-standing exception for bookstores and similar enterprises. We do not expect bookstore and magazine rack managers to be personally responsible for every word and every picture in their entire inventory. Similarly, if person A spreads a libelous remark about person B in a phone conversation with person C, we do not hold the telephone company liable. Whether cyberspace service providers such as America Online or CompuServe can ever be held liable for things that their customers say to and about each other is a question that has also been litigated in recent years and is discussed in Chapter 13.

Another way for the media to avoid liability after having republished a libelous statement is to invoke the **neutral reportage** defense. This defense, which is accepted in only a few jurisdictions, permits the press to report in a fair and unbiased manner newsworthy allegations made by any prominent and responsible speaker about public officials or well-known public personalities. Neutral reportage was first recognized by the federal Court of Appeals for the Second Circuit in 1977, in a case where the *New York Times* and the National Audubon Society defended themselves against a libel suit from a small group of scientists whose opposition to a ban on the pesticide DDT led an Audubon official to accuse them of being "paid to lie." The *Times* reprinted the charge in a story it did on the controversy surrounding pesticides. In ruling for the media organizations, Judge Kaufman argued that the public would be the ultimate loser if the press were not permitted to report that "a responsible, prominent organization" had made such serious charges against a public figure.[30]

Another privilege, sometimes called **fair report,** can protect the media from a libel judgment when the defamatory statements republished were first made in an official government proceeding or document. The privilege seems logically consistent with the **Speech and Debate Clause** (Article I, Section 6, of the U.S.

---

[27]*Gay v. Williams,* 486 F. Supp. 12 (Alaska 1979).

[28]*Layne v. Tribune Co.,* 146 So. 234 (Sup. Ct. Fla. 1933).

[29]*Howe v. Detroit Free Press,* 555 N.W.2d 738, 741 (1996).

[30]*Edwards v. National Audubon Society,* 556 F.2d 113, 129 (2d Cir. 1977).

Constitution), and similar provisions in many state constitutions that give legislators absolute privilege to say whatever they please when conducting their official duties. If representatives cannot be prosecuted or sued for any utterance they make in their official capacities, should not the news media that tell us about those utterances also be protected?

Constitutional provisions such as the Speech and Debate Clause are often said to be sources of **absolute privilege.** The word *absolute,* however, may be misleading in that courts will ask how closely tied to a legislator's official functions were the circumstances surrounding a libelous utterance. Certainly the legislator will enjoy absolute immunity for utterances made during the course of floor debate or during committee hearings. Senator William Proxmire of Wisconsin, though, learned the hard way that the privilege does not extend absolutely to all utterances on political issues. Proxmire was in the habit of publicizing from time to time what he liked to call his "Golden Fleece Awards." His goal was to shed light on government expenditures that seem especially wasteful. Proxmire gave one of his awards to federal agencies that had funded the primate aggression research conducted by Dr. Ronald Hutchinson of the Kalamazoo State Mental Hospital. The *Congressional Record* reveals Proxmire's having charged that Hutchinson's "transparently worthless" research "should make the taxpayers as well as his monkeys grind their teeth."[31]

When Hutchinson's libel suit against Proxmire reached the Supreme Court, the majority held that the means used by the senator to publicize his Golden Fleece Award—issuing press releases, sending a newsletter to a mailing list of approximately 100,000 and appearing on at least one television interview program—were not closely enough tied to his speech making in the Senate chamber itself to warrant absolute immunity. It was not clear from the *Congressional Record* whether Senator Proxmire actually delivered on the Senate floor the words attributed to him. If he had, the fair report privilege could protect the media that chose to reprint the speech from libel suits.

Three somewhat overlapping rationales have been cited over the years in support of the fair report privilege.[32] The **agency rationale** emphasizes the press's role as representatives of those members of the public who might be interested in attending a governmental meeting but who do not have the time or resources to do so. The media report back to us, as our agents. Closely related is the **supervisory rationale,** which posits that one of the media's most important functions is to encourage the public to scrutinize, or "supervise," their elected representatives. This rationale suggests that the public's supervisory role will be accomplished most effectively if the electorate is provided with as much information as possible about their representatives' day-to-day functioning. The **informational rationale** is the

---

[31]*Hutchinson v. Proxmire,* 443 U.S. 111, 116 (1979).

[32]Scott E. Saef, "Neutral Reportage: The Case for a Statutory Privilege," 86 *Northwestern University Law Review* 417, 422–25 (1992).

broadest of the three in that it does not require that the initial utterer of a libelous remark be a public official at all. If voters are to make intelligent choices *as* voters, informational theory argues, they must be educated on a broad range of public issues, the kinds of issues likely to be discussed by any of the participants in official public proceedings. The informational rationale would be the most likely of the three to cover statements made by ordinary citizens at gatherings of any organization, governmental or private, that becomes deeply involved in political issues. School board meetings would qualify, as would PTA meetings. The meetings of a legislative committee considering health care reform would be covered, as would meetings of the American Medical Association.

The fair report privilege applies to the proceedings of any legislative body, from Congress to the local school board, that is empowered to make public policy. The privilege protects accurate reports of statements made by those who convene such meetings and any member of the public who is authorized to speak to them. It also covers defamatory statements that originate in citizen petitions or similar documents that are recognized and "received" by legislative bodies.

The privilege is a qualified one. It can be overcome by a finding that the media's report of a proceeding was not "fair and accurate." Even if the report of official governmental proceedings is accurate, if a news story goes beyond those facts to offer commentary on the credibility of the participants, the privilege may still fail. A 2000 decision from the Minnesota Supreme Court, for example, concerned a newspaper article correctly reporting that a private citizen attending a city council meeting alleged that a local police officer sold illegal drugs. Summary judgment awarded to the newspaper was overturned by the court, because the newspaper also reported on a follow-up interview with the police chief and reminded readers that the citizen who had first made the accusation was a frequent contributor to the paper's editorial pages.[33]

Accurate reports of defamatory utterances or documents from the executive branch of government are also often covered. Certainly reports of presidential, gubernatorial, and mayoral press conferences and press releases are protected. In some jurisdictions, even far less public documents from the executive branch may be covered. A California appellate court, for example, exonerated a San Francisco newspaper for articles it had written about alleged financial improprieties in the Center for Pre-Hospital Research and Training at the University of California at San Francisco. The Center had been created to provide support for nonphysicians, such as EMTs and firefighters whose roles often require that they be proficient in performing some kinds of emergency medical procedures. The articles, which accused the center of having created secret checking accounts for improper expenditures and having billed some clients for services never rendered, were deemed privileged because they were based on a confidential report done by the state auditor.[34]

---

[33]*Moreno v. Crookston Times Printing Company,* 610 N.W.2d 321 (Minn. 2000).

[34]*Braun v. Chronicle Publishing Company,* 52 Cal. App. 4th 1936 (1997).

Be careful about quoting the cop on the beat, however. Earlier it was suggested that the Atlanta newspaper reports that Richard Jewell was the FBI's primary suspect in the Olympic bombing case *might* be deemed privileged. The court would consider, among other things, whether the reporters saw some kind of official, although internal, FBI memoranda or if they were simply paraphrasing something said by one or more agents informally. Indeed, with respect to the fair report privilege and the executive branch, reporters should be more and more cautious the lower-ranked the source for the reprinted libels and the less formal the communication in which the libels originated.

That the fair report privilege is also applicable to judicial proceedings is especially important to the press in that virtually every comment made about a defendant in open court beyond name, address, and age is likely to be defamatory in some way. Fortunately for the media, the privilege applies to any statements or official documents issued by any of the participants, including witnesses, jurors, the judge, and the litigating parties themselves. Moreover, the privilege has often been held to apply to judicial documents that are never read in open court. Consider, for example, a very colorful libel case from Pennsylvania prompted by HarperCollins' publication of a book called *Masters of Deception: The Gang That Ruled Cyberspace*. The book tells of nefarious activities engaged in by a group of college-age computer hackers, one of which was to break into private computer systems to obtain and then fraudulently use others' long-distance calling card codes. Here is how the book described the group's having rationalized the crime:

> It seemed victimless to them. They needed the numbers to fund calls to further their education. Who was being hurt? Not the person whose calling card number got used, because that person would dispute the bill and never have to pay. Not the phone company, because the filched phone calls emanated from a reservoir of limitless capacity. It was like riding the rails. The trains were running anyway, and a hobo wouldn't displace any cargo in the boxcar.[35]

These comments were among many that the plaintiffs thought defamatory. The court held, however, that these statements, to the extent they were accurate, were protected by the fair report privilege in that they had been obtained from such official documents as a presentencing report done on one of the hackers and a letter from the assistant district attorney to the judge.

Whether the fair report privilege extends to republications of documents from foreign countries is an issue that has produced contradictory results. The federal appellate court in the Fourth Circuit was the first to rule on the question. *Lee v. Dong-A Ilbo*[36] involved several Korean-American media that had written or broadcast a report, based on documents from the South Korean government, that a

---

[35]*Wilson v. Slatella*, 970 F. Supp. 405, 410 (E.D. Pa. 1997).

[36]849 F.2d 876 (4th Cir. 1988).

South Korean citizen living in the United States was viewed by that regime as an enemy North Korean agent. The court held that the fair report privilege did not apply to documents from foreign governments. That narrow reading of the fair report privilege has been criticized by other federal courts. In 1997, a federal district court in Pennsylvania (part of the Third Circuit) protected the *Boston Globe* and other media from a defamation suit stemming from its having reported that U.S. citizen Howard Friedman would be denied future entry into Israel. The report was based on a press release issued by three ministers of the Israeli government, claiming that Friedman had been "associated with planning illegal activities in Israel."[37]

It is important to remember that the fair report privilege is qualified, not absolute. The press forfeits its rights to the privilege if its story goes beyond in independently defamatory ways the official proceedings or proclamations from which it draws facts. If the government document upon which you base your story says that Jones "has troubles at home" and you report that "Jones is a spouse abuser," the privilege will not work for you. The privilege also is restricted to situations in which you make obvious to your readers the source of your facts. You must make a clear attribution in your story and, ideally, in your headline as well. Although there are many times when the media may use anonymous sources, using the fair report privilege against a libel judgment should not be one of them.

The old journalistic admonition to "get it *right*" is of special import here in that the fair report privilege is forfeited if your story is not an accurate report of an otherwise protected government proceeding or document. The Supreme Court of Ohio allowed a libel suit to go forward against a newspaper for having reported that "Amherst attorney James Young is facing a contempt of court citation." As it turns out, there was an Amherst attorney named James Young, and an attorney named James Young had in fact been held in contempt of court a few days prior

---

[37]*Friedman v. Israel Labour Party,* 957 F. Supp. 701 (E.D. Pa 1997).

 # Things to Remember

### THE PUBLICATION ELEMENT

- Only one additional person needs to hear the libel.
- Republication of a libel can be just as actionable as the original publication.
- Wire services, common carriers, and bookstores are generally excluded from republication liability.
- Some jurisdictions also offer the neutral reportage defense, protecting the press broadly against liability as long as they report the fact of person A's having criticized person B in a fair and unbiased way.
- A fair report privilege is also recognized concerning republications of libels initially made in an official meeting or publication.

to the story's run. The attorney who had been found in contempt, however, was a James H. Young, and *his* usual place of business was Cleveland.[38] Making the right criticisms of the wrong person can not only defeat the chance to fall back upon the fair report privilege; such mistakes can also serve to establish for the plaintiff the third element of a libel case, identification.

## Identification

The third element of libel in the common law is identification. While one might think intuitively that this element would be rather straightforward, it in fact carries its own complications. Three such complications are explored here: the relationship between naming and identifying, the special problems posed by fictional writing, and problems that emerge when libels are attributed to only some members of indentifiable groups of various sizes.

*Naming and Identifying.*   The case of the Cleveland (not Amherst!) attorney just mentioned serves as a powerful reminder that libel suits are often prompted by an omitted middle initial, a misspelling, or some other misidentification. Misidentify one person and you may succeed in defaming another. Generally, reporters are wise to identify with a vengeance whenever anything potentially defamatory is being associated with a named individual. Such identification means to use a person's full name (with middle initial where appropriate), age and full address, and perhaps even occupation.

As you begin to read full texts of court opinions, either on the job or as a requirement of this course, the phrase you will most frequently encounter when judges make reference to the element of identification is that the allegedly libelous statements must be "of or concerning" the plaintiff. It is important to recognize that the element of identification can be proven even if you never once use the plaintiff's name in your story. In one case, for example, a Philadelphia police captain serving on the city's Sex Crimes squad implied that a young woman, described only as a "Bryn Mawr student," may have filed a false report alleging she had been carjacked, robbed, and raped. The woman sued not only the police captain, but also the local media that had broadcast his allegations. In denying the defendants' motion for summary judgment, based in large part on the plaintiff never having been named, the court reminded us that naming and identifying are two different things. There were simply too many details about the young woman in the story—that she had reported being raped on a particular day, after having attended a party at the University of Pennsylvania; that she was a student at a well-known and relatively small college; that she drove a Nissan; and so on—to deny the likelihood that she would be identifiable.[39]

---

[38]*Young v. The Morning Journal,* 669 N.E.2d 1136 (Sup. Ct. Ohio 1996).

[39]*Weinstein v. Bullick,* 827 F. Supp. 1193 (E.D. Pa. 1993).

***Identification in Fiction.***    No doubt you have noticed the sentence that appears toward the end of a film's credits advising that you have just seen a work of fiction and that "any resemblance" between the characters depicted therein and "real persons, living or dead," is "purely coincidental." The film's producers insert these words because they hope that any real persons who feel they have been depicted in the film, and defamatorily so, will not sue. In fact, however, libel suits elicited by films and books that are marketed as fiction do get filed. An expert witness testifying in a 1960s libel trial admonished the publishing industry, at least with some seriousness, that any writer's first novel should be given an especially thorough review by the legal department. "They tend to be autobiographical," he pointed out, "and twentieth century fiction is replete with examples of writers whose first novel…leaned heavily on the author's (usually unflattering) portrayal of and judgment on his family."[40]

One of the most often cited fictive libel cases will likely provoke the reaction "only in California, and only in the 1970s."[41] Writer Gwen Mitchell became a member of one of Dr. Paul Bindrim's "nude marathon" psychotherapy groups. In that Mitchell had already published a best-selling book, Bindrim was suspicious enough to insist that she would be welcome as a client like any other, but not if she intended to write about the experience. He had her sign a contract to that effect, but shortly thereafter she signed another contract, this one with Doubleday for a six-figure advance on a novel about the nude encounter group movement. The book, called *Touching,* depicted "Dr. Simon Herford" as a psychotherapist who conducted nude encounter groups. One of the scenes Bindrim felt most defamed him was a discussion in group between Herford and a minister who lamented that his wife was not amenable to coming to the encounter group. Although Bindrim's own recordings of the sessions showed that such a scene took place, the novel's version has Herford using highly vulgar language to insist that the minister exercise some more authority over his wife ("You better grab her by the cunt and drag her here!").

The defendants argued unsuccessfully that Herford could not be viewed by reasonable jurors as a Bindrim surrogate. The court found the differences between the real and fictional therapists too few and too inconsequential. Herford was a psychiatrist, Bindrim a psychologist; Herford had long white hair and sideburns, Bindrim was clean shaven with short hair. Because a comparison of the book with Bindrim's tape recordings of the real sessions persuaded the court that the novel was based almost entirely on Mitchell's participation in the encounter group, the case was permitted to go forward for a jury to decide if Bindrim could establish all the elements of libel.

The *Bindrim* case serves as an example of a fascinating paradox that emerges when libel suits flow from fiction. The more disparate the actual events and those depicted in a fictional work, the less likely will a protagonist be identified in the

---

[40]*Felter v. Houghton Mifflin,* 364 F.2d 650, 651 n.3 (2d Cir. 1966).

[41]*Bindrim v. Davis,* 92 Cal. App. 3d 61 (1979).

readers' minds as anything but a fictional character. Yet it is that very distortion in fiction that might be the basis for the claim that the book or film being adjudicated is defamatory. In other words, that a scene does indeed depart from reality can serve as an argument for either the plaintiff or the defendant.

In *Geisler v. Petrocelli*,[42] the Court of Appeals for the Second Circuit ruled that Melanie Geisler's libel suit against the author and publisher of the novel *Match Set* could go forward. The book tells the tale, as the court put it, of "the odyssey of a female transsexual athlete through the allegedly corrupt and corrupting world of the women's professional tennis circuit." The book's main character is described in a way that the court found very similar to Geisler's appearance. Moreover, the author, who had made the plaintiff's acquaintance when the two of them had worked at a small publishing house, named the character—you guessed it!—Melanie Geisler.

***The Numbers Game.*** Sometimes, libel plaintiffs cannot prove that they have been identified in a defamatory utterance *as an individual* and assert instead that they have been libeled by dint of their membership in a particular group. Predicting whether such plaintiffs will prevail sometimes may seem more art than science,[43] but some general principles can be culled from the case law.

First is the general principle that membership in a very large group will not give one standing to sue for libel as a result of the group having been defamed. No individual attorney or group of attorneys would be able to win damages by suing any of the authors or publishers of the various "dead lawyer joke" compilations we find in most larger bookstores. Senator Jones could not win a suit against a radio talk show host for making the bald assertion that "all politicians are crooks." Do these examples sound outlandish and fantastic? Consider that in 1980 one court was called upon to rule that no individual of Polish descent could by law have been defamed by the Polish jokes in a popular film,[44] and another ruled that no individual Muslim can claim to having been defamed by a film (*Death of a Princess*) alleged to have insulted hundreds of millions of the faithful worldwide.[45] Or consider two more recent controversies. In New York, a suit involving the CBS program *60 Minutes* was halted when the court held that a broadcast story's general admonishment about dealing with Nigerian businessmen could not be viewed as defamatory of any individual member of the class.[46] And in Florida, two appellate courts have held that TV stations broadcasting a political advertisement in support

---

[42]616 F.2d 636 (2d Cir. 1980).

[43]Jeffrey S. Bromme, "Group Defamation: Five Guiding Factors," 64 *Texas Law Review* 591 (1985).

[44]*Mikolinski v. Burt Reynolds Production Company*, 409 N.E.2d 1324 (Mass. App. Ct. 1980).

[45]*Khalid Abdullah Tariq Al Mansour Faissal Fahd Al Tahd v. Fanning*, 506 F. Supp. 186 (N.D. Cal. 1980).

[46]*Anyanwu v. CBS*, 887 F. Supp. 690 (S.D.N.Y. 1995).

of new regulations of the commercial fishing industry cannot be said to have libeled any particular fisherman.[47]

As a general rule, then, the larger the group, the more difficult it is for an individual plaintiff to prove identification. Similarly, the smaller the number of people in the group alleged to have a defamatory trait, the more difficult it will be for individuals within the group to prevail. Defamations alleging that "one" or "a few" members of a group manifest a particularly loathsome quality will be less likely to lead to liability than claiming that "all" or "the vast majority of" a group's members can be so characterized. In some states, including New York, courts have fashioned what is called an **intensity of suspicion test** that seems as elegant a summary as one will find of the conjunction of the two principles just mentioned.[48] The larger the group, the less likely that any individual member of it will have been singled out for suspicion. Similarly, if the size of the group is held constant, more suspicion is aroused about any particular member to the extent that a large percent of the group is alleged to have a negative characteristic.

What happens if one unnamed member of a relatively small group is defamed? Such was the case when all twenty-one members of the Bellingham, Massachusetts, police force took umbrage at a column in the weekly *Woonsocket Call and Evening Reporter* that closed with the query, "Is it true that a Bellingham cop locked himself and a female companion in the back of a cruiser in a town sandpit and had to radio for help?"[49] The federal district court that first heard the case dismissed it, finding that there was no actionable identification. "If you say 11 out of 12 people are corrupt, or if you said 20 out of 21 police officers or maybe even 12 out of 21 are corrupt, or even one out of six is corrupt," the lower court judge admitted, "you would have a different situation." The appellate court affirmed the lower court's ruling, reasoning that "here we deal with a defamatory statement aimed at only one unidentified member of a group of 21. By no stretch of imagination can it be thought to suggest that the conduct of the one is typical of all. Noting the individual's membership in the group does not suggest a common determinant of character so much as simply a practical reference point." In a bit of dicta suggesting that the entire police department having shown up as coplaintiffs could be viewed as a manifestation of esprit de corps rather than selfishness, the court added: "This is not to say that each member of a small group does not feel some unease whenever a co-member comes in for criticism, shame, or obloquy. But to predicate liability to all members of a group on such an associational attitude would chill communication to the marrow."

If the lesson of the case involving the Bellingham, Massachusetts, police is that the media can rest easy should they only libel one out of twenty-one, a more

---

[47]*Thomas v. Jacksonville TV, Inc.*, 699 So. 2d 800 (Fla. Ct. App. 1st Dist. 1997); *Adams v. WFTV. Inc.*, 691 So. 2d 557 (Ct. App. Fla. 5th Dist. 1997).

[48]*Brady v. Ottaway Newspaper*, 445 N.Y.S.2d 786, 793–95 (2d Dept. 1981).

[49]*Arcand v. Evening Call Publishing Company*, 567 F.2d 1163 (1st Cir. 1977).

recent decision from North Carolina will give an added measure of comfort in that the odds improved to one out of nine. It seems that the owner of a commercial building ran a deli and a florist shop and rented out space to several other small businesses. When a group of medical technicians was planning to go for lunch at the deli, one of their colleagues discouraged them from doing so in that "someone over there" (of the nine persons employed at the deli) has AIDS. Rumors about the unnamed AIDS-infected deli employee were eventually covered in local print and broadcast media. When the various workers sued for libel, their claim was denied on the grounds of a failure to establish identification.[50]

The arithmetic does not always work in the media's favor, however. Consider the case of the retired U.S. Bureau of Prisons officer against the producers of the 1960s ABC series *The Untouchables*.[51] A two-part episode of the series told the predominantly true story of gangster Al Capone's transfer in 1934 from a prison in Georgia to the infamous Alcatraz Prison in San Francisco Bay. The producers, however, added fictional scenes depicting one of the two guards assigned to Capone taking a bribe from the gangster, apparently as a down payment on expected help with a planned escape. When the other guard demands to be cut in on the deal, he is instead gunned down by Capone's cohorts. The plaintiff was one of the two guards who really had been assigned to Capone's railway car (out of fifteen or sixteen guards altogether who were involved in some way with the transfer). In this case, which could just as easily have fit in the earlier discussion of defamation through fiction, the court first determined that the relevant ratio was one in two, not one in sixteen. Having made this preliminary decision, the court had no difficulty determining that the case could go forward to a jury.

A federal district court in Massachusetts, in a case involving the Church of Scientology, was called on to determine if the entire church could bring suit after an attorney had publicly made some defamatory conjecture about some unnamed church members. In the course of what apparently had been longstanding litigation between attorney Raymond Flynn and the church's Florida branch, Flynn needed to file motions defending himself against contempt citations issued by a Clearwater, Florida, judge. Having learned that the filing fees had not arrived in Florida, Flynn hypothesized to a reporter from that state during a telephone interview that "someone at that end infiltrated the courthouse and intercepted the mailed check, someone like a Scientologist." The court, while reminding us that corporations (including churches) can normally sue for libel, held that here the church as a whole had not been defamed, that the defendant's statement was directed only at one or a few of its members.[52]

Perhaps you are enrolled at a campus that has a "hate speech" code. Such regulations seem at first blush to have much in common with libel law in that

---

[50]*Chapman v. Byrd,* 475 S.E.2d 734 (Ct. App. N.C. 1996).

[51]*American Broadcasting-Paramount Theatres, Inc. v. Simpson,* 126 S.E.2d 873 (Ga. Ct. App. 1962).

[52]*Church of Scientology of California v. Flynn,* 578 F. Supp. 266 (Mass. 1984).

Things to Remember

**THE IDENTIFICATION ELEMENT OF LIBEL**

- It is possible to be identified for the purposes of a libel case without having been explicitly named.
- Even purportedly fictional accounts, such as movies and novels, can lead to libel suits if an unsympathetically drawn character can be shown to be identifiable as a living real person.
- No single individual member will succeed as a libel plaintiff if a huge category of persons (such as lawyers, politicians, or Jews) is defamed.
- When dealing with smaller groups, the rules are a bit more murky, with some courts having depended on an "intensity of suspicion" test suggesting that plaintiffs become more likely to prevail when the number in the whole group is small and the number alleged to have a particularly unsavory characteristic is a high proportion of that larger group.

they typically prohibit speech that expresses very negative things about a person (because of that person's race, religion, gender, sexual orientation, or some similar combination of categories). These regulations are actually not libel provisions, however, for a number of reasons. First, such regulations are not designed to protect victims' reputations, but rather their feelings. Indeed, the rules often will not be triggered unless an insulting epithet is directed to a specific individual's face, not to others *about* that individual. Second, many commentators believe that such speech codes, if they have any chance of being found constitutional, must be restricted to situations in which a violent breach of the peace is likely to occur. Although libel law may be thought of in a grand, historical way as an evolution away from such violence as dueling, contemporary libel plaintiffs need not establish the likelihood of violence as an element of their suits. Finally, whereas libel has been a respected area of tort law for centuries, with every state in the country boasting a libel statute, a complex mosaic of case law, or both, those few court decisions involving campus hate speech codes have uniformly struck down the rules as violations of the First Amendment.[53]

**Fault**

Suppose that you are the owner of a duplex, occupying one unit, leasing the other, in a relatively temperate climate, such as in North Carolina. You go away on a vacation in October, and during your absence, your hometown experiences a freak ice

---

[53]*Doe v. University of Michigan,* 721 F. Supp. 852 (E.D. Mich. 1989); *UWM Post, Inc. v. Board of Regents of the University of Wisconsin,* 774 F. Supp. 1163 (E.D. Wis. 1991).

storm. Your tenant's child slips and falls on the ice in front of your property. Does it seem fair that you can be sued in such a circumstance? You were not home and were thus unable to clear the sidewalk, and you had no reason to make arrangements for anyone else to do it for you. Yet in some jurisdictions in the United States, you could indeed be held liable for the child's injuries under the doctrine of **strict liability,** the notion that a person who causes injury to another should make retribution, even if no negligence is involved. A few generations ago, this doctrine was embraced throughout the country, and it has by no means disappeared from U.S. law. In some instances, such as product liability, the tendency over time has been to embrace strict liability rather than a demand that the plaintiffs prove an article was manufactured negligently.[54] Other contemporary examples include workers' compensation laws as well as any doctrine "that makes employers responsible for negligent acts of their employees, even where the employer himself is totally free from negligence."[55]

Now imagine for a moment a world in which the doctrine of strict liability were applied to defamation. Hurt someone's reputation by something you print or broadcast, even if your error is an innocent one, and you must pay. Misidentify a criminal suspect by using the wrong middle initial, and no amount of apologizing will get you off the hook.

In fact, libel law operated this way in many jurisdictions prior to the Supreme Court's landmark decision in 1964, *New York Times v. Sullivan.*[56] Although there are many ways of describing the significance of the case, one way is to say the Court constitutionalized the fault element of libel. An examination of *Sullivan* and its progeny is the subject of Chapter 4. Before that, however, we examine some of the arguments available to libel defendants even before the Supreme Court made this whole area of the law more "speaker friendly."

## Some Common-Law and Statutory Defenses to Libel

You have already been exposed to at least some defenses available to communicators who are sued for libel. To argue that the plaintiff has failed to establish one or more of the elements of libel is, after all, a defense. Defendants, as seen in the discussion of the identification element, might argue that the seemingly libelous remarks were not "of or about" the plaintiff. Then, too, the fair report and neutral reportage privileges are often used to suggest that although *re*publication may have taken place, the libel suit should not be permitted to go forward. Several other libel

---

[54]Robert J. Samuelson, "Streamlining Product-Liability Suits," *Los Angeles Times,* 24 June 1994, p. B7.

[55]Lawrence P. Katzenstein, "Liability without Negligence" [Editorial], *St. Louis Post-Dispatch,* 15 May 1995, p. 7B.

[56]376 U.S. 254 (1964).

defenses are available to litigants, some unique to this particular tort, others more globally available to defendants in any kind of civil case.

One of the surest ways to defeat a libel suit is to point out that the plaintiff failed to honor the applicable **statute of limitations.** To avoid clogging the courts with "stale" claims—witnesses die, memories fade, evidence is lost—virtually all civil and criminal actions must be brought within a statutorily prescribed time limit. Statutes of limitations for libel vary from state to state, typically extending for one or two years after publication. A few states recognize a three-year limitation. In most jurisdictions, the clock starts running the moment the defamation is published, not when the potential plaintiff learns about the publication. In this context, "published" refers to when the material was made generally available. In the case of broadcast stations, this time is easy to figure out. The first broadcast is the date of publication. Things are a little bit more complex with printed materials. We cannot always go by the copyright date or the cover date. Books that reach the bookstores late in the year often list the following year on the copyright page. Similarly, magazines are often postdated several weeks in advance so that they appear "fresher" on newsstands and in subscribers' homes.

The truth defense, demonstrating that allegedly defamatory statements are true, is a very powerful defense in defamation cases. It may seem puzzling to describe truth as merely a *defense* in libel law, thus suggesting that the communicator is presumed guilty, that the article is presumed false. Should not the burden be on the plaintiff to *prove* that the story is false?

The courts have not yet provided a uniform answer to this question. Traditionally, in common law, a libel *was* presumed false. If that tradition seems quirky and unfair by today's standards, try thinking about it another way. In common law, Americans' reputations were presumed unsullied and pure until proven otherwise. For an added sense of perspective, consider that the Alien and Sedition Acts discussed in Chapter 2, although viewed as reprehensible in retrospect, at the time could be seen as a step forward for freedom of the press in that they, unlike libel law at the time, at least permitted truth to be used as a defense.[57] In any event, because the Supreme Court has held in recent years that the First Amendment places some limitations on the common-law tradition of requiring the defendant to prove truth, much more about this issue is discussed in the next chapter. For now, suffice it to say that in those situations where the plaintiff must prove falsity to prevail, it will not do to point out one or a handful of inconsequential errors extraneous to the libel alleged. If my story alleges that you have been prosecuted for embezzling $30,000 from one employer and $400,000 from another, you will not have proven falsity by showing that my figures are ever so slightly off or that I spelled one of the employers' names wrong. You must prove that the gist or the "sting" of the article is false (see Figure 3.3).

---

[57]Norman L. Rosenberg, *Protecting the Best Men: An Interpretive History of the Law of Libel* (Chapel Hill: University of North Carolina Press, 1986), 86–87.

**Figure 3.3**

## Doonesbury

BY GARRY TRUDEAU

Were a libel suit to result from these allegations, the difference between using thirteen-year-olds and fourteen-year-olds would not be seen as a large enough one to establish falsity.

*Doonesbury copyright © 1997 G. B. Trudeau. Reprinted with permission of Universal Press Syndicate. All rights reserved.*

**Consent** is a rarely encountered but still respected libel defense. Should you interview a subject who, knowing full well the nature of the allegations you intend to print, expressly gives you permission to go ahead, the subject will not be able to prevail in a libel suit against you stemming from those allegations. Courts sometimes infer consent based on the plaintiff's conduct. For example, if it can be shown that a plaintiff herself has told others of the yet-unpublished defamations against her, some courts might hold that a defamation suit cannot stand. If the supposed libels had the power to damage her reputation, the reasoning goes, she would have kept them to herself. In one case involving relationships between an employer and an employee rather than a reporter and source, a state appellate court held that there can be no defamation in an employee's personnel file if the only additional pairs of eyes to have seen the alleged libels belonged to persons shown the file by the employee personally.[58]

In our earlier discussion of the element of defamation, we encountered cases where the defendant successfully argued that the alleged libel could not possibly have hurt the plaintiff's reputation because they were "mere hyperbole," not to be taken literally. Hyperbole is really a special instance of the more general common-law defense called **fair comment,** which posits that, to be defamatory, an utterance must make a specific factual claim. Opinions, if offered without any personal animus toward the person being judged (thus the "fair" in fair comment), cannot be the cause of a libel action. The fair comment privilege can be abused and thus

---

[58]*Pressley v. Continental Company, 250* S.E.2d 676 (Ct. App. N.C. 1978).

disallowed if your opinion is presented in such a way as to suggest that you have certain facts at your disposal that you are choosing not to share with your readers and that these important but undisclosed facts form the basis for your negative assessment of a potential plaintiff. This approach might be called the "if you only knew what I know" posture. If, however, you either forthrightly reveal the facts that led you to your opinions or have cause to believe that those facts are already known to your readers (for example, if this one article concerns an incident so much in the news that only a hermit could have missed earlier accounts), the privilege will generally be respected.

Here, too, the Supreme Court (and some lower courts trying to make sense of relevant Supreme Court decisions) has made some moves toward constitutionalizing this common-law defense. Thus, we discuss the fact versus opinion distinction again in Chapter 4, this time from a First Amendment perspective.

## Chapter Summary

Libel law has been around for many centuries and exists to enable persons who feel their reputations have been sullied to recover damages from anyone who has spread untruths about them.

Plaintiffs must generally establish four elements to prevail: that a specific allegation is in fact likely to damage reputation, that the defamation was published (seen by at least one third party), that the plaintiff was identified in some way, and that the publisher manifested some degree of fault. Traditionally, falsity did not have to be proven; it was assumed, with truth being a common-law defense.

Phrases amounting to mere rhetorical hyperbole are not actionable. Republication of libels from other sources can be as actionable as the publication of the original statements. Exceptions are often made for the fair reporting of libelous statements made in official proceedings.

Not only individuals but also corporations can sue for libel. If a company's product rather than its officers has been

maligned, the proper cause of action is product disparagement rather than libel itself.

Identification can exist even if the plaintiff has not been explicitly named in the offensive publication and can result from the publication of a fictional work. A plaintiff's chances of prevailing in the case of a defamation aimed at a group of which he or she is part diminishes as the group grows larger and the proportion of its members alleged to possess the defamatory quality grows smaller.

Plaintiffs can receive compensatory damages to make themselves whole. Sometimes such damages are presumed, or they might be actual damages, requiring at least some proof of harm. Special damages demand the most specific and tangible proof of harm. In some jurisdictions, punitive damages are also permitted.

Even before the Supreme Court constitutionalized libel—the subject of the next chapter—several defenses were available to defamation suits. Defendants might be able to show that their publication was substantially true. It might be alleged that a plaintiff consented, explicitly or implicitly, to the publication. The defense called fair comment, which argues that the publication consisted of nothing more than opinion rather than assertions of fact, might be invoked. Then, too, defendants can always show that plaintiffs had failed to establish one or more of the tort's elements or that the suit was not filed timely (i.e., that the statute of limitations had run out).

# chapter

# *Defamation: First Amendment Limitations*

Today, at the beginning of the third millennium, consider for a moment that we in the United States began to dismantle the system of *institutional* racial discrimination sometimes called Jim Crow two generations ago, in the 1960s. The time is rapidly approaching when not only traditional college-age students, but also their parents, will have little or no firsthand memory of life in a time of legally imposed segregation, of signs on retail store entrances that made clear whether "Whites Only" or "Coloreds" were permitted inside.

Recall too that the 1960s were before CNN, before the ability of TV news organizations to switch instantly to "live satellite feeds" from locations all over the globe, even before all the major networks had expanded to thirty minutes of nightly news. Most Americans received three or four TV stations total. It is perhaps no surprise, then, that we were so dependent on newspapers of record, such as the *New York Times,* to stay abreast of the Civil Rights struggle being waged in the South.

## Introducing *New York Times v. Sullivan*

It is against this backdrop that the U.S. Supreme Court found a vehicle by which to impose constitutional limitations on the tort of defamation. That vehicle was a jury award for libel in the amount of $500,000 to L. B. Sullivan, a city commissioner in Montgomery, Alabama, whose duties included oversight of the local police department. Sullivan's suit was prompted by the *New York Times* publication in March 1960 of a full-page paid political advertisement placed by a group of civil rights leaders calling themselves "the Committee to Defend Dr. Martin Luther King and the Struggle for Freedom in the South" (see Figure 4.1).

There were several inaccuracies in the advertisement, including the following:

- The students sang *The Star-Spangled Banner,* not *My Country, 'Tis of Thee.*
- Police did not "ring" the campus (although they were deployed there in large numbers).

Figure 4.1

**HEED THEIR RISING VOICES**

As the whole world knows by now thousands of Southern Negro students are engaged in widespread non-violent demonstrations in positive affirmation of the right to live in human dignity as guaranteed by the U.S. Constitution and the Bill of Rights. In their efforts to uphold these guarantees, they are being met by an unprecedented wave of terror by those who would deny and negate the document which the whole world looks upon as setting the pattern for modern freedom.

In Montgomery, Alabama, after students sang "My Country, 'Tis of Thee" on the State Capitol steps, their leaders were expelled from school, and truckloads of police armed with shotguns and tear-gas ringed the Alabama State College campus. When the entire student body protested to state authorities by refusing to register, their dining hall was padlocked in an attempt to starve them into submission.

Small wonder that the Southern violators of the Constitution fear this new, non-violent brand of freedom fighter. Small wonder that they are determined to destroy the one man who, more than any other, symbolizes the new spirit now sweeping the South—the Reverend Dr. Martin Luther King, Jr.

Again and again the Southern violators have answered Dr. King's peaceful protests with intimidation and violence. They have bombed his home, almost killing his wife and child. They have assaulted his person. They have arrested him seven times—for "speeding," "loitering," and similar "offenses." And now they have charged him with "perjury"—a felony under which they could imprison him for ten years.

We urge you to join hands with our fellow Americans in the South by supporting, with your dollars, this combined appeal for all three needs—the defense of Martin Luther King, the support of the embattled students, and the struggle for the right to vote.

- Students were not expelled for leading this particular state capitol demonstration, but for demanding service at a lunch counter in the county courthouse.
- The follow-up student protest against the expulsions involved most (but not all) the student body and consisted of a one-day "strike," not a mass refusal to register.
- The student dining hall was never padlocked.
- The local police dispute the allegation that King had been "assaulted."
- King had been arrested only four times, not seven.
- Sullivan had not been police commissioner at the time of three of these arrests, nor did he have anything to do with the perjury indictment against King.

Perhaps you found some of these errors substantive ones and others so innocuous as to be a waste of the Court's time. Would Sullivan's reputation have been damaged by the factual errors in the advertisement? The Court's review of the trial record suggests that Sullivan did not do a very good job of showing how he was harmed. He only produced one relevant witness on the point, a former employer who indicated that the allegations made in the advertisement were serious ones and that he would be hesitant to hire anyone who was guilty of those allegations. This same witness, however, testified that he did not believe in the truth of the allegations. Add into the equation that Sullivan's name is not mentioned once in the advertisement, and you may think that the Court could have overturned the Alabama jury's damages award of $500,000 without producing a memorable, landmark decision. Might the Supreme Court simply have decided that the plaintiff had not met his burden of proving the libel elements of defamation or of identification?

The Court could not have simply ruled that the Alabama courts did a bad job of applying that state's own law of defamation. There would then be no federal constitutional issue involved. The Supreme Court, if it wanted to reverse the damages award, would have to say something about the relationship of the First Amendment to the law of defamation. Still, it is fair to say that the Court went much further than it had to if overturning the lower court decision were its only goal.

## The Birth of the Actual Malice Rule

The U.S. Supreme Court unanimously overturned the libel judgment against the *Times* on the grounds that plaintiff had not established that the newspaper's level of fault was sufficient to justify liability. Writing for the Court, Justice Brennan set forth the central holding of the case.[1] When a **public official** sues for damages because of an allegedly defamatory falsehood concerning his or her **official conduct,** the First Amendment demands that the plaintiff prove, with **convincing clarity,** that the statement was made with **actual malice,** that is, with knowledge that it was false or with reckless disregard as to whether it was true or false. Several of these phrases require explication. Because later court cases have attempted to clarify the definitions of *public official, official conduct,* and even *actual malice* itself, those terms are discussed further when we look at *Sullivan's* progeny.

The term *convincing clarity* is a general legal term of art that tells us what the plaintiff's level of proof must be. You are likely already familiar with one or both of the other two levels of proof that together govern the vast majority of court proceedings in the United States: proof "beyond a reasonable doubt" and proof "by a preponderance of the evidence." The government, when it prosecutes a criminal defendant, must establish its case beyond a reasonable doubt.

---

[1]*New York v. Sullivan,* 376 U.S. 254 (1964). Justices Black, Douglas, and Goldberg wrote or joined concurring opinions in which they argued for a more absolute rule than that espoused by Brennan. The concurrences interpreted the First Amendment so as to provide absolute immunity for any and all statements made about public officials' official conduct, or even (in Justice Black's words) "about public affairs" generally.

# Things to Remember

---

### CONCEPTUALIZING THE *NEW YORK TIMES V. SULLIVAN* HOLDING

- *New York Times v. Sullivan* established the "actual malice" rule, which can be *expressed as*

$$PO\ (OC) \rightarrow AM\ (CC)$$

- Translation: When Public Officials sue because of criticism about their Official Conduct, they must prove Actual Malice with Convincing Clarity.

- Actual malice is defined as publishing a knowing falsehood, or publishing with "reckless disregard of truth or falsity."

- Convincing clarity is a level of proof somewhere between that required for a criminal prosecution ("beyond a reasonable doubt") and for an ordinary civil suit ("by a preponderance of the evidence").

---

How much doubt is "reasonable" doubt? There really is no one right answer to this question. Beyond *any* doubt would mean that you are 100 percent sure of the defendant's guilt. Does reasonable doubt mean 99 percent sure? Or 95 percent sure? Judges' instructions to jurors tend not to provide such mathematical equivalents. It is fair to say, however, that if your own internal mental rule translates into a probability of guilt much lower than 90 percent, a good criminal defense lawyer will do anything possible to keep you off the jury.

The level of proof called "preponderance of the evidence" is that which plaintiffs in most civil suits—the kinds that show up on the syndicated TV program *People's Court*—must establish to prevail. This level of proof has an intuitive, mathematical feel to it. Preponderance means "more than not," or any amount of proof larger than 50 percent.

What, then, is "convincing clarity"? You have probably already guessed correctly that it is defined as a standard somewhere in between "preponderance of the evidence" and "beyond a reasonable doubt." Sometimes it is defined as a level of evidentiary proof so clear as to leave no *substantial* doubt in your mind to the contrary. Although "substantial" doubt is clearly more than "reasonable" doubt, how much more is anyone's guess.

### The Court Applies the Actual Malice Standard to the *Sullivan* Facts

In finding that the *New York Times* did not manifest the high level of fault demanded by the actual malice standard, the Court emphasized two factors. First, the newspaper staff genuinely believed at the time of publication that the charges made in the advertisement were "substantially true." Second, the Court found that the most stinging charges did not refer to Sullivan, even obliquely.

Sullivan's attorneys successfully established at trial that, had the *Times'* staff responsible for accepting the advertisement taken the time to fact-check—simply using the paper's own previous editions—they would have identified many of the falsities in the ad. The failure to check facts was not sufficient evidence of actual malice, the Court held, in part because many of the signatories to the advertisement were very well-respected civil rights leaders.

*New York Times v. Sullivan* is remembered as a landmark decision not only because of the establishment of the actual malice rule, but also because much of Justice Brennan's language in other parts of the opinion has proven so very influential over the years. The next few sections describe the further significance of the *Sullivan* ruling, beyond the holding itself.

## The Relationship between Libel and Sedition Laws

The Alien and Sedition Acts, discussed in Chapter 2, prescribed jail terms of up to five years for "false, scandalous and malicious" statements made against the president, members of Congress, or the government itself. Libel suits brought by public officials angered by criticisms of their official conduct, Justice Brennan says in *Sullivan,* are uncomfortably reminiscent of such sedition prosecutions. The imposition of sanctions against those who criticize the government is "inconsistent with the First Amendment," he says. The spirit of the First Amendment is "a profound national commitment to the principle that debate on public issues should be uninhibited, robust, and wide-open, and that [such debate] may well include vehement, caustic, and sometimes unpleasantly sharp attacks on government and public officials."

That *Sullivan* was a civil libel case rather than a criminal prosecution was immaterial from the Court's perspective. "What a State may not constitutionally bring about by means of a criminal statute," Brennan admonished the Alabama's public officials, "is likewise beyond the reach of its civil law of libel." To hold otherwise would open up "the possibility that a good-faith critic of government will be penalized for his criticism, [a] proposition [that] strikes at the very center of the constitutionally protected area of free expression."

## Two Famous Metaphors: "Breathing Space" and the "Chilling Effect"

The actual malice test does not permit recovery of damages anytime defamatory falsehoods appear. Indeed, the test provides a high degree of protection for errors, as long as the publishers are neither liars nor wholly irresponsible. In *Sullivan,* Justice Brennan develops two metaphors to help explain why it is so important to permit citizen-critics such a high degree of latitude.

The first metaphor—"breathing space"—describes the latitude that must be provided to journalists commenting on public affairs. As Justice Brennan put it in

# Things to Remember

---

### *NEW YORK TIMES V. SULLIVAN:* BEYOND THE HOLDING

- The First Amendment is "a profound national commitment to the principle that debate on public issues should be uninhibited, robust, and wide-open."
- Allowing public officials to sue for libel too easily is inconsistent with this commitment and uncomfortably reminiscent of sedition prosecutions.
- The press must be granted a certain amount of wiggle room, called "breathing space," to make innocent errors.
- Without such breathing space, the press will experience the "chilling effect" of self-censorship, and we will all be deprived of valuable *true* speech.

---

*Sullivan,* "Erroneous statement is inevitable in free debate," and "it must be protected if the freedoms of expression are to have the breathing space that they need to survive."

The second metaphor—a "chilling effect"—is the opposite side of the coin. It represents journalistic timidity, making the avoidance of publishing any falsity one's most important governing principle. "There can be little doubt," Brennan warns, that reporters not given a bit of leeway will feel this chilling effect, and that "public debate and advocacy will be constrained."

## Some Unanswered Questions from *Sullivan*

*New York Times v. Sullivan* is certainly the most important U.S. libel decision to date. Indeed, much of contemporary libel doctrine can be seen as a fine-tuning or an elaboration of issues raised in the 1964 landmark.

For that reason, the majority of this chapter is devoted to examining a number of questions left unanswered in *Sullivan* but that have since received some additional guidance from the Court. This posing of questions is thematic rather than in any kind of chronological order.

### Who Is a Public Official?

The actual malice rule only applies when libel plaintiffs are public officials. Who, though, among those on the government payroll are public officials? Must they be elected, or can they be appointed? Is anyone who draws a public paycheck, from a state university president on down to each of the school's department secretaries and janitors, to be included? The *Sullivan* Court decided not to decide. The 1964 decision was not the occasion "to determine how far down into the lower ranks of government employees the 'public official' designation would extend for purposes of this rule, or otherwise to specify categories of persons who would or would not be included," Justice Brennan says.

The truth is that there is no national consensus about who is and who is not considered a public official for the purpose of the actual malice rule. Still, the Supreme Court has given some guidance, in a case decided shortly after *Sullivan*, and the pattern of lower court decisions can provide additional insights. The Supreme Court case came about because a columnist for the *Laconia Evening Citizen* in New Hampshire, in the course of praising the new supervisor of the Belknap County Recreation Area, seemed to imply—the relevant section began, "What happened to all the money *last* year? And every other year?"[2]—that the former supervisor was a poor financial manager at best, an embezzler at worst. Reversing the jury's damage awards imposed against the columnist, the Supreme Court sent the case back to the lower court to determine if the former recreation supervisor should be considered a public official, if he should have had to prove actual malice. (That he was a *former* supervisor was not deemed relevant in that the allegedly libelous remarks were made about his tenure as supervisor. Later cases make clear that *candidates* for public office can also be considered public officials for the purposes of applying the actual malice test.)

In the course of remanding the case, the Court reminds us that the earlier *New York Times v. Sullivan* decision requires that Americans must enjoy freedom to criticize "those responsible for government operations." This concern dictates a broad definition of "public official," Justice Brennan says. The phrase must apply, "at the very least, to those among the hierarchy of government employees who have, or appear to the public to have, substantial responsibility for or control over the conduct of governmental affairs.... The employee's position must be one which would invite public scrutiny and discussion of the person holding it, entirely apart from the scrutiny and discussion occasioned by the particular charges in controversy."

This definition posits two related but distinguishable criteria. First, the government employee must occupy a responsible enough position so as to have an effect on policies, to have "responsibility" or "control." The local director of Animal Control probably would be covered, although not the individual "dog catchers" who do the rounding up of dangerous creatures.

The second criterion is perhaps best understood by conjuring up an image of two neighbors gossiping (about weighty public affairs, of course!) at the backyard fence. Public officials are those who occupy positions with responsibilities of sufficient concern that we are likely to gossip about them long before anyone publishes an allegedly libelous article about them, and certainly long before they ever bring suit for libel.

---

[2]*Rosenblatt v. Baer,* 383 U.S. 75, 78 (1966).

# Things to Remember

> ### WHO IS A PUBLIC OFFICIAL?
>
> ■ Not all public employees are public officials for purposes of the *Sullivan* rule.
> ■ Public officials are persons who:
>   • Have substantial responsibility over the conduct of governmental affairs.
>   • Occupy positions that invite public scrutiny.

These criteria seem clear enough, but that does not mean that courts around the country have always been in agreement about how to apply them. Thus, although a police officer is almost certain to be deemed a public official, there has been disagreement across jurisdictions as to whether public school teachers, or even principals, are to be so designated.

### What Is Official Conduct?

The paid advertisement that formed the basis of L. B. Sullivan's libel suit against the *New York Times* made specific allegations about police conduct in Montgomery, Alabama. To the extent that the commissioner in charge of the police force there was thus being criticized, such allegations surely concerned his "official conduct." Beyond that we learn nothing from the Supreme Court's 1964 decision to help future litigants determine the difference between criticisms of official conduct and more personal attacks that would presumably not trigger the actual malice rule.

In a pair of later decisions, however, the Court does provide some guidance. The first of these, decided just shortly after *New York Times v. Sullivan,* involved New Orleans area district attorney Jim Garrison (the same Garrison played by Kevin Costner in Oliver Stone's film *JFK*), who was the defendant in a criminal libel prosecution stemming from a press conference during which he criticized several local criminal court judges.[3] Their huge backlog of cases, he alleged, could be attributed to their "inefficiency, laziness, and excessive vacations," and the difficulty in prosecuting local vice cases a direct result of their failure to reimburse the expenses incurred by undercover police officers. The *Garrison* decision overturning the criminal libel conviction is remembered today for two reasons. First, the Court used the occasion to apply the actual malice rule to criminal libel cases. In so doing, the Court recognized, but did not answer, the larger question of whether criminal libel statutes could ever be constitutionally applied against those who criticize public officials. More important for our present purposes is how the Court handled the state's argument that the actual malice rule should be inapplicable,

---

[3]*Garrison v. Louisiana,* 379 U.S. 64 (1964).

Things to Remember

---

**WHAT IS OFFICIAL CONDUCT?**

■ Some attributions of personal characteristics (such as laziness) have clear implications for the performance of one's official conduct.

■ Any allegation of criminal behavior, not matter how long ago, is relevant to one's official conduct.

---

in that Garrison's criticisms—especially the charge of "laziness"—dealt not only with the judges' official conduct but also with their overall personalities. "Any criticism of the manner in which a public official performs his duties will tend to affect his private, as well as his public, reputation," Justice Brennan wrote for the Court. "Few personal attributes are more germane to fitness for office than dishonesty, malfeasance, or improper motivation, even though these characteristics may also affect the official's private character."

Seven years later, the Court gave a bit more guidance as to what constitutes "official conduct" for the purposes of applying the actual malice doctrine. The *Monitor Patriot,* a Concord, New Hampshire, newspaper, referred to United States senatorial candidate Alphonse Roy as a "former small-time bootlegger," that is, as someone who had profited from the illegal sale of hard liquor during the Prohibition era.[4] In overturning the jury's $20,000 damages award to Roy, Justice Stewart concluded that "a charge of criminal conduct, no matter how remote in time or place, can never be irrelevant to an official's or a candidate's fitness for office."

### Who Else Should Be Required to Prove Actual Malice?

One of the Supreme Court's chief rationales for constitutionalizing the libel tort is our national commitment to the principle "that debate on public issues should be uninhibited, robust, and wide-open." Public issues, of course, do not always involve public officials. They might involve captains of industry and scientists, and both celebrities and obscure persons caught up in a controversial matter. The Supreme Court showed its recognition of this fact when, in ruling simultaneously on two cases in 1967, it extended the actual malice rule to allegedly libelous statements made about "public figures." The two cases—*Curtis Publishing v. Butts* and *Associated Press v. Walker*—share the same citation,[5] but have very different facts and produced opposite outcomes. The first case came about because the *Saturday Evening Post* had accused Wally Butts, then athletic director of the University of

---

[4]*Monitor Patriot v. Roy,* 401 U.S. 265 (1971).

[5]380 U.S. 130 (1967).

Georgia, with fixing a football game between that school and the University of Alabama. Butts could not be considered a public official, because the athletic program at Georgia was administered by a corporation funded wholly by the private sector.

The article, "The Story of a College Football Fix," quotes an Atlanta businessman who claims that his phone's wires got crossed with those of Butts, thus allowing him to listen in on the Georgia coach's revealing to his counterpart at Alabama what sounded like the kinds of team secrets that can determine game outcomes. At trial, however, it came out that the overheard phone conversation had been greatly misunderstood by the eavesdropper, that the substance of the two coaches's banter did not involve any kinds of inside facts or "trade secrets" about game plans. By a 5–4 vote, the Supreme Court upheld the lower court's awarding of almost a half million dollars to Butts, having concluded that the magazine had engaged in reprehensibly shoddy journalism, failing to take even "elementary precautions." Their main source had a criminal background, yet his story was accepted without independent support. Then, too, the magazine should have made at least some attempt "to find out whether Alabama had adjusted its plans after the alleged divulgence of information." When the Court added into the equation that the *Post* writer assigned to the story knew very little about football, the majority concluded that the magazine's conduct represented "an extreme departure from the standards of investigation and reporting ordinarily adhered to by responsible publishers."

The companion case resulted from a reporter's eyewitness dispatch to the Associated Press (AP) wire service describing a riot at the University of Mississippi in response to the National Guard's having been called out to help smooth James Meredith's enrollment there in the autumn of 1962. Meredith, of course, was the university's first black student. The account said that former Major-General Edwin Walker—who had a long and distinguished military career, but who was a private citizen at both the time of the riot and of the publication by AP—had "taken command of the violent crowd and had personally led a charge against federal marshals." It also described Walker as encouraging rioters to use violence and giving them technical advice on combating the effects of tear gas. At his libel trial, Walker testified that he was on the university campus and did talk to a group of students, but that his message to them was to exercise self-constraint and to remain peaceful. The jury awarded him $500,000 in compensatory damages; the trial judge reversed the jury's further award of $300,00 in punitive damages.

The Supreme Court unanimously overturned the award to Walker in its entirety. The Court emphasized that the story of the events on the University of Mississippi campus, unlike the one about coach Butts, was "news which required immediate dissemination." Also unlike the situation in the companion case, the AP's news source was a correspondent who "gave every indication of being trustworthy and competent," especially to staffers "familiar with General Walker's prior publicized statements on the underlying controversy."

These companion cases are remembered today for at least three issues related to the actual malice standard. First and most important, the Court used the cases as a vehicle to make clear that the *New York Times* rule would apply not only to public officials but to public figures as well. The second point is that the Court also begins to offer judges guidance for determining whether or not a journalist is guilty of actual malice. Specifically, the Court will be a bit more forgiving of journalistic errors if the news being disseminated to the public is "hard" news about important political events, if it is "hot" news that needs to be gotten out quickly, and perhaps too if the specific media outlet's tight deadline precludes careful verification of every single last fact.

The third and last point is that the breakdown of the various justices' opinions in these companion cases serves as one of the best examples in communication law in support of the point made in Chapter 1, that court watchers must be very careful to note the differences among majority, plurality, concurring, and dissenting opinions and equally careful to count up the votes for any particular point in an opinion. These cases did not produce a majority opinion. If one were to read only the four-judge plurality opinion written by Justice Harlan (joined by Justices Clark, Stewart, and Fortas), one would surmise incorrectly that the Court intended to apply a watered-down version of the actual malice test to public figures. Indeed, this position is the one taken by Harlan and the others; instead of demanding a finding that the defendant published a knowing falsehood or with "reckless disregard" of falsity, they would also permit plaintiffs who are public figures to prevail if they can prove that the defamations resulted from "highly unreasonable conduct constituting an extreme departure from the standards of investigation and reporting ordinarily adhered to by responsible publishers." Although it may be argued that this phrase seems to be simply a paraphrase of the actual malice test or that it describes a degree of fault equally damning, Justice Harlan and his cosigners clearly intended it to be a lesser showing than that required by public officials.

Harlan and the others did not prevail on this point, however. All the other justices rejected his suggestion that different standards be set for public officials and public figures. Chief Justice Warren says in his concurring opinion that "differentiation between public figures and public officials and adoption of separate standards of proof for each have no basis in law, logic, or First Amendment policy." Justice Black, joined by Justice Douglas in his opinion accepting the Court's decision concerning Walker but dissenting from the *Butts* decision, also rejects Harlan's suggestion. So, too, does Justice Brennan (together with Justice White), who wanted to send the *Butts* case back to the lower court for a new trial precisely to ensure that the actual malice test is described accurately in the instructions to the jury.

If the *Butts* and *Walker* cases together serve to emphasize that the identity of the plaintiff will go a long way toward determining who will prevail in a libel suit, the Court injected some confusion into the issue a few years later. In 1971, the Court was unable to produce a majority opinion in a case resulting from a Phila-

# Things to Remember

## APPLICATION OF THE ACTUAL MALICE RULE TO PUBLIC FIGURES

Within three years of the *Sullivan* case, the Court decided to demand that not only public officials, but also public figures, prove actual malice to establish a libel claim.

delphia area radio station having referred to a local businessman as a "smut merchant," but a plurality opinion signed by three of the justices argued for extending the "actual malice" protection to any publication focusing on a topic of public interest, regardless of the identity of the plaintiff.[6] Three years later, in the landmark *Gertz v. Welch, Inc.*[7] decision discussed at more length later in this chapter, a clear majority of the Court rejected the *Rosenbloom* plurality's logic and reaffirmed that it is primarily whether the plaintiff is a public official or public figure that determines whether the actual malice standard applies.

### What Are the Actual Malice Rule's Implications for the Truth Defense?

In the common tort law of libel, it will be recalled from Chapter 3, one of the most powerful defenses was to establish that the gist or "sting" of the defamatory remarks was substantially true. Recall, too, that when we call truth a *defense,* we emphasize that the plaintiff need not prove falsity as an element of libel. In common law, defamatory statements are presumed to be false. The alternative—because arguments require presumptions and burdens of proof—is that we presume the plaintiff really is a scoundrel, or a liar, or a spouse beater.

How does the *New York Times* actual malice rule affect the place of truth and falsity in libel law? Plaintiffs who are able to prove actual malice by the first of the two options provided in the Supreme Court's definition—that the defendant published a "knowing falsehood"—will obviously have laid to rest any ambiguity about the truth or falsity of the defamations. It also seems that the second route, proving actual malice as the dissemination of libels with "reckless disregard" as to their truth or falsity, carries with it at least a strong implication that the publication's allegations must have been false. Why sue someone for recklessly publishing the *truth,* for getting it *right* (even if by accident or sheer luck)?

To prove actual malice, then, is to prove falsity, but what of plaintiffs who do not have to prove actual malice? These plaintiffs are neither public officials nor

---

[6]*Rosenbloom v. Metromedia,* 403 U.S. 29 (1971).

[7]418 U.S. 323 (1974).

public figures. Public officials who sue because of defamations that have nothing to do with their official conduct are also under consideration. Do they have the burden of proving falsity, or does the common-law rule prevail?

The Supreme Court gave at least a partial answer to this question in 1986, when it decided *Philadelphia Newspapers v. Hepps.*[8] At issue were articles in the *Philadelphia Inquirer* linking local businessman Maurice Hepps to organized crime and alleging that his company exercised a measure of control over the State Liquor Control Board. The Pennsylvania Supreme Court, overturning a lower court finding for the newspaper, held that the jury should have been explicitly instructed that Hepps did not have the burden of proving falsity. By a 5–4 vote, the U.S. Supreme Court reversed the state high court. Writing for the majority, Justice O'Connor admits that an ironclad rule requiring all libel plaintiffs to prove falsity would be imperfect in that there will be times when defamations, although untrue, cannot be proven untrue. Yet always placing the burden of showing truth on the defendants would stifle too much speech. She emerges with a compromise position, holding that "the common-law presumption that defamatory speech is false cannot stand *when a plaintiff seeks damages against a media defendant for speech of public concern"* (emphasis added).

The holding in *Hepps* provides a clue to a larger truth about the Supreme Court's post–*New York Times v. Sullivan* defamation jurisprudence generally. That body of case law can be understood and organized far more easily if three important questions are kept in mind:

- Who is the plaintiff (a public official or figure, or private individual)?
- Who is the defendant (media or nonmedia)?
- What was the libel about (an issue of public importance or a private matter)?

The Court has in essence set up a $2 \times 2 \times 2$ matrix, creating eight possible combinations of situations. More often than not, the answer to a question about the constitutional dimension of libel law is "it depends," and what it depends on is how these three questions are answered. If the question is "Who has the burden of proof regarding truth or falsity," the answer seems to be that in at least five of the eight situations, the burden is shouldered by the plaintiff. Why five of eight? In all four situations where the answer to the first question is that the plaintiff is a public person (assuming for public officials that their official conduct is at issue), that plaintiff has the burden of proof. In at least one set of circumstances, even purely private plaintiffs must prove falsity: when the defendant is the media, *and* the offending publication is about a matter of public interest. With respect to the remaining three boxes—private plaintiffs suing nonmedia entities (regardless of the subject matter of the defamation) and private plaintiffs suing the media over a

---

[8]475 U.S. 767 (1986).

# Things to Remember

## THE FIRST AMENDMENT AND THE TRUTH DEFENSE

- Proving actual malice includes the proof of falsity.
- Those who do not have to prove actual malice will still have to prove falsity if they sue a media defendant about a story on a topic of public concern.

publication on a topic not of public concern—the First Amendment as interpreted by the Supreme Court offers no guidance as to who shoulders the burden of proof regarding truth or falsity.

### Is the Presence of Actual Malice a Legal or a Factual Question?

In Chapter 1, the distinction between questions of fact and questions of law was introduced. That distinction becomes crucial in the Supreme Court's libel jurisprudence; it becomes a big money issue in that the vast majority of libel suits are lost by the media at the trial level, but the majority of those are overturned in favor of the defendants at the appellate level. Libel defendants are therefore hungry to find plausible and fruitful grounds for appeal.

Given that so much of the constitutionalized tort of libel focuses on the level of fault manifested by defendants, whether a trial court finding of actual malice is a question of fact (generally not appealable) or a question of law (easily appealable) was a crucial question left unanswered in *New York Times v. Sullivan* itself. Twenty years later, the Court did provide an answer, one that lawyer and author Floyd Abrams hailed as a reaffirmation of "one of the most important pillars on which *Sullivan* stands: the constitutional requirement of independent appellate review to assure that juries and trial courts do not overcome or circumvent the First Amendment."[9]

The facts in *Bose Corporation v. Consumers Union*[10] will likely seem not nearly as exciting as the lofty language often used to describe the legal doctrine the case created. The case resulted from what Justice Stevens described in his majority opinion as "an unusual metaphor in a critical review of an unusual loudspeaker system." The speaker system was Bose's 901 model, the review published in the May 1970 issue of *Consumer Reports*. The reviewers, after offering some positive comments about the speaker system, cautioned that listeners "could pinpoint the location of various instruments much more easily with a standard speaker than with the Bose

---

[9] Floyd Abrams, "The Supreme Court Turns a New Page in Libel," 70 *American Bar Association Journal* 89 (1984).

[10] 466 U.S. 485 (1984).

system." With this system, the reviewers added, "individual instruments...seemed to grow to gigantic proportions and tended to wander about the room." Prospective buyers might not be very happy with the system, "after the novelty [wears] off."

The trial court ruled that the Bose Corporation would be considered a public figure for the purposes of this product disparagement suit owing to the unusual nature of the speaker system and the aggressive advertising by the company to promote it. Thus, actual malice was the required level of fault, and the court was satisfied that this level of fault had been demonstrated at trial. Where the magazine's panel of listeners reported that sound from the speakers seemed to "wander about the room," the court took it to mean "all over the room," not simply (as the evaluators *said* at trial that they meant) "along the wall," *between* the two speakers. The court concluded that the difference between what the evaluators meant and what they actually wrote was substantial enough to constitute actual malice.

If you find this discussion a bit silly, you are not alone. In his dissenting opinion, Justice Rehnquist disparagingly refers to this whole Bose speakers controversy as "The Case of the Wandering Instruments" and suggests that it would be much more at home in the *Adventures of Sherlock Holmes* than in the Court's official proceedings. In any event, the trial court assessed damages against the magazine publisher and the federal appellate court reversed, finding that the editors were guilty at most "of using imprecise language in the article—perhaps resulting from an attempt to produce a readable article for its mass audience."

The question in front of the Supreme Court, then, was whether the appellate court had overstepped its bounds by assessing anew and independently the question of whether the magazine manifested actual malice. Is actual malice a question of law or of fact?

Intuitively, one might suppose that actual malice can be either a question of fact or of law. A jury that finds the defendant published a "knowing falsehood"—that is, that he lied—would seem to be making an inference of fact. Trying to guess what was going on in another person's mind at some relevant time in the past is difficult to do; it is more art than science, but it is an issue of fact. Either he knew or he did not know that he was publishing a falsehood.

Conversely, the intuitive approach would also suggest that if the jury depends instead on the alternate definition of actual malice, that the defendant published with "reckless disregard as to truth or falsity," it will have settled a question of law rather than of fact. How far must a publisher deviate from accepted journalistic practices before we are ready to say that she crossed over the line between mere negligence and actual malice? This kind of judgment is precisely what is normally thought of as a question of law.

As it turns out, only Justice White's dissenting opinion embraced this perspective. Dissenting Justices Rehnquist and O'Connor went further, arguing that the question of actual malice is at its core a factual question in all circumstances.

The majority opinion does not really answer the question, but it does provide a rule to guide lower courts in the future. Writing for the majority, Justice Stevens emphasized that independent appellate review has been held by the Court to be required by the First Amendment in many contexts, from commercial speech to obscenity. Here, similarly, the Court concludes that "the question whether the evidence in the record in a defamation case is of the convincing clarity required to strip the utterance of First Amendment protection is not merely a question for the trier of fact." Taking on the responsibility for determining the issue of fault for itself, the majority finds that testimony offered by Consumer Union's chief engineer may have manifested a "capacity for rationalization," but not a degree of culpability approaching actual malice. As if in response to Justice Rehnquist's expressed disdain for the banality of the dispute before it, the majority further concludes that "the difference between hearing violin sounds move around the room and hearing them wander back and forth fits easily within the breathing space that gives life to the First Amendment."

The majority does not ever explicitly tell us that actual malice is a legal as opposed to a factual question, and this failure to settle the question forthrightly has been much criticized. Still, the Court concludes that the strong First Amendment interests involved outweigh the interests reflected in the "clearly erroneous rule," Rule 52(a) of Federal Civil Procedure, which was discussed briefly in Chapter 1. That rule tells federal appellate judges that they should defer to the lower-level court on matters of fact and that this deference should be especially strong when assessments of witness credibility are at issue. After all, only the trial level participants see and hear firsthand the demeanor of witnesses and are thus in a far better position to determine veracity than are appellate judges reading trial transcripts months or years later. The clearly erroneous rule, Justice Stevens holds for the majority, "does not prescribe the standard of review to be applied in reviewing a determination of actual malice in a case governed by *New York Times Co. v. Sullivan*." Rather, "appellate judges in such a case must exercise independent judgment and determine whether the record establishes actual malice with convincing clarity."

 # Things to Remember

**APPEALING ACTUAL MALICE**

- A trial court finding that a libel defendant has manifested actual malice with convincing clarity is an appealable finding.
- This finding has significant financial implications for media libel defendants, which tend to lose most libel cases at the trial level, but win on appeal.

### Can Editorial Pressure to Produce Sensational Stories Constitute Partial Evidence of Actual Malice?

In the spring of 1985, media outlets nationwide were using their editorial pages to express dismay and even a bit of panic over a decision issued by the federal appellate court for the D.C. Circuit. Mobil Oil CEO William Tavoulareas had sued the *Washington Post* for suggesting, in an article published in November 1979, that he had improperly used his influence to help set up his son Peter as a partner in a huge shipping business that had multimillion dollar contracts with Mobil.[11] The majority of the three-judge appellate panel hearing the case in 1985 made much of *Post* editor Bob Woodward putting his staff under great pressure to produce, in his words, the kind of "holy shit story" for which he himself became famous during Watergate. Might not reporters who are under the gun to write such "high-impact investigative stories of wrongdoing" be likely to see an international scandal where others would see only a father trying to help out his son? The appellate panel concluded that Woodward's colorful phrase "is relevant to the inquiry of whether a newspaper's employees acted in reckless disregard of whether a statement is false or not."

The *Post*'s appeal to the full appellate court produced a very different result. The *en banc* court overturned its own panel, holding that "managerial pressure to produce [hard-hitting investigative] stories cannot, as a matter of law, constitute evidence of actual malice" and adding that investigative reports serve "one of the highest functions of the press in our society."

The Supreme Court never heard the *Tavoulareas* case, and the media celebration of the *en banc* decision may have been both overly jubilant and premature. In the years since *Tavoulareas,* the notion that juries must never use the fact that reporters felt obliged to write hard-hitting investigative pieces as evidence of actual malice has not spread beyond the D.C. Circuit. Even before *Tavoulareas,* then Chief Justice Warren's concurring opinion from the case discussed earlier involving University of Georgia football coach Wally Butts had suggested one reason the plaintiff there correctly prevailed: the *Saturday Evening Post* staff had been under enormous pressure to increase circulation and advertising revenues through stories that Warren described as "sophisticated muckraking," those that are designed to "provoke people," to "make them mad." That this language was later cited with approval by an opinion signed by eight members of the Court would seem to suggest further that the relevant language from the *en banc* decision in *Tavoulareas* stands virtually alone.[12]

Moreover, in 1988, the federal appellate court for the Sixth Circuit, although superficially expressing agreement with the D.C. Circuit's reasoning in *Tavoulareas,* ultimately rejected that which had so comforted the press about the earlier deci-

---

[11]*Tavoulareas v. Piro,* 759 F.2d 90 (D.C. Cir. 1985), *overturned en banc,* 817 F.2d 762 (D.C. Cir. 1987).

[12]*St. Amant v. Thompson,* 390 U.S. 727, 732 n.3 (1968).

# Things to Remember

**INVESTIGATIVE JOURNALISM AND THE FIRST AMENDMENT**

■ The Court of Appeals for the D.C. Circuit has held that juries may not consider that reporters may have been under pressure to produce hard-hitting investigative pieces as evidence of likely actual malice.

■ The Sixth Circuit seems to have rejected this approach, and it is not yet clear how the Supreme Court would rule on the issue.

sion by adding that libel juries should not be required to "blind [themselves] to evidence of editorial pressure for sensationalistic stories."[13] This was admittedly *dicta,* which the Supreme Court never cited even while upholding the Sixth Circuit's decision.

### What Other Journalistic Behaviors Might Constitute Actual Malice?

The Supreme Court decision in the *Harte-Hanks* case is worthy of study for reasons that go beyond the implicit rejection of the *Tavoulareas* logic. The case was an important and disturbing one from the perspective of many commentators, who emphasized that here was the first time the Court permitted a finding of actual malice largely on the basis of what the press did *not* do or say rather than on what it actually published. Whether or not one accepts the validity of the media's assessment, the Court used the case as a vehicle to give further guidance as to what kinds of newsroom practices might constitute actual malice. A brief review of the facts gives a better understanding of how the Court did so.

*Harte-Hanks* stemmed from accusations that Daniel Connaughton, a candidate for municipal judge, had offered financial rewards of various kinds to two women who had testified at a grand jury investigating the incumbent judge's staff for, ironically enough, bribery. A jury awarded Connaughton $200,000 in damages, but the trial judge reversed that award, finding that the plaintiff had not proven actual malice. The appellate court, although not conducting as thoroughly independent a review of the actual malice question as the Supreme Court would have preferred, concluded that there was actual malice and reinstated the jury award. The Supreme Court affirmed this judgment and in so doing identified a number of factors that led it to conclude that the newspaper had manifested actual malice. Among these factors was relying on a highly questionable source while

---

[13]*Connaughton v. Harte Hanks Communications, Inc.,* 842 F.2d 825, 834 (6th Cir. 1988), *aff'd,* 491 U.S. 657 (1989).

failing to interview easily identifiable persons likely to present evidence at odds with the paper's eventual accusations. Then, too, the paper failed to listen to a tape recording it knew to exist of the conversation in which Connaughton allegedly offered tangible rewards to the grand jury witnesses. These factors and others led the Court to conclude that the paper had made a "deliberate decision not to acquire knowledge" of important facts. It was this "purposeful avoidance of the truth" that Justice Stevens's majority opinion says compelled the Court to find actual malice.

Additional guidance concerning the kinds of behaviors juries trying to assess communicators' level of fault might consider comes from a Louisiana case involving a televised political speech, but in which the speaker rather than the medium was the defendant.[14] Phil St. Amant, candidate for sheriff in Baton Rouge, strongly hinted in his speech that his opponent, deputy sheriff Herman Thompson, was guilty of accepting bribes from the president of the local Teamsters Union. Although the result of the case was to overturn a modest libel judgment against St. Amant on the ground that he had no reason to doubt the veracity of his source, Justice White's majority opinion also provided the following list of transgressions that might constitute actual malice:

- A story is fabricated by the defendant, is the product of his imagination, or is based wholly on an unverified anonymous telephone call.
- The publisher's allegations are so inherently improbable that only a reckless man would have put them in circulation.
- There are obvious reasons to doubt the veracity of the informant or the accuracy of the informant's reports.

In 1991, the Supreme Court was called on to determine whether a reporter's attribution to an interviewed source of direct quotes that were never actually uttered could be evidence of actual malice. *Masson v. New Yorker*[15] arose out of an article written by Janet Malcolm about Dr. Jeffrey Masson that appeared in two consecutive issues of the magazine in 1983. Both litigants agreed that the articles, which told the story of how Masson lost his position as the director of the Freud Archives as a result of his outspoken criticism of Freudian psychoanalysis, were largely based on forty hours of tape recorded interviews. The picture Malcolm painted of Masson was hardly flattering. As one reviewer put it, Masson was depicted as "a grandiose egoist—mean-spirited, self-serving, full of braggadocio, impossibly arrogant and, in the end, a destructive fool."[16]

The lower federal courts granted summary judgment to Malcolm and the magazine, finding that the six alleged misattributions had not altered the "substantive content" of Masson's actual remarks or were at least "rational interpretations"

---

[14]*St. Amant v. Thompson,* 390 U.S. 727 (1968).

[15]501 U.S. 496 (1991).

[16]Robert Coles, "Freudianism and Its Malcontents," *Boston Globe,* 27 May 1984, p. 58.

# Things to Remember

---

**NAILING DOWN THE ACTUAL MALICE CONCEPT**

- Juries might find actual malice if the media:
  - Depend on a single, anonymous phone call as their source.
  - Publish without checking a charge that seems very likely, on its face, to be false.
  - Show no skepticism toward a source who is almost certainly lying.
- Juries may not find actual malice in the inaccuracy of exact quotes attributed to a source unless the meaning of the source's words has been materially changed.

---

of some of Masson's more ambiguous comments. The Supreme Court reversed with respect to five of the six quotes and in so doing fashioned a slightly different rule from that embraced by the lower courts. Summary judgments based on allegedly defamatory misquotes should be permitted, Justice Kennedy wrote for the majority, as long as the printed account does not represent "a material change in the meaning conveyed" by the actual utterance.

### Is There Such a Thing as a Defamatory Opinion?

In Chapter 3, mention was made of the common-law libel defense known as fair comment, which reminds us that defamation plaintiffs must be able to prove that the damaging utterances made about them contained specific *factual* allegations. Pure opinions, at least theoretically, would not be actionable. The Supreme Court—and lower courts attempting to apply relevant Supreme Court doctrine—has in recent years applied a First Amendment analysis to the fact versus opinion distinction.

The somewhat confusing story of the Court's "protected opinion" doctrine began with an off-the-cuff bit of dicta in a 1974 decision. *Gertz v. Welch*[17] involved a conservative magazine publisher accusing a civil rights attorney of being part of a Communist conspiracy to discredit law enforcement officials. The majority opinion included the following words: "We begin with the common ground. Under the First Amendment there is no such thing as a false idea. However pernicious an opinion may seem, we depend for its correction not on the conscience of judges and juries but on the competition of other ideas."

At least two questions arise from this passage. The first, to which the Court would not provide any answer until sixteen years later, was whether it meant by its dramatic tone to create absolute immunity from liability for any utterance that could plausibly be called an opinion. Many lower courts took the Court to mean

---

[17]418 U.S. 323 (1974).

precisely that. The second question was, whatever special measure of First Amendment protection against libel suits would be granted to opinions, how would one *distinguish* facts from opinions? In the years following *Gertz,* several lower courts offered their own thoughts regarding this second question. One of the most influential suggestions was provided by the Court of Appeals for the D.C. Circuit, ruling *en banc,* in *Ollman v. Evans.*[18]

Columnists Rowland Evans and Robert Novak had written an editorial opposing the impending appointment of Bertell Ollman, a well-known professor of political science, to a department chair position at the University of Maryland. Ollman, who blamed the university's ultimate decision not to hire him on the fallout from the editorial, was depicted not only as a Marxist, but also as someone who believed in using the classroom to proselytize in support of Marxist ideology. It was another assertion that gave the appellate court the most difficulty. Was it an assertion of fact or of opinion when Evans and Novak quoted an unnamed colleague of Ollman's—described as a "political scientist in a major eastern university whose scholarship and reputation as a liberal is well known"—for the proposition that Ollman "has no status within the profession, but is a pure and simple activist"?

The *Ollman* court was a very divided one. The eleven judges produced seven separate opinions and a 6–5 vote concluding that the "no status" allegation as well as all the other remarks that offended Ollman were protected opinion. In his plurality opinion, Judge Kenneth Starr (later of Whitewater and "Monicagate" fame) lamented that "the Supreme Court provided little guidance in *Gertz* itself as to the manner in which the distinction between fact and opinion is to be discerned." Such a distinction, he added, "is by no means as easy a question as might appear at first blush." He suggests that courts trying to distinguish facts from opinions should pose these questions:

- **What is the common usage or meaning of the words?**    Generally, there will be a definiteness about facts that are missing from opinions. "He is a convicted felon" is thus much less likely to be deemed protected opinion than "He is a fascist." Accusing a journalist of "sloppy and irresponsible reporting" would surely not be actionable, but to accuse the same journalist of "making up fictitious sources whenever it suited her" might be.
- **How verifiable is the statement?**    Is the statement objectively capable of proof or disproof? Although there might be some overlap between this inquiry and the one above, verifiability raises important constitutional issues. "Insofar as a statement is unverifiable, the First Amendment is endangered when attempts are made to prove the statement true or false."

---

[18] 750 F.2d 970 (D.C. Cir. 1984).

- **What is the immediate context in which the words appear?** Look at the paragraphs before and after the allegedly libelous remark. Perhaps look at the entire article or column for guidance. Recall *Greenbelt Cooperative Publishing Association v. Bresler,*[19] discussed in Chapter 3. Plaintiff was referred to as a "blackmailer" in a local newspaper, but the immediate context of the article made clear that the commentator meant only that Bresler, a real estate developer, had driven a hard bargain with the city council, not that he was guilty of extortion.
- **What is the larger social context in which the words appear?** Consider, for example, the mind-set with which readers approach the various sections of a newspaper. In an editorial column, readers are conditioned to expect opinions rather than hard facts. Other courts have said the same of newspapers' editorial cartoons, sports sections, and restaurant reviews.

Although the *Ollman* test became quite influential, Judge Starr was the first to admit that any such calculus designed to help judges work through the immeasurably complicated issue of the meaning of words was bound to be imperfect. In 1990, the Supreme Court weighed in again on the fact versus opinion distinction in *Milkovich v. Lorain Journal Co.*[20] There is much ambiguity in the case. One commentator has suggested that lower courts have been so confused by the decision that they have gone in at least eight different directions in trying to apply it.[21] Still, it is fair to say that *Milkovich* has resulted in many libel suits going to trial that previously would have resulted in summary judgments for defendants.

The case stemmed from a lawsuit against the Ohio High School Athletic Association, which had conducted an investigation into an altercation resulting in some injuries that took place at a high school wrestling match. Maple Heights High School wrestling coach Michael Milkovich testified at that judicial proceeding, which resulted in the lifting of sanctions that had been imposed by the association. A local newspaper article commenting on the proceedings seemed to accuse Milkovich of perjury (see Figure 4.2).

Writing for a 7–2 majority, Chief Justice Rehnquist expressed concern that lower courts had made too much of the dicta from *Gertz* to the effect that "there is no such thing as a false idea." That passage was never intended "to create a wholesale defamation exemption for anything that might be labeled 'opinion,'" Rehnquist added. A contrary reading would "ignore the fact that expressions of 'opinion' may often imply an assertion of objective fact." Rehnquist further chides

[19]398 U.S. 6 (1970).

[20]497 U.S. 1 (1990).

[21]Kathryn Dix Sowle, "A Matter of Opinion: Milkovich Four Years Later," 3 *William and Mary Bill of Rights Journal* 467 (1994).

Figure 4.2

## MAPLE BEAT THE LAW WITH THE "BIG LIE"

Yesterday in the Franklin County Common Pleas Court, judge Paul Martin overturned an Ohio High School Athletic Association decision to suspend the Maple Heights wrestling team from this year's state tournament....

But there is something much more important involved here than whether Maple was denied due process by the OHSAA, the basis of the temporary injunction.

When a person takes on a job in a school, whether it be as a teacher, coach, administrator or even maintenance worker, it is well to remember that his primary job is that of educator.

There is scarcely a person concerned with school who doesn't leave his mark in some way on the young people who pass his way—many are the lessons taken away from school by students which weren't learned from a lesson plan or out of a book. They come from personal experiences with and observations of their superiors and peers, from watching actions and reactions.

Such a lesson was learned (or relearned) yesterday by the student body of Maple Heights High School, and by anyone who attended the Maple-Mentor wrestling meet of last Feb. 8.... A lesson which, sadly, in view of the events of the past year, is well they learned early. It is simply this: If you get in a jam, lie your way out.

If you're successful enough, and powerful enough, and can sound sincere enough, you stand an excellent chance of making the lie stand up, regardless of what really happened.

The teachers responsible were mainly head Maple wrestling coach, Mike Milkovich, and former superintendent of schools H. Donald Scott.

Last winter they were faced with a difficult situation. Milkovich's ranting from the side of the mat and egging the crowd on against the meet official and the opposing team...resulted in...a brawl....

Naturally,...the two men were called on the carpet to account for the incident. But they declined to walk into the hearing and face up to their responsibilities.... Instead they chose to come to the hearing and misrepresent the things that happened to the OHSAA Board of Control....

I was among the 2,000-plus witnesses of the meet at which the trouble broke out, and I also attended the hearing before the OHSAA, so I was in a unique position of being the only non-involved party to observe both the meet itself and the Milkovich-Scott version presented to the board. Any resemblance between the two occurrences is purely coincidental.

Anyone who attended the meet, whether he be from Maple Heights, Mentor, or impartial observer, knows in his heart that Milkovich and Scott lied at the hearing after each having given his solemn oath to tell the truth.

But they got away with it. Is that the kind of lesson we want our young people learning from their high school administrators and coaches? I think not.

*From the* Lorain News-Herald, *8 January 1975. Copyright © 1975 News-Herald Company. Reprinted with permission.*

the defendants for proposing that "a number of factors developed by the lower courts (in what we hold was a mistaken reliance on the *Gertz* dictum) be considered" in distinguishing facts from opinions. Clearly Rehnquist has in mind here such formulas as the *Ollman* four-part test. Such tests are unneeded, he says, in that "the breathing space which freedoms of expression require in order to survive is adequately secured by existing constitutional doctrine without the creation of an artificial dichotomy between 'opinion' and 'fact.'"

Perhaps there is a bit of irony in the *Milkovich* majority, even while criticizing lower courts for trying to fashion rules to distinguish facts from opinions, needing itself to determine if the charges leveled against the wrestling coach carried factual elements, in other words, to separate fact from opinion. Many commentators have thus suggested that the Court "simply jettisoned the terminology rather than the essence of the fact-opinion distinction."[22] In any event, Rehnquist had little difficulty concluding that the newspaper article did raise very specific factual allegations about Milkovich that should be considered by a jury rather than subject to summary judgment for the defendant. "The dispositive question in the present case," he says, is "whether a reasonable fact finder could conclude that the statements…imply an assertion that petitioner Milkovich perjured himself in a judicial proceeding. We think this question must be answered in the affirmative."

Although Chief Justice Rehnquist rejected the defense's argument that the First Amendment always "mandates an inquiry into whether a statement is 'opinion' or 'fact,'" he went out of his way to remind us that in many situations, existing Supreme Court precedents already serve to protect statements of opinion. Certainly in any case where actual malice is the required level of fault, a finding of false fact is necessarily a part of the plaintiff's burden. So too, after the *Hepps* case discussed earlier, plaintiffs suing media defendants over matters of public concern have the burden of proving that *false* allegations of fact have been made. *Milkovich's* effects would thus chiefly be felt by defendants, especially nonmedia defendants, whose utterances are not deemed to touch on matters of public concern. A 1997 decision from the Court of Appeals in the First Circuit involved such a defendant.

Levinsky's is a small chain of Portland, Maine, clothing retail stores that was feeling a great deal of competition from Wal-Mart stores that had recently opened in the area. It embarked on a playful radio advertising campaign with "David v. Goliath" elements aimed at preserving its market share. (The copy for one such ad read, "Levinsky's has a great selection and the lowest prices in Maine on Levi's jeans, Dockers and denim shirts. Wal-Mart doesn't carry Levi's—but we did get a good buy on a toaster."). A reporter for *Portland Business* magazine decided to do a

---

[22]Martin F. Hansen, "Fact, Opinion, and Consensus: The Verifiability of Allegedly Defamatory Speech," 62 *George Washington Law Review* 43, 45 (1993). See also Nat Stern, "Defamation, Epistemology, and the Erosion (But Not Destruction) of the Opinion Privilege," 57 *Tennessee Law Review* 595, 614 (1990); Jerry J. Phillips, "Opinion and Defamation: The Camel in the Tent," 57 *Tennessee Law Review* 647, 675 (1990).

story about the "store wars"; a couple of criticisms aimed at Levinsky's made to the reporter in an interview with a Wal-Mart official formed the basis for the resulting lawsuit.[23] The Wal-Mart spokesperson alleged first that one of the Levinsky outlets was "trashy" and that customers who call the local outlet are "sometimes put on hold for 20 minutes, or the phone is never picked up at all." Although the court determined that the "trashy" remark is sufficiently vague so as not to carry any clear factual allegations, the "20 minutes" remark was not deemed to be protected opinion. The statement uses a "specific time frame," one that is not so implausible as to constitute rhetorical hyperbole. Indeed, the assertion could be "verified or rebutted by objective evidence of how Levinsky's staff handled telephone calls."

Suppose that the Wal-Mart spokesperson had not referred to a specific time frame? What if he instead said something like, "You can be kept on hold *forever* when you try to reach those folks by phone"? Clearly such an utterance would be protected as rhetorical hyperbole, as a form of opinion so outlandish as to never be taken literally. Should not then the second half of the actual "20 minutes" utterance—the suggestion that the phone might "never be picked up at all"—go a long way toward protecting the entire assertion? The court rejected this argument, finding that the second portion of the statement might be taken quite literally to mean that, at least on some occasions, workers "did not bother to answer the telephone."

In the end, the case was remanded back to the district court, in part to determine if it concerned speech on a matter of public concern (in which case the

---

[23]*Levinsky's v. Wal-Mart,* 127 F.3d 122 (1st Cir. 1997).

 # Things to Remember

### FACTS AND OPINIONS

- In an offhand comment from *Gertz v. Welch* (1974), the Supreme Court implied that libel suits could never succeed against pure statements of opinion.

- Several lower courts then tried to find ways of distinguishing facts from opinions. One of the more influential tests emerged in the appellate decision in *Ollman v. Evans,* which said that courts should look at the following:
  - The everyday meanings of the words in question.
  - Whether the words are verifiable.
  - The immediate context.
  - The larger social context.

- In 1990 (*Milkovich v. Lorain Journal Co.*), the Supreme Court tried to put the matter in perspective by emphasizing that libel defendants cannot escape liability simply by prefacing their defamatory utterances with "I think that…"

- Courts still struggle with the distinction between facts and opinions.

$600,000 in presumed damages that had been awarded could not stand without a finding of actual malice).

### Can Libel Plaintiffs Use the Tort of Intentional Infliction of Emotional Distress to Avoid the Actual Malice Requirement?

In the early 1980s, the makers of Campari liqueur embarked on a clever ad campaign designed to capitalize on what might otherwise be considered a shortcoming of the product. The drink—which has been described as "distinct," "bittersweet," and "strictly an acquired taste"—often does not appeal to persons tasting it for the first time.[24] Madison Avenue's solution was to produce slick print ads featuring a celebrity talking about his or her "first time." On the surface, such personalities as actor Tony Roberts would be talking about their first time tasting Campari, but there would always be a naughty double entendre suggesting that the spokesperson's first sexual experience was the real subject under discussion.

Someone at *Hustler* magazine determined that a parody of the Campari campaign, using the Reverend Jerry Falwell as the celebrity spokesperson, would be a handy vehicle for expressing the publication's distaste for the well-known leader of the Christian Right. The parody, which appeared on the inside front cover of the magazine's November 1983 issue, boasted Falwell's photo alongside the caption, "Jerry Falwell talks about his first time." The "ad" was presented as the transcript of a fictitious interview with its subject. Unlike the Campari ads, here the double entendre was more than a hint. Indeed, the text made clear that Falwell's first time sampling the liqueur was also his first time having sex, with his mother, as it turns out, in an outhouse.

Falwell was not amused, and he instructed his attorneys to sue the magazine and publisher Larry Flynt. They employed three legal theories in their quest for damages: libel, invasion of privacy, and a third tort called intentional infliction of emotional distress. Invasion of privacy is the subject of the next chapter and need not be of concern here save to say that the state of Virginia, where Falwell brought his suit, did not recognize the category of privacy invasion for which he sought recovery. Then, too, the jury ruled against Falwell on his libel claim, finding unsurprisingly that no one could possibly take the text of the ad parody seriously and that his reputation was therefore not damaged.

It is the playing out of the third claim that makes the case an important one beyond the mere fact of the litigants' celebrity. The jury provided Falwell with a fairly sizable damages award on his emotional distress claim, and this award was in front of the U.S. Supreme Court on appeal.[25] Would Falwell be permitted to keep the award even though the jury held that there was no libel here?

---

[24]Rodney A. Smolla, *Jerry Falwell v. Larry Flynt: The First Amendment on Trial* (Chicago and Urbana: University of Illinois Press, 1988), 21.

[25]*Hustler Magazine v. Falwell,* 585 U.S. 46 (1988).

Figure 4.3

# Jerry Falwell talks about his first time. *

FALWELL: My first time was in an outhouse outside Lynchburg, Virginia.

INTERVIEWER: Wasn't it a little cramped?

FALWELL: Not after I kicked the goat out.

INTERVIEWER: I see. You must tell me all about it.

FALWELL: I never really expected to make it with Mom, but then after she showed all the other guys in town such a good time, I figured, "What the hell!"

INTERVIEWER: But your mom? Isn't that a bit odd?

FALWELL: I don't think so. Looks don't mean that much to me in a woman.

INTERVIEWER: Go on.

FALWELL: Well, we were drunk off our God-fearing asses on Campari, ginger ale and soda—that's called a Fire and Brimstone—at the time. And Mom looked better than a Baptist whore with a $100 donation.

INTERVIEWER: Campari in the crapper with Mom . . . how interesting. Well, how was it?

FALWELL: The Campari was great, but Mom passed out before I could come.

INTERVIEWER: Did you ever try it again?

FALWELL: Sure . . .

lots of times. But not in the outhouse. Between Mom and the shit, the flies were too much to bear.

INTERVIEWER: We meant the Campari.

FALWELL: Oh, yeah. I always get sloshed before I go out to the pulpit. You don't think I could lay down all that bullshit sober, do you?

© 1983—Imported by Campari U.S.A., New York, NY 48°proof Spirit Aperitif (Liqueur)

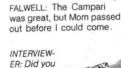

Campari, like all liquor, was made to mix you up. It's a light, 48-proof, refreshing spirit, just mild enough to make you drink too much before you know you're schnockered. For your first time, mix it with orange juice. Or maybe some white wine. Then you won't remember anything the next morning. **Campari. The mixable that smarts.**

# CAMPARI® You'll never forget your first time.

*AD PARODY—NOT TO BE TAKEN SERIOUSLY

A little history of the emotional distress tort will help us to answer that question. Emotional distress is a relative newcomer to the American scene, having been recognized only sporadically, in the past hundred years or so. As its name implies, the tort is supposed to provide a remedy for persons whose feelings have been hurt by the malicious, intentional acts of others. That the tort sometimes goes by the name "outrage" serves to remind us that the conduct of the perpetrator—typically, an overly zealous bill collector or a prankster with a perverse sense of humor—has to be truly outlandish. Sometimes the offensive behavior is much more *conduct* than *communication*. If you shoot my treasured family pet in my presence and in the presence of my young child, you will certainly have caused us both enormous emotional distress. Falsely telling someone that a loved one has died is also another example of the tort in action.

The *Falwell* case did not present the typical emotional distress set of facts, and indeed the plaintiff's attorneys added the claim almost as an afterthought. Yet it seemed a sensible legal strategy. In Virginia, and in many jurisdictions, the tort has four elements:

- The wrongdoer's conduct is intentional or reckless.
- The conduct is so "outrageous" as to offend generally accepted standards of decency.
- The conduct is in fact the cause of the plaintiff's emotional distress.
- The emotional distress thus caused is severe.

It is probably not surprising that Falwell's attorneys were able to persuade the jury that the four elements had been satisfied. In one deposition, Flynt candidly admitted that he had set out to "get" Falwell, to "assassinate" his reputation. Then, too, how many acts that could be attributed to a man would be more "outrageous," more beyond any reasonable standards of decency, than that he had sex with his mother in a stinking, fly-infested toilet? Would not seeing oneself, and one's mother, so depicted, cause severe emotional distress, even if we know "intellectually" that no one would actually believe that the outlandish allegation is true? As Chief Justice Rehnquist allowed in his opinion for a unanimous Supreme Court, the *Hustler* ad parody was obviously offensive to Falwell, "and doubtless gross and repugnant in the eyes of most others."

Nonetheless, the Court ruled against Falwell. "There is no doubt," Rehnquist allowed, that the *Hustler* ad parody was "at best a distant cousin" of the kinds of political cartoons and commentaries, caustic though they often have been, that have enriched civil discourse since the nation's birth. "Public discourse would probably suffer little or no harm" if it were possible to outlaw the *Hustler* ad without also abridging valuable political speech, but simply calling the ad "outrageous" does not help create a workable standard.

The Court thus held that public figures and public officials may not recover damages for intentional infliction of emotional distress resulting from publications

# Things to Remember

**INTENTIONAL INFLICTION OF EMOTIONAL DISTRESS**

- Sometimes called the tort of outrage, emotional distress suits are designed to protect plaintiffs from hurt feelings rather than damaged reputations.
- If an emotional distress suit is prompted by a publication about the plaintiff, he or she can only prevail if actual malice is first proven.

concerning them unless they are first able to demonstrate actual malice. In other words, if your libel suit fails, so too must your cause of action for emotional distress. The damages award was reversed.

### May Libel Plaintiffs Ask Reporters about Their "State of Mind" When They Went to Press?

Certain catchphrases are born in Washington and are well known to political news junkies. From Justice Clarence Thomas's confirmation hearings came the reference to "high-tech lynching"; the one-liner best remembered from the Iran/Contra hearings is probably the protestation of Oliver North's attorney that he was not just a "potted plant." Then there was Tennessee Senator Howard Baker's famous recurring question from the Watergate hearings: "What did the President know, and when did he know it?"

Baker's question reminds us that an agent's state of mind is often more important than his or her actual conduct. The *New York Times* actual malice test is an example of just such an instance. That a media outlet published a false and defamatory remark does not alone make the publisher liable for damages; we need to know more. To paraphrase Baker, the actual malice inquiry seeks to learn, "What did the reporters and editors know (regarding the truth or falsity of that which they were about to publish), and when did they know it?"

Libel plaintiff Anthony Herbert thought it only fair that he be able to ask reporters these questions directly as he was preparing his case against the producers of CBS's *60 Minutes* program. By a 6–3 vote, the Supreme Court agreed.[26] A retired army officer, Herbert had served extended duty in Vietnam. He came to public attention when he accused superiors of covering up various wartime atrocities. *60 Minutes* did a piece about the accusations, suggesting they were invented by Herbert as a way of rationalizing his having been disciplined by the army, including having been relieved of his command.

In pretrial discovery, *60 Minutes* producer Barry Lando refused to answer questions aimed at gauging his state of mind during the preparation of the story. How, for

---

[26]*Herbert v. Lando,* 441 U.S. 153 (1979).

Figure 4.4

"... And Just What Were Your Thoughts, Mr. Madison, When You Were Writing That Stuff About Making '... No Law ... Abridging The Freedom ... Of The Press ...'?"

Like many members of the working press at the time, cartoonist Tom Englehardt expressed his fear that Justice White's majority opinion in *Herbert v. Lando* would result in dangerous intrusions on the editorial process.

*From the* St. Louis Post-Dispatch, *Thursday, April 19, 1979. Copyright © 1979 Englehardt in the St. Louis Post-Dispatch. Reprinted with permission.*

example, did he evaluate the credibility of his sources for the story when they gave him conflicting accounts of events? Answers to inquiries such as this one would be crucial to Herbert's case in that he clearly would need to prove actual malice.

To agree with Lando's assertion that the First Amendment protects him from having to answer such questions, Justice White wrote for the Court majority, "would constitute a substantial interference with the ability of a defamation plaintiff to establish the ingredients of malice as required by *New York Times*." Plaintiffs must be able to delve "into the thoughts, opinions, and conclusions of the publisher."

The defendants also argued that the inquiries being made of them would lay bare the substance and tone of internal communications among *60 Minutes* staffers and that such conversations and exchanges of memoranda would necessarily become less candid in the long run. White was unimpressed with this argument, finding instead that the very structure of the actual malice test would almost always foster, rather than inhibit, media introspection. Under *New York Times v. Sullivan,* only recklessly published errors are sources of potential liability; thus, given exposure to liability when there is knowing or reckless error, "there is even more reason to resort to prepublication precautions, such as a frank interchange of fact and opinion. We find it difficult to believe that error-avoiding procedures will be terminated or stifled simply because there is liability for culpable error and because the editorial process will itself be examined."

## Things to Remember

### May the Press Print Things It Learns in the Pretrial Discovery Process?

Pretrial discovery, including the compelled disclosure of documents and of deposed testimony, can be a harrowing process. In 1984, the Supreme Court was asked whether a media outlet being sued for libel could use the materials it was learning about the plaintiff through the discovery process in follow-up articles about the controversy that occasioned the lawsuit. Perhaps not surprisingly, the Court's answer was no. *Seattle Times v. Rhinehart*[27] resulted from a series of articles in the 1970s that focused critical attention on a local religious group called the Aquarian Foundation, of which Keith Rhinehart was spiritual leader. As part of the pretrial discovery, the newspaper sought disclosure of the Foundation's financial records, including the names and addresses of the group's donors. Rhinehart argued that such compelled disclosure would violate the donors' privacy and their First Amendment rights (of association, and of religion) and might subject them to violent reprisals. Rhinehart sought further a protective order prohibiting the newspaper from disseminating any information learned from the entire pretrial discovery process.

Writing for a unanimous Court, Justice Powell distinguished between the compelled disclosure of the sought information to the newspaper in its role as

---

[27]467 U.S. 20 (1984).

## Things to Remember

a libel defendant and the newspaper's desire to share any such information with the public. "As in all civil litigation," he wrote, "petitioners gained the information they wish to disseminate only by virtue of the trial court's discovery processes.... Litigants have no First Amendment right of access to information made available only for purposes of trying this suit." The Court further held that the newspaper could publish any information it obtains from sources apart from the discovery process.

### What Is the Plaintiff's Burden of Proof in Combating a Defendant's Motion to Dismiss?

Journalists these days are about as unpopular with the masses as are public officials. Jury libel judgments in the millions are not the novelties that they used to be. As such, the media are anxious to resolve libel litigation at the pretrial stage, to avoid actually going to trial. The Supreme Court provided much comfort to the press when it ruled in 1986 that libel plaintiffs who would in the normal course of events have to prove actual malice *with convincing clarity* at trial must meet that same burden of proof when arguing that they should have a right to go to trial, that is, when they are combating a defendant's motion for summary judgment.[28]

Columnist Jack Anderson, in his *Investigator* magazine, described the Liberty Lobby's director as "an American Hitler": a neo-Nazi, an anti-Semite, a racist, and a fascist. The director sued for libel, alleging that there were over two dozen factually inaccurate and defamatory statements in the series of three articles. The crucial issue posed by the case was whether, at the pretrial stage, the plaintiff would have to persuade the judge of his ability to establish actual malice to a jury's satisfaction at the level of proof known as convincing clarity or if he need only demonstrate actual malice by a preponderance of the evidence (i.e., that it was simply *more likely than not* that Anderson's magazine had published with actual malice). By a 6–3 vote, with Justice White writing for the majority, the Supreme Court decided that the higher burden of proof is the appropriate one, in that the judge's role at this stage of the litigation is to mirror a hypothetical jury's decision making.

Technically, the *Liberty Lobby* doctrine applies only to libel cases decided in federal courts. Still, the vast majority of the states embrace the doctrine themselves. Only two states—Alaska[29] and Texas—have explicitly rejected the rule. The Texas Supreme Court, in 2000, reaffirmed its belief that summary judgment in libel cases brought against a media defendant is appropriate only where the defendant successfully refutes one of the elements of libel.[30]

---

[28]*Anderson v. Liberty Lobby,* 477 U.S. 242 (1986).

[29]*Moffatt v. Brown,* 751 P.2d 939, 943 (Alaska 1988).

[30]*Huckabee v. Time Warner Entertainment Company,* 19 S.W.3d 413 (Tex. 2000).

# Things to Remember

### MOTIONS TO DISMISS A LIBEL CLAIM

■ The same "convincing clarity" burden of proof that applies to actual malice trials also dictates the level of proof that libel plaintiffs must demonstrate to defeat a defendant's motion to dismiss.

■ This ruling is important from the media's perspective because it is very expensive to go to trial, even if one is destined to ultimately prevail.

### May Libel Plaintiffs Shop Around for a Favorable Jurisdiction?

When Montgomery, Alabama, police commissioner L. B. Sullivan sued the *New York Times* for libel, he did so in Alabama, rather than in New York. It would be a very foolish plaintiff's attorney who would advise him to do otherwise. A New York jury would have almost certainly refused to award damages to Mr. Sullivan.

Are a libel plaintiff's choices of jurisdictions limited to his and the defendant's states of residency? The Supreme Court, by a unanimous vote in 1984, gave plaintiffs many more choices. Indeed, they can bring suit anywhere that the libelous statements were circulated.

Kathy Keeton, a resident of New York State, wished to sue *Hustler* magazine, which was officially incorporated in Ohio and which had its main offices in California. So, naturally she brought suit in…New Hampshire.[31] There was a method to the madness in that New Hampshire was the only state in the union whose statute of limitations—a full six years—had not run out. Further, although New Hampshire was by no means the state in which the magazine had its most subscribers, between 10,000 and 15,000 copies of *Hustler* were regularly distributed there. The Supreme Court held that the district court had improperly dismissed the suit. "The tort of

---

[31]*Keeton v. Hustler Magazine*, 465 U.S. 770 (1984).

# Things to Remember

### FORUM SHOPPING

■ Libel plaintiffs may bring their suits in any state where the allegedly defamatory statements were generally circulated.

■ Plaintiffs will often use this latitude to "forum shop," to choose a jurisdiction where the law, the judges, or the jury pools are especially likely to be sympathetic to their cases.

libel," Justice Rehnquist wrote, "is generally held to occur wherever the offending material is circulated. The reputation of the libel victim may suffer harm even in a State in which he has hitherto been anonymous." Rehnquist makes clear too that libel plaintiffs' right to "forum shop" is not limited to a search for states with the longest statutes of limitation. Keeton's decision to sue in New Hampshire "is no different from the litigation strategy of countless plaintiffs who seek a forum with favorable substantive or procedural rules or sympathetic local populations."

### May a Newspaper Be Forced to Publish a Reply Submitted by a *Potential* Libel Plaintiff?

Pat Tornillo was a candidate for the Florida House of Representatives. After the *Miami Herald* published two editorials opposing that candidacy, Tornillo invoked a Florida statute that provided that candidates who are "assailed regarding [their] personal character or official record by any newspaper" have a right "to demand that the newspaper print, free of cost to the candidate, any reply the candidate may make to the newspaper's charges." The newspaper refused Tornillo's request and sought a judicial determination of the statute's constitutionality.

Professor Jerome Barron of the George Washington University School of Law, one of the nation's leading access theorists, argued in front of the Supreme Court that the spirit of the First Amendment is furthered rather than inhibited by such **right of reply statutes.** A unanimous Court, with Chief Justice Burger writing, rejected the argument. "The Florida statute," he wrote, "exacts a penalty on the basis of the content of a newspaper." Worse yet, publishers not willing to incur the costs of printing that which they would prefer not to print "might well conclude that the safe course is to avoid controversy." It is important to keep separate in our minds the category of right of reply statutes invalidated here by the Court and another category of laws called **retraction statutes.** The latter kind of law does not *demand* that the media publish anything. Rather, it gives the press a measure of protection from a later libel suit if it *chooses* first to publish a retraction (i.e., its own admission that the defamatory statements it had disseminated were in error). A majority of the states have such laws on the books. Typically, they limit the kinds of damages that libel plaintiffs may collect if the offending media outlet publishes a retraction. Some states even demand that potential libel plaintiffs first request a retraction before they may bring a full-blown libel suit.

Yet another legislative response relevant to the interactions of replies, retractions, and defamation suits is the Uniform Correction or Clarification of Defamation Act. This act was a proposal for libel reform offered in 1993 by the National Conference of Commissioners on Uniform State Laws. As of 1999, only one state, North Dakota, had adopted the statute, which enjoys the support of the American Bar Association. The Act differs a bit from traditional retraction statutes in that it provides immunity from any but special damages if the original libel is corrected in a later issue and also if the requestor fails to demonstrate the falsity of the defamatory remark.

# Things to Remember

## RIGHT OF REPLY STATUTES

■ The print media cannot be forced by statute to publish a reply from an aggrieved party.
  • Publishing such coerced replies costs valuable space and money.
  • To avoid such costs, editors might timidly avoid offending *anyone.*

■ Right of reply statutes should not be confused with retraction statutes, which provide media with some forms of relief in libel suits if they first publish a requested retraction.

Wholly apart from its relationship to libel reform efforts, the *Tornillo* case is an important document because it emphasizes that our nation's regulatory philosophy varies tremendously depending on the specific communication medium involved. This particular case involved a newspaper, an example of the print media, which traditionally enjoy the largest measure of First Amendment freedom. Broadcast media enjoy far less freedom. Indeed, in a case decided by the Court several years earlier (but never once cited by Burger's *Tornillo* decision, a fact that itself has certainly not escaped critical commentary), the Court had affirmed the constitutionality of federal legislation applying to broadcast media the same kind of right of reply at issue here. More is said about *Red Lion Broadcasting v. FCC*[32] in Chapter 12, which focuses on the electronic media.

## *Gertz v. Welch, Inc.:* The Supreme Court's Other Landmark Libel Decision

Lower court judges were beseeching the Supreme Court for a bit of clarity. In 1971, the Court produced anything but when, in *Rosenbloom v. Metromedia,*[33] its members penned five separate opinions, no one of which commanded more than three votes. Looking back at those opinions, Justice Powell wrote for the *Gertz* majority that they "not only reveal disagreement about the appropriate result; they also reflect divergent traditions of thought about the general problem of reconciling the law of defamation with the First Amendment." The upshot was that Justice Brennan's plurality opinion, which rejected the rule from *New York Times v. Sullivan* that the identity of the plaintiff would determine if actual malice need be proved in favor of letting the public interest in the subject matter of the alleged libel determine the required proof of fault, was treated by many lower courts as if it were majority doctrine. The confusion ended in 1974, when the Court reaffirmed the originally articulated *New York Times* actual malice rule.[34]

---

[32]395 U.S. 367 (1969).

[33]403 U.S. 29 (1971).

[34]*Gertz v. Welch, Inc.* 418 U.S. 323 (1974).

Here, briefly, are the facts of the case. Chicago-based civil rights attorney Elmer Gertz was hired by the family of a young man who had been killed by the police. The officer at fault had already been convicted of second-degree murder; Gertz was to handle the family's civil litigation against him. Robert Welch's magazine, *American Opinion,* an organ of the John Birch Society, published an article alleging that testimony against the cop was perjured and that Gertz was part of a Communist conspiracy to discredit law enforcement officials. The article called Gertz a Leninist, a "Communist fronter," and a former leader of the "Marxist League for Industrial Democracy."

When Gertz sued for defamation, he was awarded $50,000 in damages by the jury. The trial judge, however, threw out the award. By the time the case first reached the appellate level, the Supreme Court's *Rosenbloom* decision had been handed down. Thus, the appellate court also rejected the jury award in that the jury might not have understood that the constitutional privilege from *New York Times v. Sullivan* should now apply to *any* article about a public issue.

In a 5–4 ruling, the *Gertz* Court held that the civil rights attorney was a private figure who should not have to prove actual malice. The Court thus reversed the lower court judge's directed verdict for the defendant. The Court opted for a new trial rather than simply reinstating the jury award because the jury apparently was instructed that it could find for a private plaintiff even in the absence of any level of fault on the part of the publisher. This logic the Court soundly rejected in *Gertz.* Let us look at the several principles that *Gertz v. Welch, Inc.* added to the law of libel.

### A Reaffirmation of the "Who Is the Plaintiff" Question

Earlier in this chapter it was suggested that much of the Supreme Court's libel doctrine can be organized around three issues: who is the plaintiff, who is the defendant, and did the alleged libel concern a matter of public interest. In *Rosenbloom,* the Court flirted with discarding the question of the plaintiff's identity, letting instead the subject matter of the defamatory remarks determine the appropriate level of fault. As Justice Brennan's plurality opinion in *Rosenbloom* put it, "If a matter is a subject of public or general interest, it cannot suddenly become less so merely because a private individual is involved."

The *Gertz* majority opinion rejects the *Rosenbloom* plurality position and emphasizes the continued wisdom of looking toward the identity of the plaintiff as the proper gauge of the level of fault required to recover for libel. Focusing on the kind of libel plaintiff, Justice Powell says, is the best means of establishing the proper balance "between the needs of the press and the individual's claim to compensation for wrongful injury."

It is appropriate to focus on whether the plaintiff is a public or a private individual, Powell explains, for two reasons. First, public plaintiffs do not need to sue to be vindicated in that they can engage in "self-help" remedies instead. If they call a press conference to combat charges made against them, people will come. Powell's second reason for treating public plaintiffs differently is that they usually have *chosen* to be media personalities. People who seek public office, or fame, "run the risk of closer public scrutiny."

## Two Kinds of Public Figures

In the *Butts* and *Walker* cases decided together in 1967, the Supreme Court extended the *New York Times* actual malice rule to public figures. The *Gertz* decision clarifies and extends those holdings by pointing out that there are actually two kinds of public figures. "For the most part those who attain this status," Justice Powell says, "have assumed roles of special prominence in the affairs of society." These people are household names, the truly famous. Criticize them, and they will have to prove actual malice to recover damages from you, regardless of the specific subject matter of the defamatory remarks. Since *Gertz,* these plaintiffs are often referred to as "general" or "all-purpose" public figures to distinguish them from the second category.

The second group, "limited" or "limited-purpose" public figures, might not be truly famous, but they have "thrust themselves to the forefront of particular public controversies in order to influence the resolution of the issues involved," thus inviting both "attention" and "comment." When these personalities become libel plaintiffs, the First Amendment demands that they prove actual malice only if the defamatory remarks concern the specific political issue in which they have become involved. An automobile company middle manager who gives speeches around the country on driving safety will have to prove actual malice if you accuse her of having a string of traffic violations on her record, but not if you point out she has had an abortion. The reverse would be true of a prolife activist. Accuse her of having had an abortion and the actual malice rule will be triggered, but allegations about driving while intoxicated will be considered more private libels.

## The States Retain (Almost) Complete Control
## over the Fault Element in Private Libels

Public officials always have to prove actual malice when they sue for libel, as do general public figures. Limited public figures will at least sometimes have to prove actual malice. What, though, does the First Amendment say about the degree of fault that a truly private plaintiff—or a limited public figure who is maligned in an area of life wholly unrelated to his or her political activism—must prove? Very little, Justice Powell tells us. Consider Powell's assessment of the truly private libel plaintiff's plight: "He has not accepted public office or assumed an influential role in ordering society. He has relinquished no part of his interest in the protection of his own good name, and consequently he has a more compelling call on the courts for redress of injury inflicted by defamatory falsehood." The Court majority therefore interprets the First Amendment so as to give the individual states enormous latitude should they wish to tip the scales in favor of private parties' reputational interests. As long as states do not permit recovery on a strict liability standard (one requiring no finding of fault at all), they will be on sound constitutional footing. The majority of states require that private plaintiffs prove that defamatory remarks were made with negligence. About a dozen states demand a somewhat higher demonstration of fault, which they call "gross negligence." In some jurisdictions—New York among them[35]—which of these two standards will be applied to private plaintiffs is a function of whether the article triggering the libel suit is deemed to be on a matter of public or private interest. A small handful of states demand that all libel plaintiffs, public or private, prove actual malice.

In Figure 4.5, the vertical line represents different levels of fault. It extends from just above Strict Liability (remember from high school geometry class that an unfilled point means that the line jutting out from it comes very close to the point but does not actually touch it), through Negligence and Gross Negligence, all the way to the infinity sign at the top of the drawing. The infinity sign reminds us that the U.S. Constitution does not say anything about a right to sue for libel. Thus, if any individual state decided to get rid of libel law altogether—depicted whimsically here as a requirement that plaintiffs prove an impossible, infinite level of fault—there would be no First Amendment transgression. (Recall from Chapter 1, however, that some *state* constitutions do provide a right to sue for libel.)

---

[35]*Huggins v. Moore,* 726 N.E.2d 456 (Ct. App. N.Y. 1999).

 **Figure 4.5** *The Fault Dimension for Private Plaintiffs after* **Gertz v. Welch, Inc.**

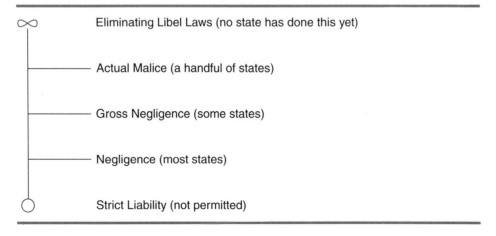

∞      Eliminating Libel Laws (no state has done this yet)

Actual Malice (a handful of states)

Gross Negligence (some states)

Negligence (most states)

Strict Liability (not permitted)

## If You Want Punitive or Presumed Damages, You Must Prove Actual Malice

"The common law of defamation," Justice Powell's majority opinion reminds us, "is an oddity of tort law, for it allows recovery of purportedly compensatory damages without evidence of actual loss. Under the traditional rules pertaining to actions for libel, the existence of injury is presumed from the fact of publication. Juries may award substantial sums as compensation for supposed damage to reputation without any proof that such harm actually occurred."

The awarding of presumed and punitive damages must be kept in check, Powell argues, because it can inhibit the vigorous exercise of First Amendment freedoms and because it invites juries to punish those who hold unpopular political opinions. The *Gertz* majority opinion will thus limit the damages available to libel plaintiffs who do not prove actual malice to an award designed to compensate for "actual injury." Powell does not try to provide a single definition for actual injury, but he makes clear that it is not limited to "out of pocket loss" (the kinds of damages described in Chapter 3 as "special damages"). States may feel free to include within actual injury such harms as "impairment of reputation and standing in the community, personal humiliation, and mental anguish and suffering"; moreover, there "need be no evidence which assigns an actual dollar value to the injury."

The "if you want punitive or presumed damages, you must prove actual malice" rule articulated in *Gertz* was limited in a later decision to those situations where the allegedly libelous remark is on a matter of public interest. (Again the 2 × 2 × 2 matrix is in play.) The case, *Dun & Bradstreet v. Greenmoss Builders,*[36] involved an erroneous report appearing in a financial newsletter with limited circulation to the effect that a local business was in bankruptcy. Although the Court voted 5–4 and failed to produce a majority opinion, five of the justices determined that the false report concerned a matter of private rather than public interest and distinguished the *Gertz* rule concerning punitive or presumed damages. The original judgment from the trial court, consisting of $50,000 in compensatory damages and $300,000 in punitive damages (the latter amount may have stemmed from the jury's shock at Dun & Bradstreet's having depended on the unchecked and unedited report from a 17-year-old high school student it had hired as a "stringer"), would be permitted to stand. Interestingly, the Vermont Supreme Court had also distinguished the *Gertz* rule and had itself reinstated the original damages award, but it did so on the grounds that *Gertz*'s rule about punitive damages should apply only to media defendants, whereas this particular financial newsletter's circulation was too small to qualify as a mass medium. The Supreme Court's needing to find that the state supreme court was right but for the wrong reasons is largely a result of a lack of precision in the *Gertz* decision itself. At several places in the 1974 decision, reference is made to "publishing" and "broadcasting" of defamations, but

---

[36]472 U.S. 749 (1985).

the Court majority had never indicated clearly whether it intended the decision to be restricted to suits involving media defendants. One thing is clear, though: the *Gertz* majority nowhere indicated that its decision should be limited to defamations concerning matters of public interest. To the extent that the *Dun & Bradstreet* plurality suggests otherwise, it is revisionist history and has been soundly criticized on that account.

### All Libel Plaintiffs Must Prove Harm to Receive Damages (the End of *Libel Per Se?*)

In the Chapter 3 review of the elements of the common law of libel, the distinction between *libel per se* (utterances that are obviously defamatory) and *libel per quod* (statements whose defamatory nature is not apparent unless the audience has additional facts at its disposal) was introduced. Traditionally, in *libel per se* situations, the plaintiff did not need to prove damages. It was assumed that a person falsely accused of being a criminal or an incompetent had been damaged.

Certainly, the *Gertz* majority opinion does express concern that the ready availability of presumed damages (the kind of award that most logically fits *libel per se* situations) gives juries too much freedom to stifle debate on important issues of the

 # Things to Remember

### *GERTZ V. WELCH, INC.*

- Reinforces the importance of the plaintiff's identity (public figure or public official, or private citizen) as the main determinant of whether actual malice must be proven.
- Gives two public policy reasons for treating public plaintiffs differently:
  - They generally chose the limelight.
  - They often have access to the media to refute any damaging remarks.
- Establishes that there are two kinds of public figures:
  - All-purpose or general public figures, who always must prove actual malice.
  - Limited public figures, who must only prove actual malice if the libelous remarks concerned the controversy they sought out.
- Emphasizes that, with respect to private plaintiffs, individual states are free to determine what level of fault they must show (mere negligence, actual malice, or something in between).
- Tells us that all plaintiffs must prove harm to win damages (dilutes the *libel per se* category from common law).
- Holds that plaintiffs who wish to receive punitive damages must prove actual malice. (In a later case, the Court limited this rule to situations involving libels on a matter of public interest.)

day. The Supreme Court fashioned a two-part remedy. First, it established the rule, from which it retreated a bit in the later *Dun & Bradstreet* decision, requiring plaintiffs seeking presumed damages to prove actual malice. Second, it required plaintiffs not otherwise needing to prove actual malice to show some kind of actual harm. Only the second rule is relevant to the libel per se category, and it surely represents a partial repudiation of the category. Under the first rule, however, presumed damages are still permitted, and proving actual malice is really quite irrelevant to whether or not the plaintiff has been harmed. Thus, the majority opinion does not sound the death knell for the distinction between *libel per se* and *libel per quod.*

A fascinating feature of *Gertz,* however, is that Justice White's dissenting opinion makes clear that he assumed the Court *had* in fact gotten rid of presumed damages, and thus the whole category of *libel per se.* "The impact of today's decision on the traditional law of libel is immediately obvious and indisputable," he wrote. "No longer will the plaintiff be able to rest his case with proof of a libel defamatory on its face or proof of a slander historically actionable per se." For whatever combination of reasons, Justice White's interpretation of what the *Gertz* majority had done has been accepted by most courts and commentators alike. Section 569 of the *Restatement of Torts,* for example, assumes that *Gertz v. Welch, Inc.* has discredited traditional notions of libel per se.

## A Final Word on Avoiding Libel Suits

An individual sees a description of herself in the media that she finds false and defamatory. She steams about it for a time and then retains an attorney and files suit against the offending publisher. That may be the way we presume libel suits happen, but it omits a crucial step. A large majority of potential libel plaintiffs pay a visit to the media outlet that defamed them before they even seek out legal advice. How the editors there treat the aggrieved individual before them often determines whether a libel suit ever gets filed.[37] At least three characteristics of the mass media tend to result in the potential plaintiff being so dissatisfied with the encounter that the person becomes a real-life plaintiff:[38]

- **Future orientation.** News organizations tend to be focused on what is going into the paper tomorrow and do not always have mechanisms in place to deal with controversies from previous editions. Individuals who complain about yesterday's news (rather than offering a tip about what might be tomorrow's news) thus tend to be shunted from department to department and put on hold indefinitely.

---

[37]Randall Bezanson, Gilbert Cranberg, and John Soloski, *Libel Law and the Press: Myth and Reality* (New York: Free Press, 1987); Edward A. Adams, "Does Alternative Dispute Resolution Work with Libel Suits? Iowa Program Hopes to Find Out," *National Law Journal,* 21 Mar. 1988, p. 4.

[38]Gilbert Cranberg, "The Libel Alternative," *Columbia Journalism Review,* Jan.–Feb. 1986, pp. 6–9.

- **Naysaying habit.** Editors become very accustomed to saying no, especially to turning down reader-generated story ideas that more often than not amount to "vanity press" about family members. They develop a siege mentality and then apply it inappropriately to very legitimate requests for retractions or some other kind of vindication from persons who have been harmed by the media's errors.
- **Reluctance to admit mistakes.** Because journalists' work output is by its very nature open to public scrutiny, reporters and editors may be especially defensive about their errors. This defensiveness, applied to an aggrieved individual seeking redress, often results in escalation, a shouting match likely to drive the complainant to an attorney's office.

Professor Gilbert Cranberg suggests that media outlets will increase the chances of persuading unhappy parties not to sue by adopting the following policies:

- Sensitize writers to the power they wield over people's lives.
- Emphasize the importance of handling complaints in a humane manner.
- Consider the use of an ombudsman to serve as an independent, readers' advocate.
- Fire anyone who tries to hide a serious complaint.

Of course, the single best way to avoid libel suits is to breathe life into that which has become cliché, the journalistic credo admonishing reporters and editors to "get it right." Still, factual error is unavoidable, and the most highly reputable newspapers usually have more than a few errors in every single issue. That libel juries nowadays so frequently emerge from their deliberations with a decision awarding huge amounts of damages to plaintiffs means that professional communicators should know more than a bit about the law of defamation.

## Chapter Summary

The landmark 1964 libel case *New York Times v. Sullivan* establishes that public officials who sue for libel because of criticisms relevant to their official conduct must prove actual malice—that is, that the defendant either knew the accusations were false or at least published with "reckless disregard of truth or falsity"—with "convincing clarity." The Supreme Court emphasized that making it too easy for governmental officials to recover damages for libel is too hauntingly reminiscent of criminal prosecutions for sedition. Journalists must be given enough "breathing room" to make honest errors, the Court said, or they will experience the "chilling effect" of self-censorship.

Later cases have fine-tuned and extended the actual malice rule in many ways. "Public officials" include those who have policy-making authority and whose positions invite public scrutiny. Criticisms of "official conduct" include any accusations of criminal wrongdoing as well as attributions of certain kinds of personal characteristics that have clear implications for public life. Not only public officials but also "public figures" must prove actual malice. So, too, must anybody who wants punitive damages (if the alleged libel touches on a matter of public importance).

Even private plaintiffs, if suing the media over a matter of public importance, must prove falsity as an element of their cases. Independent appellate review is required on the question of actual malice. Statements of pure opinions, ones that do not carry explicit or implicit factual allegations, cannot be the impetus for a libel suit.

Plaintiffs who must prove actual malice may have access to reporters' notes and outtakes as part of the pretrial discovery process.

"Convincing clarity" denotes the burden of proof on plaintiffs seeking to defeat a motion to dismiss. Libel plaintiffs may bring suit in any state where the allegedly libelous remarks were in general circulation.

All libel plaintiffs must prove some degree of harm to win damages. Individual states are given much leeway to determine what level of proof of fault is required of private plaintiffs.

chapter

# *Invasions of Privacy*

Ask a witty youngster what she wants to be when she grows up, and the reply might be, "Rich and famous." Would you really want to be famous, though? Celebrities often complain about seeing the most outlandish things written about them in supermarket tabloids and about being hounded by photographers anxious to obtain a marketably candid shot. Many people believe that overzealous photographers were a contributing cause of Princess Diana's death.

Very few of us, of course, will ever experience the kind of fame that makes us a source of fascination to the masses. Even so, the privacy of even the least noteworthy among us is subject to invasion. Consider your own reaction to having your dinner hour interrupted by a telemarketer. Perhaps you are one of the many people who uses one technology to trump another, depending on an answering machine or caller ID to reassert your need for privacy. If you choose the latter, insistent callers might use a dialing prefix that prevents their phone number from appearing on your display unit. You in turn have the option of sending out a message prerecorded by the phone company, alerting the caller that you are unwilling to receive calls from anyone choosing to hide their identifying data from you. What an elaborate dance this is, testimony to how very much we think and strategize about issues of privacy.

Perhaps telephones do not represent nearly as large a threat to personal privacy as do computers. We fear all those government agencies and credit bureaus that maintain in their computer files gobs of information, and perhaps *mis*information, about us. We resent supermarket "shopper clubs" as the pacts with the Devil that they are; in return for a few cents off on our grocery bills, we permit the cashier to create a computer record that links our personal identity with a list of every purchase we made.

## A Tale of Two Law Review Articles

Concerns over technology's potential for invading our privacy are not new. Indeed, it is not too much of an exaggeration to say that when two prominent lawyers wrote about their similar concerns over a hundred years ago,[1] they laid the foundation for modern U.S. privacy law. Compared with the centuries-old body of libel law, then, privacy is a relative newcomer to the American legal scene, even if it does predate the microchip. Boston attorneys Samuel Warren and Louis Brandeis—the latter of whom would later achieve lasting fame as a U.S. Supreme Court justice—expressed their concern that such *"recent inventions"* as *"instantaneous photographs…have in-vaded the sacred precincts of private and domestic life."* The italicized phrase does not refer to digital cameras or to Polaroids, but rather to photographic technol-ogy having advanced to the point where subjects did not have to remain motion-less for twenty minutes to have their images captured on film. At the time, this advance seemed a huge encroachment on personal privacy. In the early days of photography, subjects may have always appeared stiff and ghostlike, but at least the potential for being photographed in a "candid" moment had not yet arrived.

Warren and Brandeis recognized that technological advances were not the only cause of privacy invasion. Indeed, citizens' privacy was most threatened by the combination of the "prurient taste" of the masses and the willingness on the part of the working press to satisfy that taste by filling "column after column…with idle gossip," by "overstepping in every direction the obvious bounds of propriety and of decency." To combat these journalistic excesses, Warren and Brandeis concluded, nothing less than the creation of a new legal cause of action aimed at protecting the right to privacy, the "right to be let alone," would do.

Whereas Warren and Brandeis's essay was *pre*scriptive, telling readers what the law *should* do, a second law review article written seventy years later served as a *de*scriptive model of how the American law of privacy had developed in the first half of the twentieth century. William Prosser, then the dean of the University of Cali-fornia Law School, reviewed thousands of court cases and concluded that privacy law had really become four separate torts.[2] **Appropriation** occurs when our name or "likeness" (i.e., our face, voice, or anything so closely associated with us so as to transmit our identity) is used without permission for commercial purposes. The ag-grieved party's interest in such conflicts seems to be more a proprietary one—"How dare you make money by exploiting me?"—rather than the more psychological harm to one's feelings that we normally associate with privacy invasions. As such, this category of cases really is more closely aligned to the issue of copyright (the subject of Chapter 6) than to any intuitive notion of privacy. **Intrusion** refers to an invasion of one's personal space. The use of telephoto lenses or hidden micro-phones, or the incessant shadowing and stalking of a subject, might be deemed actionable intrusions. Such excesses, whether committed by media employees or others, would seem to have much in common with ordinary trespass. **False light** invasions of privacy, as we see later, closely resemble libel actions, with the key dis-tinction being that the statements made about the unwilling subject need not be

---

[1]Samuel Warren and Louis Brandeis, "The Right to Privacy," 4 *Harvard Law Review* 193, 195–196 (1890).

[2]William Prosser, "Privacy," 48 *California Law Review* 383 (1960).

technically defamatory. The final tort is the one that Warren and Brandeis themselves seem to have had in mind. It has come to be called the "public disclosure of true but embarrassing facts," or, more succinctly, the **public disclosure** tort. This category expresses the proposition that there are some kinds of highly personal but true information that no one has a right to publicize about us.

Two caveats are in order before we examine these four torts in more depth. First, we must remember that privacy law varies tremendously from state to state. Only about half the states recognize all four torts identified by Prosser in 1960. If you have a very specific question about the privacy implications of a story you are preparing, you will need to know which of the torts is recognized in your own jurisdiction.

The second caveat serves as a reminder that this book's subject matter is communication law, not constitutional law. We often use the word *privacy* to refer not to communication law, but to the delicate relationship between individual autonomy and the need for governmental regulation. Thus, people who want to ride their motorcycles without a helmet,[3] or who argue for a right to "die with dignity,"[4] or who think that laws against smoking marijuana are senseless,[5] all claim that the state is violating their right to privacy. They are referring to the constitutional right of privacy. In part because the word *privacy* does not appear anywhere in the U.S. Constitution, the evolution of the Supreme Court's privacy doctrine is long and complicated, one of the most intriguing tales in the modern history of constitutional law. The constitutional right of privacy, however, is generally beyond the purview of this book. We now turn to a more complete description of the tort law of privacy, knowledge of which is of more direct relevance to members of the working press.

---

[3]*Easyriders Freedom v. Hannigan,* 92 F.3d 1486 (9th Cir. 1996).

[4]*Vacco v. Quill,* 521 U.S. 793 (1997).

[5]*United States v. Kiffer,* 477 F.2d 349 (2d Cir. 1973).

 # Things to Remember

### THE DEVELOPMENT OF PRIVACY LAW IN THE UNITED STATES

- Compared with libel, the law of privacy is a newcomer to American law.
- It can be traced to the 1890 publication of a *Harvard Law Review* article by Samuel Warren and Louis Brandeis.
- Most states now recognize at least one of the four distinct privacy actions identified by William Prosser in 1960:
  - Appropriation of one's name or likeness for commercial gain.
  - Intrusion into another person's personal space.
  - False light invasions (similar to libel).
  - The public disclosure of true but embarrassing facts.
- All four of these actions are part of the tort law of privacy, which should not be confused with the constitutional right to privacy.

# Appropriation

Appropriation, sometimes called misappropriation, consists of the unauthorized use of a person's name or likeness for commercial purposes. This tort was the first of the four to develop in U.S. law following the publication of the famous Warren and Brandeis law review article. The first state to officially recognize the tort was New York, which did so by statute in 1903 in response to a ruling from that state's highest court the year before. The suit was brought on behalf of young Abigail Roberson against a milling company that had used the infant's photo without permission in advertisements for the company's flour.[6] The court, all the while expressing sympathy for the child, ruled against her, in part out of fear that the right to privacy it was being asked to create would have dangerous implications far beyond this one case: "While most persons would much prefer to have a good likeness of themselves appear in a responsible periodical or leading newspaper rather than upon an advertising card or sheet, the doctrine [sought here] would apply as well to the one publication as to the other," the court feared. A bit later in the decision, the court explicitly invited the legislature to create new law that would recognize a right of privacy, but only as applied to defendants who use another's name or likeness for purely commercial purposes.

The first state court to recognize a common-law right (i.e., prior to passage of any explicit statutes) to sue for misappropriation was Georgia.[7] The defendant in this case was held liable for using an artist's photograph in a newspaper testimonial advertisement for its life insurance policies. The Georgia Supreme Court concluded that to have one's likeness used without authorization is to be "under the control of another…held to service by a merciless master." The Georgia decision proved very influential. By 1939, so many states had been swayed by that court to themselves recognize a right of privacy against unauthorized appropriations that the tort was included in the American Law Institute's treatise called the *Restatement of Torts.*[8]

### Two Actions or One?

Appropriation is actually a hybrid tort. There are two different kinds of grievances involved. First is the feeling of shame, humiliation, or even damaged reputation associated with having one's name or photo disseminated widely in ways over which we have no control. The harm is likely most severe when our name is associated with a cause or a product with which we wholly disapprove, as in a strict vegetarian endorsing a fast-food hamburger chain.

---

[6]*Roberson v. Rochester Folding Box Company,* 64 N.E. 442 (Ct. App. N.Y. 1902).

[7]*Pavesich v. New England Life Insurance Company,* 50 S.E. 68 (Ga. 1905).

[8]Irwin R. Kramer, "The Birth of Privacy Law: A Century since Warren and Brandeis," 39 *Catholic University Law Review* 703, 718 (1990).

The second kind of harm alleged by appropriation plaintiffs is simply lost income. If you steal my name or photo to sell your product, you will thus have enriched yourself unfairly at my expense. If anyone deserves to make money off my name, it is me. Sometimes this claim is referred to separately in the law as the **right to publicity,** and it tends to apply primarily to celebrities. More than half the states have explicitly embraced the right to publicity.[9]

In some situations, plaintiffs are able to argue plausibly both that the commercial value of their name has been stolen and that the nature of the theft is one that personally embarrasses them. This was comedian Johnny Carson's dual claim when he sued the manufacturer of a line of portable toilets called—you probably guessed it—"Here's Johnny!"[10] The entrepreneur defendant in this case continued the word play by labeling his product "the world's foremost commodian." Carson was not amused, arguing that it went beyond embarrassing to "odious" to be associated with such a product. Although the court determined that the applicable right to privacy did not protect celebrities' hurt feelings in such commercial situations, it ruled for Carson on the more tangible publicity claim. Carson had shown over the years his awareness that he could profit from the commercial exploitation of his own celebrity status, as through his marketing of a line of sportswear bearing his name.

### What Is a Likeness?

In a sense, the *Carson* case staked out new ground, in that the product did not usurp the comedian's name, but rather a phrase that had come to be closely associated with that name (and with Ed McMahon's slow, rising-pitched delivery). Indeed, the appellate majority emphasized, there would have been no violation of Carson's right of publicity had the defendant called his product the "John William Carson Portable Toilet," which would have been a more literal taking of Carson's name but would not have amounted to a taking of his identity as a celebrity.

Anything likely to make readers conjure in their minds a particular individual can constitute that person's "name or likeness" for the purpose of misappropriation actions. Conversely, not every use of a celebrity's name will be closely enough associated with the marketability of the person's identity to be the focus of an appropriation lawsuit. For example, there was a somewhat famous "T. J. Hooker" long before the television series of that name ever showed up on the air. An artist well known for his carvings of ducks and other fowl, Hooker sued the producers of the TV series. The court rejected his claim, however, finding that the television producers surely had not chosen the name for their series "in order to avail themselves of his reputation as an extraordinary woodcarver."[11]

---

[9]Arlen W. Landvardt, "The Troubling Implications of a Right of Publicity 'Wheel' Spun Out of Control," 45 *Kansas Law Review* 329, 338 (1997).

[10]*Carson v. Here's Johnny Portable Toilets, Inc.,* 698 F.2d 831 (6th Cir. 1983).

[11]*Hooker v. Columbia Pictures,* 551 F. Supp. 1060, 1062 (N.D. Ill. 1982).

What other kinds of entities may be treated as a "likeness"? Certainly an identifiable photo of an individual can be a likeness. The early *Roberson* case against the flour milling company, discussed earlier, makes this much clear. A sketch or drawing can also be actionable, as the publishers of *Playgirl* magazine discovered when their February 1978 issue included a drawing of a nude black male seated in the corner of a boxing ring.[12] "Even a cursory inspection of the picture," a federal district court in New York concluded, "strongly suggests that the facial characteristics of the black male portrayed are those of Muhammad Ali. The cheekbones, broad nose and wideset brown eyes, together with the distinctive smile and close cropped black hair are recognizable as the features of the plaintiff, one of the most widely known athletes of our time." The court also took note of the ad's use of the phrase "the Greatest," long associated with Ali.

Even a fictional character can constitute a likeness. The Groucho Marx estate, for example, sued producers of the Broadway musical *A Day in Hollywood, A Night in the Ukraine.* Defendants eventually prevailed on the grounds that the right of publicity could not, in the state of California, be passed on to Marx's heirs. More important for our purpose is the federal district court's having made clear that the right of publicity is broad enough to protect the fictional characters audiences worldwide know as "the Marx Brothers," characters which "hav[e] no relation to [the] real personalities" of Julius (Groucho), Leo (Chico), or Adolf (Harpo) Marx.[13]

An infringement can be found even when the actors are less than human. The Samsung Corporation created a series of humorous TV ads that pictured one of the company's 1980s models of audio and video products in whimsical futuristic scenes, as if to suggest that such equipment would still be working many years hence. One ad featured a robot dressed in a wig, gown, and jewelry reminiscent of Vanna White posed next to a game board like that featured in *Wheel-of-Fortune.* The caption read "Longest-running game show. 2012 A.D." White sued. The federal appellate court recognized that this case could not be handled as a "name or likeness" dispute. A "likeness" must truly resemble the original, and no sane viewer would think that the robot in the ad really *was* Vanna White. As such, the court expanded the right of publicity (in California, at least) to cover celebrities' "identities."[14] The 2–1 decision—Judge Alex Kosinski wrote a stinging dissent—has been much criticized as overly broad, giving Hollywood celebrities virtual veto power over any satiric representations of them in commercial messages.[15] In another case,

---

[12]*Ali v. Playgirl,* 447 F. Supp. 723 (S.D.N.Y. 1978).

[13]*Groucho Marx Productions v. Day and Night Company,* 523 F. Supp. 485 (S.D.N.Y. 1981), *overturned on other grounds,* 689 F.2d 317 (2d Cir. 1982); see also *Chaplin v. Amador,* 93 Cal. App. 358, 360 (1st App. Dist., Div. 2, 1928).

[14]*White v. Samsung Electronics America, Inc.* 971 F.2d 1395 (9th Cir. 1992), *petition for reh'g denied,* 989 F.2d 1512 (1993).

[15]See, for example, Patricia B. Frank, "*White v. Samsung Electronics America, Inc.*: The Right of Publicity Spins Its Wheels," 55 *Ohio State Law Journal* 1115 (1994).

actors George Wendt and John Ratzenberger—best known for their long-running portrayals of Norm and Cliff, respectively—sued the creators of those *Cheers*-like bars one sees at airports.[16] These bars boast three-dimensional animatronic figures (called "Bob" and "Hank") designed to look very much like Norm and Cliff. Interestingly, the actors could not prevail on this ground alone, in that one of the defendant companies owns the copyright to *Cheers* and to all the fictional personages who patronized it. The plaintiffs did prevail, however, over defendants' motion for summary judgment. "While it is true that [Wendt and Ratzenberger's] fame arose in large part through their participation in *Cheers*," the court reasoned, "an actor or actress does not lose the right to control the commercial exploitation of his or her likeness by portraying a fictional character."

## Look-Alikes and Sound-Alikes

As you have probably already sensed, this misappropriation tort is very complex and varied. Some jurisdictions accept the tort as a viable cause of action; others do not. Some treat the right of publicity as part of the tort, some treat it as a separate entity, and some reject it entirely. Even among those jurisdictions that embrace the right of publicity, whether a defendant is being charged with stealing the plaintiff's "likeness," or "identity" varies from state to state.

Do not be overly concerned, then, if the line between the "name or likeness" cases already discussed and the cases to be reviewed in this section seems fuzzy. Still, the law in this area has developed so as to recognize separately situations wherein defendants have not misappropriated an *actual* image of a celebrity, but rather have done their best to create an *ersatz* image of that celebrity, often using the services of persons who make their living as celebrity imposters. We usually refer to these as the "look-alike" and "sound-alike" cases. In one such case, Jackie Onassis won a judgment against the Christian Dior company for employing the services of Jackie O. look-alike Barbara Reynolds in a slick magazine ad campaign appearing in such publications as *Esquire*, *Harper's Bazaar*, the *New Yorker*, and the *New York Times Magazine*.[17] The New York statute governing the case addressed only situations in which a plaintiff's "name, portrait or picture" is used without consent for a commercial purpose. The court, however, in ruling for Onassis, concluded that the use of look-alikes could not be permitted as a means of skirting the intent of the law, that "the commercial hitchhiker seeking to travel on the fame of another will have to learn to pay the fare."

Film director Woody Allen was a plaintiff in a similar case, prompted by print ads for the National Video chain using celebrity look-alike Phil Boroff.[18] That

---

[16]*Wendt v. Host International, Inc.*, 125 F.3d 806 (9th Cir. 1997), *petition for reh'g denied*, 197 F.3d 1284 (9th Cir. 1999).

[17]*Onassis v. Dior*, 472 N.Y.S. 254 (Sup. Ct. New York County 1984).

[18]*Allen v. National Video, Inc.*, 610 F. Supp. 612 (S.D.N.Y. 1985).

readers would think of Allen was ensured not only by his physical resemblance to Boroff, but also by the *Annie Hall* and *Bananas* videotapes shown on the store counter. U.S. District Judge Constance Baker Motley allowed that celebrity look-alikes such as Boroff enjoy their own rights to publicity, a right to sell *his* likeness to anyone perceiving a commercial value in it. Thus, Judge Motley had to address "the almost metaphysical question of when one person's face, presented in a certain context, becomes, as a matter of law, the face of another." She granted summary judgment to Allen, but on the grounds that the advertisement was a violation of the federal Lanham Act prohibiting such unfair business practices as the untruthful suggestion that a product has received a particular endorsement. Resolving the dispute in this manner freed Motley from having to rule definitively on Allen's publicity claim. The judge does give some indication, however, that the situation here might be distinguishable from the Barbara Reynolds photograph in the Onassis case. In that earlier case, Motley concluded, readers were led to no other possible conclusion than that Onassis herself had chosen to appear in the ad campaign. Boroff's depiction of Allen might be seen as merely *evocative* of the latter's persona or image in that the two men do not look identical. Another Phil Boroff photo—this one holding a clarinet, thus further evocative of Woody Allen for readers who know that the actor/director frequently plays the instrument in a New York tavern—led to further litigation a few years later. This photo appeared in an ad for Men's World clothing stores. Again, the court ruled for Allen, on Lanham Act grounds, having been unimpressed by the fact that the ad included a "small lightface type" disclaimer to the effect that the person depicted was a celebrity look-alike.[19]

Celebrities have also brought suit complaining about advertisements that mimic their distinctive speaking or singing voices. Early cases, involving such celebrities as actor Bert Lahr, singer Nancy Sinatra, and the '60s rock group The Fifth Dimension, were unsuccessful.[20] In each of these cases, courts ruled that the plaintiffs had no cause of action, that the right of appropriation in the jurisdictions involved was not designed or intended to cover such sound-alike situations. The legal climate seems to be changing, however, largely owing to Bette Midler's suit against Ford Motor Company and its advertising agency for hiring one of her former backup singers to imitate the Divine Miss M's rendition of the Beach Boys' tune, "Do You Want to Dance," in a Mercury Sable commercial.[21] The appellate panel ruling in favor of Midler distinguished the facts before it from those in the earlier Nancy Sinatra case by emphasizing that Sinatra's claim was much more

---

[19]*Allen v. Men's World Outlet,* 679 F. Supp. 360 (S.D.N.Y. 1988).

[20]*Lahr v. Adell Chemical Company,* 195 F. Supp. 702 (Mass. 1961), *aff'd,* 300 F.2d 256 (1st Cir. 1962); *Sinatra v. Goodyear Tire and Rubber Company,* 435 F.2d 711 (9th Cir. 1970), *cert. denied,* 402 U.S. 906 (1971); *Davis v. TWA,* 297 F. Supp. 1145 (C. D. Cal. 1969).

[21]*Midler v. Ford Motor Co.,* 849 F.2d 460 (9th Cir. 1988).

closely tied to her association in the public mind with a particular song to which she did not own the rights ("These Boots Were Made for Walking"), whereas Midler claimed that her distinctive singing voice had been misappropriated. The *Midler* court saw its ruling as a relatively narrow one, having demanded that the plaintiff establish both that the imitation was deliberate and that the plaintiff's vocal style was distinctive and well known.

### Some Folks Who Can't Sue: The "Political Figures" Exception

*Contact,* the faith versus science parable in which Jodie Foster spends her professional life listening for extraterrestrials, then goes traipsing off to meet them, boasts guest appearances, "as themselves," of several CNN journalists and of President Clinton. While the CNN folks' talking heads contracted to appear on film, Clinton appeared against his will. Footage of actual speeches were cleverly spliced into the film's narrative. White House Counsel Charles Ruff, presumably with the president's knowledge and approval, fired off a letter to *Contact* director Robert Zemeckis, complaining of the "improper" use of Clinton's public statements. The White House made clear that it had no intention to sue the movie maker; the pattern of relevant precedents suggest that Clinton could not have prevailed in any case. One such precedent involved *Smothers Brothers Comedy Hour* regular Pat Paulsen, who announced on air in 1967 that he was definitely *not* running for president, all the while conducting a fully orchestrated yet wholly tongue-in-cheek campaign under the auspices of the "Straight Talking American Government" ticket (yes, that's right—the "Stag Party"). Comic candidate Paulsen sued the distributors of a poster that bore a blow-up of his photo that depicted him with a banner reading "1968" draped across his chest, "in the manner, if not with the style, of a beauty pageant contestant." Paulsen asked a state court in New York to prevent any further distribution of the poster, which he claimed was a violation of, among other things, his statutory right to privacy. The court refused on the grounds that Paulsen had entered the political arena, "where the sensibilities of the participants must bow to the superior public interest in completely unfettered and unabridged free discussion of whatever persuasion, merit or style."[22] More recently, the producers of the Rush Limbaugh radio program were unable to shut down a competing, liberal-bent radio talk show that called itself "After the Rush."[23] Although the court determined that enough factual questions remained unresolved to require a trial on the merits, it did grant summary judgment to the defendants on the narrow question as to whether the use of this name constituted a misappropriation of Limbaugh's celebrity identity.

---

[22]*Paulsen v. Personality Posters, Inc.,* 299 N.Y.S. 501, 503 (Sup. Ct. New York County 1968).

[23]*Pam Media, Inc. v. American Research Corporation,* 889 F. Supp. 1403 (D. Colo. 1995).

That political figures will almost certainly lose their misappropriations suits does not always deter them from trying to silence those who use their name or likeness without permission. In late 1997, for example, New York City Mayor Rudolph Giuliani ordered the local transit company to remove ads that had been placed on the side of buses by the publishers of *New York* magazine. The ad campaign's theme took advantage of the mayor's reputation for self-aggrandizement, in that the caption read *"New York* magazine—possibly the only good thing in New York Rudy hasn't taken credit for." The magazine sued the Metropolitan Transit Authority and obtained an injunction precluding the agency from refusing the ads.[24] Three years later, the mayor's image was used without his permission in a much-criticized public education campaign conducted by People for the Ethical Treatment of Animals (PETA). A takeoff on the dairy industry's famous "Got Milk?" campaign, PETA's ad boasted a milk-mustached Giuliani (see Figure 5.1) to make a serious point about a posited correlation between dairy product intake and prostate cancer. News reports indicated that Giuliani considered suing, but that a sheepish PETA promptly withdrew the campaign and apologized to the mayor for making light of his own cancer diagnosis. As tasteless as this particular use of the mayor's likeness may have been, it is highly unlikely that a lawsuit for misappropriation would have succeeded.

---

[24]*New York Magazine v. Metropolitan Transportation Authority,* 136 F.3d 123 (2d Cir. 1998).

 **Figure 5.1**

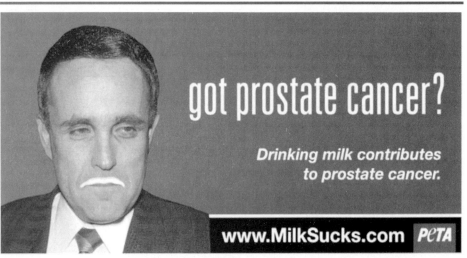

*© 2000 People for the Ethical Treatment of Animals. Reprinted with permission.*

### Folks Who Cannot be Sued?
### The Newsworthiness (and Other) Defenses

The holdings in the Pat Paulsen and Rush Limbaugh cases together suggest that what might otherwise seem an actionable misappropriation of a celebrity's name or likeness can be deemed protected speech if it entails some kind of political commentary. Consider, for example, an image circulated widely during the 1992 presidential campaign on T-shirts, postcards, and advertisements. The image was a photograph of two young men with gym-toned, bare torsos, arm in arm, with Clinton's and Gore's faces superimposed on top of the scantily clad bodies. This was a clever image, one that would appeal (for obvious reasons) to those who support the gay rights movement, but also to those very opposed to gay rights (who would perceive the photo as a harsh criticism of the Democratic team). Would the Democratic Party standard-bearers have been able to win a suit for misappropriation? Almost certainly not.

Courts have sometimes taken a shorthand route to the same conclusion, creating what has come to be known as the "newspaper exception" to misappropriation torts. Newspapers and other news media are often permitted to create artifacts the marketing of which would likely be actionable if engaged in by any other entity. San Francisco 49ers quarterback Joe Montana found out about this exception when he unsuccessfully attempted to enjoin the *San Jose Mercury News* from selling posters bearing an artist's drawing of him that had previously appeared in a special section of the newspaper celebrating the team's record of four Superbowl championships in ten years.[25] The court ruled that, just as the publisher surely had the right to print the drawing shortly after the 1990 Superbowl, so too the publisher has the right to republish it a few weeks later still.

The pattern of judicial results involving the highly litigious Elvis Presley estate is also instructive. Elvis Presley Enterprises has aggressively litigated against those it perceived to be infringing on "the King's" name and likeness, the offenses having ranged from the unauthorized marketing of posters to the naming of a bistro "The Velvet Elvis." In general, whenever the presiding court has applied the laws of a state that itself recognizes a right of publicity descendible to one's heirs or estate, Presley has prevailed.[26] A striking counterexample is found in a legal conflict surrounding Elvis's famous Madison Square Garden concerts in 1972.[27] RCA had an exclusive contract with him to market recordings stemming from

---

[25]*Montana v. San Jose Mercury News,* 34 Cal. App. 4th 790 (6th App. Dist. 1995).

[26]*Elvis Presley Enterprises v. Elvisly Yours, Inc.,* 936 F.2d 889 (6th Cir. 1991); *Elvis Presley Enterprises v. Capece,* 950 F. Supp. 783 (S.D. Tex. 1996); *Estate of Presley v. Russen,* 513 F. Supp. 1339 (N.J. 1981); *Factors Etc., Inc. v. Creative Card Company,* 444 F. Supp. 279 (S.D.N.Y. 1977); cf. *Factors Etc., Inc. v. Pro Arts, Inc.,* 652 F.2d 278 (2d Cir. 1981) (applying Tennessee law and finding no inheritable right of publicity).

[27]*Current Audio, Inc. v. RCA,* 337 N.Y.S. 2d 949 (Sup. Ct., N.Y. County, 1972).

those events, but this contract was deemed unenforceable against *Current Audio* magazine, which planned to include an audio recording of excerpts from the press conference given by Presley on the evening of one of the New York performances. Whatever might be the scope of Presley's right of publicity, the court concluded, it "has no application to the use of a picture or name in connection with the dissemination of news or public interest presentations, notwithstanding that such activities are also carried on for a profit."[28]

Courts have also recognized a more specialized news media defense that protects promotional materials. Sometimes known as the *Booth* rule after actress Shirley Booth (TV's *Hazel*), this doctrine tells media outlets that they are free to use materials they have already published in future advertisements for the same magazine or newspaper. Your local TV news no doubt does this all the time in slick spots containing short sound bites from previous stories, trumpeting its ability to get the news "first" and "best." In Booth's case, *Holiday* magazine, which had run an authorized photo of the actress vacationing in Jamaica in one issue, the next year reprinted that photo in a full-page ad for the magazine.[29] The court held that such media self-promotions are protected speech that cannot be the subject of misappropriation suits. Former New York Jets quarterback Joe Namath encountered the same result when he sued *Sports Illustrated* for having used a photo of him that had previously appeared in its own pages to drum up subscriptions in a later advertising campaign run in *Cosmopolitan* (the heading was "The Man You Love Loves Joe Namath").[30]

There are exceptions to the newsworthiness defense. Suppose that a magazine article, or an entire book, does in fact deal with a newsworthy issue, but a photo of an identifiable individual is used without the subject's consent on the publication's cover. The overall work's newsworthiness likely will not cover the unauthorized use of the photo. For example, suppose that a magazine does a story about the controversy concerning the dismantling of college admissions affirmative action programs. Using without permission a cover photo depicting a specific and identifiable African American of college age might be actionable as a misappropriation ("You have no right to make money off my image when I myself have not been involved in doing anything newsworthy") or for false light, another of the four Prosser torts, discussed later in this chapter ("This photo suggests, inaccurately, that I myself am the beneficiary of an affirmative action policy").

A second exception to the newsworthiness defense flows from the very strange set of facts that produced the U.S. Supreme Court's only decision to date in a misappropriation case. That *Zacchini v. Scripps-Howard Broadcasting Company*[31]

---

[28]337 N.Y.S. 2d at 954.

[29]*Booth v. Curtis Publishing,* 182 N.E.2d 812 (Ct. App. N.Y. 1962).

[30]*Namath v. Sports Illustrated,* 363 N.Y.S. 2d 276 (Sup. Ct. New York County 1975), *aff'd,* 371 N.Y.S. 10 (App. Div. Dept. 1 1975), *aff'd.,* 352 N.E. 584 (Ct. of Appeals 1976).

[31]433 U.S. 562 (1977).

# Things to Remember

## APPROPRIATION

- There are two distinct grievances:
  - Purely financial ("How dare you profit from my good name?").
  - Personal dignity ("You could not pay me enough to be associated with that particular product!").
- A "likeness" for purposes of appropriation suits is anything that conjures up in readers the image of the plaintiff.
- An otherwise actionable appropriation can be saved if it is part of a legitimate news story.
- Even fictional characters can have recognizable "likenesses."
- A new category of appropriation suits has emerged in recent years, protecting against look-alike and sound-alike "takings."
- Politicians who sue over appropriations of their likenesses almost always lose, usually because courts conclude that the resulting "speech" is a form of political commentary.
- Some courts have created a "newspaper exception" to the tort, permitting the media to sell posters or similar items that would almost certainly be considered commercial misappropriations if marketed by nonmedia companies.

is typically referred to in the literature as "the human cannonball case" gives some indication of the unusual dispute involved. Circus performer Hugo Zacchini was in the habit of allowing himself to be shot out of a cannon into a net some 200 feet away. In the late summer of 1972, he was slated to perform his act, which takes approximately fifteen seconds from start to finish, at the Geauga County Fair in Burton, Ohio. A local TV reporter, without Zacchini's permission, filmed the act, which was broadcast on the 11 P.M. news. By a 5–4 vote, the Supreme Court determined that the First Amendment would not protect the news media here from an otherwise legitimate suit for misappropriation. "Wherever the line in particular situations is to be drawn between media reports that are protected and those that are not," Justice White wrote for the majority, "we are quite sure that the First and Fourteenth Amendments do not immunize the media when they broadcast a performer's entire act without his consent. The Constitution no more prevents a State from requiring [the TV station] to compensate [Zacchini] for broadcasting his act on television than it would privilege respondent to film and broadcast a copyrighted dramatic work without liability to the copyright owner." Although the *Zacchini* case has been much criticized—when an entire "act" lasts only fifteen seconds, after all, how can one do a TV story about it *without* "appropriating" the whole thing?—the general rule espoused is in most circumstances quite sensible. That the middle-age version of the Rolling Stones were enjoying several successful concert tours in the late 1990s certainly gave the media license to report on the performances as news events, but no TV station would think it could get away with broadcasting its videotaped version of an entire concert as a "documentary special" without paying Mick and the boys big bucks. In any event, precisely because the factual situation from *Zacchini* was so unusual, it has been virtually ignored over the years except when courts have felt the need to distinguish it from the conflict being adjudicated at the time.

# Intrusion

In a speech delivered at Texas Christian University, ABC-TV correspondent Jeff Greenfield pointed out that the public gets much more exorcized over invasions of privacy perpetrated by members of the broadcast, as opposed to the print, media. Television, he argued, cannot help but bring viewers into the process of news gathering. Both a newspaper reporter and a TV news producer assigned to cover a crime victim's plight may intrude upon the subject's space and ask offensive and hurtful questions. The key difference is that the public will actually *see* the TV reporter shove the microphone into the subject's face. Viewers' disgust at this phenomenon underscores their (and the courts') belief that the intrusion itself should sometimes be an actionable wrong.

### Why the First Amendment Is Not Much Help

Unique among the four privacy torts, intrusion concerns news *gathering* rather than news *reporting*. If shoving a microphone into a subject's face can ever be an actionable intrusion, it will be so even if no news story ever results. The *Restatement (Second) of Torts* (a scholarly treatise compiled and periodically updated by the American Law Institute) says that we can be held liable for intrusion if we "intentionally intrude, physically or otherwise, upon the solitude or seclusion of another or his private affairs or concerns."[32] Depending on the jurisdiction—about four-fifths of the states recognize the tort—actionable intrusions may consist of the use of telephoto lenses, hidden recording equipment, or even surveillance that is so incessant as to not permit the target a moment of peace.

Precisely because the actionable harm in intrusion cases occurs via the news *gathering* process, the First Amendment offers the press only very limited, if any, protection. The reason, UCLA Law Professor Melville Nimmer suggested many years ago, is because intrusions result from "the physical or mechanical observation of the private affairs of another, and not by the publication of such observations."[33] To many commentators, judicial reluctance to honor the media's free

[32]*Restatement (Second) of Torts* sec. 652B (1977).

[33]Melville Nimmer, "The Right to Speak from *Times* to *Time:* First Amendment Theory Applied to Libel and Misapplied to Privacy," 56 *California Law Review* 935, 957 (1968).

speech and free press claims in these cases is simple common sense. As one writer put it, "To deny holding the tabloid media liable for an intrusive invasion of privacy is similar to holding a local television news crew immune from tort liability for its van intentionally running over someone on its way to cover a big story."[34]

One of the earliest cases to discuss the issue of media intrusions found Senator Thomas Dodd of Connecticut suing newspaper columnists Drew Pearson and Jack Anderson for publishing information that had been culled from documents leaked to them without permission by congressional staffers. The columnists prevailed, in that they themselves had not thus intruded upon the senator's privacy. The court went out of its way, however, to point out that journalists in future cases could be held liable were they to engage in "unauthorized bugging," "tapping a telephone," "snooping through windows," or even "overzealous shadowing" of a subject.[35]

Two years later, a federal appellate court upheld a judgment against a pair of *Life* magazine reporters who, acting pursuant to an agreement with the Los Angeles District Attorney's Office, pretended to be potential patients and entered the premises of a disabled veteran who apparently was practicing medicine without a license.[36] The magazine's liability was based not so much on the reporters' lack of candor with the plaintiff as on their having used a hidden camera and audio recording device. "One who invites another to his home or office takes a risk that the visitor may not be what he seems," the court allowed, "and that the visitor may repeat all he hears and observes when he leaves. But he does not and should not be required to take the risk that what is heard and seen will be transmitted by photograph or recording, or in our modern world, in full living color and hi-fi to the public at large or to any segment of it that the visitor may select."

### No "Intrusion" If *Anyone* Could Have Seen or Heard

In Chapter 1, the Fourth Amendment's protection against unconstitutional searches and seizures was mentioned briefly. One exception to the general principle that police must first obtain a warrant to conduct a search is that law enforcement officers are permitted to search and seize things that are not hidden, that are in plain sight.[37] Analogously in the tort law of privacy, courts have held that there is no intrusion when the media photograph or record, from a public place, that which disinterested passersby could just as easily have seen or heard for themselves. In *Mark v. Seattle Times*,[38] a KING-TV cameraman had set up

---

[34]Eduardo W. Gonzalez, "'Get That Camera Out of My Face!' An Examination of the Viability of Suing 'Tabloid Television' for Invasion of Privacy," 51 *University of Miami Law Review* 935, 952 (1997).

[35]*Pearson v. Dodd*, 410 F.2d 701 (D.C. Cir. 1969), *cert. denied*, 395 U.S. 947 (1969).

[36]*Dietemann v. Time, Inc.*, 449 F.2d 245 (9th Cir. 1971).

[37]*Coolidge v. New Hampshire*, 403 U.S. 443 (1971).

[38]635 P.2d 1081 (Wash. 1981).

his equipment against the window of a locked pharmacy—it is not clear from the court record whether the camera itself was on public or private property—to record the actions inside of pharmacist Albert Mark, who had recently been indicted for Medicaid fraud. The Washington Supreme Court determined that the cameraman's conduct was not actionable in that he merely made a record of "a public sight which anyone would be free to see."

An Ohio court reached a similar result when a Cleveland TV station filmed, in the county sheriff's department building, a drug felony suspect being transported from his interrogation to the booking room. "Liability for intrusion does not exist," the court held, if the media "merely observe, film, or record a person in a public place, such as a courthouse or a police station."[39] Another reporter, this time in Arkansas, was not held liable for making and later broadcasting audio recordings of a DWI suspect who happened to be an attorney and former judge. The reporter had set up his equipment with police consent in the cell block housing the suspect. The court emphasized that the suspect was behaving in a loud and abusive manner that could readily have been overheard by anyone in the area.[40] Then, too, a New York area TV reporter could not be held liable for intrusion in taping a New Jersey manufacturing company president on the grounds immediately outside the front entrance of the firm's headquarters. The court noted that the plaintiff, from whom the TV reporter sought information about chemical dumping that had apparently been taking place near the company's site, was filmed in "a semi-public area...visible to the public eye."[41]

Members of the press do not enjoy absolute immunity from liability simply because they engage in news gathering in public or semipublic places. Particularly outrageous conduct can still result in liability even if there is no intrusion on private property. Consider the result of two separate sets of protracted litigation involving the close surveillance of two celebrities. The first of these involved consumer advocate Ralph Nader, whose pursuers were not the press but rather sleuths hired by General Motors, which had apparently been concerned about Nader ever since the late 1960s when his classic *Unsafe at Any Speed,* a scathing review of the auto industry's safety track record, was in press.[42] Many, but not all of the activities engaged in by the private eyes were deemed actionable, some criminally so, some on the basis of tort law. Simply conducting interviews with persons acquainted with Nader in the hope of uncovering salacious information about him was not a violation of Nader's right of privacy. Because Nader himself had revealed any such information to the interviewees, he had taken the risk that

---

[39]*Haynik v. Zimlich,* 508 N.E.2d 195, 200 (Cuyahoga County, Ohio 1986).

[40]*Holman v. Central Arkansas Broadcasting Company,* 610 F.2d 542, 544 (8th Cir. 1979).

[41]*Machleder v. Diaz,* 538 F. Supp. 1364, 1374 (S.D.N.Y. 1982). Some of the court's holdings on other claims apart from that for intrusion were later overturned. See 801 F.2d 46 (2d Cir. 1986), *cert. denied,* 479 U.S. 1088 (1987).

[42]*Nader v. General Motors,* 255 N.E.2d 765, 770 (Ct. App. N.Y. 1970).

his confidences would be breached. Neither was having attractive women accost Nader in an attempt to record him accepting their illicit proposals a violation. The manner of the surveillance itself, however, was viewed as a possibly actionable intrusion on Nader's privacy, as on one occasion when a General Motors stalker stood close enough to Nader in a bank "to see the denomination of the bills he was withdrawing."

The second celebrity who had to go to court to be granted some peace of mind in her public comings and goings (as well as those of children Caroline and John Jr.) was Jacqueline Onassis. Her nemesis for years had been freelance photographer Ronald Galella, who trailed Onassis everywhere, hiding in bushes and behind coatracks in restaurants and even intruding into her children's schools. The remedy applied by the court was an injunction against further harassment by Galella; it did not prohibit him from photographing the family, although it required that he stand as far as 100 yards away from his subjects.[43] An appellate court later affirmed the order, but lowered the distance for most situations to twenty-five feet. Although the legal controversy ultimately turned on the question of whether Galella was guilty of violating New York's criminal harassment statute, Judge Cooper made clear that the photographer's conduct also constituted "tortious invasion of privacy."

In both the *Nader* and *Onassis* cases, a long pattern of media misconduct was alleged. Liability can also stem from a single incident. CBS-TV's Channel 2 in New York discovered this when they sent a camera crew to a Manhattan restaurant that had been cited for health code violations. As a state court described the scene, the station's employees "burst into" the restaurant with lights and cameras running, and, in the ensuing chaos, some patrons left without paying their checks, while others "hid their faces behind napkins or table cloths." The restaurant was awarded damages for CBS's trespass. That the restaurant is a public accommodation is irrelevant, the court held, because the camera crew was not there to partake of that which was being offered to the public, that is, food and drink.[44]

## "Ride-Along" Intrusions

One of the more popular genres of television fare in recent years has been "reality programs" that show live footage of police officers stopping, questioning, searching, and arresting suspects, or of emergency fire and medical teams responding to calls for assistance. Sometimes the events take place in public places, such as on city streets. At other times, law enforcement or other emergency workers may be called into private residences. In a unanimous 1999 decision,[45] the Supreme Court held that law enforcement agencies may be found in violation of the Fourth

---

[43]*Galella v. Onassis,* 353 F. Supp. 196 (S.D.N.Y. 1972), *aff'd,* 487 F.2d 986 (2d Cir. 1973).

[44]*Le Mistral, Inc. v. CBS, Inc.,* 402 N.Y.S.2d 815 (App. Div. 1978).

[45]*Wilson v. Layne,* 526 U.S. 603 (1999).

Amendment for inviting media to observe their activities conducted in a private residence. Dominic Wilson was wanted by federal authorities for violating his probation on previous charges of robbery, theft, and assault with intent to rob. The U.S. Marshall's office obtained a warrant authorizing a predawn storming of Wilson's home in Rockville, Maryland, and invited the *Washington Post* along. As it happens, the police had the address wrong and wound up pointing several guns not at the suspect, but at his father. Chief Justice Rehnquist's opinion for the Court makes clear that police may invite to such events as the execution of search and arrest warrants only nonparticipants who have a direct stake in the event, such as crime victims who can identify their stolen property. The individual law enforcement agents executing the warrant were immune from liability, the Court held, largely because the relevant case law had been contradictory, thus not giving them sufficient notice as to their constitutional obligations. The Wilsons did not sue the *Post* itself; thus, lower court decisions must be examined to see what liability the media may have when they participate in ride-alongs.

In a relatively early case of this type, the widow of a heart attack victim sued NBC and its Los Angeles affiliate KNBC after they had accompanied the paramedics called to treat the victim. A segment of the resulting video appeared on the *NBC Nightly News* as well as in an on-air advertisement for a future "minidocumentary" about the paramedics, despite the family never consenting either to the taping or to the physical intrusion into their home on the part of the media. A state appellate court found that the plaintiff had stated a sufficient claim for invasion of privacy to defeat the defendant's motion for summary judgment. In doing so, the court admitted that the quality of performance on the part of emergency medical personnel is a very newsworthy subject matter, but emphasized that newsworthiness is wholly irrelevant to the intrusion tort.[46]

Another California case, this time involving CBS's *Street Stories,* found that a victim of domestic violence could proceed against the media company for some of her tort claims. She would not be able to have her intrusion claim aired in court, however, in that she consented to the film crew's having accompanied the county Mobile Crisis Intervention Team onto her property. Because that consent, however, was based on the crew's having falsely represented to her that the video would be used only for internal training purposes, rather than national broadcast, she would be permitted to pursue her fraud claim.[47]

Also unsuccessful in her intrusion suit was an Oregon resident who sought damages against KATU-TV of Portland. The station's crew had accompanied local police officers in their execution of a search warrant at the home of the plaintiff, who did not consent to the filming. Even though the crew might very well be guilty of trespass, the court reminded us that the tort of intrusion requires that the alleged invasion on a complainant's privacy must be "highly offensive." The appel-

---

[46]*Miller v. National Broadcasting Company,* 232 Cal. Rptr. 668 (Cal. Ct. App. 2d Dist. 1986).

[47]*Baugh v. C.B.S., Inc.,* 828 F. Supp. 745 (N.D. Cal. 1993).

late court here refused to overturn the jury's finding that this particular trespass was not sufficiently offensive so as to constitute tortious intrusion.[48]

CBS's *Street Stories* program was also the subject of a New York case wherein the camera crew was invited by the Secret Service to observe their agents' executing a search warrant at the home of a man suspected of credit card fraud. The crew ignored the suspect's wife and child's objection to their filming. Instead, they followed the Secret Service's clear instructions to continue filming, especially while the agents interviewed the wife about articles found during the search. None of the footage was ever broadcast by CBS. The federal district court concluded that CBS had become so closely intertwined with the Secret Service's functioning as to be considered a "state's agent" that could be sued for violating citizens' *constitutional* right to privacy.[49] Similarly, the Court of Appeals for the Ninth Circuit declared that CNN could be sued not only for trespass but also for violating a Montana plaintiff's civil rights. The network had accompanied U.S. Fish and Wildlife agents, who suspected Paul Berger of poisoning endangered species, on a search of Berger's ranch. The court was especially concerned at CNN's having entered into an elaborate agreement with the government agency, being granted permission to film as long as it promised not to air the footage until a jury was empaneled or a plea bargain struck.[50]

By way of contrast, a police search of a St. Louis, Missouri, home, one of whose residents was suspected of keeping illegal weapons, produced a federal appellate ruling relieving the media of any constitutional liability. The court emphasized that the crew from local station KSDK, although *invited* by the police to accompany them as they executed a search warrant, were not in any way *directed* by the officials to enter or not to enter, to film or not to film.

In short, the more the media presence and on-site conduct are controlled directly by the police, the more likely that presence can lead to media liability. An exception to this generalization may by found in cases where the search warrant explicitly authorizes videotaping or similar recording of evidence.[51]

## Intrusions and Fraud

In the *Dietemann* case, it will be recalled, the *Life* magazine reporters were held liable not because they engaged in deception so as to obtain their story (by pretending

---

[48]*Magenis v. Fisher Broadcasting, Inc.,* 798 P.2d 1106 (Or. Ct. App. 1990).

[49]*Ayeni v. CBS, Inc.,* 848 F. Supp. 362 (E.D.N.Y. 1994), *aff'd sub nom, Ayeni v. Mottola,* 35 F.2d 680 (2d Cir. 1994), *cert denied,* 514 U.S. 1062 (1995). *Note:* The change in the case's name at the appellate level reflects CBS's having been removed as a defendant in that the network reached an out-of-court settlement with the plaintiff.

[50]*Berger v. Hanlon,* 129 F.3d 505, 515 (9th Cir. 1997); technically, the Supreme Court, in *Wilson v. Layne,* affirmed this decision as well, although no separate discussion of the case's facts are presented.

[51]*Prahl v. Brosamle,* 295 N.W.2d 768 (Wis. Ct. App. 1980).

to be in need of medical attention), but rather because of the surreptitious use of recording equipment. Does this mean that the media are always free to lie with impunity to obtain access to a residence or business? Does a newsworthy end justify a deceptive means?

As several courts have pointed out, deception is a necessary component of some kinds of reportage, from the restaurant critic who dons a disguise so as not to receive VIP treatment, to the use of paired "testers" to uncover discriminatory housing and employment practices. In a 1995 decision, Judge Richard Posner of the Seventh Circuit Court of Appeals concluded that reporters could not be held liable for trespass as long as their deceptions do not grant them access to truly private areas, and they do not reveal "intimate details" of their subjects' lives.[52]

A few years later, a damage award of over $300,000 was assessed against producers of the ABC news magazine program, *Prime Time Live,* owing to their reporters' fraudulently obtaining employment as Food Lion meat wrappers to research a story on unsafe meat preparation and marketing practices. On appeal, only a nominal award of two dollars for "breach of loyalty" (taking wages from one employer while engaged in practices designed to hurt the interests of that employer) was permitted to stand. The Fourth Circuit Court of Appeals threw out the huge punitive damages based on the reporters' fraudulent misrepresentation of their employment and educational backgrounds, finding that the real harm suffered by Food Lion was a function not of those false statements, but of the broadcast story resulting from the undercover operation. The court held further that if Food Lion wanted to be compensated for the harm caused to its reputation, it would have to sue for libel (and to prove that ABC published with actual malice).[53]

### A Note about Wiretapping

As we have already seen, one cannot discuss the privacy tort called intrusion without also talking about such related torts as trespass and fraud. It is also important to realize that certain kinds of news gathering practices, whether or not they technically meet the definition of the intrusion tort in your state, might open you up to criminal prosecution. Chief among these are the use of mechanical devices to monitor or record conversations (whether live or telephone) or to read another person's e-mail or similar computer communications. Both federal and state statutes can govern these behaviors.

The law generally recognizes a difference between **third-party monitoring** (wherein person A records a conversation between persons B and C) and **participant monitoring** (person A records her own conversation with person B). An example of the former category became a miniscandal in 1997 when a Florida couple, using a police scanner, intercepted House Speaker Newt Gingrich's private cellular phone conversations and made recordings of them available to the news media.

---

[52]*Desnick v. American Broadcasting Company,* 44 F.3d 1345 (7th Cir. 1995).

[53]*Food Lion v. Capital Cities Cable/ABC,* 194 F.3d 505 (4th Cir. 1999).

Gingrich, it will be recalled, was under investigation by the House Ethics Committee for questionable fund-raising practices surrounding a college course he offered by teleconference. The intercepted conversations seemed to contradict Gingrich's promise to the committee not to contest its decision to reprimand him. Although the *New York Times* and other media likely were not in violation of the law for publishing excerpts of the conversations, the Florida couple pled guilty to violating the Electronic Communications Privacy Act (ECPA) of 1986. In 1999, a federal appellate court determined that a civil suit against the Democratic congressman who had received the tapes from the couple and made them available could go forward.[54]

The ECPA criminalizes the interception of oral messages as well as those sent by e-mail,[55] satellite, and cellular phones. A U.S. Attorney in New York used the statute to prosecute the Fort Lee, New Jersey–based "Breaking News Network" for intercepting beeper messages sent by the police and other emergency crews as well as by the mayor's office. BNN, whose clients included the Associated Press wire service as well as several New York newspapers and TV stations, was known for providing useful leads for fast-breaking crime stories. The company and three of its executives pled guilty, and BNN was fined $500,000.

The Act was also at issue in a 1990 case involving the syndicated TV program, *Inside Edition,* which had surreptitiously videotaped a New York physician then under investigation by the New York State Department of Health, Office of Professional Medical Conduct for his highly unusual and allegedly fraudulent manner of treating overweight patients. The doctor obtained a ten-day temporary restraining order against the TV producers, prohibiting them from broadcasting the footage obtained in a manner likely prohibited by the Act. An appellate court overturned the order, however, finding that even if the TV staff was guilty of violating the Act, that issue is wholly separable from the First Amendment right to share whatever information they had obtained with their viewers.[56]

Laws against the recording of conversations by one of the participants are generally less strict than the ECPA. Most media representatives would agree that to tape-record other people's comments without their permission is ethically questionable at best. If you decide that you have a compelling need to engage in such behavior, you certainly will want to know if your jurisdiction criminalizes participant monitoring. Under federal law there is no criminal liability for surreptitious participant taping. Your local phone company, however, acting under directions from the FCC, likely has a policy prohibiting you from taping conversations unless all parties consent.

The majority of states use the same rules as the federal model, permitting recording of phone conversations as long as at least one party is aware of the taping. About ten states, however, require that all parties consent to the taping of phone

---

[54]*Boehner v. McDermott,* 191 F.3d 463 (D.C. Cir. 1999).

[55]It should be kept in mind, however, that in the workplace, your employer, not you, owns the e-mail system; thus, it is not illegal under current law for businesses to monitor and store transmissions sent to and by their employees.

[56]*In re King World Productions,* 898 F.2d 56 (6th Cir. 1990).

conversations. One such state is Maryland. Thus, when Linda Tripp taped Monica Lewinsky's tales of White House sexual escapades without the latter's knowledge, she was probably in violation of the law (although the prosecutor dropped his case in May 2000 because so much of it was built around testimony for which Tripp had already been granted immunity by Special Prosecutor Kenneth Starr). A similar statute in Florida was upheld by that state's Supreme Court against a First Amendment challenge brought by a Miami TV station and newspaper. "The ancient art of investigative reporting was successfully practiced long before the invention of electronic devices," the court wrote, adding that "hidden mechanical contrivances" have not become, even in the modern age, "indispensable tools of investigative reporting."[57]

At least one court has held, even in the face of a state statute seeming to prohibit participant taping, that any party who does not manifest an objective expectation of privacy in the conversation—for example, by lowering his or her voice, closing doors, or otherwise demonstrating that it is a "private" conversation—forfeits the right to recover damages. At issue was the surreptitious audio and video recording of conversations with the manager of a fish market by the producers of ABC-TV's *Prime Time Live,* which was investigating allegations of unsanitary conditions in the industry.[58]

Whether wiretapping laws can make reporters liable for the broadcasting or other disclosure of illegally taped conversations, even if the media had no role in the taping, was still an open question as this book was going to press. A radio station in Wyoming Valley, Pennsylvania, broadcast excerpts of cellular telephone conversations between a local high school teacher and the head of the teachers' union negotiating team. In the conversation, the union official expresses anger at the school board for leaking too many details of the negotiations to the local newspaper rather than sitting down with the union in good faith. In what we can presume was a bit of rhetorical hyperbole, the union official planned to "blow off the front porches" of some of the board members' homes. An unknown individual intercepted and taped the conversation and then left the tape in the mailbox of the president of the local taxpayers' association, who in turn gave it to a local radio talk show host. After the tapes were broadcast, the teacher and the union representative sued the radio talk show host under federal and state wiretapping laws.

After the federal district court refused to grant summary judgment to the radio station, the Third Circuit Court of Appeals reversed. Wiretapping statutes cannot be constitutionally applied to persons who disclose illegally taped conversations, the court held, unless there is also evidence to suggest that the defendants had at least an indirect role in the taping. The U.S. Supreme Court heard arguments on the case in December 2000, and a decision was pending as this book was going to press.[59]

---

[57]*Shevin v. Sunbeam Television Corporation,* 351 So. 2d 723, 727 (Fla. 1977).

[58]*Russell v. American Broadcasting Co., Inc.* 1995 WL 330920 (N.D. Ill.), cited in "Major Court Decisions of 1995," 4 *CommLaw Conspectus* 271, 290 (1996).

[59]*Bartnicki v. Vopper,* 200 F.3d 109 (3d Cir. 1999).

# Things to Remember

### INTRUSION

- Uniquely among the four privacy torts, intrusion does not require that anything be published. Therefore, the First Amendment is not a very helpful defense.
- There is generally no intrusion if the media capture images of scenes that any passerby could have seen (unless the media otherwise act egregiously).
- The Supreme Court has ruled that law enforcement officials may be in violation of suspects' constitutional privacy rights when they invite the media on "ride-along" observations; some courts have held that the media themselves may be sued for both tortious claims and for civil rights violations when they participate in the execution of a search warrant.
- That employees of news organizations sometimes lie to their subjects to gain access to property and obtain information is usually not sufficient to create an actionable intrusion.
- Reporters who surreptitiously record phone conversations with subjects run the risk not only of civil suit; they may be in violation of state statutes.

## False Light

The next of the four privacy torts identified by Prosser has much in common with libel. False light plaintiffs, like libel plaintiffs, sue because falsehoods have been spread about them. There is one very important difference between false light and libel, however. Plaintiffs in false light privacy suits need not prove that the falsities told about them are actually defamatory, only that they are offensive. In actuality, the vast majority of false light plaintiffs sue because of defamatory statements about them. In such cases, the false light claim seems to be a fallback option in controversies that should be litigated as libel actions. Indeed, when these plaintiffs prevail, it is usually on the defamation claim.

Still, the definition of the false light tort does not require a finding of defamation. Indeed, in the leading Supreme Court false light case, the falsity at issue might be interpreted as laudatory, as painting the plaintiffs in an inappropriately heroic light.[60] The factual situation in *Time, Inc. v. Hill* began in 1952, when James Hill and his family were held hostage in their own Philadelphia area home by three escaped convicts. A novel called *The Desperate Hours,* loosely based on the Hill family's ordeal, came out soon afterwards. The novel was turned into a Broadway play starring Robert Montgomery. The February 1955 *Life* magazine article that became the subject of the lawsuit also reported on the then upcoming movie

---

[60]*Time, Inc. v. Hill,* 385 U.S. 374 (1967).

version. The magazine article caused his family anguish, Hill alleged, not only because it exposed them anew to national attention for an episode of their lives that they would have preferred to put behind them, but also because the article was fundamentally false. *Life* readers were led to the incorrect belief that the play was a completely factual retelling of the Hill family's experiences. As awful as the real ordeal was, Hill claimed, the *Life* account made it appear far worse. The magazine took the cast of the play, then in performance in Philadelphia, to the original site of the crime. (The Hill family had since moved to Connecticut.) There they reenacted scenes from the play, captured by *Life* photographers. One such photo, labeled "Brutish Convict," pictured Hill's son being "roughed up"; a picture captioned "Daring Daughter" showed Hill's daughter biting the hand of a convict to make him drop a gun; a third photo depicted Hill himself throwing the convict's gun through a door in a "Brave Try" to rescue his family.

None of the incidents depicted in the photos ever really happened. Indeed, in an interview with the press shortly after the convicts were captured in 1952, Hill emphasized that they "had treated the family courteously, had not molested them, and had not been at all violent." Hill could not sue for libel, of course. Where is the defamation in being depicted as being a bit more heroic in an adverse situation than you really were?

In overturning a lower court's award of $30,000 in compensatory damages to Hill, the Supreme Court unanimously held that false light privacy actions involving newsworthy events could not stand in the absence of a finding of actual malice, that is, that the defendant knew the story was false or published with reckless disregard as to its truth or falsity. By constitutionalizing the tort in this way, the Court demonstrated its concern that false light plaintiffs not be able to circumvent too easily the First Amendment protections granted the press three years earlier in the landmark *New York Times v. Sullivan* libel decision. Some but not all states require a finding of actual malice even when private citizens (i.e., persons who are neither public officials nor public figures) sue about depictions of events eventually deemed to be nonnewsworthy. The other states require at least a finding of negligence in such instances.[61]

Many commentators agree that false light cases come in three varieties (although there can be overlap among the categories). They are distortion, embellishment, and fictionalization.[62]

## Distortion

Distortion results when text or photos appear out of context or in ways that omit key information. Let us look at two early cases from California that both stemmed

---

[61]Ronald Smolla, *The Law of Defamation* (St. Paul, MN: West Group, 1990), 13.

[62]Michael Sewell, "Invasion of Privacy in Texas: Public Disclosure of Embarrassing Private Facts," 3 *Texas Wesleyan Law Review* 411, 414 (1995).

from publication of the same photograph. The opposite rulings in the cases are a function of the photo being used appropriately by one publication, but in a distortive manner by the other.

John Gill and his wife were photographed without their knowledge while they were "seated in an affectionate pose" at a candy and ice-cream stand in the Los Angeles Farmers' Market. In one of the two cases, the Gills sued *Harper's Bazaar* magazine, which used their photo to illustrate a whimsical article titled "And So the World Goes Round, " described by Justice Spence of the California Supreme Court as "a short commentary reaffirming the poet's conviction that the world could not revolve without love."[63] With respect to this use of the photo, the magazine publishers prevailed. The photo was not used in a context that would offend persons of reasonable sensibility.

The very same photo also showed up in the *Ladies' Home Journal,* but this time it was part of an article the theme of which was that only some kinds of love— those based on an enduring affection rather than simply physical attraction—are desirable and praiseworthy. Associated with the Gills' photo was a caption reading, "Publicized as glamorous, desirable, 'love at first sight' is a bad risk." The article refers to this kind of love as "wrong," as "founded upon 100 per cent sex attraction" and as likely to lead to divorce. The Gills claimed that the article cast them, a "happily married" couple of "high moral reputation," in a hurtfully false light. The California Supreme Court agreed, finding that this use of the photo was "seriously humiliating and disturbing" in that it calls to mind "the intimate and private relationship between the opposite sexes and marriage."[64]

Another example of distortion is found in what might be called "the case of the maligned pedestrian." It seems that a ten-year-old girl was struck by a careless motorist in the streets of Birmingham, Alabama. A newspaper photographer happened by and got a shot of a bystander lifting the girl to her feet. That the photo appeared the next day in the local paper was hardly remarkable and could not have become the basis for a lawsuit. The photo reemerged about two years later, however, as an illustration for a *Saturday Evening Post* article on traffic accidents, with emphasis on pedestrian carelessness, under the title, "They Ask To Be Killed." The plaintiff's damage award was upheld in that the title, and the text surrounding the picture, erroneously implied that the girl was careless of her own safety.[65]

In another case, the U.S. District Court for the District of Columbia found ABC's affiliate station, WJLA, to have misemployed video footage so as to cast a local woman in a false light. Linda Duncan was one of several persons shown standing on a crowded downtown Washington street while 11 P.M. anchorperson David Schoumacher made reference to "the 20 million Americans who have

---

[63]*Gill v. Hearst Publishing Company,* 253 P. 2d 441, 442 (1953).

[64]*Gill v. Curtis Publishing Company,* 239 P.2d 630 (1952).

[65]*Leverton v. Curtis Publishing Company,* 192 F.2d 974 (1951).

herpes."[66] Although the damages awarded Duncan were minimal—$750 of the $2.1 million she had sought—the case does suggest an important rule for TV journalists. If the spoken text of your story deals with potentially embarrassing subjects, make sure that none of the people you might use in your "establishing shots" are recognizable. If need be, use footage of feet, not faces.

In New York, even an inarguably distortive use of a photograph will generally not be actionable, if the overall context is a newsworthy one. The leading case on this point involved a professional model who had consented to her photos being used in *YM* magazine, but who was shocked at the specific nature of the use. Three photos of the plaintiff illustrated the magazine's "Love Crisis" column, a letter ostensibly written by a 14-year-old reader who had "gotten trashed and had sex with three guys." New York's Court of Appeals (the state's highest court) held the state privacy law inapplicable to such a clearly newsworthy use (confronting such issues as underage drinking and date rape).[67]

## Embellishment

The second category of false light cases results from journalistic accounts that are knowingly "enhanced" by falsehoods that might seem on the surface to be innocuous, but that nonetheless cause the subjects of such stories great anguish. The leading case is a Supreme Court decision involving a *Cleveland Plain Dealer* article about the death of Melvin Cantrell, who perished along with forty-three other people when the Silver Bridge across the Ohio River at Point Pleasant, West Virginia, collapsed. A follow-up story published about eight months after the accident emphasized the "abject poverty" in which Cantrell's widow and children lived. At one point, the article says of Mrs. Cantrell herself that she "will talk neither about what happened nor about how they are doing," that she "wears the same mask of non-expression she wore at the funeral."[68]

Where is the embellishment here, you may wonder? It turns out that Mrs. Cantrell was not at home when the reporter and photographer came by to pursue their story. In other words, all references to what she looked like or to what she would or would not agree to talk about were, depending on one's perspective about such matters, either examples of poetic license or just plain lies. The Supreme Court thus had no difficulty ruling, in an 8–1 vote, that the original jury award of compensatory damages was a proper one.

---

[66]*Duncan v. WJLA-TV,* 10 Media Law Rptr. 1395 (D.D.C. 1984), *new trial denied,* 1984 U.S. Dist. LEXIS 21273.

[67]*Messenger v. Gruner + Jahr Printing and Publishing,* 727 N.E. 2d 549 (N.Y. 2000). A federal appellate court accepted this reasoning in a later decision stemming from the same facts and bearing the same name. 208 F. 3d 122 (2nd Cir. 2000).

[68]*Cantrell v. Forest City Publishing Company,* 419 U.S. 245, 248 (1974).

### Fictionalization

The last category of false light cases, fictionalization, results from the deliberate use of falsehood for the purpose of creating fictional accounts. TV docudramas, movies whose plots are based on real events but that take liberties with events, and historical novels have been the typical artifacts to prompt such lawsuits.

Supermarket tabloids have a reputation for creating wholly fictional works more for the entertainment than the edification of their readers. It is not surprising that they have frequently been defendants in libel and invasion of privacy suits. A particularly hilarious case involved the publishers of the *Sun,* which ran a completely fictitious story about one "Audrey Wiles," described as having quit her paper route—at the age of 101!—because an extramarital affair with a millionaire client on her route had left her pregnant. Because there was no Audrey Wiles, nor a millionaire client, one would think that the article would have resulted in nothing more than a few chuckles. The newspaper, however, made the mistake of illustrating the story with photographs of the very real Nellie Mitchell, who was herself just a few years shy of the century mark and who was well known in her Baxter County, Arkansas, home as the operator of a local newsstand who did indeed deliver papers. The newspaper apparently obtained the photos from its own files, having been one of many media outlets that had done a factual account of Mitchell's longevity and industriousness some ten years earlier. Although Mitchell's libel claim against the newspaper was rejected by the jury, she prevailed in her false light privacy suit. Refusing to overturn the jury's finding, the court emphasized that readers who looked only at the cover page of the newspaper would not necessarily realize that the story to be found inside was a complete fiction. Then, too, the court held, the newspaper could not avoid liability by dint of the implausibility of the facts asserted in the story.[69]

---

[69]*People's Bank and Trust Company of Mountain Home v. Globe International,* 978 F.2d 1065 (8th. Cir. 1992).

 # Things to Remember

### FALSE LIGHT

- The false light tort is similar to libel except that the remarks that cast the plaintiff in a false light need not be defamatory; they can simply be embarrassing (and false).
- In 1967, the Supreme Court ruled that false light plaintiffs who sue over stories on a matter of public interest must prove actual malice, just as if they had sued for libel.
- Courts generally recognize three varieties of false light suits: distortion, embellishment, and fictionalization.

## Privacy in Only One of Four Torts?

Before introducing the last of the four torts, a point made much earlier in this chapter—that concerns about media invasions of privacy are viewed by many commentators as much more questions of ethics than of law—must be emphasized again. A two-pronged argument is often offered in support of this idea. The argument begins by recognizing that the first three torts discussed already in this chapter add very little to the body of law that existed before the famous Warren and Brandeis article encouraged the judiciary to respect privacy as an independent tort claim. Privacy law skeptics complete their argument by pointing out that the only true privacy tort—the public disclosure category originally proposed by Warren and Brandeis—almost always results in victories for defendants.

We have already seen how closely intertwined the intrusion tort is to ordinary trespass. Whereas we traditionally think of trespasses as unauthorized presence on another's property, intrusions are more akin to stalking in that they intrude on a personal bubble of privacy that travels with the possessor. A 1997 Supreme Court decision may make this distinction even less tenable in the future. In *Schenck v. Pro-Choice Network of Western New York*,[70] the Court upheld an injunction issued against prolife demonstrators as applied to a "fixed buffer zone" around clinic driveways and entranceways but rejected application of the injunction as applied to a "floating buffer zone" surrounding the clinic patients themselves. In other words, the demonstrators were told that they could not trespass but that they could intrude. Should lower courts interpret that decision broadly, they may refuse to sanction intrusions that do not also involve trespasses. (Note that *Schenck* did not involve the federal Freedom of Access to Clinic Entrances Act, which provides for civil suits against persons who "intimidate," "harass," or "threaten" women trying to enter an abortion clinic.[71])

The misappropriation tort also adds very little to the law not already present in statutory and common-law copyright protections. Copyright is discussed in the next chapter. For now, suffice it to say that copyright is designed to protect an artist or writer's finished product (a book, a play, choreographic notations, etc.). At first blush, it would thus seem that the misappropriation tort is conceptually distinct from copyright in that the former protects us from the unauthorized use of our "name or likeness," of our identity. We do not usually think of our name or our identity as finished products, as things we have created. Consider, though, that the most typical misappropriation cases involve celebrity plaintiffs who have worked hard to instill a commercial value to their name or likeness. That which is sought to be protected by these kind of misappropriation suits is thus every bit as much a "product" of the celebrity's sweat equity as is the artist's painting or the author's monograph. Indeed, it has been suggested that those who achieve celebrity status

---

[70]519 U.S. 357 (1997).

[71]See, for example, *U.S. v. Gregg* 226 F.3d 253 (3d Cir. 2000).

by happenstance rather than by design—Kato Kaelin's fame, for example, stems from his having been O. J. Simpson's houseguest—should not be permitted to recover damages for misappropriation of their name or likeness.[72]

Chapter 6 also discusses trademark law. For purposes of the present discussion, we need only know that trademarks are designed to protect consumers from confusion, to ensure that the products they purchase are indeed what they believe them to be, manufactured by the company they believe to be the producer. Recall, however, that misappropriation plaintiffs often argue that consumers will be confused, that they will mistakenly believe that a celebrity has lent his or her name to a product. Again, the tort adds little to the law that was not there before.

False light invasion of privacy suits have frequently been maligned as attempted end runs around the constitutional protections accorded to libel defendants. One commentator says that "false light is but a small corner of the tort of defamation that in no sense needs its own niche in the law of privacy."[73] Another reports that several courts have rejected the tort altogether because it seeks to "evade first amendment protections applicable in defamation cases" and concluded that false light is "merely an imperfect and less-defined duplication of the long-recognized tort of defamation."[74] The Supreme Court, of course, expressed its own skepticism about false light when, in *Time, Inc. v. Hill*,[75] it applied the *Sullivan* "actual malice" rule[76] to false light suits whenever the revelation prompting the suit is a newsworthy one.

The public disclosure tort, then, is the only one of the four that truly adds anything new to the law. The remainder of this chapter is devoted to an explication of that tort. While it is important for communications professionals to understand the nature of the tort, it should be admitted at the outset that plaintiffs rarely win these suits. Writing in the early 1980s, Professor Diane Zimmerman reported that her exhaustive search of the literature uncovered only eighteen successful public disclosure suits since the tort's birth in the beginning years of the twentieth century. Several of these suits were reports of defendants' unsuccessful motion for summary judgment; such defendants may have ultimately prevailed at a trial unreported in the literature.[77] A few years later, a detailed statistical analysis of libel and privacy suits revealed that mass media defendants ultimately win public disclosure

---

[72]Landvardt, "The Troubling Implications," 337.

[73]Richard A. Epstein, "A Taste for Privacy? Evolution and the Emergence of a Naturalistic Ethic," 9 *Journal of Legal Studies* 665, 668 (1980).

[74]Terence J. Clark, "The Right to Privacy One Hundred Years Later: When Privacy Rights Encounter First Amendment Freedoms," 41 *Case Western Reserve L Rev* 921, 926 (1991).

[75]385 U.S. 374 (1967).

[76]*New York Times v. Sullivan*, 376 U.S. 254 (1964).

[77]Diane L. Zimmerman, "Requiem for a Heavyweight: A Farewell to Warren and Brandeis's Privacy Tort," 68 *Cornell Law Review* 291, 293 n.5 (1983).

suits more than 97 percent of the time.[78] Successful public disclosure suits have likely become even less frequent in that both surveys reported data that predate an important Supreme Court decision, *Florida Star v. B. J. F.,* which is discussed later in this chapter.

As we review the structure and history of the public disclosure tort, you may want to consider the ethical, not just the legal, questions posed by the case law. If we ask only if we *may* publish truths that will embarrass the subject of our disclosures, the answer is almost always yes. The more interesting question is almost always going to be, *Should* we publish?

## Public Disclosure

In April 1992, tennis star Arthur Ashe held a news conference to reveal that he was infected with the AIDS virus. The immediate impetus for Ashe's decision to go public with information that had previously been known only to his wife and a small number of close friends was *USA Today*'s editors confronting him upon hearing rumors of his illness. Suppose Ashe had not decided to preempt the paper's scoop, that he instead implored the media to keep his secret, a request that surely would not have been uniformly honored? Suppose further that he had brought a public disclosure suit against any and all media outlets that chose to reveal this highly intimate information. Such a suit, as will soon become apparent, would almost certainly have failed.

Although the public disclosure tort is not recognized in all American jurisdictions, those that do recognize it generally agree on its elements. A plaintiff must prove the following:

- That defendant publicly disclosed information about the plaintiff.
- That information was private (i.e., previously unknown to others).
- That disclosure would be highly offensive to a reasonable person.
- That information is not newsworthy.

Let us examine each element in turn.

### *Publicly* Disclosing Information

Unlike in defamation law, where all that is required is for one third party to hear the libelous statement, here the private facts must be made available to a wide audience in order to be actionable. This does not mean that the mass media are the only potential defendants in such cases, however. Employers who reveal intimate

---

[78]Randall Bezanson, Gilbert Cranberg, and John Soloski, *Libel Law and the Press: Myth and Reality* (New York: Free Press, 1987), 116.

details of an employee's life to her coworkers, for example, have sometimes been found liable for damages under this tort. Or consider the case of *Boyles v. Kerr*,[79] wherein a teenager and several of his friends set up a hidden video camera to tape him having sex with his girlfriend. Her suit against the amateur videographers succeeded, even though they had apparently shown the tape to fewer than a dozen others.

## Information That Was Previously *Private*

One cannot be held accountable for violating another's privacy if that which is revealed was already widely known or readily available to all who wished to see. An often-cited case for this point is *Neff v. Time, Inc.*[80] in which a particularly enthusiastic Pittsburgh Steelers fan was upset enough about a *Sports Illustrated* photo narrative about him to bring suit against the magazine's publisher. Neff and several other fans were, in the court's words, "jumping up and down in full view of the fans in the stadium" and "waving Steeler banners and drinking beer." They also seemed to be "slightly inebriated" on beer, "screaming and howling" and "hamming it up" for the photographer. Neff apparently did not realize that his trouser fly was completely open, not to the point "of being revealing," but enough for the court to charge the magazine's editors, who selected for publication that one particular photo from among thousands available to them, with "utmost bad taste." Neff could not recover damages, the court concluded, because he "was photographed in a public place for a newsworthy article."

Another unsuccessful privacy plaintiff was Oliver Sipple, who achieved a degree of fame in the autumn of 1975 when President Ford was visiting San Francisco. Sipple foiled Sara Jane Moore's attempt to shoot Ford by grabbing her arm and deflecting the shot. As one can imagine, the national news media were abuzz with the story. When newspapers in San Francisco and elsewhere reported that Sipple happened to be gay—the first time most of his family learned of his sexual orientation—he took umbrage and sued. His invasion of privacy lawsuits failed, at least in part[81] because that which was revealed about him was not deemed sufficiently *private* to meet the tort's demands. He was well known within the gay community, the courts pointed out, having participated in numerous Gay Pride parades and even having developed a friendship with openly gay San Francisco Board of Supervisors member Harvey Milk.[82]

---

[79]806 S.W.2d 255 (Ct. App. Tex. 1991).

[80]406 F. Supp. 858 (W.D. Pa. 1976).

[81]The court also emphasized the newsworthiness of Sipple's sexual orientation, especially in that President Ford apparently had not made any effort to express his gratitude toward the man. Whether the president was thus manifesting some kind of antihomosexual bias was deemed by the court an important question worthy of pursuing.

[82]*Sipple v. Chronicle Publishing Company,* 201 Cal. Rptr. 665 (Ct. App. 4th App. Dist. 1984).

Sipple's sexual orientation was known to many people, even if not to his family. Other court decisions have emphasized the other side of the coin, that a plaintiff's having revealed his secrets to a select group of close ones will not alone defeat an invasion of privacy suit. Consider the case of *Multimedia WMAZ, Inc. v. Kubach.*[83] A Georgia television station invited Kubach, who had AIDS, to discuss his disease on a live call-in show, promising him that his face would be sufficiently disguised through computer digitization so as to be unrecognizable. For at least the first seven seconds of the broadcast, however, the digitization was faulty and Kubach was easily identifiable to the entire Macon audience. When Kubach brought suit against the station, it argued that the information revealed about him was not truly private in that he had shared the fact of his illness with family members, friends, medical personnel, and members of his AIDS support group, likely as many as sixty people in all. The court rejected this argument, emphasizing that even such a relatively large number of confidants pales in comparison to "the entire television viewing public."

Some courts have had a slightly different take on the public disclosure tort's requirement that the facts revealed be *private* ones. Instead of focusing on how readily available the information was prior to the offensive disclosure, these courts concentrate on the nature of the information itself. For example, Minnesota gubernatorial candidate Jon Grunseth, whose high-level lobbying position frequently brought him to Washington, D.C., brought suit against a Marriott hotel there for releasing to Minnesota newspapers a copy of a receipt that helped the media corroborate an allegation of a long-time affair he had apparently conducted with a Washington-area woman. Although the ruling against him was ultimately based on his having failed to file his suit before the statute of limitations had run out, the court volunteered that his invasion of privacy suit could not have succeeded anyway. The receipt at issue did not contain "private facts," the court pointed out. "The only facts the hotel receipt can be said to show," Judge Kessler wrote, "are that Plaintiff arrived at the J. W. Marriott on July 12, 1989, departed on July 13, 1989, made three long distance and four local calls (with no indication of to whom), placed a modestly priced order with room service, ordered a movie, and made a purchase from the refreshment center."[84]

## Highly Offensive Revelations

The public disclosure tort also requires that the private information revealed be of a kind that would be found highly offensive by reasonable people. Consider the text of a *Time* magazine article from March 13, 1939 (Figure 5.2), which resulted in one of the most often-cited invasion of privacy suits.[85]

---

[83]443 S.E.2d 491 (Ct. App. Ga. 1994).

[84]*Grunseth v. Marriott Corporation*, 872 F. Supp. 1069, 1075–76 (D.C. 1995), *aff'd*, 79 F.3d 169 (D.C. Cir. 1996).

[85]*Barber v. Time, Inc.*, 159 S.W.2d 291, 292 (Sup. Ct. Mo. 1942).

Figure 5.2

## STARVING GLUTTON

One night last week pretty Mrs. Dorothy Barber of Kansas City grabbed a candy bar, packed up some clothes, and walked to General Hospital. "I want to stay here," she said between bites. "I want to eat all the time. I can finish a normal meal and be back in the kitchen in ten minutes eating again."

Dr. R. K. Simpson immediately packed her off to a ward, and ordered a big meal from the hospital kitchen while he questioned Mrs. Barber. He found that although she had eaten enough in the past year to feed a family of ten, she had lost 25 pounds. After a preliminary examination Dr. Simpson thought that Mrs. Barber's pancreas might be functioning abnormally, that it might be burning up too much sugar in her blood and somehow causing an excessive flow of digestive juices, which sharpened her appetite. While he made painstaking laboratory tests and discussed the advisability of a rare operation, Mrs. Barber lay in bed and ate.

*From* Time *magazine, March 13, 1939.*

Accompanying the brief article was a photo of Dorothy Barber in bed in a long-sleeved hospital gown, a close-up picture showing only her face, head, and arms, with the bedclothes over her chest. The caption read, "Insatiable Eater Barber—She Eats Enough For Ten." The Missouri Supreme Court, while allowing the need to educate the public about even unusual medical conditions, noted that medical textbooks typically preserve the anonymity of the afflicted persons depicted within. "If there is any right of privacy at all, it should include the right to obtain medical treatment at home or in a hospital for an individual personal condition (at least if it is not contagious or dangerous to others) without personal publicity."

In another early and often-cited case, an Alabama newspaper ran on its front page an embarrassing photo of Flora Bell Graham, who, while attending the Cullman County Fair, accompanied her children to the "Fun House." While leaving the building, her dress was blown up by air jets and "her body was exposed from the waist down, with the exception of that portion covered by her panties." It was at that moment that the paper's photographer snapped the shot, unbeknownst to Graham. In ruling for the plaintiff, the court engaged in what we would likely today think of as a bit of rhetorical excess. "Not only was this photograph embarrassing to one of normal sensibilities," Justice Harwood wrote for the Alabama Supreme Court, "we think it could properly be classified as obscene, in that obscene means 'offensive to modesty or decency' or expressing to the mind or view something which delicacy, purity, or decency forbid to be expressed."[86]

Another case frequently cited in support of the principle that unconscionable intrusions into individuals' privacy should be restrained concerned film

---

[86]*Daily Times Democrat v. Graham*, 162 So. 2d 474, 477 (Sup. Ct. Ala. 1964).

documentarian Fred Wiseman's *Titicut Follies.*[87] The film depicted conditions in the Massachusetts Correctional Institution at Bridgewater, which housed "insane persons charged with crime, and defective delinquents." As a result of the suit, for many years showings of the film were restricted to audiences of mental health and similar professionals. Only in recent years, largely owing to the death of most or all of the patients depicted, has the film been made available for general release. Although the court's decision was apparently based on its fear that the film would subject the inmates to intense humiliation, several commentators suggested that the real impetus behind the suit was government officials' fear that the unconscionable conditions at Bridgewater would be exposed to public view.

*Graham* and *Barber* are rather old cases, and the *Titicut Follies* case is open to conflicting interpretations. Nowadays, even on the few occasions when a publication of private information is so revealing as to seem "offensive," courts rarely impose liability, due in large part to the impact of the tort's final element—a lack of newsworthiness.

## Newsworthiness: Has the Defense Swallowed the Tort?

Newsworthiness is often referred to somewhat inaccurately as a defense to public disclosure suits. This statement is in error because it misplaces the burden of proof. In actuality, the burden is on the plaintiff to demonstrate that the offensive revelations of private information are *not* newsworthy, are *not* of public concern. In any event, it is clear that courts have made it very difficult indeed for plaintiffs to establish that revelations of embarrassing truths about them lack newsworthiness.

One of the leading cases on this point concerned young William Sidis, who might be described as the "Doogie Howser" of his day, although his field of endeavor was mathematics rather than medicine. At the age of eleven, Sidis lectured to distinguished mathematicians on the subject of four-dimensional bodies. When he was sixteen, he was graduated from Harvard College, amid considerable public attention. Then Sidis dropped out of public sight for many years and became something of a recluse, at least until the *New Yorker* found him.

The magazine often included within its pages a feature called "Where Are They Now?" which, as its name implies, sought to bring readers up to date on the once famous. The article's subtitle, "April Fool," neatly encapsulates what the Second Circuit Court of Appeals saw as the piece's condescending and abusive tone. The magazine focused on the "bizarre ways" in which Sidis's genius was manifested, such as his penchant for collecting streetcar transfers.

Although the court concluded that the essay was "merciless in its dissection of intimate details of its subject's personal life," Sidis's privacy claim was rejected. There are times, Judge Swan wrote, when "the public interest in obtaining

---

[87]*Commonwealth of Massachusetts v. Wiseman*, 49 N.E.2d 610 (1969), *cert. denied*, 398 U.S. 960 (1970).

information becomes dominant over the individual's desire for privacy."[88] This was surely such a case, the court concluded, in that the *New Yorker* piece had at least the potential for answering a very important question: whether Sidis had lived up to his earlier promise. The answer to that question cannot help but have implications for public policy. After all, how better to determine if society's treatment of child prodigies is for the good than to examine the lives of such persons when they are no longer children?

Just to give a sense of how felicitous courts have been to claims of newsworthiness in recent years, consider Carl DeGregorio's unsuccessful invasion of privacy suit against CBS. The plaintiff, a construction worker, was upset at the station's having included in a story on "Romance in New York" video footage of him walking hand in hand with an unmarried female coworker. The court surmised that "the perceived novelty of these two hard hats walking in romantic linkage apparently triggered the camera crew's interest." DeGregorio pleaded with the CBS crew to not run the footage. "It would not look good," he pleaded, in that he was married, and the young woman was herself engaged to be married. His plea was not heeded, thus his suit for invasion of privacy. In dismissing the claims against the television network, the court interpreted "newsworthiness" as broad enough to include "an exploration of prevailing attitudes towards [romance.]."[89]

Does newsworthiness wear off over time, or do persons whose fame has faded have a right to live in relative anonymity? Although the *Sidis* case seems to stand for the principle "once newsworthy, always newsworthy," it is possible that the public policy implications discussed earlier—that we need to follow up on former child prodigies to assess how well or poorly education of the gifted is conducted—makes the precedent a limited one.

Some courts have decided that people have a right to turn over a new leaf, to transcend past mistakes, and to get on with their lives in relative solitude. The issue in *Briscoe v. Reader's Digest*[90] was the magazine's story about the crime of truck hijacking, a small part of which reminded readers of Briscoe's conviction years before for this offense. The California Supreme Court, in overturning a lower court's having granted summary judgment in favor of the magazine, emphasized that plaintiff had "abandoned his life of shame and become entirely rehabilitated and has thereafter at all times lived an exemplary, virtuous and honorable life," that he had "assumed a place in respectable society and made many friends who were not aware of the incident in his earlier life." Protection of the privacy interests of such a plaintiff would be in the public interest, the court found, in that doing so would foster "the state's interest in the integrity of the rehabilitative process."

---

[88]*Sidis v. F-R Publications,* 113 F.2d 806 (2d Cir. 1940). Interestingly, the author of the *New Yorker* essay retained a bit of privacy himself. The interviewer was noted humorist James Thurber, writing under the pseudonym Jared Manley. See Richard S. Murphy, "Property Rights in Personal Information: An Economic Defense of Privacy," 84 *Georgetown Law Journal* 2381, 2394 (1996).

[89]*DeGregorio v. CBS,* 473 N.Y.S. 922 (Sup. Ct. New York County 1984).

[90]483 P.2d 34 (1971).

Correctional systems, the court suggested, are predicated on faith that "the rehabilitated offender can rejoin that great bulk of the community from which he has
been ostracized for his anti-social acts. In return for becoming a 'new man,' he is
allowed to melt into the shadows of obscurity."

Although the court recognized the public's legitimate desire to learn about
the criminal justice system and allowed that even criminal *suspects* necessarily for-
feit some of their rights of privacy, it emphasized that the public interest is most
strong when the crime is a recent one. Identification of individuals involved in
crimes long ago serves neither "to bring forth witnesses" nor to "obtain succor for
victims." Indeed, the only public "interest" served is that of curiosity.

If *Briscoe* had stood for the broad principle that newsworthiness fades over
time, a more recent California Supreme Court decision makes clear that the earlier
case's scope should be limited to its facts, to situations involving the reporting
of long-forgotten criminal wrongdoing. *Forsher v. Bugliosi*[91] is a complicated libel
and invasion of privacy suit against the authors and publishers of the book *Helter
Skelter* by a plaintiff who apparently played a very tangential role in the Manson
family. In upholding the granting of summary judgment to the defendants, the appellate court looked back on *Briscoe* as "an exception to the more general rule that
once a man has become a public figure, or news, he remains a matter of legitimate
recall to the public mind to the end of his days."

Professor Diane Zimmerman reports that *Briscoe* and cases like it are indeed
historic artifacts, and she is pleased by this turn of events. "It is difficult to imagine how the passage of time could constitute a serious consideration in determining newsworthiness," she argues. "Such a standard would make the exploration of
modern history a hazardous enterprise."[92]

The media have little to fear from public disclosure suits these days, Zimmerman argues, because, more often than not, courts asked to adjudicate the issue
of newsworthiness have come to embrace a model that she calls "leave it to the
press." The familiar *New York Times'* enduring masthead boasts that readers will
find within "all the news that's fit to print." Courts that are called on to adjudicate
the media's newsworthiness defense in public disclosure suits seem to take these
words to heart, ruling in perhaps circular fashion that if a subject matter has appeared in the news media, it must be news, that is, must be news*worthy*. Zimmerman sees this view as only appropriate. The press "has a better mechanism for
testing newsworthiness than do the courts," she argues, in that media outlets' economic survival "depends upon their ability to provide a product that the public
will buy."

There are at least two more reasons why public disclosure cases have become
all but unwinnable. The first requires us to recognize that the law has not always
treated the elements of the tort as independent; rather they sometimes are allowed

---

[91]608 P.2d 716 (Cal. 1980).

[92]Zimmerman, "Requiem for a Heavyweight," n.75.

to flow together. Thus a court's adjudication of the newsworthiness issue often leads it to make conclusions about other elements, such as whether the revelations were truly private, or whether they were highly offensive.

It is hard to imagine a category of revelation both more private and more highly offensive than allegations of childhood sexual abuse. In a case decided in the early 1990s by a federal district court in Pennsylvania, the offensiveness of the revelations was compounded; the mother and daughter who had accused the father were promised falsely by the media that their names would not be used and that their silhouetted picture would be unrecognizable. Their invasion of privacy suit was unsuccessful because the court found that the story was highly newsworthy, especially given that the accused was a former police chief. For a court to rule in favor of the media in such a case is hardly remarkable. What is puzzling, however, is that the court allowed the newsworthiness of the information to compel the conclusions that the revelations were neither private information nor highly offensive ("except in the abstract," the court allowed).[93]

A second reason that it might be time to bury the public disclosure tort is that the Supreme Court has weighed in on the issue of the tort's constitutionality. Although the Court has stopped short of immunizing the press for reports of the truth, it has come mighty close to doing just that.

## The Supreme Court and the Public Disclosure Tort

No suit for public disclosure has ever withstood U.S. Supreme Court scrutiny. Although there have been only two such cases, a careful reading of them provides further support for the principle that the public disclosure tort has been virtually removed from the law.

Both cases involved press reports of rape that included the victim's name. In *Cox Broadcasting v. Cohn*,[94] WSB-TV in Georgia reported the name of the victim of a vicious gang rape and homicide, information its reporter had obtained from the official indictment provided to him by the clerk of the court. The deceased's father then brought a privacy suit against the owner of the broadcast station.

The Court declined in *Cox* to rule on the central question—"whether truthful publications may *ever* be subjected to civil or criminal liability consistently with the First Amendment" (emphasis added)—instead emphasizing the specific facts of the case to produce a narrow holding. Cohn may not prevail, the Court held, but only because the broadcaster obtained the private information from a governmental source.

*Florida Star v. B.J.F.*[95] also involved reporting of a rape victim's name, but there were two important differences between the facts here and in the earlier *Cox*

---

[93]*Morgan by and through Chambon v. Celender,* 780 F. Supp. 307, 310 (W.D. Pa. 1992).

[94]420 U.S. 469 (1975).

[95]491 U.S. 524 (1989).

*Broadcasting* case. First, the rape victim was still alive (and her rapist still at large). Indeed, as a result of the publication from which the suit flowed, the rapist phoned the victim's mother, threatening to attack her again. Second, although here too the media obtained the victim's name from a governmental source, the reporter clearly was on notice from the outset that the information was being given to him by mistake. To be sure, BJF's name was included in the sheriff department's incident report, but prominently displayed in the same court room where that paper was distributed to reporters was a sign reminding the media that Florida law prohibited publication of the names of sex crime victims.

Here, as in *Cox Broadcasting*, the Court makes clear that it does not intend to close the door on the possibility that a future public disclosure plaintiff might prevail against the press for its reporting of admittedly true information. "Our cases have carefully eschewed reaching [the] ultimate question of [whether] truthful publication may [e]ver be punished consistent with the First Amendment," the majority further cautioned.

The Court came rather close to reaching that ultimate question, however. Whereas it could simply have followed *Cox Broadcasting* to rest its holding on the basis that the *Florida Star* reporter had obtained the victim's name from a governmental source, it chose not to do so. The earlier case was different, the Court tells us, in that a trial was under way, thus tipping the First Amendment scales in favor of the public's right to observe the judicial process. Here, there was only a police report; a trial had not begun, a suspect had not yet even been identified. The Court held instead that the *Star*'s story could not be sanctioned because the victim's name was "lawfully obtained." Although the Court later suggests that even truthful, lawfully obtained information might be the impetus for a successful public disclosure suit, it emphasizes even here that the state would need to be furthering

 # Things to Remember

**PUBLIC DISCLOSURE**

- Public disclosure is the only one of the four privacy torts that really added anything new to the law.
- The tort consists of these elements:
  - Information is published.
  - That information was previously private.
  - The revelation offends public sensibilities.
  - The revelation is not newsworthy.
- In recent years, the newsworthiness defense seems to have swallowed the tort.
- It is virtually impossible for public disclosure plaintiffs to prevail against the media.

a "narrowly tailored" interest of "the highest order." If helping to protect the life of a rape victim whose assailant has not yet been apprehended does not constitute such a compelling state's interest, one wonders if anything possibly could.

## I *May* Publish it, but *Should* I Publish It?

If the public disclosure tort is the only privacy tort that added something truly new to the law and if plaintiffs rarely prevail on their public disclosure claims, privacy is best thought of as an *extra*legal, ethical question. It is not surprising that the two leading U.S. Supreme Court public disclosure decisions have both dealt with the naming of rape victims. Recall that one of the elements of the public disclosure tort is that the revelation be highly offensive. Traditionally, there are few factual revelations viewed as more likely to offend than the naming of a rape victim. The executive director of a rape crisis center in Florida put it this way:

> Sexual assault is the most underreported crime in our society. Yet it is one of the most damaging. Years after the crime occurs victims still suffer from the shame, embarrassment, degradation, nightmares and flashbacks.… If the victims are shamed into silence when we are not printing the names, what will they resort to if their names are available for public scrutiny? Why should we have access to some of the most private issues in a person's life? Because they were victimized by another and forced into a role they never would have chosen for themselves? What good does it do for individuals to know who has been humiliated by another? Does this not further degrade them? There is no benefit to this disclosure.[96]

Another letter to the editor of the same newspaper takes to task those who argue in favor of disclosing rape victims' names on the grounds that we should not treat this crime differently from any other:

> Society still has a victim-blaming mentality. How many victims of a burglary are asked what they were wearing at the time of the crime and then hear whispered that they "probably were looking for it"? How many victims of scams and frauds have their underwear passed around for inspection by a jury? There is a very big difference between rape and other crimes.[97]

While she was editor of the *Des Moines Register,* Geneva Overholser offered an eloquent argument in favor of naming names. "Does not our very delicacy in dealing with rape victims subscribe to the idea that rape is a crime of sex rather

---

[96]Nancy A. Moores, "Rape Victims' Names Should Be Kept Secret" [Letters to Editor], *St. Petersburg Times,* 24 Jan. 1995, p. 2.

[97]Judi Barrett, "Rape Victims' Names Should Not Be Published, Say Readers," *St. Petersburg Times,* 15 Jan. 1995, p. 3D.

than the crime of brutal violence that it really is?" Editors, in her opinion, should therefore encourage rape survivors to come forward and tell their tales without the shield of anonymity. Even Overholser, however, stopped short of suggesting that the media should publish the names of unwilling subjects:

> If I seek a world in which newspapers routinely print rape victims' names, it is also a world in which rape victims are treated compassionately, the stigma eradicated. So I am unwilling to sacrifice today's unwilling victims for long-term good. Yet I believe that we will not break down the stigma until more and more women take public stands. I will go on with the general rule, as most newspapers do, despite my dislike of it.... Rape is an American shame. Our society needs to see that and attend to it, not hide it or hush it up.[98]

---

[98]Geneva Overholser, "Why Hide Rapes?" *New York Times,* 11 July 1989, p. A19.

## Chapter Summary

The tort law of privacy is a relative newcomer to the United States, owing much of its birth to an 1890 law review article. Generally, states now recognize some of or all four distinct privacy torts: appropriation, intrusion, false light, and public disclosure.

Appropriation means the exploiting of another person's name or likeness for commercial gain. Suits can be prompted by the use of models chosen to look like or sound like a celebrity. Uses that can plausibly be considered political speech rarely can result in liability. Then, too, the media have virtual carte blanche to commercially exploit images that they have once before used in a legitimate news context.

The intrusion tort does not necessarily involve publication at all. The offense occurs at the news gathering stage, as in stalking news subjects or otherwise intruding relentlessly into their personal space. News media have been put on alert by a number of recent decisions that if they cooperate too closely with law enforcement officials in the live coverage of the execution of search warrants or police raids, they might be sued along with the government for violation of the subject's civil rights.

False light actions are similar to libel except that the publication need only be embarrassing, it need not be defamatory. When suing over revelations of matters of public concern, false light plaintiffs must prove actual malice.

Appropriation is very similar to copyright and trademark infringements. Intrusion is an offshoot of trespass law. False light suits are often thought of as attempts to circumvent the constitutional protections offered to libel defendants. As such, the public disclosure tort, which makes actionable the reporting of true but embarrassing, previously private, nonnewsworthy facts, is the only one of the four torts that adds much to the law. Since at least the early 1990s, in large part because the courts embrace the newsworthiness defense so wholeheartedly, public disclosure plaintiffs almost never prevail against the media.

chapter

# *Copyright and Trademark*

An old folk song in the trade labor movement asks, "Which side are you on?" From this vantage point, the subject matter of the current chapter is unique. Professional communicators, from journalists to film producers and musicians, are just as likely to be plaintiffs as defendants in copyright infringement suits (and, to a lesser extent, in trademark litigation as well). Authors are sued by other authors, musicians by other musicians, film producers by playwrights or novelists who claim the basis for today's blockbuster was really their lesser known but equally worthy work. Then, too, consider how conflicted most universities feel about their own role in this area of law. On one hand, institutions of higher learning will embrace the rights of their faculty who write books and other creative works that qualify for copyright protection. University libraries, however, also argue strenuously for the right to make photocopies for scholarly use of book chapters or journal articles without seeking out the permission of or feeling the need to reimburse *those* authors.[1]

The federal constitution, in Article I, Section 8, tells Congress that it may create laws to protect "for limited times to authors and inventors the exclusive right to their respective writings and discoveries." That body of law designed to protect inventors is patent law. Most patents remain in force for seventeen years, although patents issued after 1995 extend for twenty years. Although a patent can be awarded to the inventor of an improved printing press, the inventor of the proverbial "better mousetrap" can also receive one. Patent law thus does not inherently concern the act of communication and for that reason is beyond the scope of this book.

The two other areas of law that stem from the Article I, Section 8, excerpt cited in the previous paragraph are copyright and trademark. Copyright protects a creative work itself, such as a book, movie, play, photograph, or song. Trademark is designed to protect the slogans, logos, and trade names used by companies to identify their products so as to avoid consumer confusion. If you think you are buying a pair of Nike footwear, you would be very upset if your purchase was not in fact manufactured by that particular company. Although the two bodies of law

---

[1]Kenneth D. Crews, *Copyright, Fair Use, and the Challenge for Universities* (Chicago: University of Chicago Press, 1993).

protect different things, the philosophy behind them is remarkably similar. Both copyright and trademark are designed to protect the interests of the public itself, although the immediate beneficiary may be an individual artist or corporation. In the case of copyright, protection for the financial interests of authors and other creative artists exists to encourage them to produce so that we all can enjoy the fruits of their labors. Trademark also creates a financial incentive for businesses to create worthwhile goods and services. Such companies want the public to have pleasant mental associations with their brand name and logo. Again, a body of law designed in the end to benefit the public at large does its work by giving financial incentives to others who will then create things we will want to consume.

One key difference between the two bodies of law is that copyright lasts for a fixed period of time, whereas trademark protection can continue as long as a company is in the business of marketing the products identified by a particular trademark. Indeed, this contrast may itself have been an impetus behind Congress's decision in 1998 to extend copyright duration. Ever since the major overhaul of copyright law conducted in 1976 took effect, protection lasted for the life of the author or artist plus fifty years, or for a total of seventy-five years in the case of a corporate owner. So it was that copyright protection was set to expire on some early Disney creations, including several of the first Mickey Mouse films, in the late 1990s and early 2000s. Yet Mickey Mouse himself could have been used as an exclusive trademark by the Disney company. If this sounds a bit confusing, rest assured you are not alone. Indeed, lawyers who specialize in these areas of the law are not quite sure what will happen if and when, for example, a vendor wishes to sell T-shirts or other merchandise bearing a still photo of Mickey taken from one of his early films, such as "Steamboat Willie." The film itself will have reverted back from the copyright owner to the public, but the use of Mickey's image to sell merchandise would theoretically be seen as an infringement of Disney's continuing trademark interest. Such a scenario is neither whimsical nor fanciful. In 2000, a federal appellate court dealt with precisely this issue when the company owning the rights to market the Three Stooges sued the producers of *The Long Kiss Goodnight,* a popular film that used without permission a 30-second segment of the Stooges' film, *Disorder in the Court,* as one scene's visual background. The court ruled for the defendant corporation, in that the copyright on the Stooges's film had long since expired. The court opinion indicates, however, that a different case would have been presented had the defendant instead been in the business of selling T-shirts with Moe, Larry, and Curly's pictures on them.[2]

The need to clarify such matters was postponed a bit when, in late 1998, Congress passed the Copyright Term Extension Act[3] (opponents derided it as the "Steamboat Willie Rule"). The Act provides that copyright now lasts twenty years longer than had been provided for in 1976. For works created by individuals, this

---

[2]*Comedy III Productions, Inc. v. New Line Cinema,* 200 F.3d 593 (9th Cir. 2000).

[3]P.L. 105-298, amending 17 U.S.C.S. secs. 108, 203, and 301–4.

# Things to Remember

**BASICS OF INTELLECTUAL PROPERTY LAW**

- Article I, Section 8, of the U.S. Constitution gives Congress the right to protect intellectual property.
- The three main branches of intellectual property law are patent, trademark, and copyright:
  - Patent protects functional devices and is beyond the scope of this book.
  - Copyright protects creative works such as writing, music, and art.
  - Trademark protects words, slogans, and other devices used to identify a company's goods.

extension will generally mean for the life of the creator plus seventy years. Works with corporate authorship will now be protected for ninety-five years after the date of first publication, or 120 years after the work's creation, whichever comes first.

The Act provided a measure of retroactivity in that works already created and otherwise due to enter the public domain will also enjoy an extension for a period of twenty years. This latter provision seemed to some constitutionally suspect. After all, Article I, Section 8, tells Congress that it may enact copyright laws "to promote" the creation of artistic and literary works. Retroactive extensions of a copyright's term promotes nothing, in that the affected works are already in existence. Federal courts have rejected this argument, however, holding that Congress had enormous discretion to determine the duration of copyright.[4]

## The Law of Copyright

Let us suppose that, twenty years from now, you have achieved a level of fame in your chosen field that makes yours a household name as much as the best-known and admired movie stars, sports figures, or political leaders. Imagine further that a former boyfriend or girlfriend, out of spite or greed, decides to write a "kiss and tell" book in which you will feature prominently, and that this author intends to reprint several love letters from you still in his or her possession. You bring suit, seeking an injunction against the use of your letters in the book as well as the return of the original letters to you. The chances are that your first wish will be honored but not your second, because the love letters, the actual papers with your handwriting on them, are the physical property of your ex-flame. You gave them freely, and a gift is a gift. The words you used to express your feelings at the time

---

[4]*Eldred v. Reno,* 74 F. Supp. 2d 1 (D.C. 1999), *aff'd,* 239 F.3d 372 (D.C. Cir. 2001).

may still belong to you, however, and only you can decide if and when they will ever be published. That is the essence of the law of **intellectual property,** of which copyright is part. We use the word *property* to describe it, even if that which is possessed is somewhat ethereal or intangible.

The first copyright law in the United States was adopted in 1790. Copyright law was significantly revised in 1909 and again in 1976. Most of the discussion in this chapter is based on the 1976 law, although it too has been revised in some ways since then, largely to make allowances for new technologies and to help bring the U.S. body of law in better sync with the international law of copyright.

## Copyright's Scope

U.S. copyright law protects "original works of authorship, fixed in any tangible medium of expression." The statute enumerates many general categories of creative works, including literary works; musical works (both the musical notes and the lyrics, if any); dramatic works (i.e., plays, including musicals); pantomimes and choreographic works; pictorial, graphic, and sculptural works; motion pictures and other audiovisual works; sound recordings; and architectural works.

A few clarifying points are in order. First, do not get carried away by the word *literary* in the first category. Yes, works of great literature are protected here, but so too is the letter a college student writes to her parents asking for more money. This book you are reading is copyrighted, and so too are the sample examination questions in the instructor's manual. In other words, *words* is the key. The first category protects creative works that are made up of words.

Although it may not seem intuitive, computer programs are treated as literary works. The history, as well as the politics, of how software came to be accepted by federal copyright examiners is long and fascinating. For our purposes, suffice it to say that the silicon chip industry realized early on that the patent application process can drag on far longer than the useful life of the software itself, whereas copyright protection is born with the creation of the product. In any event, the argument can be made that computer programs are, in essence, a set of instructions (from the programmer to the computer itself) and that these "communications" should be protected just as would any textual, "literary" work.

As with literary works, we should not assume that "pictorial," "graphic," and "sculptural" works will always be the kinds of high art creations collected by museums. Copyright also covers such useful art as clothing design. In a suit involving competing dress designers, for example, the Court of Appeals for the Second Circuit accepted as copyrightable a design consisting of "a geometric arrangement of color blocks banded in heavy lines" used on women's pullover tops.[5]

With respect to musical works, it is important to note that copyrights can apply to the composition itself (as expressed typically in sheet music) and also to a particular performance of the composition (on a cassette or CD). Also, if music is

---

[5]*North Coast Industries v. Jason Maxwell, Inc.,* 972 F.2d 1031 (2d Cir. 1992).

considered a function of rhythm, harmony, and melody, courts tend to emphasize melody as the heart of a musical work most likely to make it copyrightable.[6] A particular arrangement of a well-known melody can itself be copyrightable and indeed quite valuable, however, as is the case, for example, with Nelson Riddle's arrangements of many of the tunes made popular by Frank Sinatra.

What does it mean to say that a work must be "fixed" in some kind of "tangible medium of expression" to be copyrightable? Consider the "pantomimes and choreographic works" category as an example. If you dance up a storm at a party, no matter how much you impress the other guests and how many of them try to mimic your steps, your creation is not yet copyrightable. The reason is not just because it was live and spontaneous. It will not be copyrightable even if you can repeat it step by step, move by move, on command. If, however, you commit to writing something resembling choreographic notation for your dance steps—and you need not be very professional about it—you will have a potentially copyrightable work. The same requirement that a work be set down in some fixed medium applies to all the categories.

To be copyrightable, a work must also be "original." Being original does not mean that it needs to be the expression of an earth-shattering, paradigm-shifting revelation. The law is not nearly so strict. Think of the many times you have seen the proverbial "feeding frenzy" of media coverage of a live media event. Dozens of flash cameras go off again and again. Each photograph that results is eligible for copyright protection, even if a particular photo is barely distinguishable in terms of lighting, angle, and composition from several other photos.

That which is original in your work might be simply the way you have organized others' materials. Perhaps your local newspaper, in addition to offering its own reviews of new movies, provides a summary of what other well-known film critics have had to say about the film. The *Boston Globe* offers this kind of service through syndication to other publications (see Figure 6.1). The presentation of these comparisons among many movie critics' comments is itself copyrightable, even though the simple fact that "Ebert gave it a thumbs up" is not copyrightable. Or, think of newspaper sports pages that often include very detailed information about the records of two baseball pitchers about to face each other in an important game. The statistics that comprise such a feature—overall win–loss record, more focused win–loss record against this particular opponent, and so on—are themselves not copyrightable in that they are readily available facts. The writer's choice of which statistics to present and how to present them, however, may enjoy copyright protection.[7] These kinds of situations are referred to by the U.S. Copyright Office as **compilations,** which the Copyright Act defines as "a work formed by the collection and assembly of preexisting materials or of data that are selected, coordinated, or arranged in such a way that the resulting work as a whole constitutes an original work of authorship."

[6]*Northern Music Corp. v. King Record Distributing Co.,* 105 F. Supp. 393 (1952).

[7]*Kregos v. Associated Press,* 3 F.3d 656 (2d Cir. 1993).

## Figure 6.1  *Boston Globe Movies Chart*

| CRITICAL CHOICES | BOSTON GLOBE | TIME | NEW YORK TIMES | PEOPLE | NEWSWEEK | LOS ANGELES TIMES | HOLLYWOOD REPORTER | BOSTON PHOENIX |
|---|---|---|---|---|---|---|---|---|
| AIR BUD: GOLDEN RECEIVER | ● | | | | | | ● | |
| UN AIR DE FAMILLE | ★ | ★ | | ● | | ★ | | ● |
| ARMAGEDDON | ● | ○ | ○ | ★ | ★ | ○ | ★ | ○ |
| BASKETBALL | ○ | ★ | ● | ○ | ○ | ○ | ★ | ○ |
| BILLY'S HOLLYWOOD SCREEN TEST | ★ | ★ | | ★ | | ★ | ★ | ● |
| BUFFALO 66 | ● | ★ | ★ | ○ | | ★ | ○ | ● |
| DISTURBING BEHAVIOR | ● | ○ | ○ | ● | ○ | ○ | ○ | ○ |
| DR. DOLITTLE | ● | ★ | ○ | ★ | ★ | ○ | ● | ● |
| EVER AFTER | ★ | ○ | | ★ | ★ | ● | ★ | ○ |
| FIRST LOVE, LAST RITES | ○ | | | | | ○ | ● | |
| THE GOVERNESS | ● | ★ | | ○ | | ● | ★ | ★ |
| HALLOWEEN: H2O | ○ | ○ | | ● | ★ | ★ | ● | ● |
| HIGH ART | ★ | ● | | ○ | | ● | ★ | ★ |
| HOMEGROWN | ○ | . | | | | ○ | ★ | |
| HOW STELLA GOT HER GROOVE BACK | ★ | | ★ | | ★ | | ★ | |
| LETHAL WEAPON 4 | ○ | ★ | | | ○ | ○ | ★ | ○ |
| MADELINE | ★ | ● | ○ | ● | | ● | ★ | ● |
| MAFIA! | ○ | ● | | | | ○ | ○ | ★ |
| THE MASK OF ZORRO | ★ | ★ | ★ | ★ | ★ | ★ | ○ | ★ |
| MULAN | ★ | ○ | ★ | ★ | ★ | ● | ★ | ★ |
| THE NEGOTIATOR | ● | ○ | ● | ★ | ★ | ● | ★ | ○ |
| THE OPPOSITE SEX | ★ | ★ | ★ | | | ★ | ★ | ○ |
| THE PARENT TRAP | ● | ● | | ★ | ★ | ★ | ★ | ★ |
| π | ★ | ★ | | | | ★ | ★ | ★ |
| POLISH WEDDING | ○ | ○ | | ○ | | ● | ★ | ○ |
| RETURN TO PARADISE | ● | | | | | ● | | |
| SAFE MEN | ● | ○ | | | | ● | ○ | ● |
| SAVING PRIVATE RYAN | ★ | ★ | ★ | ★ | ★ | ★ | ★ | ★ |
| SMALL SOLDIERS | ★ | ○ | | ○ | ○ | ● | ★ | ★ |
| SMOKE SIGNALS | ★ | ★ | | ★ | ★ | ★ | ★ | ★ |
| SNAKE EYES | ● | ● | | ○ | ● | ○ | ○ | ● |
| THERE'S SOMETHING ABOUT MARY | ★ | ★ | ● | | ★ | ★ | ★ | ★ |
| THE THIEF | ★ | ★ | | ★ | | ★ | ★ | ● |
| THE TRUMAN SHOW | ★ | ★ | ★ | ★ | ★ | ★ | ★ | ★ |
| WESTERN | ★ | ★ | | ★ | | ★ | ○ | ★ |

KEY
★ RECOMMENDED
● A MIXED BAG
○ DON'T BOTHER

This chart is legitimately copyrightable as a compilation, even though it consists of the mere fact that this or that reviewer liked or disliked a particular film.

*Reprinted courtesy of the* Boston Globe.

Not every collection of preexisting materials will be copyrightable, however. The organizer-author must demonstrate at least a modicum of creativity. The Supreme Court said as much in 1991 when it held that the names and phone numbers in an ordinary telephone directory (white pages) are not protected by copyright. A small publishing company in Kansas decided to create a multiarea white pages that would encompass about a dozen local phone company dialing areas. This way, users would avoid the hassle of having to consult multiple directories and the expense of having to make large numbers of directory assistance calls. One of the telephone companies in the area, however, refused to sell the publisher the rights to use its directory's listings as a basis for the larger book. When the publishing company decided to use the data anyway, without permission, a lawsuit resulted. The Court held that the telephone company's own listings were not legitimately copyrightable in the first place. All that the company did was to "take the data provided by its subscribers and list it alphabetically by surname." The resulting book was "a garden-variety white pages directory, devoid of even the slightest trace of creativity."[8]

**Collective works** are special kinds of compilations in which the individual components are themselves original works of authorship eligible for copyright (and, indeed, that may have been granted a copyright previously). A collection of previously published short stories or poems is a good example. The collection itself becomes copyrightable, although the editor of the compilation will not then take over ownership of the copyrights already accruing to the individual contributors to the volume. Note, too, that the editor must obtain permission to reprint each of the works still covered by copyright.

What about movie adaptations of novels or stage plays? These works fit into a category called **derivative works,** which build on preexisting works by recasting, transforming, or adapting them. A colorized version of a previously black-and-white movie is such a derivative work, as can be a movie or TV program that has been made accessible to the deaf or the blind through the addition of closed captioning or descriptive video services. The creator of the derivative work is granted a copyright

---

[8]*Feist Publications v. Rural Telephone Service Company,* 499 U.S. 340, 362 (1991).

## Things to Remember

### COPYRIGHT'S SCOPE

- Even the most mundane "literary works" are protected by copyright.
- Computer software is treated as a literary work.
- A work must be set down in some fixed medium before it becomes eligible for protection.
- At least a modicum of creativity in the work is also required.
- Mere facts are not copyrightable.
- A creative compilation of facts may sometimes be copyrightable.
- A collection of others' previously copyrighted works may itself be copyrightable.
- "Derivative" adaptations of earlier works can be copyrightable.

only for those creative elements that he or she added to the original, however. The people who add closed captioning to a TV program, for example, do not by this action earn a copyright to the program itself, only to the captioned version of it.

### Things That Cannot be Copyrighted

Not everything that can be set down into some fixed medium of communication is copyrightable. The *Feist* case discussed in the previous section—the one involving the competing telephone directories—serves as a reminder that mere facts cannot be copyrighted.

Consistent with the Copyright Act's insistence that the law is designed to protect works that are already created (rather than in the nascent planning stages), mere ideas are not copyrightable. Suppose that you read about the discovery of the remains of the *Titanic* back in 1985 and—creative soul that you are—began to imagine creating a screenplay about an actual *Titanic* survivor who also read about that discovery and contacted the scientists involved to tell her tale. That *idea* for a screenplay, even if you shared the idea in writing with others, does not allow you to sue the producers of the blockbuster film of the 1990s. Copyright law does not protect mere ideas.

Also excluded from copyright protection are formulas or methods of instruction. Consider a musical example. Hungarian composer Zoltán Kodály developed a method of teaching youngsters how to sight-read. Students were given a hand shape to associate mentally with each note of the octave. Eventually, the teacher could establish the key, and, upon seeing the conductor make the appropriate hand shape, the students would sing each desired new pitch. Could Kodály or one of his followers obtain a copyright for this brilliant pedagogical advance? Of course not. Anyone caring to write an article or textbook using the method or teaching teachers how to use the method, however, could be granted a copyright for such a literary work.

Also not copyrightable are works that the case law often refers to as "trivial," which is simply another way of emphasizing that originality is one requirement for copyright. The Copyright Office of the Library of Congress has set forth three categories of such trivial materials.[9] The first category consists of words and short phrases such as names, titles, and slogans. There are, for example, several songs by the name of "Goodnight, My Love." The "blank forms" category includes time cards, graph paper, scorecards, and address books, which are all designed for recording information but do not themselves convey any information. Finally, there are those works entirely dependent on information that is common property. Included here are standard calendars, height and weight charts, tape measures, and rulers. Obviously, if the author does add some originality to the commonplace, as we see in the decorative calendars sold by numerous companies, copyright can accrue to the unique design features involved.

---

[9]37 C.F.R. 202.1 (1998).

## How Can You Protect Your Copyright?

It was a classic *Seinfeld* episode. The "Soup Nazi," the owner-manager of a small carryout restaurant serving only soup, had a maddeningly authoritarian nature. He demanded that his customers enact a highly scripted routine for ordering their lunch, lest they be banished from the premises ("Out! OUT! No soup for YOU!"). It seems that Jerry Seinfeld's pal Elaine incurred the Soup Nazi's wrath, but managed to get back at him when she discovered that an armoire once belonging to the proprietor had dozens of his handwritten recipes in its drawers. "Why, I can copy these and deliver them to every restaurant in town. I can *publish* them!" she exclaims. In the episode's closing sequence, we learn that the Soup Nazi saw the handwriting on the wall and was going out of business.

Would copyright law really have permitted Elaine to copy and publish the recipes? The earlier example of the love letters and the kiss-and-tell book should give you the answer. Elaine may own the paper on which the recipes are written, but she does not own the recipes themselves. Would the Soup Nazi have had to take some affirmative steps, however, to establish his copyright? The shortest correct answer to that question is—yes and no. At least since 1989, when the United States brought its own copyright law more in line with the international conventions collectively known as the Berne Convention, it has been clear that a copyright is born the moment a creative work—which would include original recipes for different kinds of soup—is written down. Despite the ubiquity of copyright notices on everything from books to CD liner notes, the copyright holder is not legally required to take any affirmative steps to "earn" a copyright.

It would be foolish, however, *not* to register a copyrightable work to which the writer attributes significant value. Should you ever need to bring suit against another person who has infringed on your copyright, registration of your work enables you to obtain money damages and sometimes attorneys' fees as well. Prominent notice of such registration also puts potential infringers on notice that this work is, in fact, protected.

Registration is very easy. One need only pay a modest fee to the federal Copyright Office, fill out the appropriate form depending on the specific medium involved, and place a copyright notice on existing copies of the work. You will also be asked to provide the office with two copies of the work to be copyrighted. More information can be obtained from the Public Information Office, Library of Congress, Copyright Office, 101 Independence Avenue, SE, Washington, DC 20559-6000.

Copyright notices generally consist of these elements:

- The internationally accepted symbol © [℗ for sound recordings], and/or the word "copyright" or abbreviation "copr."
- The date of the copyright (typically the date of publication).
- The name of the copyright holder.

The Copyright Office gives detailed suggestions concerning *where* to place a copyright notice.[10] For books, the following places are appropriate for the copyright notice: the title page or the page immediately following it, either side of the front cover or of the back cover, or the first (or last) page of the main text. Any of these are also fine for a periodical, which might instead feature the copyright notice as part of its masthead. For computer disks and other works that require the use of some kind of machine to read, it is acceptable to have the copyright notice appear to the user the moment he or she logs on or indeed to have the notice visible as long as the program is running. Also acceptable is the use of some kind of gummed label on the disk itself. Motion picture copyright notices generally appear with or near the title or credits, and either at the beginning or the very end of the film. Three-dimensional works of art, such as sculpture, become a bit tricky. The regulations suggest that artists affix copyright notices in some appropriate manner (such as cementing) either to the work itself or to its base or mounting.

### Who Owns the Copyright?

Usually, the answer to the question of who owns a copyright is rather straightforward. The creator of a work—the author or artist—is the natural owner of a copyright to his or her work. Authors and artists do not always work alone, however. They may have collaborators, such as a lyricist joining forces with a composer, or a small group of writers who coauthor a book. In such cases, in the absence of a contract to the contrary, the creators will jointly and equally own a copyright.

Who owns the copyright to a motion picture? In the United States, even though film critics are fond of using the French word *auteur* (as in "writer" or "creator") when speaking of a film's director, typically the film studio insists that *it* be granted the copyright to the finished work before it will risk its millions of dollars and take on a project. Most other countries recognize what is called *le droit moral* (the "moral rights") of artists, which protects film directors' reputational interests in the integrity of their work even if they have signed away their *financial* rights to the studios. In those countries, directors have a great deal to say about whether or how their work can be altered, such as in the colorization of black-and-white films, the editing of films for television, or the creation of interactive CD-ROM versions of the movie narrative. The United States generally does not recognize such rights. The clash between the U.S. copyright system and *le droit moral* emerged most clearly when media mogul Ted Turner purchased the MGM Studios film library and made clear his intention to colorize many of the collection's older black-and-white films. Directors and other artists cried foul and unsuccessfully lobbied Congress to bring U.S. law in line with the international standard. When Turner contracted with a French television station to air a colorized version of John Huston's *The Asphalt Jungle,* the director obtained an injunction—in France, based on French law—that prevented the distribution of the colorized film in that one country.

---

[10]Copyright Office and Procedures, General Provisions, 37 C.F.R. 201.20 (1998).

Another complication affecting the ownership of copyrights is the **work for hire doctrine.** The general principle is quite straightforward. If your job description includes creating works that are copyrightable—such as drafting speeches for your company's president, or writing and editing the company newsletter—your employer rather than you will be the owner of the copyright.

The issue becomes a bit more complex when the artist or author is a contractor rather than an employee. In this context, a contractor can be anyone from a freelance reporter to an advertising agency hired to create a marketing brochure to a photographer asked to take appetizing photos of a restaurant's main dishes for its Web site. The Supreme Court provided some guidance for such situations in a rather poignant 1989 decision, *Community for Creative Non-Violence v. Reid.*[11] CCNV, an organization dedicated to advocacy on behalf of the homeless, approached sculptor James Earl Reid to create a Nativity scene featuring, in lieu of the traditional Holy Family, two adult and one infant African-American figures huddled for warmth on a steam grate. Reid donated his services, but was to be reimbursed for materials. Neither he nor CCNV founder Mitch Snyder apparently ever discussed the issue of copyright. After the completed statue had been placed on display for a few weeks in the winter of 1985–1986, it was sent to Reid for some needed repairs. A few months later, CCNV's request for the statue's return was denied, and both Reid and Snyder, in that order, filed competing certificates of registration for the sculpture with the Copyright Office.

In holding that Reid should not be considered an employee of CCNV, the unanimous Court concluded that many factors should go into such determinations, including the hiring party's right to control the manner and means by which the product is accomplished, the nature of the skill required to complete the

---

[11]490 U.S. 730 (1989).

 # Things to Remember

### RECOGNITION OF COPYRIGHTS

- Things that are generally not copyrightable include the following:
  - Mere ideas.
  - Methods of instruction.
  - "Trivial works" such as name, titles, and slogans.
- Copyright attaches to a work the moment it is set down.
- Registering a work is necessary, however, to win damages against an infringer.
- The Copyright Office provides detailed instructions for posting copyright notice on or near the work.
- The artistic creator is the "natural" owner of the copyright, but often the "work for hire" doctrine dictates that the person or group footing the bill is the true owner.

project, and the extent of the hired party's discretion over when and how long to work. Using these criteria, the Court concluded that Reid should be considered an independent contractor rather than an employee.

### Bringing a Copyright Infringement Suit

The word *copyright* seems to say it all. It grants the owner the right to "copy" the protected work. Copyright infringement is thus the unauthorized copying of that protected work. It can refer to such obviously illegal actions as marketing bootleg copies of CDs or movies. The creation of adaptations of protected works (e.g., making a movie of a popular novel) without permission is similarly forbidden. So, too, is the "public performance" of a work without permission. This part of the Copyright Act means that it is technically a violation of law for a family restaurant, if it fails to pay licensing fees to the appropriate music clearinghouse, to have its staff sing "Happy Birthday" to its patrons on that special day.

In the real world, most copyright conflicts do not result in litigation. More typically, a letter is drafted by the potential plaintiff to the suspected infringer, demanding that the infringement stop. If the case does come to court, typical remedies are an injunction as well as damages that can include both the plaintiff's lost income *and* the income illegally obtained by the infringer. These two broad categories of monetary damages are not necessarily the same thing. If, without your permission, I create a movie based on your book, I might create more income for you than you had been enjoying on your own, in that viewing my film might encourage viewers to "read more about it." You may nonetheless be entitled to receive my profits as part of your damages award. Then, too, there are statutorily provided damage awards that plaintiffs may fall back on. Currently, these awards range from $500 to $20,000, with some exceptions. For example, judges have the discretion, in the case of defendants who can prove that they *innocently* infringed ("I obtained permission from the person listed on the copyright notice. How was I to know that he did not really own the work?"), to reduce the minimum award to $200. At the other end, especially egregious violations, such as the kind of willful taking involved when the copyright holder explicitly rejects your request for rights to reprint a protected work but you do it anyway, the maximum award can be as high as $100,000. The extreme case of systematic marketing of bootlegged works can be a criminal offense, punishable by a hefty fine and some jail time.

Copyright owners who choose to bring suit must prove three elements: originality, access, and substantial similarity.

*Originality.*    A copyright infringement plaintiff must first establish that the material alleged to have been stolen was original enough to have been legitimately copyrightable in the first place. This lesson was driven home by the Supreme Court majority in *Feist Publications v. Rural Telephone Service Company,*[12] a case mentioned in

---

[12]499 U.S. 340 (1991).

the earlier discussion of compilations. Here a phone company sued a publisher for copying its subscriber listings in the course of compiling its own phone directory designed to cover a wider territory. The key issue in front of the Court was whether the alphabetical listings in the Rural Telephone Service Company's book should ever have been granted a copyright. Writing for the majority, Justice O'Connor concluded that the phone company's listing of its subscribers' names, addresses, and telephone numbers were not sufficiently original to be copyrightable.

*Access.*    The element of access in copyright infringement suits is somewhat analogous to proving that a criminal defendant had the opportunity to commit the crime. One cannot steal that which one never knew existed. It is not often possible to *prove* access in the sense of producing a witness to testify that the defendant became aware of the plaintiff's original work at a certain place and time. Often, access is demonstrated more inferentially. Thus, when former Beatle George Harrison was sued because his song "My Sweet Lord" seemed to be an unauthorized copying of the earlier hit song "He's So Fine," the plaintiff pointed to how popular the Chiffons hit had been in its day (it had been at the top of the Billboard charts for five weeks).[13]

*Substantial Similarity.*    Except in those instances where a defendant has clearly marketed bootleg or otherwise unauthorized copies of an original work, it is necessary for plaintiffs to demonstrate that the fruits of the infringer's labors are so similar to their own copyrighted work as to constitute the theft of intellectual property. Courts typically employ a form of the familiar "reasonable person" test: Are the two artifacts being compared so very similar as to suggest to a reasonable person that the one was copied from the other?

The substantial similarity element looms large in many copyright infringement suits involving musical works, and courts often rely on the testimony of musicologists to establish similarity. In the case against George Harrison mentioned above, the court found it helpful to actually reprint short snippets from the sheet music to "He's So Fine" and "My Sweet Lord."

In another case that turned on the issue of similarity, U.S. District Judge Gesell had no difficulty determining that the publishers of the then-fledgling *Conservative Digest* had copied the cover design from the far more established *Reader's Digest*.[14] He thus issued an injunction against further infringement as well as nominal damages. The cover design was protected both by copyright law (as an artistic work in its own right) and by trademark law (as a way of letting consumers know that this was indeed the popular magazine with which they are familiar). Judge Gesell analyzed such design features as composition (the

---

[13]*Bright Tunes Music v. Harrisongs Music,* 420 F. Supp. 177 (1976).

[14]*Reader's Digest Association v. Conservative Digest, Inc.,* 642 F. Supp. 144, 145 (D.D.C. 1986), *aff'd,* 821 F.2d 800 (D.C. Cir. 1987).

placement of the table of contents, magazine name, date, and cover price) and the choice of fonts and use of boldface type. Make your own judgment by examining Figure 6.2.

Let us look at how one court dealt with the issue of substantial similarity between two films. All these years after its release, the motion picture industry still ranks *Jaws* among the top twenty grossing films of all time. It is no surprise, then, that Universal Studios was and is very protective of the copyright to the film. Universal brought suit against a company that was planning to market a film called *Great White*. The federal district judge, who issued an injunction against the distribution of the latter film, was dumbstruck by the numerous similarities between the works. Indeed, several full pages of the court's opinion are taken up with descriptions of those similarities. That the creators of *Great White* originally planned to call their work *The Last Jaws* and that a main character in the film was named Peter Benton (author Peter Benchley wrote the novel upon which *Jaws* was based) suggested that they wished for their work "to be as closely connected with [the

 **Figure 6.2**

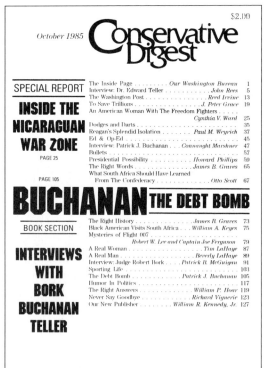

*From* Reader's Digest Association v. Conservative Digest, Inc., *642 F. Supp. 144, 149 (D.D.C. 1986) © 1981, 1983 by the Reader's Digest Assn., Inc. © 1985 by* Conservative Digest. *Reprinted with permission.*

Figure 6.3

| **Substantial Similarity between Two Films** | |
| :---: | :---: |
| **Jaws** | **Great White** |
| ■ The opening scene includes many underwater shots of a swimmer, repeated bass tones to indicate the approach of the shark and to build tension, and the swimmer's becoming the first victim of the shark. | ■ The opening scene includes many underwater shots of a windsurfer, repeated musical bass tones to indicate the approach of the shark and to build tension, and the windsurfer's becoming the first victim of the shark. |
| ■ There is a boat scene in which, to the sound of bass tones, the shark approaches the boat, bumps it, and causes a boy to fall into the water. The boy is rescued before the shark attacks. | ■ There is a boat scene in which, to the sound of bass tones, the shark approaches the boat, bumps it, and causes a girl to fall into the water. The girl is rescued before the shark attacks. |
| ■ A bathing cap, which looks like the head of a shark, floats through the water. | ■ A broken surfboard, which looks like the fin of a shark, floats through the water. |
| ■ The local mayor plays down the news of the shark in the interest of local tourism. | ■ A gubernatorial candidate plays down the news of the shark in the interest of local tourism. |
| ■ After the police chief's child has gone into a state of shock because of the shark, the politician apologizes to the father in the hospital and as an act of contrition signs a contract hiring the salty skipper to hunt the shark. | ■ After the shark expert's child is injured by the shark, the politician apologizes to the father in the hospital and as an act of contrition personally hunts for the shark. |
| ■ The action revolves primarily around a salty English-accented skipper, a shark expert, and the local police chief who go out in a boat to hunt the shark. | ■ The action revolves primarily around a salty, English-accented skipper and a local shark expert who go out in a boat to hunt the shark. |
| ■ In the finale, the skipper is eaten by the shark, and then the police chief kills the shark by exploding a canister of compressed air which the shark has swallowed. | ■ In the finale, the skipper is eaten by the shark, and then the shark expert kills the shark by detonating dynamite which the shark has swallowed. |

*From* Universal City Studios v. Film Ventures International, *543 F. Supp. 1134 (C. D. Cal. 1982).*

original] *Jaws* as possible." Figure 6.3 presents some of the main similarities between the two films identified by the court.

There are at least two circumstances in which a court will permit a great deal of similarity between artifacts without finding infringement. The first kind of situation arises when a central idea common to both works (recall that *ideas* may not be copyrighted) can only be expressed in a very small number of ways. This is referred to in copyright law as the doctrine of **idea/expression merger.** In one case, a jewelry company that had marketed a pin with a jeweled bee as its major design feature sued a competitor that had also created a jeweled bee pin. The court concluded that, once we grant that the *idea* of encrusting a bee with jewels for a pin is not itself copyrightable, it is hard to imagine that any two such pins could be sufficiently distinctive such that one would be the infringement of the other's protected expression.[15] More recently, the U.S. Court of Claims had to decide whether the U.S. Postal Service's "LOVE" stamp (featuring a heart-shaped globe on a background of navy blue with white stars, with the word *love* in the upper right corner) constituted an infringement of a competing copyright. The court determined that the idea of enclosing the globe within a heart shape was just that—an idea—and not properly copyrightable, even when set down in a tangible form.

The second doctrine, called **scenes à faire,** is employed most typically in litigation involving motion pictures. The doctrine posits that when directors choose a particular locale for their story, they commit themselves to including a number of highly predictable filmic moments. Thus, for example, the author of a series of children's books about a park filled with dinosaurs was unsuccessful in his suit alleging that *Jurassic Park* was an infringement of his copyright. That both the plaintiff's and defendant's works took place in a "dinosaur park" meant that such features as electrified fences, automated tours, dinosaur nurseries, and uniformed workers were virtually unavoidable.[16] Similarly, the producers and screen writers of the movie *Fort Apache, the Bronx* successfully defended against a lawsuit by the author of a book called *Fort Apache.* The two works were inarguably simi-

---

[15]*Herbert Rosenthal Jewelry Corp. v. Kalpakian,* 446 F.2d 738 (9th Cir. 1971).

[16]*Williams v. Crichton,* 84 F.2d 581 (2d Cir. 1996).

 # Things to Remember

**PROVING COPYRIGHT INFRINGEMENT**

- Copyright infringement plaintiffs may be awarded both their own lost profits and any profits illegally accrued by the defendant.
- The Copyright Act itself also provides specific dollar amounts.
- Especially egregious infringements can also be a criminal offense.
- The main elements of an infringement suit are originality, access, and substantial similarity.
- The idea/expression merger and *scenes à faire* doctrines may excuse artifacts that would otherwise be considered substantially similar to the plaintiff's work.

lar in theme. Both took place in the New York City Police Department's 41st Precinct in the South Bronx. The plaintiff pointed to several deeper similarities between the two works, including the use of third- or fourth-generation Irish policemen from Queens as central characters, and also such dramatic elements as cockfights, drunks, stripped cars, prostitutes, rats, and unsuccessful foot chases of fleeing criminals. Such components of the two works, the court ruled, could not constitute copyright infringement in that they "would appear in *any* realistic work about the work of policemen in the South Bronx" (emphasis added).[17]

### Defending against a Copyright Infringement Suit: The Fair Use Doctrine

As we have seen, plaintiffs in copyright infringement suits must prove three elements: originality, access, and substantial similarity. Thus, we already know some of the arguments that defendants in such suits are likely to make, that is, "the plaintiff has failed to establish one or more elements, and here is why." Technically, because the burden of proof in establishing these elements is on the plaintiff, defendants' counterarguments do not constitute legal "defenses." A defense in this context is better thought of as an admission of copying, with an explanation. By far the most important defense in copyright infringement suits is the one that invokes the **Fair Use** doctrine, which is codified as section 107 of the Copyright Act. The basic philosophy underlying Fair Use is that there are some instances of copying that must be protected, either because they provide some societal good or at least because they do not do a great deal of harm to the copyright holders. Many commentators have suggested that if the Act did not provide this kind of defense, courts would have had to create it as a kind of First Amendment counterweight in favor of speech.

Section 107 is structured as a list of four questions (see Figure 6.4) that courts must ask as they try to determine if a particular taking that would otherwise be seen as an actionable copyright infringement should be excused as a fair use. The first question focuses on the actions of the alleged infringer. What is the nature of the use to which the defendant has put this copyrighted work? Some kinds of uses—such as for nonprofit, educational purposes or to make critical commentary on the original artifact—are especially deserving of protection. The second question shifts the court's focus to the nature of the original, copyrighted work. Here, too, the thrust of this question is that certain kinds of works are more protected than others. The third question asks how much was taken, reflecting Congress's belief that writers should almost always be able to quote small sections of others' work without seeking permission. Finally, courts must ask what often turns out to be the most important inquiry of all: what is the likely financial effect of this unauthorized taking on the potential value of the original copyright?

---

[17]*Walker v. Time Life Films,* 784 F.2d 44, 50 (2d Cir. 1986).

## Figure 6.4    *The Fair Use Doctrine*

[T]he fair use of a copyrighted work...for purposes such as criticism, comment, news reporting, teaching (including multiple copies for classroom use), scholarship, or research, is not an infringement of copyright. In determining whether the use made of a work in any particular case is a fair use the factors to be considered shall include

- **The purpose and character of the use,** including whether such use is of commercial nature or is for nonprofit education purposes

- **The nature of the copyrighted work**
- **The amount and substantiality of the portion used** in relation to the copyrighted work as a whole
- **The effect of the use upon the potential market** for or value of the copyrighted work. The fact that a work is unpublished shall not itself bar a finding of fair use if such finding is made upon consideration of all the above factors.

*From Section 107 of the Copyright Act.*

The four questions are somewhat interdependent. Thus, for example, some kinds of uses (the first question) may permit a larger amount of taking from the original work (the third question) than would otherwise be the case.

***Setting the Stage: Three Supreme Court Decisions.***    Although we examine many examples of case law in the explication of the Fair Use questions to follow, three specific Supreme Court decisions are referred to over and over again. Therefore, a short description of the facts and rulings for each of the decisions is in order.

*Home Videotapers Are Not Criminals: the* Sony *Case.*    If you assume that you have the right to use a VCR at home to record broadcast TV programs, even though such programs' on-air copyright notice typically advises viewers that "unauthorized copying" is strictly prohibited, you are correct. What you may not realize is how very close you came to losing this right in 1984, when the Supreme Court produced a 5–4 decision in favor of the home tapers.[18] In more recent years, scholars who have pored over the papers of the late Justice Thurgood Marshall have discovered that the case was almost decided the other way.[19]

The "Betamax" case—a charmingly anachronistic nickname, given the victory of the VHS format over Sony's Beta format for VCRs—was filed because TV and movie production studios were afraid that large-scale home taping of their

---

[18]*Sony Corporation of America v. Universal City Studios,* 464 U.S. 417 (1984).

[19]Paul Goldstein, *Copyright's Highway: The Law and Lore of Copyright from Gutenberg to the Celestial Jukebox* (New York: Hill and Wang, 1994), 149.

programs would greatly diminish the value of their copyrights. If you tape a day-time soap opera for viewing when you return home from work (a practice called **time shifting**), you may be tempted to "zap" through the commercials. Copyright owners worry about this phenomenon because the fewer people known to view the commercials, the less advertisers will be willing to pay the TV networks for air time, and thus the less TV networks will be willing to pay the program producers. Then, too, you might like this specific episode of your favorite soap opera so much that you keep the tape to watch again and again. This practice, intuitively enough called **"library building,"** will have obvious implications for the market value of a TV series in that reruns will have an even smaller audience than they otherwise would have.

Naming millions of VCR purchasers as defendants would have been more than a bit unwieldy, of course, so the plaintiffs instead went after Sony Corporation, one of the major manufacturers of home taping equipment, as well as a small sample of retail outlets known to sell VCRs. Sony's advertising agency was also named as a defendant, because it was alleged that the marketing campaign for Betamax machines encouraged purchasers to tape copyrighted programs from broadcast stations. Universal City and Disney, the main plaintiffs, sought an injunction against the sale of video recorders, or, barring that, some form of mandatory royalties on the sale of each machine (and perhaps on the sale of blank videotapes as well). The Supreme Court denied the injunction. The majority's reasoning, which we examine in more detail when we return to an explication of Section 107, was based largely on the first and fourth Fair Use inquiries, that is, the nature of the infringer's use of the copyrighted material, and this use's effect on the value of the copyright.

*Newsworthiness and Copyright Infringement: President Ford's Memoirs.* The underlying facts in *Harper & Row v. The Nation*[20] could have been part of a mystery novel. Victor Navasky, publisher of the *Nation* magazine, received a mysterious stranger one evening in March 1979, a stranger who had in his or her possession a copy of former President Gerald Ford's memoirs, scheduled to be published in the next few weeks by Harper & Row (jointly with *Reader's Digest*) under the title *A Time to Heal*. Harper & Row had also contracted with *Time* magazine to publish excerpts from the book timed so as to increase sales. The mysterious stranger made clear that Navasky might look at the manuscript but not keep it or make photocopies from it. Over the next twenty-four to seventy-two hours, Navasky took detailed notes from the Ford memoirs, including several hundred words of direct quotes. Believing that some of the revelations in the memoirs were so newsworthy that they should be brought to the public without delay, the *Nation* scooped the other publishers by including in its April 3, 1979, issue an article of about 2,250 words based on President Ford's manuscript.

---

[20]471 U.S. 539 (1985).

Not surprisingly, the copyright owners sued the *Nation,* which defended itself in part by arguing that the specific words taken from Ford constituted a kind of contemporary history and were thus uncopyrightable *facts.* The Court rejected this argument as well as several the defendant made based on the Fair Use doctrine. The majority ruling, as we shall see, says much about the Court's current interpretation of this most frequently raised defense to copyright infringement.

*A Pretty (Hairy) Decision: Roy Orbison and 2 Live Crew.*    The rap group 2 Live Crew took Roy Orbison's 1960s hit, "Oh, Pretty Woman" and, depending on one's point of view, either created a work of biting social commentary on the work and upon the hypocritical culture from which it sprang or simply ripped off the original for their own enrichment. The Orbison song tells the tale of a lonely man who, while walking the street late at night, encounters a woman who seems much too beautiful to consider spending time with him. "Don't walk on by," he pleads with her. "Don't make me cry." Just as he is about to leave for another lonely night at home, he finds he has guessed wrong and that the pretty woman is indeed walking his way.

The Luther Campbell version recorded by 2 Live Crew has a quite different theme. Their "pretty woman" is likened to Cousin It of Addams Family fame, transmogrified into a "bald-headed," "hairy," and "two-timing" creature. This latter description carries with it a silver lining of sorts, as the lead vocalist expresses relief that there is a good chance "the baby ain't mine."

Fundamentally, *Campbell v. Acuff-Rose Music*[21] is about the relationship between the Fair Use doctrine and the long accepted notion that comedians who use satire or parody should be allowed to point their audience's attention at various other cultural artifacts without having to obtain permission from those who own the copyright to such artifacts. Yet there has always been tremendous disagreement among courts as to the proper scope of the parodist's license. Should it cover *any* work that borrows from the original and that also happens to be funny, or must the comedy stem from a statement *about the original work*? Moreover, is the parodist's protection from copyright infringement suits something separate from and greater than the Fair Use doctrine, or should the defendant's satiric intent be simply one of the bits of data used in answering the four questions? The Supreme Court ruled unanimously in favor of 2 Live Crew, although it embraced the narrower definition of parody and made clear that defenses based on comedic intent will be handled as part of traditional Fair Use analysis.

***Fair Use Inquiry 1: The Purpose and Character of the Use.***    As the discussion of the 2 Live Crew case indicates, one of the categories of "uses" often at issue in copyright infringement litigation is parody. In that 1994 decision, Justice Souter's unanimous opinion makes clear that the Court's definition of parody is narrow.

---

[21]510 U.S. 569 (1994).

Those comedic works most likely to be protected by Fair Use analysis are the ones that comment on the original work. Writers who borrow from earlier works only to make their own job easier will likely not enjoy any special degree of protection. As Justice Souter put it, if the new work "has no critical bearing on the substance or style of the original composition," if the only reason the defendant borrowed from the original was "to get attention" or "to avoid the drudgery" of creating something truly new, the fairness of the use "diminishes accordingly, if it does not vanish." It is important to realize that most parodists, and perhaps especially most parody songwriters, will not enjoy automatic protection based on the Court's reasoning. Let us take the example of the popular songwriting and performing troupe called the Capitol Steps, a Washington-based group whose founding members are all current or former Congressional staffers. When they sing about "The Bimbo Collection," they mean to make fun of Bill Clinton, not Kermit the Frog (of "Rainbow Connection" fame). Similarly, "Breaking Knees Is Hard to Do" is aimed straight at controversial ice-skater Tonya Harding, not at songwriter Neil Sedaka ("Breaking Up Is Hard to Do"). The Capitol Steps' "I Want a Man with a Slow Mind" is a commentary on former Vice President Dan Quayle, not the Pointer Sisters' desire for a man with a slow *hand,* and their "The Fools on the Hill" is a critique of Congress, not of the similarly titled Lennon-McCartney tune.

Why do such parodists borrow other's melodies? Probably for two reasons. First, there is a higher probability that listeners will remember the lyrics if they already know the melody. Doesn't this reason, however, fit into the category of using the original work to "get attention," as Justice Souter put it? Second, it is plainly easier to write lyrics alone, which is another way of saying, again borrowing from Souter, that one "avoids the drudgery" of writing an accompanying melody. Most musical parodists will thus not find automatic refuge in the *Campbell* decision.

Luther Campbell and 2 Live Crew are not the only comedic artists who have survived a copyright infringement suit stemming from their parodies of others' works. The producers of the long-running NBC program *Saturday Night Live* successfully defended against a copyright infringement suit stemming from a skit depicting the city fathers of the Biblical town of Sodom devising a public relations campaign for their town reminiscent of the one that New York had recently embarked on. The skit's finale had the participants singing "I Love Sodom" to the tune of "I Love New York," the centerpiece of the New York campaign. The court got the joke and recognized that it was at the expense, at least in part, of the earlier tune's creators. Thus the SNL team had achieved a pure parody.[22] In another musical example, disk jockey Rick Dees was sued, unsuccessfully, for having written and performed "When Sonny Sniffs Glue," which the courts understood to be a send-up both of the 1950s jazz standard "When Sunny Gets Blue" and of Johnny Mathis's distinctive version of the earlier tune.[23]

---

[22]*Elsmere Music, Inc. v. National Broadcasting Company,* 623 F.2d 252 (2d Cir. 1980).

[23]*Fisher v. Dees,* 794 F.2d 432 (9th Cir. 1986).

Consider a more recent court case involving visual images (see Figure 6.5). The magazine *Vanity Fair* made quite a splash when it featured a nude and very pregnant Demi Moore on its August 1991 cover. Judge Newman of the Court of Appeals for the Seventh Circuit commented that photographer Annie Leibovitz posed Moore "in profile, with her right hand and arm covering her breasts and her left hand supporting her distended stomach—a well-known pose evocative of Botticelli's *Birth of Venus.*" When Paramount Pictures, as part of its publicity campaign for the Leslie Nielsen film *Naked Gun 33⅓ The Final Insult,* superimposed Nielsen's face on a torso chosen to closely resemble Moore's—the composite photo's caption was "Due this March"—Leibovitz sued. She could not prevail against Paramount Pictures, in that the studio's promotional photo was at least partially a comment on her own work. If the message of the *Vanity Fair* photo was, as Leibo-

## Figure 6.5

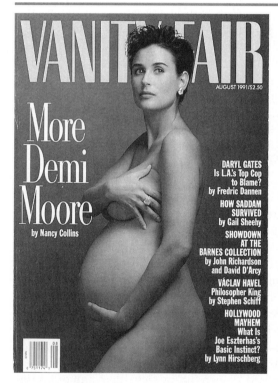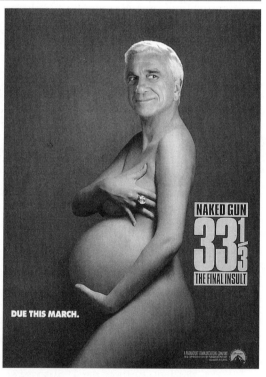

Photographer Annie Leibovitz was unsuccessful in her lawsuit against the producers of the Leslie Nielsen film, who clearly intended to conjure up in readers' minds an image of the earlier Demi Moore photograph.

vitz allowed, one woman's "self-confidence or feeling of pride in being beautiful and pregnant," Paramount's "ridiculous image of a smirking, foolish-looking pregnant man" was clearly designed to offer a differing view of the subject matter.[24]

Parody is really just a subset of a larger category of potential fair uses of copyrighted material: the excerpting from another's work to *comment* on it. Thus, a drama critic does not need to obtain permission to quote from a play's dialogue. A film critic can show excerpts from a copyrighted film in the course of doing a movie review for the TV news. In an especially ironic contemporary example, the Reverend Jerry Falwell and the Moral Majority organization were permitted to send copies of the famous Campari parody ad, the same one that upset Falwell enough to prompt him to sue *Hustler* magazine for libel (see the discussion of the case in Chapter 4), to his supporters as part of a direct mail solicitation. Although the court concluded that the mailing had commercial elements in that it was designed to raise money to defray Falwell's legal expenses, the unauthorized copying of the offensive ad was done primarily "to rebut the personal attack upon Falwell and make a political comment about pornography."[25]

In the Sony Betamax case, the Supreme Court was asked to rule not on a particular use of a specific copyrighted material, but rather on a technology's potential for performing a whole host of "uses." One reason the Court refused to stop the manufacturing and marketing of VCRs was its having found that the machines can be used in many ways that do not violate the Copyright Act. Some broadcast programs, such as very old movies, are no longer protected by copyright. Other programs are "born in the public domain," such as C-SPAN's live coverage of Congressional floor debates. Then, too, some copyright holders would not be at all upset to learn that consumers were time shifting their programs for later viewing. For example, Fred Rogers, the host of *Mister Rogers' Neighborhood* on PBS, testified at trial that he encourages parents to tape his program and then view it at a more convenient time, in the company of their children. The Court also determined that the use of VCRs to do nothing more than time shift (rather than to make multiple copies of tapes and sell them to others, or even to build a permanent home library) is a nonprofit use consistent with the Copyright Act.

Defendants who can demonstrate that their use of another's copyrighted materials was for a nonprofit, educational purpose are given much deference in Fair Use analysis. The Copyright Act does not itself provide clear guidance as to how to balance the interests of copyright holders with those of teachers wishing to present examples in their classes or to distribute varied readings to their students. The House of Representatives created a report called the "Agreement on Guidelines for Classroom Copying in Not-for-Profit Educational Institutions" (usually referred to more succinctly as the Classroom Guidelines) at around the time of the 1976 Act's adoption. Although this report is not formally part of the statute

---

[24]*Leibovitz v. Paramount Pictures,* 137 F.3d 109 (2d Cir. 1998).

[25]*Hustler Magazine v. Moral Majority,* 796 F.2d 1148, 1152 (9th Cir. 1986).

itself, courts have sometimes employed the Guidelines in Fair Use analyses. The Guidelines are built around three main issues: brevity, spontaneity, and cumulative effect.

The **brevity** requirement permits teachers to make a single copy of a book chapter or an article for their own scholarly use or to prepare to teach a class about the work. Making multiple copies to distribute to students, however, triggers overall length limits (e.g., 250 words for a poem, 2,500 words for an article, a book chapter that is no more than 10 percent the total length of the book) that are quite rigid. **Spontaneity** means that a teacher is more likely to be permitted to make multiple copies if there is not enough time to contact the copyright holder for permission. The **cumulative effect** requirement limits teachers to copying no more than two works by the same author, no more than three from the same anthology, and no more than nine artifacts total for classroom distribution during any single semester.

The Guidelines make certain explicit prohibitions above and beyond the matters of brevity, spontaneity, and cumulative effect. Perhaps most important is that at no time should copying be used as a substitute for anthologies, compilations, or collective works. Then, too, no copying would be permitted of works designed to be "consumable," such as workbooks, exercises, and standardized tests. All copying must be a result of the individual teacher's inspiration rather than directions from any higher administrative authority. Finally, students may not be charged any fees beyond the actual cost of the copying.

Separately created guidelines govern the use by teachers of homemade videotapes from broadcast programs. The general rule here is that educators may retain and use any such videos only for forty-five days, after which the videos must be erased or destroyed. These guidelines are also not officially part of the Copyright Act, although Congress has endorsed them and placed them in the *Congressional Record.*

Sometimes the most hotly contested issue in a copyright infringement dispute is whether or not the use should be considered nonprofit or commercial. This question was central to two important lower federal court cases governing professors' use of commercial photocopying shops to create customized textbooks for their students. In both cases, courts emphasized that the copy outlets made a profit and that this profit was enhanced by their failure to pay royalties to the copyright holders of the individual works being compiled. The first case involved the Kinko's chain, whose outlets are found in cities and college towns nationwide. From the students' perspective, such "Professor's Publishing" anthologies may have been educational uses, but the court found that they were a primarily commercial enterprise.[26] The second case involved a more local but equally commercial copying enterprise in Ann Arbor, Michigan, run by a self-taught legal scholar who persuaded himself, to his detriment, that the earlier Kinko's decision was an aberration. The

---

[26]*Basic Books, Inc. v. Kinko's Graphics Corporation,* 758 F. Supp. 1522 (S.D.N.Y. 1991).

federal appeals court for the Sixth Circuit, ruling *en banc,* used much the same reasoning as that earlier decision by allowing that the students' use of the copied materials may have been an educational one, but that the plaintiffs were complaining about the for-profit intermediary, the copy shop. The court majority explicitly refused to decide whether there would have been copyright infringement if the professors or students themselves had made the desired copies rather than contracting with the photocopy shop.[27]

In the Supreme Court case concerning President Ford's memoirs, discussed earlier, the *Nation* magazine argued that its unauthorized use of purloined excerpts from the yet unpublished Harper & Row book should be protected as news reporting. The Court majority, however, emphasized that the magazine's motivation was commercial, that it intended to "scoop" the copyright holders. Moreover, the opinion rejects the newsworthiness defense outright, finding that "the public's interest in learning this news as fast as possible" does not necessarily outweigh the author's right to control the timing and circumstances of his work's publication. "The promise of copyright would be an empty one," Justice O'Connor wrote, "if it could be avoided merely by dubbing the infringement a fair use 'news report' of a book."

Uses of copyrighted works that are "incidental" or "fortuitous" have often been protected as fair uses. UCLA Law Professor Melville Nimmer uses the example of a motion picture in which an actor is seen reading a magazine such that its cover is clearly visible. The magazine would not be able to sue the film's producers for copyright infringement.[28] A case from New York City is instructive. WABC-TV televised the annual San Gennaro Festival from the Little Italy section of Manhattan, which included footage of a band playing a song called "Dove sta Zaza" by the Italian composer Giuseppe Cioffi. The owners of the copyright to the song sued the station, but the court ruled that the news crew had no advance knowledge that this particular song was to be played, that they had come to cover a bona fide news event, and that their use of the excerpts from the song was "incidental to the overall, informative purpose of the newscast."[29]

Although this area of the law is quite unsettled, it is fair to say that defendants who specifically seek out particular copyrighted artifacts will not be as readily protected by the Fair Use doctrine as was WABC-TV. In 1997, for example, HBO and BET unsuccessfully sought summary judgment against a plaintiff whose artistic poster was used as part of the set in an episode of the sitcom *ROC*. The court emphasized that the TV producers purposely chose to use this specific piece of art for the same reason the artist created it: to be decorative.[30] A different result was reached by the same federal appellate court, however, in a case involving the

---

[27]*Princeton University Press v. Michigan Document Services,* 99 F.3d 1381 (6th Cir. 1996).

[28]*Nimmer on Copyright,* sec. 13.05(D)3 (1997).

[29]*Italian Book Corporation v. ABC,* 458 F. Supp. 65, 68 (S.D.N.Y. 1978).

[30]*Ringgold v. Black Entertainment Television,* 126 F.3d 70, 79 (2d Cir. 1997).

motion picture *Seven,* about a deranged photographer, a serial killer who does his deeds in the manner of the seven deadly sins. At one point in the film, detectives search the photographer's apartment and encounter on the wall a light-box with a number of transparencies attached to it. Jorge Antonio Sandoval claimed that the transparencies were images of several of his own black-and-white photos, and New Line Cinema did not contest this allegation. The court ruled for the movie producers nonetheless, emphasizing that the images were seen on screen for such a short time and in such an obscured way so as to make them almost unidentifiable as Sandoval's creations. Technically, this was not a Fair Use finding at all. Rather, the court found that the film's use of the images was such that, from the perspective of viewers, they were no longer "substantially similar" to the originals.[31]

In another dispute that never came to trial, sculptor Frederick E. Hart settled out of court with the producers of the Warner Brothers' film *The Devil's Advocate,* starring Keanu Reeves and Al Pacino. In the film, Pacino's Lucifer is a high-powered attorney who has followed young attorney Reeves's career from a

---

[31] *Sandoval v. New Line Cinema,* 147 F.3d 215 (2d Cir. 1998).

Sculptor Frederick E. Hart settled out of court with Warner Brothers, producers of the film *The Devil's Advocate,* in a copyright dispute alleging that his *Ex Nihilo* had been used in the movie without his permission.

*Photograph by Tracy A. Woodard.* **Copyright © 1997, The Washington Post. Reprinted with permission.**

# Things to Remember

### THE NATURE OF THE USE

- Parody, comedic works that make fun of an earlier copyrighted work, may be protected as a Fair Use.
- Nonprofit and educational uses receive an extra weighting in Fair Use analysis.
- It is not always easy to determine if a use is commercial or educational (or both).
- The Classroom Guidelines accompanying the Copyright Act provide highly specific and rather strict rules for educators.
- Unauthorized uses that are so incidental or unintended as to be "fortuitous" will generally be excused.

distance for reasons that only become apparent in the final scene. In that scene, Pacino's office wall is dominated by a large sculpture, one that Hart thought a little too reminiscent of his own famous *Ex Nihilo* (Out of Nothing). In this climactic scene, the wall comes to life, its component characters engaging in a wide variety of sexual acts. Had the suit gone to trial, Warner Brothers might have argued that its use of the Hart sculpture was only incidental to the film narrative. If you have seen the film, you know that this argument would likely have failed, in that the final scene employs the sculpture as a kind of Greek chorus commenting on the Faustian offer Pacino extends to Reeves.

***Fair Use Inquiry 2: The Nature of the Work.*** Recall that the *Harper & Row* case's outcome was based in part on President Ford's memoirs having not yet been published. The majority reasoned that, because one of the rights that the Copyright Act explicitly protects is authors' choice of if, when, and how their work will come to press, unauthorized takings of not yet published works are especially troublesome.

A small handful of lower court cases following on the heels of the Ford memoirs case applied the same strictness against defendants who planned to quote from works the authors of which likely did not intend ever to be published. Thus, biographer Ian Hamilton, contracted to write a book about the reclusive literary figure J. D. Salinger, was not permitted to quote from any of the personal letters written by his subject that had found their way into various university archives. The court quotes from Justice O'Connor's *Harper & Row* opinion for the proposition that "under ordinary circumstances, the author's right to control the first public appearance of his undisseminated expression will outweigh a claim of fair use.[32] Similarly, a biography of Church of Scientology founder L. Ron Hubbard was found in

---

[32]*Salinger v. Random House,* 811 F.2d 90, 95 (2d Cir. 1987).

violation of the Copyright Act, owing to the unauthorized inclusion of Hubbard's unpublished correspondence.[33]

A biography of the late African-American writer Richard Wright was permitted to go forward, notwithstanding his heir's protestations at the biographer's unauthorized use of some of Wright's unpublished letters. Even here, however, the court's Fair Use analysis counted against the defendant with respect to the unpublished nature of the original work. The court distinguished this case from the one involving Salinger on the relatively narrow grounds that here the writer paraphrased loosely more than quoted directly, and depended on the letters more for (uncopyrightable) facts than for protected expression.[34] Largely out of concern that lower courts were misinterpreting the *Harper & Row* decision so as to suggest that defendants should almost never prevail if they disseminate others' yet unpublished works, Congress amended the Copyright Act in 1992, inserting in Section 107 this admonition: "The fact that a work is unpublished shall not itself bar a finding of fair use." Still, it is a fair bet that the unpublished status of a protected work will more often than not count against defendants who plan to publish the writings without authorization.

Note also that a not yet published work is distinguished in copyright law from a work that is out of print. With respect to the latter kinds of books, the Classroom Guidelines suggest an extra measure of leeway in copying. After all, consumers would likely not be able to buy even a single copy of the book, much less multiple copies for classroom distribution.

Another way that courts handle the "nature of the work" inquiry is to determine whether the original work was laden with facts and statistics or was rather a highly expressive and artistic one. At the extreme, the taking of purely factual material is necessarily a fair use, in that such material is not itself copyrightable in the first place. Such was the lesson of the *Feist* case, discussed earlier, involving the competing telephone directories. An interesting case from the 1970s concerned a company that proposed to create a specialized index that would list all persons ever named in *New York Times* articles. The company used the newspaper's own indices to cull the information they required. The novel question posed by the case was, in the court's words, "whether or not millions of names scattered over more than one hundred volumes and integrated with a great mass of other data" constitutes a copyrightable compilation (and whether employing such data to create a new index can be a fair use). That the newspaper's own indexes were "rather in the nature of a collection of facts than in the nature of a creative or imaginative work" meant that the defendants had "greater license to use portions of the *Times Index* under the Fair Use doctrine than they would have if a creative work had been involved," the court added. The newspaper was not granted the injunction it sought against the defendant's new index.[35]

---

[33]*New Era Publications International v. Henry Holt & Company,* 873 F.2d 576 (2d Cir. 1989).

[34]*Wright v. Warner Books,* 953 F.2d 731 (2d Cir. 1991).

[35]*New York Times Company v. Roxbury Data Interface, Inc.,* 434 F. Supp. 217 (N.J. 1977).

A special method of adjudicating the "nature of the work" issue arises when the work is truly unique and when its dissemination is of clear public interest. The long and complicated history of litigation and legislation surrounding the famous Zapruder film of President Kennedy's assassination is the most often cited example. Dallas dressmaker Abraham Zapruder just happened to be making a home movie of the JFK motorcade at the precise time the fatal shots came. His eight-millimeter film is surely one of the most important pieces of archival footage of the twentieth century. The publisher of *Life* magazine purchased the rights to the film from Zapruder for $150,000. A book critical of the government's investigation of the assassination called *Six Seconds in Dallas* appeared in 1967. The author of the book, who did not have hands-on access to the Zapruder film itself, instead used line sketches, each one copied from a different frame from the film, as reprinted earlier in *Life* magazine. The magazine publisher's resulting infringement suit was dismissed, because the public interest "in having the fullest information available on the murder of President Kennedy" necessitated that this particular film be made available to writers wishing to comment on this defining historical event.[36] Time, Inc. sold the rights to the film back to the Zapruder family for the token sum of one dollar in 1975. In 1992, Congress passed the JFK Assassination Records Collection Act,[37] and in 1997, a special review board created by that Act declared the Zapruder film an official record that the government would thus be entitled to confiscate.[38] The board told the Zapruders to make whatever arrangements were necessary to transfer ownership to the government by August 1998. A year of negotiations resulted in payment of $16 million to the Zapruders. During those negotiations, the family arranged to have an Illinois company market

---

[36]*Time, Inc. v. Bernard Geis Associates,* 293 F. Supp. 130 (S.D.N.Y.1968).

[37]44 U.S.C. sec. 2107 (1992).

[38]62 F.R. 27008 (1997).

 **Things to Remember**

### THE NATURE OF THE WORK

- Not yet published works are especially deserving of protection so as to preserve the author's right to determine how, when, and if they will be published.

- Works that are out of print are given a bit less protection from unauthorized copying than are other works.

- The courts also give fact-laden works less protection than more artistic works.

- If the dissemination of a work is judged to be of strong public interest or if it is the only way of bringing important information to the public (the Zapruder film of the JFK assassination being the best-known example), such determination will also be factored into the inquiry.

a digitally enhanced copy of their original film. Thus, "Image of an Assassination," a forty-five-minute documentary incorporating a new version of the twenty-six-second film, became available in video stores.

***Fair Use Inquiry 3: The Amount Taken.***    It has already been mentioned that the four Fair Use inquiries are interdependent, that the answer to one may affect the court's adjudication of others as well. This fact is very clear in the way that judges deal with the third inquiry, the "how much was taken?" issue. How much you are allowed to take depends on both the nature of the original work and the nature of your use.

If copyrighted works vary along a continuum from the factually heavy to the more artistically creative, it is no surprise that defendants are permitted greater latitude in taking from the former than from the latter kinds of artifacts. Call to mind again the *Feist* case involving the rural telephone books. The defendant in that case took virtually the entire book compiled by the plaintiff, minus a few pages of introduction and a certain percent of alphabetical listings that were discarded because they did not fit into the geographic scope of the new book. The Court permitted this taking, however, on the grounds that the material that was taken was purely factual.

Clearly, the length of the original work is important to consider as well. Indeed, in Section 107 of the Copyright Act, the precise wording of the third question asks courts to consider "the amount and substantiality of the portion used *in relation to the copyrighted work as a whole*" (emphasis added). This is Congress's way of saying that taking fifty words from a hundred-word poem is less likely to be considered a Fair Use than is taking 500 words from a full-length novel.

In the *Sony* case, the Court refused to enjoin the production or marketing of VCRs even though they are often used to make copies of 100 percent of an original work. That case was unusual, however, because, in a sense, the machines themselves were the defendants. The basis of the decision was that VCRs can be used in ways that are not violations of the Copyright Act. At most, the manufacturers of the units might have been guilty of **contributory infringement,** rather than **direct infringement,** on anyone's copyright.

The *Harper & Row* case posed an intriguing problem for the Court. If the wording of section 107 was to be taken as a purely quantitative issue, the *Nation* magazine surely should have won. After all, it only quoted a few hundred words from a soon to be published full-length book. The Court's explanation of its ruling against the magazine is relevant to the "how much did you take?" inquiry in at least two ways. First, Justice O'Connor makes clear that this part of the Fair Use analysis has not only quantitative but also qualitative dimensions. Quoting from an earlier decision, she chided the defendant that "no plagiarist can excuse the wrong by showing how much...he did *not* pirate." That which the *Nation* took from President Ford's memoirs was the heart of the book, she emphasized. The magazine editor's testimony made clear that he purposely chose the book's most powerful passages, the ones that would convey the "absolute certainty with which [Ford] expressed himself."

A second important feature of the *Harper & Row* decision is that O'Connor's Fair Use analysis seems to deviate from the instructions, such as they are, in the Copyright Act itself. Whereas Section 107 tells courts to adjudicate the third Fair Use inquiry by comparing that which was stolen to the length of "the copyrighted work as a whole," O'Connor also considered the length of the resulting *Nation* magazine story. At one point she reports that 13 percent of the magazine article consisted of quotes from President Ford himself. Thus, the vast majority of the *Nation* essay was at least original enough not to have been lifted verbatim from someone else. Even here, though, her analysis becomes more qualitative than quantitative, as she concludes that the article "is structured around the quoted excerpts," that they "serve as its dramatic focal points," that they play a "key role in the infringing work."

The general topic of how parodies are treated within fair use analysis has already been introduced. With respect to the third inquiry, the general rule, not surprisingly, is that a parody is permitted to "take" more from the original than might other kinds of works. Parodists may, minimally, take whatever is necessary to "conjure up the original" in the minds of the listeners. Clearly, this standard is not very precise. It is fair to say, however, based on the "Oh, Pretty Woman" and "When Sonny Sniffs Glue" cases discussed earlier, that musical parodists may with impunity use the complete melody of the original, if the new lyrics are indeed a critical commentary on the earlier work rather than a more general comedic statement about society in general or aimed at some specific entity other than the original.

# Things to Remember

## THE AMOUNT TAKEN

- How much defendants are allowed to "take" is often a function both of the nature of their use and of the original work.

- Although Section 107 directs courts to consider "the amount and substantiality of the portion used in relation to the copyrighted work as a whole," courts often add into the equation the ratio of unoriginal to original words in the defendant's creation.

- There is also a qualitative dimension to the test, in that defendants are likely to be held liable for taking the "heart" of a work, no matter how few words are actually taken.

- Parodists are permitted to take, minimally, whatever is necessary to "conjure up the original" in the minds of readers.

***Fair Use Inquiry 4: The Effect of the Taking on the Copyright's Value.***   Copyright law is at its heart a way of protecting a property interest. It is therefore not surprising that this fourth inquiry, where courts are to determine how much the value of the original work's copyright has been damaged, is crucial. Indeed, Justice O'Connor's opinion in the *Harper & Row* case makes clear that this fourth and last inquiry "is undoubtedly the single most important element of fair use." In that same case, the Court was presented with an unusually clear and measurable example of harm. After the *Nation* went to press, *Time* magazine canceled its contract with Harper & Row (which had been for the *exclusive* rights to print excerpts from the book) and refused to pay the remaining money due the book publisher.

In the *Sony* case, the Court had to deal with the VCR manufacturer's argument that their machines actually *enhanced* the value of the plaintiffs' copyrights. After all, the reasoning went, many people use video recorders primarily as video players and depend on professionally prerecorded movies for their in-home video entertainment. Were there no VCRs, the whole home video market never would have developed, and the video rental and sales industry represents a tremendous new stream of revenue for Universal City and other movie studios. Although it will be recalled that the Court ultimately ruled for the VCR manufacturers on other grounds (the machines' potential for noninfringing uses), Justice O'Connor made clear that this argument must be rejected. Successful plaintiffs in an infringement suit are entitled not only to any revenues they may have lost, but also to profits the defendants have illegitimately earned. The fourth Fair Use inquiry, then, allows plaintiffs to say to defendants, "How dare you make money off of my copyright, without my permission, even if your so doing makes money for me as well!"

The fourth Fair Use inquiry concerns not only the copyright holders' financial interests in the work already created and marketed but also in any future derivative works they may choose to market in the future. That is one of the key reasons the Court in the 2 Live Crew case was not able to settle every issue before it and had to remand the case to a lower court. What if Acuff-Rose had decided to license a rap music version of Roy Orbison's "Oh, Pretty Woman" itself? Would the 2 Live Crew parody supplant the market for such a work, thus diminishing *its* value? The Court correctly expressed its skepticism at such a scenario, realizing that a straightforward rap version of a song and a parody of a song that happens to be sung in a rap idiom probably would appeal to different markets. Then, too, one reason parodies are given special deference within Fair Use analysis is that parody is precisely the kind of derivative work that artists and authors are least likely to market. Very few writers choose to make fun of their own work.

Parody's potential for dampening the market for the original might be a function of the satire's bite. Ray Stevens, for example, has written a parody of Barry Manilow ("I Need Your Help, Barry Manilow") that makes fun of the megastar and his fans ("No one knows how to suffer quite like you"). If listeners were to be swayed by Stevens's musical "argument" that Manilow is an overly sentimental songwriter whose devotees have a maudlin, masochistic streak, the value of the latter's copyrights would surely be diminished. This diminution is not the kind the law is designed to protect.

This situation is true not only of parodies. Any "taking" of a copyrighted work, assuming it would not otherwise be actionable, cannot become so simply because the defendant's use of the work results in people buying less of the original creator's artifacts. Perhaps the leading example of this phenomenon is a 1977 decision involving the *Miami Herald* and *TV Guide.* The newspaper had decided to expand its coverage of television by offering a free weekly TV magazine. It launched the new supplement with an advertising campaign in the newspaper itself, the thrust of which was to suggest that here was quite a bargain compared with subscribing to *TV Guide,* in that consumers get a thick, multifaceted newspaper *plus* a viewing guide. The ads included a pictorial comparison of the covers of the two magazines. In response to *TV Guide*'s resulting copyright infringement suit, the court allowed that the ads "may have had the effect of drawing customers away," but concluded that any such result would stem from the logic of the *Herald*'s arguments to consumers, not from the *TV Guide* covers being used.[39]

When diminution of the original copyright's value flows from the taking itself, the defendant is almost certain to lose both the fourth Fair Use inquiry and the litigation. This situation has been apparent in a number of cases involving book publishers seeking to capitalize on the popularity of a motion picture or a television series. In one case, a company marketed a book called *Twin Peaks: A Complete Guide to Who's Who and What's What,* aimed at the somewhat cultish devotees of the highly stylized TV serial. Obviously, such a book is unlikely to dampen the market for the program itself—the reruns, the home videos, and so forth—but that was not the point, the court held. The crucial issue was that the producers of the TV program had already licensed some books related to the show and might have wanted to license more.[40] Similarly, the publishers of *The Seinfeld Aptitude Test* trivia book—in homage to the TV show, they organized the questions into five categories of increasing difficulty, from "Wuss" to "Master of Your Domain"—were held to be in violation of the Copyright Act. It mattered not, the court held, that the *Seinfeld* producers had thus far chosen not to exploit the derivative market themselves. That is an economic choice that copyright law must respect.[41] A similar result was reached in a 1998 suit by Paramount Pictures against a company marketing *The Joy of Trek,* a book designed to "explain the *Star Trek* phenomenon to the non-*Trek*ker, particularly someone who finds him or herself involved in a relationship with a *Trek*ker."[42]

---

[39]*Triangle Publications, Inc. v. Knight-Ridder Newspapers, Inc.,* 626 F.2d 1171 (5th Cir. 1980).

[40]*Twin Peaks Productions, Inc. v. Publications International, Ltd.,* 996 F.2d 1366 (2d Cir. 1993).

[41]*Castle Rock Entertainment v. Carol Publishing Group,* 150 F.3d 132 (2d Cir. 1998).

[42]*Paramount Pictures Corporation v. Carol Publishing Group,* 25 F. Supp. 2d 372 (S.D.N.Y. 1998), *aff'd,* 181 F.3d 83 (2d Cir. 1999).

# Things to Remember

## THE EFFECT OF THE TAKING ON THE COPYRIGHT'S VALUE

- Most courts treat this last Fair Use inquiry as the most important of the four.
- Infringers will be held liable even for profits they have earned from marketing works to new markets the original copyright owner may never have intended to reach or profit from.
- Even if an infringement can be shown to have increased the monies flowing to the copyright holder, the defendants will still be held liable for the amount of their own profits.
- Diminution of the original copyright's value is actionable only if the taking itself (rather than, say, criticism hurled within the new work at the original work) is the cause of the diminished value.

## The Law of Trademarks

Imagine you are taking a long car trip, alone. You have been on the road for over ten hours, and your body is telling you to start seeking lodging for the night. You pass a number of motels with names that suggest a bit of local color, but nothing about the cleanliness or overall quality of the property. Indeed, a few of them look a bit scuzzy. Then your eyes catch sight of a familiar name and logo—it really does not matter for present purposes whether it is *Holiday Inn* or *Ramada* or any of their well-known competitors—and you pull into the driveway, confident that you will enjoy a comfortable stay. If this narrative rings true for you, you already have a good intuitive feel for the law of trademark. Trademarks exist to give consumers a sense of predictability, and thus to help businesses earn a deserved brand loyalty.

### Kinds of Marks

In the United States, **trademark** is protected by the Lanham Act of 1946. The Act defines trademarks as any word, name, symbol, or device that a company may use to distinguish its products or services from its competition. Marks can be familiar brand names. They can also be slogans, such as American Express's admonition, "Don't Leave Home Without It." Distinctive shapes can also be marks, the best-known example probably being the shape of Coca-Cola bottles. Even a color can be protected under trademark law.[43]

---

[43]*Qualitex Company v. Jacobson Products,* 514 U.S. 159 (1992); *In re Owens-Corning Fiberglass Corp.,* 774 F.2d 1116, 1128 (Cal. Fed. 1985).

The word *trademark* is used somewhat generically here. Technically, trademarks apply to a company's products, whereas a company that offers primarily a service (such as the hotel chains in the example above) seek protection instead for its **service marks.** The law also recognizes an interest in protecting **collective marks,** which serve the needs of associations of businesses. The Chamber of Commerce, the National Restaurant Association, the National Association of Broadcasters all represent many companies with overlapping interests and all are eligible to register their own marks. You have probably also seen **certification marks,** which do not refer to a product in its entirety but rather to a feature of that product. Probably the best known is that provided by Underwriters Laboratory ("UL approved") to appliance manufacturers. The promise of "REAL" cheese on a frozen pizza is another example. Certification marks can also be used to indicate a product's origins, as in Idaho potatoes or New Zealand wool. Finally, the Lanham Act provides for protection of the overall packaging through which a product or service line is marketed.[44] This protection is called **trade dress.**

## What Makes a Mark Protectable?

In copyright law, a creation is protected from the moment it is set down in some kind of finished form. Trademark law is quite different in this respect. You might create a terribly clever slogan or an eye-catching logo. Neither is protectable under trademark law until you actually establish a track record of using it in commerce or at least what the Patent and Trademark Office calls a "bona fide intention" to use your mark within the next six months.

Just as not every conceivable "creation" is copyrightable, so too not every possible mark is protectable by trademark law. The law of copyright demands a measure of originality. Trademark law requires **distinctiveness,** which means that the mark does something more than simply describe the product or service. You cannot register the exclusive right to market "Lead" pencils because being made of lead is part of the definition of any pencil. Even purely descriptive terms can sometimes become distinctive, and thus protectable, over time. A **descriptive mark** is protected if a company can demonstrate that it has been marketing its wares under a specific name for so long and with such success that the public has developed a mental association between the name and the product. The Steak and Brew restaurant chain, for example, has chosen a name for itself that *describes* its menu offerings fairly well, yet the name is now a protected service mark because of a demonstrable history of public acceptance. American Airlines is another example. The name at first blush seems to designate any airline company that happens to be based in the United States or even somewhere in the Western Hemisphere, yet most people clearly associate the name with a specific company. When a word or

---

[44]*Wal-Mart v. Samara Brothers,* 529 U.S. 205 (2000); *Two Pesos, Inc. v. Taco Cabana, Inc.,* 505 U.S. 763 (1992).

phrase that would otherwise be considered merely descriptive becomes distinctive in this way, it has acquired a **secondary meaning,** sometimes referred to instead as **acquired distinctiveness.** Company owners' surnames generally must acquire distinctiveness before they can be protected. Such names as "Perdue" chickens and "Kingsford" charcoal are generally protected only to the extent their parent companies can demonstrate that the public strongly associates the names with a specific product line.[45]

One currently unsettled area of the law is the extent to which "800" telephone numbers or Internet domain names employing words that would otherwise be purely descriptive may nonetheless enjoy a degree of protection as the public comes to associate the number or the name with a particular company.[46] Can only one company that sells flowers, for example, make a point of telling customers that its phone number is easy to remember because it spells out "F-L-O-W-E-R-S"?

It is generally preferable from the marketer's perspective if a mark can be distinctive from its very creation. Trademark law refers to such marks as "inherently distinctive," sometimes called "strong" marks. Generally, a mark can be inherently distinctive in three ways. The first way is if the mark is *fanciful,* if it has no life apart from its association with the product it seeks to market. Such marks are found in no dictionary, but are created out of thin air, often with the help of a high-power advertising agency. The name "Prell" applied to a shampoo is a fanciful name. So, too, are such marks as "Xerox" copying machines and "Clorox" bleach. A mark can

---

[45]*The Kingsford Products Company v. Stephen T. Kingsford,* 931 F.3d 63 (10th Cir. 1991).

[46]*Dial-A-Mattress Franchise Corp. v. Page,* 880 F.2d 675 (2d Cir. 1989); *Dranoff-Perlstein Assocs. v. Sklar,* 967 F.2d 852 (3d Cir. 1992); *CD Solutions Inc. v. CDS Networks Inc.,* Civil No.97-793-HA (D.Ore. Apr. 22, 1998); W. Scott Petty, "Can a 'Generic' Domain Name Infringe a Registered Mark?" *Intellectual Property Today,* August 1998, p. 39.

 # Things to Remember

## THE BASICS OF TRADEMARK LAW

- The Lanham Act protects trademarks, service marks, collective marks, certification marks, and trade dress. The word *trademark* is often used to refer to any of these categories of emblems.

- A trademark is any word, logo, slogan, or similar device used to call to mind a specific manufacturer's goods or services.

- The law protects only distinctive marks, those that do something more than simply describe the product or service.

- Marks can be distinctive from their birth (as in the case of fanciful, arbitrary, and suggestive marks), or they may be otherwise merely descriptive terms that have become distinctive over time through the acquisition of a secondary meaning.

also be inherently distinctive if it is *arbitrary*. Arbitrary marks do have established dictionary meanings, but the specific product or service is not inherently related to that dictionary meaning. "Boston" as applied to contact lens supplies is one such example; others are "Apple" computers and "Camel" cigarettes. Finally, inherently distinctive marks can be *suggestive*, referring to a mark's ability to suggest, without explicitly describing, a product or service's qualities or features. "Head and Shoulders" shampoo is such a mark, and a rather clever one, aimed at suggesting that this product will help you prevent dandruff (the "shoulders" part). If the product were instead called "Antidandruff Shampoo," the mark would be merely descriptive and thus unprotectable.

## Trademark Infringement

*Likelihood of Confusion.*   Generally, plaintiffs can establish that their trademarks have been infringed in two ways. The first way is to show that the public is likely to be confused by the defendant's use of a highly similar mark, that it will presume incorrectly that the products or services are the plaintiff's or at least that the plaintiff authorized use of the mark. This is called the **likelihood of confusion** standard. Historically, it has been limited both by geography and product line. A trademark infringement is less likely to be found if the alleged infringer is marketing goods or services in a geographic region far removed from where the plaintiff conducts business. Although this limitation is not as important with respect to large companies that market their goods nationally or internationally, it still comes into play when litigants are relatively local concerns. Thus, for example, the famous Sardi's Restaurant in New York City was unable to enjoin the owner of a small neighborhood pub in California from using a highly similar name.[47]

Also traditionally, the law only protected companies' trademarks from those who sought to market product lines highly similar to their own. Often referred to as **product proximity,** this general rule says that trademark infringement is more likely to be found if the two products at issue are similar enough to compete plausibly with each other. To cite one early example, the manufacturer of "V-8" vitamin supplements was successfully sued by the manufacturer of the famous vegetable juice of the same name.[48]

*Dilution.*   The second way a company might infringe on a competing company's trademark is through dilution. The distinction between dilution and the more traditional likelihood of confusion standard in trademark law is not always easily discernible and can seem confusingly circular. This confusion emerges because the accepted definition of dilution, as articulated first only in state statutes but as of 1996 in the federal Lanham Act as well, does not require that the plaintiff's

---

[47] *Sardi's Restaurant v. Lyle Sardie,* 755 F.2d 719 (9th Cir. 1985); cf. *Good Earth Corporation v. M. D. Horton and Associates,* 1998 U.S. App. LEXIS 12572 (9th Cir. 1998).

[48] *Standard Brands, Inc. v. Smidler,* 151 F.2d 34 (2d Cir. 1945).

and defendant's product lines be at all similar. Dilution statutes have been supported on the grounds that *any* unauthorized use of another's trademarks can diminish the value of those trademarks via a process sometimes called **blurring.** In the trademark infringement literature, a hypothetical example of "Buick aspirin tablets" is often used. If the public began to believe mistakenly that the Chrysler Corporation had begun to sell analgesics, there would be a traditional likelihood of confusion suit. But what if the market were simultaneously flooded with a host of other "Buick" products, from toothbrushes to hammers? Infringement still might exist, but on the alternative theory—blurring—that consumers would no longer think only of cars when they encounter the trademark "Buick."[49]

Thus, even though dilution claims do not technically require a finding of likely confusion, the plaintiffs' chances of success tend to be better the more their and the defendant's product lines are similar. For example, the company then owning the rights to the LEXIS computer database was not able to enjoin the car manufacturer from using the Lexus mark. The court emphasized that not only were the two companies in very different enterprises, but also that the plaintiff's service mark, very well known to attorneys and similar professionals, was not at all familiar to the lay public.[50]

One category of dilution claim is more clearly distinct from ordinary trademark infringement cases: the "**tarnishment**" claims against uses that tend to disparage the plaintiff's trademarks. Consider, for example, the Coca-Cola company's suit against the distributors of a popular counterculture poster depicting an "exact blown-up reproduction of plaintiff's familiar 'Coca-Cola' trademark and distinctive format except for the substitution of the script letters 'ine' for '-Cola,' so that the poster reads 'Enjoy Cocaine.'"[51] In the course of granting the plaintiff the requested injunction, the court emphasized that in the highly competitive soft drink industry, "even the slightest negative connotation concerning a particular beverage" may have a significant effect on market share.

***Trademark Parody.***    A tarnishment claim will generally not succeed, however, if the defendant can demonstrate that the unauthorized use of plaintiff's trademark was for the purpose of parody or some other related kind of political commentary. Thus, the L. L. Bean Company was not able to enjoin publication of a spoof called *L. L. Beam's Back-To-School-Sex-Catalog,*[52] and the "San Diego Chicken" sports mascot was permitted to make fun of PBS's "Barney" the dinosaur, by having a stand-in for the purple creature perform an athletically demanding dance sequence.[53]

---

[49]Eric Prager, "The Federal Trademark Dilution Act of 1995: Substantial Likelihood of Confusion," 7 *Fordham Intellectual Property, Media, and Entertainment Law Journal* 121, 123 n.8 (1996).

[50]*Mead Data Central v. Toyota Motor Sales,* 875 F.2d 1026 (2d Cir. 1989).

[51]*Coca Cola Company v. Gemini Rising,* 346 F. Supp. 1183 (E.D.N.Y. 1972).

[52]*L. L. Bean, Inc. v. Drake Publishers, Inc.,* 811 F.2d 26 (1st Cir. 1987).

[53]*Lyons Partnership v. Giannoulas,* 179 F.3d 384 (5th Cir. 1999).

In the summer of 2000, MasterCard International sued presidential candidate Ralph Nader for copyright and trademark infringement. The candidate was running a thirty-second TV ad (duplicated on his Web site) borrowing the credit card company's successful "priceless" tag line to argue for the pricelessness of "the truth," which the ad argued would emerge only if Nader were permitted to participate in the presidential debates. A federal district court in New York produced an unpublished decision for Nader, finding that the credit card company had failed to establish how it was being harmed.[54]

## Use It or Lose It: The Fear of "Going Generic"

A company whose marketing of a protected product or service ceases for two years will generally be presumed to have abandoned the related trademark. In such a case, the trademark will become part of the public domain, and any competitor can use it in commerce. Often, corporations place advertisements in the *Columbia Journalism Review* and similar trade magazines in an effort to remind opinion leaders of the companies' continued interest in their trademark because abandonment can also be inferred from a marketer's failure to police *others's* inappropriate use of its trademarks. Thus, it is not at all unusual for a reporter who publishes an article that carelessly misuses a trademark somewhere in the text—such as, for example, using "Xerox" as a noun or a verb instead of as an adjective describing one particular company's photocopying machines—to receive a letter from one of the offended corporation's officers or attorneys. Although such letters sometimes read like threats of litigation, in fact corporations almost never sue reporters about these careless lapses. Indeed, the more important reason for sending the letter is that the company's file copy of it and other similar correspondence may become an important part of the company's proof, if it ever needs such proof, that it has *not* abandoned its trademarks.

Sometimes a company will lose the protection of a trademark through no fault of its own. This loss occurs if the trademark becomes "generic," if the word itself becomes so well accepted by the public that the mental association with a particular company dissipates. There is a certain irony to all this, of course. The most successfully marketed trademarks are perhaps the most likely to become generic over time. Regardless of how and why this reality of language evolution happens, the logic behind ending trademark protection is straightforward enough. If the public perceives that a certain word denotes a whole category of products rather than a particular company's goods, continuing to protect the trademark would result in the originator's monopoly not only in the use of the word, but also in the ability to market that category of products. It may surprise you to learn some of the names for products currently on the market that once were the exclusive trademarks of a specific company. Aspirin is one example;[55] other examples

---

[54]Valerie Sieminski, "First Amendment Priceless," *The National Journal,* 2 Oct. 2000, p. B12.

[55]*Bayer Co. v. United Drug Co.,* 272 F. 505 (N. Y. 1921).

# Things to Remember

## PROTECTING ONE'S TRADEMARK

- Trademarks are infringed on when the likelihood of confusion is introduced as to whose products or services a customer is actually buying.
- Even actions that do not necessarily create confusion may still result in liability if they diminish a trademark's distinctiveness by diluting it.
- Courts generally recognize two varieties of trademark dilution: blurring and tarnishment.
- Unauthorized uses that might otherwise be considered tarnishing dilutions may be protected nonetheless as trademark parodies.
- A trademark may lose its protectability if, over time, consumers come to perceive the mark as a generic word describing the entire product category. Words such as *kleenex, aspirin,* and *escalator,* all once trademarks of specific companies, have gone this route.

include escalators,[56] yo-yos,[57] thermoses,[58] "the pill" (as applied to contraceptive pills),[59] cola (not "Coca-Cola," just "cola"),[60] and cellophane.[61] It is no wonder that corporations spend so much energy and resources protecting their valuable trademarks. Who among us, after all, has not misused such brand names as Xerox, Kleenex, or Post-it?

---

[56]*Haughton Elevator Co. v. Seeberger,* 85 U.S.P.Q. 80 (1950).

[57]*Donald F. Duncan, Inc. v. Royal Tops Mfg.,* 343 F.2d 655 (7th Cir. 1965).

[58]*King-Seeley Thermos Company v. Aladdin Industries,* 321 F.2d 577 (2d Cir. 1963).

[59]*In re G. D. Searle & Company,* 360 F.2d 650 (1956).

[60]*Coca Cola Co. v. Snow Crest Beverages,* 162 F.2d 280 (1st Cir. 1947).

[61]*DuPont Cellophane Company v. Waxed Products Company,* 85 F.2d 75 (2d Cir. 1936).

## Chapter Summary

Copyright law is designed to protect the rights of authors and artists and to encourage them to create. It covers everything from music to literary works, from architectural drawings to computer software. A work must be set down in some fixed medium and must manifest some degree of creativity to be eligible for protection. Mere facts are not copyrightable, although a creative compilation of facts may sometimes be copyrightable. In some instances, the natural owner of a copyright will be an employer rather than the actual creative artist.

Copyright infringement suits must establish originality (that the plaintiff's work was legitimately copyrightable in the first place), access (that the defendant was aware of the plaintiff's work), and substantial similarity (that the defendant's work actually does constitute an infringement on the plaintiff's work).

The most important defense to a lawsuit is the Fair Use doctrine, which asks courts to make four inquiries: the nature of the use (whether for purely commercial or for educational or other productive purposes), the nature of the work (already published or not, factual or artistic), how much was taken, and the likely effect on the potential value of the original copyright.

Trademark law's province is commerce, and it is designed to avoid consumer confusion in the marketplace. The word *trademark* is often used as a shorthand to refer to trademarks, service marks, collective marks, certification marks, and trade dress, which are all protected by the Lanham Act.

The law protects only distinctive marks, those that do something more than simply describe the product or service. Marks can be distinctive from their birth (as in the case of fanciful, arbitrary, and suggestive marks), or they may be otherwise merely descriptive terms that have become distinctive over time through the acquisition of a secondary meaning.

Typically, trademark infringement lawsuits seek to establish that consumers are likely to be confused by the defendant's conduct as to the true source of goods or services. Antidilution actions do not require such proof, especially in the case of tarnishment claims. Even a use that may tarnish the public image of a trademark may be protected speech if it serves as a parody on the original.

Trademark holders' biggest fear is that their marks will be so successful that they become generic, that the public starts associating them with the entire industry's offerings, rather than just that of one company. For example, kleenex, escalator, and yo-yo are now generic terms, although at one time they were protected trademarks.

chapter

# Access to Information

The First Amendment's guarantees to freedom of speech and freedom of the press, the U.S. Supreme Court has said on a number of occasions, at least imply a corollary right to hear, to listen, to read. A group of concerned students successfully challenged a Long Island, New York, school board's decision to remove books from high school and junior high school libraries. Announcing the decision of the court in *Board of Education v. Pico*[1] (there was no majority opinion), Justice Douglas remarked that the justices have frequently held, "in a variety of contexts," that the First Amendment protects not only the right to speak, but also "the right to receive information and ideas." Within the realm of sexually oriented speech (see Chapter 11), although states are free to pass antiobscenity laws that comport with certain federal guidelines, no state may make criminal the mere act of *reading* obscene materials.[2] In the 1960s, when the postmaster general sought to prevent the use of the mails for sending "Communist propaganda" to any persons who did not explicitly request it, the Court ruled that he had overstepped his bounds by placing such a requirement on readers. "It would be a barren marketplace of ideas that had only sellers and no buyers," Justice Brennan wrote. In another case, although choosing to defer to the attorney general's refusal of an entry visa to a well-known Marxist scholar who wished to offer a series of lectures at American universities, the Court went out of its way to say that whatever First Amendment interests were involved here were those of the potential audience members.[3]

These cases all have something in common: the pairing of a willing speaker and an equally willing listener. Whatever First Amendment right to hear might exist, it cannot compel others to speak. Reporters assigned to cover a local crime story understand that the victim's relatives and friends have no obligation to answer their questions. A press credential is not a subpoena.

---

[1]457 U.S. 853 (1982).

[2]*Stanley v. Georgia,* 394 U.S. 557 (1969).

[3]*Kleindeinst v. Mandel,* 408 U.S. 753 (1972).

Suppose, however, that you are a reporter assigned to cover not one particular crime, but rather overall violent crime statistics in your community. Do you have a First Amendment right to compel your government—local, state, or federal—to release to you the information you seek? It may surprise you to learn that the answer is no. Justice Stewart, in a famous lecture at the Yale Law School, explained that "there is no constitutional right to have access to particular government information," that "the Constitution itself is neither a Freedom of Information Act nor an Official Secrets Act."[4]

In that same speech, Justice Stewart allows that "Congress may provide a resolution," if it wishes. As it turns out, Congress and the individual state legislatures have stepped in to provide a measure of statutory support for the news gathering process. Much of this chapter is therefore devoted to a discussion of legislation designed to promote openness, especially the federal Freedom of Information Act. After considering some additional federal legislation (the Government in the Sunshine Act and the Federal Advisory Committee Act), we examine the general pattern of state laws designed to mirror and sometimes go beyond the federal legislation. Finally, we consider ways in which media outlets themselves sometimes stand in the way of the "public's right to know."

A small caveat is in order first: it has become increasingly difficult to distinguish between news gathering and news reporting. Some media activities seem to fit into both categories simultaneously. Among these are the televising of live and unedited events. Examples include C-SPAN's gavel-to-gavel coverage of floor debates in both houses of Congress and the bizarre slow motion "chase" of O. J. Simpson's white Bronco on the Los Angeles freeways. So too is the even more bizarre and disturbing live image, again in the Los Angeles area, of Daniel Jones stopping traffic to unfurl a banner protesting that "HMOs are in it for the money!" and eventually to take his own life on camera. The technological ability of the electronic media to cover events live either around the corner or halfway around the world cannot help but have significant implications for the traditionally accepted distinctions between news gathering and news reporting.

News media sometimes choose to forgo their traditional editorial role so as to get the story as quickly as possible. Thus, in the late summer of 1998, many media outlets chose to transmit whole President Clinton's videotaped grand jury testimony as fed to them by the House of Representatives staff. That the line between news gathering and news reporting was being blurred was driven home when the feed was delayed by several minutes because House members apparently had failed to indicate in what order the staff should play the four tapes. Recall also that this media event followed closely the release of the Starr Report itself. The House of Representatives made the text available on its own Internet site, and innumerable Internet Service Providers and more traditional media outlets' online versions chose to serve as real-time conduits for the materials. When viewers saw

---

[4]Potter Stewart, "Or of the Press," 26 *Hastings Law Journal* 631, 636 (1975).

reporters reading that huge document and thinking aloud about what they were reading, was it news gathering, news reporting, or something else entirely?

# News Gathering: The Constitutional Framework

"I don't have to tell you that it gets mighty hot in Philadelphia in July!" So said columnist and author George Will to the Senate Rules Committee back in 1985. Will was testifying—unsuccessfully, as it turned out—against a bill that was about to open Senate floor debates to regular gavel-to-gavel TV coverage (thus also indirectly creating what is now known as the C-SPAN2 cable network). Will feared that bringing the TV cameras into the Senate, which the Founders designed as the more deliberative body of Congress, would greatly diminish the quality of the debates. It is very clear that the Founding Fathers would not support this degree of openness, Will argued. After all, when the Continental Congress was convened in Philadelphia in the summer of 1787 for the purpose of writing the Constitution, the doors and windows were bolted shut.

There is much evidence from the records such as there are of those debates in Philadelphia to the contemporaneous writings of Thomas Jefferson and James Madison and others suggesting that Will was right. The Founders did not presume that the right to report news includes a constitutional right to gather news. That would not necessarily prevent the more modern Supreme Court, of course, from interpreting the First Amendment more expansively. As we see in Chapter 8, the Court has fashioned a fairly extensive First Amendment right to attend court proceedings and to write about what transpires in the courtroom. Yet the Court has refused to create a more inclusive First Amendment right to gather news from the government.

### No Special Access Rights for the Press: A Tale of Three Prisons

It was in 1972 that the Court came closest to suggesting that the First Amendment, properly interpreted, includes at least a qualified right to gather news. In *Branzburg v. Hayes,* the Court ruled that a reporter for the *Louisville Courier-Journal* did not have a First Amendment right to disobey a subpoena to testify in front of a grand jury about stories he had written about local trafficking in illegal drugs. Even though the decision ultimately went against Paul Branzburg, Justice White allowed that "freedom of the press could be eviscerated" if there were no First Amendment protection for seeking out the news.[5] Whatever solace the press may have taken from these words began to seem misplaced two years later, when the Court handed down two cases on the same day that both rejected reporters' claims that their First Amendment right to gather news had been abridged. The first, *Pell v.*

---

[5]*Branzburg v. Hayes,* 408 U.S. 665, 681 (1972).

*Procunier,*[6] concerned a California Department of Corrections regulation providing that reporters would have access to prisons and might be able to interview inmates of the prison staff's choosing, but that they could not themselves identify any particular inmates for interviews. Prison officials argued that the policy was necessary to prevent certain prisoners from becoming celebrities within their institutions, thus able to influence other prisoners to emulate their own noncooperative conduct. Writing for the Court's majority, Justice Stewart upheld the prison regulation. The Constitution, he concluded, does not impose on government "the affirmative duty to make available to journalists sources of information not available to members of the public generally.... The right to speak and publish does not carry with it the unrestrained right to gather information."

The second case from 1974, *Saxbe v. Washington Post,*[7] involved a Federal Bureau of Prisons regulation virtually identical to the California rule against requesting a specific prisoner to interview. Writing for the same 5–4 majority, Justice Stewart emphasized that there were ample alternative means by which reporters could gather information about the correctional systems without enjoying carte blanche to interview anyone they chose. They could carry on correspondence with inmates. They could tour the prisons, even the most secure sections of the facilities, and interact with any inmates they happened to encounter. And, of course, they could always interview *former* prisoners.

Four years later, the Court dealt with yet another prison access case.[8] KQED sought radio and television access to a particular portion of the Alameda County Jail (in the San Francisco Bay area) that had been the site of an inmate suicide as well as a number of alleged beatings and rapes. The litigation that ensued produced a fragmented Court decision, with two justices not participating and the remaining seven unable to agree on a majority opinion. Taken together, the plurality opinion (Chief Justice Burger writing for himself, Justice Rehnquist, and Justice White) and Justice Stewart's separate concurrence nonetheless make clear that the Court was again unwilling to put much stock in the notion of a First Amendment right to gather news. The plurality opinion allows that there is a strong public benefit to be derived from access to information about jail conditions. Chief Justice Burger, however, makes equally clear that there is "no basis for reading into the Constitution a right of the public or the media to enter these institutions, with camera equipment, and take moving and still pictures of inmates for broadcast purposes." The First Amendment does not mean that the media are guaranteed "a right of access to all sources of information within government control."

Justice Stewart's separate concurring opinion provided the needed fourth vote in this case. He agreed that KQED personnel were legitimately denied access to specific sections of jail, precisely because the public was denied the same access.

---

[6]417 U.S. 817 (1974).

[7]417 U.S. 843 (1974).

[8]*Houchins v. KQED,* 438 U.S. 1 (1978).

In those portions of the jail where the public had been granted access, however, Stewart insisted that broadcast media representatives must be permitted to bring in their electronic equipment.

## Access to Other Places

The Supreme Court's decisions in these three prison cases are very consistent with more general principles governing the relationship between the press and government authorities empowered to control the security of specific spaces. Thus, even though both the press and the public are generally free to traverse public streets and parks, anyone who disobeys a police officer's legitimate order to disperse in an emergency (such as the site of an automobile accident) may be prosecuted for such crimes as obstructing the law, resisting arrest, or criminal trespass. More typically, media personnel with appropriate identification are permitted to cross police barricades, although in most jurisdictions this practice is entirely at the discretion of the officers on the scene.

In the case of spaces that might be *owned* by the public but generally not *open to* the public (such as military bases or power-generating plants), trespassers are even more likely to be arrested, their newsgathering motives notwithstanding. Also, elaborate procedures exist for determining how and when reporters will be permitted access by the military to international war zones. There have been ongoing tensions between the media and Pentagon officials about this issue for many years. Media organizations expressed much dissatisfaction, for example, with the degree and timeliness of access to war zones during the Grenada and Panama military actions and the Gulf War. A 1991 lawsuit challenging the tight control maintained over the media during the Gulf War, however, was unsuccessful.[9]

That the First Amendment provides at best very limited protection for news gathering is also consistent with the case law involving the mixture of privacy and trespass claims examined in Chapter 5. Recall, for example, the case involving the New York City restaurant that won damages against CBS-TV for trespass because reporters had caused a great commotion when they intruded on the premises with cameras rolling to do a story about local health regulations. There, too, reporters argued unsuccessfully that the court should base its decision on an argued First Amendment right to gather news.[10]

## Equal Access to News as a First Amendment Right

Although courts have been very reluctant to find in the First Amendment an implicit right to gather news, several courts have held that once the government *does* choose to provide access to the news media, it may not discriminate among friendly and unfriendly media outlets. In one case, a federal judge held that a sher-

[9] *Nation Magazine v. U.S. Department of Defense,* 762 F. Supp. 1558 (S.D.N.Y. 1991).

[10] *Le Mistral, Inc. v. CBS, Inc.,* 402 N.Y.S.2d 815 (App. Div. 1978).

iff in the New Orleans area, who was at the time involved in libel litigation with the *Times-Picayune* newspaper, had trampled on the First Amendment when he announced that reporters for that particular media company would no longer receive advance word of upcoming press conferences and would be turned away at the door if they attempted to participate in any such press conferences. The sheriff further advised his staff not to provide any information or answer any questions for employees of the newspaper, except through a highly restricted process in writing through his public information office.[11]

A similar result was reached in Hawaii, where Honolulu Mayor Frank Fasi sought to bar one particular reporter from the *Honolulu Advertiser* (the largest general circulation newspaper in the state) from official press conferences. That the mayor described it as a personal grudge against only one man (reporter Richard Borreca) and that he was willing to welcome any reporter from the same newspaper other than Borreca made no difference to the judge. Granting access to individual reporters on the basis of compatibility with the mayor is as much an act of censorship, Judge King concluded, as would be requiring a newspaper to submit its proposed news stories for prepublication clearance.[12]

Even the White House is not relieved of the obligation to treat media representatives evenhandedly. Reporter Robert Sherrill from the *Nation* magazine brought suit against the Secret Service for denying him access to the White House as a "security risk." Although the appellate court for the D.C. Circuit did not require that the Secret Service's decision be reversed, it did insist that the Service must give any reporter denied a pass written notice and an opportunity to rebut whatever evidence was used to support the government's decision. The court made clear, however, that its decision should not be read so as to require "that the White House must open its doors to the press, conduct press conferences, or operate press facilities."[13]

## Hearing from Criminals and Bureaucrats

In two instances, the Supreme Court has struck down laws aimed squarely at reporters' potential sources rather than at media outlets themselves, at least in part because of the laws' effect on the "public's right to know." The word *newsgathering* appears nowhere in either case, yet the philosophical bases for the decisions is very consistent with the media's often repeated argument that the news gathering process deserves special protection precisely because the public will otherwise be deprived of important information about weighty political matters.

The first of these cases involved New York State's "Son of Sam" law, named after serial killer David Berkowitz's nickname. The law required that any profits

---

[11]*Times-Picayune Publishing v. Lee,* 15 Media Law Rptr. 1713 (E.D. La. 1988).

[12]*Borreca v. Fasi,* 369 F. Supp. 906 (Haw. 1974).

[13]*Sherrill v. Knight,* 569 F.2d 124 (D.C. Cir. 1977).

derived from writing about criminal wrongdoing be placed in a special escrow account for a period of five years, during which time the identifiable victims of any such crimes would be able to seek payment from that fund in partial compensation for their injuries. Justice O'Connor's majority opinion struck down the law as classic, content-based censorship, finding that a financial disincentive to publish, when aimed only at some topics of discussion, is just as odious as an outright ban on the speech. Her opinion argues that such statutes also can deprive the public of important information, that such classic works as *The Autobiography of Malcolm X* (which describes crimes committed by the civil rights leader before he became a public figure) and Henry David Thoreau's *Civil Disobedience* might never have been written under the law's restrictions.[14]

---

[14]*Simon & Schuster v. New York State Crime Victims Board,* 502 U.S. 105 (1991).

 Figure 7.1

Although the Supreme Court struck down New York's "Son of Sam" law, trial court judges are with increasing frequency including in their sentences a prohibition against defendants' profiting from telling their stories.

*Reprinted by permission of Johnny Hart and Creators Syndicate, Inc.*

Similarly, the Court in 1995 struck down portions of the federal Ethics Reform Act, which had forbade the vast majority of federal employees from receiving honoraria for writing or lecturing in their spare time, even if the topic of their communications was not at all related to their official duties. Here, too, the Court emphasized the law's effect on the public's right to know. "Federal employees who write for publication in their spare time have made significant contributions to the marketplace of ideas," wrote Justice Stevens for the Court. "They include literary giants like Nathaniel Hawthorne and Herman Melville, who were employed by the Customs Service; Walt Whitman, who worked for the Departments of Justice and Interior; and Bret Harte, an employee of the mint."[15]

Note, however, that neither of these cases seeks to establish an affirmative constitutional right to *compel* criminals or government employees to share their wisdom with us. In this sense, perhaps, they are best thought of as anticensorship decisions that happen to include a bit of pro–news gathering dicta.

---

[15]*United States v. National Treasury Employees Union,* 513 U.S. 454, 464–65 (1995).

 **Figure 7.2**

"THIS IS PERFECTLY LEGAL. THEY'RE ONLY LIMITING OUR OUTSIDE INCOME FROM SPEECHES AND ARTICLES."

That Congress chose to forbid certain federal employees from making money only from engaging in speech and writing was a fatal flaw, the Court held in the *National Treasury Employees Union* case.

© *1988 Sidney Harris. Reprinted with permission.*

# Things to Remember

---

**A CONSTITUTIONAL RIGHT TO GATHER NEWS?**

- The U.S. Supreme Court has at least hinted on several occasions that freedom of speech implies freedom to hear and to read.
- The Court has, however, refused to find an explicit First Amendment right to force the government to reveal information or to allow the press access to governmental venues.
- If, however, the government does grant press access to an event, it will not be allowed to discriminate among media outlets on the basis of a reporter's politics.

---

## Access to Public Information: The Statutory Framework

Although the First Amendment does not provide the media an affirmative right to obtain government documents, the federal and all state governments have passed laws that give varying degrees of such access. Many of the state laws are modeled after the federal statute; therefore, this section begins with a detailed examination of the federal Freedom of Information Act.

### The Federal Freedom of Information Act

Congress passed the Freedom of Information Act (FOIA) in 1966, although it has been amended several times since.[16] The philosophy undergirding the Act, as interpreted by the federal judiciary, is that government works best when its work is open to public inspection.

The Act requires that federal agencies' records that do not fit one of the law's nine exemptions be made available to requestors. Moreover, most of the exemptions tell agencies only what they *may* withhold; government officials can usually choose to reveal more than the FOIA demands. Each year, hundreds of thousands of requests for government information are made under the Act. Because requesters who are denied the information they seek are explicitly given the right in the Act to bring suit in federal court, hundreds of federal FOIA cases are decided annually.

Those cases typically involve the process of statutory construction introduced in Chapter 1, as the courts' main role is to decide what the Act means and whether a specific federal agency has conducted itself in ways consistent with the Act. The courts do not look to the First Amendment to decide these cases in that there is no *constitutional* obligation for the government to open its records to the public.

---

[16]The federal FOIA can be found at 5 U.S.C.S. sec. 552 (1998).

It is also important to note that the Act depends very much on the good will of the various federal agencies and the executive branch in fostering an atmosphere of openness. Each administration has interpreted the FOIA in ways consistent with the president's own philosophies. There are myriad ways for agencies to violate the spirit of the Act. They may interpret the Act's various exemptions broadly, they may not hire enough staff for their agencies' FOIA units, or they may have sufficient staff but create an incentive system that rewards the staff for maintaining secrecy more than for fostering openness. As reporter Carl Stern once explained, although the Act includes nine statutory exemptions to the presumption of disclosure, in fact there always has been a tenth, unwritten exemption: the individual bureaucrat who has decided that "I don't want to give it to you, so I won't give it to you."

In any event, it is inarguable that some rather dramatic stories have been made possible over the years due to FOIA requests. Because of reporters' diligent pursuit of information under the Act, such matters as the Ford Pinto's dangerously faulty gas tank, the details of the federal savings and loan crisis, and the government snafus involved in the launching of the Hubble telescope were learned. It is important to note, however, that the vast majority of FOIA requests are not made by reporters seeking to check on governmental abuse. As one commentator has said, "The typical FOIA request is made by a wily civil litigant circumventing traditional discovery rules, a corporate counsel in search of competitors' financial information, or a conspiracy theorist demanding operational files of the Central Intelligence Agency (CIA) on himself or other players in covert intelligence maneuvers in Cuba."[17]

***What Is an "Agency"?***   The Act defines a federal agency as "any executive department, military department, Government corporation, Government controlled corporation, or other establishment in the executive branch of the Government (including the Executive Office of the President), or any independent regulatory agency." Conspicuously missing from this list is Congress itself as well as the federal judiciary. The president is also not considered an "agency," nor is the presidential staff or any group whose sole function is to advise the president. Thus, for example, the records of President Reagan's "Task Force on Regulatory Relief" were properly withheld from an FOIA request, notwithstanding that individual members of the task force (including Vice President Bush and several cabinet officers) certainly had functions beyond that of simply advising the president.[18] Similarly, the National Security Council has been held to be beyond the reach of FOIA. The council's function, as set forth in the National Security Act that created it, is "to *advise* the President with respect to the integration of

---

[17]Amy E. Rees, "Recent Developments Regarding the Freedom of Information Act: A Prologue to a Farce or a Tragedy; Or, Perhaps Both," 44 *Duke Law Journal* 1183, 1184 (1995).

[18]*Meyer v. Bush,* 981 F.2d 1288 (D.C. Cir. 1993).

domestic, foreign, and military policies relating to the national security" (emphasis added).[19]

The definition of "agency" in the Act does cover many entities, however. It includes the departments of government headed by the various cabinet officers, such as the Department of the Treasury and the Department of Defense. The Act also covers the various agencies that report to cabinet members. For example, the FBI, which reports to the attorney general, is covered. The many agencies whose work is especially relevant to communication industries anyway, such as the Federal Communications Commission, the Federal Trade Commission, and the Food and Drug Administration, are also included in the Act.

***What Is a Record?***   The FOIA does not define the word *record*, but the case law makes clear that it is to be interpreted broadly so as to include papers, reports, manuals, letters, and computer files as well as audiotapes and other sound recordings, films, and photos. One thing that all these categories of materials have in common is their reproducibility. Physical objects that do not share this quality are beyond the scope of the FOIA. Thus, a reporter might obtain ballistic records from the FBI but will not be given access to actual guns and bullets. You may get reports on the efficacy of competing diet pills from the FDA, but you will not get samples of the pills studied by the agency.

Only materials that have been created or otherwise obtained by an agency and that are under the agency's possession and control are covered by FOIA. A 1980 Supreme Court decision, *Kissinger v. Reporters Committee for Freedom of the Press,*[20] exemplifies this feature of the Act. The Reporters Committee had requested transcripts of some of former Secretary of State Henry Kissinger's conversations. Although such materials might otherwise have been revealable under FOIA, the Supreme Court held that Kissinger's having donated them to the Library of Congress prior to the filing of the committee's FOIA request meant that they were not "agency records." Because the library is itself not covered by FOIA, and because Kissinger's agreement with the library included substantial limitations on public access to the materials being donated, this decision effectively prevented their disclosure.

That same decision also included a request by *New York Times* columnist William Safire for some written notes made by Kissinger about his phone conversations. Because the notes were made while Kissinger had been an advisor to the president rather than secretary of state, they would not normally be disclosable under FOIA. Safire, however, hoped that they would be released anyway because they were housed at the State Department, which is within FOIA's scope. The Supreme Court refused Safire's request, holding that the physical location of data cannot alone make them into "agency records." To be considered agency records,

---

[19]*Armstrong v. Executive Office of the President,* 90 F.3d 553 (D.C. Cir. 1996).

[20]445 U.S. 169 (1980).

materials must be created by a covered agency or otherwise obtained in the course of carrying out its official functions. For example, the Department of Justice was ordered to release numerous records of federal court decisions involving tax laws. Although the department does not create such records—they are created by the trial courts themselves—it keeps them on file because it provides the attorneys to represent the government in court on tax matters. This fact was enough to have the opinions considered Department of Justice agency records for the purposes of an FOIA request.[21]

***Making an FOIA Request.*** Perhaps the most difficult part of making a request under the FOIA is to identify the federal agency most likely to house the information sought. There is no single, government-wide FOIA clearinghouse, so a fairly thorough understanding of the kinds of functions performed by the various agencies is needed. If you are interested in learning whether a particular toy is suspected by the government of being a safety hazard, the Consumer Product Safety Commission is a logical place to start. A reporter desiring the latest report on the conditions at a specific nursing home receiving Medicare payments would likely contact the local Social Security Office. If you are unsure which agency to contact, a good place to begin your research is the *Federal Register*, where each agency provides a description of its functions as well as any FOIA contact information. Many federal agencies also have Web sites that provide varying degrees of helpfulness to potential FOIA requestors. The Reporters Committee for Freedom of the Press's Web site <www.rcfp.org> also provides much help in using the FOIA, including sample letters of request.

Once you identify the specific agency most likely to house the information you seek, a short letter to that agency's FOI officer is the next step. Indicate early on (probably in the opening paragraph) that you are making a request "pursuant to the federal Freedom of Information Act," and, in as much detail as you possibly can, specify the precise information you seek. Mention if you are a representative of the news media, because FOIA instructs agencies to give special consideration to reporters who intend to disseminate the information they gather. Perhaps most important is that agencies are supposed to charge such requestors only the cost of duplicating the records (waiving the often much larger cost involved in researching and organizing the records). Indeed, the Act provides that *all* fees may be waived if the release of the information sought will be in the public interest. So, add a sentence or two explaining why you believe the articles you intend to write will indeed benefit the public.

Because we are living in a digital age, indicate also in what form you would like the information (old-fashioned paper, floppy disks, CD-ROM, etc.). FOIA was amended in 1996 by passage of the Electronic Freedom of Information Act, which requires that agencies comply with such instructions as long as the records sought

---

[21]*Department of Justice v. Tax Analysts*, 492 U.S. 136 (1989).

are "readily reproducible" in the format requested. In other words, an agency FOI officer will not be required to *create* a database according to the parameters you prefer, but if the database has already been created, it is considered an agency record every bit as much as is the hard paper version of the same data.

The FOIA requires that agencies respond to requests for information within twenty days of receipt. This requirement, however, does not necessarily mean that you will have the information you seek in twenty days. Often the response is in the form of a request for additional specificity or an alert that the request is a huge one that will take a fair amount of time to fill. If the agency's FOI officer concludes that the information you seek falls into one of the nine exemptions enumerated in the Act, your request may be denied in full. Or, some material may be deemed releasable, other portions subject to withholding. In that case, a redacted version of your request will be released, which often takes the decidedly low-tech form of sheets of paper with the exempted information blacked out. Agencies that deny requests either in whole or in part are generally required to provide descriptions of the kinds of documents being withheld, together with precise reasons for the withholding.[22] This detailed listing of the kinds of documents in the agency's possession that are and are not being released is often referred to in the case law and commentary as a **Vaughn index,** named after an appellate decision from 1973.[23] If, however, an agency can demonstrate that the mere listing of the kinds of information available in the file will itself result in the same kind of serious harm that disclosure of the

---

[22]*King v. Department of Justice,* 830 F.2d 210, 224 (D.C. Cir. 1987).

[23]*Vaughn v. Rosen,* 484 F.2d 820 (D.C. Cir. 1973).

# Things to Remember

## FUNDAMENTALS OF THE FEDERAL FOIA

- Passed in 1966 and amended several times since, the Freedom of Information Act tells government officials that they must make their agency records available to requestors, unless the requests fall into a handful of statutory exemptions.

- Under the Act, "agencies" include departments headed by or reporting to cabinet officials as well as many other kinds of executive offices; the president and Congress itself, and the judiciary, are exempted, as are entities whose sole function is to advise the president.

- Virtually any reproducible entity can be considered a "record" under the Act, whether in the form of paper, films, photos, or computer records.

- Agency records must have been created by a covered agency or otherwise obtained in the course of carrying out its official functions.

- The Act specifies the time frame in which FOIA staff must respond to requests for information as well as fees to be charged for searching and photocopying.

full documents themselves would cause, the agency may be permitted to answer a request by refusing to indicate even whether the requested documents exist. Such answers are called **Glomar responses,** named after a commercial vessel the records for which had been the subject of an FOIA request in a 1976 decision.[24]

***Exemptions to Disclosure.***   The Freedom of Information Act provides nine exemptions to the presumption that requests for information should be honored. Except for exemption 3, these exemptions are discretionary: FOI officers who conclude that a requested record falls within the scope of an exemption may withhold the information, but they do not have to withhold it.

*Exemption 1: National Security.*   This first exemption permits agencies to withhold records that are "specifically authorized under the criteria authorized by an Executive order to be kept secret in the interest of national defense or foreign policy" if the secret classification is done properly.[25] Perhaps more than any other exemption, this one lends itself to each administration's imprimatur in that modern presidencies have varied widely in terms of their enthusiasm for classifying documents "secret" and "top secret."

Federal judges who hear Exemption 1 appeals are permitted to review the classified material to determine if the decision to classify was a proper one. In practice, judges very rarely exercise their option to perform such *in camera* reviews, relying instead on detailed affidavits from the government explaining why the material had been kept secret.

In 1986, Congress amended the FOIA so as to explicitly permit the FBI to refuse to confirm or deny the existence of a requested file if the agency's invocation of Exemption 1 would itself threaten the national security. The material in question must have been properly classified, and the agency's freedom to deny the existence of the files will last only so long as that classification remains in force.

*Exemption 2: Internal Agency Personnel Rules.*   Records "related solely to the internal personnel rules and practices of an agency" need not be released to the public. Exemption 2 is designed to protect some admittedly trivial materials from disclosure, such as the agency's rules for coffee or cigarette breaks and personal leave days. This exemption does not exist to protect delicate information, the kind that would violate employees' privacy. (Exemption 6 covers the more personal kinds of personnel files.)

The Supreme Court has held that Exemption 2 seeks to "relieve agencies of the burden of assembling and maintaining for public inspection matter in which the public could not reasonably be expected to have an interest."[26] Still, at times

---

[24]*Phillippi v. Central Intelligence Agency,* 546 F.2d 1009 (D.C. Cir. 1976).

[25]*Baez v. United States Department of Justice,* 647 F.2d 1328 (D.C. Cir. 1980).

[26]*Department of Air Force v. Rose,* 425 U.S. 352, 369–70 (1976).

the public may have an interest in an agency's "internal" regulations. Suppose, for example, that you were assigned to do a story about the kinds of training that FBI agents receive in hostage negotiation techniques or in dealing with media personnel covering hostage-taking incidents. It is highly unlikely that a federal judge would compel the FBI to reveal such information to you. In 1981, the D.C. Circuit Court of Appeals permitted the Bureau of Alcohol, Tobacco and Firearms to withhold under Exemption 2 portions of its training manual used to teach new agents how to conduct "surveillance of premises, vehicles and persons." While admitting that there might be much legitimate public interest in such matters, the court concluded that the information in the training manual was created predominantly for internal personnel reasons. The court also emphasized that disclosure might give undue aid to persons with a criminal intent.[27]

Some federal agencies have taken the position that *any* information in their files that can assist the agency's employees in performing their duties should fall within Exemption 2. Courts have generally rejected such a broad interpretation of the exemption. In two similar cases from 1997, the Ninth and Tenth Circuits rejected the U.S. Forest Service's somewhat comical assertion that maps showing the nesting sites of certain birds were the kinds of internal personnel files encompassed by Exemption 2.[28]

*Exemption 3: Withholding Mandated by Other Federal Laws.*   Perhaps this part of the FOIA should be known as the "We bow down to other laws" exemption. It is sometimes referred to as the "catch-all" exemption, and it is the only one of the nine wherein nondisclosure of requested files may be mandatory rather than discretionary. Agencies seeking to withhold data under this exemption must point to a specific federal law that either demands that this kind of information be kept secret or that establishes clear criteria for determining whether the material needs to be withheld. Often courts are called on to referee what might be described as a "dance of deference" in that some federal statutes generally calling for nondisclosure include provisions rendering that presumption inoperable if another law (such as the FOIA) would otherwise mandate disclosure. The Privacy Act of 1974—which grants a qualified right to find out what information the government has about us, to correct such information where necessary, and to limit the ways in which the government may use that information (and to whom it may release it)—is one such statute.[29] In 1984, Congress amended the Privacy Act to clarify that the FOIA's presumption in favor of openness should prevail whenever the two laws might seem to conflict. Nonetheless, agencies will sometimes err on the side

---

[27]*Crooker v. Bureau of Alcohol, Tobacco, and Firearms,* 670 F.2d 1051 (D.C. Cir. 1981).

[28]*Audubon Society v. United States Forest Service,* 104 F.3d 1201 (10th Cir. 1997); *Maricopa Audubon Society v. United States Forest Service,* 108 F.3d 1082 (9th Cir. 1997).

[29]Cordell A. Johnston, "*Greentree v. United States Customs Service:* A Misinterpretation of the Relationship between FOIA Exemption 3 and the Privacy Act," 63 *Boston University Law Review* 507 (1983).

of nondisclosure in that persons may bring suit under the Privacy Act against any government agency that improperly reveals personal information about them to others. Such suits, if successful, can result in payment not only of court costs and attorney's fees, but also of compensatory damages. By contrast, an FOIA requestor who sues an agency for improperly withholding data cannot receive damages.

A good example of Exemption 3 at work is found in *CIA v. Sims*,[30] decided by the Supreme Court in 1985. At issue was an FOIA request that sought information about "MKULTRA," a multifaceted initiative in the 1950s and 1960s through which the CIA sought data on "the use of biological and chemical materials in altering human behavior," or "brainwashing." Part of the experiments had the government administering consciousness-altering drugs such as LSD to unwitting subjects, two of whom died during the course of the studies. The FOIA request sought copies of the grant proposals and contracts awarded under the MKULTRA program as well as the names of the individuals, research universities, and other institutions that had performed the research. In denying that request, the CIA pointed to the National Security Act of 1947, which instructs the director of the agency to "protect intelligence sources and methods."

The Supreme Court ruled unanimously in favor of the agency and had no difficulty in determining at the outset that the National Security Act was precisely the kind of law to which Congress intended agency FOIA officers to defer when it wrote Exemption 3. The legislative history of the FOIA indicated that Congress knew the Act's sponsors intended that the National Security Act would trigger FOIA's Exemption 3. Lower courts called on to rule on the issue had also so held.

The more complicated part of the Court's deliberations concerned whether this particular FOIA request was covered by the National Security Act's call for nondisclosure, whether the names of the individuals and institutions sought should be categorized as "intelligence sources." The lower court fashioned a definition limited to sources of information that the agency "could not reasonably expect to obtain without guaranteeing confidentiality," but Chief Justice Burger's majority opinion concluded that the decision as to when promises of confidentiality are necessary should be left to the director of the CIA, not to the courts.

*Exemption 4: Confidential Commercial Information.* Often in the course of conducting an investigation of a company or an industry (such as in deciding whether or not to approve a merger or to block it on antitrust grounds), the government will learn things about one company that its competitors would love to learn but have no right to know. Exemption 4 reflects Congress's belief that neither competing companies nor the public in general necessarily has a right to learn such data, which after all had not started off as *government* information at all. For an FOIA request to be denied on the grounds that it includes such confidential commercial or financial information, the agency must conform to either of two rules set

---

[30]471 U.S. 159 (1985).

forth in a pair of decisions from the D.C. Circuit Court of Appeals. These rules are often referred to as the *National Parks* test,[31] as modified by the more recent *Critical Mass*[32] decision. The *National Parks* test governs information that a company has been *required* to provide to the government. When another entity makes an FOIA request for such data, an agency that seeks to deny the request under Exemption 4 must be able to demonstrate that disclosure will either make it more difficult for the government to obtain such data in the future (because corporations will be less forthright) or that revelation will do substantial harm to the competitive stance of the company that originally made the data available to the government.

Data that a company has *voluntarily* submitted to the government are administered instead under the rule set forth in the *Critical Mass* decision. There, the D.C. Circuit Court of Appeals applied the first prong of the *National Parks* test, but substituted for the second prong a new test: that the information sought be of a kind that would not "customarily" be revealed by a corporation to the public in general.

Exemption 4 also provides for the withholding from FOIA requestors of "trade secrets," which the D.C. Circuit Court of Appeals defines as "a commercially valuable" formula or process that was created from much innovation.[33] Examples are KFC's combination of spices in its fried chicken and the formula for Coca-Cola syrup.

*Exemption 5: Internal Agency Policy Discussions and Memoranda.* The philosophy behind exemption of the FOIA—often called the "working papers" or "executive privilege" exemption—is that the public has a right to know what policies a government agency has adopted, but not all details of the discussions that helped shape the completed policy. Such revelations would "chill" the speech of agencies' employees and advisors—who will fear that their words may come back to haunt them—and thus jeopardize the quality of decision making. The exemption is consistent also with a sense that public servants "should be judged by what they decided, not for matters they considered before making up their minds."[34]

Exemption 5 also permits withholding data related to a government agency's legal consultations with its own or outside attorneys (the "attorney–client privilege")[35] as well as, more generally, any strategizing done by attorneys who are contemplating litigation on behalf of a government agency (the "attorney work-product privilege").[36] This latter privilege reflects the belief that the FOIA should not result in disclosure of information that would not normally be revealed to

---

[31]*National Parks and Conservation Association v. Morton,* 498 F.2d 765, 770 (D.C. Cir. 1974).

[32]*Critical Mass Energy Project v. NRC,* 975 F.2d 871 (D.C. Cir. 1992).

[33]*Public Citizen Health Research Group v. FDA,* 704 F.2d 1280, 1288 (D.C. Cir. 1983).

[34]*Jordan v. Department of Justice,* 591 F.2d 753, 773 (D.C. Cir. 1978).

[35]*Mead Data Central v. United States Department of the Air Force,* 566 F.2d 242 (D.C. Cir. 1977).

[36]*FTC v. Grolier,* 462 U.S. 19 (1983).

an adversary in litigation via the discovery process. In 1988, the Supreme Court issued a ruling on this facet of the exemption in the context of an FOIA request by a group of federal prisoners for their "presentencing reports," which are made at the request of probation officers to the district court judge and which often include testimony from neighbors, therapists, and others who may have some knowledge about the circumstances surrounding a defendant's crimes. In a 5–3 vote, the Court determined that such reports might be withheld under exemption 5 from release to third parties, but that the data should be given to the prisoners themselves.[37]

*Exemption 6: Personnel, Medical, and Similar Files.* As seen earlier, Exemption 2 permits the nondisclosure of the kinds of trivial personnel matters (parking space allocations, coffee break policies) in which the public has no interest. Exemption 6 also provides for the nondisclosure of personnel matters, but those of a more personal nature. The latter exemption is not restricted to information about government personnel, but extends to any individual about whom highly private information is included in a file.

The specific wording of the exemption tells FOI officers they may withhold information from "personnel and medical files and similar files the disclosure of which would constitute a clearly unwarranted invasion of privacy." There are thus two steps in Exemption 6 adjudication. First, it must be determined whether the file is indeed a personnel or medical or "similar" file. Then courts must assess how "unwarranted" the privacy invasion would be if the files should be revealed.

Concerning the initial inquiry, it is not surprising that the word *similar* has been problematic. The key to determining relevant similarity is that the information sought is "of the same magnitude, as highly personal, or as intimate in nature, as that at stake in personnel and medical records."[38] Using this formula, the First Circuit Court of Appeals found that the names of scientists who had submitted unsuccessful proposals for National Cancer Institute grants would not be as "personal" a revelation as is envisioned by the Exemption. The court pointed out that being rejected for such grants was "not so rare an occurrence as to stigmatize the unfunded applicant." Moreover, those in a position to affect the careers of these applicants would tend to be rather sophisticated themselves about the scientific grant-making process and would thus know that failure to obtain a particular kind of funding is not necessarily a negative reflection on the objective merits of a proposal.[39]

Probably one of the most closely watched instances of Exemption 6 litigation involved the explosion of the *Challenger* space shuttle, which killed all the

---

[37]*United States Department of Justice v. Julian,* 486 U.S. 1 (1988).

[38]*Board of Trade of the City of Chicago v. Commodity Futures Trading Commission,* 627 F.2d 392, 398 (D.C. Cir. 1980).

[39]*Kurzon v. Department of Health and Human Services,* 649 F.2d 65 (1st Cir. 1981).

astronauts aboard, including high school teacher Christa McAuliffe. The *New York Times* sought from NASA the audiotape of the astronauts' voice recorder. One of the threshold issues the courts had to confront was whether, given that NASA had already released what it claimed were the full printed transcripts of the tapes, the release of the requested tape recordings would provide enough *additional* "personal" information so as to trigger Exemption 6. In an *en banc* ruling, the D.C. Circuit Court of Appeals found the tapes were in fact covered by the exemption. "While the taped words do not contain information about the personal lives of the astronauts," Judge Douglas Ginsburg wrote for the majority, "disclosure of the file would reveal the sound and inflection of the crew's voices during the last seconds of their lives." He went on to compare the *Challenger* disaster with the *Apollo 1* cockpit fire that claimed the lives of three astronauts back in 1967. The transcripts of that tragedy ended with Roger Chafee yelling, "We're on fire! Get us out of here!" As Judge Ginsburg explains: "The description alone is chilling. One can hardly doubt that the horror in the voices on the tape would convey additional information that applies to the astronauts in the throes of their deaths."[40]

The second Exemption 6 inquiry asks whether the feared privacy invasion will be "unwarranted." The *Challenger* tapes were ultimately withheld from the *New York Times* because of the feared privacy invasion that would be suffered by the families of the perished astronauts.[41] Also, in 1994, the Supreme Court adjudicated an FOIA request by union affiliates that wished to organize federal workers in several agencies and thus sought workers' home mailing addresses.[42] Disclosure of this information would constitute an unwarranted invasion of privacy, Justice Thomas concluded for the majority, in that its revelation would lead to an "influx of union-related mail, and, perhaps, union-related telephone calls or visits" that at least some employees would prefer to avoid.

*Exemption 7: Law Enforcement.* The purpose of Exemption 7 is to prevent the premature disclosure of materials that would jeopardize criminal or civil investigations or cause some kind of demonstrable harm to informants who have assisted law enforcement personnel. This is the most wordy of the FOIA exemptions. Because it is set forth within the statute as subsections (a) through (f), it is often thought of as six exemptions in one. Courts called on to adjudicate Exemption 7 claims follow a two-part analysis. First, they must determine whether the sought information has been "compiled for law enforcement purposes." If that is in fact why the information has been compiled, the courts must ask if revealing the information will result in any of the following: interference with law enforcement proceedings, jeopardizing someone's right to a fair trial, invasion of privacy rights,

---

[40]*NASA v. New York Times,* 920 F.2d 1002 (D.C. Cir. 1990).

[41]*NASA v. New York Times,* 782 F. Supp. 628 (D.C. 1991).

[42]*United States Department of Defense v. Federal Labor Relations Authority,* 510 U.S. 487 (1994).

disclosing a confidential source's identity, revealing investigatory techniques, or endangering someone's life or physical safety.

Courts have generally been very deferential in their handling of the first inquiry, the question of whether the information sought has been "compiled for law enforcement purposes." In 1982, for example, the Supreme Court held that the FBI files and other possibly derogatory materials that the Nixon Administration had gathered to hurt persons on Nixon's famous "enemies list" should be considered exempt from FOIA disclosure. Even though the immediate reason for compiling the information may have been for rather shallow, and perhaps even illegal, political ends, the data had been originally gathered for legitimate law enforcement reasons.[43]

In another case, the Court held that materials not initially gathered for a law enforcement purpose can be exempted from FOIA disclosure if later used for such a purpose.[44] As part of a routine government audit—*not* as part of a law enforcement investigation—Grumman Aircraft had made financial data available to the Defense Contract Audit Agency in 1978. Several years later, the government was investigating Grumman for allegedly fraudulent practices, and the company sought from the government the data it had provided earlier, hoping the information would help in its defense.

The government refused the FOIA request. Emphasizing that the statute demands only that the information had been "compiled," not necessarily "*originally* compiled," for law enforcement purposes, Justice Blackmun concluded for the majority that Exemption 7 is appropriately invoked as long as the information requested has been "compiled" for such a purpose at any time prior to the filing of the FOIA request itself.

*Exemption 8: Financial Institutions.*    The purpose of the rather infrequently used exemption 8 is to foster continued public confidence in banks, trust companies, securities exchanges, and similar entities. Experience has shown, after all, that an unsupported belief in a financial institution's insolvency can become a self-fulfilling prophecy. Yet the exemption also covers institutions that do not receive deposits and are not subject to mass withdrawals in the way ordinary banks are. For example, the consumer group Public Citizen was unsuccessful in its FOIA request for the annual credit examinations of the National Consumer Cooperative Bank, chartered by Congress to provide "specialized credit and technical assistance to nonprofit cooperatives." Deposits made to that bank are not subject to withdrawal on demand, thus undermining the governmental interest in avoiding a "run on the bank." The D.C. Circuit Court of Appeals, however, concluded that the phrase "financial institutions" in Exemption 8 is not limited to depository institutions.[45]

---

[43]*FBI v. Abramson,* 456 U.S. 615, 631–32 (1982).

[44]*John Doe Agency v. John Doe Corporation,* 493 U.S. 146 (1989).

[45]*Public Citizen v. Farm Credit Administration,* 938 F.2d 290 (D.C. Cir. 1991).

# Things to Remember

## THE NINE FOIA EXEMPTIONS

- National security
- Routine personnel records
- Deference to other federal laws
- Confidential commercial information
- Internal agency discussions
- Personnel, medical, or similar files
- Law enforcement
- Confidential data from financial institutions
- Geological and geophysical data

*Exemption 9: Geological and Geophysical Data.*    Exemption 9 is designed to protect the financial interests of companies that have filed with the government data concerning oil wells and natural gas deposits. It is the least used of all the nine FOIA exemptions; it has been cited in only a handful of court cases. Moreover, claims under this exemption often overlap with Exemption 8 (financial data)[46] or Exemption 4 (trade secret)[47] arguments.

## The Government in the Sunshine Act

In 1976, Congress passed the Government in the Sunshine Act, which requires generally that those federal agencies normally covered by the FOIA and at least two or more of whose governing body members have been appointed by the president (with Senate approval) shall conduct their meetings in public. Most, although not all, the agencies covered by FOIA are thus also covered by the Sunshine Act.

That a federal body's leadership is composed of rather high-power government officials is not alone sufficient to trigger the Sunshine Act. For example, the ad hoc Chrysler Loan Guarantee Board—its name is a reminder of its function, to administer the federal government's "bail out" of the financially troubled auto manufacturer—was exempt from the law, even though it boasted the chairman of the Federal Reserve and the Secretary of the Treasury among its leadership and even though all members of the board had been appointed to their more permanent federal positions via presidential appointment and Senate consent.[48] To

---

[46]*NBC v. Small Business Administration,* 836 F. Supp. 121 (S.D. N.Y. 1993).

[47]*Black Hills Alliance v. United States Forest Service,* 603 F. Supp. 117 (D.S.D. 1984).

[48]*Symons v. Chrysler Corporation Loan Guarantee Board,* 670 F.2d 238 (D.C. Cir. 1981).

be covered by the Sunshine Act, a governing body must also have some policy-making powers. Thus, the Council of Economic Advisers—again, the name suggests the function—is exempt from the Act precisely because its role is only to *advise* the president on economic matters.[49]

Agencies that are covered by the Sunshine Act must conduct their meetings in public. A "meeting" is defined in the Act as anytime a quorum of its members talk together about their official business. A meeting can thus be in a government hearing room or in a coffee shop. It can be live or via telephone conference call. Future litigation will likely hold that "chat room" consultations can also be considered meetings.

Under the Act, agencies must make an announcement of an upcoming meeting at least one week in advance. Should the agency determine that the upcoming meeting need not be opened because its subject matter is listed among the Act's explicit exemptions, that determination must be included in the announcement. Persons who wish to appeal the agency's proposed closing can immediately bring suit in federal district court. Aggrieved parties can also sue after a closed hearing has been held, although such suits must be filed within sixty days. While the burden of proof is always on the agency to justify closure, even a successful suit will typically result only in release of a transcript or tape recording of the closed hearing. (Agencies are always required to produce such records and to retain them for at least two years.) There is no provision for damage awards, and the awarding of attorneys' fees and court costs is infrequent.

The statutory exemptions to open meetings under the Act are designed for the most part to mirror FOIA exemptions, including an exemption for meetings at which trade secrets will be discussed or where an open meeting will jeopardize a national security interest. A few of the Sunshine Act's exemptions are different from those of the FOIA, however. For example, the Act includes an exemption for meetings that "involve accusing any person of a crime, or formally censuring any person."[50] Meetings can also be closed if companies or individuals likely to be subject to a proposed regulation would want to attend only to learn ways of evading the law.[51]

## The Federal Advisory Committee Act

"Vote for me, and you get two for one!" So said Bill Clinton during the 1992 presidential campaign as a way of reminding voters that Hillary Rodham Clinton would be the nation's first First Lady reared in the feminist era, that she would spearhead important policy initiatives in a Clinton White House. Some voters undoubtedly applauded this new kind of First Lady, while others were wary. As it turned out,

---

[49]*Rushforth v. Council of Economic Advisors,* 762 F.2d 1038 (D.C. Cir. 1985).

[50]5 U.S.C. sec. 552 b (c) (5). There has been no published case law interpreting the provision.

[51]*Common Cause v. Nuclear Regulatory Commission,* 674 F.2d 921 (D.C. Cir. 1982).

her status as First Lady helped her prevail against a lawsuit brought under an infrequently used federal law.

Not long after Inauguration Day in 1993, President Clinton appointed his wife chair of the President's Task Force on National Health Care Reform, a small group consisting mostly of Cabinet-level officers that was asked to make a report within 100 days. With the exception of one high-profile public hearing, the Task Force conducted its work in closed session. This fact disturbed a coalition of doctors and allies who thought that the meetings should be open to the public. Their suit against Mrs. Clinton was unsuccessful, however. As the D.C. Circuit Court of Appeals pointed out, the Federal Advisory Committee Act was designed to open up the meetings of groups composed of private citizens. The Act specifically exempts committees "composed wholly of full-time, or permanent part-time, officers or employees of the Federal Government." Despite Mrs. Clinton's unpaid status, the court emphasized, she must be considered the equivalent of a federal employee for at least two reasons. First, elsewhere in the Federal Code, Congress had specifically authorized presidents to pay their spouses out of the treasury funds for providing assistance in the carrying out of presidential duties. Second, to rule otherwise would have absurd and unwanted effects on the functioning of the executive branch. Were a First Lady to attend and participate in Cabinet meetings regularly, suddenly the entire Cabinet would be converted to a FACA "advisory group" and would thus not be normally able to conduct its deliberations in private.[52]

The Clinton administration produced another headline-making Federal Advisory Committee Act precedent when it set up the Presidential Legal Expense Trust to gather private donations toward the Clintons' private legal fees from the

---

[52]*Association of American Physicians and Surgeons v. Clinton,* 997 F.2d 898 (D.C. Cir. 1993); *Association of American Physicians and Surgeons v. Clinton,* 989 F. Supp. 8 (D.D.C. 1997).

# Things to Remember

### FEDERAL OPEN MEETINGS LAWS

- The Government in the Sunshine Act of 1976 generally requires meetings conducted by agencies covered by the FOIA to be open to the public.
- Meetings need not be in person, nor in formal meeting rooms.
- Exemptions generally mirror the FOIA's own exemptions.
- Agencies wishing to meet in private must first alert the public of this intention, which is itself appealable.
- The Federal Advisory Committee Act, which also requires that certain meetings be open to the public, was deemed inapplicable to Hillary Rodham Clinton's Health Care Reform group.

Whitewater investigations and the Paula Jones sexual harassment suit.[53] When a private citizens' committee brought suit, alleging that the Trust was not behaving in accordance with FACA, the federal district court determined that the Act was not implicated, that "a trust established by a government officer in his personal capacity without use of public funds, and which renders absolutely no advice on official government policy, simply is not within FACA's scope."[54]

## State Freedom of Information Acts

All fifty states and the District of Columbia have some form of legislation providing for access to government records. In that the federal law was adopted so early (1966), it is not surprising that many states have modeled their own statutes after the federal law. Moreover, it is not at all unusual for state supreme courts to cite federal case law interpreting FOIA as precedents when they are called on to interpret their own state statutes.

State statutes typically define records rather broadly so as to include not only papers but also most other methods in which information might be retained, including computer databases. Several state laws make an explicit distinction between the information contained in a database (revealable) and the computer software that helps to organize that information (not necessarily revealable). Perhaps the most dramatic example of a state FOIA law at work in recent years has been the application of Florida's law so as to include the individual ballots from the 2000 election, thus enabling a consortium of news media to conduct a post-election statewide recount of all ballots not correctly processed by vote tally machines.

A minority of states restrict informational access to citizens of that particular state. Most states do not allow agencies to base access decisions on the requestors' motives (personal, educational, commercial), although several states do provide for a higher fee structure in the case of purely commercial uses. Within this framework, reporters seeking information for dissemination to the public are not considered commercial users, the profit motive of their employers notwithstanding. In 1999, the Supreme Court saw no constitutional impediment to a California statute permitting the release by law enforcement agencies of arrestees' home addresses only to persons willing to declare that the information would not be used for commercial purposes. (The company challenging the law routinely made the addresses available to attorneys, who would presumably contact the individuals named to solicit business).[55] Although most states charge requestors only for photocopying costs, some also assess a fee for the agency's expenditure of human and other resources in researching a request. Overall fee waivers are common when requestors

---

[53]Ruth Marcus, "Clintons Establish Fund to Meet Legal Expenses," *Washington Post,* 29 June 1994, p. A1.

[54]*Judicial Watch v. Clinton,* 880 F. Supp. 1, 8 (D.D.C. 1995), *aff'd,* 76 F.3d 1232 (D.C. Cir. 1996).

[55]*Los Angeles Police Department v. United Reporting Publishing Corporation,* 528 U.S. 32 (1999).

are able to demonstrate a public benefit in the release of the information sought. In practice, the result is that the media often do not have to pay fees.

Not surprisingly, all state access laws provide for exceptions to the general presumption of openness. Often these exemptions are part of the statute itself, as is the case with the federal FOIA. Sometimes it has instead fallen to the state courts to create categories of exemptions over the years. Whether an exemption requires or merely permits nondisclosure varies from state to state. Although many states have fashioned their own lists of exemptions after the federal statute, clearly some FOIA provisions make little sense in the context of a state law. For example, how often does the revelation of records held by a state agency have the potential to endanger "national security," as provided for in the FOIA's Exemption 1?

Requestors who are dissatisfied with a state agency's response may appeal, either initially via some administrative process or directly to state court. Many states provide for an expedited appeals process so that these kinds of cases can be moved to the front of a court's calendar. Successful litigants will generally receive only the information they sought, not money damages, although attorneys' fees may be awarded under some circumstances.

Requests for certain categories of information have generated much public interest and litigation under state law. One such recurring issue has been the need to balance the public's right to know the details of searches to fill high-level job vacancies against the danger of discouraging the candidacies of applicants who fear publicity. State universities want to attract the very best candidates to become administrators and often argue that the most attractive candidates might not want to have their current employers know that they are considering moving.[56]

There has also been a fair amount of litigation seeking the disclosure of test results on exams used for identifying candidates for promotion within state or local civil service systems. Generally, state courts have ruled in favor of disclosing test scores in the aggregate, but not scores of any individual employee. The exams themselves have generally not been subject to disclosure so as to maintain their integrity and to permit the reuse of items in future testing.[57] Some courts have required even more disclosure. In Wisconsin, for example, test scores on a physician licensing exam were ordered disclosed as well as the scores of individual physicians asked to retake the exams because questions had been raised about their professional skills.[58]

Individuals' medical records and birth certificates are generally not disclosable under state FOIA provisions. Coroners' records, however, are generally revealable (unless they are part of an ongoing police investigation) on the grounds that our privacy rights expire along with us.

---

[56]*Arizona Board of Regents v. Phoenix Newspapers,* 806 P.2d 348 (Ariz. 1991); *Wood v. Marston,* 442 So. 2d 934 (Fla. 1983); *Booth Newspapers v. Board of Regents,* 507 N.W.2d 422 (Mich. 1993).

[57]*DeLamater v. Marion Civil Service Commission,* 554 N.W.2d 875 (Iowa 1996).

[58]*Munroe v. Braatz,* 549 N.W.2d 451 (Ct. App. Wis. 1996).

Until 1994, it had been up to each state's discretion whether to keep information found in driver license records open to the public. The public policy implications of this question had become controversial for at least two reasons. First, there was growing resentment in some quarters at the states' profiting from selling their motor vehicle license databases to commercial users, such as in letting Toyota have a list of the state's Honda owners. To many, this policy was seen as an unwarranted invasion of privacy. Much concern was also expressed that states making driver license records available to any requestor were acting as unwitting accomplices to criminal wrongdoing. An actress in California had been murdered by a stalker who had obtained her address from the state, because he already knew the woman's license plate number. Antiabortion protesters can similarly obtain names and addresses not only of clinic physicians and staffs, but often of their clients, which has often led to harassing mail and phone calls.

Concerns such as these led to passage of the federal Driver's Privacy Protection Act in 1994,[59] which requires that states give motorists the option of keeping their data confidential. In 1998, the Fourth Circuit Court of Appeals held the federal law unconstitutional as a violation of the states' autonomy rights articulated in the Tenth Amendment. The Supreme Court unanimously reversed this decision in 2000, finding that Congress had acted within its legitimate power to regulate interstate commerce.[60]

## State Open Meeting Laws

All fifty states and the District of Columbia also have some kind of legislation providing for the opening up of governmental meetings to the press and public. The majority of these laws predate the federal Government in the Sunshine Act of 1976, which was itself modeled after the law in Florida. The statutes also require that some form of advance public notice be provided of an upcoming meeting, often in the form of a formal announcement in the local newspaper. In some but not all states, openness means not only that the public and press may attend, but that citizens may address the meeting during a public comment period. Some statutes also explicitly provide for a right to broadcast meetings live. Typically, state-level laws govern meetings held by city, county, and town entities as well. Factors weighing in favor of a given group being covered by an open meetings law include that it performs government-like functions or has policy-making authority, that it was created by state law (or the state constitution), that its membership consists mostly of public officials, and that public funds pay its expenses.

Reporters often complain that public officials will try to skirt their state's open meeting law by having informal or "spontaneous" gatherings over lunch or in some other seemingly social milieu. State laws and judicial interpretations vary

---

[59]18 U.S.C. sec. 2721–725.

[60]*Reno v. Condon,* 528 U.S. 141 (2000).

in the zeal with which they will try to prevent such abuses. Most open meeting laws provide that any gathering of a quorum (the smallest number needed to take official action) of a governmental body will be considered a "meeting," wherever such gatherings may take place, as long as some official business is discussed. The Texas Supreme Court held that when two of the state's three water commissioners had discussed a case before them while in the men's room on recess, they had held a "meeting" that should have been open to the public (although not necessarily in the men's room, one can assume).[61] Another popular way of trying to evade the law's demand for openness is the use of "serial communication," a succession of private communications each one of which involves a number of participants fewer than necessary to trigger the statute, but where the cumulative effect is to conduct via this "telephone game" the equivalent of a prohibited meeting of the whole. Some state statutes specifically prohibit this procedure, and in other states the judiciary has stepped in to accomplish the same thing.

Not surprisingly, state statutes provide for exceptions to the assumption of openness. Public bodies can meet in secret, "executive session," when the matters they intend to discuss fall into certain specified categories, such as consultations with an attorney about ongoing litigation or internal personnel matters that would likely result in an unwarranted invasion of privacy. Typically, the decision to move into executive session must itself be in the form of a motion that is made and voted on in open session. Moreover, many states dictate that executive sessions are designed for discussions only, that any formal actions taken by the government body after participating in such private discussions must then again be voted on in public.

Although the kinds of matters that can justify an executive session vary from state to state, a good rule of thumb is that the more general the discussion, the more likely it is to be kept open, that closed sessions tend to deal with specific individuals. Thus, discussion of welfare reform would be public, but fact-finding about a specific welfare recipient's alleged abuse of benefits is more likely to be done in private.

States vary in the kinds of sanctions to be applied against public officials who hold closed meetings that should have remained open to the public. Some statutes provide for criminal fines and even imprisonment, but these penalties are rarely invoked. It is also possible in several jurisdictions to have a state court nullify any government actions that had been taken in an improperly convened executive session.

Suppose that you are a reporter covering a public hearing, when the presiding officer announces that the participants will be going into executive session and that all members of the public and press should leave. What should you do? Certainly, it would not be wise to physically resist an order to leave, but do insist that

---

[61]*Acker v. Texas Water Commission,* 790 S.W.2d 299 (Tex. 1990); *Newspaper Guild v. Sacramento County Board of Supervisors,* 69 Cal. Rptr. 280 (Cal. Ct. App. 1968) (a luncheon at the Elks Club deemed a "meeting" under the state law).

# Things to Remember

---

### STATE FOIA AND OPEN MEETING LAWS

- All fifty states and the District of Columbia have FOIA and open meeting laws.
- State FOIA laws, although generally modeled after the federal law, vary greatly in terms of who may obtain information and for what purposes and whether any statutory exemptions require, or merely permit, nondisclosure.
- Most state open meeting laws predate the federal law, and many give the public a right not only to attend, but also to speak.
- States have often been called on to apply their laws to "spontaneous, off-the-record" meetings.

---

you be told precisely what provision of the applicable open meetings law permits the proposed closure. A prompt call to your employer, who may be able to obtain a lawyer's opinion as to the legality of closing the hearing, would be in order next. In the event that the closure is improper, it is sometimes possible to shame the officials into reopening the proceedings simply by publishing an account of the closure.

## Private "Censorship" of Information

The *New York Times'* famous masthead boasts that the paper includes "All the news that's fit to print"; it does not say, "All the news we know."

When media organizations make judgments about whether to report or withhold information on the basis of its perceived news value or on the editors' comfort level concerning the reliability of a reporter's sources, few eyebrows are raised. For example, in the reporting of the Monica Lewinsky saga, Jackie Judd of ABC News was virtually the only employee from a mainstream news organization who reported on the existence of the infamous "blue dress"—long before the Starr Report confirmed such evidence—even though the artifact was common knowledge within the Washington press corps. Such "should we go with it or hold it?" decisions are the essence of editorial judgment.

Suspicions are often aroused, however, when a news organization's decision to withhold information from the public seems to be based on criteria other than ordinary news judgment. In this concluding section, we discuss four categories of such criteria that often lead to controversy. Each can be described as behavior that appears to some observers as bowing to pressure: from advertisers, from sources, from the news organization's owners, and from employees' possibly competing financial incentives. It should be admitted at the outset that virtually none of the situations to be described here involves media *law* per se; rather, they are problems in media *ethics*. They are presented here because, from the consumers' perspective, it often matters not whether information is being withheld by the government or by the media themselves.

### Pressure from Advertisers

Many of our parents likely taught us the adage, "If you have nothing good to say about someone, it is best to say nothing at all." What happens, however, when media outlets try too hard to accentuate the positive, at least when writing about companies upon whose advertising support they depend?

Writing in the *Columbia Journalism Review*, Russ Baker reported that the Chrysler Corporation's advertising agency had put dozens of major magazines on notice that it must be alerted in advance about any content in news and editorials "that might be construed as provocative or offensive." Apparently, the car manufacturer feared having a major advertising piece appear in a magazine issue that produced too much controversy of any kind. The memorandum had dramatic repercussions at *Esquire* magazine, which killed a short story by writer David Leavitt at the last minute out of fear that the piece's somewhat risqué content might offend Chrysler. The magazine's literary editor handed in his resignation in protest.[62]

Sometimes news outlets make a point of toeing the line without having to be put on such explicit notice by their larger advertisers. Thus, for example, several newspapers in Toronto refused to accept ads offered by a company that provided its call-in subscribers with information about dealer invoice costs on new cars and average trade-in prices of used cars. The media were afraid of offending their larger and more long-term advertisers, the local auto dealerships. Also fearing the ire of the auto industry, an executive of the *Tribune-Democrat* newspaper in Johnstown, Pennsylvania, wrote to apologize to local car dealerships after it had run a first-person account by one of its reporters about the stresses involved in trying to get a good price on a car.[63]

Clearly, news and advertising content are interdependent. In a small town, that a major department store has just opened is legitimate news, even though feature stories about the opening may do more for the store's bottom line than its initial paid advertising budget. We also would not expect a newspaper or magazine that had just run a favorable review of a restaurant to *refuse* to run an ad from the eatery, touting excerpts from the review as reasons for patronizing the place. Ethical questions arise when news and editorial judgments seem to be based primarily on the need to please advertisers. Yet, given that most media make most of their

---

[62]Russ Baker, "Some Major Advertisers Step Up the Pressure on Magazines to Alter Their Content; Will Editors Bend?" *Columbia Journalism Review,* September-October 1997, p. 30.

[63]"Darts and Laurels," *Columbia Journalism Review,* Nov.-Dec. 1994, p. 25.

revenues from advertisers, how can they help but have one eye tentatively focused on the possible financial repercussions of running any given story? If you are the editor of a magazine aimed at new parents, for example, will you devote a special issue to Sudden Infant Death Syndrome, even though you know that diaper manufacturers and baby-food distributors prefer to have their ads surrounded by more upbeat stories? The answers are not easy ones, but it is important to recognize the advertiser's influence on that which we call news.

### Pressure from News Sources

It is not at all unusual for a person interviewed for a news story to try to kill the story prior to publication. Sometimes the request may be quite reasonable. The news outlet may have the facts all wrong. The narrative it is planning to present may be libelous. At other times, there may be no allegation at all as to the untruth of a planned story, although some legal action other than libel may be threatened. Such was the case when former tobacco company executive Jeffrey Wigand's 1995 interview on CBS's *60 Minutes* was canceled because Wigand's former employer threatened CBS with a multibillion dollar lawsuit for "tortious interference." Wigand had a confidentiality agreement with Brown and Williamson, and CBS feared that it could be held liable for inducing Wigand to break that agreement. After details of one of Wigand's depositions in a Mississippi suit against the tobacco giant were published in the *Wall Street Journal,* CBS decided its own potential liability was greatly diminished, and it finally aired a version of the original interview three months late. The story formed the basis for the 1999 feature film, *The Insider.*

 Figure 7.3

Cartoonist Jimmy Margulies tweaks CBS's *60 Minutes* for allowing tobacco companies to influence its news coverage about their industry.

*© 1995 Jimmy Margulies, The Record (N.J.). Reprinted by permission.*

More mundane pressure from sources to postpone publication of news comes in the form of "news embargoes." Often, an organization will widely disseminate a press release with some presumed news value and ask that the information in the mailing not be published until a specific date in the near future. One of the main reasons an organization uses this means of public relations is when it does not want the substance of the story to leak prior to its own planned press conference, yet the story is too complex to expect accurate coverage without giving the media some lead time to do their own research. News outlets that violate the terms of the embargo will not have committed any crime, nor will the organization that drafted the press release have any legal cause of action against them. The main incentive for obeying the embargo is to stay on the organization's mailing list for future announcements.

An ethical dilemma emerges when the news sought to be embargoed is so very important that it might literally be a matter of life and death. In 1998, for example, several news outlets pleaded unsuccessfully with the British medical journal *Nature Medicine* for permission to publish immediately details about a dietary supplement sold in health food stores that might have been contaminated with a highly dangerous chemical.[64] The *New England Journal of Medicine* has also been the source of highly controversial news embargoes. It has a rather strict policy to the effect that media outlets that violate the terms of an embargo will be cut off for an indefinite period from future announcements and that researchers scheduled to be published in the journal who dare to discuss their findings prematurely with the media may have their manuscripts killed at the last moment. In the 1980s, the policy was enforced against physicians who wished to go public with their data showing the efficacy of taking an aspirin pill daily in the reduction of the risk of second heart attacks.[65] The *Journal* waived this policy in the case of a 1997 report on the potentially fatal cardiac complications associated with taking a particular combination of prescription diet pills.[66]

## Pressure from Management

A. J. Liebling once wrote in the *New Yorker* that "freedom of the press is guaranteed only to those who own one." Judicial interpretation of the First Amendment has generally been consistent with this appraisal. Reporters and editors who are terminated because their work angers their bosses do not have any legal recourse, at least not under the First Amendment. In the 1990s, for example, it was widely reported that Michael Kelly was fired from his position as editor of the *New Republic*

---

[64]Howard Kurtz, "Journal Resisted Calls to Lift News Embargo," *Washington Post,* 1 Sept. 1998, p. A2.

[65]I. Herbert Scheinberg, "When a Medical News Embargo Caused Harm" [Letter to Editor], *New York Times,* 30 Apr. 1994, p. 22.

[66]Kenneth Walker, "Pills Never the Best Way to Reduce Weight," *Chicago Sun Times,* 23 Nov. 1997, p. 47.

because he was too critical in print of Vice President Al Gore, a personal friend of Martin Peretz, the magazine's publisher. *Philadelphia Enquirer* reporter Ralph Cipriano claimed that he was fired because his reporting about financial improprieties within the local Catholic archdiocese was making life a bit too uncomfortable for his bosses.[67] In neither situation would the aggrieved employee have a First Amendment claim against the former employer. Actually, Cipriano did sue the *Enquirer*—though not on First Amendment grounds—and the case was settled out of court in late 2000.

More troublesome are allegations of a media outlet's institutional self-censorship aimed at preventing negative publicity about the outlet itself. Such allegations have been on the rise ever since large conglomerates whose major assets are not journalism holdings have bought media companies. Thus, for example, concerns are often expressed that the NBC network is especially reluctant to criticize its parent company, General Electric, and that Disney films and Disney company practices are very unlikely to be panned on ABC, which it owns. In 1998, ABC's *20/20* killed a planned exposé of unfair labor practices at Disney World.[68] When NBC forced reporter Bob Costas to apologize for mentioning China's human rights abuses on air during the 1996 Olympics, critics wondered if the network's motivation was that its parent company, GE, has enormous investments in China.[69]

Management at the *Los Angeles Times* had to conduct an extraordinary business meeting in the fall of 1999 to apologize to its staff for having kept them, and thus the public, in the dark about one of the paper's financial interests. It seems that the newspaper, unbeknownst to any of its own editors, had entered into a financial arrangement with the owners of the city's new sports arena whereby the two entities would split the advertising revenues from the Sunday magazine supplement devoted to coverage of the arena's opening. As one media critic put it: "Journalists are not supposed to have financial arrangements with the people or institutions they cover. That's a conflict of interest, clear and simple."[70] Some observers wondered if the incident was caused in part by Times Mirror (the paper's parent company) having brought in a General Mills executive with no particular media experience to serve as its board chairperson.

Finally, sometimes allegations of financial conflicts are made against the media industry as a whole. For example, you probably have heard much about the advent of high-definition television (HDTV), the digital technology that produces movie theater-quality visual images. There is a good chance, however, that you did not hear or read much about the enormous lobbying campaign that the mass

---

[67]Howard Kurtz, "Crossed Agendas: Church vs. Reporter," *Washington Post,* 13 June 1998, p. E1.

[68]Lawrie Mifflin, "An ABC News Reporter Tests the Boundaries of Investigating Disney and Finds Them," *New York Times,* 19 Oct. 1998, p. C8.

[69]"Muzzled by Murdoch," *Boston Globe,* 6 Mar. 1998, p. A18.

[70]Richard Cohen, "No Way to Do Business," *Washington Post,* 11 Nov. 1999, p. A43.

media waged in Washington to ensure that the new electromagnetic spectrum bandwidths needed to transmit in HDTV—worth scores of billions of dollars—would be *given away* to the holders of more traditional TV licenses. If you have not heard about the spectrum giveaway or if you did not know much about the issue before, might it be because media companies preferred that you not know? The issue was never featured on any of the nightly news program segments that focus on the wasting of government dollars, such as NBC's "The Fleecing of America" or ABC's "It's Your Money."

### Pressure from Employees' Competing Financial Interests

Government officials are required by a wide array of federal, state, and local regulations to file highly detailed public documentation of their financial holdings. The purpose behind such laws, of course, is to help the public ensure that their elected (and, in many cases, appointed) representatives do not abuse their positions of power by making decisions that will benefit them financially. Indeed, officials are often called on to put their financial holdings into a blind trust so that they will not know when their decisions may help or hurt their own financial health. Not surprisingly, then, the question has often arisen as to whether similar concerns about potential conflicts of interest should be applied to our "representatives" in the Fourth Estate (the news media).

Sometimes the concerns may seem mundane, such as when travel reporters accept free trips to vacation spots. Will they not feel compelled to report positively about the locales they visit, the inns where they stay, the area's restaurants and other diversions? The number of raised eyebrows aimed at reporters' financial dealings has undoubtedly increased with reports of the media superstars' multimillion dollar contracts and speaking fees in the tens of thousands of dollars.[71] When such reporters are called on to write stories that in some way affect the interests of the industry groups that have paid these fees, their own credibility might be jeopardized.

Sometimes a concern has been expressed about reporters who are working on longer book-length manuscripts without taking a leave of absence from their employers. Might such reporters sometimes be tempted to withhold from their newspaper audience the most truly newsworthy facts they uncover out of fear that they will steal their own thunder and undermine the eventual market for their upcoming book? Perhaps the best-known instance of this kind of controversy surrounded the *Washington Post*'s Bob Woodward, who in the 1980s was working on a book about the CIA and managed to obtain some rather intimate access to the agency's former director, William Casey. Those interviews led to some startling revelations about the CIA's role in various covert operations, but *Post* readers did not learn the details until Woodward's book appeared. The news media were abuzz with allegations that Woodward's dual roles as reporter and author may have done journalism a disservice.

---

[71]James Fallows, *Breaking the News: How the Media Undermine American Democracy* (New York: Pantheon, 1996).

# Things to Remember

**PRIVATE "CENSORSHIP"**

■ The line between "censorship" and "editorial discretion" can be hard to draw.

■ Ethical questions arise when the decision to withhold information is based on pressures from advertisers, inappropriate use of news embargoes, or financial conflicts of interest within the media themselves.

 ## Chapter Summary

Although Supreme Court decisions have often included dicta to the effect that the First Amendment has some relevance to the news gathering process, it has also held that there is no constitutional right to obtain information from the government. Congress and the state legislatures have created a limited statutory right through the passage of Freedom of Information Act and open meeting laws. These laws all provide categories of exemptions from disclosure, which have in turn resulted in a voluminous case law seeking to determine if a specific information request is exempted.

From the media consumer's perspective, it often matters not whether information is withheld by the government or by the media themselves, and the line between improper self-censorship (stemming from identifiable sources of conflicts of interest) and ordinary editorial judgment is sometimes hard to discern.

chapter

# *Reporting on the Judiciary*

You may wonder why there is a separate chapter on media coverage of the courts. Shouldn't the judiciary be treated as just one more topic of government information to which the press would want to gain access? In other words, couldn't the subject matter of this chapter have been handled in the previous chapter instead, the one dealing with access to information?

The main reason is one of happenstance: that the law in this area has developed separately from the "access to information" case law. Then, too, the kinds of issues encountered in this chapter concern not only access to judicial venues and information, but also the core right to publish that which the press already knows.

## A Clash of Rights

In many legal disputes concerning information about the judiciary, both litigants favoring disclosure and those seeking secrecy have constitutional arguments on their side. Indeed, these disputes are often referred to as "First v. Sixth Amendment" clashes in that the free press guarantee is pitted against the various "fair trial" rights—to a speedy trial, to an impartial jury of one's peers, and so forth—enumerated in the Sixth Amendment. Although presidents may occasionally argue that the Constitution itself—rather than just a Freedom of Information Act exemption—gives them the right to withhold information, the case law examining the constitutional underpinnings of such an "executive privilege" is scant. By contrast, the U.S. Supreme Court has handed down dozens of cases involving the clash between the First and Sixth Amendments. Thus, the case law from the previous chapter dealt most often with statutory construction, the process of figuring out what laws mean. By contrast, litigation involving access to and freedom to report information about a court case is at its core a battle over competing constitutional rights. The Supreme Court's interpretation of these competing claims has resulted in more of a constitutional right of access to judicial venues and documents than to other public spaces and information. Thus, there is a constitutional right to attend a criminal suspect's trial, even though there is not a right (as we saw in Chapter 7) to interview that same suspect in jail. On the other hand, media are often prohibited to publish that which they already know about a judicial proceeding, whereas such a restriction on publishing information about other governmental proceedings is almost unthinkable.

## The Contempt Power

It is especially important for professional communicators to understand their obligations under the Sixth Amendment because those who disobey orders from trial judges risk being issued a contempt citation. To be held in **contempt of court** means to be fined or imprisoned for taking any action that a trial judge perceives as disobedient or disrespectful. The judiciary is not the only branch of government that can hold an offender in contempt. Congress held in contempt several uncooperative witnesses called before it during the McCarthy era and has often threatened to hold presidential appointees in contempt for failing to give complete and accurate testimony. The contempt power, however, is wielded most often by the judiciary. Most forcefully, too, in that the Founders borrowed from the English common law the power of judges to issue **summary contempt** orders via which persons disrupting the courtroom can be cited and punished on the spot, without a right to any further due process.

The law recognizes two broad categories of contempt citations. **Civil contempt citations** are designed to persuade ("coerce" might be a better word) a reluctant party to do something she or he has thus far failed to do. In the case of reporters, this most typically means to reveal the identity of one's sources. Many reporters have incurred daily fines and even been imprisoned as part of a judge's efforts to compel disclosure.

**Criminal contempt citations** are issued as a punishment for actions already taken. Overzealous attorneys may incur the wrath of trial judges in this way if they disobey the trial judge's orders. The order might be to "stop badgering a witness" or to accept an adverse ruling from the bench without any vocal complaints. On at least one occasion, Judge Lance Ito warned attorneys in the O. J. Simpson criminal trial, "Get out your checkbooks—Now!" One of the attorneys in the 1998 defamation case stemming from young Tawana Brawley's apparently having concocted a story about having been gang-raped was sentenced to a short jail term by the trial judge after an especially heated courtroom exchange.

When media professionals are found in criminal contempt of court, it is most frequently for publishing information that had been subject to a judge's **gag order** prohibiting such publication. Reporters have gotten into trouble in other ways as well. In Louisiana, a cameraman was held in contempt for disobeying an order prohibiting filming in the halls of the criminal justice building.[1] In Texas, a cameraman was arrested after having filmed jurors leaving the courtroom.[2]

---

[1]*State v. Angelico,* 328 So. 2d 378 (La. 1975).
[2]*Duffy v. State,* 567 S.W.2d 197 (Tex. Crim. App. 1978).

## Trial Judges' Burden of Proof

In the law, the phrase "burden of proof" often comes up. Usually, we think in terms of a prosecutor's burden of proof in a criminal case, to establish the defendant's guilt "beyond a reasonable doubt." This chapter is about a special kind of burden of proof, imposed by appellate courts (and especially by the U.S. Supreme Court) on trial judges who wish to rein in press coverage of trial proceedings. Sometimes judges try to do so by explicitly forbidding the dissemination of particular facts related to a trial. Such gag orders (judges usually prefer to call them restrictive orders) might be imposed directly on the media or on the trial participants—lawyers, witnesses, jurors—from whom the media might gather news. Judges often instead determine that the best way to retain some control over courtroom proceedings is to close the press and the public out of the courtroom altogether. **Closure orders** may apply to a trial itself or to any of several steps in the pretrial process. Trial judges may also deny press access to certain categories of court documents.

As it turns out, the Supreme Court has heard numerous cases involving closure orders and a small number of cases involving gag orders. To varying degrees, the doctrines that emerge from those cases give trial judges a sense of what burden of proof they incur when they contemplate issuing such orders. Sometimes it is the press that brings suit against the trial judge, either because they have been "gagged" or closed out of the courtroom or because gag orders placed on trial participants arguably infringe on the press's right to *gather* news. Sometimes the trial participants themselves, most frequently attorneys or witnesses, will seek to have a gag order lifted. Then, too, sometimes criminal defendants will argue that their convictions should be overturned because a judge's closure order (or refusal to issue a closure order) resulted in an unfair trial. Whatever the specific legal posture of a case, it makes sense to think in terms of the trial judge's burden of proof when answering to a higher judicial authority.

## The Unusual American Balancing Act

Although this book is about communication law in *America,* a bit of international perspective concerning these issues is in order. You may recall the 1997 Massachusetts trial involving British au pair Louise Woodward, who was convicted of second-degree homicide—later reduced to involuntary manslaughter—in the "shaken baby syndrome" death of young Matthew Eappen. Coverage of the trial was even more intense in England than it was in the United States. One of the British tabloids even provided readers with the White House's phone number, urging them to call and express their outrage at the jury's verdict.[3]

Had Woodward been accused of harming an English child, in an English court, the coverage would have been quite different, and not just for what may seem the obvious reasons. British law generally does not permit the media to offer

[3]Justin Dunn, "Now Call Clinton," *The Mirror,* 3 Nov. 1997, p. 1.

# Things to Remember

**AN OVERVIEW OF FIRST VERSUS
SIXTH AMENDMENT CONTROVERSIES**

- Conflicts wherein the press is prevented from learning or reporting information about the judiciary usually pit the First Amendment against the Sixth Amendment.
- Judges may hold reporters in contempt of court for violating their orders.
  - Civil contempts are designed to produce compliance.
  - Criminal contempts are designed to punish noncompliance.
- Trial judges assume a "burden of proof" when they consider either closing their courtrooms or placing gag orders on those who are permitted in.
- That burden of proof is far higher in the United States than in most other democratic nations.

commentary about ongoing court cases. This policy is not an aberration, from an international perspective. Indeed, the United States is very much in the minority among Western democracies in its *not* having such a legal restriction. As it turns out, just a few months after the case's resolution, a strikingly similar case was working its way through the English judiciary, this one involving an Australian nanny working in London who, like Woodward, was charged with shaking a baby to death.[4] Media coverage was limited to matter-of-fact reportage of actual court proceedings, with no commentary.[5]

Consider also this contrast between the U.S. model of covering the courts and that of its neighbor to the north. For most of a three-year-long Canadian trial involving a particularly grisly homicide, the judge ordered that the press report virtually nothing about the case, in which Paul Bernardo, with his wife as accomplice, was convicted of the rape and murder of two teenage girls. Much to the chagrin of the trial judge, media in the United States provided extensive coverage of the trial proceedings, and many Americans faxed stories to their Canadian friends.

## What's a Judge to Do?
## The Supreme Court and the Fugitive

Sometimes First and Sixth Amendment values work well together. The First Amendment, of course, includes among its provisions the constitutional guarantees

[4]Stephen Wright, "Dead Baby Girl 'Had Signs of Being Shaken,'" *Daily Mail* (London), 12 Aug. 1998, p. 17.

[5]T. R. Reid, "On New Au Pair Trial, 'No Comment, We're British,'" *Washington Post,* 28 Apr. 1998, p. A13.

for freedom of speech and freedom of the press. The Sixth Amendment promises to criminal defendants the right to "a speedy and public trial, by an impartial jury." The Sixth Amendment's guarantee of a public trial seems wholly consistent with freedom of the press. Then, too, to the extent that unfettered public and press access to the workings of the judiciary can uncover governmental abuses, such access would seem to be at least one means of giving breath to the Sixth Amendment's promise of a trial by "impartial" jurors.

Yet the two amendments do sometimes conflict. Before enumerating the ways in which this can occur, a bit of perspective is in order. The vast majority of criminal cases nationwide attract little or no media attention. In the absence of a pretrial media spectacle, there is no conflict between First Amendment values and the also compelling interest in empaneling an impartial jury. Another truth about the criminal justice system also needs to be factored into the equation. More than 90 percent of criminal prosecutions do not result in a trial at all. Rather, the typical defendant, after having been given a sense of the kinds of evidence the state will be able to present should a trial be held, will choose instead to plea bargain. In return for saving the state the time and expense of a full-blown trial, the district attorney's office, with the cooperation of the presiding judge, will accept a guilty plea to some lesser offense or will promise to seek a less harsh penalty than might otherwise be requested. The infamous Unabomber, Theodore J. Kaczynski, for example, reached a plea agreement with federal prosecutors that resulted in successive life terms instead of the death penalty.

We should realize, then, that the discussion of conflicts between First and Sixth Amendment provisions involves a tiny portion of criminal prosecutions. That being said, what are some of the ways that media coverage of the criminal justice system may make it difficult for a suspect to receive a fair trial? Consider the plight of Dr. Sam Sheppard, whose conviction for the murder of his wife provided the basic source material for the TV series and later movie, *The Fugitive*. After several unsuccessful appeals in the Ohio state court system, and after he had spent a dozen years in jail, the U.S. Supreme Court overturned Sheppard's conviction on the grounds that the media circus surrounding his prosecution made a fair trial impossible.[6]

Within a few days of Marilyn Sheppard's death, newspaper stories made clear that the doctor was the prime suspect and that local police were frustrated by his refusal to take a lie detector test or be injected with "truth serum." Such accounts were followed by what Justice Clark's majority opinion referred to as the "editorial artillery," the first of which asserted boldly that Sheppard was "getting away with murder." Prejudicial pretrial publicity continued. One story reported a detective's assertion that "scientific tests" had "definitely established" a particular trail of blood that would conflict with Sheppard's account of the murder. Yet no such evidence was produced at trial. Other articles reported on Sheppard's alleged

---

[6]*Sheppard v. Maxwell*, 384 U.S. 333 (1966).

extramarital affairs with numerous women, although only one such relationship was ever discussed at trial. Sheppard's difficulties with the media followed him into the trial courtroom as well in that the press were seated so close to him that he and his attorney often needed to leave the room to confer in confidence.

It was not difficult for the Supreme Court to conclude that jurors had been tainted by both pretrial publicity and by events in the courtroom. Justice Clark thought it highly relevant that jurors' photographs and life stories showed up frequently in the media and that they were not questioned about their own media consumption habits once they were chosen.

Justice Clark's majority opinion amounted to a public scolding of the trial judge. He has allowed the courtroom to become a circus, Clark charged, and failed to take any meaningful actions to minimize the effects of pretrial publicity on the jury pool or media coverage of the trial itself on the jurors. The Court also made clear that the vast majority of avenues available to trial judges seeking to ensure that defendants receive a fair trial do not infringe on the First Amendment at all. Before examining the development of Supreme Court doctrine concerning closures and gag orders, we first consider some of these other remedies.

## Remedies That Do Not Infringe on Freedom of the Press

As we shall see, the Supreme Court has imposed a rather strict burden of proof on trial judges who seek to further Sixth Amendment interests in a fair trial by methods such as courtroom closures or gag orders. With respect to the latter kind of remedy, there exists a problem above and beyond any First Amendment counterweights to be applied. Most of the truly damaging material, from the defendant's perspective, is likely to emerge long before a trial is held, long before a trial judge is even selected. Trial judges cannot prevent dissemination of such TV images as the defendant being handcuffed and arrested, often juxtaposed with "sound bites" of community members expressing outrage at the heinousness of the crime. Let us consider some of the actions trial judges can take to remedy the effects of pretrial publicity.

### Continuance

A fair amount of social science evidence suggests that news media stories are rather ephemeral things, soon forgotten.[7] Defendants who seek a **continuance** (i.e., a delay) of their trial are banking on the forgetfulness of community members from whom the jury pool will be drawn. Any harmful effects of prejudicial pretrial publicity should diminish, the reasoning goes, as citizens cease to focus on the sordid details of any particular crime and return to their normal day-to-day concerns.

---

[7]John P. Robinson and Mark R. Levy, *The Main Source: What People Learn from Television News* (Beverly Hills, Calif.: Sage, 1986).

Courts are reluctant to grant motions for a continuance. Delaying a trial places a burden on the judicial system. Witnesses may become unavailable and their memories may fade, records may be lost or otherwise become less usable. Another problem with trial delay is that the Sixth Amendment provides that defendants should be granted a "speedy" trial. The Speedy Trial Act provides quantitative definitions of "speedy" judicial proceedings, at least for defendants in the federal courts. The Act requires, with some flexibility, that defendants generally be indicted within thirty days of arrest and brought to trial within seventy days of indictment.[8]

## Change of Venue

In extraordinary circumstances, where a community is so saturated with prejudicial publicity that a trial judge concludes it will be impossible to impanel an impartial jury, the trial may be moved to another jurisdiction (see Figure 8.1). For example, the trial of Timothy McVeigh for the bombing of the Alfred P. Murrah Federal Building in Oklahoma City took place in Denver, Colorado. The court had considered moving the trial instead to Tulsa, but determined that pretrial publicity had been so intense that a fair trial was unlikely anywhere in the state.[9]

The McVeigh example notwithstanding, trial judges very rarely grant defendants' motions for a **change of venue.** It is a very difficult thing for judges to make a ruling admitting they are powerless to ensure a fair trial in their own jurisdiction. Even the judge presiding over the original trial of Jack Ruby for murdering accused JFK assassin Lee Harvey Oswald refused to grant the defendant a change of venue, even though so many millions had seen Ruby shoot Oswald on television. (This decision weighed heavily in an appellate court's overturning the conviction.[10] Ruby died of cancer while awaiting retrial). Then, too, a change of venue is an extremely expensive remedy. The transportation, housing, and boarding expenses for attorneys, court personnel, and an often lengthy group of witnesses can be staggering.

There is an additional problem associated with changes of venue. Defendants who accept a new venue as a means of maximizing their chance of obtaining a fair trial must by so doing waive their Sixth Amendment right to a trial of their peers, at least as the Constitution's drafters envisioned it. The Sixth Amendment promises the accused a jury of "impartial" citizens "of the State and district wherein the crime shall have been committed." Defendants are thus guaranteed both an impartial jury and a *local* one, and often they must choose between the two guarantees.

Finally, trial judges may be incorrect in their faith that the news media in the new locale will avoid the kind of sensationalist coverage that prompted the defense to seek the change. Because there is typically a delay of several weeks or even

---

[8]18 U.S.C. sec. 3161–74 (1996).

[9]*United States v. McVeigh,* 918 F. Supp. 1467, 1474 (W.D. Okla. 1996).

[10]*Rubenstein v. State,* 407 S.W.2d 793 (Tex. Crim. App. 1966).

months between the granting of a venue change request and the actual commencing of a trial, the problem of pretrial publicity may simply start all over again.

Some of these problems can be avoided through a **change of venire** instead of a change of venue. This means to conduct a trial in the locale where the crime was committed, but to do so with a jury imported from another jurisdiction. A change of venire is generally less costly than a change of venue, although the living and traveling expenses of the jury have to be considered. It also is no less violative of the Sixth Amendment guarantee of a local jury than is a change of venue. Whether the imported jurors will themselves be bombarded by prejudicial publicity back in their hometowns will be jointly a function of media interest and the delay between revelation of the trial judge's decision to change the venire and the actual seating of the jurors. Changes of venire are even rarer than changes of venue. In one study, not one of the judges surveyed had ever even received a motion for a change of venire.[11]

---

[11]Fred Siebert, *Free Press and Fair Trial: Some Dimensions of the Problem* (Athens: University of Georgia, 1970).

 Figure 8.1

"MOST EXTREME CHANGE OF VENUE I'VE EVER HAD."

*© 1988 Sidney Harris. Reprinted with permission.*

## Sequestration of the Jury

Sequestration is a remedy that does not prevent bias caused by *pre*trial publicity but does effectively shield jurors already impaneled from any ongoing news coverage of the trial itself. To sequester jurors is to house them in seclusion, at the government's expense, monitoring their media consumption so as to make sure that the trial itself is their only source of information. The O. J. Simpson homicide jury was sequestered; the jury in his later civil trial was not. Neither was the Timothy McVeigh jury sequestered.

The life of a sequestered juror resembles that of an inmate in a minimum security prison. Long trials can take a hefty toll on jurors' morale, mental health, and family relationships. Juror pay is minimal, and although employers are generally required to make their workers available for jury duty, they are not typically required to pay them their full salaries during the trial. Because sequestration is a remedy disproportionately used in trials that are predicted to be quite lengthy, the financial burden on individual jurors can be immense. In addition, jurors may come to blame the defendant for the inconveniences to which they are being subjected and thus become more prone to convict.

## Voir Dire

Mark Twain once quipped that the U.S. criminal jury system is the best in the world, its only blemish being "the difficulty of finding twelve everyday men who don't know anything and can't read." More recently, commenting on the trial of Lieutenant Oliver North for his activities related to the Iran Contra scandal in the Reagan administration, Professors Peter D'Errico and Richard Moran questioned the trial judge's practice of dismissing all potential jurors who had read or heard anything about North's previous congressional testimony. Anyone at the time who literally had no knowledge of North was either a recluse or a dolt. Is this the kind of person we want sitting on juries, they wondered?[12] Both Twain and the pair of professors were reacting to excesses in the voir dire process. Voir dire refers to the process of questioning potential jurors in an effort to identify any sources of bias. It is by far the most frequently employed technique for ensuring that defendants—and the state—receive a fair trial. Voir dire is also used in civil trials.

The process may be as simple as a judge addressing the entire group of potential jurors, asking them if there is any reason they will not be able to render a verdict based solely on the evidence to be presented in the trial itself. Or, voir dire can include having every potential juror fill out a lengthy questionnaire drafted jointly by counsels for both sides, under the judge's supervision.

Twain and the other critics notwithstanding, voir dire, when conducted properly, does not need to result in the impaneling of ignoramuses as jurors.

---

[12]Peter D'Errico and Richard Moran, "An Impartial Jury or an Ignorant One?" *Boston Globe,* 21 Feb. 1989, p. A18.

Indeed, the Supreme Court has made clear on a number of occasions that jurors need not be ignorant of the matter before them. As long ago as 1878, in refusing a convicted bigamist's appeal, the Court found that the seating of a juror who had admitted during voir dire that he had an "opinion" about the defendant's guilt or innocence was not a violation of the defendant's rights, because the juror also indicated that he would be able to set aside his opinion and make his final judgment based on the evidence to be presented.[13] Chief Justice Waite even cautioned trial judges that potential jurors will not infrequently feign bias to avoid having to serve. In a more recent case, the Court suggested that because we live in an era of "swift, widespread and diverse methods of communication"—these words were written in the early 1960s, so the point is surely even more true today—it is unrealistic to expect to find many jurors who have heard nothing about a particularly notorious crime. All that is necessary to insure a fair trial, Justice Clark wrote, is that a juror be able to "lay aside his impression or opinion and render a verdict based on the evidence presented in court."[14] In a 1991 decision, the Supreme Court held that trial judges need not ask each potential juror about his or her exposure to media accounts of the crime to be presented to them. It is sufficient, Chief Justice Rehnquist ruled, that jurors be questioned about their ability to render a verdict based solely on the courtroom evidence.[15]

What happens when a jury pool member's potential bias is uncovered? An attorney for either side can have that juror removed **for cause** if the trial judge is persuaded of the likely bias. Attorneys are granted an unlimited number of such motions for removal. In addition, attorneys for both sides are permitted to seek the exclusion of other jurors whose bias is not alleged. These **peremptory challenges** form the art of jury selection. Those who can afford it often hire highly paid jury consultants to help identify the kinds of jurors, in terms of demographic variables or patterns of answers to specific questions, who are likely to be predisposed either for or against their client's case. In addition to the limit on the number of such challenges, which varies from venue to venue and among types of cases, the Supreme Court has said that attorneys may not systematically use their peremptory challenges to exclude jurors based on either race[16] or gender.[17] The Court has also held that a defendant's Sixth Amendment rights are violated by a racially discriminatory pattern of jury foreman selection. The case came from Louisiana, where such selections are made by trial judges.[18]

The voir dire process is designed to work hand in hand with the use of clearly worded instructions to the jurors by the trial judge. Except in the rare cases where

---

[13]*Reynolds v. United States,* 98 U.S. 145 (1878).

[14]*Irvin v. Dowd,* 366 U.S. 717, 722, 723 (1961).

[15]*Mu'Min v. Virginia,* 500 U.S. 415 (1991).

[16]*Batson v. Kentucky,* 476 U.S. 79 (1986).

[17]*J. E. B. v. Alabama,* 511 U.S. 127 (1994).

[18]*Campbell v. Louisiana,* 523 U.S. 392 (1998).

Things to Remember

---

**TRADITIONAL SIXTH AMENDMENT INTERVENTIONS**

■ In *Sheppard v. Maxwell,* the Supreme Court expressed displeasure with a trial judge's failure to keep control over the courtroom.

■ Traditionally, trial judges have numerous strategies at their disposal to minimize the effects of prejudicial publicity:
  • Continuance.
  • Change of venue.
  • Change of venire.
  • Sequestration of the jury.
  • Careful voir dire.
  • Instructions to jurors.

---

juries are sequestered, judges must rely on juror compliance with such admonitions as "Do not discuss the case with friends or family members" and "Do not permit yourselves to view any news accounts of this trial." Judges may insist that jurors not read newspapers or magazines at all for fear that a headline alone will prove prejudicial. Although jurors probably take such admonitions quite seriously, social science evidence suggests that the more forceful the instructions from the judge, the *less* likely jurors will be able to ignore "evidence" from beyond the courtroom.[19] This reaction might be a function of what social psychologist Jack Brehm calls reactance: that if we coerce people into doing things that they were planning to do anyway, resentment and noncompliance may result.[20] A perhaps more benign explanation is that focusing on the instruction itself necessitates focusing on that which the instruction forbids, an adult version of the childhood admonition, "Don't think of pink elephants."

## Preventing Prejudicial Publicity: Gag Orders

There are at least some disadvantages in each of the traditional remedies trial judges may use to minimize the effects of prejudicial publicity. It is not surprising, then, that judges have sometimes tried to employ the seemingly more efficient strategy of simply forbidding the press to report potentially prejudicial information. Judges call these instructions restrictive orders, although the decrees are

---

[19]Geoffrey P. Kramer, Norbert L. Kerr, and John S. Carroll, "Pretrial Publicity, Judicial Remedies, and Jury Bias," 14 *Law and Human Behavior* 409 (1990); J. Alexander Tanford, "The Law and Psychology of Jury Instructions," 69 *Nebraska Law Review* 71 (1990).

[20]Jack Brehm, *A Theory of Psychological Reactance* (New York: Academic Press, 1966).

often referred to as gag orders. Judges also sometimes impose gag orders on trial participants. For example, the trial judge preparing to preside over the trial of fifteen-year-old Michael Carneal in the shootings at West Paducah High School in Kentucky imposed a gag order (eventually overturned) on some of the victims' parents. This section considers both kinds of restrictions.

### Gag Orders Applied to the Press

One autumn evening in 1975, police in the town of Sutherland, Nebraska (population 850) found six members of the Henry Kellie family murdered in their home. Suspect Erwin Charles Simants was arraigned the next morning. Both the prosecutor's office and Simants's attorney asked the court to issue a gag order to minimize the extent of pretrial publicity. The county judge issued a rather broad one, forbidding the press from publishing "any testimony given or evidence adduced." A group of media entities appealed the order. The Nebraska Supreme Court modified and narrowed the order, still prohibiting discussion of the suspect's confession to police as well as of any other matter that would be "strongly implicative of the accused." The court emphasized that specific provisions of Nebraska criminal law made it difficult for the trial judge to entertain remedies other than a gag order. A continuance would be improper in that state law required a trial be held within six months of a suspect's arrest. Similarly, a change of venue would be ineffective in that Nebraska trial judges could move proceedings only to contiguous counties, and the extraordinary pretrial publicity in this case had already permeated the neighboring counties.

The U.S. Supreme Court held unanimously that the restrictive order, even as construed by the state's highest court, was a violation of the First Amendment.[21] Chief Justice Burger's opinion emphasized that gag orders, although they sometimes seem the best way to ensure a fair trial, are still prior restraints on communication, which come to the Court with a presumption of their unconstitutionality. In this particular case, the trial judge failed to demonstrate that remedies less restrictive of the First Amendment—such as careful voir dire coupled with clear and strict judicial instructions to the jurors—could not have produced a fair trial. Burger also rejected the state's refusal to consider a change of venue. The Nebraska practice of restricting such changes to neighboring counties may have had to give way to the larger Sixth Amendment interests.

The gag order in the Simants case was especially troublesome for three other reasons, Burger concluded. First, the amended order's prohibition on stories containing "implicative" information was plainly too vague. Second, the order prohibited discussion of the suspect's confession, which had been presented in a preliminary hearing open to the press and public. It is a "settled principle," he wrote, that "once a public hearing had been held, what transpired there could not be subject to prior restraint." The final feature of the gag order that compelled its

---

[21]*Nebraska Press Association v. Stuart,* 427 U.S. 539 (1976).

invalidation was its likely ineffectiveness. This homicide took place, after all, in a town of 850 residents, where "rumors would travel swiftly by word of mouth."

Chief Justice Burger's opinion was a relatively narrow one, emphasizing again and again the particular facts of the case before him. If only the trial judge had more systematically entertained less restrictive remedies, if only the gag order had been worded more clearly, if only the order's likely success could have been better predicted, the outcome might have been different. "Of necessity," Burger cautioned, the Court's holding should be "confined to the record before us." Several justices wrote separate concurring opinions that, taken together, depicted a majority of the Court at least flirting with an *absolute* ban on gag orders. Over time, the most influential of all the *Nebraska Press* opinions was the concurrence offered by Justice Powell. Whereas Chief Justice Burger's opinion emphasized the unique features of this particular gag order, Powell went out of his way to offer lower court judges what they hunger for from the high Court: a set of rules to apply in future cases. A gag order would only be permitted, Powell suggested, if there is a "clear threat" to a fair trial posed by precisely the narrowly crafted categories of publicity the order seeks to contain, and if no less restrictive alternatives are available. At least some courts have quoted portions of Powell's concurrence as if it were majority doctrine.[22]

The *Nebraska Press* decision has been interpreted by lower courts as a requirement that trial judges demonstrate a "clear and present danger" to the fairness of a trial before a gag order on the press can be entertained. It is now very rare for an appellate court to uphold restrictive orders applied against the media. For example, a criminal defendant was unsuccessful in his attempt to enjoin the NBC network from airing a docudrama called *The Billionaire Boys Club,* which depicted a homicide for which the defendant had not yet been tried.[23] Lyle and Erik Menendez, the California brothers who were eventually convicted of first-degree murder in the deaths of their parents, were also refused their request to enjoin a documentary (*Honor Thy Father and Mother*) about their legal problems.[24] They were awaiting retrial at the time. In another case, the Supreme Court of Arizona overturned a trial judge's requirement that courtroom sketch artists clear their output with him prior to broadcast. The judge's motivation may have been noble—protecting jurors from outside influence and possible retribution—but the order restricted more speech than necessary.[25] And, in an especially convoluted bit of litigation, an order restraining *Business Week* magazine from publishing sealed court documents it had legally obtained from parties to a multimillion dollar civil suit between Procter & Gamble and the Banker's Trust Company was allowed to stand for ap-

---

[22]See, for example, *Sherrill v. Amerada Hess Corp.,* 504 S.E.2d 802 (Ct. App. N.C. 1998).

[23]*Hunt v. NBC,* 872 F.2d 289 (9th Cir. 1988).

[24]Alberto Bernabe-Riefkohl, "Prior Restraints on the Media and the Right to a Fair Trial: A Proposal for a New Standard, 84 *Kentucky Law Journal* 259, 290 (1995).

[25]*KPNX Broadcasting Co. v. Superior Court,* 678 P.2d 431 (Sup. Ct. Ariz. 1984).

proximately six months before finally being overturned by an appellate court.[26] The same appellate court, and the Supreme Court, had earlier refused to intervene, because at that point in the litigation the judge's order was a temporary restraining order as opposed to a permanent injunction. Temporary restraining orders are generally issued only on an emergency basis, when a magistrate is persuaded that irreparable harm will be done to one or more litigants should unauthorized publication take place prior to the court's having an opportunity to fully air the constitutional issues involved. In addition, as the name implies, permanent injunctions are issued only after a judge has had a chance to hold a full hearing.

In only a tiny handful of instances in recent years have appellate courts upheld gag orders applied to the press itself. Certainly the best known example involved Manuel Noriega, the former leader of Panama who was brought to the United States to face drug trafficking charges. When Judge William Hoveler learned that prison officials had surreptitiously taped conversations between Noriega and his attorneys and that CNN had copies of the tapes, he enjoined the cable network from broadcasting any excerpts from them. An appellate court upheld Judge Hoveler, and the U.S. Supreme Court, by refusing to hear the case, let the gag order stand.[27] After listening to the tapes and satisfying himself that Noriega's rights to a fair trial would not be jeopardized by their dissemination, Judge Hoveler rescinded his own order.[28] CNN had already aired English translations of some of the tapes while Hoveler's gag order was still in place. As a result, the network was held in contempt of court, which was eventually settled in 1995 when it ran an on-air apology and reimbursed the government the approximately $85,000 incurred in prosecuting the case. Gag orders have also been upheld in recent years by both the North Carolina[29] and Utah[30] Supreme Courts, but again, these are exceptions to the general rule that the press prevails in these kinds of cases.

The CNN case is but one example of a body of case law that places the media on warning: Disobey a judge's order at your own peril. Even if the original judicial decree is later found unconstitutional, the contempt of court citation issued to punish the press for its disobeyal will often be upheld. This is called the **collateral bar rule,** or the "Dickinson rule," referring to a federal appellate decision from 1972.[31] The case concerned two reporters for a Baton Rouge, Louisiana, newspaper who disobeyed a local judge's order by printing details of a federal hearing convened to examine an indictment for conspiracy to kill the city's mayor. This

---

[26]*Procter & Gamble v. Banker's Trust Company,* 78 F.3d 219 (1996).

[27]*United States v. Noriega,* 752 F. Supp. 1032 (S.D. Fla.), *aff'd sub nom., In re Cable News Network,* 917 F.2d 1543 (11th Cir. 1990), *cert. denied,* 498 U.S. 976 (1990).

[28]*United States v. Noriega,* 752 F. Supp. 1045 (S.D. Fla. 1990).

[29]*The State Record v. South Carolina,* 504 S.E.2d 592 (S. C. 1998).

[30]*KUTV v. Wilkinson,* 686 P.2d 456 (1984).

[31]*United States v. Dickinson,* 465 F.2d 496 (5th Cir. 1972).

rule has been accepted in some jurisdictions and rejected in others. In a 1987 decision, another federal appellate court determined that disobeying a "transparently invalid" court order could not serve as the basis for a contempt citation,[32] but a later *en banc* ruling emphasized that the press would be far wiser to obey even a blatantly unconstitutional ruling while appealing it to a higher court.[33]

## Gag Orders Applied to Trial Participants

As we have seen, the U.S. Supreme Court has placed a very high burden of proof on trial judges who seek to ensure a fair trial by imposing restrictive orders on the media. The Court's *Nebraska Press* decision, however, had very little to say concerning the appropriateness of imposing gag orders instead on the media's most likely news sources: lawyers, witnesses, litigants, and jurors. Indeed, the Supreme Court has never dealt with a case involving this precise issue. As a result, lower courts are in disagreement as to the burden of proof demanded of trial judges who contemplate the use of gag orders aimed at trial participants rather than the media. At least in some jurisdictions, a trial judge's showing of a "reasonable likelihood" of an unfair trial is often sufficient to support the issuing of such a gag order.[34] Other courts, emphasizing the First Amendment right to hear, have concluded that gag orders imposed on those likely to speak to the press are indistinguishable from those imposed on the press directly.[35] In this section, we look first at gag orders aimed at attorneys and then at those orders targeted at other trial participants (such as jurors and witnesses).

*Attorneys.*    Although the U.S. Supreme Court has never heard a case involving a gag order issued against an individual attorney, it did, in 1991, assess the constitutionality of a state supreme court rule governing the out-of-courtroom speech of all Nevada lawyers. The appellant in that case was Las Vegas criminal defense attorney Dominic Gentile, who had been disciplined for holding a press conference in which he not only proclaimed his client's innocence, but also suggested that the guilty party may have been a specific police detective who Gentile had concluded was a cocaine addict. Although the U.S. Supreme Court held that the state rule was improperly applied to Gentile's speech, it did not find the rule itself unconstitutional.[36]

Most states have such rules, modeled after the rules of professional conduct of the American Bar Association (ABA) that warn lawyers not to make any "extra-

---

[32]*In re Providence Journal Company,* 820 F.2d 1342, 1347 (1st Cir. 1986).

[33]*In re Providence Journal,* 820 F.2d 1354, 1355 (1st Cir. 1987).

[34]*In re Dow Jones & Company, Inc.,* 842 F.2d 603, 610 (2d Cir. 1988).

[35]*Journal Publishing Co. v. Mechem,* 801 F.2d 1233 (10th Cir. 1986); *CBS, Inc. v. Young,* 522 F.2d 234 (6th Cir. 1975); *Connecticut Magazine v. Moraghan,* 676 F. Supp. 38 (D. Conn. 1987).

[36]*Gentile v. State Bar of Nevada,* 501 U.S. 1030 (1991).

judicial statement that a reasonable person would expect to be disseminated by means of public communication if the lawyer knows or reasonably should know that it will have a substantial likelihood of materially prejudicing an adjudicative proceeding." The ABA rules offer several categories of statements that might result in such prejudice, such as references to a suspect's confession or refusal to take a polygraph test, or the possibility of a plea bargain.[37] It is not surprising, then, that trial judges' gag orders aimed at attorneys are a far more acceptable part of the legal landscape than similar orders targeting the press directly. Attorneys, after all, are often referred to as "officers of the court," a label that emphasizes their special responsibility to avoid behaving in ways that will likely result in an unfair trial. Thus, it was seen as relatively unremarkable when Judge Richard Matsch prohibited attorneys and other court personnel in the Timothy McVeigh and Terry Nichols Oklahoma City bombing trials from engaging in categories of communications closely paralleling those enumerated in the ABA Code.[38] Similarly, a gag order was upheld as applied against attorney Bruce Cutler, who at the time was representing Mafia figure John Gotti.[39]

None of this discussion is to suggest that trial judges have *carte blanche* to issue extraordinarily broad gag orders against attorneys or other trial participants. This lesson was learned in *United States v. Salameh,*[40] in which the trial judge presiding over the World Trade Center bombing prosecutions tried to prevent attorneys from making *any* public utterances about the case. The appellate court that invalidated the order concluded that even restrictions on attorney speech may be "no broader than necessary to protect the integrity of the judicial system and the defendants' right to a fair trial." The court also took note of the potentially astronomical fines that would have been levied against any attorneys the trial judge thought to be in violation of the order.

***Jurors and Witnesses.*** Often, restrictive orders are targeted at jurors and witnesses instead of—or, more frequently, in addition to—attorneys. There is no U.S. Supreme Court majority opinion giving trial judges clear guidelines as to whether restrictions placed on witnesses and jurors should be granted more or less deference than those aimed at attorneys. In the *Gentile* case involving the Nevada attorney, Justice Kennedy argued that trial judges should be able to "require an attorney's cooperation to an extent not possible of nonparticipants," but that section of his opinion was joined by only three other justices. Jurors and witnesses are not "officers of the court" in the same way that attorneys are, and thus one might suppose that gag orders aimed at trial participants other than attorneys would be less likely to be upheld on appeal.

---

[37]ABA Model Rules of Professional Conduct, Rule 3.6 (1994).

[38]*United States v. McVeigh,* 931 F. Supp. 756 (1996).

[39]*United States v. Cutler,* 58 F.2d 825, 838 (2d Cir. 1995).

[40]992 F.2d 445 (2d Cir. 1993).

Such a presumption, however, would ignore the long tradition in this country of *secret* jury deliberations. Part of what it means to have a fair trial is that jurors feel comfortable to express themselves openly and candidly during their deliberations. If jurors fear that their statements and their votes will be revealed publicly by other jurors, might their candor be thus diminished? Keep in mind, of course, that we are considering restrictions on the *post*trial statements of jurors. During trials, jurors are always required not to speak to anyone about the case before them.

The other side of the equation is that jurors are uniquely qualified to set the record straight about controversial trials. Several of the O. J. Simpson criminal trial jurors felt the need to explain their Not Guilty verdict. Indeed, three of them coauthored a book toward that end.[41] Similarly, ABC's *Nightline* devoted more than one program to a comparison of the juries in the Rodney King beating (involving a group of predominantly white police officers subduing a black suspect) and the Reginald Denny beating (black youths attacking a white truck driver during the civil unrest stirred by the verdict in the first case against Rodney King's arresting officers).

Not surprisingly, courts have come down on both sides, and often the result has been a function of the breadth of the gag order. In both the Third[42] and Fifth[43] Circuits, trial judges' orders forbidding reporters from asking jurors how other jurors had voted or what other jurors had said during deliberations have been upheld. Litigation in the Fifth Circuit has been especially confusing. In 1982, in a case involving the illegal transporting of undocumented aliens, the court overturned a gag order that forbade reporters to talk with any jurors about any aspect of their deliberations. The gag order was overly broad, the court held, in that it applied "equally to jurors willing and anxious to speak and to jurors desiring privacy, forbidding both courteous as well as uncivil communications, and foreclosing questions about a juror's general reactions as well as specific questions about other jurors' votes."[44] Sixteen years later, the same court upheld an order forbidding the press from even attempting to contact jurors who had served in a celebrated corruption case without advance authorization from the state trial judge. The gag order here was distinguishable from that in the earlier case, the court held, in that it was limited to interviews concerning jury *deliberations;* it did not apply to questions about the jury verdict itself.[45]

The Ninth Circuit, in a case stemming from an armed bank robbery prosecution, overturned a gag order that prohibited the media or anyone else—one of the defendants had sent letters to jurors' homes—from attempting to contact jurors.

---

[41]Amanda Cooley, Carrie Bess, and Marsha Rubin-Jackson, *Madame Foreman* (Beverly Hills, CA: Dove Publishing, 1996).

[42]*United States v. Antar,* 38 F.3d 1348 (3d Cir. 1994).

[43]*United States v. Harrelson,* 713 F.2d 1114 (5th Cir. 1983).

[44]*In re Express-News Corporation,* 695 F.2d 807, 810 (5th Cir. 1982).

[45]*United States v. Cleveland,* 128 F.3d 267 (5th Cir. 1998).

Although preventing harassment of jurors was deemed an important state's interest, this particular gag order was overly restrictive on the press's right to gather news.[46] Also, the Tenth Circuit threw out a gag order that forbade jurors to discuss with anyone their verdict in a civil rights case against the Albuquerque, New Mexico, police. Contacts between reporters and jurors do not pose "a danger to effective justice," the court concluded, in that the media have no incentive "to upset a verdict."[47]

On occasion, witnesses have incurred the wrath of trial judges for disobeying a gag order. In a Texas case that received much news coverage, Dallas Cowboys football player Michael Jerome Irvin was on trial for possession of illegal drugs. The trial judge drafted a gag order designed to cover the same kinds of extrajudicial statements covered in the ABA Code and applied it to all trial participants. Dennis Pedini, at one time a friend of Irvin's, violated the order in dramatic fashion, first by producing a hidden video that purported to show Irvin purchasing cocaine and talking about his drug habit, and then by selling the video to the syndicated TV program *Hard Copy* and appearing on the show to describe the action. Judge Alvarez held Pedini in contempt of court, and this sanction was upheld in federal court.[48]

---

[46]*United States v. Sherman,* 581 F.2d 1358 (9th Cir. 1978).

[47]*Journal Publishing Company v. Mechem,* 801 F.2d 1233, 1236 (10th Cir. 1986).

[48]*Pedini v. Bowles,* 940 F. Supp. 1020 (N.D. Tex. 1996).

# Things to Remember

## GAG ORDERS

- In the *Nebraska Press* case, the Supreme Court ruled that trial judges may impose gag orders on the media only when
  - There is a clear threat to the fairness of trial.
  - The gag order is narrowly tailored, to remedy just that threat.
  - The more traditional means would not work.
  - It is not too late for the gag order to be effective.
- Gag orders placed on the press are now quite rare.
- In most jurisdictions, trial judges have a far lower burden of proof when they impose a gag order on trial participants rather than on the media.
- This lower burden of proof applies especially to attorneys, whose own ethical code demands that they refrain from out-of-court utterances likely to make a fair trial more difficult.
- Contempt citations issued against reporters who disobey even an obviously unconstitutional order from a trial judge may still be upheld by an appellate court.

Some state courts, even while concluding that the First Amendment only demands a relaxed standard of review for gag orders issued against trial participants, have found in their state constitutions a more exacting standard. A good example is found in *The Missoulian v. Montana Twenty-First Judicial District Court*,[49] which involved a gag order applied to all participants in a homicide trial. The state supreme court, in ruling on a local newspaper's challenge, held that the order was not the kind of prior restraint that would require the exacting level of scrutiny prescribed in the *Nebraska Press* case. The court went on to find in the Montana state constitution a public "right to know" beyond that implicit in the First Amendment, including a requirement that the press and public be granted a full hearing before any gag order is issued. The court also embraced a "substantial probability" of prejudice standard, which represents an intermediate level of scrutiny, somewhere between the "clear and present danger to a fair trial" test implicit in the *Nebraska Press* case for gag orders applied directly to the press and the much less demanding "reasonable likelihood of unfairness" standard embraced by some courts that have reviewed gag orders aimed at trial participants.

## Closing Reporters Out

Restrictive orders seek to prevent the media from reporting that which they already know. Sometimes, judges have instead tried to ensure a fair trial by preventing the media from learning potentially prejudicial information in the first place. Language from two Supreme Court decisions handed down not long after the *Nebraska Press* case may have emboldened some trial judges to issue such closure orders. In the first case, decided in 1978, the Court ruled that a Virginia newspaper had a right to publish a story identifying a state judge whose conduct had been the subject of hearings conducted by the state's judicial review committee. A gag order was not at issue in *Landmark Publications v. Virginia*,[50] but rather a state statute specifically prohibiting dissemination of information concerning the committee's investigations. Writing for the Supreme Court's majority, Chief Justice Burger allowed that the committee certainly had the right to conduct its business secretly, but concluded that the press could not be forbidden to publish whatever it learns about the committee's work (even if the source who "leaked" the material may have been in violation of the statute). The majority decision seems to be telling the states, "If you want to keep certain judicial proceedings secret, make sure that they are indeed secret."

The second case, *Smith v. Daily Mail Publishing Company*,[51] also concerned a state statute rather than a gag order. West Virginia law prohibited the publication

---

[49]933 P.2d 829 (Sup. Ct. Mont. 1997).

[50]435 U.S. 829 (1978).

[51]443 U.S. 97 (1979).

of juvenile defendants' names without prior written approval of the juvenile court. When newspapers in Charleston published the name of a fourteen-year-old accused of killing a junior high school classmate—the information was obtained by interviewing witnesses at the scene—the state prosecuted them for violation of the statute. When the appeal reached the Supreme Court, Chief Justice Burger concluded that the statute was in violation of the First Amendment. Yet he added that this ruling was a narrow one in that the Court had not been asked to determine whether the state could legitimately close juvenile proceedings to the press and public, nor was this case one of a newspaper reporter somehow gaining "unlawful access" to such proceedings.

This section examines judicial closure orders as applied to trials and to various kinds of pretrial hearings. We also look at orders sealing court documents from press and public inspection. In addition, we consider the history and current status of televising trials.

## Closing the Trial Itself

The U.S. Supreme Court has given trial court judges fairly clear guidance concerning when closing an actual criminal trial to the press and public can be permitted. The burden of proof demanded by the Supreme Court is a rather strict one, especially considering the circumstances surrounding the closure order resulting in the leading precedent. The closure at issue in *Richmond Newspapers v. Virginia*[52] was imposed in a homicide case. The unusual feature about the case was that this trial was defendant John Stevenson's *fourth*. His first trial had resulted in a conviction, but this judgment was reversed on the grounds that some inadmissible evidence had been presented to the jury. His second and third trials ended in mistrial. If ever a trial judge could be excused for a bit of zealotry in his attempt to ensure a fair trial, this case would seem to be such a situation, especially because the defense sought the closure order and the prosecution had no objection to it. That zealotry was manifested in at least one rather ironic way. When two newspaper reporters demanded a hearing on the closure order, the trial judge complied, but determined that the hearing should be considered a part of the trial itself, thus subject to the closure order. As such, the reporters were closed out of their own hearing! Their interests were represented at the hearing by their attorneys.

Chief Justice Burger announced the judgment of the Court, a 7–1 decision that the public and the press have a First Amendment right to attend criminal trials. Burger's opinion was joined only by two other justices; thus, it was not a majority opinion. It has been treated as such, however, because the pattern of concurring opinions was such that a clear majority actually did support his reasoning, as far as it went. "The right to attend criminal trials," Burger wrote, "is implicit in the guarantees of the First Amendment; without the freedom to attend such trials, which people have exercised for centuries, important aspects of freedom of speech

[52]448 U.S. 555 (1980).

and the press could be eviscerated." Could criminal trials ever be closed? Burger maintained that trial judges must have an "overriding interest" in doing so and that the interest must be "articulated in findings" that includes an inquiry as to whether remedies less intrusive on First Amendment interests might have sufficed. The various concurring opinions manifested the Court's lack of consensus as to whether the right to a *public* trial is a Sixth Amendment right, a First Amendment right, or both and whether the right should extend to civil trials as well.

The only other case in which the Supreme Court has dealt with closure of a criminal trial itself was in the context of a closure order issued by a Massachusetts judge presiding over a sex-crime trial. The trial judge was required by state law to issue such an order in that the victims were juveniles. When the *Boston Globe* appealed the order, the state supreme court interpreted the statute so as to require clearing the courtroom only during times when a juvenile victim was actually testifying. That interpretation would not help the *Globe* in this particular instance in that the rape trial had already been completed, with the press and the public completely closed out of the proceedings. The newspaper pursued the litigation to the U.S. Supreme Court, which held that statutes *requiring* closure are violative of the First Amendment. Writing for the majority, Justice Brennan admitted that although at least one of the state's interests involved—"the protection of minor victims of sex crimes from further trauma and embarrassment"—was a compelling one, it did not justify a broadly sweeping statutory requirement of closure. Rather, he said, the trial judge must be permitted to determine these matters case by case, taking into account the victim's willingness to testify in open court, tempered by his or her age and psychological maturity.[53]

Overall, the impact of the *Richmond Newspapers* and *Globe Newspapers* cases together is that actual trials are almost always kept open to the press and the public, except when the trial is part of the juvenile justice system. At least since the 1820s,[54] juvenile law in the United States has been premised on the belief that youthful offenders can and should be rehabilitated. Several differences between the adult and juvenile justice systems have thus been part of the U.S. legal landscape for much of the country's history. Although juveniles are incarcerated, they are sent to separate detention centers rather than prisons. The residents of such facilities are typically referred to as "delinquents" or "juvenile offenders" rather than "criminals." Punishment for crimes committed as a juvenile typically ends at the attainment of the age of majority, at which time the individual's record is expunged. Seen in this light, that trial proceedings involving juvenile defendants have traditionally been conducted in secret is just one more difference.[55]

---

[53]*Globe Newspapers v. Superior Court,* 457 U.S. 596 (1982).

[54]Sanford J. Fox, "Juvenile Justice Reform: An Historical Perspective," 22 *Stanford Law Review* 1187 (1970).

[55]"Media Access to Juvenile Justice: Should Freedom of the Press Be Limited to Promote Rehabilitation of Youthful Offenders?" 68 *Temple Law Review* 1897 (1995).

It is possible for an individual to be tried as a *federal* juvenile delinquent, as in the case of underage defendants charged with violating federal hate crimes laws under the provisions of the Federal Juvenile Delinquency Act.[56] Although the Act does not clearly set forth whether proceedings conducted within its scope should be open to the press, at least two courts have interpreted the Act so as to provide discretion in this regard to the trial judges.[57]

Juvenile proceedings are more typically a matter of state law. In most states, anyone who does not have a "direct interest" in the outcome of a juvenile proceeding, or at least in the judicial operations of the court, is excluded from attending. There is tremendous variation across jurisdictions, however, as to whether the media are considered to have such an interest. Many statutes explicitly invite trial judges to make this determination on a case-by-case basis. The wording of other statutes seems to suggest to judges that, when in doubt, they should exclude the media. In Connecticut, for example, judges are instructed to exclude from hearings anyone whose presence is not "necessary."[58] Several other states, even while granting discretion to trial judges, show a bias toward opening proceedings to the press and the public. Then, too, some statutes cite circumstances in which trial judges will not be given any discretion. In California and in Massachusetts, for example, the press and public must be granted access if the crime committed is an especially serious one. The California statute lists dozens of crimes that are considered serious enough to trigger the open access presumption,[59] whereas Massachusetts limits the presumptions to cases of first- or second-degree homicide.[60]

---

[56]18 U.S.C. sec. 5031–42 (1988).

[57]*United States v. Three Juveniles,* 61 F.3d 86 (1st Cir. 1995); *United States v. A. D.,* 28 F.3d 1353 (3d Cir. 1994).

[58]Conn. Gen. Stat. sec. 46b-122 (1997).

[59]Cal. Wel. & Inst. Code sec. 676 (1997).

[60]Mass. Ann. Laws ch. 119, sec. 65 (1998).

 # Things to Remember

### CLOSING ACTUAL TRIALS

- In the *Richmond Newspapers* case, the Supreme Court told trial judges that they may close the courtroom to the press and public only for an "overriding interest."
- Later, in the *Globe Newspapers* case, the Court indicated that, even in highly sensitive sex-crime trials, closures must be made on a case-by-case, perhaps even a moment-by-moment, basis; they cannot be mandated by statute.
- Actual trials, other than juvenile trials, are very rarely closed to the public these days.

Given the great variety of statutory approaches to the question of whether juvenile proceedings should be closed, it is no surprise that the courts called on to interpret the statutes have not produced a consistent body of case law. Thus, the best advice that can be given to professional communicators is that they become familiar with the applicable law in their own jurisdictions.

## Closing Pretrial Hearings

The vast majority of what the Supreme Court has had to say about conflicts between First and Sixth Amendment rights emerges from a handful of decisions governing public and press access to pretrial hearings. Because it is important to understand the evolution of that case law, in this section the cases are discussed in chronological order.

***The Defendant Seeks Closure:* Gannett v. DePasquale.**    The Court's doctrine concerning when pretrial hearings can be closed began with its 1979 decision in *Gannett v. DePasquale.*[61] At issue was whether the press had a right to attend a pretrial suppression hearing, even when the defendant has asked that it be closed and the prosecution and trial judge have agreed. The case surrounding the dispute was a homicide trial from the Rochester, New York, area; the trial judge, Daniel DePasquale, conducted the suppression hearing with the public and press excluded and further denied the local newspapers' request to be provided immediately with a transcript of that hearing. The enveloping homicide case ended quickly with a plea bargain, at which point the transcript to the suppression hearing was released. The newspapers decided to press the constitutional issue further, however, a decision that resulted in a 5–4 vote upholding Judge DePasquale's original closure order.

Writing for the majority, Justice Stewart concluded that the most important right at stake in the dispute was that to a public trial. Such a right is granted by the Sixth Amendment to the accused, not to the press and the public. In situations such as this one, where the defendant specifically requests closure, the Sixth Amendment inquiry would be concluded. None of this discussion is to deny that the public may have interests that generally coincide with the rights enumerated in the Sixth Amendment. A public trial benefits the public in many ways, Stewart admitted, but that does not mean that the public has a Sixth Amendment *right* to a public trial.

Justice Stewart allowed that the press and the public *might* be able to argue under the First Amendment for an open suppression hearing, but he was not ready to commit himself to the proposition that such a right exists. Even if such a right does exist, Stewart continued, the defendant's Sixth Amendment rights would prevail, at least in this case. After all, the press was granted a hearing to present through counsel its interests in keeping the hearing opening. Also, the closure did

---

[61]443 U.S. 368 (1979).

not amount to a permanent denial to the press and public of information about the judiciary in that the transcript of the suppression hearing was released immediately upon the entering of the defendant's plea bargain.

The majority opinion was thus a narrowly written one from two perspectives. First, Justice Stewart did not commit himself one way or the other as to whether a First Amendment right to attend pretrial hearings exists. Second, he felt no need to create a general rule to the effect that a defendant's Sixth Amendment interest in having a closed hearing would always trump whatever First Amendment interest the public may have in keeping the hearing open.

Justice Powell wrote a separate concurring opinion, destined to become majority doctrine a few years later.[62] Although agreeing with the majority that the defendant's wishes must prevail in this particular case, Powell went one step farther than Stewart, committing himself to the view that there *is* a First Amendment right on the part of the press and the public to attend even pretrial hearings. Access to suppression hearings is especially deserving of protection, Powell asserted, precisely because such hearings are often the only trial; depending on their outcome, they most often lead either to a defendant very anxious to plea bargain or to a district attorney dropping a prosecution in frustration. Powell's concurring opinion also provided lower courts with a set of guidelines to use in determining whether a suppression hearing should be closed to the press and public. Upon receiving a defendant's motion for closure, trial judges should consider whether any of the more traditional means of preserving a fair trial might work as well as closure. Should they be leaning toward closure, they must make sure that the closure order extends no farther than necessary. They must also permit any press representatives present to express their views on the matter. Although these suggestions were not majority doctrine, many lower courts have since quoted the "Powell standard" with approval, and it has been adopted by both the Judicial Conference of the United States and the Department of Justice.

As it turns out, there had been a newspaper reporter in the courtroom when Judge DePasquale entertained the defense motion for closure, and she did not object to the motion. Largely as a result of that reporter's acquiescence—she was not an attorney, after all, and may not have felt comfortable rising to object— mass media companies soon got into the habit of providing their reporters on the "courtroom beat" a carefully worded statement that would enable them to object immediately and more effectively to any proposed courtroom closure. Printed on what are often called "Gannett cards," these statements are designed to prevent a closure order from being instituted before the media's attorneys have had a chance to make legal arguments against it. Typically, the reporter will make clear in delivering the statement that he or she is not prepared to make the necessary arguments, rather that a short break is requested so that attorneys can be called in. In at least one case involving a motion to close a suppression hearing, the reading of the Gannett card backfired. The Kansas Supreme Court upheld a trial judge's decision

---

[62]*Press-Enterprise Company v. Superior Court* (II), 478 U.S. 1 (1986).

to close a suppression hearing in a homicide case, partly on the basis that the judge had conducted a hearing on the matter. That "hearing" consisted of a *Kansas City Times* reporter's standing up and reading her Gannett card to the judge![63]

***Voir Dire Hearings:* Press-Enterprise Company v. Superior Court *(I).*** Technically, the process of jury selection and questioning (voir dire) is the beginning of a trial. Still, the Supreme Court's case law concerning motions to close voir dire proceedings has developed separately from cases involving closure of full-blown trials themselves. The first of two otherwise unrelated pretrial closure cases bearing the same name, *Press-Enterprise Company v. Superior Court* (I),[64] stemmed from a racially tinged (white victim, black defendant) rape and homicide trial in California. In this case, it was the prosecution that sought to close the voir dire proceedings, fearing that media presence would make it difficult for potential jurors to answer candidly the highly personal questions likely to be posed to them. The trial judge decided to close virtually the entire voir dire hearing, which lasted six weeks, to the press and public.

Immediately after the selection of the jury, the *Riverside Press-Enterprise* sought a transcript of the hearing. This request the trial judge denied, on the grounds that the privacy of individual jurors would be otherwise compromised. A second request for the transcripts, made after the trial itself had concluded—the defendant had been convicted and sentenced to death—was similarly denied. The newspaper then commenced litigation to obtain the transcripts and have the original closure order ruled unconstitutional. By a unanimous vote, the Supreme Court sided with the press on both counts. Chief Justice Burger wrote the opinion for the Court. In it, he reviewed the available historical evidence dating back to even before the Norman Conquests to demonstrate that the jury selection process had been a presumptively open one in English law for many centuries. "The process of juror selection is itself a matter of importance," he explained, "not simply to the adversaries but to the criminal justice system." Openness helps the community see "that offenders are being brought to account for their criminal conduct by jurors fairly and openly selected."

Because the defendant in this case had wanted the voir dire hearing open as much as the press did, Burger did not need to determine whether the right to this openness was enjoyed only by the accused (as a Sixth Amendment right) or by the press and the public as well (whether as a Sixth Amendment or a First Amendment right). He did, however, give trial judges some kind of guidance as to their burden of proof should they contemplate closing a voir dire hearing: "The presumption of openness may be overcome only by an overriding interest based on findings that closure is essential to preserve higher values and is narrowly tailored to serve that interest. The interest is to be articulated along with findings specific enough that a reviewing court can determine whether the closure order was properly entered."

---

[63]*Kansas City Star Company v. Fossey,* 630 P.2d 1176 (Sup. Ct. Kan. 1981).

[64] 464 U.S. 501 (1984).

Much of this language is familiar, but at least one thing is new. Notice the deliberately vague reference to "higher values" rather than a more concrete reference to "a fair trial." The protection of individual jurors' privacy rights may itself constitute such a "higher value." Although the trial judge's desire to produce an impartial jury and to protect participants' privacy was laudable, Burger concluded, the closure order was overkill. A more narrowly tailored closure might have been permissible, he added. For example, if a juror were to tell the judge and attorneys of her own or a loved one's experience as a rape survivor, that specific part of the voir dire might legitimately be held in the judge's chambers, away from the press and public. As part of the voir dire process, the trial judge could explicitly invite any jurors who have any reluctance to answering specific questions in the open courtroom to request the same level of privacy. The closure of virtually the entire hearing to the press and public, however, was a far greater encroachment on the presumption of openness than was warranted.

Chief Justice Burger's suggestions to trial courts should be seen as just that. In several instances since *Press-Enterprise* (I) was handed down, trial judges have succeeded in closing most of or all the voir dire process without being overturned on appeal. When boxing promoter Don King was on trial for wire fraud, the trial judge sealed the questionnaires filled out by prospective jurors as well as transcripts of follow-up questions posed in the judge's chambers. Media plaintiffs protested, arguing that, at a bare minimum, the burden should have been on individual jurors to request having their follow-up questioning be conducted in private. The Second Circuit Court of Appeals disagreed.[65] The trial judge's goal here was not the protection of juror privacy, as was the case in *Press-Enterprise*; rather, the judge wanted to ensure a fair trial in a highly charged atmosphere. An HBO movie highly critical of King had just come out. There had already been a mistrial, which local press headlines blamed on the defendant's having "played the race card" when all King had done was to challenge the prosecution's alleged use of peremptory challenges to get rid of a disproportionate number of African-American jurors. One of the New York newspapers, reacting angrily to the earlier mistrial, referred to King as "another Teflon Don," thus analogizing him to Mafia kingpin John Gotti. The appellate court ruled that *Press-Enterprise* requires only that trial judges "make supportable findings, consider alternatives, and frame a limited form of relief." They need not follow each and every one of Chief Justice Burger's suggestions.

***Closures Ignoring the Defendant's Wishes:* Waller v. Georgia.** A few months after the *Press-Enterprise* (I) case was decided, the Court handed down a decision that is unique in that the appeal for an open pretrial hearing came to the Court from the criminal defendant himself rather than from the press. Guy Waller appealed his conviction on commercial gambling charges on the grounds that the closing

---

[65]*United States v. Don King Productions,* 140 F.3d 76 (2d Cir. 1998).

of the pretrial hearing convened to assess the admissibility of wiretap evidence was a violation of his constitutional right to a fair trial.[66] It was the state that had moved for closure, on two grounds. First, publicly playing some of the wiretap tapes would invade the privacy of some innocent persons whose names or voices appeared. Conversely, yet other persons identified on the tapes had been indicted but not yet tried, and the playing of the tapes in open court might, under Georgia law, make it difficult or impossible for the state to use such "tainted" evidence in later trials with other defendants. The suppression hearing was closed for its entire seven-day duration, even though only a few hours were taken up in actually playing tapes from the wiretaps.

Writing for a unanimous Court, Justice Powell concluded that Waller's constitutional rights had indeed been violated. Powell's opinion emphasizes the importance of suppression hearings in the overall judicial system in that such hearings are often the only "trial" a suspect will experience. He here repeated the point he had made in his concurring opinion from *Gannett v. DePasquale:* suppression hearings usually end in either plea bargains or in the dismissal of charges, with no trial to follow.

Perhaps the most interesting part of the *Waller* case was the Court's struggle to fashion an appropriate remedy. To set Waller free seemed a bit extreme, as did the suggestion that he be granted a new trial. Principles of equity demanded only that Waller be given that which he had been denied: a new suppression hearing, this time open to the press and public. If and only if that new hearing were to result in some significant evidence that had earlier been deemed admissible now being suppressed would Waller be granted a whole new trial.

### Closing a Preliminary Hearing:
### *Press-Enterprise Company v. Superior Court* (II)

Two years later, the Court ruled in what has come to be known as *Press-Enterprise Company v. Superior Court* (II).[67] The case stemmed from a multiple homicide case involving a nurse named Robert Diaz, who was accused of killing a dozen patients in California via the administration of overdoses of a heart drug. The defendant's preliminary hearing was closed to the press and public at his own request. In California's penal system, these hearings function very much like full-blown trials; the prosecution produces evidence and witnesses, and the defense is invited to do so also. Witnesses can be cross-examined by either side. Indeed, almost the only differences between the preliminary hearing and a trial is the absence of a jury and the lower standard of proof of guilt ("probable cause" to proceed to trial, where the state's burden of proof rises to the familiar "beyond a reasonable doubt" standard).

---

[66]*Waller v. Georgia,* 467 U.S. 39 (1984).

[67] 478 U.S. 1 (1986).

By a 7–2 vote, the U.S. Supreme Court ruled that the decision to close Diaz's preliminary hearing was made using a standard not sensitive enough to the public's First Amendment interest and that, in any event, a transcript of the proceedings should have been made available to the press at the first possible moment. Chief Justice Burger's majority opinion is notable for at least three reasons. First, he commits the Court for the first time to the principle that the interest in keeping judicial proceedings in general open to the press and public is primarily a *First* Amendment issue.

Second, the Court comes about as close as it possibly could to overturning the *Gannett* case without explicitly doing so. *Gannett,* it will be recalled, also involved a motion from the defendant to close a pretrial hearing. No doubt Burger did not feel compelled to overturn *Gannett* precisely because the majority decision in that 1979 case—by leaving open the possibility that there *might* be a First Amendment right to attend pretrial hearings that *might* in some circumstances outweigh a defendant's wish for closure—left future Court majorities enough "wiggle room." Still, if *Gannett* ever stood for the principle that a defendant's wish for closure necessarily trumps the media's desire for openness, that notion was now rejected.

Finally, and perhaps most important, *Press-Enterprise* (II) represents the Court's first attempt to give trial judges a rule that should cover *all* kinds of judicial hearings. This attempt is all the more important when we consider that the Supreme Court has only reviewed cases to date involving three kinds of judicial hearings beyond actual criminal trials themselves: voir dire proceedings, suppression hearings, and the kind of quasi-trial that California's preliminary hearings resemble. Trial judges, however, have to deal with all sorts of other hearings as well, such as bail hearings, competency hearings, plea bargain hearings, or post-trial hearings alleging prosecutorial or jury misconduct. The *Press-Enterprise* test asks trial judges to consider first whether the category of hearing involved is one that should be considered "presumptively open." To be considered presumptively open, a category of hearings must meet at least one of two criteria. Either it has historically been conducted in public (such as criminal trials themselves and voir dire hearings), or openness will make for a better hearing (i.e., it will enhance the hearing's "function in the judicial process").

Once it is determined that a category of judicial hearing is, in fact, presumptively open, then a burden of proof applies to any persons seeking to close the proceeding. Before approving a motion for closure, a trial judge must be able to demonstrate that there is a *substantial probability* of jeopardizing a "higher value" and that the closure is narrowly tailored to preserve that higher value.

In 1993, the Supreme Court had occasion to consider application of the *Press-Enterprise* test to preliminary hearings conducted in the Commonwealth of Puerto Rico.[68] The hearings were structured very similarly to those in California,

---

[68]*El Vocero de Puerto Rico v. Puerto Rico,* 508 U.S. 147 (1993).

but local law explicitly stated that they were to be conducted in secret unless the defendant requested otherwise. Puerto Rico's highest court upheld this provision against a challenge by local newspaper reporters, having concluded that the hearings function differently in the commonwealth's "unique history and traditions, which display a special concern for the honor and reputation of the citizenry." The court also emphasized that the openly conducted preliminary hearings were far more likely to result in biased trial juries given the commonwealth's small size and dense population. In a relatively short, *per curiam* opinion, a unanimous U.S. Supreme Court rejected Puerto Rico's analysis, emphasizing that when the *Press-Enterprise* test asks that trial courts look at whether certain categories of hearings have historically been "presumptively open," that inquiry is to be based on U.S. history as a whole, not the history of any smaller jurisdiction within.

### Lower Courts Apply the *Press-Enterprise* Test

As we have seen, the Supreme Court has heard closure order cases involving only suppression hearings, voir dire hearings, and the kind of elaborate preliminary hearings conducted in California and some other jurisdictions. In this section, we examine the pattern of lower court case law in which other kinds of hearings were at issue.

***One-Sided Preliminary Hearings.***    Recall that the preliminary hearing conducted in the *Press-Enterprise* case from California was itself very similar to a trial, especially in that both sides were permitted to present evidence and to question each other's witnesses and that the defendant had an absolute right to such a hearing. In most states, however, preliminary hearings are far more one-sided. They are times for the prosecution to present a truncated version of its case to a magistrate, who will then decide if probable cause exists to hold the defendant over for trial. Given the kinds of damaging evidence often heard in such hearings, it is no surprise that defendants often move for closure. The pattern of post–*Press-Enterprise* lower court decisions suggests, however, that trial judges are very reluctant to approve these motions, in part because the preliminary hearing, like a suppression hearing, typically results in either a plea bargain or in the dismissal of charges and may thus be the only opportunity for the press and the public to monitor the criminal justice system. The Idaho Supreme Court feared that closure denies the public "the opportunity to observe the criminal justice system at work." "Public access to the preliminary hearing," the Iowa Supreme Court has similarly emphasized, functions as "a curb on prosecutorial and judicial misconduct."[69]

---

[69]*Rivera Puig v. Garcia Rosario,* 785 F. Supp. 278 (D.P.R. 1992); *Cowles Publishing Company v. Magistrate Court,* 800 P.2d 640 (Idaho 1990); *Des Moines Register & Tribune Company v. District Court,* 426 N.W.2d 142 (Iowa 1988).

***Hearing on a Motion to Disqualify a Judge.*** In the 1980s, officers of the Teamsters Union being prosecuted on embezzlement charges moved to disqualify Judge Ann Aldrich from hearing the case, alleging that her past conflicts with one of their attorneys would bias her. Defendants requested further that the hearing on this motion be conducted in secret, and a district court judge chosen to hear the motion agreed. The Sixth Circuit Court of Appeals overturned this ruling, finding that these kinds of hearings met both parts of the *Press-Enterprise* test for presumed openness. First, the court reviewed many decades of history within the circuit and found that all such hearings had been open in the past. Writing for the appellate panel majority, Judge Lively concluded also that openness served a valuable societal function. "The background, experience, and associations of the judge are important factors in any trial," Lively wrote. "When a judge's impartiality is questioned, it strengthens the judicial process for the public to be informed of how the issue is approached and decided."[70]

***Bail Hearings.*** Probably some of the most dramatic recurring media narratives about the judiciary are tales of violent criminal acts committed by persons out on bail while awaiting trial on wholly unrelated charges. Thus, there is tremendous public interest in at least the end results, if not the mechanics, of bail hearings, and courts have often held that such hearings are presumptively open.[71]

The Court of Appeals for the First Circuit has emphasized that, just as pretrial hearings are often a defendant's only trial, a bail hearing may represent the public's only chance to witness a suspect's interaction with the criminal justice system. This situation would occur, of course, if bail is granted and the suspect then flees. Conversely, the decision not to grant bail, or to set it so high as to effectively ensure that suspects will remain in jail pending trial, necessarily deprives defendants of their liberty before they have been convicted of any crime.[72] The First Amendment right to attend bail hearings is not absolute. Limited closure has often been permitted when inadmissible evidence, such as tapes or transcripts from improperly conducted wiretaps, is to be presented as part of the prosecution's argument for denying bail.[73]

***Competency Hearings.*** Although there have not been many cases involving the issue of closing competency hearings, courts that have addressed the matter have generally found a First Amendment interest in favor of openness. Some of these cases predate the *Press-Enterprise* rule. In one case from 1979, New York's highest court ruled that a competency proceeding in preparation for a rape trial had been

---

[70]*Application of National Broadcasting Company,* 828 F.2d 340, 345 (6th Cir. 1987).

[71]*United States v. Chagra,* 701 F.2d 354 (5th Cir. 1983).

[72]*In re Globe Newspaper Company,* 729 F.2d 47 (1st Cir. 1984).

[73]C. Thomas Dienes, Lee Levine, and Robert C. Lind, *Newsgathering and the Law* (Charlottesville, Va.: Michie, 1997), 87.

improperly closed, especially in that the trial judge made no attempt to articulate what specific pieces of evidence to be presented at the hearing were likely to prejudice the defendant's interests in a fair trial. The decision, which resulted in the release of transcripts from the competency hearings, was based on state constitutional provisions. The court emphasized that competency hearings should be open because they may "eliminate the need for a trial" in that "either the charges are dismissed or the determination at the hearing substantially affects or destroys a party's chance of succeeding at trial."[74]

Also predating the *Press-Enterprise* test was *Miami Herald Publishing Company v. Chappell*[75] in which a Florida appellate court ruled that a trial judge who had closed a competency hearing because the public disclosure of mental health professionals' assessment of the defendant's status would violate his privacy was misreading the scope of the applicable state confidentiality statutes. Here, too, the appellate court emphasized that competency hearings should be presumptively open in that they more often than not are the only trial.

Not surprisingly, those lower court rulings that came after *Press-Enterprise* have continued the trend toward openness of competency hearings. "Given [the] strong public policy against trying an incompetent person for a criminal offense," the Utah Supreme Court wrote in a 1987 case, "it seems plain that the proceeding at which competency is determined is a significant one in the criminal process."[76] At issue was a series of three hearings held to determine the competency of a suspect accused of killing his sister-in-law and her child. The state supreme court ruled that the hearings had been improperly closed and ordered transcripts released. More recently, a state appellate court in Virginia held that the press must be given access to a videotape of the competency hearing already held for a multiple homicide defendant. "Public access can play a significant positive role in criminal competency hearings," the court wrote, in that such hearings "can postpone, sometimes indefinitely, the trial of an accused."[77]

## Access to Judicial Documents

Some of the same Supreme Court precedents that have established a qualified First Amendment right to attend judicial proceedings have also had something to say about access to judicial documents. The transcript of a voir dire proceeding is, after all, a judicial document. In *Press-Enterprise Company v. Superior Court* (I), one of the issues before the Supreme Court was whether the press should have at least been given a transcript of the voir dire proceeding in a timely fashion. The Court's

---

[74]*Westchester Rockland Newspapers Corp. v. Leggett*, 399 N.E.2d. 518, 523 (N.Y. 1979).

[75]403 So. 2d 1342 (Fla. Dist. Ct. App. 1981).

[76]*Society of Professional Journalists v. Bullock*, 743 P.2d 1166, 1178 (Utah 1987).

[77]*In re Times-World Corporation*, 488 S.E.2d 677, 682 (Ct. App. Va. 1997).

majority came out strongly in favor of such disclosure. Similarly, in *Press-Enterprise Company v. Superior Court* (II), the Supreme Court concluded that, by denying the press's repeated requests for a transcript of the elaborate preliminary hearing, the trial judge had frustrated "the community therapeutic value of openness."

The trial of former Attorney General John Mitchell for Watergate-related offenses provided the occasion for the Court to look a bit more directly at the issue of press access to judicial records.[78] Several hours of Oval Office tape recordings had been admitted into evidence and played at Mitchell's trial. The Supreme Court denied a request by the media for the right to broadcast the tapes and to sell copies to the public. In his majority opinion, Justice Powell emphasized that the press was not being closed out completely from the information on the tapes. The media were in the courtroom when the tapes were played, after all, and were provided transcripts.

This case was unusual, Powell admitted, in that Congress had already instituted a process for orderly release of the Nixon tapes to the public when it passed the Presidential Recordings Act. Lower courts have thus been free to find a right—most frequently a common-law right based on tradition rather than a First Amendment right—for broadcasters to copy and broadcast copies of audiotapes or videotapes played as evidence in court. The Abscam FBI sting in which local, state, and federal elected officials were caught on videotape accepting bribes from actors playing the role of international merchants resulted in court decisions responding to media requests to broadcast the tapes.[79] The Second Circuit Court of Appeals concluded that the videotape record necessarily provides more information than raw transcripts, that the public will want to see and hear their elected representatives's behavior.

If a witness makes a request to provide testimony via videotape rather than live in the courtroom, the resulting video will not necessarily be considered a judicial record, even if it is played in open court. Thus, when President Clinton provided a videotape deposition in the Arkansas trial of his Whitewater associate Jim McDougal, the media were not permitted to copy and broadcast the tape.[80] After all, the Eighth Circuit Court of Appeals reasoned, cameras are generally not permitted into federal courtrooms, so why should they be given a video record of this one witness's testimony? The court also shared the president's concern that the tape might improperly be used for partisan purposes, such as campaign advertisements.

Some courts have been rather stingy in determining what it means for a document to have actually been "admitted into evidence" and thus presumably made a part of the official record open to the press. In 1998, a federal district

---

[78]*Nixon v. Warner Communications, Incorporated,* 435 U.S. 589 (1978).

[79]*In re Application of NBC* (Criden), 648 F. 2d 814 (3d Cir. 1981); *In re Application of National Broadcasting Company* (Myers), 635 F.2d 945 (2d Cir. 1980).

[80]*United States v. McDougal,* 103 F.2d 651 (8th Cir. 1996).

court in Illinois honored the request of former Archer Daniels Midland executives on trial for conspiracy to deny press access to transcripts from audiotapes and videotapes produced by a "wired" government informant. Because the defendants planned to challenge the accuracy of the tapes, the court found that the materials would be ultimately found inadmissible. Moreover, transcripts used by jurors merely as a guide to help them listen to tapes that are not ultimately admitted into evidence are themselves not revealable, the court found.[81]

The First Circuit has found a right to open judicial records in the First Amendment, striking down a Massachusetts statute that permitted courts to seal court records permanently in any criminal case that did not result in conviction. The statute would thus be triggered any time a defendant was found not guilty, a grand jury failed to indict, a judge determined there was not probable cause to hold a defendant for trial, or the prosecution decided to dismiss charges. The statute amounted to a serious violation of the First Amendment, the court reasoned, because a press that is unable to report on past court cases could not provide any meaningful perspective on today's litigation.[82]

Years before the Supreme Court provided any relevant guidance, the Ninth Circuit Court of Appeals concluded that whatever rules govern closure of judicial hearings must also govern access to court documents. Overturning a trial judge's order sealing all documents concerning the drug prosecution of flamboyant auto manufacturer John DeLorean, the appellate court reasoned that it makes no sense "to distinguish between pretrial proceedings and the documents filed in regard to them."[83]

Lower courts have dealt with motions to open sealed records dealing with everything from wiretap records[84] and presentencing reports to applications for search warrants,[85] from plea agreements[86] and documents filed in support of a motion for a change of venue[87] to an accounting of expenses incurred by the public in paying for the Oklahoma City bombing defendants' legal costs.[88] In one instance, a federal prosecutor was chastised for posting to the Internet the text of a presentencing report on a group of defendants convicted of taking part in a kickback scheme.[89]

---

[81]*United States v. Andreas,* 1998 U.S. Dist. LEXIS 11347 (N.D. Ill. 1998).

[82]*Globe Newspaper Company v. Pokaski,* 868 F.2d 497 (1st Cir. 1989).

[83]*Associated Press v. United States District Court,* 705 F.2d 1143 (9th Cir. 1983).

[84]*United States v. Rosenthal,* 763 F.2d 1291 (11th Cir. 1985).

[85]*In re Search Warrant for Secretarial Area Outside Office of Thomas Gunn,* 855 F. 2d 569 (8th Cir. 1988).

[86]*Washington Post Company v. Robinson,* 935 F.2d 282 (D.C. Cir. 1991); *United States v. El-Sayegh,* 131 F.3d 158 (D.C. Cir. 1997).

[87]*In re Charlotte Observer,* 882 F.2d 850 (4th Cir. 1989).

[88]*United States v. McVeigh,* 918 F. Supp. 1452 (W.D. Okla. 1996).

[89]*United States v. Smith,* 992 F. Supp. 743 (N.J. 1998).

Trial judges have a burden of proof when they seek to close judicial records that closely mirrors that which they assume when they wish to close judicial hearings. Often this means demonstrating that there is not a history of openness with respect to a particular category of judicial document (such as details of the negotiations that may lead to a plea agreement). Sometimes the judge meets the burden of proof by identifying reasons for closure compelling enough to override whatever common-law or constitutional interests may exist in openness.

Given the traditional secrecy surrounding grand jury proceedings, it is no surprise that judges overseeing such matters are given great deference should they wish to deny media access to related documents. This became painfully clear to the array of media outlets that conducted a daily stakeout of the courthouse in Washington, D.C., where the grand jury looking into whether Monica Lewinsky should be tried for suborning perjury and otherwise obstructing justice in Paula Jones's suit against President Clinton. Although it was obvious to all concerned that the press had no First Amendment right to grand jury proceedings themselves, the media thought they should be given access to documents related to several "ancillary proceedings" flowing from the grand jury.

Several witnesses called before the grand jury had decided to challenge their subpoenas. President Clinton's attorneys filed papers asking that Kenneth

 # Things to Remember

### CLOSURE OF OTHER COURT PROCEEDINGS

- In 1979, in *Gannett v. DePasquale,* the Court ruled that a defendant's wish to exclude the press from a pretrial hearing might outweigh whatever rights the press may have to attend.

- In *Press-Enterprise Company v. Superior Court* (I) (1984), the majority ruled that voir dire hearings may be closed only when an "overriding interest" is established by "findings" (i.e., the judge must prove it, not just say it) and that closure is "essential." The "overriding interest" might be something other than a fair trial; it might be to protect jurors' privacy.

- In *Press-Enterprise Company v. Superior Court* (II) (1986), the Court tells trial judges that they should consider whether this kind of hearing has historically been open or if the function of the hearing will be enhanced by openness.

- Presumptively open categories of hearings may only be closed if the closure is narrowly tailored to ward off a "substantial probability" of jeopardizing a "higher value."

- This *Press-Enterprise* test has since been applied by lower courts to several additional categories of pretrial hearings.

- Lower courts have fashioned similar rules to determine whether judicial documents may be sealed.

Starr's Office of the Independent Counsel be compelled to show cause why it should not be held in contempt of court for leaking confidential materials to the press, thus compromising the grand jury's function. Should the press have been granted access to paperwork associated with such matters? The D.C. Circuit Court of Appeals, in two separate decisions,[90] ruled against the press. The First Amendment, and relevant federal and local rules of judicial procedure, dictated that the press could be denied not only full text copies of any grand jury documents, but also a docket of the kinds of motions before the judge overseeing the grand jury. The appellate court threw one bone to the plaintiff media organizations, however: if the trial judge refused a formal request for a docket of matters related to a specific grand jury proceeding, that denial must include a clear justification that "must bear some logical connection to the individual request." The court cannot simply claim that the "administrative burdens" would be too cumbersome; unsubstantiated and general fears of leaks would be insufficient to justify denial.

## TV Cameras in Court

Trial judges may assume a burden of proof to higher courts when they seek to gag the press or close the press out of judicial proceedings. The question of whether television cameras should be permitted in courtrooms is quite different. A trial judge's discretionary decision to prohibit cameras in the courtroom is generally not appealable. From the perspective of those who favor televised coverage of the judiciary, even this state of affairs represents a major step forward from the 1960s.

It was in 1965 that the Supreme Court overturned the fraud conviction of Billy Sol Estes, a friend of President Johnson who had apparently "sold" farmers imaginary tanks of fertilizer and other agricultural equipment.[91] The majority accepted Estes's argument that his constitutional rights had been violated by the introduction of TV cameras into the courtroom. Writing for a 5–4 majority, Justice Clark expressed dismay over the cables and wires that "snaked across the courtroom floor" and to the "considerable disruption" caused by the dozen cameramen and their equipment. Clark dismissed the argument made in the *amicus* briefs filed by the National Association of Broadcasters and the Radio and Television News Directors Association. The First Amendment was not violated by the discriminatory exclusion of *broadcast* media from the judicial process, Clark wrote. TV reporters are allowed into the courtroom; they simply may not bring their cameras, just as print reporters were not permitted to bring their typewriters.

---

[90]*In re Motions of Dow Jones & Company,* 142 F.3d 496 (D.C. Cir. 1998); *In re Sealed Case,* 199 F.3d 522 (D.C. Cir. 2000).

[91]*Estes v. Texas,* 381 U.S. 532 (1965).

Only four of the five justices in the *Estes* majority felt that TV in courts neces-sarily violated suspects' rights. Justice Harlan, who provided the majority with its needed fifth vote, made clear that the *Estes* decision should be read narrowly as a suggestion that bringing cameras into criminal trials generating "great notoriety" could be violative of the defendant's rights.

Thus, the individual states felt free to experiment cautiously with television in the courtroom. By 1980, twenty-eight states had already permitted some trials to be televised, and another dozen states were studying the issue. In 1982, the American Bar Association abandoned its own decades long opposition to TV in courts.

The amount of such experimentation increased dramatically after a second Supreme Court decision handed down sixteen years after *Estes. Chandler v. Florida*[92] involved two Miami Beach police officers appealing their burglary conviction on the grounds that the trial judge's decision to permit the televising of portions of their trial had violated their constitutional rights. In a unanimous ruling, the Su-preme Court upheld the conviction and determined that the televising of a trial, even over a defendant's objections, is not itself a violation of the right to a fair trial. *Chandler* was not an outright overturning of the earlier *Estes* doctrine, however. Using the vocabulary from Chapter 1, we might say that the 1981 decision is best thought of as having *modified* the 1965 precedent. The introduction of TV cameras into a courtroom was no longer deemed inherently violative of the defendant's rights because something in the real world had changed: technology had improved to the point that TV cameras were no longer automatically intrusive. They had become smaller, as well as quieter, and they were now less dependent on the glare of high-intensity lighting.

If anything, the pace with which state judiciaries have moved TV into court-rooms since *Chandler* has been so fast that it no longer makes sense to even speak of "experimentation" with the technology. The vast majority of states now permit television coverage of both trial and appellate courts, both in civil and criminal litigation. In only a tiny number of states is the defendant in a criminal matter permitted veto powers over a trial judge's decision to admit cameras.

In federal courts, the story is quite different. There has never been a chief jus-tice of the Supreme Court who has been a supporter of TV in courts; indeed, the last few persons to occupy that position have been strongly opposed to the idea. Because the chief justice also serves as the head of the Judicial Conference of the United States, which promulgates rules governing the federal judiciary, television cameras have typically not been invited into federal courtrooms. In the early 1990s, the Conference initiated a three-year experiment, with cameras being permitted into appellate courts in two federal appellate circuits as well as district courts in a hand-ful of states. Although the Conference staff report was highly positive, the Confer-ence itself decided to continue the ban on television cameras. There have been only

---

[92]449 U.S. 560 (1981).

some modest inroads since, as a handful of federal district judges have been persuaded that the Conference's stance is merely a recommendation, that the individual district's rules, which may be more flexible, govern instead. In the 106th Congress (1999–2001), Senate bill 721, which would have empowered the chief judge of any federal district or appellate circuit to permit cameras into the courtrooms of their own jurisdictions, was introduced. The bill, however, never received a floor vote.

Even in state courts, broadcast media do not have a free rein. Trial judges are the ultimate arbiters in this arena. *Chandler* stands only for the principle that trial judges *may* have cameras in court; it does not instruct them to do so. The various state supreme rules that govern audio and video technologies in courtrooms typically provide rather strict guidelines. Jurors are not to be shown, nor may private consultations among attorneys and the judge be broadcast. There may be strict limitations on the number and positioning of cameras, which may not bear the name or logo of any particular network or station.

To be sure, many trial judges and commentators continue to view cameras and courtrooms as fundamentally incompatible. Some people argue that the dignity of the courtroom cannot help but be compromised by the televising of trials, especially when the coverage is interrupted by commercials or by the kinds of commentary on lawyers' strategies associated with sportscasters' second-guessing of coaches. Others fear that no matter how physically unobtrusive a camera may be, the behavior of trial participants who know they are being televised cannot help but be changed. A truthful witness made unusually nervous by the presence of the camera may appear fidgety and unresponsive, leading some jurors to conclude incorrectly that the witness is lying.

Some skeptics express a special concern for jurors who go home each night after listening to the evidence or after a long day of deliberating a verdict. Although trial judges admonish jurors to avoid having any conversations about the case with outsiders, such conversations, however fleeting, do occur. If those outsiders have had access to nonstop TV coverage of the trial, they may wield undue influence as they challenge jurors to justify their perceptions and their decisions.

The appeal of anti-TV arguments varies with the nature of the judicial proceeding and the coverage. The Sixth Amendment concerns about a criminal defendant's right to a fair trial are inapplicable when television cameras are invited into civil trials. Concerns about commercial interruptions, or pundits offering play-by-play critiques of trial strategies, would not be at issue if a nonprofit network known for gavel-to-gavel coverage *sans* commentary (such as C-SPAN) were to be the source of information. First Amendment and Equal Protection considerations would require, however, that if one news outlet is to be given access to the "feed" of a public trial, all news outlets be provided it as well.

Arguments that focus on how TV changes the behavior of trial participants seem not to apply with much force at the appellate level, where there are no witnesses and no jurors. An appellate case typically consists of attorneys for opposing sides making oral arguments for an hour or so to a panel of experienced judges. If lawyers at such proceedings begin to "grandstand" for the cameras, the judges can keep them in check. C-SPAN has been on record for years with its offer to create a "C-SPAN3" network devoted to the judiciary, if only the U.S. Supreme Court would permit gavel-to-gavel coverage of its own oral arguments. Most observers believe that it will require several personnel changes on the Court before such an offer would be accepted.

In the aftermath of the 2000 presidential election, the Cable News Network and other media organizations beseeched the Supreme Court to permit live coverage of its own two sets of oral arguments involving the tallying of votes in Florida. On both occasions, the Court denied CNN's request, but did permit audiotapes of the proceedings to be made available to news media nationwide within a few minutes of the arguments' conclusion. Many news organizations immediately broadcast those tapes in their entirety, enhanced by either photographs or artists's sketches of the lawyers and the justices.

Many arguments exist in support of televising trials. Because television is the primary means by which most Americans receive their news, the denial of electronic access effectively shuts off one branch of government from public scrutiny. Some argue that the meaning of a *public* trial under the Sixth Amendment needs to be redefined in such a technology-dependent age as ours, that the availability of the few dozen public seats in the average courtroom no longer satisfies the spirit of this important constitutional provision. Others point to the tremendous educational benefits of television, that just as the C-SPAN cable networks have greatly enhanced public understanding of the legislative branch, so too the level of public appreciation of the judicial branch's functions can surely be enhanced by the introduction of cameras.

The 1990s saw the birth of a for-profit cable network called Court TV. The brainchild of entrepreneur Steven Brill, the network covered over 500 trials from thirty-eight states and four foreign countries in its first seven years of operation. Although many of the cases were selected in part because of the celebrity litigants, Court TV's viewers have also been exposed to judicial proceedings dealing with a wide variety of societal conflicts, from Bosnian war crimes to smokers' claims against cigarette companies. Some argue that Court TV is an imperfect means of educating the public; it is a commercial network, after all, and it does boast many legally trained pundits who are in fact paid to offer "Monday morning quarterbacking" critiques of trial participants' performances. Similarly, CNN's *Burden of Proof* program consists mostly of such critiques (and commercials), with only very brief snippets from courtroom proceedings. Other models are being developed, however. In the state of Washington, a former state legislator in 1995 began a twenty-four-hour nonprofit cable network called TVW, which provides viewers with, among other things, oral arguments at the state supreme court. A similar network called MGTV began in Michigan the year after.

Things to Remember

### TV IN COURTS

- There is no First Amendment right to have a trial televised.
- Nonetheless, in most states, television cameras are permitted at the trial level, the appellate level, or both and at both civil and criminal cases.
- State trial judges retain complete discretion to refuse a request to televise a trial.
- TV is virtually unheard of in federal courtrooms, despite generally positive feedback from an experimental program in the 1990s.

 ## Chapter Summary

Reporters covering the judiciary often confront a clash between First Amendment and Sixth Amendment values. If a trial judge issues an order that unconstitutionally restricts the press, wise reporters obey the order even while taking an appeal to a higher court, lest a contempt citation be upheld.

Trial judges have many strategies at their disposal to minimize the damage caused by pretrial publicity. Among these options are a continuance, a change of venue or of venire, or sequestering the jury. By far the most common techniques are a carefully conducted voir dire together with clear instructions to the jurors selected.

Sometimes trial judges also embrace one of two other strategies: either preventing the press from publishing that which it already knows (a "gag" order) or closing the press and the public out of the judicial proceedings at which they might learn potentially prejudicial information. In a number of decisions handed down since the late 1970s, the Supreme Court has set forth rules governing what burden of proof trial judges assume if they choose to use either strategy.

Although the Court has said that there is a qualified First Amendment right to attend and report about judicial proceedings, there is no such constitutional right to bring TV cameras into courtrooms. Nonetheless, the vast majority of states do permit cameras into their court systems (as long as the trial judge does not object). Cameras are virtually unheard of, however, in federal courts.

# *Protecting News Sources*

The previous two chapters dealt primarily with reporters seeking information from the government. We examined federal and state Freedom of Information Acts and open meeting laws in Chapter 7 and the complex First Amendment doctrine governing access to judicial proceedings and documents in Chapter 8. In this chapter, we look instead at what happens when the government seeks information from reporters. Although some of the earliest case law deals with congressional investigatory committees, the more typical situation involves a party in civil or criminal litigation seeking compelled disclosure of information from a media representative. When will reporters be able to challenge successfully an order to testify or to turn over materials? The short answer is, not surprisingly, that it depends.

Whether reporters will have to turn over information to the government depends on a number of variables. One consideration is the kind of information sought. Is the reporter merely being asked to tell what he or she has seen first-hand as a witness to an event, or does the government instead want the reporter to repeat data that an informant has provided? A related variable is whether the government seeks disclosure of an informant's identity. Whether reporters will be compelled to disclose information will also often be a function of their having explicitly promised anonymity to their sources.

This area of law is complicated further in that whatever rights reporters may have to avoid compelled disclosures come from a patchwork of federal and state case law interpreting First Amendment and state constitutional provisions, state "reporter shield laws," judicial rules, and even attorney general guidelines.

We begin by looking at the interdependent relationship between the media and their informants.

## Reporters and Confidential Sources

Look in any major newspaper, especially one well known for doing investigative reporting, and you will find frequent references to "sources in a position to know," "highly placed sources," "administration sources," and sources who spoke "upon a promise of anonymity." Often the passive voice is used to avoid even suggesting the existence of a source. Thus, we may hear only that "CNN has learned…" (from intense meditation?) some important news tidbit.

It is fair to say that the media have a love–hate relationship with confidential sources. The dangers of overreliance on such sources are obvious; it is equally obvious, however, that many important stories would never be reported without promises of anonymity. Perhaps the best example in modern American journalism is "Deep Throat," Bob Woodward's anonymous source without whom the Watergate scandal might never have been reported by the *Washington Post.* More recently, the same newspaper needed to rely at least in part on anonymous sources to report on Vice President Gore's zealous and possibly illegal fund-raising activities. The paper's ombudsman at the time took the writer—Bob Woodward, again, as it turns out—to task for failing to name sources. Robert Kaiser, then the paper's managing editor, defended Woodward's decision. It is highly unlikely, Kaiser suggested, that the sort of person who gives hundreds of thousands of dollars to the Democratic Party would go *on the record* with their feeling that Gore's fund-raising tactics were inappropriate, earning him the nickname of "Solicitor-in-Chief."

A whole lexicon has developed governing the degree of anonymity a source may expect when conversing with a reporter. There is no ambiguity about the meaning of talking "on the record"; hence, the reporter is free to use everything the source says, and to quote the source directly. "Off the record" means, minimally, that the source is not to be quoted. Some assume that it also means that paraphrases are equally forbidden, and still others think that the reporter should pretend that off the record conversations never took place.

If a source insists on speaking "on background," the reporter can repeat everything that is said, and attribute it, although somewhat vaguely. Certainly the source's name should not be associated with any quotes. Sources sometimes will speak only "on deep background," which most reporters take to mean that paraphrasing is permitted, but no attributions at all, even to such vague entities as "informed sources."[1]

---

[1]Jo Mannies, "The Background on Sources," *St. Louis Post-Dispatch,* 17 Feb. 1993, p. C1.

 **Things to Remember**

**REPORTERS AND CONFIDENTIAL SOURCES**

- Reporters, especially in Washington, have a love–hate, interdependent relationship with confidential sources.
- A special lexicon exists describing the degree of anonymity demanded by a source, including such phrases as speaking "off the record," "on background," and "on deep background."

Most of the remainder of this chapter concerns the legal conflicts that arise when government officials ask reporters to break their bonds of confidentiality with their sources. We begin that exploration by looking closely at the one time the U.S. Supreme Court has issued an opinion on the question of whether the U.S. Constitution protects reporters who wish to keep confidential the identity of their sources.

## The First Amendment and Confidential Sources: *Branzburg v. Hayes*

It all began with a story written by reporter Paul Branzburg of the *Louisville Courier-Journal* in November 1969 (see Figure 9.1). The subject was a pair of local residents—given the pseudonyms Larry and Jack—and their partnership in the synthesis of hashish from marijuana plants, "a weird business that is a combination of capitalism, chemistry, and criminality."

Unsurprisingly, the local district attorney was interested in learning the informants' true identities. Thus, Branzburg was subpoenaed to appear before a Jefferson County grand jury. Although the reporter did appear as ordered, he refused to answer any questions he felt would tend to reveal the identities of his sources.

The *Courier-Journal* published another Branzburg article, this one about marijuana use by residents of Frankfort, Kentucky, and here also the reporter's work

 Figure 9.1

**COULD BE A POT OF GOLD**
**The Hash They Make Isn't to Eat**

*By Paul M. Branzburg*

Larry, a young Louisville hippie, wiped the sweat off his brow, looked about the stuffy little room and put another pot on the stove over which he had been laboring for hours. For over a week, he has been proudly tending his pots and pans.... Larry and his partner, Jack, are engaged in a weird business that is a combination of capitalism, chemistry, and criminality.

They are operating a makeshift laboratory in south-central Louisville that may produce them enough hashish, or "hash," a concentrate of marijuana, to net them up to $5,000 for three weeks of work,...

"I don't know why I'm letting you do this story...To make the narcs (narcotics detectives) mad, I guess. That's the main reason..."

"The trouble we're having is finding the right base," Larry said, as he continued to chop stems. "The hash we've produced gets you stoned, but it doesn't smoke the same as foreign hash. I tried to use incense as a base, but it gives too much of a sweet taste. In the Middle East they use camel manure, so I'm thinking of going out to the zoo..."

*Excerpts from* Louisville Courier-Journal, *15 November 1969. Reprinted with permission. Courier-Journal and Louisville Times Company.*

attracted the attention of local law enforcement officials. This time Branzburg refused to testify at all before the grand jury. It is a very difficult thing, Branzburg
argued, for a reporter to build trust between himself and informants with firsthand information about the extent of illicit drug use in a community. Such sources
would never trust him again were he to appear before a grand jury. Because grand
jury proceedings are traditionally sealed, the moment it became known that he had
appeared before the body, he would have no way of persuading his informants that
he did *not* betray them.

The Supreme Court consolidated the two disputes involving Paul Branzburg
with two other appeals involving reporters with information sought by law enforcement officials. In one, photographer Paul Pappas had been summoned to appear
before the Bristol County, Massachusetts, grand jury to provide both his film and
his testimony concerning possible criminal actions engaged in by a chapter of the
Black Panthers Party in New Bedford. Although Pappas had visited the Party's headquarters, he never produced or broadcast a story about whatever he learned there.
Pappas appeared before the grand jury and answered some of their queries, but he
refused to answer any questions about events that may have transpired inside the
party's headquarters. The other case involved *New York Times* reporter Earl Caldwell,
who also had researched the Black Panthers (in the Oakland, California, area) and
who also was summoned by a local grand jury to testify. He refused and was held in
contempt of court. The contempt citation was eventually overturned.

## Counting the Votes

*Branzburg v. Hayes*[2] resulted in a 5–4 split among the justices. Much of Justice
White's opinion for the Court was majority doctrine, having been joined by Justices Blackmun, Powell, and Rehnquist and Chief Justice Burger. Yet the odd
nature of Justice Powell's separate concurring opinion leads to the conclusion that,
although Powell officially voted with the majority, some sections of Justice White's
opinion really commanded only a plurality of four votes. Moreover, because Justice
Powell's concurring opinion shared some common ground with those of the four
dissenters, *Branzburg* represents one of those quirky situations where a Supreme
Court dissenting opinion has been followed by lower courts much more than has
been the majority opinion.

Looking first at the majority opinion, we note that Justice White rejected the
reporters' claim that confidential sources whose identities reporters are compelled
to reveal to a grand jury "will be measurably deterred from furnishing publish-
able information, all to the detriment of the free flow of information protected by
the First Amendment." Only when reporters' sources are suspected of criminal
wrongdoing would the question of compelled testimony surface. To rule for the
reporters here would send the message that "it is better to write about crime than
to do something about it."

---

[2]408 U.S. 665 (1972).

The imposition placed on the reporters in these cases by the respective grand juries was minimal, Justice White concluded. The reporters were not prohibited from publishing, nor were they told that they had to eschew the use of confidential sources. "The sole issue before us," he wrote, "is the obligation of reporters to respond to grand jury subpoenas as other citizens do and to answer questions relevant to an investigation into the commission of crime." Reporters, he added, "are not exempt from the normal duty of appearing before a grand jury and answering questions relevant to a criminal investigation." The majority thus made clear that it did not see this as a First Amendment case at all. Indeed, White added, for the judiciary to find a constitutional right on the part of reporters to refuse to testify in front of grand juries would create a logistic nightmare. "Sooner or later," he warned, "it would be necessary to define those categories of newsmen who qualified for the privilege, a questionable procedure in light of the traditional doctrine that liberty of the press is the right of the lonely pamphleteer who uses carbon paper or a mimeograph just as much as of the large metropolitan publisher who utilizes the latest photo composition methods." As we see later in this chapter, state legislatures have had to deal with this precise issue—defining who is a "reporter"—in their enacting of reporter shield laws.

Let us examine the dissenting opinions. Justice Douglas, writing only for himself, argued that reporters should enjoy an *absolute* right to refuse to testify in front of grand juries. In those rare circumstances in which reporters themselves are suspected of criminal wrongdoing, the Fifth Amendment's guarantee against self-incrimination would provide the protection. The First Amendment should serve as the reporter's security against forced disclosure about any other matters, Douglas concluded. Starting with these premises, he expresses amazement at media representatives who concede too much by allowing that the rights of their reporters need to be balanced against other competing interests. The only "balancing" called for had already been done by the Constitution's Framers, he wrote. Their having written the First Amendment in absolute language ("Congress shall make *no* law…") provides sufficient guidance.

The other three dissenters were not willing to go quite as far as Justice Douglas. Justice Stewart, writing for himself as well as for Justices Brennan and Marshall, offers lower courts a set of principles by which to balance a reporter's interest in keeping information confidential with the grand jury's interest in compelling disclosure. The reporter's interest should prevail, Justice Stewart suggests, unless the government can prove three elements:

- There is probable cause to believe that the reporter possesses information relevant to a criminal investigation.

- The government has a compelling need for this information (i.e., its disclosure or nondisclosure will likely affect the outcome of the case).

- The reporter is the only identifiable source of the needed information.

Why, though, should the government have to meet such a high burden of proof? For Justice Stewart, the special, interdependent relationship between informants and reporters provides the answer. "The promise of confidentiality," he proposed, is "a necessary prerequisite" to the nurturance of that relationship. The institutionalized press needs such informants "if it is to perform its constitutional mission." Without them, the media will be reduced to "printing public statements" and "publishing prepared handouts."

Justice Powell's brief concurring opinion in *Branzburg* is the key to understanding how and why the three-part test from Justice Stewart's dissenting opinion has been so very influential. Powell cautions that the majority "does not hold that newsmen, subpoenaed to testify before a grand jury, are without constitutional rights." Should a reporter called before a grand jury conclude that "the investigation is not being conducted in good faith," that the information sought has "only a remote and tenuous relationship to the subject of the investigation," a motion to quash (i.e., to invalidate) the subpoena would appropriately be sought. A court asked to intervene in this way would make its decision by "striking a proper balance" between the reporter's First Amendment claims and competing state's interests.

At its core, Justice Powell's opinion was far more consistent with the philosophy espoused by the dissenters than it was with the majority. He, unlike the majority, accepted that the First Amendment is implicated when reporters are called on by the government to reveal confidential information. Like Justice Stewart, he argued for a balancing test. Perhaps it should not be surprising, then, that many lower court judges counted up the *Branzburg* votes and concluded that a majority of the Court—the four dissenters plus Justice Powell—insisted that reporters' First Amendment claims of confidentiality be taken seriously.

 # Things to Remember

### BRANZBURG V. HAYES

- In *Branzburg v. Hayes* (1972), the Supreme Court held that, even if reporters do enjoy some such First Amendment protection, their claims must yield to the need of grand juries investigating criminal wrongdoing.

- Justice Stewart's dissenting opinion—which has proved more influential than the majority opinion—argued that states wishing to compel reporter testimony must prove: (1) that there is probable cause to believe that the reporter possesses information relevant to a criminal investigation; (2) that the government has a compelling need for this information (i.e., its disclosure or nondisclosure will likely affect the outcome of the case); and (3) that the reporter is the only identifiable source of the needed information.

## The Lower Courts Apply *Branzburg*

In the decades since *Branzburg* was decided, courts in all the federal appellate circuits that have confronted the issue have recognized at least a limited First Amendment privilege for reporters who wish to avoid compelled disclosure of information in their possession. Only the Seventh Circuit, covering Illinois, Indiana, and Wisconsin, has not handed down a decision on the point. A 1987 decision from the Sixth Circuit, with jurisdiction over Kentucky, Michigan, Ohio, and Tennessee, seemed to reject such a privilege,[3] but later cases from the same circuit have interpreted the decision very narrowly and have allowed that reporters do have some constitutional confidentiality rights.[4]

Because the Supreme Court has never clarified the confusing array of opinions from the *Branzburg* case and has never heard a similar dispute, lower courts have fashioned their own assessments as to the scope of any First Amendment protection for journalists' sources. How much protection courts grant is a function of three variables: (1) Is the judicial proceeding at issue a grand jury? (2) Is the information sought truly "confidential"? (3) Is the person being asked to testify really a "reporter"? Let us examine each variable in turn.

***What Kind of Judicial Proceeding?*** Lower courts have applied the *Branzburg* precedent in three different circumstances. First are those situations in which a reporter is compelled to testify in a criminal trial. The second category of cases involves civil litigants who seek such information from reporters. Finally, we look at compelled grand jury testimony, the same situation that was at issue in *Branzburg* itself.

*Criminal Trials.* In Chapter 8, we considered conflicts between the media's First Amendment interest in reporting on judicial proceedings and the accused's Sixth Amendment right to a fair trial. Those two constitutional provisions are again in conflict here. Reporters claim a First Amendment privilege in keeping information from the judiciary, but criminal suspects also have a Sixth Amendment interest in compelling disclosure of such information. The relevant portion of the Sixth Amendment says that the accused has a right "to have compulsory process for obtaining witnesses in his favor."

That criminal defendants enjoy an explicit constitutional right has resulted in some courts being especially skittish about recognizing a confidentiality privilege for reporters seeking to quash a subpoena to testify at criminal trials. Consider the case of *Los Angeles Herald Examiner* reporter William Farr, who went to jail rather

---

[3] *Storer Communications v. Giovan,* 810 F.2d 580 (6th Cir. 1987).

[4] *Southwell v. The Southern Poverty Law Center,* 949 F. Supp. 1303 (W.D. Mich. 1996); *King v. Photo Marketing Association International,* 327 N.W.2d 515 (Mich. Ct. App. 1982); *Marketos v. American Employers Insurance Company,* 460 N.W.2d 272 (Mich. Ct. App. 1990).

than reveal the source of an inadmissible bit of evidence improperly leaked to him during the infamous Charles Manson "family" homicide trial.[5] The Ninth Circuit Court of Appeals ruled against the reporter, finding that whatever First Amendment interests may be involved were trumped by "the paramount interest...of the power of the court to enforce its duty and obligation relative to the guarantee of due process to the defendants in the on-going trial."

A similar result was reached in *United States v. LaRouche Campaign,*[6] which emerged from an investigation by the government of fraud charges against some operatives in Lyndon LaRouche's presidential campaign. NBC was told that it would have to produce video outtakes of a relevant interview. Although the court allowed that the network had legitimate First Amendment interests, it concluded that these were outweighed. "At stake on the defendants' side of the equation," the court reasoned, "are their constitutional rights to a fair trial under the Fifth Amendment and to compulsory process and effective confrontation and cross-examination of adverse witnesses under the Sixth Amendment."

In most American jurisdictions, however, at least a qualified reporter's privilege has been recognized even in the context of criminal trials. Indeed, even within the Ninth Circuit a qualified privilege has been recognized, though not by application of the First Amendment. The Supreme Court of Washington, for example, has held that the tradition of that state's common law provides for a qualified reporters' confidentiality privilege, even with respect to criminal trials.[7]

In the criminal realm, some of the federal circuits apply a balancing test not too different from that proposed by Justice Stewart's *Branzburg* dissent. In *United States v. Burke,* involving a conspiracy prosecution on a charge of "fixing" college basketball games, the Second Circuit held that media representatives may be compelled to reveal confidential information in criminal proceedings only when the government can first demonstrate that the information cannot be obtained from any other source. The material sought must also be "highly material and relevant," and "necessary or critical" to the trial outcome.[8] This is not an impossible burden of proof. Bruce Cutler, one of Mafia chieftain John Gotti's attorneys, met the burden when he sought reporters' notes and TV news outtakes to defend himself from a contempt of court charge alleging he had made forbidden out-of-court statements. The appellate court found Cutler's logic compelling: Because "the allegedly contemptuous conduct...is precisely what the reporters observed and wrote about, and what the TV stations recorded on videotape," how could he defend himself without gaining access to those materials?[9]

---

[5]*Farr v. Pitchess,* 522 F.2d 464 (9th Cir. 1976).

[6]841 F.2d 1176 (1st Cir. 1988).

[7]*State v. Rinaldo,* 689 P.2d 392 (Sup. Ct. Wash. 1984).

[8]*United States v. Burke,* 700 F.2d 70 (2d Cir. 1983).

[9]*United States v. Cutler,* 6 F.3d 67 (2d Cir. 1993).

In the Third Circuit, the press has been told that its qualified confidentiality privilege applies with equal force in civil and in criminal proceedings. The relevant ruling emerged from a case involving a subpoena of statements made to CBS's *60 Minutes* program by likely government witnesses in a fraud prosecution against the owners of a chain of fast-food restaurants in the Newark, New Jersey, area. As the appellate court put it, "the interests of the press that form the foundation for the privilege are not diminished because the nature of the underlying proceeding out of which the request for the information arises is a criminal trial."[10] Criminal defendants' Fifth Amendment due process rights and Sixth Amendment right to compel the testimony of witnesses could be weighed against the press's First Amendment rights, case by case, but they did not count as reasons for denying the existence of the journalistic privilege.

*Civil Proceedings.*   When the person seeking to compel a reporter to testify is a civil litigant rather than a criminal defendant, there is no Sixth Amendment right to balance against the journalist's asserted First Amendment interests. As such, we find that courts are especially likely to embrace the media's qualified privilege and typically to apply some form of the test suggested in Justice Stewart's dissenting opinion from *Branzburg.* Moreover, the case-by-case application of such a test is more likely to result in a finding for the press when a civil litigant is involved. Judges are less likely to find that the private interests of civil litigants rise to a level of "compelling interest" manifested by a criminal suspect seeking to avoid a prison term. To the extent that the larger public interest factors into the judge's reasoning, disputes among private parties are unlikely to tip the scales against reporters quite as easily as the societal interest in ensuring that all criminal defendants obtain a fair trial.

A qualified privilege against disclosure in civil litigation was recognized very soon after the *Branzburg* decision itself was handed down. The precipitating incidents were the Watergate break-in and the Democratic National Committee's subpoena issued against several media outlets. Perhaps the media had information that would help the DNC in its civil suit against the burglars themselves. A federal district court in the District of Columbia quashed the subpoena.[11]

Several years later, the federal appellate court for the District of Columbia produced a decision very strongly supportive of the reporters' privilege. In the early 1970s, *Detroit News* reporter Seth Kanter published a series of articles about organized crime's influence on that city. Local residents Anthony T. Zerilli and Michael Polizzi, whose phones had been illegally tapped by the Justice Department, concluded that some of the factual assertions in those articles could only have been obtained from transcripts of their recorded conversations. To aid them in their civil lawsuit against the Justice Department, the plaintiffs sought the identity

---

[10]*United States. v. Cuthbertson,* 630 F.2d 139, 147 (1980).

[11]*DNC v. McCord,* 356 F. Supp. 1394 (D.C. 1973).

of Kanter's sources. The D.C. Circuit Court of Appeals denied the request. Although the information sought was unquestionably crucial to their case, the court reasoned, the plaintiffs had not exhausted all other possible ways of obtaining it, especially in that the Justice Department had already provided them with a list of other persons who had had access to the transcripts. The court also concluded that, when balanced against civil litigants' interests, reporters' privilege should prevail in "all but the most exceptional cases."[12]

The Second Circuit has also recognized a qualified privilege against revealing confidential sources soon after *Branzburg* was handed down. At issue was a July 1962 *Saturday Evening Post* article written by Alfred Balk that exposed discriminatory real estate practices in Chicago. The headline read, "Confessions of a Block-Buster—a Chicago Real-Estate Agent Who Moves Negro Families into All-White Blocks Reveals How He Reaps Enormous Profits from Racial Prejudice." The article relied heavily on the pseudonymous Norris Vitcheck, who made money by frightening white residents into racially motivated panic selling at reduced prices and then selling those homes at much higher prices to black buyers. A few years later, a group of African Americans brought suit against local realty companies and individual landlords, alleging that they had been induced by false and excessive appraisals to pay exorbitant prices for their homes, in violation of relevant civil rights law. The plaintiffs determined that the anonymous informant featured in the magazine article would be a good source of information for their lawsuit, and they asked the court to compel disclosure of his identity. The request was denied, in part because the plaintiffs had many other ways to obtain the kinds of information that the mystery source might have provided. The *Saturday Evening Post* article itself could provide valuable leads, the court said, as could "a search of the title records and the mortgage records in the county in which plaintiffs claim the unlawful activities took place." The court did not commit itself as to whether its ruling was based on the First Amendment or on relevant Illinois and New York statutes.[13]

As a general rule, reporters will not be compelled to disclose confidential information to civil litigants unless it can be shown that the material sought is of clear relevance to the litigation, that the case's outcome will likely be determined by the disclosure, and that the information is not available from any other source. Again, these criteria parallel closely the guidelines offered by Justice Stewart in his *Branzburg* dissent.

A bit more complicated are those civil cases in which the reporters are themselves litigants. Most typically, this situation would occur in a libel suit stemming from an article that relied on one or more anonymous sources. We already know from *Herbert v. Lando*[14] (discussed in Chapter 4) that libel plaintiffs who need to prove actual malice will be granted access to reporters' notes and outtakes as part

---

[12]*Zerilli v. Smith,* 656 F.2d 705 (D.C. Cir. 1981).

[13]*Baker v. F & F Investment,* 470 F.2d 778 (2d Cir. 1972).

[14]441 U.S. 153 (1979).

of the pretrial discovery process. The same logic often dictates that the media reveal the identity of their confidential sources to libel plaintiffs. Thus, comedian Rodney Dangerfield finally got some respect when he sued the publishers of the *Star* tabloid, which quoted several unnamed employees of Caesar's Palace in Las Vegas in an article that depicted the comic as quite a party animal. He trashed his hotel room, the article said, breaking a marble shower; he was wildly drunk in his flooded hotel room, standing in ankle-deep water with two naked girls and chasing a female employee around his room with ice tongs, saying he wanted to rip her clothes off. The court granted Dangerfield's request to compel disclosure of these confidential sources in that questioning whether the sources did in fact exist and were at all credible would have to form the heart of his proof of actual malice.[15]

Media outlets that find themselves as libel defendants and that refuse to reveal the name of a confidential source may be subject to a specially fashioned sanction. The court adjudicating the libel claim may rule, as a matter of law, that no such source exists. The logical conclusion of such an assumption is that the media simply made up whatever libelous statements had been attributed to the unnamed source. To do so would clearly be to publish a "knowing falsehood." In other words, refuse to reveal your source, and you admit that you published with actual malice.[16] This assumption that no source exists is not embraced in most jurisdictions, however, and state reporter shield statutes may provide explicit protections against the assumption.[17]

*Grand Jury Proceedings.* Courts are least likely to recognize a confidentiality privilege when the forum seeking information from a reporter is a grand jury. This generalization is somewhat counterintuitive. One would think that reporters would be more likely to be compelled to testify at criminal trials than at grand jury proceedings. After all, the Sixth Amendment's explicit right of the accused to compel witness testimony applies to trials, not to grand juries. Then, too, we may remind ourselves that the *Branzburg* majority's admonition to the press that it is more important to *do something* about crime than to write about it dealt with grand juries rather than criminal trials. Surely, if society has an interest in *indicting* criminals (the function of grand juries), it has even more of an interest in *convicting* them.

Any logical inconsistencies suggested here can be explained by the principle of *stare decisis* introduced in Chapter 1. Supreme Court precedents, to the extent they offer clear guidance, should be followed. The *Branzburg* case itself dealt with reporters who had been compelled to testify in front of grand juries. In that the majority ruled against the journalists, the decision provides little "wiggle room" to lower court judges who might otherwise be inclined to recognize a journalistic privilege against compelled grand jury testimony. Indeed, a general rule

---

[15]*Dangerfield v. Star Editorial*, 817 F. Supp. 833 (C.D. Cal.), *aff'd*, 7 F.3d 856 (9th Cir. 1993).

[16]See, for example, *Downing v. Monitor Publishing Company*, 415 A.2d 683 (N.H. 1980).

[17]*Maressa v. New Jersey Monthly*, 445 A.2d 376 (N.J. 1982).

has developed, consistent with the majority and concurring opinions in *Branzburg,* that reporters must testify unless the grand jury is engaged in a bad faith "fishing expedition" or if it is otherwise intent merely on harassing the media.

In 1987, the Sixth Circuit Court of Appeals upheld the contempt citation (and jailing) of TV journalist Brad Stone for refusing to provide to a Detroit area grand jury videotape and other evidence he had acquired in the course of reporting about local youth gangs. To recognize any First Amendment privilege in such a case, the court concluded, would require it "to restructure the holding of the Supreme Court in *Branzburg v. Hayes."* It added that "fair and effective law enforcement aimed at providing security for the person and property of the individual is a fundamental function of government, and the grand jury plays an important, constitutionally mandated role in this process."[18]

Lisa Abraham, a reporter for the Warren, Ohio, *Tribune Chronicle,* was sent to jail for twenty-two days in 1994 for refusing to testify in front of a grand jury investigating whether a local official she had interviewed was guilty of misreporting the use of public funds for renovation of his office. An appellate court found that the state's sole burden was to ensure that its subpoena was issued "for a legitimate purpose, rather than for harassment."[19] More recently, Judge Susan Webber Wright, the judge in whose courtroom Paula Corbin Jones first filed her lawsuit against President Clinton, ruled that ABC-TV's *Primetime Live* had to turn over to the grand jury investigating the Whitewater land deal all its video and transcripts from Diane Sawyer's interview with Clinton friend Susan McDougal.[20] Media outlets typically turn over such materials only under court order, not wanting to be perceived by news sources as an arm of law enforcement.

---

[18]*In re Grand Jury Proceedings (Storer Communications v. Giovan),* 810 F.2d 580 (6th Cir. 1987).

[19]*In re Grand Jury Witness Subpoena of Abraham,* 634 N.E.2d 667 (Ct. App. Ohio 1993).

[20]*In re Grand Jury Subpoena (American Broadcasting Companies),* 947 F. Supp. 1314 (E.D. Ark. 1996).

 # Things to Remember

### APPLYING *BRANZBURG* TO VARIOUS JUDICIAL PROCEEDINGS

- As a general rule, reporters are most likely to succeed in their efforts to keep information confidential when confronting a subpoena to testify in an ordinary civil proceeding, a bit less likely to succeed if the proceeding is a criminal trial, and least likely to succeed when they wish to keep information from a grand jury.

- In some jurisdictions, reporters who refuse to reveal a confidential source when they are sued for libel risk a judicial determination that no such source exists; such a declaration virtually ensures that the plaintiff will prevail.

***What Kind of Information?*** Whether courts will recognize a qualified reporter's privilege is also in large part a function of whether the information sought is truly *confidential* information. Generally, confidential information is that which a source tells a reporter under an agreement of anonymity. Certainly this also includes the confidential source's identity.

Nonconfidential information refers to things that reporters witness for themselves firsthand as well as any other materials gathered without a promise of confidentiality. Thus, for example, if an interview with a nonconfidential source is aired on a TV news program, the footage that was shot but not aired is no more confidential than that which was broadcast. Similarly, information found in print reporters' notes that did not survive the editor's red pen are no more confidential than the words that actually were printed. (The notes may be considered confidential if they could be used to reveal the identity of an anonymous source.)

The defendants in the *Branzburg* case itself sought to keep *confidential* information—the identify of their sources—from the grand jury. That facet of the case figured prominently in all the justices' separate opinions. Thus, whatever First Amendment confidentiality right reporters enjoy is most likely to be outweighed by competing state's interests when the information sought from the journalist is not truly confidential.

A January 1997 episode of NBC's *Dateline* news magazine program featured an exposé of how a deputy sheriff on highway patrol in part of Louisiana had a reputation for pulling over out-of-state motorists and trumping up charges against them, resulting in huge fines and sometimes in confiscation of the "offending" vehicles. Albert and Mary Gonzales, in pursuit of their lawsuit against a Louisiana deputy sheriff who they alleged pulled them over from Interstate 10 and detained them for an overly long time in a discriminatory fashion—a "Driving While Hispanic" offense, they claimed—sought NBC's outtakes from the program. They had reason to assume the material would be especially helpful in that the network story featured the very same deputy named in their lawsuit. NBC refused, but the Second Circuit Court of Appeals ruled for the plaintiffs. The court concluded that there is no First Amendment privilege in withholding this kind of *non*confidential material. At least some of the media's traditional arguments in favor of a privilege have little validity with respect to nonconfidential material, the court emphasized. Almost by definition, after all, there is no danger that "the well of confidential sources will run dry." Also, because on-the-record sources have no way of knowing, at the time they are interviewed, what portions of the dialogue will be aired and what portions will become outtakes, they have no recognizable privacy interests in the unaired material.[21]

In another case, WDSU-TV New Orleans reporter Taylor Henry was told to hand over outtakes from his interview with Frank Smith, an employee of the Mac-Frugal's Regional Distribution Center. Smith was suspected by local authorities of

---

[21]*Gonzales v. NBC,* 194 F.3d 29 (2d Cir. 1998).

being the arsonist who had torched the building. Those same authorities noticed several statements made by Smith in portions of the interview already broadcast that were at odds with the facts of the case. They therefore presumed that the station's complete tapes would help them identify additional inconsistencies and thus aid the prosecution of the case. The Fifth Circuit Court of Appeals ruled against the TV station, holding that there is no reporter's privilege under the First Amendment for nonconfidential information, at least in criminal matters. There is no societal interest in protecting the sources of such information, the court said, or in ensuring the future availability of such sources, precisely because there is no asserted right of confidentiality as such. It would strain credulity to suggest that such sources would be loath to speak with reporters out of fear that law enforcement officials will obtain the information they provide. Surely the interviewees realize that the police watch TV news, too.[22]

The Fourth Circuit also refuses to recognize a privilege with respect to nonconfidential information. The leading case involves the compelled testimony from four newspaper reporters in the bribery trials of several South Carolina state legislators. The court found the subpoenas to have been legitimately issued in that the information sought was not obtained under a promise of confidentiality and because it was available only from the media representatives. The court also suggested that the only circumstances in which nonconfidential materials could survive a subpoena would be those in which law enforcement officials' motivation was to harass the news gatherers.[23]

In some jurisdictions, federal appellate courts stop short of concluding categorically that reporters enjoy no First Amendment rights in challenging a subpoena for nonconfidential information. These courts say that there is a First Amendment interest to be placed in the balance. One court has enumerated four plausible interests raised by reporters seeking to protect even nonconfidential information: (1) the threat of intrusion into the newsgathering and editorial process,

---

[22]*United States v. Smith,* 135 F.3d 963 (5th Cir. 1998).

[23]*In re Shain,* 978 F.2d 850 (4th Cir. 1992).

# Things to Remember

## APPLYING *BRANZBURG* TO VARIOUS KINDS OF INFORMATION

- Whereas the *Branzburg* case involved reporters' *confidential* information, courts are very loath to recognize a media right not to testify about *non*confidential information.

- The usual press arguments in favor of nondisclosure do not apply to such situations, courts reason; there is, for example, no danger of "the well of confidential sources running dry" when there is no *confidential* source at all.

(2) fear that the media will seem to become an investigative arm of the government, (3) giving media a disincentive to compile and preserve outtakes, and (4) the burden on journalists' time and resources in responding to subpoenas.[24] Even in those jurisdictions favoring a balancing test, however, the scales are weighted a bit more against the press when the information sought is nonconfidential.[25]

### From Whom Is the Information Sought?

> It would be unthinkable to have a rule that an investigative journalist, such as Bob Woodward, would be protected by the privilege in his capacity as a newspaper reporter writing about Watergate, but not as the author of a book on the same topic.[26]

If the lesson of *Branzburg* and subsequent cases is that there exists at least a limited First Amendment reporter's privilege, we should ask the question that the Supreme Court avoided in that case: What does it mean to be a reporter?

The question has been addressed by several courts, dating back to the 1970s. *Apicella v. McNeil Laboratories*[27] stemmed from a damages suit against the manufacturer of Innovar, a drug used as an operating room anesthetic. The defendant sought to compel testimony from the editor of a professional medical bimonthly journal called the *Medical Letter on Drugs and Therapeutics,* which had run an article critical of Innovar. That article included anonymous testimony from a physician claiming to have seen three patients die from heart problems as a result of using the drug. The federal district court denied the defendant's request, finding that the journal performed as valuable a public service as any general circulation newspaper and that the reporter's confidentiality privilege would thus apply to the publication's contributors.

The reporter's privilege was also extended to documentary film maker Arthur Buzz Hirsch, who was researching the suspicious death of Karen Silkwood, the whistle-blower who had alleged various public safety violations at a nuclear generating plant.[28] That Kerr-McGee Corporation (the target of Silkwood's complaints) was making such a "major legal effort" to obtain Hirsch's testimony was seen by a panel of the Tenth Circuit Court of Appeals as evidence that he must have been doing serious reporting.

A 1987 case involving another notoriously suspicious turn of events led the Second Circuit Court of Appeals to devise a set of guidelines to determine what categories of persons may claim the reporter's confidentiality privilege. The

---

[24]*United States v. La Rouche Campaign,* 841 F.2d 1176, 1182 (1st Cir. 1988).

[25]*Schoen v. Schoen,* 5 F.3d 1289 (9th Cir. 1993); *von Bulow v. von Bulow,* 811 F.2d 136 (2d Cir. 1987).

[26]*Shoen v. Shoen,* 5 F.3d 1289, 1293 (9th Cir. 1993).

[27]66 F.R.D. 78 (E.D.N.Y. 1975).

[28]*Silkwood v. Kerr-McGee Corporation,* 563 F.2d 433 (10th Cir. 1977).

case was an offshoot of the criminal prosecution and later civil litigation against Claus von Bulow, alleging that he assaulted his wife, Sunny, with intent to kill by injecting her with insulin and other drugs. (He was acquitted of the charges.) In the civil litigation, Sunny von Bulow's family members sought testimony and document disclosures from Andrea Reynolds, a long-term friend of Claus von Bulow's, who was at the time writing a book based on the criminal case. The court determined that a "reporter" need not be an employee of a newspaper or similarly traditional media outlet; all that was required was that she intended, at the time she was gathering information, to disseminate it to the public. Reynolds herself, however, failed even this test. Her primary motivation at the outset of her fact gathering, the court determined, was to clear Claus von Bulow's name, not to write a book.[29]

The test suggested by the *von Bulow* court has been accepted in at least two other circuits. The Ninth Circuit adopted the test in *Shoen v. Shoen,*[30] which involved the tragicomic family feud among the owners of the privately held U-Haul truck rental company. One side of the family sought disclosures from Ronald J. Watkins, who had interviewed patriarch Leonard Shoen as part of his research for *Birthright,* the book in which he deconstructs the family's travails. The court ruled in favor of Watkins, emphasizing that the reporter's privilege includes book authors. The court singled out Upton Sinclair, Rachel Carson, and Ralph Nader as examples of authors who brought more "newsworthy" information to the public than most "reporters" ever do.

The Third Circuit, although rejecting a claim of journalistic privilege made by World Championship Wrestling employee John Madden, also embraced the test proposed by the *von Bulow* court. *In re Madden*[31] flowed from an unfair trade practices suit between the two major producers of professional wrestling events in the United States. One of the litigants sought to depose Madden, whose job for the WCW was to produce tongue-in-cheek tape recordings for the company's 900-number phone lines. The *von Bulow* test requires that "reporters" must have an intention to publish at the time they gather news and that they be involved in activities traditionally associated with the gathering and dissemination of news. Madden did not pass the test in that the information he was to use in his phone recordings was provided directly by his employers. "Madden's primary goal," the court held, was "to provide advertisement and entertainment—not to gather news or disseminate information."

In ruling on a discovery motion stemming from the federal government's antitrust lawsuit against Microsoft Corporation, the First Circuit Court of Appeals also cited the *von Bulow* guidelines with approval. Microsoft sought disclosures from Professor Michael Cusumano of MIT and Professor David Yoffie of Harvard,

---

[29]*von Bulow v. von Bulow,* 811 F.2d 136 (2d Cir. 1987).

[30]5 F.3d 1289 (9th Cir. 1993).

[31]*In re Madden* [*Titan Sports v. Turner Broadcasting*], 151 F.3d 125 (3d Cir. 1998).

# Things to Remember

---

### APPLYING *BRANZBURG* TO VARIOUS KINDS OF WRITERS

- The First Amendment "reporter's privilege" has been applied not only to employees of well-known media outlets, but also to professional journals with far more limited circulation, to book authors, and to documentary film makers.

- Many courts will apply the privilege to any persons who, at the time of gathering information or "news," intended to disseminate their findings to the public eventually. Such individuals need not be employees of media organizations.

---

who were at the time finishing a book called *Competing on Internet Time* for which they had interviewed many employees of Microsoft rival Netscape. "Scholars," the court reasoned, are every bit as much "information gatherers and disseminators" as are more mainstream journalists and are thus as deserving of whatever protection the "reporter's privilege" may grant.[32]

## State Reporter Shield Laws

Reporters who wish to avoid testifying before judicial proceedings are not limited to making First Amendment arguments. In 1972, when *Branzburg v. Hayes* told the press that any First Amendment claims would necessarily be limited by the judiciary's needs, seventeen states already had statutes on the books providing reporters a limited right to keep their confidential sources confidential. The first such law was enacted by Maryland, in 1896.

Thirty-one states plus the District of Columbia have some form of reporter shield law on the books. Further, the majority of the states that do not have an actual statute governing this area of law still provide some protection for confidential sources through judicial interpretation of either state constitutions[33] or the common law.[34] In only a handful of states—Hawaii, Mississippi, North Carolina, Utah, and Wyoming—has the state supreme court not produced a ruling committing itself to at least some kind of reporters' privilege.

Specific provisions of state shield laws vary in ways that generally parallel the three criteria already seen with respect to the federal constitutional privilege. One

---

[32]*In re Cusumano and Yoffie* [*United States v. Microsoft*], 162 F.3d 708 (1st Cir. 1998).

[33]See, for example, *Winegard v. Oxberger,* 258 N.W.2d 847 (Iowa 1977); *Opinion of the Justices,* 373 A.2d 644 (N.H. 1977); *Matter of Contempt of Wright,* 700 P.2d 40 (Idaho 1985); *In re Letellier,* 578 A.2d 722 (Me. 1990) .

[34]See, for example, *Sinnott v. Boston Retirement Board,* 524 N.E.2d 100 (Mass. 1988).

is the nature of the information being sought; another is the matter of who should be considered a reporter. There is also some variation on the third dimension discussed in the earlier examination of First Amendment protections: whether the reporter is asked to testify before a civil proceeding, a criminal trial, or a grand jury.[35]

### What Kind of Information?

Shield statutes vary as to the kinds of information that are protected. Some jurisdictions—Arizona, Maryland, and the District of Columbia among them—provide absolute immunity from compelled disclosure of a source's identity.[36] The Illinois statute provides a qualified privilege to shield a source's identity, but no other protections.[37] New York's statute provides absolute immunity for both a source's identity and for any information obtained from that source in confidence.[38] California and Florida do not distinguish between confidential and nonconfidential information.[39] The privilege in New Jersey extends also to reporters' notes and outtakes in general in that the statute has been interpreted so as to protect the news gathering process itself.[40]

Although one might assume that New York and California, the two states in which media industries are especially concentrated, would boast the most far-reaching shield statutes, laws in some of the other states actually offer more protection. New Jersey, for example, provides reporters absolute immunity from having to testify in civil cases. Reporters in that state are sometimes required to testify when called before criminal proceedings, but only if they have witnessed a crime taking place or an accident happening. The privilege will remain intact, in other words, if the reporter arrived on the scene so late as to only see the *aftermath* of the crime or the accident.[41] The Nevada statute is also quite extensive, providing absolute protection for source identity and other information, even in cases where a media outlet is defending itself in a libel suit.[42]

---

[35]Laurence B. Alexander and Ellen M. Bush, "Shield Laws on Trial: State Court Interpretation of the Journalist's Statutory Privilege," 23 *Journal of Legislation* 215 (1997).

[36]See, for example, D.C. Cod Ann. secs. 16-4701-04 (1998); Md. Cts. & Jud. Proc. Code Ann. sec. 9-112 (1998); Ariz. Rev. Stat. Ann. secs. 12-2214, 12-2237 (1998).

[37]Ill. Ann. Stat. ch. 110, para. 8-901-909 (1998).

[38]N.Y. C.L.S. Civ. R. sec. 79-h (1998).

[39]Cal. Const. Art 1, sec. 2 (1998); *Davis v. Florida*, 720 So. 2d 220 (1998).

[40]N.J. Stat. Ann. secs. 2A:84A-21–21.9, 2A:84A-29 (1998).

[41]*Woodhaven Lumber and Mill Work. State v. Asbury Park Press*, 589 A.2d 135, 143 (N.J. Sup. Ct. 1991).

[42]Nev. Rev. Stat. Ann. secs. 49.275, 49.385 (1998).

## Who Is Protected?

Most state shield laws define *reporter* fairly narrowly, limiting protection to those who are "employed by" such traditional media outlets as newspapers, magazines, and broadcast stations. Such wording seems to exclude freelance writers. The Florida statute explicitly excludes from its scope "book authors and others who are not professional journalists."[43] Other statutes more broadly protect not only persons employed by the media industries, but also those "connected with" the media.[44] The Delaware statute lists "scholars," "educators," and even "polemicists" among those who enjoy the reporters' privilege,[45] whereas the law in Nebraska provides immunity to anyone "engaged in procuring, gathering, writing, editing, or disseminating news *or other information* to the public" (emphasis added).[46]

Often the question of whether freelance writers are protected is not spelled out clearly in the statute itself, requiring state courts to weigh in with their interpretations of the law's wording. An appellate court in Arizona, for example, refused to apply its shield law to author Dary Matera, who was at the time writing a book about undercover "sting" operations that had resulted in the prosecution of several state officials. One of those state officials subpoenaed Matera for materials he thought would help him in preparing his defense. Although the statute was worded broadly, the court used a Webster's dictionary definition of news, which was limited to "material reported in a newspaper or news periodical or on a newscast." Matera's motion to quash the subpoena was thus denied.[47]

Whether freelance reporters are protected by California's shield law is unclear. A 1982 lower court case held that authors who have not yet entered into a contract with a news organization or book publisher cannot claim a reporter's privilege.[48] A decade later, however, the state supreme court denied to review two rulings from lower courts; one of the cases had extended the privilege to a freelance writer, and the other held that freelancers were categorically excluded from the statute's protection.

## What Type of Proceeding?

One advantage for the press of living in a state with a strong shield law is that such statutes need not be constrained by the specific holding, from *Branzburg v. Hayes,* that there is no First Amendment right to refuse to testify in front of a grand

---

[43]Fla. Stat. sec. 90.5015 (1998).

[44]See, for example, Ala. Code sec. 12-21-142 (1998).

[45]Del. Code Ann. tit. 10, secs. 4320–26 (1998).

[46]Neb. Rev. Stat. Ann. secs. 20-144–47 (1998).

[47]*Matera v. Superior Court,* 825 P.2d 971 (Ct. App. 1992).

[48]*In re Van Ness,* 8 Media Law Rptr. 2563 (Cal. Super. Ct. 1982).

Things to Remember

---

### STATE REPORTER SHIELD LAWS

- As of 1999, thirty states plus the District of Columbia had reporter shield statutes, and the majority of the remaining states recognize a reporter's privilege either in their state constitutions or in the common law.
- The statutes vary widely with respect to what kinds of information are protected and who is considered a reporter.
- Many reporter shield statutes give the media a stronger presumption in favor of nondisclosure of information in a civil, as opposed to a criminal, proceeding.

---

jury. Still, several states do provide more protection to reporters seeking to quash a subpoena emerging from civil litigation than from a criminal prosecution. The logic here is much the same as that offered by the various federal courts that have adjudicated the issue from a constitutional perspective. Criminal defendants' right to a fair trial figure prominently in the balance. The shield law in Michigan, for example, requires reporters to produce subpoenaed materials when sought by a criminal defendant facing a possible life sentence.[49] The New Jersey statute offers absolute protection from compelled testimony in civil cases, but only qualified immunity in criminal cases.[50] Similarly, in Ohio, an otherwise absolute immunity from having to reveal one's confidential sources must yield when a criminal defendant's Sixth Amendment rights would suffer.[51]

## Federal Department of Justice Guidelines

In the wake of *Branzburg,* several bills were introduced in Congress that sought to provide some measure of protection for reporters' confidential sources, but none passed. In part, it may have been because the press itself was not united behind the statutory approach. Some media companies preferred instead to seek stronger First Amendment protection from a future Supreme Court.

The federal government does, however, impose some restrictions on its own interactions with reporters in the form of guidelines promulgated by the office of the attorney general. The guidelines, which have been in the *Federal Register* in its current form since 1973,[52] are in some ways modeled after Justice Stewart's dissent-

---

[49]MSA sec. 28.945(1) (1998).

[50]N.J. Stat. sec. 2A:84A-21.1 (1998).

[51]Ohio Rev. Code Ann. sec. 2739.04, 2739.12 (1998).

[52]28 C.F.R. 50.10 (1999).

ing opinion from *Branzburg v. Hayes*. Department of Justice officials are instructed in the guidelines to make "all reasonable attempts" to obtain needed information elsewhere before seeking a subpoena against the news media. Moreover, the information must be deemed "essential" to building the government's case.

There has not been a lot of litigation stemming from the guidelines, in large part because they provide no judicial remedy against a Justice Department official who violates them. A reporter who is issued a subpoena in violation of the guidelines cannot sue the department. Neither will a subpoena issued in violation of the guidelines be automatically invalidated, although at least one court has suggested that the Justice Department must follow its own guidelines.[53] Even in that case, though, the basis for the ruling was the First Amendment, not the guidelines themselves.

It should also be emphasized that the guidelines govern only the Department of Justice, which is not the only federal entity empowered to issue subpoenas. In one case from Charleston, West Virginia, a federal district court expressed concern over the National Labor Relations Board's having issued a subpoena to a local newspaper reporter without following the attorney general's guidelines, but the Fourth Circuit Court of Appeals vacated this ruling.[54]

## Newsroom Searches

From a law enforcement perspective, issuing a subpoena to a reluctant informant—whether a reporter or anyone else—can be a rather inefficient means of obtaining data. If the subpoena's recipient is well-heeled or well insured or both, the motions to modify or quash a subpoena can be time-consuming and expensive for both sides. No wonder, then, that police sometimes find it more expedient to knock on the media's door with search warrant in hand.

### No Constitutional Immunity: *Zurcher v. Stanford Daily*

Stanford University enjoys an international reputation as a top-ranked institution with a beautiful campus of bicyclists, inline skaters, and mission revival–style sandstone buildings with red tile roofs, the essence of "West Coast laid back." On one particular Friday afternoon in April 1971, however, the Stanford campus was the site of a violent political demonstration pressing several employee demands and protesting the firing of a janitor by the university hospital. When local police were brought in to remove the protesters, there were twenty-two arrests, several injuries, and over $100,000 in damages. The incident also resulted in a major Supreme Court decision and an important piece of federal legislation aimed at undoing that decision. The

[53]*United States v. Blanton,* 534 F. Supp. 295, 297 (S.D. Fla. 1982).

[54]*Maurice v. National Labor Relations Board,* 7 Media Law Rptr. 2221 (S.D. W. Va. 1981), *vacated and remanded,* 691 F.2d 182 (4th Cir. 1982).

campus newspaper published a special Sunday edition focusing on the demonstration. The very next day, the local district attorney obtained and executed a warrant to search the offices of the *Stanford Daily* in hope of recovering photo negatives that might serve to identify those demonstrators who had engaged in violence or vandalism. The police affidavits accompanying the application for the warrant made clear that the newspaper staff itself was not suspected of any wrongdoing.

The search was unsuccessful in that only photographs already published in the newspaper were on hand. The newspaper staff, upset that the search could have laid bare reporters' notes that had been gathered from confidential sources, brought suit against Palo Alto Police Chief James Zurcher, alleging that the search was conducted in violation of the First and Fourth Amendments.

When the case reached the Supreme Court, it resulted in a 5–3 vote (Justice Brennan did not participate) rejecting the newspaper's claims.[55] Justice White disposed of the Fourth Amendment argument first. That this was a "third-party" search—i.e., that the newspaper staff was not itself under investigation—was of no constitutional consequence, he concluded. "Under existing law," he wrote, "valid warrants may be issued to search any property, whether or not occupied by a third party, at which there is probable cause to believe that fruits, instrumentalities, or evidence of a crime will be found."

The plaintiffs had also argued that, whatever Fourth Amendment protections might apply to third-party searches in general, the First Amendment interests that come into play when the site to be searched is a newspaper office necessitated judicial recognition of an added measure of privacy. Justice White expressed sympathy for the media's First Amendment claims. Newsroom searches are often physically disruptive, he admitted, thus jeopardizing "timely publication" of the news. Then, too, confidential sources might dry up if that which they tell a reporter in confidence may be revealed to the police by coercion. The proliferation of such sources might give reporters an incentive toward sloppy journalism, because they will be reluctant to maintain detailed notes or recordings. Important though these interests might be, White concluded, there was no need to create any special measure of Fourth Amendment protection for the press against third-party searches. "Properly administered," he wrote, "the preconditions for a warrant—probable cause, specificity with respect to the place to be searched and the things to be seized, and overall reasonableness—should afford sufficient protection against the harms that are assertedly threatened by warrants for searching newspaper offices."

### The Privacy Protection Act

The *Zurcher* case prompted media industries to lobby Congress for some legislative remedy, which resulted in the Privacy Protection Act of 1980.[56] The law provides

---

[55]*Zurcher v. Stanford Daily,* 436 U.S. 547 (1978).

[56]42 U.S.C.S. sec. 2000aa (1998).

that law enforcement officials at any level of government who seek testimony from reporters or from anyone "reasonably believed to have a purpose to disseminate" information to the public should generally use subpoenas rather than search warrants. Subpoenas are far preferable from the media's perspective. They invite a chance to argue, through counsel, why some of or all the sought materials should not be turned over. More important, they do not result in a newsroom being ransacked, disrupting the reporting operation and often turning up confidential materials not at all related to the specific law investigation at hand.

The Privacy Protection Act provides that there will be occasions when law enforcement will need to conduct a search of the newsroom. These exceptions to the general rule that a subpoena should be issued instead vary according to what kinds of materials are sought. The Act recognizes two broad categories: **work product** and **documentary materials.**

To help distinguish between these two categories, let us imagine that you are a reporter assigned to cover a recurring story in the United States: the competing political protests that take place each year in late January, the anniversary of the Supreme Court's famous abortion decision *Roe v. Wade.* As you prepare to do the story, you will likely gather together many materials that have been written by others. These might include position statements from both prolife and prochoice organizations, excerpts from any of the scores of books and thousands of articles that have been written about abortion, as well as the Supreme Court opinion itself (and later abortion opinions that have cited *Roe* as a precedent). These are all examples of documentary materials as defined in the Privacy Protection Act.

Your story will likely also flow from materials you produce yourself. These might include transcripts of interviews you conduct with leaders on both sides of the abortion debate, notes you make to yourself as you observe the street demonstrations, and any early drafts of your article. These materials all fit into the category called work product.

In that your work product is unique to you and not as easily reproducible as the documentary materials you gather, the former is the more protected of the two categories. Hence, there will be fewer exceptions to the "get a subpoena, not a search warrant" rule if the law seeks your work product.

Indeed, when seeking a reporter's work product, law enforcement officials are told in the Act that they may obtain a search warrant only under two conditions. The first is the easier of the two to articulate. If the police can demonstrate that someone is likely to die or suffer serious bodily harm should the sought material not be immediately uncovered, that is sufficient proof to obtain a search warrant.

The second condition is a bit more complicated. The reporter must personally be suspected of criminal wrongdoing; in other words, this situation is not the kind of third-party search that was conducted on the Stanford University campus. The Privacy Protection Act limits this condition a bit further. The criminal wrongdoing of which the reporter is suspected cannot be simply the possession of the materials the law enforcement officials want. Rather, the investigators must persuade the magistrate from whom a search warrant is sought that the work product will provide independent evidence of some *other* kinds of wrongdoing. Now, just to complicate things a bit further, this limitation is itself limited a bit in the Act; there is an exception to the exception. It is a sufficient proof of suspected criminal wrongdoing if the police can show that the reporter has in his or her possession classified materials or similarly restricted data, or any similar "information relating to the national defense." Similarly, suspected possession of child pornography is sufficient to obtain a search warrant.

When the law enforcement officials seek a reporter's documentary materials, the same two exceptions already articulated still apply, plus two more. First, the police will be permitted to search a newsroom if using a subpoena would likely result in the materials' "destruction, alteration, or concealment." Alternatively, if the reporter has disobeyed a subpoena seeking the production of the material in question, a search of the premises may be justified. Prior to the authorization of such a search, however, the reporter must be given a chance to submit an affidavit arguing why the materials in question should not be subject to seizure.

In the real world, of course, people do not always adhere to the letter of the law. What remedies are available to news media representatives whose premises have been searched in violation of the Privacy Protection Act? The Act gives aggrieved parties the right to sue the government under the Act for the improper conduct of any law enforcement official. This could mean suing the federal government, or state or local governments, with one caveat: the Eleventh Amendment to the U.S. Constitution tells individual states that they need not permit citizens to sue them. Because the Constitution supersedes any individual piece of federal legislation, the individual states may be sued for Privacy Protection Act violations only with their consent.

Plaintiffs may obtain damage awards either large enough to reimburse them for actual losses or up to $1,000, whichever is larger. Attorneys fees and other related litigation costs are also recoverable. No damages will be paid, and the plaintiff's suit will fail, if the state is able to show that its agents acted in the "good faith" belief that they were not, in fact, in violation of the law.

If the specific facts of a case might permit a search under the Act, a failure on the part of police to state clearly in their application for a search warrant which of the Act's provisions support issuance of the warrant will not itself constitute a violation of law. This lesson was learned in a case involving WDAF-TV in Kansas City, which had purchased from a tourist one evening in August 1994 a videotape depicting a brutal murder that had been committed earlier in the day. (The tourist was not himself suspected of any criminal activity; apparently he had been walking in a public park and happened upon the crime in progress.) The local police were able to make an arrest in the homicide, but they would not be able to hold the suspect very long without the additional evidence they presumed the videotape could provide. It is at least arguable that the Act's exception aimed at preventing death or serious injury would apply to this situation; after all, here is a person suspected of homicide and who may very well commit additional crimes if released. The majority of a federal appellate court panel ruled that the district attorney should be permitted to defend herself against the station's Privacy Protection Act suit by citing this exemption, despite the defectiveness of the affidavit in support of the search warrant application.[57]

One might suppose that a search conducted in violation of the Privacy Protection Act is, by definition, an *unconstitutional* search. The Act itself, however, makes clear that the question of whether a search is constitutional or not—that is, whether it is in keeping with the Fourth Amendment's prohibition against unreasonable searches and seizures—is a completely separate issue. This point is important because it means that the fruits of a search conducted in violation of the Privacy Protection Act are not by that fact alone subject to the Exclusionary Rule of Fourth Amendment jurisprudence. They are not automatically suppressed; they can still be used in a criminal prosecution.

The federal Privacy Protection Act clearly gives media industries important rights vis-à-vis law enforcement officials. Reporters should also know that a handful of states boast their own such laws and that some of these give protections beyond those provided in the federal law. Wisconsin's statute, for example, does not contemplate the use of search warrants against news media except when the staff there is itself suspected of criminal wrongdoing.[58]

---

[57]*Citicasters DBA WDAF-TV v. McCaskill,* 89 F.3d 1350 (8th Cir. 1996).

[58]Wis. Stat. sec. 968.13

 # Things to Remember

### NEWSROOM SEARCHES

- Although there is no federal reporter shield law, the Department of Justice has issued guidelines to its own agents that greatly limit the circumstances in which media representatives should be compelled to reveal their sources or other confidential information.

- In *Zurcher v. Stanford Daily* (1978), the Supreme Court ruled that the First Amendment does not protect the media from a newsroom search that is conducted in the furtherance of a properly issued warrant.

- In response to the *Zurcher* case, Congress passed the Privacy Protection Act of 1980, which sets up a general presumption that law enforcement officials at all levels of government should use subpoenas instead of searches to compel testimony from reporters.

- The Act is especially protective of a reporter's work product (things the reporter created, such as notes or interview tapes), and a bit less protective of documentary materials gathered by the reporter from other sources.

- Searches conducted in violation of the Act are not necessarily unconstitutional under the Fourth Amendment.

## Betraying a Pledge of Confidentiality

Thus far, this chapter has focused on reporters' efforts to maintain the confidentiality of their sources' identity and the information obtained from them. In 1991, the Supreme Court ruled in a dispute that turned the usual relationship between the media and their sources on its head.[59] The case emerged out of a hotly contested gubernatorial election in Minnesota—and no, Jesse "The Body" Ventura was not one of the protagonists.

Dan Cohen, who had been working in 1982 as a public relations consultant for the Independent Republicans' slate of Wheelock Whitney and Loris Krenick (for governor and lieutenant governor), brought to the attention of several Twin Cities area reporters the fact that the Democratic Farmer Labor Party's candidate for lieutenant governor, Marlene Johnson, had been convicted many years earlier of petty larceny. With each reporter he approached, Cohen performed a ritual of sorts. Prior to opening up the envelope containing Johnson's court records, Cohen would indicate that he had "some documents which may or may not relate to a candidate in the upcoming election" and offer to hand them over only if the reporter promised "that I will be treated as an anonymous source, that my name will not appear in any material in connection with this," and that "you're not going to pursue me with a question of who my source is."

Some of the reporters shooed Cohen away, concluding that Johnson's criminal act was too minor and too long ago to be newsworthy. Reporters for the *St. Paul Pioneer Press Dispatch* and the *Minneapolis Star and Tribune,* however, felt otherwise and determined to write articles incorporating Cohen's information. They both readily agreed to their source's request for confidentiality.

The two papers, in independent editorial meetings, determined that the news about Johnson's petty larceny conviction was sufficiently newsworthy to be placed before their readers on the eve of this hotly contested election. The editors also decided that Cohen's identity was too integral to the story to be omitted. The *Star Tribune* unmasked Cohen it its very first paragraph. The article carried Wheelock Whitney and his campaign manager's denial of having prior knowledge as to Cohen's intentions; both nonetheless told the reporter that "such information about a candidate's past ought to be available to the public before an election."

On several occasions in the next few years—in depositions, at trial, and in other court documents—the *Star Tribune* staff was called on to describe the editorial process that day. In their brief before the U.S. Supreme Court, the publishers noted that several options had been open to them. They could publish no article at all, but that would be unacceptable. Not only were the allegations themselves newsworthy, but, because other local media had gone forward with the story, for

---

[59]*Cohen v. Cowles Media Company,* #79-8806 (Minn. Dist. Ct. 4th Dist., Hennepin County), *rev'd,* 457 N.W.2d 199 (Minn. 1990), *rev'd,* 501 U.S. 663 (1991).

the *Star Tribune* not to publish would open it to charges of being biased in favor of the Democratic candidate (whom the paper had endorsed editorially a few days earlier). Attributing the charge in a deliberately vague way, such as to a "Whitney supporter," was also deemed unacceptable in that the Whitney campaign denied (falsely, as it later turned out) any involvement in the dissemination of the information.

So it was that two newspapers in the Twin Cities decided to override their own reporters' promises of confidentiality to Cohen, who lost his job with a public relations firm almost immediately upon publication and who promptly brought suit in Minnesota state court for fraudulent misrepresentation and for breach of contract. A jury awarded damages totaling $700,000 on both claims. The trial judge determined that the First Amendment had nothing to say about this dispute, that it was governed instead by the purely commercial relationship between reporter and source.

The Minnesota Supreme Court overturned both judgments against the newspapers. Writing for the majority, Justice Simonett concluded that the agreement reached between Cohen and the two reporters never was a formal contract as such, but rather an "I'll scratch your back if you scratch mine" accommodation. The court especially noted that the dispute arose "in the classic First Amendment context of the quintessential public debate in our democratic society, namely, a political source involved in a political campaign." To permit the awarding of damages for such promises, he added, "chills public debate."

The U.S. Supreme Court reviewed the case, allowing at the outset that there was indeed no formal contract between Cohen and either of the reporters. The legal doctrine known as **promissory estoppel,** however, dictates that if failure to enforce an agreement would be inequitable or would otherwise be against the public interest, the state may enforce the agreement, even in the absence of a contract. From the justices' point of view, the *Cohen* case asked whether the First Amendment should preclude the state from applying the promissory estoppel doctrine against the press. Justice White, writing for the majority, concluded that the First Amendment does not bar application of the doctrine in situations such as these. Newspaper publishers have "no special immunity from the application of general laws," he wrote. They must obey the National Labor Relations Act and the Fair Labor Standards Act, as well as laws against breaking and entering. Enforcement of such general laws, White wrote, "is not subject to stricter scrutiny than would be applied to enforcement against other persons or organizations."

Nothing in the *Cohen* decision limits the promissory estoppel doctrine to guarantees of confidentiality. Reporters who mislead their sources in other ways can also incur liability. In 2000, the First Circuit Court of Appeals permitted a truck driver to sue NBC because the network's *Dateline* producers falsely promised the source that the story they were preparing would not include testimony from a group called Parents Against Tired Truckers. The producers' more general promise to the effect that the broadcast would depict the driver in a positive light was deemed too vague to be actionable.[60] A reporter can also be sued simply for asking specific questions during an interview, if an earlier agreement had included a guarantee that certain subject matters would be off limits.[61]

Dan Cohen's case was unusual in that his attorneys were able to turn against the local newspapers arguments usually embraced by the media. If confidential sources are so important to the media, Cohen's argument proceeded, anything that would dissuade such sources from telling their tales would necessarily jeopardize core First Amendment values. Cohen's Supreme Court brief pointed to studies showing that "eighty percent of national news magazine articles and fifty percent of national wire service stories...rely on confidential sources" and that the *Washington Post* often uses more than a hundred such sources in a single day's paper.

The media in general were not quite sure what to make of the *Cohen* case. On one hand, editorials appeared in newspapers around the country, distancing their own practices from those of the two Twin Cities papers. The *Baltimore Sun's* Supreme Court reporter argued that the two newspapers' conduct was "unforgivable" and amounted to "a straightforward, bald faced ethical violation." Media attorney Floyd Abrams called the newspapers' betrayal of Cohen "reprehensible and damaging to all journalists."

This does not mean that the media were happy with the Supreme Court's decision. Long Island's *Newsday* editorialized that "if disgruntled sources are free to sue under state laws because they don't like the way their stories came out in print, the media's First Amendment protection is in serious jeopardy."[62] The *Chicago Tribune* added that "there is no compelling public interest in suddenly formalizing the relationship" between newspapers and their sources "through the threat of lawsuit."[63] And the *St. Petersburg Times* concluded that "the government is on the wrong side when a newspaper can be punished for publishing the truth to inform voters about an election, even if it has to break a promise to do so."[64]

The *Cohen* case represents a cry for improved communication between reporters and editors. If reporters are not truly empowered to make promises of confidentiality to their sources, such promises should not be made, or at least they should be made conditionally. This solution is not wholly satisfying, of course. There is no way of knowing how many important stories will be lost because sources are not sufficiently comforted by a promise of confidentiality that is "contingent on my editor's signing off on it later."

---

[60]*Veilleux v. NBC,* 206 F. 3d 92 (1st Cir. 2000).

[61]Kyu Ho Youm and Harry W. Stonecipher, "The Legal Bounds of Confidentiality Promises: Promissory Estoppel and the First Amendment," 45 *Federal Communication Law Journal* 63, 77–78 (1992).

[62]"Don't Punish the Media When They Tell The Truth," *Newsday,* 27 June 1991, p. 64.

[63]"A Bad First Amendment Case," *Chicago Tribune,* 1 July 1991, p. C16.

[64]"Voters Had a Right to Know," *St. Petersburg Times,* 25 June 1991, p. 10A.

# Things to Remember

**BETRAYING A SOURCE**

■ In *Cohen v. Cowles Media Company* (1991), the Supreme Court relied on the principle that the media are not exempt from obeying laws applied to all so as to uphold a damage award against newspapers that published a source's name after having promised confidentiality.

■ The situation can recur wherever reporters on the beat are in the habit of offering unconditional confidentiality when in fact they are only authorized to offer such promises "contingent on my editor's agreement."

At least one court has concluded that a Cohen-like promise is not binding on a reporter when the source is a liar. Perhaps you recall the *60 Minutes* interview with former White House employee Kathleen Willey, who claimed that President Clinton had "groped" her in the Oval Office when she came to speak with him about a personal problem. Seeking to bolster her credibility, Willey apparently asked long-time friend Julie Steele to tell a *Newsweek* reporter, falsely, that Willey had confided in her immediately after the incident with Clinton. This Steele agreed to do only on the condition that her name never appear in print. When Steele later confessed to the *Newsweek* reporter that she had lied, the magazine felt relieved of any moral responsibility to keep its promise of confidentiality. A federal district court in Washington, D.C., concluded that the publication was also relieved of any legal, contractual obligation to keep its promise under these circumstances.[65]

---

[65]*Steele v. Isikoff,* #98-CV-1471 (U.S.D.C. 2000) (unpublished opinion).

 ## Chapter Summary

In *Branzburg v. Hayes* (1972), the Supreme Court ruled that whatever First Amendment rights reporters might enjoy in the confidentiality of their sources do not extend so far as to outweigh a grand jury's demand for testimony. Because five members of the Court agreed that the First Amendment is at least implicated, however, lower courts in many jurisdictions have concluded that there is a qualified reporters' privilege to confiden-

tiality. How much protection that privilege provides is a function of what kind of information is being sought (sources' identities, other confidential information, or nonconfidential information witnessed first hand by the reporter), what type of judicial proceeding is involved (grand jury, criminal or civil proceedings), and whether the person from whom the material is being sought is considered a reporter. Several jurisdictions have openly embraced a test endorsed by Justice Stewart in his dissenting opinion from *Branzburg*. Reporters should be compelled to testify, Stewart argued, only if they are the only identifiable source of information relevant to a criminal investigation and for which the government has a compelling need. The vast majority of the states either have a reporters' shield law in their statute books or recognize a confidentiality privilege as a matter of state constitutional or common law. Here, too, the same three variables tend to determine how much protection is provided.

Although there is no federal reporter shield law, the Department of Justice has created guidelines for its own agents that emphasize a preference for negotiating with media representatives rather than creating an adversary relationship by using a subpoena or a search warrant.

In *Zurcher v. Stanford Daily* (1978), the Supreme Court held that the First Amendment does not provide reporters with any special measure of protection against newsroom searches, that the constitution only requires such searches be conducted in accordance with standard Fourth Amendment limitations. The Privacy Protection Act of 1980, designed to undo the effects of the *Zurcher* decision, proceeds on the general assumption that law enforcement officials seeking information from reporters should use subpoenas instead of search warrants. Exceptions may be made under certain specified circumstances, depending on whether the material sought was created by the reporters themselves (their work product), or was documentary materials gathered by them but created by others.

A promise of confidentiality made and then broken to a news source was the impetus for the 1991 ruling, *Cohen v. Cowles Media Company*. There the Court held that media employees, like other citizens, may be sued for violating their promises, in accordance with the principle of promissory estoppel. That doctrine holds that the state may find it in the public interest to enforce even promises that were not part of a formal contract.

chapter

# *Regulation of Advertising*

Americans have a love–hate relationship with advertising. They express dismay at the ubiquity of commercial messages on shopping carts, on movie screens, even in public toilet stalls. In community after community nationwide, school boards have wrestled with the dilemma posed by the Channel One phenomenon: The company will provide thousands of dollars of media equipment to participating schools, but only if students are required to watch its fast-paced daily news programming, including commercials.

Yet we also cannot help but admire the art of the sell. Super Bowl viewers are often more likely to talk the next day about the commercials premiered during that annual event than about the game itself, which should not be surprising given that the production costs associated with a thirty-second commercial often exceed those incurred by the producers of the thirty-minute program during which it runs. The issue of relative costs aside, many of us embrace the world of advertising as part of the popular culture. Consider the innumerable phrases from commercials that have entered the lexicon, from "Good to the last drop!" "Just do it!" and "You deserve a break today!" to "How do *you* spell relief," "Help! I've fallen, and I can't get up!" and "Don't hate me because I'm beautiful." Then there is also the famous "Where's the beef?" line that crossed over from commercial to political speech when Walter Mondale used it against Gary Hart in a 1984 debate.

One of the major themes of this chapter is that society's legal response to advertising manifests the same love–hate relationship. Perhaps nowhere has that ambivalence been more pronounced than in the development of the U.S. Supreme Court's own commercial speech doctrine. The first part of this chapter examines the evolution of that doctrine. Supreme Court pronouncements, however, are intended only to tell the other branches of government how much regulation is consistent with the First Amendment. It is also important to understand how the government regulates advertising day to day. The second part of the chapter therefore considers statutory and regulatory approaches. That section begins by considering state and local regulation of advertising and then moves to an extensive discussion of the most important regulatory body in this area, the Federal Trade

Commission. Next is a discussion of the federal Lanham Act—which allows a company to sue a competitor it feels has hurt its market share through deceptive advertising—and a short discourse on industry self-regulation. The chapter concludes with a discussion of political campaign advertising.

# The Supreme Court and Commercial Speech

Just as there are many sources of communication law in general, so also are there many sources of law as it affects the practice of advertising. Congress, the states, and local governments may all pass laws governing some kinds of commercial speech, such as regulating the size and distance from the highway of roadside billboards. Various federal and state agencies promulgate regulations dealing with the advertising, marketing, and labeling of commercial goods. Ultimately, all these laws and regulations must comport with the First Amendment. The task of determining what that last sentence means, of telling just how much First Amendment protection advertising enjoys, is the Supreme Court's responsibility.

## Beyond the First Amendment?

"See how men live in a hell diver! Popular prices: adults 25 cents and children 15 cents." So read the brochure that colorful entrepreneur F. J. Chrestensen handed out on New York City streets to attract paying customers for a tour of his surplus Navy submarine. But it was not to be. Chrestensen was forbidden by police commissioner Lewis Valentine to dock his submarine. The problem was not the submarine, but the brochure, which would put Chrestensen in violation of a city ordinance that forbade the distribution of *commercial* handbills.

Chrestensen went back to the printing press—quite literally—and reprinted his leaflets, this time on two sides. The reverse side boasted a political message (protesting the fact that he was not allowed to distribute a purely commercial message!). Would the distribution of this leaflet similarly be prohibited? Writing for a unanimous Supreme Court, Justice Jackson concluded that even the reprinted leaflet was "purely commercial" in nature. For the Court to rule otherwise, Jackson feared, would mean that "every merchant who desires to broadcast advertising leaflets in the streets need only append a civic appeal, or a moral platitude, to achieve immunity from the law's command."[1]

Although Justice Jackson's opinion is exceedingly brief, it does make clear the Court's view at the time that advertising is completely unprotected by the First Amendment. Although many prior decisions had put government officials on notice that they may not "unduly burden or proscribe" the dissemination of political messages, he wrote, "the Constitution imposes no such restraint on government as respects purely commercial advertising."

---

[1]*Valentine v. Chrestensen,* 316 U.S. 52, 55 (1942).

## Protecting All but "Pure" Advertising?

It took the Court more than thirty years to decide that advertising should in fact receive First Amendment protection. Along the way, the justices dealt with such issues as editorial advertisements placed by political activists, the classified pages' Help Wanted ads, and the constitutionality of one state's prohibiting ads for a product or service that is legal in other states.

***Revisiting* New York Times v. Sullivan.**   The Supreme Court's next examination of advertising's place in the system of free expression came in the 1964 libel case, *New York Times v. Sullivan.*[2] Recall that the artifact prompting Montgomery, Alabama, police commissioner L. B. Sullivan to sue the newspaper was a paid advertisement. One of Sullivan's arguments at trial was that the newspaper should be prohibited from raising any constitutional defenses at all, in that this material was commercial speech, wholly unprotected by the First Amendment. Yet it was not a "*commercial* advertisement," Justice Brennan replied, in that it "communicated information, expressed opinion, recited grievances, protested claimed abuses, and sought financial support on behalf of a movement whose existence and objectives are matters of the highest public interest and concern."

***Job Hunting in Pennsylvania.***   Consider next a case from 1973 involving the classified advertising pages of the *Pittsburgh Press.*[3] As was the case with many newspapers of the day, the *Press*'s Help Wanted ads were sex-segregated into sections headed "HELP WANTED—MALE" and "HELP WANTED—FEMALE." The newspaper disavowed any discriminatory purpose, justifying the organization of the ads by pointing out that "most jobs generally appeal more to persons of one sex than the other."

The National Organization for Women filed a complaint against the newspaper with the Pittsburgh Human Relations Commission. When the case finally reached the Supreme Court, it produced a 5–4 ruling against the newspaper. Justice Powell's majority opinion makes clear that the advertisements here were purely commercial speech, unlike the political advertisement at issue in the *New York Times v. Sullivan* libel case. That should have been enough to resolve the case: If the ads were purely commercial, they enjoyed no First Amendment protection at all, thus making almost any challenge to the Human Relations Commission's findings meritless. Justice Powell, however, emphasized that these ads were incitements to "illegal commercial activity" (employment discrimination).

The press can also be held liable for more subtle communications of an intention to discriminate. Some courts have found that the disproportionate use of white faces in display ads for housing developments can itself be a violation of the

---

[2]*New York Times v. Sullivan,* 376 U.S. 254 (1964).

[3]*Pittsburgh Press Company v. Pittsburgh Commission on Human Relations,* 413 U.S. 376 (1973).

federal Fair Housing Act, in that the practice visually implies that some housing opportunities are still for "Whites Only." The Court of Appeals for the Second Circuit permitted a suit to go forward against the *New York Times* for an alleged long-term pattern of publishing real estate ads that either excluded black models altogether or used them only when dressed as maids and doormen.[4] Most such suits tend to name the real estate advertisers themselves as defendants, however, rather than the media that printed the ads.[5] Indeed, in the Sixth Circuit a formidable obstacle has been placed in the way of plaintiffs seeking to recover damages from media outlets for pictorially discriminatory advertising. Only a campaign of several ads over time by a single advertiser can be actionable, this court held. Neither a newspaper's decision to publish a particular ad, nor its many individual decisions over time to publish ads from many different advertisers, would constitute a campaign.[6] This area of the law will likely require Supreme Court resolution.

The 1973 *Pittsburgh Press* decision says that an employer's use of discriminatory language in a Help Wanted ad is inseparable from the act of employment discrimination itself. What about ads placed by job *seekers?* Consider the following examples of such ads that ran in the *Pittsburgh Press* and that resulted in a 1979 Pennsylvania Supreme Court decision:

### Situation Wanted

- College Grad—Born Again Christian with Bachelor's Degree and seven years sales and marketing management experience seeking work with Christian business or organization.
- White Woman—desires day work, office cleaning.
- Parolee—White, needs employment to be released. Licensed steam boiler and engineer.
- Salesman, age 30, looking for career in Pittsburgh, start immediately, 15 years selling experience.

Justice Manderino concluded for the court that the newspaper could accept these ads with impunity in that they "proposed no illegal transactions, [but] simply ask that prospective employers hire the respective individual advertisers." That the advertisers sought to bring to employers' attention such "prohibited employment criteria" as age, race, and gender, was irrelevant, the court majority concluded; after all, employers could easily obtain that same information simply by scheduling a job interview.[7]

---

[4]*Ragin v. New York Times,* 923 F.2d 995 (2d Cir. 1991).

[5]*Ragin v. Harry Macklowe Real Estate Company,* 6 F.3d 898 (2d Cir. 1993); *Spann v. Colonial Village, Inc.,* 899 F.2d 24 (D.C. Cir. 1990); *Tyus v. Urban Search Management,* 102 F.3d 256 (7th Cir. 1997); *Arkansas Acorn Fair Housing v. Greystone Limited,* 160 F.3d 433 (8th Cir. 1998).

[6]*Housing Opportunities Made Equal v. Cincinnati Enquirer,* 943 F.2d 644 (6th Cir. 1990).

[7]*Commonwealth v. Pittsburgh Press Company,* 396 A.2d 1187 (Pa. 1979).

***Out-of-State Abortion Services.*** Jeffrey Bigelow was the editor of a weekly "underground" newspaper focusing on events at the University of Virginia community. In February 1971, two years before the Supreme Court's *Roe v. Wade* abortion decision, Bigelow accepted a paid advertisement from the Women's Pavilion in New York City, an abortion referral center. At the time of the ad's placement, not only was abortion illegal in Virginia, but the state also forbade any communications that might "encourage" or "prompt" women to receive abortions anywhere. Bigelow was successfully prosecuted under the statute, and appealed his conviction all the way to the Supreme Court.[8] Writing for a 7–2 majority, Justice Blackmun found for Bigelow, holding that the abortion ad was reminiscent of the advocacy advertisement in *New York Times v. Sullivan.* In the context of a highly contentious national debate about reproductive freedom, this simple ad "conveyed information of potential interest and value" and was thus "newsworthy."

The *Bigelow* decision created much confusion concerning the place of commercial speech in the system of free expression. Surely the Court did not mean to suggest that advertisements only for controversial products and services were to enjoy First Amendment protection. All would have been so much easier had the Court simply admitted that its real goal was to overturn *Chrestensen,* bringing advertising as a broad category of speech within the First Amendment. The next term would confront the Court with a controversy that virtually demanded a more candid overturning of the decades-old precedent.

## Bringing Commercial Speech under the Umbrella

The state of Virginia forbade not only advertising for abortions, but also advertising by pharmacists of prescription drug prices. A successful court challenge of this latter provision led the Supreme Court to finally overturn the 1942 *Chrestensen* decision, holding that the First Amendment does cover even purely commercial speech.[9] Justice Blackmun's majority opinion pointed out that the case was postured as a right to hear issue in that the plaintiffs were consumers rather than pharmacists. "Freedom of speech presupposes a willing speaker," Blackmun wrote; the First Amendment protects "the communication," both its source and its recipient. Predictably, the state felt its most powerful argument was that this was purely commercial speech, wholly unprotected by the First Amendment. Blackmun admitted that the "idea" sought to be communicated here—"I will sell you the X prescription drug at the Y price"—was a purely commercial one. The Court must thus finally answer whether such a message is "wholly outside the protection of the First Amendment. Our answer is that it is not."

Thus, the Court overturned *Chrestensen* and brought commercial speech within the protection of the First Amendment. It is understandable that Blackmun

---

[8]*Bigelow v. Virginia,* 421 U.S. 809 (1973).

[9]*Virginia State Board of Pharmacy v. Virginia Citizens Consumer Council,* 425 U.S. 748 (1976).

felt a need to provide some justification for the Court's having simply changed its mind after thirty-four years. It was not difficult to do. Surveys of local prescription drug prices provided to the trial court uncovered tremendous disparity among drug dispensers, as much as 650 percent for some drugs. Keeping consumers ignorant as to who in town offered the best prices served only to bilk the poor. Surely that would have been enough, but Blackmun went further, and in so doing demonstrated the Court's continuing ambivalence about *pure* advertising by purposely blurring the line between commercial and political speech. "So long as we preserve a predominantly free enterprise economy," he wrote, "the allocation of our resources in large measure will be made through numerous private economic decisions. It is a matter of public interest that those decisions, in the aggregate, be intelligent and well informed." What better way to ensure that public benefit is achieved than through "the free flow of commercial information"? Seen this way, advertising must be protected even by a First Amendment narrowly construed so as to apply only to speech that "enlightens public decision-making in a democracy." *Virginia Pharmacy*, then, says that commercial speech is protected even if it has no political elements. Yet the reason for this change of heart seems to be precisely because commercial speech has very strong political elements. Hasn't Justice Blackmun, after all, equated smart shopping with patriotism?

 # Things to Remember

### COMMERCIAL SPEECH DOCTRINE: EARLY HISTORY

- *Valentine v. Chrestensen* (1942). The Supreme Court holds that commercial speech is wholly unprotected by the First Amendment.
- *New York Times v. Sullivan* (1964). That the offending material in this landmark libel case appeared in a paid advocacy *advertisement* did not make it any less protected by the First Amendment than any other political speech.
- *Pittsburgh Press Company v. Pittsburgh Commission on Human Relations* (1973). Although the Court begins to suggest that it might be ready to overturn *Chrestensen,* this case would not be the right one. The HELP WANTED ads at issue here were an inextricable part of illegal activity (employment discrimination).
- *Bigelow v. Virginia* (1973). As in the *New York Times* case, the Court here also emphasizes the political elements in an ad for an out-of-state abortion clinic. We know that the Court is closer to being ready to overturn *Chrestensen* in that this was an advertisement for a service, admittedly a very controversial service. It was not an advocacy ad like the one the civil rights workers paid to have the *New York Times* publish.
- *Virginia State Board of Pharmacy v. Virginia Citizens Consumer Council* (1976). Forced finally to determine whether *Chrestensen* is still good law, the Court overturns the 1942 precedent, holding for the first time that even purely commercial speech is protected by the First Amendment.

In its next term, the Court continued its tendency to emphasize the political elements of commercial messages, even though it had already extended First Amendment protection to purely commercial speech.[10] At issue was a Willingboro, New Jersey, town ordinance—designed to stem the flow of "white flight" and to retain its integrated community—which forbade the use of "FOR SALE" and "SOLD" signs on residential lawns. The Court unanimously struck down the ordinance, in part because it stifled the flow of information "of vital interest to Willingboro residents, since it may bear on one of the most important decisions they have a right to make: where to live and raise their families." Here, too, we see the elevation of the commercial ("I have a house for sale here") to the political (a statement about racial harmony?). Justice Marshall's opinion is especially ironic in that, in a racially charged atmosphere of unscrupulous realtors inducing panic selling, the presence of a "FOR SALE" sign would not necessarily signal to a black family that this was, indeed, a place where *they* could live.

### How Much Protection? The *Central Hudson* Test

The *Virginia Pharmacy* case said that commercial speech enjoyed at least some First Amendment protection, but not how much. The answer to that question emerged a few years later in a case involving a New York law, borne of the 1970s energy crisis, prohibiting advertising by any electric company that would tend to promote the increased use of electricity.[11] Writing for an 8–1 majority, Justice Powell struck down the law as unconstitutional (see Figure 10.1). In so doing, he established the four-part "*Central Hudson* test," intended to give lower courts guidance as to how to adjudicate disputes involving regulation of commercial speech. In step one, courts ask if the advertisement is misleading or if it is promoting an illegal product or service. If so, any law regulating or prohibiting it is constitutional. If not, courts pose three queries about the state's interest in regulating this kind of speech: (1) Is that interest a substantial one? (2) Does the regulation really further that interest? and (3) Does the regulation abridge no more speech than necessary?[12]

Applying the test to the law before it, Justice Powell found initially that electricity is a legal product and that Central Hudson's ads were not misleading. Moving to the second inquiry, he allowed that the state did in fact have a substantial interest at stake: energy conservation. Did the law under review further that substantial interest, as the third inquiry demands? Powell felt so. Common sense

---

[10]*Linmark Associates v. Township of Willingboro,* 431 U.S. 85 (1977).

[11]*Central Hudson Gas & Electric v. Public Service Commission of New York,* 447 U.S. 557 (1980).

[12]In 1989 (*Board of Trustees of the State University of New York v. Fox,* 492 U.S. 469), the Court substituted a less stringent fourth query, asking only that there be a "reasonable fit" between the regulation and the state's interest; the Court, however, has since returned to its original *Central Hudson* formulation.

Figure 10.1    *The Central Hudson Test*

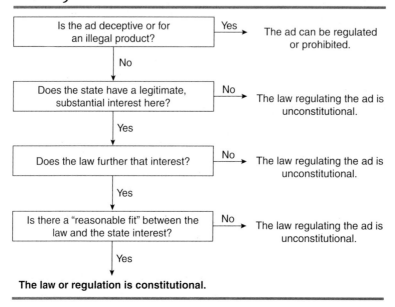

 Things to Remember

**THE *CENTRAL HUDSON* TEST**

- Is this a misleading advertisement, or an advertisement for an illegal product?
  - Yes → The ad can be regulated, or banned.
  - No → (Go to the next question.)
- Does the state have a substantial interest here?
  - No → The regulation is unconstitutional.
  - Yes → (Go to the next question)
- Does this regulation further the state's interest?
  - No → The regulation is unconstitutional.
  - Yes → (Go to the next question)
- Is the regulation no more extensive (i.e., no more restrictive of speech) than necessary?
  - Yes → The regulation is constitutional.
  - No → The regulation is unconstitutional.

suggests that advertising for a product will result in more demand for that product. Why would Central Hudson contest the advertising ban unless it believed it could increase its own sales via advertising?

The fourth inquiry, regarding how extensive the regulation, whether it abridged more speech than necessary to achieve the state's legitimate goals, proved the state's downfall. The prohibition on advertising was more extensive than necessary for two reasons, Powell concluded. First, the ban covered *all* promotional advertising, thus even prohibiting utility companies from marketing energy-*saving* devices such as heat pumps. Second, the state's interest was in saving *energy,* not electricity, yet some people (depending on what systems they already were using) might waste less energy overall by switching to electricity.

### Illegal, Misleading, or *Dangerous*?
### Smoking, Drinking, and Gambling

The late 1990s saw a tremendous flurry of legal activity involving tobacco companies. Dozens of states' attorneys general prepared lawsuits against the big tobacco conglomerates, seeking reimbursement for billions of dollars in health care costs. In early 2000, the major tobacco companies entered into a "Master Settlement Agreement" that put to rest dozens of those suits in return for billions of dollars, plus several concessions concerning the future marketing of tobacco products. Among the concessions were the companies' promise to stop targeting the underage youth market, to cease using cartoon figures such as Joe Camel, and to refrain from any further outdoor advertising (such as highway billboards or ads placed on the exterior of buses). By signing the Agreement, the tobacco companies thus hoped to avoid judicial resolution of a question that has stymied jurists and scholars for decades: Would the First Amendment permit the government to forbid tobacco advertising altogether? The Agreement, however, cannot resolve all outstanding issues concerning advertising of tobacco products. For example, although it covers outdoor advertising placed by the tobacco companies themselves, it is mute with respect to such advertising placed by retail establishments that sell tobacco products. That issue—and others concerning perceived conflicts between state and federal regulations in this area—were due to be heard by the U.S. Supreme Court in April 2001, with a decision expected a few months later.[13]

Unless you are more than a bit older than the typical undergraduate student, your only familiarity with TV commercials for tobacco products will be through archival footage. Yet tobacco companies were among the biggest spenders on TV and radio air time until the early 1970s. Indeed, in decades past, broadcast personalities often stepped out of role for a few moments to hawk cigarettes on their own

---

[13]*Consolidated Cigar Corporation v. Reilly,* 218 F. 3d 30 (1st Cir. 2000).

programs. Lucille Ball and Desi Arnaz did it, as did the voices behind the Flint-stones. That all stopped with the passage of the Public Health Cigarette Smoking Act, which as of 1971 forbade the advertising of cigarettes on television and radio. A special three-judge panel of the federal district court for Washington, D.C., upheld the constitutionality of that Act, and the Supreme Court, without writing an opinion, upheld the lower court ruling.[14] Although the decision was based upon the government's unique relationship to the electronic media, the district court majority added in dicta that "Congress has the power to prohibit the advertising of cigarettes *in any media*" (emphasis added). How much weight this statement should be given is unclear. That broader question was not presented to the lower court. Moreover, the decision was written prior to the *Virginia Pharmacy* ruling, thus at a time when lower courts had no reason to expect that advertising enjoyed *any* First Amendment protection.

Those who support the complete banning of tobacco advertising across all media took much solace from a 1986 Supreme Court decision. Recall that the first part of the *Central Hudson* test from 1980 asks whether an advertisement is misleading or is for an illegal product or service. The 1986 ruling in *Posadas de Puerto Rico v. Tourism Company,*[15] a 5–4 vote, prompted many to wonder whether the justices had secretly added a third prong to that inquiry. The decision seemed to say that a very diluted version of the commercial speech doctrine would apply when the product or service being advertised was a *dangerous* (although legal) one. At issue was a Puerto Rico law that forbade some forms of advertising for casinos. More specifically, ads aimed at Puerto Ricans were banned, but ads aimed at tourists from elsewhere were permitted.

Writing for a 5–4 majority, Justice Rehnquist made clear that the governmental interests—wishing to avoid increases in prostitution and in other local and organized crime—were substantial. Justice Rehnquist went on to find that the law directly advanced the governmental interest, employing the same commonsense rationale used in *Central Hudson* itself: that advertising tends to increase consumption. The law was not overly restrictive, he said, precisely because it was applicable only to ads aimed at island residents.

The most puzzling part of the Rehnquist opinion was his addition of another reason, beyond the mechanics of the *Central Hudson* test, for upholding the statute. He placed gambling in the category of products and services—he included cigarettes, alcoholic beverages, and prostitution—that governments may legitimately "deem harmful." Puerto Rico could surely have prohibited its residents from engaging altogether in such a harmful activity as casino gambling, Rehnquist suggested, and this broad power must surely include "the lesser power" to ban advertising designed to stimulate demand for the casinos.

---

[14]*Capital Broadcasting Company v. Mitchell,* 333 F. Supp. 582 (D.C. 1971), *aff'd mem.,* 405 U.S. 1000 (1972).

[15]478 U.S. 328 (1986).

Did Rehnquist thus mean to suggest that governments would be given carte blanche to regulate (or indeed, to prohibit) advertising for any "products or activities deemed harmful"? Two more recent cases indicate that the *Posadas* decision is perhaps best seen as an aberration, even though it has not yet been explicitly overturned.

The first of these involved the Coors Brewing Company, which industry analysts suggest has been plagued by a reputation that its products have too *low* an alcohol content.[16] The company sought governmental permission from the Bureau of Alcohol, Tobacco and Firearms (BATF), which governs such matters, to tell consumers the alcohol content of its beer in both advertisements and in product labeling. The BATF concluded that portions of the Federal Alcohol Administration Act of 1935 required it to deny the request. The federal district and appellate courts upheld the government's action with respect to advertising, but insisted that the company be permitted to list the alcohol content on the beer containers themselves.

Writing for a unanimous Court, Justice Thomas accepted the state's argument that there was a substantial government interest in discouraging liquor companies from engaging in "strength wars," trying to lure potential customers to their brands by dint of their high alcohol content. But would the governmental action here further that state's interest, as the *Central Hudson* test demands? In finding against the government on this crucial point, Thomas made much of the BATF choosing not to appeal its defeat below on the issue of advertising (as opposed to bottle labeling). Considering also that the vast majority of states permit advertising of alcohol content, brewers are thus allowed in most regions to disclose alcohol content in advertisements, but not on labels. "The failure to prohibit the disclosure of alcohol content in advertising, which would seem to constitute a more influential weapon in any strength war than labels," Justice Thomas concluded, "makes no rational sense if the government's true aim is to suppress strength wars."

Thomas also found suspect the overall pattern of federal regulation of liquor labeling in that the law treats wines and spirits in precisely the opposite manner as it treats beer. Not only *may* distilled spirits containers include statements about alcohol content, but such disclosures are *required* in the case of both spirits and wines that have more than 14 percent alcohol: "If combating strength wars were the goal," he wrote, "we would assume that Congress would regulate disclosure of alcohol content for the strongest beverages as well as for the weakest ones."

The *Rubin* decision struck down regulations on advertising for one of the "harmful" products listed by Justice Rehnquist in his *Posadas* opinion. If *Rubin* represents a step back from *Posadas,* a decision from the Court's very next term

---

[16]*Rubin v. Coors Brewing Company,* 514 U.S. 476 (1995).

looks more like a full-throttle retreat. At issue in *44 Liquormart v. Rhode Island*[17] were two statutes, both dating to 1956. The first prohibited licensed vendors of alcoholic products from advertising their prices (except in the form of in-store displays not visible from the street), and the other prohibited the media in Rhode Island from publicizing liquor prices, even prices offered by out-of-state retail outlets.

Although the Supreme Court unanimously struck down the statutes, the justices could not agree on a single rationale and thus did not produce a majority opinion. Some of Justice Stevens's plurality opinion speaks for one group of four justices, some for another four, some for only three. Stevens expresses skepticism as to whether the laws will further the state's legitimate interest in encouraging temperance. Even accepting the commonsense assumption that the regulations here will drive prices up and demand down, temperance may not be the result, in that the most abusive drinkers are not much swayed by price.

Stevens also argues that the *Central Hudson* test does not give sufficient protection to speech against state regulations that completely ban a truthful message about a legal product. Such rules "rest solely on the offensive assumption that the public will respond irrationally to the truth," that it is a legitimate function of government to keep the citizenry ignorant. Regulations that manifest this kind of paternalism, he suggests, should be subject to a level of scrutiny approaching that applied to laws abridging political speech.

Stevens shows an awareness that the *Posadas* decision seems to argue for upholding the Rhode Island statutes, for two reasons. First, alcohol is one of the harmful products or services mentioned in *Posadas* the market for which the state should be free to damper, even if its strategy includes regulation of advertising. Second, just as Puerto Rico could have banned casino gambling altogether, so also Rhode Island could have chosen to become a dry state, and in both situations, *Posadas* stands for the principle that regulating advertising for the product or service is less restrictive than banning the activity itself.

Instead of honoring the precedential value of *Posadas,* Stevens reports that he and the three justices joining this section of his opinion are "persuaded that *Posadas* erroneously performed the First Amendment analysis." Moreover, his reading of the various concurring opinions persuades him that "the entire Court apparently now agrees [that] the statements in the *Posadas* opinion on which Rhode Island relies are no longer persuasive." None of the other justices expressed disagreement with this sentiment.

What does all this bode for restrictions on tobacco advertising beyond those that might survive *Central Hudson* scrutiny anyway, or even for an outright ban on advertising for this still-legal product? The question cannot be answered with total certainty, but it would seem that the *Rubin* and *44 Liquormart* cases together signal the Court's reluctance to permit the censoring of true commercial informa-

---

[17]517 U.S. 484 (1996).

# Things to Remember

## POSADAS DE PUERTO RICO V. TOURISM COMPANY

- Justice Rehnquist seemed to add two very new rationales, above and beyond the *Central Hudson* test, for upholding the commonwealth's ban on casino advertising:
  - The state's inarguable freedom to ban the activity altogether surely includes the "lesser" right to ban advertising for the activity.
  - Governments should have a large amount of leeway in regulating advertising for products or services deemed harmful, such as gambling, smoking, and drinking.
- *Posadas* has since been discredited, although not explicitly overruled

tion based on the fear that readers will act on the information.[18] The argument could be made, of course, that most tobacco advertising either does not impart any information or imparts mostly a kind of nonverbal misinformation. Do not most print ads for tobacco products, after all, seek to create a mental association of the product with athletic endeavors engaged in by healthy, young models with impeccably white teeth? Surely this is quite different from such mundane and verifiable kinds of information as the price of a bottle of beer or its percent of alcoholic content. Whether that difference is one that makes a difference from the perspective of First Amendment analysis is a question for possible future litigation.

### Advertising by Lawyers and Other Professionals

Back in the landmark *Virginia Pharmacy* decision that first held purely commercial speech protected by the First Amendment, some of the justices tried carefully to limit the ruling to pharmacists only. In his majority opinion, Justice Blackmun went out of his way to say that he would "express no opinion as to other professions." He hinted, however, that lawyers and doctors would likely be treated differently in that they "do not dispense standardized products" but rather "render professional services of almost infinite variety and nature." Chief Justice Burger's concurring opinion emphasized that he was voting with the majority only because he predicted it would be possible to restrict this ruling to pharmacists. He pointed to data showing that 95 percent of prescriptions are already in dosage units when they arrive at the pharmacy—thus implying that pharmacists spend most of their time simply pouring pills from big bottles into little bottles—and concluded that the druggist "no more renders a true professional service than does a clerk who sells law books."

---

[18]Such an inference finds further support in *Greater New Orleans Broadcasting Association v. United States,* 527 U.S. 173 (1999).

***Not Only Pharmacists.***    Only Justice Rehnquist's crystal ball seems to have been working. He alone, in his *Virginia Pharmacy* dissenting opinion, argued that there would be no way to avoid opening the door to advertising by all categories of professionals, including lawyers. "I cannot distinguish," he taunted his colleagues, "between the public's right to know the price of drugs and its right to know the price of title searches or physical examinations." Why "title searches" and "physical examinations"? Clearly this was his way of throwing the majority's words back at Justice Blackmun. Pharmacists are not the only professionals who render "standardized products."

It did not take very long for Justice Rehnquist to be proven right. In its very next term after deciding *Virginia Pharmacy,* the Court ruled 5–4 to strike down Arizona's law banning lawyer advertising.[19] A Phoenix law firm called Bates and O'Steen placed an ad in a local newspaper describing itself as a "legal clinic" offering "very reasonable rates." The ad went on to indicate the actual rates charged for such services as uncontested divorce or separation, adoption, change of name, and bankruptcy.

Among the state's arguments in defense of the law was that lawyer advertising would have an adverse effect on attorney professionalism and that lawyer ads are inherently misleading. With respect to the first concern, Justice Blackmun likened it to a prediction that a client who perceives that the lawyer is motivated by profit will lose confidence that the attorney is acting out of a commitment to the client's welfare. How absurd, he exclaimed, given that the ABA code of ethics

---

[19]*Bates v. State Bar of Arizona,* 433 U.S. 350 (1977).

 Figure 10.2    *Frank and Ernest*

Frank and Ernest

When Justice Blackmun, in his *Bates* majority opinion, suggested that lawyers and clients should come to a mutual understanding at the outset about legal fees, this is likely not what he had in mind.

explicitly advises attorneys to "reach a clear agreement" with clients about fees as early on as possible (see Figure 10.2). If the obvious fact that the attorney–client relationship is at least in part a commercial one must be disclosed once the client is in the office, how can the state condemn "the candid revelation of the same information" in advertising, prior to the client's arrival?

Justice Blackmun took the state's second argument to mean that lawyers could not possibly advertise without deceiving potential clients, "in that attorney services are so individualized as to prevent informed comparison." In response, he admits that it would be rare for an attorney to advertise a fixed price for a nonroutine service ("No matter what crime you have committed, I will keep you out of jail, for $5000 or less!"). After all, attorneys know they cannot predict how much work, and of what variety, such complicated cases will entail. If and when attorneys do choose to include their price lists in their ads, Blackmun contended, the state's only concern should be that they "do the necessary work at the advertised price," that they keep whatever promises they make.

***"High-Quality" Professionals?***   Having determined that the state could not forbid attorney advertising across the board, Blackmun next had to consider whether this particular law firm's advertising campaign was deceptive. Despite the state's allegation to the contrary, he found that the lawyers' calling themselves a "legal clinic" was not necessarily misleading, that the phrase does not suggest some kind of government subsidy is at work here to keep prices down. Nor was it unreasonable for Bates to call his fees "reasonable." Indeed, they were towards the low end of the Phoenix market at the time. The majority cautioned, however, that lawyers should be very cautious about making global pronouncements in their ads about the "quality" of their services, because such claims would not be "susceptible to measurement by verification."

In two more recent decisions, the Court elaborated on, and perhaps stepped back a bit from, its concern about advertisements touting a professional's "quality" of service. In 1990, by a 5–4 vote, the Court overturned the censuring of Illinois attorney Gary Peel for having advertised, on his personal letterhead, that he held a "Certificate in Civil Trial Advocacy from the National Board of Trial Advocacy."[20] The state was concerned nonetheless that readers would assume (incorrectly) that the NBTA is a government agency, and, in any event, that Peel's boasting of his certificate was an impermissible statement, at least implicitly, about the quality of his services. Four of the five justices in the majority emphasized the difference between unsubstantiated promises of quality based on nothing more than a lawyer's own assessment of how wonderful he or she is, and statements of objective facts that may support an inference of quality. Although Justice Marshall did not join in the plurality opinion, his separate opinion did not contradict the plurality on this point.

---

[20]*Peel v. Attorney Registration and Disciplinary Commission of Illinois,* 496 U.S. 91 (1990).

Four years later, a similar case presented itself. Florida attorney Silvia Safille Ibanez, who also happened to be both an accountant and a "certified financial planner," advertised these latter qualifications in her Yellow Pages advertisement (under "Attorneys").[21] The state agency regulating the practice of accountancy took issue with her listing her certification as a financial planner on the grounds, reminiscent of the *Peel* case just discussed, that readers would incorrectly presume such certification came from the state itself. This time a clear majority of the Court, with Justice Ginsburg writing, concluded that there was nothing inherently misleading in Ibanez's description of her qualifications.

***State-Prescribed Wording.*** The Court had more to say about lawyer advertising in a case involving a St. Louis attorney—identified in the court proceedings only as R. M. J.—who had been disciplined by the Missouri Supreme Court's Advisory Committee for placing advertisements the text of which deviated from the group's strict guidelines.[22] Chief among R. M. J.'s sins were his having strayed from the precise wording demanded by the state to describe his practice—"personal injury" instead of "tort law," and "real estate" instead of "property law"—and his having indicated that he was a member of the U.S. Supreme Court Bar. Writing for a unanimous Court, Justice Powell overturned the reprimand issued against R. M. J., telling the states that they may not "place an absolute prohibition" on whole categories of "*potentially* misleading information," but must instead target advertising practices that are in fact deceptive.

R. M. J.'s having used slightly different wording to describe his areas of specialty from that which the state had preferred him to use was not inherently misleading and thus was protected by the First Amendment. The attorney's having indicated his membership in the Bar of the Supreme Court of the United States was "somewhat more troubling," Powell admitted. Consider for a moment what it would mean to *you* to learn that an attorney had such membership. Would you be impressed? You probably should not be, at least not very much. Membership in the Supreme Court Bar means that you are permitted to make oral arguments in front of the nation's highest court, but there is no test to take or interview to pass. One must simply have been a practicing attorney for three years, pay a fee, and have a current member of the Bar attest that one is "of good character." That R. M. J. chose to include this relatively uninformative fact about his qualifications was "at least bad taste," Powell concluded, but the Missouri rules did not specifically prohibit the disclosure, and in any event the state did not present clear evidence to support its contention that this particular boast was deceptive. Moreover, as R. M. J.'s attorneys argued in his defense, potential clients with a case that raises federal constitutional issues may want to seek out a member of the Bar to repre-

---

[21]*Ibanez v. Florida Department of Business and Professional Regulation, Board of Accountancy*, 512 U.S. 136 (1994).

[22]*In re R. M. J.*, 455 U.S. 191 (1982).

Figure 10.3

This ad is from the January/February issue of *West End Word,* which resulted in the *R. M. J.* case. Notice that the lawyer mentions, although not in an especially dramatic way, that he is a member of the Supreme Court bar.

sent them, and such membership is routinely listed in the kinds of legal directories available at public libraries.

Shifting for a moment from the practice of law to that of optometry, consider the plight of Dr. Jay Rogers, a Texas optometrist who challenged unsuccessfully his state's rule prohibiting members of his profession from doing business under a trade name.[23] A trade name in this context would mean virtually any wording on the shingle other than "Jay Rogers, O.D." You are probably familiar with numerous trade names used by optometrists; sometimes they are clever puns such as "For Eyes" or "Make a Spectacle." Rogers's chosen trade name was the more mundane "Texas State Optical."

Writing for a 7–2 majority, Justice Powell upheld the constitutionality of the state's prohibition, contrasting the Texas rule here with the Virginia rule that had prohibited pharmacists from advertising their prescription drug prices. It is difficult to imagine any commercial information more crucial to consumers than the prices of goods and services, Powell suggested. The speech Texas prohibits here, by contrast, is not valuable information and indeed "has no intrinsic meaning" at all." Perhaps more important is that trade names are at least as likely to deceive

---

[23]*Friedman v. Rogers,* 440 U.S. 1 (1979).

consumers as to inform them. A company can continue to use a trade name even after one or more optometrists whose reputation first attracted the public to the practice have departed. Conversely, an optometrist with a terrible reputation, perhaps owing to his or her own "negligence or misconduct," can simply change the name of the practice. Then, too, an optometrist can, "by using different trade names at shops under his common ownership, give the public the false impression of competition among the shops." None of these situations should be seen as whimsical hypotheticals, Powell warned. Indeed, they came from the pages of a real investigation of a Texas optometrist by the state's Board of Examiners.

In 1985, the Court dealt with two incidents stemming from a Columbus, Ohio, attorney's having advertised for DUI defendants and IUD plaintiffs.[24] In the first episode, attorney Philip Zauderer had sought clients with an ad that promised that "your full legal fee will be refunded if you are convicted of drunk driving." The deceptiveness in this ad, Ohio claimed, was its failure to inform readers that most criminal cases ripe for trial end in plea bargains. Any of Zauderer's clients who chose to plead guilty to a lesser offense would have to pay his full fee. As soon as the state expressed its displeasure to Zauderer, he withdrew the ad and pledged not to take on as clients any person who might respond to it.

The second instance involved Zauderer's elaborate ad seeking women who had been hurt by intrauterine devices. The ad featured a drawing of the Dalkon Shield and the caption, "Did you use this IUD?" The text went on to enumerate the many health problems that had been associated with this particular IUD, admonished possible victims that it is "not too late to take legal action," and informed them that "our law firm is presently representing women on such cases." The ad also promised that "no legal fees" will be owed unless a suit is successful.

The Dalkon Shield ad attracted the attention of the Supreme Court of Ohio's Disciplinary Committee for several reasons. First, the state had a clear rule against drawings or any other illustrations in lawyer advertisements. Second, Ohio had an anti–"ambulance chasing" rule that it interpreted so as to forbid attorneys recommending themselves to any potential client who has not specifically sought out their advice. In other words, attorneys were forbidden to give unsolicited legal advice including both the messages "You need an attorney" and "You ought to consider hiring *me*." Third, Zauderer's promise that "if there is no recovery, no legal fees are owed" seemed vague. Apparently, the client would not have to pay the attorney his fee. But what about fees due to the court itself, such as filing fees or fees for photocopying official documents? Moreover, if the client wins—and thus has to pay the attorney's fee—will that fee be calculated as a percentage of the gross amount awarded to the client, or the net (after the client pays all court costs out of pocket)?

Writing for the Court, Justice White had no trouble overturning the state's blanket prohibition against drawings or illustrations. "The use of illustrations or

---

[24]*Zauderer v. Office of Disciplinary Counsel,* 471 U.S. 626 (1985).

pictures in advertisements," he wrote, "serves important communicative functions: it attracts the attention of the audience to the advertiser's message, and it may serve also to impart information directly."

Concerning the contingency fees issue, Justice White's opinion upheld the judgment of the state, in a manner very consistent with Justices Holmes and Brandeis's famous dicta—see the discussion of *Whitney v. California* in Chapter 2—that the proper remedy to be applied to bad speech is "more speech rather than enforced silence." The Court's ruling might have been different had Ohio prohibited attorneys from advertising that they are willing to accept clients on a contingency fee basis, but all that Ohio demanded of Zauderer was that he make more clear what the fee arrangement truly would be. The reprimand on this point would therefore remain in force, because to laypeople unaware of the distinction between "legal fees" and "costs," the ad would falsely suggest "that employing Zauderer would be a no-lose proposition."

***Solicitation, Advertising, and the Mails.*** One key issue remained in the *Zauderer* case: the state's application of its antisolicitation rules to Zauderer for having both suggested to readers that they might need an attorney *and* that he might be a good one to hire. "All advertising is a plea for the audience's patronage," Justice White reminded the Disciplinary Committee. More to the point, there was nothing deceptive either in the ad's suggesting that women who have been hurt by the Dalkon Shield might need an attorney to help them recover damages or in its reporting that Zauderer's firm was experienced in this particular kind of litigation. Justice White made clear that it is quite legitimate for state regulations to protect the public from *in-person* attorney solicitations (from true "ambulance chasers"). Print advertising is different, however, in that it lacks "the coercive force of the personal presence of a trained advocate" and thus is "more conducive to reflection."

A few years later, the Court revisited the distinction between attorneys' in-person solicitation of business and attorney advertising. The case concerned a Louisville, Kentucky, attorney named Richard Shapero who was in the habit of culling through public records for lists of persons whose homes were being foreclosed upon. He would then write to these individuals and offer his services.[25] The Kentucky Bar Association had strict rules forbidding most kinds of direct mail advertising, and their logic was interesting. States can surely prohibit attorneys from mailing an individually targeted letter of solicitation to a specific individual, Kentucky reasoned, in that such a communication is very similar to in-person solicitation. As the science of information retrieval and direct mail list development grows more precise, lawyers may know so much about the persons on a carefully created mailing list that writing a letter to the entire list might also come to approximate in-person self-promotions. The Kentucky Bar Association therefore prohibited attorneys from writing direct mailings to any group of people

---

[25] *Shapero v. Kentucky Bar Association,* 486 U.S. 466 (1988).

who are somehow systematically different from the general public because of some "specific event or occurrence" (such as an auto accident or, indeed, a home foreclosure).

The wording of the rule was not terribly clear, which is part of the reason the Supreme Court struck it down. The rule prohibited mailings to persons "known to need legal services of the kind provided by the lawyer in a particular manner," but permitted mailing to persons "who are so situated that they *might* in general find such services useful" (emphasis added). Perhaps, then, Shapero could have mailed to whole zip codes in the poorer parts of town? Justice Brennan's opinion for the Court, like Justice White's in the earlier *Zauderer* case, emphasizes the key difference between in-person solicitations and direct mail appeals. "A letter, like a printed ad," Brennan reminds us, "can readily be put in a drawer to be considered later, ignored, or discarded."

Justice Brennan admits that a targeted mail campaign does carry with it the danger that recipients will overestimate the lawyer's qualifications—"He knows so much about me, he must be a good attorney!"—but this danger counts as a reason for carefully monitoring direct mail, not for banning it altogether. The Court suggests here that states may require all attorneys who wish to send direct mailings to have them prescreened by an appropriate regulatory body.

If the *Shapero* decision tells attorneys that it is all right to target for direct mail someone who may need their services because of a specific, catastrophic life event, a 1995 decision cautions that they may have to sit out a suitable waiting period before posting any letters.[26] In a 5–4 ruling, the Court upheld a Florida statute prohibiting attorneys from sending targeted direct mail solicitations to accident or natural catastrophe victims or their relatives for thirty days following the event. Justice O'Connor applied the *Central Hudson* test on behalf of the Court. The state's purported interest in "protecting the privacy and tranquility of personal injury victims and their loved ones against intrusive, unsolicited contact by lawyers" was clearly substantial. Moreover, the state's regulation served to further that interest in a narrowly tailored way. After all, attorneys do not have to wait thirty days to do other kinds of outreach, such as newspaper ads, billboard placements, or broadcast spots.

An interesting twist on attorney direct mail solicitations surfaced in Maryland in 1997. A group of lawyers had sent mailings to Marylanders revealed by a law enforcement computer database to have outstanding arrest warrants. In some instances, the receipt of the direct mail offer of professional services was the recipients' first tip-off that they were under investigation by the police. An outraged state judge promptly removed the attorneys' access to the law database, and a state judicial panel recommended keeping all unserved arrest warrants sealed for at least the first ninety days after issuance.[27]

---

[26]*Florida Bar v. Went for It, Inc.,* 515 U.S. 618 (1995).

[27]Del Quentin Wilber, "Keeping Unserved Warrants Secret for 90 Days Advised," *Baltimore Sun,* 10 Jan. 1998, p. 4B.

The whole issue of in-person solicitation was treated somewhat differently by the Supreme Court when the professional involved was an accountant rather than an attorney.[28] Florida was one of a tiny handful of states that forbade accountants from engaging in "direct, in-person, uninvited solicitation" to obtain new clients. Accountant Scott Fane wanted to do just that and so sought a declaratory judgment on the rule's constitutionality. Writing for an 8–1 majority, Justice Kennedy rejected the state's argument that any accountant who thus solicits clients "is obviously in need of business" and might be a bit too willing to bend the rules when it comes time each year to certify that the client's accounting practices are appropriate. Indeed, the opposite—that accountants with *long-standing* clients would be most likely to bend reality a bit at certification time—is equally plausible. Despite the Court's often-expressed fears about in-person solicitation by *attorneys,*[29] Kennedy had some rather laudatory comments about the benefits of commercial solicitation in general. Only in-person solicitations, after all, permit "direct and spontaneous communication between buyer and seller." Why, then, should in-person solicitation by attorneys be considered dangerous? Because attorneys are almost unique among professionals, in that they are "trained in the art of persuasion" and because their clients are very often "unsophisticated, injured or distressed lay persons." Initial contacts between attorneys and potential clients often occur "at a moment of high stress and vulnerability." By contrast, most

---

[28]*Edenfeld v. Fane,* 507 U.S. 761 (1993).

[29]See, for example, *Ohralik v. Ohio State Bar Association,* 436 U.S. 447 (1978).

 # Things to Remember

### ADVERTISING BY LAWYERS AND OTHER PROFESSIONALS

- The 1977 *Bates* case first opened the door to lawyer advertising.
- The Court has since *said* it would be very leery of attorneys whose ads were designed to tout the high quality of their services, yet the justices have never upheld any state sanction against an attorney for doing just that.
- The only sanctions the Court has upheld were for advertising in potentially deceptive ways with respect to fees.
- There is a long history of forbidding attorneys to do in-person solicitations for their services; neither traditional mass media advertising nor direct mail appeals are considered solicitation.
- States may, however, insist that attorneys wait a suitable time after an accident or other catastrophic event before doing a mailing to the victims.
- States may not constitutionally prohibit accountants (nor, presumably, other professionals who are not "trained in the art of advocacy") from engaging in in-person solicitation.
- States may prohibit professionals from doing business under a trade name.

accountants' clients are "experienced business executives," and meetings between accountants and such businesspeople tend to take place "in their [the client's] offices at a time of their choosing."

## Statutory and Regulatory Approaches

The First Amendment, as interpreted by the Supreme Court in such landmark decisions as *Virginia Pharmacy* and *Central Hudson,* puts the government on notice as to how much regulation of advertising will be permissible. One thing that has remained constant throughout and even before the development of the Supreme Court's commercial speech doctrine is the commonsense notion that government should protect us from deceptive advertising. Not surprisingly, most of the ongoing regulatory interactions between government and advertisers are aimed at identifying and eliminating deceptive statements from commercial messages. This section looks first at state and local regulations of advertising, then at the most important source of federal regulation—the Federal Trade Commission (FTC). We then examine the federal Lanham Act, which permits one competitor to sue another for damages, without having to persuade the FTC to intervene. After considering nongovernmental efforts at self-regulation by media and by the advertising industry, we conclude with a brief look at Supreme Court decisions concerning corporate advertising that seeks to "sell" political candidates rather than products and services.

### State and Local Regulations

In the late 1990s, dozens of states and even more individuals were engaged in litigation against the nation's major tobacco companies, attempting to recover billions of dollars of health care related expenses as well as other kinds of damage awards. One argument appearing in several of these cases was that the companies had been guilty of using deceptive advertising—failing to disclose the addictive nature of their products—in violation of relevant state laws.

None of this should be surprising, actually. State regulation of advertising predates any meaningful intervention by the federal government. A magazine based in New York, reacting to an array of newspaper and magazine exposés of medical quackery, proposed in 1911 that individual states draft laws criminalizing the use of deceptive advertising. Such **Printer's Ink statutes,** named after that magazine, were eventually passed by the majority of states.

Many state laws governing advertising practices are fashioned after federal laws and regulations. At times, state laws have been ruled in violation of the federal constitution's **Supremacy Clause** prohibiting state and local governments from enacting laws that conflict with federal law. In 1992, the Supreme Court prevented a group of state attorneys general from enforcing their own guidelines governing price advertising by airlines. The federal Airline Deregulation Act of 1978, the Court held, explicitly preempted state regulation in this area.[30] In another case, the Supreme Court held that the state of Oklahoma could not enforce a law prohibiting wine advertising on cable television stations, because doing so would conflict with federal laws and regulations.[31] The question of whether Massachusetts's regulations of tobacco advertising are preempted by relevant federal legislation is squarely before the Supreme Court in its 2000–2001 term.

Where state provisions do not conflict with or usurp federal regulations, the Supremacy Clause does not apply, and the individual states therefore often do take actions against advertisers that, for whatever reasons, the federal government is slow to take. In 1998, for example, American Family Publishers had to pay damages totaling over $1 million to several states that had sued the magazine subscription service best known for its annual sweepstakes using Ed McMahon and Dick Clark as pitchmen. The large print in mailings from the company trumpeted that the recipient "has won" millions of dollars; only by reading the very fine print would one learn that this joyful event will only have come to pass if "you have and mail in the winning number. Some recipients of the mail piece, convinced that they were millionaires, had flown cross-country at their own expense to pick up their prize!"[32] Publicity generated from state prosecutions spurred the federal government into

---

[30]*Morales v. Trans World Airlines,* 504 U.S. 347 (1992).

[31]*Capital Cities Cable v. Crisp,* 467 U.S. 691 (1984).

[32]Diane Bell, "Sweeping Changes in Sweepstakes," *San Diego Union-Tribune,* 12 May 1998, p. B1.

 Figure 10.4

The kinds of sweepstakes pitches that so upset Broom Hilda here could lead to sanctions at the state level and are also prohibited by the federal Deceptive Mail Prevention and Enforcement Act.

action. In December 1999, President Clinton signed into law the Deceptive Mail Prevention and Enforcement Act;[33] among its provisions is a requirement that qualifying language contradicting the bold assertion that the recipient "has won" must be "clearly and conspicuously displayed." (This wording is a rather watered-down version of the original bill's mandate that any qualifying language be the same size as the very largest font used anywhere in the mailing.) The law also requires sweepstakes mailings to make clear that participants' odds of winning are not affected by whether or not they purchase the promoter's products, such as magazine subscriptions.

Municipal governments have also gotten involved in the regulation of commercial messages. The *Pittsburgh Press* case discussed earlier in this chapter concerned *local* statutes forbidding discriminatory advertisement for employment. In another case, the city of Cincinnati required news racks on city streets to be used only for the distribution of "real" newspapers rather than the "commercial" newspapers one often finds publicizing local real estate offerings, alternative "learning exchange" educational institutions, or even dating services.[34] That the Supreme Court struck down this particular local law is not surprising in that the factual situation was so very similar to that of *Valentine v. Chrestensen* (involving handbills inviting folks to pay a few pennies to come aboard a submarine), which had itself been overturned in the landmark *Virginia Pharmacy* decision. Then, too, many cities and towns have some kind of regulations governing the placement of signs and billboards. A San Diego statute was struck down by the Supreme Court in part because it, ironically enough, provided *more* freedom of speech for commercial messages than for political ones.[35] Some antibillboard laws in other locales that did not manifest this fatal flaw have been upheld.[36]

---

[33]106 P.L. 168 (1999).

[34]*City of Cincinnati v. Discovery Network,* 507 U.S. 410 (1993).

[35]*Metromedia v. City of San Diego,* 453 U.S. 490 (1981).

[36]*Major Media, Inc. v. City of Raleigh,* 792 F.2d 1269 (4th Cir. 1986); *National Advertising Company v. City of Denver,* 912 F.2d 405 (10th Cir. 1990); *Messer v. City of Douglasville, Georgia,* 975 F.2d 1505 (11th Cir. 1992).

 # Things to Remember

### STATE AND LOCAL REGULATIONS OF ADVERTISING

- State Printers' Ink statutes were adopted early in the twentieth century to protect consumers from deceptive advertising.
- The Supremacy Clause of the U.S. Constitution prevents states or localities from passing regulations in conflict with federal law.

## The Federal Trade Commission

The main vehicle for the day-to-day federal regulation of advertising is the FTC, created appropriately enough by the Federal Trade Commission Act of 1914. The FTC has five commissioners, appointed by the president with the consent of the Senate, who serve for seven-year, staggered terms. The FTC was originally empowered only to police business practices whereby one company's behavior would unfairly hurt a competing company's bottom line. Congress's passage of the Wheeler–Lea Amendments to the Federal Trade Commission Act, in 1938, gave the Commission the power to protect consumers too from unfair and deceptive business practices.

A word is in order about that phrase from the preceding sentence—"unfair and deceptive." Much of what the FTC does is not actually concerned with deceptive advertising. The Commission's definition of unfairness, as laid down by Congress, points to any business practice that "causes or is likely to cause substantial injury to consumers which is not reasonably avoidable by consumers themselves and not outweighed by countervailing benefits to consumers or to competition." There is nothing in the Act that restricts the Commission to consider only issues related to advertising messages. Thus, for example, in 1973, the Philip Morris Company, which even then was a conglomerate that sold many kinds of products other than cigarettes, got into trouble with the FTC for giving away free razor blades as part of newspaper home delivery inserts. The Commission had no trouble concluding that the serious safety hazard inherent in the practice constituted the kind of "substantial injury to consumers" Congress sought to prevent.[37]

*Deceptive Advertising.*  The Commission uses a three-step process to determine whether it should move against an allegedly deceptive advertisement. The first step involves a textual analysis of the ad and its context to determine just what it is saying, whether it appears on the surface to be deceptive. The second step, almost inseparable from the first in practice, requires the Commission to consider whether a *reasonable* consumer would be deceived by the ad. Assuming that there is some deception at work, the last inquiry is whether or not that inaccuracy is *material*—that is, is it likely to affect the purchasing decision. Let us examine these three inquiries in turn.

*Finding the Meaning of the Ad.*  Some advertisements, such as one that falsely claims the Surgeon General has endorsed a product, are obviously deceptive. More typically, deceptive messages are implied rather than expressly stated. Professor Ivan Preston of the University of Wisconsin, one of the country's most prolific writers on FTC policies, has suggested that advertisers who study Commission decisions

---

[37]*Philip Morris, Inc.,* 82 F.T.C. 16 (1973). Notice that citations to FTC opinions most frequently name only the company involved. Only if and when a company appeals an FTC decision to a federal court does the citation then acquire the form "Company X v. FTC."

carefully will discover that there are recurring categories of implied deception employed by the agency. Preston identifies fifteen such categories.[38] Although the pages that follow owe much to Preston's work, several of his categories have been collapsed together and renamed, to make them easier to remember. Four categories of implied deception result: "And I can prove it!," "More than I can say," "Did I hear that right?," and "Who said that?"

- **"And I Can Prove It!"**  At one level, almost all advertising copy includes the implication "And I can prove it!" Make virtually any factual claim about your product, and consumers will assume that you have some reasonable basis for making the claim, that you can prove it. Sometimes ads teasingly go a step further, hinting at a particular kind of proof for their claims. Suppose an advertiser said that "90 percent of all teachers surveyed recommended the Grok Reading Program." That seems like pretty compelling testimony, doesn't it? But what if the 90 percent figure refers, literally, to nine out of ten teachers, and that all ten were employees of the company? The deceptiveness then becomes apparent. The moment survey data or other statistical evidence are offered as proof for a claim, consumers have a right to expect that the figures were gathered in a scientifically valid way. Thus, for example, the makers of Fleishmann's margarine were told by the FTC to stop advertising that twice as many doctors recommended their margarine as any other brand. The manufacturer failed to include the sobering caveat that almost 70 percent of the physicians surveyed did not express a preference for any particular brand.[39]

When a company offers "proof" of its product effectiveness in the form of an actual demonstration, the FTC requires that the demonstration not be rigged in any material way. Campbell Soup company, for example, concerned that the solid chunks of meat and vegetables in their product would tend to sink to the bottom of the bowl over time, dropped a number of marbles into soup bowls so that the TV camera would not make it seem as if the soup was merely broth. The FTC charged Campbell's with using a visually deceptive claim.[40] The makers of Kava coffee, seeking to emphasize that their brand was less bitter and less acidic than the competition, used a pH meter to demonstrate.[41] The problem? As you may know, substances' pH levels can range from zero (acidic) to fourteen (completely lacking in acidity). The Kava pH meter had been dramatically recalibrated so that a mere two-point difference in pH level was made to take up the entire instrument. As Professor Ivan Preston has explained, "It was as if a household thermometer, typically about ten inches high and calibrated from 120 degrees to minus

---

[38]Ivan Preston, "The Federal Trade Commission's Identification of Implications as Constituting Deceptive Advertising," 57 *University of Cincinnati Law Review* 1243 (1989).

[39]*Standard Brands, Inc.,* 97 F.T.C. 233 (1981).

[40]*Campbell Soup Company,* 77 F.T.C. 150 (1970).

[41]*Borden Company,* 78 F.T.C. 686 (1971).

50 degrees, was revised to show a range of only 70 to 75 degrees in the same 10 inches."[42] So when Kava made the needle move to the extreme right of the meter and the competing brands to the extreme left, consumers should not have been nearly so impressed as the company wanted them to be.

Probably the most famously deceptive advertising demonstration to attract the FTC's attention was that engaged in by the makers of Rapid Shave, who wanted to show viewers that their lather made shaving so effortless that it could strip sandpaper of its grain. Apparently, it would have been possible for the product to shave very fine sandpaper, if said paper had been soaking long enough in advance of the demonstration. Fine sandpaper, however, does not "read" like sandpaper at all on TV—you can't see the grain. Very coarse sandpaper would produce the right picture for the cameras, except that it would be clearly impossible to actually shave it. So the manufacturer instead affixed grains of sand onto a piece of Plexiglas. The announcer then informed the audience that the purpose of the demonstration was "to prove Rapid Shave's supermoisturizing power" and that the process was as simple as "apply, soak, and off in a stroke." The FTC ordered the company to take the ads off the air, and the manufacturer appealed all the way to the Supreme Court, which upheld the Commission's decision. The commercial included three misrepresentations, the Court held: that sandpaper could be shaved by Rapid Shave, that an experiment had been conducted verifying this claim, and that the viewer was seeing this experiment for themselves.[43]

• **"More than I can say!"** Advertisements fit into the "More than I can say" category when their text is cleverly crafted so as to imply erroneous conclusions. For a tire company to claim that its tires passed all the manufacturer's inspections, for example, would seem to imply that the product must be wholly without defects. It is not what the text *says,* but the message is surely implied.[44] The makers of Geritol, who for many years sponsored the *Ted Mack Amateur Hour* on television, touted its product as a miracle dietary supplement for those who suffer from the lethargy caused by "iron poor blood." Such a claim, the Commission concluded, was misleading in its failure to point out that very few cases of fatigue are caused by anemic blood.[45]

Sometimes a disclaimer is provided in a commercial specifically asking consumers *not* to jump to the erroneous conclusions that the rest of the advertisement's text would otherwise imply. The Commission, however, will still need to determine if that qualification or disclaimer is adequate to prevent the consumers' leap of faith. Thus, when in the 1970s Ford Motor Company used a dramatic

---

[42]Ivan L. Preston, *The Great American Blowup: Puffery in Advertising and Selling* (Madison: University of Wisconsin Press, 1996), 174.

[43]*FTC v. Colgate-Palmolive,* 380 U.S. 374 (1965).

[44]*Firestone Tire & Rubber Company v. FTC,* 481 F.2d 246 (6th Cir. 1972).

[45]*J. B. Williams & Company v. FTC,* 381 F.2d 884 (6th Cir. 1967).

advertising campaign, including a test drive from Phoenix to Los Angeles, to show that its cars get excellent mileage, the Commission felt that the company's disclaimer—"the mileage you get may be less or even more depending on many factors"—was inadequate.[46]

Sometimes, by touting a specific property inherent to its product, an advertiser may suggest that this brand is the only one on the market with that quality. For example, Whirlpool Company got the Commission's attention when it boasted that its air conditioners had a "special Panic Button to cool you off extra fast." The FTC found that such a button was hardly unique to Whirlpool's products, but was "merely a control which activates the highest of the three fan speeds, substantially similar to controls on comparable air conditioners made by other companies."[47]

Sometimes the way a company emphasizes an advantage its product truly does have may create a "halo effect," implying falsely that the product has other, related benefits as well. When Anacin is touted as having more of a specific but unnamed pain reliever (aspirin) than the competition, isn't it likely that consumers will infer that the product is therefore superior overall as a painkiller? The inference may not be logical. It ignores the possibility that competing brands' formulas, which may include some aspirin plus some other drugs, might produce better results. Yet the inference is a likely one and is one that the Anacin ad almost demands we make.[48] Another example is found in the ad campaign run by Sun Oil Company for its high-octane Sunoco 260 gasoline. In meticulous detail, the ads explained how there were two kinds of gasoline stored underground at Sunoco stations, regular 190 octane and the high-premium 260 octane. Customers could pump gasoline labeled 190, 200, 210, and so on, all the way to 260, and for the intermediate grades an appropriately proportioned blend from the two tanks would be delivered. The company's transgression, from the Commission's perspective, was its emphasizing that all its blends save for pure 190 would thus have "260 action." Were consumers thus not being led to conclude that whatever sterling qualities pure 260 gas had would somehow also be enjoyed by those pumping lesser grades?[49] Indeed, Professor Ivan Preston found that 80 percent of students he surveyed had inferred precisely that.[50]

Cornelia Pechmann, a University of California at Irvine marketing professor, studied consumer interpretations of a United Parcel Service (UPS) advertisement. On its face, the ad promised only that UPS was the cheapest service provider if one needed to have a package delivered by 10:30 the next morning and if one was willing to deliver the package to the local UPS collection site. A fairly sizable number of Pechmann's subjects concluded falsely from this premise that UPS would also

[46]*Ford Motor Company,* 87 F.T.C. 756 (1976).

[47]*Whirlpool Company,* 83 F.T.C. 1830 (1974).

[48]*American Home Products Corporation,* 98 F.T.C. 136 (1981).

[49]*Sun Oil Company,* 84 F.T.C. 247 (1974).

[50]Preston, *The Great American Blowup,* 106–108.

be cheapest in other circumstances, such as if the customer needed pickup service or if delivery was not essential until the end of business the next day.[51]

A related type of distortion occurs when advertisers offer, often in a dramatic way, true but not terribly important information about their product. One of the best-known examples was when the makers of Carnation Instant Breakfast emphasized in their ads that their product has "as much mineral nourishment as two strips of crisp bacon." How many consumers realized that bacon has very few mineral nutrients, so that the comparison was not terribly meaningful?[52]

The FTC released a major report in September 2000 on the marketing of violent entertainment (movies, music, and video games) to children. A key finding was that even media that the industries themselves claimed to be targeted exclusively at adults—such as R-rated movies, to which minors unaccompanied by a parent or guardian are to be denied admission—were in fact heavily advertised during TV programs with heavy youth viewership (e.g., *The Simpsons,* professional wrestling, and *Xena: Warrior Princess*). Might such marketing strategies constitute a kind of deceptive advertising, the Commission wondered, in that they would cause viewers to doubt the industry's seriousness about restricting certain kinds of content to mature audiences only?

• **"Did I Hear That Right?"** Advertisers will often choose their words carefully, perhaps even injecting new words into the lexicon, to lead consumers to make conclusions based on a kind of auditory confusion. If you heard that a sweater was made of "cashmora," for example, isn't it likely that you will free-associate to "cashmere"?[53] Or, consider "plyhide" as a descriptive name for an upholstery material. Does it not suggest some kind of leather, or at least the hide of some unnamed animal, rather than the vinyl it really was?[54]

Advertisers do not have to invent new words to create linguistic ambiguity. Thus, the Commission's suspicions were aroused by America Online's ubiquitous offers of ten "free hours" of online time. Consumers would easily miss the barely visible warnings that the hours must all be used in one month, that any use exceeding the ten hours or going beyond the one month trial would result in automatic charges to their credit card, and that users needed to take the affirmative step of contacting the company to cancel their membership prior to the month's passage or they would begin to incur hourly fees.[55]

If advertisers can get into trouble for offering their wares "free," they certainly can attract the Commission's attention when they offer merchandise at sale prices.

---

[51]Cornelia Pechmann, "Do Consumers Overgeneralize One-Sided Comparative Price Claims, and Are More Stringent Regulations Needed?" 33 *Journal of Marketing Research* 150 (1996).

[52]*Carnation Company,* 77 F.T.C. 1547 (1970).

[53]*Elliot Knitwear,* 59 F.T.C. 893 (1961).

[54]*Robbin Products,* 62 F.T.C. 1461 (1963).

[55]*America Online,* 1998 F.T.C. LEXIS 25, Docket no. C-3787 (1998).

Look at the typical full-page department store ad in your local newspaper, telling readers that this or that product is now "on sale" for a hefty "percent off." What does this wording mean? The Commission demands that the percent be a comparison with a bona fide "regular" price, and that the regular price shall have been in place for a reasonable period of time prior to the beginning of the special sale days. Ideally, too, a substantial number of sales will have resulted from the offering at the regular price. If not, this very fact must be affirmatively disclosed in the ad. Thus, if you look at the fine print of such ads, you will often see words to the effect that "our regular and original prices are offering prices only and may or may not have resulted in sales."[56]

- **"*Who* Said That?"** Advertisements often rely just as heavily on the attributed source for their message as on the text itself. Madison Avenue is constantly on the lookout for appropriate spokespersons, celebrity or otherwise, to endorse their clients' goods and services. FTC regulation in this area is rather complex.

The Commission does not consider all instances of people saying nice things about products in commercials "endorsements." Advertising narratives in which one character teaches another about a product, whether food storage bags or laxatives, would not usually be of Commission concern. Viewers understand that these are fictional relationships depicted by paid actors. Nor does a spokesperson who does not enjoy any special brand of notoriety beyond appearing in a commercial typically count as an endorser. The famous "Where's the beef?" commercials did not make actress Clara Peller into an endorser, for the purpose of Commission policies.

An endorsement must represent the genuine beliefs and experiences of the person or group to whom it is attributed. In a classic case on this point, a cigarette company advertised in such a way so as to imply that a *Reader's Digest* article had endorsed its product line. The appellate court that upheld the FTC's order to cease the advertisement campaign referred to the ads as "a perversion of the meaning of the *Reader's Digest* article." Whereas the article itself emphasized that the differences in tar and nicotine levels of competing cigarette brands were so negligible that a smoker could be confident that any of them could "effectively nail down his coffin," the manufacturer made it seem as if the magazine had endorsed Old Gold cigarettes as an especially healthful brand.[57]

Endorsers who claim to be users of products they advertise must in fact be users. Thus, singer Pat Boone's hawking of Acne-Satin skin medication was seen as deceptive because, among other reasons, he claimed falsely that all his daughters used it.[58] Advertisers have the responsibility to keep in touch with endorsers periodically, to make sure that they still are users of products they endorse for as long as the campaign runs.

---

[56]*Home Centers, Inc.,* 94 F.T.C. 1362 (1979).

[57]*P. Lorillard Co. v. Federal Trade Commission,* 186 F.2d 52 (4th Cir. 1950).

[58]*Cooga Mooga,* 92 F.T.C. 310 (1978).

If an endorser's experience with a product is more dramatically positive than most consumers should expect, that fact must be disclosed. In 1998, the FTC filed a complaint against the Jenny Craig company, asking it clearly indicate that the "success story" testimonials appearing in the company's ads are unusual, that most people will not lose so many pounds so quickly, and that many people regain the weight they lose on such plans.[59]

When an advertisement purports to be using ordinary consumers rather than paid actors, that representation must itself be truthful. In its guide to advertisers, the FTC uses the example of a company seeming to have a hidden camera catch real consumers in a candid scene at a cafeteria to seek out spontaneous testimonials about a new brand of breakfast cereal. Such a production technique would itself be deceptive if the on-screen spokespersons are instead paid actors.

The Commission employs a special measure of scrutiny concerning the use of "experts" giving testimonials. When an advertisement either expressly or implicitly states that an endorser has some special expertise vis-à-vis a product, commission policy is that "the endorser's qualifications must in fact give him the expertise that he is represented as possessing." Beatrice Foods, makers of Milk Duds candies, got into a bit of trouble with the Commission for its TV ads depicting baseball player Lou Brock getting a base hit, catching an opponent's fly ball, and stealing second base. The voiceover interviewer asks Brock his "secret for stealing second," and Brock replies that as soon as the pitcher winds up, "I take off like a sprinter. I take off running like I'm going for the last box of Milk Duds in town."

The FTC forced Beatrice Foods to stop using this narrative. From the Commission's perspective, the commercial implied that the consumption of Milk Duds "is linked to and necessary for the instilling, improving and maintaining of athletic ability and performance." The implication is untrue, the Commission held, and Brock, despite his inarguable athletic abilities, was not qualified as an expert to make such a claim.[60] Interestingly, the FTC has not gotten involved in advertising campaigns exploiting the "expertise" attached to actors because of particular roles with which they are best associated. The Commission never asked the Sanka people to refrain from using actor Robert Young to tout the benefits of drinking decaffeinated coffee, yet it is clear that the manufacturer was primarily interested in exploiting the public's identification of Young as *Marcus Welby, M.D.* Similarly, American Express embarked on its famous "Don't leave home without it" campaign with actor Karl Malden, best known at the time for playing a cop on *Streets of San Francisco.*[61]

---

[59]*Jenny Craig,* 1998 F.T.C. LEXIS 13 (27 Feb. 1998).

[60]*Beatrice Foods,* 81 F.T.C. 830 (1972).

[61]Michael Madow, "Private Ownership of Public Image: Popular Culture and Publicity Rights," 81 *California Law Review* 125 (1993); Michael Schudson, *Advertising: The Uneasy Persuasion: Its Dubious Impact on American Society* (New York: Basic Books, 1986), pp. 212–213.

*Deceptive to a "Reasonable" Consumer?*   In fulfilling its mission to protect the consumer against deceptive advertising, the FTC has at times presumed complete gullibility on the part of the citizenry. In one often criticized case, the Commission refused to permit a cosmetics company to advertise that its product could "color hair permanently." The Commission felt this was misleading because hair that had not yet grown in would emerge in one's natural color.[62] The Commission abandoned that entirely paternalistic approach some years later. In 1963, for example, it determined that a company marketing a device called Swim-Ezy to help novice swimmers stay afloat had not advertised deceptively by describing the small device as "invisible"; obviously, the product was not "invisible or impalpable or dimensionless," the FTC allowed, and consumers would be no more likely to think so than they would assume that "Danish pastry" must, as a matter of law, come from Denmark.[63]

Whether a reasonable consumer—the language currently favored by the Commission is "consumers acting reasonably under the circumstances"—is likely to be misled can sometimes become a numbers game. What percentage of consumers need to be led astray before an ad will be found deceptive? Indeed, sometimes the Commission has entertained survey or experimental research data to determine whether an ad is deceptive. The research cited earlier in this chapter on the UPS ads followed carefully the kinds of designs that expert witnesses have often employed in gathering statistics for presentation to the FTC. In recent years, however, the courts have been more deferential to the Commission, in essence saying that its staff's educated guesses as to whether an ad is likely to deceive will be enough justification.[64]

Do consumers even have an opportunity to behave "reasonably" when an advertisement sneaks up on them, when it does not seem to be a commercial message at all? The question is relevant to the issue of **product placements** through which movie production companies recoup some of their costs by accepting payments from corporations for the chance to have their products appear on screen.

Product placements are big business. The scene from Steven Spielberg's *E.T.* in which the wide-eyed extraterrestrial is lured out of hiding by young Elliott's lovingly placed trail of Reese's Pieces is one of the best-known moments from contemporary American cinema. The scene also resulted in a dramatic increase in sales for the candy morsels manufacturer. Then, too, a Disney studios memorandum once established rates for placements in one of its films at $20,000 to have a product visibly identifiable, $40,000 to have the brand name mentioned in the story line, and $60,000 to have an actor using or holding the product.[65]

---

[62]*Gelb v. FTC,* 144 F.2d 580 (2d Cir. 1944).

[63]*Heinz W. Kirchner,* 63 F.T.C. 1282 (1963).

[64]Dennis P. Stolle, "The FTC's Reliance on Extrinsic Evidence in Cases of Deceptive Advertising: A Proposal for Interpretive Rulemaking," 74 *Nebraska Law Review* 352 (1995).

[65]Randall Rothenberg, "Is It a Film? Is It an Ad? Harder to Tell," *New York Times,* 13 Mar. 1990, p. D23.

Movie producers point out that the use of real brand name products in films makes dramatic sense. Would it not be jarring, disruptive of the suspension of disbelief necessary to enjoying any theatric experience, to see characters using generically labeled products, drinking "Fruit Juice" or eating "Breakfast Cereal" or splashing on a few drops of "Cologne?" So who is hurt, the producers argue, if the reality we see on the screen is a strategically placed reality, and why should it matter to the viewers whether or not money has changed hands so as to sway the producers to choose one brand over another? Certainly viewers know that product placement is going on, and Hollywood enjoys making fun of us knowing, as in such films as *Wayne's World* and *The Truman Show.*

Many people find the practice of product placement disturbing. In 1991, a coalition of consumer advocacy groups petitioned the FTC, imploring it, minimally, to require that all product placements be prominently disclosed to movie viewers at the beginning of films. Product placement, the groups alleged, amounted to a kind of subliminal advertising in that viewers do not recognize the placements as commercials and thus fail to employ the kinds of cognitive and psychological defenses they would use if they were consciously aware of the filmmaker's persuasive intent. Companies who pay for product placements "openly seek to exploit the relaxed and artificial atmosphere created by the cinema," they told the Commission.[66] But the Commission saw no compelling reason to engage in any kind of rule making.

Two more recent product placement developments are worthy of mention. First, in 1998, the FTC asked several large liquor manufacturers to give the Commission a full accounting of their advertising and product placement practices, with an eye toward ensuring that the industry remain true to its self-imposed prohibitions on commercials aimed at children. Second, the "Master Settlement Agreement" agreed to between the major tobacco companies and the majority of the states' attorneys general in 2000 includes a "prohibition on payments related to tobacco products and media" that promises to end the industry's use of product placements "in any motion picture, television show, theatrical production or other live performance, live or recorded performance of music, commercial film or video, or video game." An exception is provided for "adults-only" events. The Agreement does not, however, prohibit a tobacco conglomerate from actually buying a TV or movie production company. On-screen depictions of characters smoking the company's brand of cigarettes in its own studio's movie would likely not be considered a "product placement" in that no one would have paid for the placement.

During the 2000 presidential campaign, an amusing instance of allegedly subliminal advertising occurred. The Republican National Committee placed a TV ad critical of Al Gore's prescription medicine plan for senior citizens. At one point in the ad a frame emerges with the word *RATS* taking up most of the screen. Democratic members of Congress promptly requested that the FCC investigate whether the ad violated its rules against subliminal advertising.

---

[66]In the Matter of Unfair and Deceptive Acts and Practices in the Placement of Product Advertisements in Motion Pictures, Complaint and Request for Investigation and Rulemaking, F.T.C. Docket no. P914518 209-59 (1991).

Figure 10.5

The Doonesbury gang provides a humorous approach to the issue of product placement. Is it important from your perspective whether movie viewers are told when producers "get some sort of consideration" or some "free stuff"?

*Doonesbury © 1994 G. B. Trudeau. Reprinted with permission of Universal Press Syndicate. All rights reserved.*

The Commission recognizes also that some ad campaigns are targeted to very specific markets. If the persons targeted are likely to be particularly vulnerable, the FTC may employ a more fluid definition of what it means to be "reasonable" or to be "likely to deceive." In 1975, the Commission forced a company to stop advertising travel packages to the Philippines to undergo "psychic surgery," a kind of faith healing purported to be a treatment by which the body is entered without surgical instruments, using only bare hands. The FTC complaint charged that these ads "prey upon and exploit the frustrations and hopes of people who are seriously ill," that such people are "vulnerable to the influence" of the promotions because they "hold out a tantalizing hope which the medical profession, by contrast, cannot offer."[67] More recently the Commission indicated its concern about companies that aggressively market loans to persons who may have very

---

[67] *Travel King, Inc.,* 86 F.T.C. 715 (1975).

poor credit histories but lots of equity built up in their homes. Such persons may be in need not only of money but also the chance to improve their credit ratings. Often these "predatory" mortgage companies, as the FTC calls them, make loans that they surmise will lead to default, thus allowing them to foreclose on their clients' homes.[68]

Not surprisingly, the Commission has often expressed concern about children as an especially vulnerable target audience. Youngsters are, in the Commission's words, "unqualified by age or experience to anticipate or appreciate the possibility that representations may be exaggerated or untrue."[69] Perhaps you have noticed that TV spots for toys often include the disclaimer that this or that accessory is "sold separately." That practice is very much in keeping with an FTC complaint filed against Lewis Galoob Toys Company, whose ads visually implied falsely that the "Transport Chopper," "Aircraft Carrier," and "Air Cargo" playsets came prepackaged with all the accessories depicted in the commercials. The Commission also expressed its concern that the ad's depiction of a toy missile launcher made it appear that the missile would travel a great distance at a high speed and that the company's "Bouncin' Kid Ballerina" was deceptively depicted to "stand on one foot and twirl by herself without human assistance." Future disclaimers in the company's ads would have to be written "in language understandable to children."[70] In another relevant action, the Commission published an opinion letter concerning online companies that target children. Prompting the FTC's concern were the actions of a company called KidsCom, whose Web site was billed as a "communications playground for kids ages 4 to 15." Children visiting the site had to register by completing a survey that asked for their name, gender, birthday, e-mail address, home address, number of family members, and school grade. Only then could the respondents enter the site and chat with each other (or answer more questions, or read about new products). The very process of gathering this information from children is inherently deceptive, the Commission claimed, especially without disclosing the marketing purpose in a way that would be understandable to the target audience.[71]

*"Material" Information.*   Not all potentially deceptive marketing messages are actionable. Only those that are material, that will likely affect the consumer's purchasing decision, will catch the FTC's attention. In practice, the FTC considers any factual claim about a product expressed in words to be material. The logic seems

---

[68]"FTC Charges D.C. Mortgage Lender with Deception and Unfairness Against Borrowers" [Press Release, 30 Jan. 1998, www.ftc.gov].

[69]*Ideal Toy Corporation,* 64 F.T.C. 297 (1964).

[70]*Lewis Galoob Toys,* 1991 F.T.C. LEXIS 74 (27 Feb. 1991).

[71]Chris Brewster, "FTC Issues Guidelines for Marketers Targeting Kids Online," *Marketing News,* 8 Dec. 1997, p. 7.

## Figure 10.6

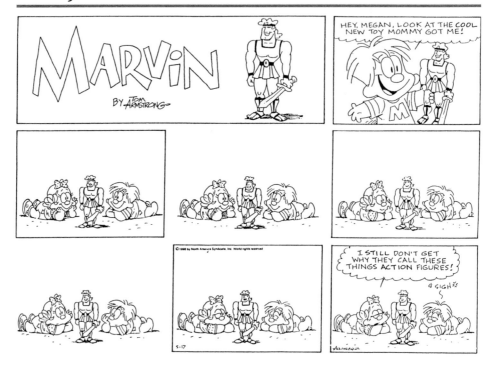

Since the label "action figure" has become so common (as a way of allowing boys to play with "dolls" without being teased), the FTC would likely not bring a complaint against the toy manufacturer depicted here.

*© 1998 North America Syndicate. Reprinted with special permission of King Features Syndicate.*

to be that if the advertiser chooses to make a claim, it is likely doing so to influence the consumer's purchasing decision. That is the whole point of running the ad in the first place.

Nontextual, visual elements become a bit trickier. If your product line is children's sportswear and your TV ads depict kids running around having fun while wearing your product, the FTC will not be terribly concerned that the ice-cream cones the child actors seem to be consuming with such glee are actually filled with colored mashed potatoes. Ice cream just does not hold up very well to the hot lights in the television studio. Indeed, even if you are selling ice cream itself, you will be able to use mashed potatoes in your ads as long as you do nothing special to make the switch material. Thus, for example, if your ad touts the large number of flavor choices your company offers, there is no problem. If, however, your ad instead emphasizes the rich color and texture of the ice cream and the "fact" that it will help keep your kids neat and clean because it does not melt as quickly as other brands, you will have serious problems with the Commission.

There is a special category of assertions about products that the Commission has determined would not be used by reasonable consumers in making purchasing decisions. This is called **puffery,** those unsubstantiated statements of opinion about a product's overall quality that consumers theoretically listen to with only one ear and do not take very seriously. We buy Hallmark greeting cards when we "care enough to send the very best." We are told that Carnival cruises are "the most popular in the world." If we "bring out the Hellmann's" mayonnaise, we "bring out the best." The FTC presumes that such claims about products serve no higher purpose than to keep the brand names alive in the collective consciousness, that they do not affect purchasing decisions in a material way.

 Figure 10.7

**DENNIS THE MENACE**

"I WANT MY QUARTER BACK! THIS ALL-DAY SUCKER LASTED ONLY *TWO HOURS!*"

Dennis would likely not have a legal claim here in that calling the lollipop an all-day sucker is the permissible form of playful exaggeration called puffery.

*Dennis the Menace ® used by permission of Hank Ketcham and © by North America Syndicate.*

***Procedures and Powers of the FTC.***    The totality of the FTC's powers and responsibilities go far beyond the subject matter of this book. Over the years, Congress has asked the agency to enforce no fewer than three dozen federal statutes, many of which have nothing to do with communication. We limit the consideration here to the Commission's actions against deceptive advertising. How does the FTC decide what cases to pursue? It often makes these determinations independently, as a result of its own staff having monitored a specific ad campaign or concluded that a whole industry could benefit from the Commission's guidance concerning consumers' likely inferences from the claims made in a category of advertising. Then, too, sometimes the Commission first learns about a potentially deceptive practice from a company's competitors or even from a member of the public.

However an advertising campaign comes to the Commission's attention, the FTC staff may, if it believes a violation of the law has occurred, attempt to obtain voluntary compliance. The staff will thus seek to enter into what is called a **consent order** with the company. This is similar to a consent decree except that there is no judge and no court of law in charge of enforcing the order. A company that signs a consent order need not admit that it violated the law, but it must agree to stop the disputed practices, which the Commission will have outlined in an accompanying complaint. The vast majority of FTC actions against particular advertisers are such consent orders.

Sometimes a company will be unwilling to sign a consent order. It may dispute the FTC's findings, believing that its advertising is not deceptive and should not be subject to any governmental sanctions. In this event, the Commission staff will often issue an **administrative complaint.** This will result in a formal proceeding that is much like a court trial except that the judge hearing the dispute is not an ordinary federal district judge but rather an **administrative law judge** (or ALJ). Should the ALJ determine that the advertisement in dispute is indeed deceptive, a **cease and desist** order—the label is self-explanatory—will typically be issued.

If the defendant advertiser is dissatisfied with the ALJ's initial ruling, it may bring an appeal, which will initially go to the five FTC commissioners themselves. Commission rulings are also appealable, first to the federal appellate court (usually the one for the District of Columbia) and ultimately to the Supreme Court (if it chooses to hear the case).

The FTC may in some circumstances opt to circumvent the often laborious administrative process of seeking a consent order and going to an ALJ. It can instead apply directly to a federal district judge for an injunction ordering the advertising to cease. The direct adjudicative route has the advantage of surprise in that offending advertisers will not learn of the FTC's interest in them until the suit is actually filed. The Commission typically reserves this action for very egregious and continuing ad campaigns and for those that may have direct and immediate implications for consumers' health.

The FTC is empowered not only to stop the use of an advertisement's deceptive wording, but also to require advertisers to insert specific language, called **af-**

**firmative disclosures,** into future advertisements. Consent orders (agreements between the FTC and an advertiser) and **consent decrees** (issued by a federal court at the Commission's request) frequently include such a requirement. In 1997, for example, the FTC reached an agreement with a sunscreen lotion company that the Commission's staff felt had made unrealistic claims about its product's ability to protect users from dangerous rays. The final order required, among other things, that the company's future advertising include such caveats as "tanning in sunlight or under tanning lamps can cause skin cancer and premature skin aging—even if you don't burn" and (with respect to lotions not having at least an SPF value of 2) that "this product does not contain a sun screen and does not protect against sunburn."[72]

The vast majority of disclaimers found in commercial messages, however, are offered voluntarily by the individual advertiser, with no direct input from the FTC or any other regulatory body. As a practical matter, marketers know that consumers are often unable to make sense of such disclaimers, especially in TV ads, in that they flash on the screen too quickly and in print far too small to read.[73]

In very rare circumstances, an advertiser will be required to insert specific language into future advertising to undo a long history of past deceptions. Such **corrective advertising** was required by the FTC only twice since its creation. The first case involved Warner-Lambert Company, makers of Listerine mouthwash, which had for many years suggested in its advertisements that the product could prevent the common cold. In 1975, the FTC ordered the company to insert into its next $10 million worth of advertising the admission that the mouthwash "will not help prevent colds or sore throats." The Commission also wanted the company to precede that admission with the words, "contrary to prior advertising"—thus forcing Warner-Lambert to explicitly admit that it had lied in the past—but the federal appellate court held that this latter language was unnecessarily punitive.[74] When the corrective ads eventually ran on TV, Warner-Lambert cleverly deemphasized the forced disclaimer by making it the dependent clause in a compound sentence, thus turning a negative into a positive: "Although Listerine will not help prevent colds or sore throats or lessen their severity, it kills germs on contact, the germs that can cause bad breath."[75]

In May 1999, the FTC voted to require that the manufacturer of Doan's Pills, which the commissioners felt had implied falsely for many years that its product was superior to other analgesics for the relief of back pain, insert in its next $8 million of advertising a candid admission that there is no such evidence. The ruling

---

[72]*California Suncare,* 1997 F.T.C. LEXIS 24.

[73]Paul Farhi, "The Big Business of Small Type," *Washington Post,* 6 Mar. 2000, p. C4; Darrel D. Muehling and Richard H. Kolbe, "Fine Print in Television Advertising: Views from the Top," 26 *Journal of Advertising* 1 (1997).

[74]*Warner-Lambert Company v. FTC,* 562 F.2d 749 (D.C. Cir. 1977).

[75]"Turning Warner-Lambert into a Marketing Conglomerate," *Business Week,* 5 Mar. 1979, p. 60.

was a vehicle for the Commission to assert that corrective advertising is an appropriate remedy whenever prior advertising has "substantially created or reinforced a misbelief, and the misbelief is likely to linger into the future."[76]

The Commission need not wait until a specific company's advertising campaign comes to its attention. Often the agency acts prospectively, offering general guidelines concerning advertising of particular products or within a particular industry. Such **industry guides,** as they are called, offer highly specific instructions concerning the proper use of product claims and may have relevance for manufacturers of many kinds of products rather than just one. In 1998, for example, the Commission issued a lengthy policy statement concerning when products may legitimately be marketed as "recyclable" or "made from recycled materials."[77] A related kind of prospective action is the **trade regulation rule,** which looks very much like an industry guide but which carries the force of law. The Commission is therefore required to follow elaborate public notice procedures in advance of issuing such rules. The last few decades have been characterized by a complicated relationship between the FTC and Congress with respect to how much autonomy the Commission should wield in creating such rules. In the 1970s, for example, Congress pressured the Commission to create rules that would protect children from being manipulated by advertisements. When the FTC responded by proposing that no television advertising should ever be directed toward children in that they are often unable to discern the commercial nature of messages, Congress objected that the rule was far too broad.[78]

Laws passed by Congress often explicitly instruct the Commission to promulgate rules in the furtherance of the legislation's objectives. For example, when Congress passed a law aimed at protecting consumers from being inappropriately billed for calls to "900" numbers, it instructed the FTC to devise mechanisms to implement the legislation.[79] The FTC's resulting rules require most businesses using such call-in phone services to provide a clear audio message at the outset, informing the caller what the charge per minute will be, and permitting a period of time during which callers can hang up without incurring any charges.[80] Then, in the Telecommunications Act of 1996, Congress instructed the Commission to create new rules that would expand the definition of "900" numbers to reflect the fact that consumers might not actually dial that specific prefix yet still find themselves being charged an excessive per-minute fee.

---

[76]Final order, In the Matter of Novartis Corporation and Novartis Consumer Health, Inc., Docket no. 9279, 13 May 1999 <http://www.ftc.gov/os/1999/9905/novaord.htm>.

[77]Guides for the use of environmental marketing claims, 16 C.F.R. 260.1–260.8 (1998).

[78]Mark E. Budnitz, "The FTC's Consumer Protection Program during the Miller Years: Lessons for Administrative Agency Structure and Operation," 46 *Catholic University Law Review* 371 (1997).

[79]Telephone Disclosure and Dispute Resolution Act of 1992 (TDDRA), 15 U.S.C. sec. 5701.

[80]16 C.F.R. 308.2.

# Things to Remember

## THE FEDERAL TRADE COMMISSION

- When created in 1914, the Commission was only able to protect competing companies from each other's excesses; today the FTC is also empowered to protect consumers from unfair and deceptive practices.

- To determine if an advertisement is deceptive, the Commission first does a textual analysis of the ad, then determines whether a reasonable consumer is likely to be misled, and finally decides whether any such deception would be material to the purchasing decision.

- Deceptiveness can be explicit or implicit, it can appear in text or in visual demonstrations.

- Powers wielded by the FTC include the consent order (whereby the FTC staff itself typically requires, at a bare minimum, that the offending company cease making a particular claim that the Commission has decided is deceptive), the cease and desist order (issued by an administrative law judge after a full hearing), and a demand that the advertiser engage in affirmative disclosures or corrective advertising in future commercial messages.

- The Commission can also issue industry guides and trade regulation rules, both of which put companies on notice about the kinds of claims the FTC staff is likely to find deceptive.

Despite the many powers it wields, the FTC is often criticized by consumer groups and others for being ineffectual, and much too slow. Ordering a company to cease and desist last year's campaign is hardly an effective remedy. Then, too, fines imposed by the Commission are so small that huge corporations often choose to simply absorb them as part of the cost of doing business. Finally, the specific changes in wording demanded by the FTC in any given case may be so slight so as to not truly undo the deceptive impact of an ongoing campaign.[81]

### The Lanham Act: Suits by Competitors and Consumers

The FTC investigates what it wishes and passes on any issue it does not have the staff or the enthusiasm to pursue. Bringing a claim of deceptive advertising to the attention of the Commission, however, is not the only remedy available to aggrieved parties. Another important provision is the federal Lanham Act, adopted

---

[81]"Seeing Is Believing: False Advertising Should Be Investigated by Federal Trade Commission, but Some Ads Still Run with Only Small Changes and May Still Mislead Consumers," NBC Transcripts, *Dateline NBC,* 16 Nov. 1997.

in 1946. The Act, initially designed to protect against trademark infringements, also includes prohibitions against deceptive advertising. Section 43(a) of the Act forbids advertisers to "misrepresent the nature, characteristics, qualities, or geographic origin of [their] or another person's goods, services, or commercial activities." Perhaps the section's most important feature is that it allows "any person who believes that he or she is or is likely to be damaged" by the misrepresentation to sue. Certainly that wording means that competing companies may bring suit. In a small number of jurisdictions, the courts have interpreted the Act so as to give individual consumers a right to sue as well. Consumers rarely litigate under the Act, however. Indeed, they rarely take advantage of state or common-law remedies against deceptive advertising because the harm they might be able to prove generally is not large enough to justify the expense of hiring an attorney.[82]

Perhaps the most frequent category of Lanham Act advertising claims concern comparative advertising, in which one company's commercial mentions and criticizes the competition by name. Will you save the most money on your long-distance phone bills by signing up with AT&T, Sprint, MCI, or one of the other handful of smaller players to enter the market in recent years? It would be hard to find a definitive answer by observing the companies' multimillion dollar national advertising campaigns. All one learns from ads is that corporations vying for consumers' dollars are not at all shy about naming and criticizing their competitors. The days of comparisons with "Brand X" seem to be long passed.

Lanham Act suits can result in an injunction against the defendant company's ads. Damage awards can also be made and can include the defendant's full profits attributable to the deception, the plaintiff's damages (such as lost market share), plus court costs. In especially egregious cases, the award can be triple the actual amount of damages and can include attorneys' fees. Corrective advertising can be ordered as well.

---

[82]Lee Goldman, "The World's Best Article on Competitor Suits for False Advertising," 45 *Florida Law Review* 487, 505 (1993).

 ## Things to Remember

**THE LANHAM ACT**

- Created in 1946, the Act permits a company to sue a competitor for deceptive advertising.
- A successful suit can result in forfeiture of profits attributable to the deception, damages, court costs, attorney's fees, and compelled corrective advertising.

## Industry Self-Regulation

Companies that think their competitors are engaged in deceptive advertising campaigns but that wish to avoid the costs and long delays inherent in litigation and governmental intervention may instead choose to bring a complaint to the National Advertising Division. The NAD is a self-regulatory system created by major advertising associations and the Council of Better Business Bureaus in 1971 to hear such complaints. Comparative advertising cases have always been a large part of the Division's docket.

The procedure of bringing an NAD complaint is in some ways very similar to that of going to court. After the complaint is filed, an investigation ensues, and a process like pretrial discovery takes place. The NAD's inquiry will generally be limited to determining whether or not the company whose advertising is the target of the complaint can offer sufficient substantiation of the claims made in the advertisement. If the NAD determines that the ad lacks substantiation, it will request that the campaign be stopped or changed. This remedy is the only one available. There are no money damages to be awarded, no attorney's fees, no court costs. Of course, because the NAD regularly publishes the results of its hearings, and these findings appear regularly in such outlets as the *Wall Street Journal* and *Advertising Age,* adverse publicity must also be considered a remedy inherent in this self-regulatory process. If either party to an NAD decision is dissatisfied with the ruling, it can appeal to the next and final level of decision making, the five-member National Advertising Review Board. This is a relatively infrequent occurrence.

Compared with litigation or waiting for ultimate FTC action, the NAD/NARB process is timely, informal, and relatively inexpensive. Advertisers also often prefer to use this procedure because the decision makers are all experts in the fields of advertising and marketing. The industry self-regulatory procedure is not a panacea, however. The NAD restricts its inquiries to national advertising campaigns. Also, the Division reserves the right to refuse to hear any complaint that

 Things to Remember

**INDUSTRY SELF-REGULATION**

- The National Advertising Division was created in 1971 to provide a forum for companies to complain about competitors' allegedly deceptive national advertising campaigns.
- The NAD can request that an offending advertiser cease and desist, and it will publish its findings in outlets that reach the advertising community as well as the general public.

does not raise issues of public interest. That one company is losing market share to another is usually insufficient to trigger an investigation.[83]

# Regulation of Political Campaign Advertising

Not all advertising engaged in by corporate America is designed to sell a particular product or service. Mobil Oil's weekly *New York Times* "advertorials," through which the company expressed its opinion on various political issues—not all directly related to the oil industry—are studied in university business schools and public relations programs nationwide.[84] It is perfectly legal for corporations to use the advertising space or time they pay for to participate in the nation's political dialogue. Some legal restrictions apply, however, when the focus of the speech is on a particular election, whether on behalf of a candidate or of a public referendum issue. Before discussing those legal restrictions, three preliminary points need to be made about the limited scope of that discussion. First, we need to understand that there is a body of case law governing political campaign advertising that applies only to television and radio, largely owing to specific provisions of the legislation that set up the Federal Communications Commission. We postpone a discussion of that case law until Chapter 12, which deals with content regulations of the broadcast media. Second, although there is also a body of case law based on the Federal Elections Campaign Act and parallel state laws that addresses the issue of limitations on financial *contributions* to political campaigns[85]—as well as cases dealing with contributions to committees set up to work for or against referendum proposals[86]—that area of law is beyond the scope of this book. After all, even though candidates do spend a high proportion of contributions on political advertising, they might also spend donations on travel expenses or on any number of other things not directly related to communication. Suffice it to say that, in general, there are far more restrictions on contributions to political campaigns than on independent expenditures in support of those campaigns. The third preliminary matter to keep in mind is that the discussion of *corporate* expenditures in this section refers to monies taken directly from a company's treasury. Restrictions on such political expenditures have generally been upheld, but corporations and other entities are free to establish and solicit contributions for separate funds, often called political action

---

[83]Paul Pompeo, "To Tell the Truth: Comparative Advertising and Lanham Act Section 43(a)," 36 *Catholic University Law Review* 565 (1987).

[84]Herb Schmertz, *Good-bye to the Low Profile: The Art of Creative Confrontation* (New York: Little Brown, 1986).

[85]*Nixon v. Shrink Missouri Government PAC,* 528 U.S. 377 (2000).

[86]*Citizens Against Rent Control, Coalition for Fair Housing v. Berkeley,* 454 U.S. 290 (1981).

committees (or PACs), and to use these funds in the furtherance of political causes or candidates.[87]

We focus now on the rights of corporations to pay from their general treasuries for advertising aimed at swaying public opinion concerning either upcoming referenda issues or the relative merits of competing political candidates. In general, the Court has been more deferential to governmental restrictions on expenditures related to candidacies than to citizen referenda. In part this is because of the fear that candidates, if successful, will be inappropriately beholden to the interests of corporations that have used their general funds to advertise on their behalf.

Approximately half the states permit some form of direct referenda whereby citizens can circumvent their legislatures and create law themselves.[88] State referenda have in recent years covered such matters as term limits, use of recycled materials, and the right to die. Several states embracing the referenda process enacted laws that prohibit corporations from spending money trying to influence their outcome. The Supreme Court ruled on such a statute in 1978, when the First National Bank of Boston wanted to buy newspaper ads opposing a referendum that would amend the state constitution so as to permit the creation of a graduated personal income tax in Massachusetts. The proposed ads would violate a state law prohibiting corporate expenditures on referenda not directly related to the specific company's area of business. In overturning this state law, the Court focused primarily on the rights of the citizens to hear what the bank's officers had to say. Justice Powell wrote for the majority that information about a tax referendum is "indispensable to decision-making in a democracy" and that "the inherent worth of the speech in terms of its capacity for informing the public does not depend upon the identity of its source, whether corporation, association, union, or individual."[89] Nowhere did the Court suggest, however, that corporations' right to free speech would necessarily be equal to those of the citizens themselves. If the state had successfully demonstrated that corporate speech was likely to dominate the referendum process and thus to jeopardize the integrity of the electoral process itself, the decision would have been a different one.

The Court has also on occasion ruled on the matter of corporate expenditures in the furtherance of particular candidates for elected office. In a 1986 decision, the Court held that a portion of the Federal Election Campaign Act prohibiting expenditures "in connection with" (supporting or opposing) any candidate for federal office was unconstitutional as applied to the Massachusetts Citizens for Life (MCFL). In advance of the September 1978 primary elections, MCFL

---

[87]*Federal Election Commission v. Akins,* 524 U.S. 11 (1998); *Colorado Republican Federal Campaign Committee v. Federal Election Commission,* 518 U.S. 604 (1996); *Federal Election Commission v. National Conservative Political Action Committee,* 470 U.S. 480 (1985); *Buckley v. Valeo,* 424 U.S. 1 (1976).

[88]Lawrence W. Reed, "Citizen Initiatives Fertilize the Grass Roots," *Journal of American Citizenship Policy Review,* July–Aug. 1996, p. 10.

[89]*First National Bank of Boston v. Bellotti,* 435 U.S. 765, 776 (1978).

had spent approximately $10,000 to distribute over 100,000 copies of a special edition of its newsletter. The thrust of the group's message is apparent from the newsletter's front-page headline—"Everything You Need to Know to Vote Pro-Life." The newsletter included a coupon intended to be clipped and taken to the polls to remind voters of the name of all the prolife candidates.

Writing for the majority, Justice Brennan allowed that the Act, as applied to ordinary for-profit companies using their general funds in support of candidates, furthered a compelling state's interest, but concluded that the state's interest was absent when the expenditures were made by such organizations as MCFL, which are more similar to voluntary political associations than they are to business firms. How much money groups such as MCFL have on hand to pay for political speech is a direct reflection of the popular support enjoyed by the committee's positions. By contrast, the resources available in the coffers of for-profit corporations is a function only of how many widgets the company sells.[90]

The main reason the Act was held unconstitutional as applied to MCFL, then, was that those who contributed to the prolife group clearly knew that their money would be used for very specific political ends. This situation is very different from a corporation that makes its money from selling a product or service. Such a company's customers do not presume that the profits from their purchases will be used to further any particular political cause or candidate.

A different kind of corporate entity was involved in *Austin v. Michigan Chamber of Commerce*,[91] a 1990 case in which the Supreme Court upheld a state law prohibiting corporate expenditures on behalf of candidates. At first blush, one would think that the Chamber of Commerce would be treated the same as was the MCFL. Both are nonprofit corporations, and both seem to have predictable political agenda such that their financial supporters would be on notice about the kinds of causes espoused by the groups. The Supreme Court, however, concluded that the Michigan statute could be constitutionally applied to the Chamber of Commerce, thus preventing the group from buying newspaper advertisements in support of a candidate for state office. Whereas MCFL "was formed for the express purpose of promoting political ideas," the Chamber's bylaws "set forth more varied purposes, several of which are not inherently political."

The Court emphasized also that there were no persons whose association with MCFL could be analogized to that of a shareholder to a corporation. Such a relationship creates an "economic disincentive for disassociating" with a company (i.e., for selling one's holdings) if one disagrees with its political activity. Members of the chamber, although not shareholders as such, would nonetheless be reluctant to end their membership in the organization, even if the group did support causes or candidates with which they disagreed. The resultant loss of ties with the business community, as well as the forfeiting of numerous other membership services provided by the Chamber, would be too high a price to pay.

---

[90]*Federal Election Commission v. Massachusetts Citizens for Life,* 479 U.S. 238 (1986).

[91]494 U.S. 652 (1990).

# Things to Remember

## REGULATION OF CORPORATE EXPENDITURES ON POLITICAL ADVERTISING

- There are generally far more restrictions on contributions to candidates' campaigns than on independent expenditures in support of candidates.
- Corporations are generally free to spend their own monies on advertising concerning upcoming citizen initiative (referenda) issues.
- Corporations are less free to spend their own monies on advertising for or against specific candidates for office, unless such corporations function more like political associations.
- The Supreme Court has focused in this area of law on whether contributors to the corporate general funds would expect their monies to go to support candidates and whether the contributors might be reluctant to dissassociate themselves from a corporation espousing political candidacies with which they themselves disagree.

The Chamber was also different from the MCFL in that its membership consisted primarily of for-profit businesses; approximately three-quarters of its 8,000 or so members fit into this category. Thus, to the extent that the Michigan Campaign Finance Act was designed to diminish the ability of *corporations* to influence the political process, the Chamber was an appropriate target of the legislation, in that it is simply a large group of corporations. The MCFL, by contrast, accepted no corporate contributions, but was funded entirely by individual donors.

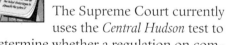

## Chapter Summary

The Supreme Court currently uses the *Central Hudson* test to determine whether a regulation on commercial speech is consistent with the First Amendment. The test requires that we ask whether the product or service being offered is itself legal or the advertisement deceptive, whether the state has a legitimate interest in this regulation, and whether there is a reasonable fit between the regulation and the interest.

The Court has on a number of occasions dealt with the issue of advertising by attorneys and other professionals. In general, the rule seems to be that we should focus on the first *Central Hudson* question: Is the advertisement inherently deceptive? If not, the Court has been very reluctant to allow much state intrusion on the content of communications between professionals and potential clients.

Although individual states and even municipalities are in the business of regulating advertising, by far the most active agent in this area is the Federal Trade Commission. To determine if a given ad is deceptive, the agency first examines the text of the ad and then considers whether a reasonable consumer would likely be deceived, and whether any such deception would be material to the purchasing decision. The vast majority of Commission investigations go no further than the consent agreement stage, at which the offending company agrees to meet certain requests by the Commission staff, such as to stop making a deceptive claim. The FTC also is empowered to require advertisers to insert specific wording into future ads. Companies can also sue competitors for advertising deceptively under such statutes as the federal Lanham Act.

As a general rule, corporations are free to engage in political speech but are regulated when they seek to comment on particular, upcoming elections. Corporations are generally more free to spend monies from their own treasuries to comment on upcoming referenda issues than on competing candidates for office.

chapter

# Sexually Oriented Speech

*Dirty books are fun! That's all there is to it. But you can't get up in the court and say that, I suppose.*

—Tom Lehrer
"Smut," *That Was the Year That Was* (Reprise Records, 1965)

Americans are often described as oversexed. In 1997, we spent over $10 billion on pornographic videos, nearly double what we spent that year on Hollywood's more mainstream offerings. Candid and highly emotional discussions of every imaginable sexual variation and fetish are the mainstay of daytime TV talk shows. The communication technologies we embrace most swiftly are those—such as self-developing film, VCRs, camcorders, and, more recently, the Internet—that allow an indulgence in sexual imagery.

Somewhat paradoxically, we Americans are also seen as highly puritanical in our approach to sexual matters. Award-winning European film directors often produce a toned-down print for distribution in the U.S. market so as to obtain an "R" rather than the dreaded "NC-17" rating. Emotional debates in the United States over what to tell youngsters about sex and morality have consumed school boards nationwide.

In the 1940s, the U.S. Supreme Court, in one of the most often quoted passages in the history of First Amendment jurisprudence, placed "the lewd and obscene" at the head of its list of categories of speech deemed "of such slight social value" as to be outside the constitution's protection.[1] Sexual speech that meets the current legal definition of obscenity can be criminalized. Even nonobscene sexual expression can be regulated in several ways. It can be banned from TV and radio[2] or zoned into certain restricted parts of town.[3] Communicators of sexual messages

---

[1]*Chaplinsky v. New Hampshire,* 315 U.S. 568, 571 (1942).

[2]*FCC v. Pacifica,* 438 U.S. 726 (1978). More recent rulings permit airing of such programming between 10 P.M. and 6 A.M.

[3]*Young v. American Mini-Theatres,* 427 U.S. 50 (1976).

might not be permitted to use their chosen mode of presentation; the state can insist, for example, that they keep their clothes on.[4]

Unless your career ambition is to become a porn star, you may wonder how this chapter on sexually oriented speech will benefit you, or even why it is included in a book aimed at professional communicators. There are at least three reasons for studying the law's interaction with sexual communication. The first is that we learn much about the Supreme Court's view of the relationship between the individual and the state from reading cases involving sexual communication, in part because the state's interest in curtailing sexual speech is probably more nebulous, more difficult to articulate, than in other areas of communication law. Libel law seeks to protect individuals' reputations. Copyright law is designed to prevent the theft of intellectual property. Federal Trade Commission policies are aimed at protecting vulnerable consumers from parting with their money in response to fraudulent advertising claims. In these and other areas of communication law, potential victims are easy to find. Obscenity law is different. The state is not required to identify a victim. Rather, regulations or outright prohibitions of sexual communication are often upheld because of a more generalized fear about the potential impact on a society's "moral fiber."

The second reason for having at least some familiarity with this area of law is also related to the nature of U.S. Supreme Court jurisprudence. Obscenity law constitutes a unique departure from the usual rule that speech is presumed protected by the First Amendment unless and until the state articulates a "compelling interest" in its suppression, an interest that survives the Court's "strict scrutiny." When dealing with sexual matters, the Supreme Court often eschews the more traditional jurisprudence in favor of a categorical exclusion. In other words, obscenity is proscribable not because it is seen as particularly dangerous speech, but rather because it is defined by the Court as something *other than* speech. Obscenity is not expression and is therefore not protected by the First Amendment.

A third reason for learning about governments' handling of sexual imagery requires a more international perspective. Totalitarian nations have often applied labels such as "obscene" and "pornographic" to political speech, as a way of making the regulation or prohibition of that speech seem more acceptable. This has been true, for example, of the Soviet Union, Nazi Germany, the apartheid South African regime, and the communist Chinese government.[5] Learning about the history and current structure of obscenity law, then, may be the best defense against governments' tendency towards rhetorical excess. If we know what it *really* means to be obscene, we will be less likely to be fooled by those who seek to demonize political speech with that label.

---

[4]*Barnes v. Glen Theatre,* 501 U.S. 560 (1991); *City of Erie v. Pap's A. M.,* 529 U.S. 277 (2000).

[5]Nadine Strossen, *Defending Pornography: Free Speech, Sex, and the Fight for Women's Rights* (New York: Scribner, 1995), 219–220.

# Thinking about the Obscene

Although this chapter is primarily about *obscenity* and the law, two related constructs that often produce confusion need to be defined first. The word *pornography* refers to any printed text, drawing, picture, film, or other communication in which the explicit depiction or description of sexual conduct occurs. Although journalists, scholars, and even lawyers and judges often use the word to refer to sexual materials, it has no *legal* definition, nor does its publication carry any legal penalty. *Indecency* is a word used to describe a wide set of sexual materials that meet some of but not all the components of the Supreme Court's current definition of obscenity. Although it would be unconstitutional for the government to ban writings that are merely indecent, such materials may be broadcast on radio and TV only between 10 P.M. and 6 A.M. Because the law affecting indecent speech is restricted to the broadcast media, we postpone a more extensive discussion of this matter until Chapter 12, which deals with regulation of the electronic media. As we see in Chapter 13, the government has also attempted, unsuccessfully, to outlaw indecent speech on the Internet.

What does it mean to be obscene? In everyday parlance, the word can attach to anything deemed outrageous or offensive, from the high price of funerals to the exorbitant salaries paid to professional sports figures. For most of us, the label is not limited to matters of sex. Philosopher Harry Clor has suggested that obscenity refers to making offensively public that which should be private. Certainly the notion of obscenity as graphic depictions of others' sexual behavior would fit within this definition, but there can also be obscene depictions of such physical acts as eating, scratching, or grooming. For Clor, the key is that the persons depicted are degraded by having their humanity reduced to animalistic behaviors. If "dining" is too genteel a word to describe the way you might attack that lamb chop when no one is watching, you can surely understand Clor's point.[6]

The idea that only certain kinds of *sexual* depictions are obscene is of relatively recent vintage. Indeed, the Supreme Court did not step in to limit the definition of obscenity to matters sexual until very near the end of the nineteenth century. For much of this country's history, and for many centuries earlier in England, persons were far more likely to be punished for religious than for sexual heresies. Indeed, it was often hard to tell the two apart. Thus, for example, Lord Chamberlin suggested in 1696 that English magistrates should "correc[t] all obscenities and other scandalous matters and such as any ways offend against ye laws of God and good manners." From the time of the reign of Henry VIII through the Elizabethan era in England, sexually explicit writings that did not also amount to religious or political heresies generally escaped the censors. So, too, all the American colonies had laws against blasphemy and heresy, but not against obscenity per se.

---

[6]Harry M. Clor, *Obscenity and Public Morality: Censorship in a Liberal Society* (Chicago: University of Chicago Press, 1966), 225.

# Things to Remember

**THINKING ABOUT OBSCENITY**

- Under the law, obscenity is viewed as something other than speech, thus wholly outside the First Amendment's protection.
- In everyday conversation, *obscenity* seems to refer to anything outrageously offensive, not narrowly to sexual matters.
- For much of U.S. history, there either were no obscenity laws or such laws aimed more often at blasphemous and profane speech than at words or images designed to elicit sexual arousal.

## Development of Obscenity Law in America

There are no recorded prosecutions in the United States for obscenity until 1815, when a Philadelphia merchant named Jesse Sharpless was accused of exhibiting "a certain lewd, wicked, scandalous, infamous...painting" depicting a man and woman in "an obscene, imprudent, and indecent posture."[7] Six years later, in the first U.S. obscenity case involving the printed word, Peter Holmes was prosecuted for publishing an edition of John Cleland's famous *Memoirs of a Woman of Pleasure,* more commonly known as *Fanny Hill.*[8] The book had first appeared in England in 1748 with no government opposition.

Both the Sharpless and Holmes prosecutions were made under the common law, because there were no applicable obscenity statutes on the books at the time. The first such written law did not show up until 1821, in Vermont. Connecticut and Massachusetts enacted obscenity laws in the 1830s, and several other states followed suit in the years leading up to the Civil War. These laws typically criminalized not only the publication of obscene materials, but also the use of profane language and such offenses as public lewdness and indecent exposure.

The first federal obscenity statute did not appear until 1842, in the form of amendments to the customs laws that forbade the importing of obscene materials. In 1865, it first became illegal to send obscene works through the U.S. mails; then, the Comstock Act, enacted in 1873, more explicitly gave post office officials the authority to open and confiscate such disapproved mailings.

A few words about that latter law's namesake are in order. Anthony Comstock probably had more influence over the development of obscenity law in the United States than any other individual. Although Comstock became a special agent of the Post Office so as to have a direct hand in the enforcement of the

---

[7]*Commonwealth v. Sharpless,* 2 Serg. & Rawle 91 (Pa. 1815).

[8]*Commonwealth v. Holmes,* 17 Mass. 336 (1821).

federal law that is his best known legacy, he began to affect public policy earlier on as a private citizen and activist. First working under the auspices of the New York YMCA, and later the New York Society for the Suppression of Vice, Comstock worked tirelessly to pressure state and local governments to pass obscenity laws and to enforce those already on the books more aggressively. In the first year of the federal statute's existence, Comstock boasted of having confiscated hundreds of thousands of pictures, photographs, and books as well as "numerous contraceptive devices and allegedly aphrodisiac medicines."[9]

## The *Hicklin* Rule

For many decades, U.S. obscenity law was modeled after a British case from the 1860s called *Regina v. Hicklin,*[10] which involved a defendant who had distributed a pamphlet highly critical of the Catholic Church. Again is seen the historic intermingling of blasphemy and sexual heresies, in that one of the publication's chief offenses was to lay bare the "questions put to females in confession." In a famous bit of dicta accompanying a decision that upheld the defendant's obscenity conviction, Lord Chief Justice Cockburn established two important points of law that together comprise the "*Hicklin* rule." The first point was that an entire work may be found obscene even if only relatively small, isolated passages are punishable. The other half concerned a work's possible effects on its audience. As Justice Cockburn put it, obscenity would be judged by the work's potential "to deprave and corrupt *those whose minds are open to such immoral influences* and into whose hands a publication of this sort may fall" (emphasis added). In the nonsexual arena, this would be akin to prosecuting director Martin Scorsese because his award-winning film *Taxi Driver* seemed to be the impetus for John Hinckley, in his deranged mind, to conclude that killing President Reagan would make actress Jodie Foster fall in love with him.

The Supreme Court first stated its approval of the *Hicklin* rule—although not mentioning the case by name—in *United States v. Rosen,* decided in 1896.[11] Lew Rosen's offense was having sent through the mails pictures of women whose clothing consisted of a kind of opaque but removable substance—similar to that used today on "scratch and win" lottery tickets—such that the models' covering could be "erased with a piece of bread." Writing for the Court's majority, Justice Harlan expressed approval for the judge's instructions to the jury, which encouraged them to consider whether the pictures would "suggest or convey lewd thoughts and lascivious thoughts to the young and inexperienced."

---

[9]Frederick F. Schauer, *The Law of Obscenity* (Edison, NJ: BNA Press, 1976), 13.

[10]3 Q. B. 360 (1868). Some U.S. cases embracing the *Hicklin* rule include *United States v. Bennett,* 24 F. Cas. 1093 (Circuit Ct., S.D.N.Y. 1879); *United States v. Clarke,* 38 F. 732 (E.D. Mo. 1889); and *United States v. Chesman,* 19 F. 497 (C.C.E.D. Mo. 1881).

[11]*United States v. Rosen,* 161 U.S. 29 (1896).

Also in 1896, the Supreme Court issued an opinion that for the first time made clear its belief that the definition of obscenity was limited to *sexual* matters.[12] That may seem self-evident, but just as obscenity and blasphemy were virtually indistinguishable offenses for many years, so too in the United States did obscenity prosecutions often go forward against defendants who merely uttered profane and insulting language. In the 1896 case, defendant Dan Swearingen had written an article in the Burlington, Kansas, *Courier*—his having mailed the offensive article made this case a Comstock Act prosecution—which used highly abusive language to describe another town resident. The target of Swearingen's ire was described as "about the meanest and most universally hated and detested thing in human shape," a "black hearted coward," a "liar, perjurer, and slanderer, who would sell a mother's honor with less hesitancy and for much less silver than Judas betrayed the Saviour, and who would pimp and fatten on a sister's shame with as much unction as a buzzard gluts in carrion." Although these insults are certainly harsh, the Court held that there was nothing "lewd" or "lascivious" about them. This was not the stuff of obscenity.

U.S. obscenity law in the first half of the twentieth century was characterized by conflicting trends, although overall by a tendency toward liberalization. On one hand, prosecutors were zealous in their pursuit of sexual materials and were often not concerned whether their targets were "dirt for dirt's sake" or literary classics. Thus, such noteworthy books as Radclyffe Hall's *The Well of Loneliness*,[13] Theodore

---

[12]*Swearingen v. United States,* 161 U.S. 446 (1896).

[13]*People v. Friede,* 233 N.Y.S. 565 (1929).

 ## Things to Remember

### EARLY OBSCENITY LAW IN THE U.S.

- The first state obscenity law (in Vermont) was passed in 1821; the first federal obscenity law (prohibiting the importing of obscene materials from overseas) was enacted in 1842.

- One of the most influential antipornography activists in U.S. history, Anthony Comstock, lobbied successfully for a federal law permitting post office workers to open and confiscate obscene mailings.

- For many years, U.S. courts embraced the British *Hicklin* rule, which held that a work's obscenity could be determined based on its most salacious passages' potential effects on particularly susceptible consumers.

- In the first half of the twentieth century, many prosecutors zealously brought obscenity charges cases against even accepted literary works; there was also a contradictory trend in other courts toward slowly rejecting the *Hicklin* rule and making it more difficult for governments to obtain convictions.

Dreiser's *An American Tragedy*,[14] and Henry Miller's *Tropic of Cancer* and *Tropic of Capricorn*[15] were all successfully prosecuted. Yet other courts began slowly to reject aspects of the *Hicklin* rule and to set the stage for the Supreme Court's ultimate repudiation, in 1957, of the British precedent. Lower courts, both state and federal, began to take such steps as taking into account a book's literary merits (and often accepting expert testimony on the matter), viewing works in their entirety (instead of condemning them for isolated passages), and considering a work's likely effect on a "reasonable" or "average" person or on the author's intended audience (rather than on the "depraved" and "susceptible" consumers envisioned in the *Hicklin* rule). Although this more liberal pattern of cases was by no means consistent across jurisdictions or over time, it did permit the Supreme Court to make it seem as if it were saying nothing dramatic or unprecedented when it articulated a new constitutional framework for obscenity.

## The *Roth* Test

Samuel Roth was a New York–based entrepreneur convicted of mailing obscene books and periodicals with such titles as *Wanton by Night* and *Wild Passion*. Unlike most convicted pornographers, Roth appealed his conviction on straightforward constitutional grounds, arguing that the Comstock Act was in violation of the First Amendment. The gist of Roth's argument was that sexual communication should be treated no differently than other categories of messages, such as political or religious speech, that the government should have a right to prohibit such speech only if a "clear and present danger" of a "substantive evil" was on the horizon. Traditionally, obscenity laws have been predicated on a felt need to avoid the encouragement of lustful thoughts by the consumers of pornography. Roth argued that this is not a legitimate state's interest, that Americans have a right to feel sexy. Alternatively, Roth allowed, the state's interest might be to prevent rape or other criminal behaviors. While this clearly would be a legitimate matter for governmental intervention, there was no evidence that reading pornographic books and magazines causes an increase in such antisocial conduct.

In his opinion for the Court, Justice Brennan rejected Roth's invitation to bring obscene writings within the protection of the First Amendment's balancing test. Rather, the *Roth* decision[16] says that obscenity is "utterly without redeeming social importance" and therefore "not within the area of constitutionally protected speech or press."

---

[14]*Commonwealth v. Friede*, 171 N.E. 472 (Mass. 1930).

[15]*United States v. Two Obscene Books*, 99 F. Supp. 760 (N.D. Cal. 1951), *aff'd sub nom.*, *Besig v. United States*, 208 F.2d 142 (9th Cir. 1953).

[16]*United States v. Roth*, 354 U.S. 476 (1957). Roth's case was decided together with another case, *Alberts v. California*, in which David Alberts appealed his conviction for violating a state obscenity statute.

Justice Brennan emphasized, however, that "the portrayal of sex…in art, literature and scientific works" should not incur the wrath of the law, that "sex and obscenity are not synonymous," that to be obscene a work must be aimed at readers' "prurient interest"—an "itching," a "lascivious longing," or "a shameful or morbid interest in nudity, sex, or excretion."

Justice Brennan's opinion moved next to a more explicit repudiation of the *Hicklin* rule. Although some courts had embraced that "early standard," which "allowed material to be judged merely by the effect of an isolated excerpt upon particularly susceptible persons," the Court now preferred the following test for defining obscenity: "whether to the average person, applying contemporary community standards, the dominant theme of the material taken as a whole appeals to the prurient interest."

It was not clear what the Court meant by the phrase "contemporary community standards." Certainly "contemporary" suggests an awareness that societal values and sexual mores change over time. But what size "community" did the Court intend? Is the entire United States one large community? Would each state set its own standard? Or, could that which is obscene in one county be accepted for distribution in a contiguous county? The Court grappled with this question in 1964, in *Jacobellis v. Ohio,*[17] but could not produce a majority opinion. The plurality opinion argued for a nationwide standard. (This case was also the vehicle for Justice Stewart, in a separate concurring opinion, to issue his famous admission that, although he was unable to articulate a coherent definition of obscenity, "I know it when I see it!") The Court finally resolved the "*community* standard" issue in 1973 on the occasion of handing down a decision that altered the *Roth* test somewhat, and produced the test for obscenity that, in slightly amended form, still governs today.

---

[17]378 U.S. 184 (1964).

 # Things to Remember

### THE *ROTH* TEST

- In *United States v. Roth* (1957), the Supreme Court explicitly rejected the *Hicklin* rule.
- The majority opinion provided these guidelines for determining whether a work is obscene:
  - The work must be judged as a whole.
  - It must appeal to the "prurient interest" in sex.
  - It is to be judged by "contemporary community standards."
  - Courts must consider the work's likely effect on the *average community member.*

## The *Miller* Test

The Supreme Court of 1973 was very different from the one that produced the *Roth* decision in 1957. Only four justices who had participated in *Roth*—Burger, Douglas, Black, and Brennan—remained on the Court. Perhaps more important is that four of the five new justices had been appointed by President Nixon, whose disdain for permissive sexuality was well known. In 1970, when the National Commission on Obscenity and Pornography, which had been appointed by President Johnson, issued a report calling for repeal of virtually all laws against pornography, Nixon issued a statement in which he "categorically reject[ed]" the group's "morally bankrupt" conclusions. "So long as I am in the White House," he intoned, "there will be no relaxation of the national effort to control and eliminate smut from our national life."[18]

The Court accepted many obscenity cases for consideration in its 1972–1973 term and handed down eight of them in June of 1973. By far the most important one was *Miller v. California,*[19] which represented the first time since 1957 that a majority of the Court would grapple with the actual definition of obscenity.

The factual situation was an unusual one. Most obscenity convictions involve the selling or mailing of materials to willing recipients, or at least to undercover police officers masquerading as such willing recipients. Here the defendant instead had mailed unsolicited brochures advertising books bearing such titles as *Intercourse* and *Sex Orgies Illustrated.* The brochure itself was not for the squeamish, consisting primarily of "pictures and drawings very explicitly depicting men and women in groups of two or more engaging in a variety of sexual activities, with genitals often prominently displayed." The prosecution commenced after a restaurant owner in Newport Beach opened the brochure (in the company of his mother) and complained to the police. The Supreme Court, by a 5–4 vote, upheld Miller's conviction.

Chief Justice Burger's majority opinion is a reminder that the Court, despite having heard dozens of obscenity cases in the interim, was unable to agree about the *definition* of obscenity since the *Roth* formulation sixteen years earlier. Although the *Miller* decision does not provide a single, comprehensive definition, it does give the individual states several important guidelines. Most fundamentally, the Chief Justice tells the states that "the permissible scope" of their regulations must be limited to "works which depict or describe sexual conduct" and that the regulations themselves, whether in statutes or in judge-made common law, must "specifically define" that which is prohibited. The First Amendment requires also that government regulations prohibit only "works which, taken as a whole, appeal to the prurient interest in sex, which portray sexual conduct in a patently offensive way, and which, taken as a whole, do not have serious literary, artistic, political, or scientific value."

---

[18]Richard F. Hixson, *Pornography and the Justices* (Carbondale, IL: SIU Press, 1996), 98.

[19]413 U.S. 15 (1973).

Some features of the *Miller* test represented significant breaks with *Roth*. First is the added requirement that a work must be "patently offensive." Kathleen Sullivan, a Stanford University law professor, has suggested somewhat playfully that the dual requirements of appealing to the prurient interest *and* being patently offensive seem to suggest that only materials that both turn us on and gross us out can be found obscene.[20] Cartoonist Mike Twohy (see Figure 11.1) shares Sullivan's assessment of this feature of the *Miller* test.

Another feature that was changed, or at least clarified, from the earlier *Roth* test is the nature of the "community" in the phrase "contemporary community standards." The *Roth* decision itself was silent on this point, but many courts since had assumed that a single nationwide standard was intended for the purposes of determining whether a work appealed to the prurient interest. The *Miller* jury, however, had been asked to apply *statewide* standards, and Chief Justice Burger agreed with this instruction, also suggesting that a smaller "community" might also be invoked.

---

[20]Jeffrey Rosen, *"Miller* Time," *The New Republic,* 1 Oct. 1990, p. 17.

 **Figure 11.1**

**THAT'S LIFE**   MIKE TWOHY

"We find the defendant guilty of violating community standards on pornography, and, may I add, we especially enjoyed exhibit 'D'."

These jurors clearly enjoyed having their prurient interest aroused (one of the components of the *Miller* obscenity test).

*© 2001 by the Washington Post Writers Group. Reprinted with permission.*

Asking jurors to apply a *local* community standard has important implications, depending in part on the technology involved. If a book or a magazine is found obscene in only a few venues in relatively conservative areas of the country, distribution can still proceed in the rest of the country. Suppose, though, that the work at issue is a film, distributed using direct broadcast satellite. The cost of maximizing the potential for delivery systems (and profits) while ensuring that potential viewers who live in parts of the country where the film has been judged obscene will not be able to access it can be large. In 1990, a New York–based film distributor called Home Dish Satellite was effectively put out of business by one successful obscenity prosecution in Alabama. The state of Alabama requested further that the company's executives be extradited from New York to stand trial. This Governor Mario Cuomo refused to do.[21]

---

[21]Sam Howe Verhovek, "Cuomo Turns Down Request to Extradite Cable Officials," *New York Times,* 21 June 1990, p. B4.

 Figure 11.2

One of the most perplexing aspects of obscenity prosecutions has been how to instruct jurors to infer their own community's standards.

*From* Herblock on All Fronts *(New York, New American Library, 1980). © 1977 Herb Block. Reprinted with permission.*

Local communities' judgments must sometimes be kept in check by appellate review, however, as the Supreme Court made clear in its very next term after handing down *Miller*. The state of Georgia had ruled that the film *Carnal Knowledge*, starring Jack Nicholson, Art Garfunkel, Candace Bergen, and Ann-Margret was obscene. This story of two male college roommates' difficulties in relating to women (after years of marriage, Garfunkel's character wonders aloud if sex is "just not supposed to be fun anymore when you love her") made many critics' best ten films of the year lists and resulted in an Academy Award nomination for Margret. The film did include brief bits of nudity. There were also several instances where the characters seemed to be engaging in sexual activity—notably in the final scene, where Nicholson's character can achieve orgasm only through a highly ritualized act of fellatio performed by high-class call girl Rita Moreno—but all these were only hinted at, with the camera focused elsewhere. The Supreme Court held that this film was plainly not obscene, that no reasonable jury could have found it patently offensive.[22]

Perhaps the *Miller* Court's most significant departure from the earlier *Roth* test was Chief Justice Burger's reference to the limiting of obscenity laws to works lacking *serious* value, whether literary, artistic, political, or scientific (the SLAPS test). States were now given far more leeway than before; the *Roth* test, you will recall, defined the obscene as that which lacks *any* redeeming value.

In a decision handed down in 1987, the Supreme Court clarified that jurors' adjudication of the "serious value" question—unlike the questions concerning whether a work is "patently offensive" and whether it appeals to the "prurient interest"—should be done according to a national standard. Moreover, when determining whether or not a work boasts enough serious value to be protected from an obscenity charge, jurors should conjure up as best they can their image of what a "reasonable" person would say, rather than an "average" person.[23] This latter

---

[22]*Jenkins v. Georgia,* 418 U.S. 153 (1974).

[23]*Pope v. Illinois,* 481 U.S. 497 (1987).

 # Things to Remember

### THE *MILLER* TEST

- In *Miller v. California* (1973), the Supreme Court created a new test for obscenity, retaining some features and rejecting others from the earlier *Roth* test.
- Under the *Miller* test, a work is obscene if:
  - The average person, applying contemporary community standards, would find that the work, taken as a whole, appeals to the prurient interest.
  - The work depicts or describes specified sexual conduct in a patently offensive manner.
  - The work lacks serious literary, artistic, political or scientific value.

point may on its surface seem a bit insulting, as if the Court is suggesting that the "average" American is not very reasonable. It also makes an already confusing set of legal instructions even more so. In any event, the clear intent of the decision is in the direction of making obscenity convictions a bit more difficult to obtain against works of value.

## Fine-Tuning the Legal Definition of Obscenity

The Supreme Court has offered additional guidelines for states trying to fashion constitutional obscenity statutes. Some of these guidelines can be culled from *Miller* itself, others from new interpretations of previous cases, and others still from cases decided in more recent years.

***What Kind of Sexual Conduct?*** Under *Miller,* obscenity prosecutions can succeed only against works that are aimed at the "prurient" interest and are "patently offensive." Neither phrase is self-defining. Even while cautioning that "it is not our function to propose regulatory schemes for the states," that is in fact what the *Miller* majority did. A constitutionally acceptable statute might be one, Burger wrote, that prohibits either "representations or descriptions of ultimate sexual acts, normal or perverted, actual or simulated" or "representations or descriptions of masturbation, excretory functions, and lewd exhibition of the genitals." Not surprisingly, approximately half the states now quote this language in their statutes.

The *Miller* Court also required that obscenity laws "specifically define" what was to be prohibited. A few years later, however, the Court made clear that whatever due process guarantees seemed to flow from such a requirement would not be strictly enforced. Defendants in *Ward v. Illinois*[24] had been convicted for selling magazines that depicted sadomasochistic sexual practices. By a vote of 5–4, the Court upheld Ward's conviction, even though the state law nowhere mentioned sadomasochistic practices. Justice Stevens's dissenting opinion lamented what he saw as the majority's having "abandon[ed] one of the cornerstones of the *Miller* test," the requirement that states put citizens on notice as to precisely what kinds of sexual expression would be criminalized.

***Thematic Obscenity.*** States may not use obscenity law to stifle debate *about* sexual matters. The leading case on this issue is from 1959, when the Supreme Court told the state of New York that it could not deny a distribution license for the showing of a film version of D. H. Lawrence's *Lady Chatterley's Lover.* One of the state's arguments had been that the film glorifies the commission of adultery, which is "contrary to the moral standards, the religious precepts, and the legal code of its citizenry." Writing for the Court, Justice Stewart chided the state for "misconceiving what the Constitution protects." The First Amendment "protects

---

[24]431 U.S. 767 (1977).

advocacy of the opinion that adultery may sometimes be proper" as well as all sorts of other views not necessarily shared by the majority.[25]

The doctrine of **thematic obscenity** means that artistic works with a sexual theme or thesis cannot be banned because the arguments they make are unpopular or unsettling. For example, in the late 1990s, Terrence McNally's play *Corpus Christi* created enormous controversy because it suggested that Jesus was gay and that he and Judas had been lovers. (Notice yet again the interrelationship between sexual and religious heresies.) The Manhattan Theatre Club received bomb threats when it was preparing to stage the work. Years earlier, Martin Scorsese's film version of *The Last Temptation of Christ* (which posited a sexual relationship between Jesus and Mary Magdalene) also sparked vociferous protests in many cities. When the lead character in the TV series *Ellen* came out as a lesbian, there also were many protests and calls for boycotts of advertisers. In none of these instances would the works have been found legally obscene on the basis of the message or theme their creators sought to convey.

***The Privacy of the Home.***    Georgia State Police suspected Robert E. Stanley of being a small-time bookmaker and obtained a search warrant for his home. They did not find any helpful evidence on the gambling charge, but while looking through a desk drawer in an upstairs bedroom, they found three reels of film. Using Stanley's own film projector, they examined the films, which they concluded were obscene. Stanley was placed under arrest for possession of obscene materials, in violation of state law. The state obtained a conviction, which was upheld by the Georgia Supreme Court. The U.S. Supreme Court, however, unanimously overturned Stanley's conviction.[26] Justice Marshall's opinion for the Court articulated a fusion of First and Fourth Amendment values, emphasizing that the government "has no business telling a man, sitting alone in his own house, what books he may read or what films he may watch."

Some lower courts, citing *Stanley*'s emphasis on a right to receive information, reasoned that the right should have a life beyond one's own four walls. Thus, for example, one federal court ruled that obscenity laws could not reach the patrons (or the owner) of a movie theater showing the film *I Am Curious (Yellow),* which the judges assumed to be obscene under the relevant local statute. "If Stanley has a constitutional right to view obscene films," the judges reasoned, it makes no sense that he can exercise that right only at the expense of a criminal prosecution against the theater owner, "the only logical source" of such films for most patrons.[27] Similarly, a federal court in California assumed that the Supreme Court's emphasis in *Stanley* on the right to own obscene films must include a right to receive them and so struck down the federal statute against

---

[25]*Kingsley International Pictures Corporation v. Regents,* 360 U.S. 684 (1959).

[26]*Stanley v. Georgia,* 394 U.S. 557 (1969).

[27]*Karalexis v. Byrne,* 306 F. Supp. 1363, 1366 (D. Mass. 1969).

Figure 11.3

"WE SAID, MADAM, THAT YOU MAY VIEW
PORNOGRAPHY IN THE PRIVACY OF YOUR HOME.
WE DIDN'T SAY YOU HAD TO!"

*© 1993 Sidney Harris. Reprinted with
permission.*

importation of such materials. The Supreme Court disagreed and reinstated the federal law.[28]

Another court used *Stanley* to strike down the federal law prohibiting the interstate transport of obscene materials. Writing for a 5–4 majority, Chief Justice Burger vacated the lower court ruling, rejecting the notion that "the right to possess obscene material in the privacy of the home…creates a correlative right to receive it [or] transport it."[29] The Supreme Court similarly vacated a lower court ruling that had cited *Stanley* logic while striking down the federal law permitting the Customs Service to seize obscene works at the border.[30] This line of cases led Justice Black to comment on what he saw as the illogic of construing *Stanley* too narrowly. "The right to read and view any literature and pictures at home is hollow indeed," Black lamented, "if it does not include a right to carry that material privately in one's luggage when entering the country."[31] Justice Douglas added, in

---

[28]*United States v. Thirty-Seven Photographs,* 309 F. Supp. 36 (C.D. Cal. 1970)., *rev'd,* 402 U.S. 363 (1971).

[29]*United States v. Orito,* 413 U.S. 139, 141 (1973).

[30]*United States v. 12 200-Foot Reels of 8 MM Film,* 413 U.S. 123 (1973).

[31]*United States v. Thirty-Seven Photographs,* 402 U.S. 363, 381 (1971).

another case, that he "fail[ed] to comprehend how the right to possession enunci-ated in *Stanley* has any meaning when States are allowed to outlaw the commercial transactions which give rise to such possession."[32]

Perhaps the death knell for broad interpretations of *Stanley* occurred in 1973, when, on the same day the Supreme Court produced the *Miller* test, it also handed down *Paris Adult Theatre I v. Slaton*,[33] upholding the constitutionality of an obscen-ity prosecution against a pair of adult movie theatre owners in Atlanta. The owners based their appeal in part on their patrons being consenting adults each of whom would, under *Stanley*, have a right to view the same films at home that they saw at the theatre. The entrance to the theatre, which the Court described as "con-ventional" and inoffensive," boasted signs saying, "Atlanta's Finest Mature Feature Films" and "Adult Theatre—You must be 21 and able to prove it. If viewing the nude body offends you, Please Do Not Enter." A 5–4 Court rejected the "consent-ing adults" defense and made clear that *Stanley* "was hardly more than a reaffirma-tion that 'a man's home is his castle,'" not the creation of a "zone of privacy that follows a distributor or a consumer of obscene materials wherever he goes."

***Variable Obscenity.***    On occasion, the Supreme Court has recognized that its definition of obscenity has to be adjusted or modified—sometimes in the direction of more strictness, sometimes a more relaxed standard—depending on a pornog-rapher's intended audience or the manner in which he advertises his wares. Collec-tively, such instances have come to be called the doctrine of **variable obscenity**.

There is a practical problem in basing the definition of obscenity in part on reference to an "average" member of a community, as do both the *Roth* and *Miller* tests. Much of the typical adult book and movie outlet's wares are aimed not at the average consumer, but at consumers with sexual interests that deviate from the statistical norm. This might mean gay erotica or an emphasis on sadomasochistic images. Fetishes may run from leather to lace, from diapers to latex, and one will be able to find pornographic materials aimed at them all and many more. To the hypothesized "average" citizen, such erotica might not appeal to the prurient inter-est at all. These more specialized images may or may not seem patently offensive to that same average person; they might instead simply confuse and amuse. What to do with the definition of obscenity, and therefore the instructions to the jury, in such situations?

The general rule the Court has fashioned, intuitively enough, says to focus on the average member of the intended target audience. Consider the case of Edward Mishkin, who was convicted in New York of selling numerous books de-picting such practices as sadomasochism, spanking, and flagellation. Mishkin's novel argument on appeal was that his publications could not possibly meet the

---

[32]*Carlson v. Minnesota,* 414 U.S. 953, 954 (1973).

[33]413 U.S. 49 (1973). The "I" in the name of the case is not an indication that there is a later court decision by the same name, but rather that there were two theatres side by side, the Paris Adult I and the Paris Adult II.

Supreme Court's definition of obscenity in that the average person, rather than being sexually stimulated by this material, would be disgusted and sickened. Justice Brennan, writing for the Court, rejected Mishkin's argument and held instead that "when the material is designed and primarily disseminated to a clearly defined deviant sexual group, rather than the public at large, the prurient appeal requirement...is satisfied if the dominant theme of the material taken as a whole appeals to the prurient interest in sex *of the members of that group*" (emphasis added).[34] Of course, ordinary jurors who are not themselves adherents to the particular fetishes exploited by an obscenity defendant's wares may be at somewhat of a loss trying to discern what such persons would find sexually stimulating. Trial courts tend to handle this problem by being a bit more open to expert testimony than they might be in more "mainstream" obscenity prosecutions.

The government claims a special interest in seeing to it that obscene materials do not fall into the hands of children. Thus, another instance of variable obscenity concerns materials that are marketed to children or at least where the purveyors do not take sufficient steps to block access by children. The leading case on this point is *Ginsberg v. New York*.[35] The defendant and his spouse found their troubles began with they sold two "girlie magazines," as the Court put it, to a sixteen-year-old patron of their ma and pa operation, Sam's Stationery and Luncheonette, on Long Island. The magazines, which were not claimed to be obscene for an adult audience, were found in violation of a state law prohibiting the distribution to minors of photos showing "female buttocks...or female breasts with less than a fully opaque covering." The Supreme Court upheld Ginsberg's conviction, with Justice Brennan finding that it is "altogether fitting and proper for a state to include in a statute designed to regulate the sale of pornography to children special standards, broader than those embodied in legislation aimed at controlling dissemination of such material to adults."

A few clarifying points about the *Ginsberg* case are in order. First, it is important to remember that Ginsberg actually sold to a minor. That is the offense for which he was prosecuted, not for publishing or selling materials that would be deemed harmful to an hypothesized minor who *might* come across them. The Supreme Court has made clear that states may not, in pursuit of the laudable goal of protecting children, create obscenity laws so restrictive that adults are limited to that which would be suitable only for children.[36]

The *Ginsberg* case did, however, put managers of bookstores and magazine stands on notice that it would be in their interests to take some actions to prevent the accessing by minors of sexually explicit materials. In recent years, statutes have sprung up in numerous locales requiring such businesspeople to cover up titillating magazine cover photos or to keep such materials physically removed from minors

---

[34]*Mishkin v. New York*, 383 U.S. 502, 508 (1966).

[35]390 U.S. 629 (1968).

[36]*Butler v. Michigan*, 352 U.S. 380 (1957).

(such as behind the retail counter). When these statutes have narrowly and carefully specified the kinds of materials within their scope, they have generally been upheld.[37] The U.S. Supreme Court has yet to rule on such a statute, however.

A final point about the *Ginsberg* case concerns how the Supreme Court asks us to interpret the decision. From Justice Brennan's perspective, the New York statute used against Ginsberg was upheld precisely because it demanded a finding of obscenity, albeit a modified or watered-down version of obscenity. States may, Brennan wrote, "adjust the definition of obscenity to social realities by permitting the appeal of this type of material to be assessed in terms of the sexual interests...of such minors." Thus, the *Ginsberg* case did for minors what the *Mishkin* case did for fetishists and others whose sexual interests are beyond the mainstream. It said that obscenity statutes may take into consideration the sexual material's audience. This is probably a legal fiction, of course; fetishist films and magazines really are targeted toward narrow groups of consumers, whereas "girlie magazines" are read by minors and adults alike. As applied to children, then, "variable obscenity" probably does not really mean obscenity at all, although the Supreme Court does not admit as much.

The doctrine of variable obscenity also permits states to take into account the manner in which sexual materials are marketed, specifically whether the defendant has engaged in what is called "pandering." The leading case is *Ginzburg v. United States*[38] (do not confuse this with the *Ginsberg* case discussed earlier). Ralph Ginzburg appealed his Comstock Act convictions for having used the U.S. mails to distribute three issues of his magazine *Eros,* which consisted of articles, essays, and photos. Some of the material in one of the issues had appeared previously in professional journals. That same issue also included "an interview with a psychotherapist who favors the broadest license in sexual relationships." In other words, this was not the sort of material one usually considers hard-core pornography.

One reason the Supreme Court upheld Ginzburg's conviction was that he had engaged in pandering, "the business of purveying textual or graphic matter openly advertised to appeal to the erotic interest of [one's] customers." The mailed advertisements, Justice Brennan wrote, "stressed the sexual candor of the respective publications, and openly boasted that the publishers would take full advantage of what they regarded as an unrestricted license allowed by law in the expression of sex and sexual matters." That Ginzburg had tried unsuccessfully to obtain mailing privileges for his wares from the postmasters of Intercourse and Blue Ball, Pennsylvania—in the end, he had to settle for Middlesex, New Jersey—also merited the Court's mention.

---

[37]*M. S. News Co. v. Casado,* 721 F.2d 1281 (10th Cir. 1983); *Upper Midwest Booksellers Association v. City of Minneapolis,* 602 F. Supp. 1361 (D. Minn. 1985); *American Booksellers Association v. Rendell,* 481 A.2d 919 (Pa. Super. Ct. 1984). See, however, *American Booksellers Association v. Virginia,* 792 F.2d 1261 (4th Cir. 1986); *Rushia v. Town of Ashburnham,* 582 F. Supp. 900 (D. Mass.1983); *American Booksellers Association v. McAuliffe,* 533 F. Supp. 50 (N.D. Ga. 1981); *Tattered Cover, Inc. v. Tooley,* 696 P.2d 780 (Colo. 1985).

[38]383 U.S. 463 (1966).

# Things to Remember

## FINE TUNING OBSCENITY

- In *Ward v. Illinois* (1977), the Court told states that their obscenity statutes need not spell out every possible component of what might make a sexual depiction obscene.
- The doctrine of "thematic obscenity" says that works cannot be found obscene because they seem to glorify or condone immoral sexual practices or values.
- The Court's decision in *Stanley v. Georgia* (1969) gives Americans the right to *own* obscene material (but not to buy, or import, or transport it across state lines).
- The mere fact that the only attendees at a viewing of obscene materials are consenting adults does not protect that proprietor of the establishment from prosecution.
- The "variable obscenity" doctrine says that the definition of obscenity can be modified to reflect the specific audience targeted (e.g., persons with unusual sexual interests, or children) or that a pornographer has marketed sexy wares in a "pandering," leering way.

The *Ginzburg* case did not create a separate cause of action or enhanced punishment for pandering (as the dissenting justices claimed). One cannot be prosecuted for advertising *non*obscene materials in a sexy manner, unless the advertisements themselves are obscene. Pandering is an indicator of crime; it is not itself a crime. In essence, the decision means that a purveyor's having marketed his or her wares in a pandering manner may be used only as one piece of evidence "in determining the ultimate question of obscenity."

## Child Pornography

The variable obscenity doctrine, as we have seen, is in part a manifestation of society's desire to protect children from sexually explicit messages. That protectiveness is apparent also in the existence of child pornography laws. These statutes, which began to spring up in the late 1970s and 1980s, generally prohibit the use of minors as actors or models in the production and later distribution of sexual images. Clearly, then, one of the government's interests in criminalizing the production of "kiddie porn," as it is often called, is to prevent the sexual abuse of children. Whereas the traditional impetus behind obscenity laws is to safeguard the morals of pornography's consumers, child pornography laws are designed to protect the actors.

It matters not, then, if child pornography meets all the components of the *Miller* test. Child abuse is child abuse, whether or not the photographic record of the event appeals to consumers' prurient interest, regardless of a lack of patent offensiveness, and despite whatever serious literary or other value the work may possess. Therefore, most child pornography statutes do not require that these issues be addressed to justify a conviction. Similarly, the finished product need not be judged as a whole, for what difference would it make whether a scene involving child abuse takes up 5 percent or 75 percent of a film's total running time?

If the only state interest in prosecuting child pornography cases were the prevention of the child abuse inherent in the production of the materials themselves, it would at least be arguable whether such statutes should reach beyond the producers to the distributors and to individual consumers. Governments, however, argue that they have other, related interests as well. The Supreme Court, in a 1982 decision upholding New York's child pornography law, pointed to several harms flowing from the production and distribution of these materials.[39] Sexually exploited children, Justice White pointed out, are often unable to develop healthy affectionate relationships in later life and are likely to become sexual abusers themselves. The existence of a photographic or filmic record of an episode of sexual abuse continues to victimize the child participants by invading their privacy as adults.

Justice White concluded that the state may legitimately criminalize not only the production but also the distribution of child pornography. One of the most efficient ways of providing a disincentive for the production of such pornographic images designed for commercial distribution is to choke off the distribution network itself. It is much easier for the state to go after marketers, because the production of this kind of material tends to be a "low-profile" and "clandestine" enterprise.

Virtually the only portion of the *Miller* obscenity test that the Court did apply to child pornography statutes is the due process requirement that such laws clearly specify precisely what kinds of representations or depictions are covered. The only guidance the majority opinion provides to the states is that the laws criminalize only "works that visually depict sexual conduct by children below a specified age" and that the phrase "sexual conduct" itself needs to be "suitably limited and described." The New York statute's definition of sexual conduct included "actual or simulated sexual intercourse, deviate sexual intercourse, sexual bestiality, masturbation, sado-masochistic abuse, or lewd exhibition of the genitals," and the Court found this precise enough to withstand constitutional challenge.

Emboldened by the *Ferber* decision, some states began to amend their child pornography statutes to criminalize not only the commercial distribution of such materials, but also the private possession of them. In 1990, the Supreme Court held that statutes prohibiting private possession are constitutional, that the *Stanley* decision finding a constitutional privacy right in the mere possession of obscene materials did not apply to child pornography.[40] Again writing for the majority, Jus-

---

[39]*Ferber v. New York*, 458, U.S. 747 (1982).

[40]*Osborne v. Ohio*, 495 U.S. 103 (1990).

tice White justified the law's reach to private possession by citing research demonstrating that pedophiles often show youngsters pornographic images involving minors as a way of convincing their victims to participate "voluntarily" in sexual conduct.

Can a journalist who claims to be doing research for a future story use that assertion as a defense to a charge of sending and receiving child pornography? In a case involving a reporter for WTOP radio in Washington, D.C.—he was prosecuted in Maryland, where he had been uploading and downloading pornographic images on his home PC—the Court of Appeals for the Fourth Circuit said no.[41]

In recent years, a complicated issue concerning the permissible definition of prohibited conduct in child pornography laws has surfaced: can pictures or videos of *fully clothed* underage models ever be criminalized? In a 1994 decision, the Third Circuit Court of Appeals ruled that such depictions may indeed constitute child pornography,[42] in violation of relevant portions of the federal Protection of Children Against Sexual Exploitation Act.[43] Penn State University graduate student Stephen Knox had in his possession several videotapes depicting teen and preteen girls in bikinis or similar attire. The court emphasized that the films, which featured extended close-ups of the children's pubic and genital areas, were clearly designed to pander to pedophiles. Such artifacts are easily distinguishable from the proverbial "infant on the bearskin rug" photos the defendant argued would seem to be equally prohibited by the statute.

---

[41]*U.S. v. Matthews,* 209 F. 3d 338 (4th Cir. 2000).

[42]United States v. Knox, 32 F.3d 733 (3d Cir. 1994).

[43]Public Law No. 95-225, 92 Stat. 7 (1977) (codified as amended at 18 U.S.C. sec. 2251–3).

 # Things to Remember

### CHILD PORNOGRAPHY

- Child pornography laws are aimed at sexually oriented materials that use children as actors or models.
- Such laws differ from obscenity statutes in that:
  - Works need not be judged as a whole.
  - There is no exemption for works with serious value.
  - The works need not appeal to the prurient interest.
  - The state may criminalize the mere possession of child pornography.
- Even photos of fully clothed youngsters may be child pornography if the children are engaged in lewd poses or conduct or if the focus is on the genital area.
- In 1996, Congress broadened the definition of child pornography to include images that *appear to be* of children in sexual poses; the constitutionality of this provision has not been definitively determined.

A new twist on the child pornography debate emerged in 1996 when Congress amended the federal statute to include video images, including computer-generated ones, that *appear to be* minors engaging in sexually provocative poses or conduct. No underage model, indeed no model at all, need be involved in the creation of such images. Congress was motivated in part by its frustration over the Justice Department's having decided in 1995 not to prosecute controversial fashion designer Calvin Klein on child pornography charges. Klein's company had produced several very sexually charged print and TV ads depicting young models who appeared to be underage but who were actually adults. Four federal appellate courts have ruled on the Child Pornography Prevention Act. The First,[44] Fourth,[45] and the Eleventh Circuits[46] upheld the statute, but the Ninth Circuit ruled that the law was unconstitutionally vague, at least when applied to images that merely "appear to be" a minor or "convey the impression" that a minor is involved.[47] The Supreme Court granted review to the Ninth Circuit decision, and will hear the case sometime during its 2001–2002 term.

## Pornography as a Civil Rights Issue: The Feminist Response

In the early 1980s, feminists Andrea Dworkin and Professor Catherine MacKinnon drafted a model ordinance that would take a novel approach to sexually explicit communications. The ordinance sought to define "pornography" rather than "obscenity" as a legal construct. It provided for civil actions rather than criminal prosecutions. Most crucially, the purported state's interest in providing for such civil actions was the promotion of equality rights rather than a desire to foster a traditional view of morality.

Pornography, the law's feminist sponsors argued, harms women in several ways. The women who appear in pornography are often physically and sexually abused in the course of producing films. As MacKinnon has written, pornography "forces, threatens, blackmails, pressures, tricks and cajoles women into sex for pictures."[48] Proponents of the civil rights approach also point to the plethora of social science research showing that people who are exposed to many pornographic images develop misogynist attitudes and beliefs (such as, for example, that women enjoy pain or that they want to be raped). Much evidence also shows that sex criminals seem disproportionately likely to have been voracious consumers of pornography.[49]

---

[44]*United States v. Hilton,* 167 F.3d 61 (1st Cir. 1999).

[45]*United States v. Mento,* 231 F.3d 912 (4th Cir. 1999).

[46]*United States v. Acheson,* 195 F.3d 645 (11th Cir. 1999).

[47]*Free Speech Coalition v. Reno,* 198 F.3d, 1083 (9th Cir. 1999).

[48]Catherine A. MacKinnon, *Only Words* (Cambridge: Harvard University Press, 1993), 15.

[49]Gail Dines, Robert Jensen, and Ann Russo, *Pornography: The Production and Consumption of Inequality* (New York: Routledge, 1998).

The city council of Minneapolis passed the model ordinance, but the law was promptly vetoed by the city's mayor. Then, conservative organizations in Indianapolis cleverly coopted the feminist model and succeeded in passing a similar ordinance. The law was challenged in court by a coalition of groups and individuals headed by the American Booksellers Association. A federal district court, affirmed by the Seventh Circuit Court of Appeals, held the statute unconstitutional.[50]

The statute defined pornography as "the graphic sexually explicit subordination of women, whether in pictures or in words" when such depictions also include any of several specified exacerbating features. Depictions of women enjoying pain or humiliation would trigger the law, as would their being tied up, mutilated, or penetrated by objects or animals. More broadly, the law also would reach depictions of "degradation," of women as "inferior," or in "postures or positions of servility or submission."

Writing for the appellate panel, Judge Easterbrook emphasized that the statute lacked many of the constitutional protections provided under the *Miller* test. First, there was no requirement that works be judged as a whole. Also conspicuously absent from the ordinance was an exception for works of serious value, akin to *Miller*'s SLAPS test. Then, too, the statutory definition required neither a finding of patent offensiveness nor of the work's appealing to the prurient interest. The statute's more fundamental constitutional flaw, however, was that it prohibited the expression of specific *ideas* about women. Speech that portrays women in positions of equality, Easterbrook pointed out, would be beyond the law's reach, no matter how graphic the content, whereas speech that presents women in submissive roles would be sanctioned, no matter how tame. Such legislation seeks to establish "an approved view of women" and thus amounts to "thought control."

Interestingly, a philosophy very similar to that undergirding the Indianapolis ordinance has been accepted in Canada. The Canadian Supreme Court's decision in *Regina v. Butler*[51] embraced the belief that pornography is primarily a civil rights issue and that the law should protect women from its "degrading and dehumanizing" depictions. The Canadian decision departed from the Indianapolis approach in several key ways, however. The *Butler* decision dealt exclusively with criminal law, not civil. Also unlike the Indianapolis ordinance, the Canadian system requires that works be judged as a whole and provides a defense for "artistic necessity," similar to the *Miller* SLAPS rule.

Finally, although the Indianapolis statute is often characterized as *the* feminist answer to sexually explicit images, in fact many women who describe themselves as feminists are strong opponents of any government censorship in this arena. Nadine Strossen's book *Defending Pornography* is probably the best-known articulation of the feminist, civil libertarian view. Members of a group called the Feminist Anti-Censorship Task Force, or FACT, also oppose obscenity laws.

---

[50]*American Booksellers Association v. Hudnut,* 598 F. Supp. 1316 (S.D. Ind. 1984), *aff'd,* 771 F.2d 323 (7th Cir. 1985).

[51]89 D. L. R. 449 (Can. 1992).

Things to Remember

---

**PORNOGRAPHY AND FEMINISM**

■ Some feminists joined forces in the 1980s with conservative groups to lobby for laws giving women the right to sue pornographers for depicting women in sexually degrading ways.

■ An Indianapolis ordinance that took this approach was held unconstitutional.

■ Canada has reinterpreted its own obscenity law consistent with the civil rights approach, concluding that the evil in pornography is in its treatment of women, not in its overall effect on a society's moral climate.

## Other Means of Regulating Sexual Materials

As we have seen, the Supreme Court defines obscenity as categorically beyond the protection of the First Amendment, as if it were not speech at all. There is also a wide variety of sexual texts and images that do not necessarily fit the definition of obscenity, but that the government has been permitted to regulate in numerous ways. In this section, we examine several kinds of such regulations, including zoning of adult businesses, declaring such businesses to be "public nuisances," and treating pornographers as practitioners of organized crime. Also included here are discussions of movie censorship, government funding of the arts and humanities, and Postal Service regulations governing the mailing of adult-oriented materials. We conclude with a brief discussion of nongovernmental actions against sexual images, either by private citizen groups or through industry self-regulation.

### Zoning Laws

Government zoning commissions wield tremendous power in the United States. They can decide where you may live, tell you that you may not convert your attic into a separate apartment, and even dictate what colors you may or may not paint your home's exterior. Many communities have used zoning ordinances either to cluster all "adult businesses" into a single red-light district or to disperse them widely so as not to become too big an eyesore for any one neighborhood. Generally, the courts have upheld such zoning plans if they further a clearly articulated and substantial state's interest, are aimed at the "secondary effects" of adult businesses (not at the adult content itself), restrict no more speech than necessary, and do not have the real-world effect of forcing the targeted businesses to go *out of business*.

The Supreme Court first ruled on this kind of zoning law in 1976.[52] At issue were Detroit statutes requiring that adult movie theaters—defined in the statute as those that present material "characterized by an emphasis" on any of a list of "sexual activities" and/or "anatomical areas" enumerated in the law itself—must obtain a city license to operate and must not locate within 1,000 feet of any two other adult theaters (or adult book stores, cabarets, bars, or hotels). Clearly, then, Detroit's aim was to prevent the creation of a red-light district. Equally clear is that the definition of affected businesses was not at all related to obscenity itself; a theater could be subject to the licensing and zoning scheme without ever having been accused of showing obscene movies. Justice Stevens's majority opinion upholding the ordinances rested in part on his assertion that nonobscene sexual speech, although it may enjoy some First Amendment protection, is not nearly as central to our system of freedom of expression as is political speech. "Few of us would march our sons and daughters off to war," Stevens wrote, "to preserve the citizen's right to see 'Specified Sexual Activities' exhibited in the theaters of our choice."

The city of Detroit had presented much evidence about the "secondary effects" of these kinds of movie houses. The Court found this significant. It would not do, the majority ruled, for a government to say that its substantial interest in zoning X-rated theaters is that it does not like such places or finds them immoral. Rather, the government must be able to articulate some additional negative impact that is not itself related to the content of the films. In the case of Detroit, this took the form of showing that "neighborhood decay" is a predictable result of allowing too many of these kinds of businesses in a limited area.

Five years after its *Young* decision, the Court struck down a zoning ordinance in Mt. Ephraim, New Jersey.[53] Although the defendant was in the business of providing coin-operated booths through which patrons could watch live, nude dancers perform, the applicable ordinance was worded so broadly as to preclude *any* live entertainment from the entire downtown area. The Court's decision was based in large part on the borough's failure to clearly articulate a substantive state's interest in preventing its citizens from partaking of such a wide variety of protected expression.

Then, in 1986, the Court upheld a zoning law from the city of Renton, Washington, which forbade adult movie houses from locating within 1,000 feet of any residential area, church, park, or school. It is in this decision that the Court most clearly articulates the criteria to be used in assessing the constitutionality of such zoning schemes. Justice Rehnquist (he had not yet been elevated to Chief Justice) admitted at the outset that these kinds of laws comprise a unique category. In a way, they are based on the content of the theater owners' message in that only movie houses that predominantly show "adult" films are affected. Traditional First Amendment jurisprudence dictates that content-based regulations come to the

---

[52]*Young v. American Mini-Theatres,* 427 U.S. 50 (1976).

[53]*Schad v. Mount Ephraim,* 452 U.S. 61 (1981).

Things to Remember

---

**ZONING ORDINANCES**

- Some local governments have decided to control the proliferation of adult-oriented businesses through the use of zoning ordinances, intended either to cluster all such businesses together into a red-light district or to disperse them so as to avoid the creation of such a zone.
- Such laws have generally been upheld if they further a clearly articulated and substantial state's interest, are aimed at regulating the "secondary effects" of adult businesses, restrict no more speech than necessary, and do not make it impossible for such businesses to exist.

---

Court with a presumption of unconstitutionality, unless the state can show a *compelling* interest furthered by the regulation. Because these zoning ordinances are aimed at the adverse "secondary effects" of adult businesses on neighborhood children and on attempts at urban development, however, rather than on the content of any specific film, the laws will be judged by a far less exacting standard. Using the same standard, the Court has also allowed communities to ban (not merely zone) nude dancing clubs, as long as the state aims at secondary effects.[54]

A new and interesting twist on zoning ordinance emerged in the state of New York in 1999, when a number of businesses featuring strippers decided to avoid the impact of local laws simply by admitting minors. They could thus no longer be considered adult-oriented businesses, or so they argued. A state judge in New York City agreed with one club's owners, whose attorney argued that if "you could take your 15-year-old to see the movie, 'Striptease,'" you should also be able to take him to see a live striptease. An appellate court reversed this ruling, however, finding that the state may legitimately base its definition of "adult" establishments on the nature of the entertainment provided within, regardless of whether admission is limited to those who have achieved the age of majority.[55]

### Public Nuisance Laws

For many years, communities have attempted to protect citizens from having unwanted sexual images thrust at them through the use of public nuisance laws. These laws have not always demanded that the images be obscene ones. A Dallas ordinance, for example, prohibited the public display of photos depicting human genitals or buttocks. Newsstand workers thus had to paste over a famous *News-*

---

[54]*City of Erie v. Pap's A.M.*, 529 U.S. 277 (2000).

[55]*The City of New York v. Stringfellows*, 253 A.D.2d 110 (Sup. Ct., App. Div., 1st Dept. 1999).

*week* magazine cover in 1975, showing a Vietnamese mother carrying her young, wounded, *nude,* daughter. In 1975, the Supreme Court struck down the Jacksonville, Florida, public nuisance law, which had been applied to a drive-in movie theater showing nonobscene films that included nudity and could be seen from a nearby church parking lot. Those who might be offended by these images could always avert their eyes, the Court held.[56]

At the other extreme, businesses that happen to sell books or rent or sell videotapes cannot find First Amendment protection when the government seeks to enjoin activity that itself would inarguably be prohibitable as a public nuisance. Thus, the operators of the Village Books and News Store in Kenmore, New York, were put out of business for violating the state's public nuisance statute by permitting their premises to be used by patrons for masturbation, oral sex, and solicitation of prostitution. Writing for the Supreme Court majority, Chief Justice Burger chided the defendants for making the "ludicrous" argument that closing the bookstore was an unconstitutional sanction: Such an assertion, he wrote, is akin to "a thief who is sent to prison...complain[ing] that his First Amendment right to speak in public places has been infringed because of the confinement."[57]

Some courts, however, have concluded that the First Amendment requires a company's "expressive activity" be permitted to continue even while activity that truly is a public nuisance is enjoined or punished. Thus, an adult establishment in Allen County, Ohio, that included a bookstore and a video arcade of private booths in which patrons would masturbate while viewing films was allowed to retain its inventory and stay in business (although the arcade area was shut down).[58] Similarly, rules in Chattanooga, Tennessee, requiring that viewing booths not provide enough privacy to engage in sex and that establishments with such booths not be permitted to remain open twenty-four hours a day, were upheld, although other rules affecting the owners and investors in the bookstore itself were struck down.[59]

Some local governments have created nuisance laws that demand an initial finding that a business has sold or distributed obscene material, triggering an injunction, often referred to as a standards injunction, forbidding the further dissemination of those *or similar* materials. The case law on these kinds of statutes is mixed, often turning on whether the court concludes that the law is aimed at punishing pornographers for past sins or at trying to prevent future dissemination of possibly obscene materials.[60] When judges conclude that the latter motivation

---

[56]*Erznoznik v. Jacksonville,* 422 U.S. 205 (1975).

[57]*Arcara v. Cloud Books,* 478 U.S. 697 (1986).

[58]*Ohio v. Elida Road Video & Books,* 696 N.E.2d 668 (Ohio App. 1997).

[59]*Broadway Books v. Roberts,* 642 F. Supp. 486 (E. D. Tenn. 1986); see also *Ellwest Stereo Theater v. Boner,* 718 F. Supp. 1553 (M.D. Tenn. 1989) concerning similar rules in Nashville.

[60]Steven T. Catlett, "Enjoining Obscenity as a Public Nuisance and the Prior Restraint Doctrine," 84 *Columbia Law Review* 1616 (1984).

# Things to Remember

### PUBLIC NUISANCES

- Some communities have used public nuisance statutes to close down adult businesses.
- Not all such laws require a requisite finding that a business has sold obscene literature.
- Nuisance laws vary with respect to whether they result in businesses losing their licenses or being shut down for a specified period of time.
- These laws are most likely to be found constitutional if they are perceived as punishments for past offenses rather than prophylactic measures designed to prevent future wrongdoing (thus falling into the category of "prior restraints" on speech).

is involved, statutes tend to be struck down as unconstitutional prior restraints on speech.[61] Some courts also look more favorably on "padlock laws," which force offending businesses to close shop for a specified period of time, than on those that include the complete revocation of the defendant's license to conduct business as part of the punishment.[62]

### Racketeering Statutes

Both the federal government and many states have embraced a new and controversial weapon against pornographers, similar to public nuisance laws but with a few twists. The federal Racketeering Influence and Corrupt Organizations Act, popularly known as RICO, was enacted in 1970 as a way of curtailing the influence of organized crime on otherwise legitimate businesses. Today, RICO is used against may different kinds of activities that at first blush might not seem the stuff of the Mafia. For example, the Supreme Court has held that RICO can be used against prolife protestors at abortion clinics to the extent that they are involved in organized conspiracies to shut down the clinics through illegal means.[63] State and federal prosecutors nationwide have used RICO laws also against persons who peddle pornography. It has been assumed for some time that organized crime has a hand in pornography industries. Still, RICO statutes are worded and interpreted broadly enough to reach even relatively mainstream publishers and bookstores. All that is usually required to obtain a conviction is to show that the accused has sold obscene materials at least two times over a ten-year period.

As in the case of public nuisance statutes, that a defendant has engaged in the peddling of obscenity is used as a means of triggering a legal action other than

---

[61]*Cohen v. City of Daleville,* 695 F. Supp. 1168 (M.D. Ala. 1988).

[62]*City of Paducah v. Investment Entertainment, Inc.,* 791 F.2d 463 (6th Cir. 1986).

[63]*National Organization for Women v. Scheidler,* 510 U.S. 249 (1993).

enforcement of an ordinary obscenity statute. When that legal action is a RICO conviction, defendants face punishments not contemplated in the typical obscenity law or public nuisance statute. A racketeering conviction can result in a twenty-year jail sentence and hundreds of thousands of dollars in fines. Moreover, any property used by the defendant in racketeering activities or purchased with the profits from such activities can be forfeitable. Not only can the defendant's place of business and entire inventory (obscene and nonobscene) be seized, but the seizure might extend to personal property such as a place of residence. After all, placing a phone call to order a supply of magazines or videotapes for the store or giving instructions to employees—activities often conducted from a store owner's private residence—are both "associated with" committing the crime of selling obscene materials.

The Supreme Court has twice had occasion to rule on RICO's applications to pornography. In 1989, it held that the state of Indiana had violated the First Amendment when, under its state RICO law, it seized an adult bookstore's inventory before any convictions had been obtained. The Court also gave its approval, however, to the use of racketeering statutes and their forfeiture provisions as long as no confiscation occurs prior to a conviction.[64] Four years later, in *Anderson v. United States,*[65] the Court made a similar ruling concerning the federal RICO law, emphasizing that the forfeiture here of the defendant's entire business and approximately $9 million in profits was not a prior restraint on feared future pornography peddling, but rather permissible punishment for past violations of the law. The majority sent the case back to the lower courts, however, to determine if this huge forfeiture was a violation of the Eighth Amendment's prohibition against

---

[64]*Fort Wayne Books v. Indiana,* 489 U.S. 46 (1989).

[65]509 U.S. 544 (1993).

# Things to Remember

### SEX AND RICO

- The federal Racketeering Influence and Corrupt Organizations Act, originally enacted in 1970, has been amended to provide for the prosecution of pornographers as one would prosecute organized crime figures.
- Many states have passed their own RICO laws as well.
- These laws provide for hefty fines and lengthy prison terms as well as forfeiture of any and all possessions purchased with proceeds from the commissions of the crimes or that have been used in the furtherance of the criminal activity.
- The Supreme Court has upheld the constitutionality of such forfeitures as long as they do not happen before any convictions are obtained.

cruel and unusual punishments. On remand, the lower courts upheld the forfeiture amount, and the Supreme Court denied to review the case again.[66]

## Movie Censorship

When motion pictures first came on the scene around the end of the nineteenth century, audiences were spellbound by the technology itself, by the optical illusion of having multiple, successive still shots of a subject seem to present the subject in motion. The idea of using the technology to tell stories did not come about until years later. The Supreme Court, when first asked to rule on the matter in 1915, decided that movies were entertainment and nothing more, and were beyond the protection of the First Amendment.[67] That decision, even though disavowed by the Court in 1952,[68] set a tone for many years thereafter consistent with treating movies as a bit more dangerous, a bit less deserving of constitutional consideration, than print media.

Cities nationwide required film distributors to present their products to local censorship boards prior to their public exhibition. This practice hardly ever happens anymore, although the Supreme Court has never explicitly said that it is unconstitutional. Rather, the Court has, in a number of decisions,[69] created a set of rules by which any such commissions must operate. The reviewing board must act swiftly (generally within two weeks) either to grant permission to exhibit or to begin litigation to stop the exhibition. In the event that litigation is commenced, there must be expedited review (i.e., within two months or so) of the case. Finally, the burden of proof will always lie with the censors, rather than with the movie's

---

[66]*United States v. Alexander,* 32 F.3d 1231 (1994) (remanding case back to district court on the Eighth Amendment question); 108 F.3d 853 (1997) (upholding district court's finding that forfeiture was constitutional), *cert. denied sub nom. Schlidt v. Souval,* 522 U.S. 869 (1997).

[67]*Mutual Film Corporation v. Industrial Commission of Ohio,* 236 U.S. 230 (1915).

[68]*Burstyn v. Wilson,* 343 U.S. 495 (1952).

[69]*Gelling v. Texas,* 343 U.S. 960 (1952); *Superior Films v. Department of Education,* 346 U.S. 587 (1953); *Times Film Corporation v. City of Chicago,* 365 U.S. 43 (1961); *Freedman v. Maryland,* 380 U.S. 51 (1965); *Teitel Films v. Cussak,* 390 U.S. 139 (1968).

 # Things to Remember

### MOVIE CENSORSHIP

- Although they are not common today, for many years cities nationwide required film distributors to permit local censor boards to preview movies.
- The Supreme Court has never explicitly struck down the use of such censorship boards, but it has imposed certain restrictions on their functioning.

distributors. The same standards have been applied by the Court to prior restraints for alleged obscenity in other settings as well, from seizures of goods by the Postal Service[70] and by the U.S. Customs Service[71] to live theatric performances.[72]

## Government Sponsorship of the Arts

There is a long and complicated body of case law on the question of what First Amendment limitations apply when the government itself is the speaker. It is clear that the government as speaker may engage in viewpoint-based discrimination that would be impermissible in other contexts. The state may not censor private speech arguing for or against drug legalization, but when was the last time you saw a government-sponsored Public Service Announcement on the issue calling for anything other than complete abstinence? In another context, the Supreme Court has said that, when the federal government pays for health care, the professionals delivering that care can be prohibited not only from performing abortions, but also from even mentioning the topic.[73]

The National Endowment for the Arts (NEA) was created in 1965. Since then, it has made over 100,000 grants to artists and arts organizations, totaling over $3 billion. Only a tiny number of the grants have resulted in political controversies. Two such controversies from 1989, however—one involving photographer Robert Mapplethorpe's sadomasochistic and homoerotic images, the other Andre Serrano's "Piss Christ," in which a crucifix is immersed in urine—were intense enough to prompt Congressional response. That action took the form of an amendment to the National Foundation on the Arts and Humanities Act, forbidding the use of federal funds "to promote, disseminate, or produce" any materials that the NEA believes might be obscene. That provision was struck down by a federal court, not because the government should be forced to fund obscene art, but because the statute placed too much administrative discretion within the NEA itself. In other words, judges determine what is obscene, not government bureaucrats.[74]

Congress tried its hand once more at amending the Act, this time instructing the NEA that it should make grants on the basis not only of artistic excellence, but also "taking into consideration general standards of decency and respect for the diverse beliefs and values of the American public." Four performance artists with reputations for doing feminist, gay, and other provocative works—Karen Finley, John Fleck, Holly Hughes, and Tim Miller—challenged the new provision. Each had previously been recipients of NEA grants and had pending proposals accepted

---

[70]*Blount v. Rizzi,* 400 U.S. 410 (1971).

[71]*United States v. Thirty-Seven Photographs,* 402 U.S. 363 (1971).

[72]*Southeastern Promotions v. Conrad,* 420 U.S. 546 (1975).

[73]*Rust v. Sullivan,* 500 U.S. 173 (1991).

[74]*Bella Lewitzky Dance Foundation v. Frohnmayer,* 754 F. Supp. 774 (C.D. Cal. 1991).

Things to Remember

---

### GOVERNMENT SPONSORSHIP

- A small handful of the thousands of grants made by the National Endowment of the Arts have been very controversial and have led Congress to demand that the funding agency include general notions of "decency" into its decision making.
- The Supreme Court has upheld this provision, but has warned the NEA that it must not engage in flagrant viewpoint-based discrimination.

---

by an endowment advisory panel but ultimately disapproved by the director. Two lower federal courts held the "decency" amendment unconstitutional, but the Supreme Court, in an 8–1 ruling, overturned these judgments in 1998. Justice O'Connor's majority opinion was based on the rather narrow grounds that the amendment was merely "hortatory," that it told the NEA director what the grants application *should* look like, rather than explicitly prohibiting the funding of indecent art. Had the NEA in fact developed an unwritten policy against funding art espousing specific political messages, the decision might have been different.[75]

Washington is not the only source of government funding for the arts, of course. From time to time, state and local funders create their own First Amendment nightmares. In 1999, the Brooklyn Museum included as part of an exhibit entitled "Sensation" a painting by Chris Ofili—an impressionistic rendering of the Virgin Mary created from, among other materials, elephant dung. Outraged by what he perceived as the artist's desecration of the Catholic faith, New York City Mayor Rudolph Giuliani promptly withheld funds already appropriated to the museum for operating expenses and maintenance. He also commenced litigation seeking to eject the museum from the city-owned land and building in which its collections had been housed for over a hundred years. Federal District Judge Nina Gerson enjoined the city from imposing any such tangible sanctions against the museum.[76]

### Postal Regulations and Sexually Oriented Junk Mail

Earlier in the chapter, we examined the federal laws making it illegal to send obscene materials through the mails, and giving post office investigators the right to open and seize obscene materials. In this section, we see two additional pieces of federal legislation that, taken together, can save homeowners the embarrassment or inconvenience of receiving any "adult" mailings.

---

[75] *National Endowment for the Arts v. Finley,* 524 U.S. 569 (1998).

[76] *Brooklyn Institute of Arts and Sciences v. The City of New York,* 64 F. Supp. 2d 184 (E.D.N.Y. 1999); see also *Cuban Museum of Arts and Culture, Inc. v. City of Miami,* 766 F. Supp. 1121 (S.D. Fla. 1991).

Under section 3010 of Title 39 of the U.S. Code, known as the Goldwater Amendment to the Postal Reorganization Act, homeowners who do not wish to receive sexually oriented mail of any kind may fill out a form at their local post office informing the postmaster of this wish. The Postal Service in turn alerts all companies that it has previously determined to be in the business of sending such mail to purchase the list—updated monthly—of all such mail patrons who have filled out the requisite paperwork. These companies are then required by law to remove your name and address from any mailing lists and to never mail *anything* to you (whether they think the particular mailing is "adult" or not). The constitutionality of this provision has been upheld.[77] That the mailings covered by the statute were not obscene and were thus protected by the First Amendment, Judge Judd wrote for a special three-judge panel, "does not mean that the mailer's right to communicate ideas supersedes the right of the addressee to be let alone."

More wide-reaching is section 3008 of the code, usually referred to as the Pandering Act. Under this provision, mail patrons who fill out a different form at the post office indicating their belief that a specific company's mailing was "erotically arousing" will thus put that company on notice that it may no longer send mail to the patron. Notice the difference. The Postal Service does not decide that the mailing is sexually oriented or that the mailer is a company in the business of sending such mailings. Only you may make that determination, and your judgment is final and unappealable. Yes, this means that you may use this law to avoid getting those bulky mail-order catalogs that take up so much room in your mailbox. The catalog need not be from Victoria's Secret; it can be from Radio Shack.

---

[77]*Pent-R-Books v. United States Postal Office,* 328 F. Supp. 297 (E.D.N.Y. 1971).

 # Things to Remember

**SEX AND THE MAILS**

- In addition to laws criminalizing the mailing of obscene materials, the Postal Service is empowered by two other congressional provisions to control the mailing of nonobscene, but sexually oriented, messages.

- Section 3010 of the U.S. Code requires companies that do mailings of "adult" materials to purchase and act on a periodically updated list from the Postal Service of all mail patrons who do not want to receive any such mailings.

- Section 3008 gives mail patrons themselves the absolute right to determine that a given mailing is "sexually arousing" and to notify the post office of this determination; such notification will result in the offending company being told by the Postal Service that it may not ever send any mail to that patron again.

Section 3008 has also been found constitutional, in a 1970 Supreme Court decision.[78] As Chief Justice Burger wrote for the Court, "whether measured by pieces or pounds, Everyman's mail today is made up overwhelmingly of material he did not seek from persons he does not know, and all too often it is matter he finds offensive."

## Private Pressure and Industry Self-Regulation

Our freedom of speech has always included the right to persuade others to shut up—as long we do so peaceably. Because the Supreme Court's legal definition of obscenity covers only a tiny portion of the sexual imagery that many people may find offensive, it is no surprise that private citizen action often fills the vacuum in an effort to shame the pornographer. Most such efforts are local and attract little or no national media attention. A typical scenario may find a citizens' group pressuring the owner of a strip shopping mall not to lease space to adult-oriented businesses; sometimes a video rental store will be persuaded to decrease or eliminate its X-rated offerings.

Sexual imagery and narratives found offensive by some groups may become the impetus for an organized boycott. Disney—owner of Capital Cities–ABC—has often become the target of boycotts in recent years. When ABC aired the famous "coming out" and subsequent episodes of the *Ellen* program, several groups called for a boycott of the network and of *Ellen*'s advertising sponsors. The program did indeed experience a noticeable drop in viewership not long after its title character's emergence as a lesbian icon, but by most accounts, that was more a reflection of stale writing than of the boycott.

One of the most dramatic examples of citizen action in the past generation was aimed at a more aural than visual medium. The Parents Resource Music Center, among whose founders was Tipper Gore, joined forces in the mid-1980s with the PTA and other groups to pressure the recording industry to help parents to prevent their children from having access to music with sexually explicit and otherwise offensive lyrics. The Recording Industry Association of America responded by instituting a system of parental advisory labels affixed to cassette and CD packaging. Former Secretary of Education William Bennett, together with Senator Joseph Lieberman, have given "Silver Sewer" awards to mass media companies they see as "purveyors of cultural filth." The pair usually do not succeed in eliminating offensive products, but they have shamed large corporations from attaching their name to the products. Thus, for example, Time Warner was pressured to sell its financial interests in Interscope Records. Among Interscope's artists was Nine Inch Nails, whose sexually explicit lyrics were harshly criticized by Bennett, Lieberman, and then Senator Bob Dole.

---

[78]*Rowan v. United States Post Office Department,* 397 U.S. 728 (1970).

The motion picture industry has for many years exercised self-regulation in the form of the Motion Pictures Association of America's movie rating system, the familiar G, PG, PG-13, R, and NC-17 labels so familiar to us all. Self-regulation in the industry far predates this particular rating system. In the 1930s, the Motion Picture Producers and Distributors Association, led by former Republican Party Chairman Will Hays, created a code to monitor movie content. The Hollywood Production Code dealt with violent and other kinds of antisocial images, but reserved its most detailed guidelines for depictions of sexual relationships. The code, which remained in effect for over thirty years, prohibited—among hundreds of other images—on-screen kisses longer than thirty seconds or with open mouths and exposure of the female leg above the knee.

## Chapter Summary

The Supreme Court says that obscenity is not speech and is thus wholly outside of the First Amendment's protection. For many years, U.S. law followed the British *Hicklin* rule, which said that pornography should be judged by its potential effects on society's most susceptible members and that even an isolated obscene passage could be enough to find an entire book obscene. The *Hicklin* rule was rejected in favor of the *Roth* test in 1957, which in turn gave way to the *Miller* test, first articulated in 1973.

The *Miller* test provides that allegedly obscene works should be judged as a whole, not by isolated passages, and by their likely effects on average, or reasonable, community members. To be judged obscene, a work must, in a patently offensive way, describe or depict sexual matters in a way that appeals to the prurient interest. Whether a work meets that definition is a determination to be made using contemporary community standards (not a single national standard). Moreover, works that have serious literary, artistic, political, or scientific value—this one issue being

judged by a national standard—cannot be found obscene. Materials cannot be found obscene because they seem to condone or glorify immoral sexual values.

There exists a right to privacy in the home that extends far enough to protect individuals' right to possess obscene materials, but not so far as to permit them to import them, carry them across state lines, or use the mails to ship them.

Child pornography laws are aimed at sexually oriented materials that use children as actors or models. Such laws differ from obscenity statutes in many ways. Works need not be judged as a whole; they are not exempted from the law by dint of having serious value; they need not appeal to the prurient interest. Moreover, the state may criminalize the mere possession of child pornography.

In the 1980s, a feminist response to pornography developed, emphasizing the material's degrading depiction of women rather than its overall effect on a society's moral tone. An Indianapolis ordinance based on this new theory was struck down as unconstitutional.

In recent years, communities have embraced legal strategies beyond a reliance on obscenity laws per se to stem the proliferation of adult-oriented businesses. These include zoning ordinances and public nuisance statutes as well as the use of federal and state antiracketeering laws. In addition, homeowners have rights under laws governing the U.S. Postal Service to avoid receiving unwanted sexual mailings, whether obscene or not.

## chapter 12

# *Broadcast, Cable, and Satellite TV Regulation*

Revisit for a moment this disclaimer encountered in Chapter 1: "This book is already out of date. So rapid are changes in the law that most any legal textbook, even assuming the speediest of production schedules, is several months out of date the moment it arrives at your bookstore."

That caution is especially applicable to these final two chapters. The current chapter reviews the complicated regulatory framework governing the electronic media—chiefly broadcast radio and TV, but also cable, satellite, and microwave means of delivery. Then, Chapter 13 explores the new and challenging field of Internet law.

A sense of humility should accompany us as we try to make sense of the rapid changes that have characterized the regulation of electronic media. New court cases and new Federal Communications Commission rules (or, more often, the discarding of old rules) emerge on the scene every week. Also of relevance are the frequent announcements of mergers among major players in the telecommunications industries and the new ways of playing out old turf wars among broadcast, cable, satellite, local and long-distance telephone, and Internet companies. The primary characteristic of U.S. media outlets is largeness; fewer than two dozen companies control almost the entirety of the media culture.[1]

We are often reminded that we live in an era not only of rapid deregulation of the electronic media, but also one of **convergence.** Industry analysts use the word to describe as best they can the not-too-distant future of telecommunications. They predict that in a few decades or sooner, the average middle-class household will not have televisions, radios, telephones, cable decoders, computers, and newspapers and magazines, but instead one single apparatus that will perform all these media functions and more. It will likely also be a home alarm system or a monitoring system to ensure we use gas and electricity efficiently, and it may perform several other functions not yet imagined.

---

[1]Robert McChesney, "A Media Deal with Plenty of Bad News," *San Diego Union-Tribune*, 19 Jan. 2000, p. B7.

Although there is broad consensus that the industry is headed in this general direction, no one knows what that single apparatus will look like or exactly by which mechanisms it will gather, store, and transmit data. Necessarily, we are therefore also looking toward a highly fluid and unpredictable regulatory environment. Traditionally, we have been content with a small handful of neatly defined and separate categories of communications media. The print media are governed by one body of law, and the broadcast media have had additional laws and regulations imposed on them. Cable TV systems have been subject to a body of regulations somewhat more restrictive than those imposed against print media, but less restrictive than those applied to over-the-air TV and radio. Rather separate has been the body of law governing telephone companies, often called "common carriers" because their traditional function has been to serve as a mere conduit for others' transmissions such that anyone able and willing to pay the price (the hook-up costs, the monthly phone bill) gets to send messages. Which model shall we use, then, to regulate this yet-unseen single home appliance that will perform all our communications functions? The short answer is that no one knows. All these cautions should be kept in mind as you read these final two chapters.

In the next section, we explore the history and general structure of electronic media regulation. The most prominent feature of that structure is the Federal Communications Commission, which governs through formal rule-making and through its interactions with Congress, the courts (especially the D.C. Circuit Court of Appeals), and industry trade groups.

This chapter next considers the traditional rationales used by the Commission, Congress, and the courts for treating print and electronic media differently. Government has regulated electronic media more strictly because of the scarceness of available frequencies (so that not everyone who wants to obtain a broadcast license may get one), the pervasiveness of TV and radio in our daily lives, and these media's unique power to influence the young.

We next focus on three broad categories of regulations governing TV and radio: those affecting licensing of individual stations; those aimed at improving the technical, engineering aspects of broadcasting (including the goal of making signals accessible to the Deaf and hard-of-hearing and to the visually impaired); and those more directly aimed at specific kinds of content. As we shall see, electronic media are subject to regulations concerning their political content (especially with respect to speech by and about political candidates), sexually oriented messages, and programming aimed at children. Content regulations applying uniquely to public broadcasters, such as NPR and PBS stations, are also discussed.

Then we will examine the complicated development of laws and regulations affecting the cable industry. Even to this day, the Supreme Court has refused to commit itself as to how much free speech cable TV operators should enjoy, save to say that it will be an "intermediate" amount, somewhere between the print and electronic media models. Finally, we look briefly at such hybrid technologies as satellite master antenna television (SMATV) systems, direct broadcast satellite (DBS) service, and multichannel multipoint distribution service (MMDS).

# Things to Remember

### A CHANGING MEDIA LANDSCAPE

- Traditionally, media in the United States are regulated by one of three models: print, broadcasting, and "common carrier" (e.g., telephone and telegraph), with cable TV fitting in somewhere between the first two models.

- Media analysts, however, predict that diverse media technologies will soon converge, so that most people will have one as-yet-unnamed appliance that will perform the functions now associated with all these media and more.

- Because it is impossible to know what model of communication law will apply to that single appliance, the body of law presented in these final two chapters must be regarded as a work in progress.

## The Birth of Broadcast Regulation

Social historians have often pointed out that two seemingly contradictory features of radio's early history together ensured that electronic media would be treated differently from print, that radio (and later, television) would not enjoy the full protection of the First Amendment. One of these forces was radio's emergence as a hobbyists' toy. The other is radio's ability, proven very early on, to save lives.

The social histories of radio and of motion pictures were very similar in that both began as media whose main function was to entertain. The first commercially produced films had no narrative, no tale to tell. Their selling point was merely the novelty of seeing images appear to move. So it was that the Supreme Court decided early on, in *Mutual Film Corporation v. Industrial Commission of Ohio*[2]—a decision it would not repudiate for many years[3]—that motion pictures were wholly outside the protection of the First Amendment. The logic undergirding the *Mutual Film* decision—that this medium was designed for entertainment, or "spectacle," and thus not "to be regarded…as part of the press of the country or as organs of public opinion"—was fresh in the minds of lawmakers in the 1920s, when the first comprehensive legislation governing the broadcast media was drafted. It seemed only natural to also deny radio the full measure of First Amendment protection granted to print media. Radio, like motion pictures, existed primarily for its entertainment value.

Sometimes, however, the specific message sent by radio was a matter of life and death. The timely transmission and retransmission of an SOS saved many lives in January 1909, when the R.M.S. *Republic,* a 600-foot luxury liner owned by the White Star Shipping Company, collided with a smaller ship, the *Florida.* Together the two ships' passengers and crew totaled over 1,500 people, yet only

---

[2]236 U.S. 230 (1915).
[3]*Burstyn v. Wilson,* 343 U.S. 495 (1962).

six perished. The event marked the first use ever of a distress signal at sea; the *Republic*'s radio operator was hailed as an international hero. It also led Congress to pass the Wireless Ship Act of 1910, which required that any steamer large enough to carry fifty or more passengers and sailing to or from a U.S. port on a journey of 200 miles or more must have radio equipment and a trained operator on board. The law also required that operators answer and retransmit ship distress signals.

White Star also owned the *Titanic,* whose sinking taught us that radio distress signals only save lives if they are received timely. An ocean liner called the *California* was fewer than twenty miles away when the *Titanic* hit the iceberg. The *California*'s radio operator, however, had gone off duty. Indeed, its captain had turned off the ship's engines. Without an auxiliary power system, the radio would not have worked. The *Titanic*'s distress signal did reach a Marconi company outpost in Newfoundland, but that station's retransmissions were blocked by many amateur hobbyists along the way. The hobbyists' interference may also serve to explain how the *Titanic* failed to receive warnings from vessels that had traversed the same route a bit earlier and had spotted many icebergs.[4]

Congress then passed the Radio Act of 1912, which provided that all radio operators had to be licensed by the federal government and which authorized the Secretary of Commerce to administer the license system and to ensure twenty-four-hour staffing of ship radio equipment. The Act had many unfortunate omissions. It provided no mechanism for choosing among competing applicants for a specific radio frequency, nor was the Secretary permitted ever to turn down a request for a license. As a result of the law's lack of teeth, it was common for licensees to take it upon themselves to broadcast at frequencies other than those assigned to them or at hours when they were not permitted to broadcast. There were also instances of a licensee moving operations to a new city, thus directly interfering with another operator already authorized there to use a certain frequency. When then Secretary of Commerce Herbert Hoover tried to bring order from chaos, a federal judge determined that he had exceeded his authority by his attempts to sanction a Chicago radio station that had been broadcasting in a manner inconsistent with its license.[5] Hoover certainly was not happy; neither were radio listeners in that they often received only the cacophony of competing signals. Radio set manufacturers General Electric and Westinghouse were perhaps least happy in that they knew the market for their product would stagnate unless a meaningful system of regulations allowed the authorized signals to get through. As Hoover himself remarked, "this is probably the only industry in the United States that is unanimously in favor of having itself regulated."[6]

---

[4]Susan J. Douglas, *Inventing American Broadcasting: 1899–1922* (Baltimore: Johns Hopkins University Press, 1987).

[5]*United States v. Zenith Radio Corporation,* 12 F.2d 616 (N.D. Ill. 1926).

[6]Sidney Head, *Broadcasting in America: A Survey of Television and Radio,* 3rd ed. (New York: Houghton Mifflin, 1976), 126.

Congress's response was the Radio Act of 1927, the first comprehensive piece of legislation aimed at the electronic media. The Act not only provided for a far more elaborate licensing scheme, but also established that a "public trustee" model would govern radio in America. Because the electromagnetic spectrum, which includes not only radio waves but also X rays, gamma rays, and the infrared and ultraviolet, is inherently limited, not every applicant who would like to obtain a broadcasting license can do so. In the Act, Congress therefore asserted that the airwaves belong to the public, that the individual licensees in their roles as trustees of that valuable public resource must use it in a manner consistent with the "public interest, convenience and necessity." The Act also created the Federal Radio Commission (FRC), a five-member board granted broad powers not only to issue licenses but also to deny applications and to revoke licenses already granted. As interpreted by the Supreme Court in a 1933 decision, the Act also clarified that regulation of the radio spectrum must be done at the national rather than at the state level, in that "no state lines divide the radio waves."[7]

In 1934, Congress entered further into the regulation of electronic media with passage of the Federal Communications Act, which, as amended over the years, still governs American broadcasting. The 1934 Act disbanded the FRC and created in its stead the Federal Communications Commission, aptly named in that its seven commissioners (since reduced to five) were to be charged with regulating not only radio, but also the common carrier technologies of the day (telephones and telegraph).

---

[7]*Federal Radio Commission v. Nelson Brothers,* 289 U.S. 266, 279 (1933).

 # Things to Remember

## EARLY BROADCAST REGULATION

- Radio's early history virtually guaranteed that it would enjoy fewer First Amendment rights than print for two reasons:
  - It was a hobbyist's toy.
  - If properly regulated, it could be used to save lives in emergencies.
- The Radio Act of 1912 authorized the Secretary of Commerce to dole out licenses, but did not authorize him to impose any sanctions against stations that operated in violation of the terms of their licenses.
- Passage of the Radio Act of 1927 created the Federal Radio Commission and first authorized the federal government to rescind licenses from those who were not operating "in the public interest."
- In 1934, Congress passed the Federal Communications Act, which, as modified over the years, is the basis for government regulation of electronic media as well as telecommunications.

## Structure and Powers of the FCC

The Federal Communication Commission's five commissioners are appointed by the president with the consent of the Senate. They serve five-year, staggered terms. No more than three of the five commissioners may be registered in the same political party. The president designates one of the five to serve as the commission's chairman. In 2001, President Bush elevated Michael Powell, who had been appointed an FCC commissioner by President Clinton in 1997, to serve as chairman. Son of Secretary of State Colin Powell, the new chairman is a graduate of Georgetown University Law School and is a former chief of staff of the antitrust division at the Department of Justice.

### The FCC's Bureaus

As with any large bureaucracy, most of the nuts and bolts work in the FCC is done by its professional staff, who are primarily attorneys, engineers, and economists. The staff is organized into seven divisions or "bureaus": the Mass Media Bureau regulates AM, FM, and television broadcast stations. The Cable Services Bureau was established as a separate entity in 1993, primarily to administer the complicated provisions of the Cable Television Consumer Protection and Competition Act of 1992. As its name would suggest, the Common Carrier Bureau's responsibilities include regulating telephone and telegraph services. The Wireless Telecommunications Bureau (formerly the "Private Radio" Bureau) deals primarily with private land mobile, aviation, marine, personal and amateur wireless transmissions; this FCC entity also oversees cellular telephone and personal communication services as well as paging systems. The International Bureau was created in 1994 to represent the Commission at international conferences involving telecommunications matters. This bureau also administers any relevant provisions of treaties and other international agreements. The Enforcement Bureau's responsibilities cut across other bureaus' domains for the purpose of investigating alleged violations of law or FCC policies by licensees. In this bureau, agents quite literally bring out the hatchets when they hear of unauthorized, "rogue" radio transmitters. In early 2000, the FCC created the Consumer Information Bureau so as to centralize the handling of public inquiries and informal consumer complaints. Further structural changes are in the offing, as the Commission becomes more organized according to function—across different media—rather than medium by medium.

### Rule Making and Enforcement

The process of creating new FCC regulations typically begins when the Commission's professional staff—sometimes on their own initiative, sometimes after spurring on by external constituencies—brings to the commissioners an outline of a problem and its proposed solution. That solution is usually in the form of a Notice of Proposed Rule Making (NPRM). If accepted by the commissioners, the NPRM is then widely disseminated to the affected industries and, through publication in the *Federal Register,* to the public at large. Public comments are sought over a period of months, and the text of those comments is also made available for review by any interested parties, which typically results in a second round of comments. At that point, the commissioners review staff reports and the public's feedback and articulate their final decision, a Report and Order.

The FCC not only creates new policies, of course; it must also enforce existing policies and relevant statutes. One might suppose that the most frequent impetus for the Commission to commence an investigation against a broadcast licensee would be a complaint from an offended viewer or listener. The FCC, however, re-quires that a *pattern* of abuse be demonstrated before it will take on a case for review, and the average consumer simply does not have the time and resources to monitor a station for a long enough period to meet this standard. More typical, therefore, are complaints from organized interest groups or from licensees whose own economic interests are tangibly affected by another station's alleged wrongdoing.

If a matter brought to the FCC staff's attention is seen as warranting investiga-tion, a typical next step is to draft a letter of inquiry (LOI) to the licensee against whom a complaint has been brought, seeking additional information. This initial inquiry is popularly known as "regulation by raised eyebrow" and is often sufficient to bring licensees' behaviors into compliance with FCC policies. The licensee's written response to the LOI might elicit a slight escalation from the FCC staff, in the form of a Notice of Apparent Liability. Sometimes, too, the "raised eyebrow" does not consist of singling out individual stations at all, but instead takes the form of a speech or other formal statement by the chairman or other commissioners, criticizing an overall in-dustry practice. In the 1970s, the FCC followed this strategy in expressing dismay over radio stations whose play lists included songs thought to glorify the drug culture.

The Commission is also empowered to issue cease and desist orders and to levy fines against offending licensees. One of the most famous examples of the latter was a series of fines totaling over $1.7 million against Infinity Broadcasting in 1995 for multiple transgressions by "shock jock" Howard Stern.

The most extreme measures available to the Commission include granting a license renewal of a probationary nature—for a shorter time than the usual eight years—and refusing to renew a license altogether. This latter action is very rarely taken and, in recent decades, almost never on the basis of broadcast content itself. Licensees found to have engaged in fraud, however, may very well lose their li-censes. Sometimes such cases involve purposeful overbilling of advertisers. Then, too, the FCC is not shy about using this harshest of punishments when a licensee has been untruthful in dealings with the Commission itself. In 1999, for example, the Commission revoked Trinity Company's license for WHFT-TV in Miami. The licensee had apparently set up a "puppet," ostensibly minority-owned company, so as to qualify for more licenses than it would have otherwise been entitled.[8]

---

[8]Harry Martin, "FCC Revokes Trinity License," *Broadcast Engineering,* June 1999.

## Ancillary Powers

Technically, the FCC is only empowered to regulate government licensees; with respect to broadcast regulation, that means only to the individuals and companies who have been granted a license to run specific, local TV or radio stations. Even more narrowly, in that Congress's right to establish the FCC in the first place flows from the Constitution's Interstate Commerce Clause, one might expect that a station whose broadcast radius is a small one, located in the middle of a huge state and thus capable of only *intra*state transmissions, would be beyond the Commission's purview. Enter the **ancillary powers** doctrine through which the courts have granted the FCC authority to regulate matters not specifically enumerated in the Federal Communications Act, but which the Commission must oversee if it is to effectively regulate interstate transmissions by individual licensees. The doctrine has been invoked to permit regulation of purely intrastate signals on the theory that such transmissions could interfere with neighboring broadcast stations whose interstate transmissions inarguably bring them into the Commission's domain.[9] The FCC has also been permitted to maintain some oversight of radio and TV *networks,* which are not themselves licensed entities. In this instance, two theories are involved. First, although networks are mostly comprised of far-flung individual stations that they do not own, each network also does have a number of "O&O" (owned and operated) stations within its portfolio. Second, the contractual relationships between networks and their affiliate stations necessarily have an impact on local broadcasting.[10] In more recent years, the doctrine has been used to give the FCC some limited jurisdiction over cable television,[11] even before Congress passed its first piece of legislation specifically governing that industry.

---

[9]*FRC v. Nelson Brothers,* 289 U.S. 266 (1933).

[10]*NBC v. FCC,* 319 U.S. 190 (1943).

[11]*United States v. Southwestern Cable Company,* 392 U.S. 157 (1968).

# Things to Remember

## FCC STRUCTURE AND POWERS

- The FCC has five commissioners, appointed by the president with consent of the Senate, no more than three of whom may be of the same political party; they serve for staggered five-year terms.
- The FCC is empowered to enforce existing regulations as well as to promulgate new regulations consistent with federal law.
- To punish stations found in violation of relevant regulations, the FCC is empowered to employ any of several sanctions, including the rarely invoked revocation of a license.
- The ancillary powers doctrine has been used to extend the Commission's authority to TV and radio networks, cable systems, and small stations with wholly *intra*state signals.

## Why Treat Broadcast and Print Media Differently?

A whole host of laws and regulations govern the broadcast media that would be clearly unconstitutional as applied to newspapers, books, magazines, or other print media. Some of these rules determine who may own a station license, others impose highly specific restrictions on message content. Over the years, several rationales have been offered in support of the differential treatment of print and broadcast media. The chief rationale has always been, as seen in the earlier discussion of the Radio Act of 1927, Congress's assertion that the airwaves belong to the public. There have been other reasons offered as well. We look here at three of them: spectrum scarcity, pervasiveness, and accessibility to children.

### Spectrum Scarcity

As we have already seen, spectrum scarcity forced the government to regulate radio broadcasting from the very beginning of the industry. It makes no sense to speak of a "right" to a broadcast license when there are not enough to go around.[12]

The spectrum scarcity argument is not without its critics. Many argue that the government creates, or at least exacerbates, the scarcity by *giving away* licenses worth tens or even hundreds of millions of dollars. If scarcity is determined by the ratio of the supply of and demand for a product, the giving away of licenses does much to increase the demand. In recent years, Congress has instructed the FCC to experiment with the use of auctions, rather than government giveaways, to distribute new kinds of licenses. The Commission raised tens of billions of dollars in the 1990s, auctioning off licenses to use portions of the spectrum for personal communication systems and other wireless telephone and radio services.

Clearly the government can affect demand for spectrum by selling rather than giving away licenses. The supply side of the equation is also at least somewhat in the government's control. Reassignment to the private broadcasting domain of a single UHF frequency now reserved by the government for other uses, for example, can create well over a hundred new radio stations in any given market. Some researchers in the field of wireless, "spread spectrum" engineering posit that it may soon be possible for many users to "share the same slice of spectrum without interfering with one another."[13] The FCC itself, although still accepting the notion that there is not enough room on the spectrum for all who want a broadcast license to have one, has in recent years downplayed the significance of that reality. We should examine the issue from the consumer's perspective, the Commission contends. Whereas most television viewers had a choice among only three

---

[12]*Red Lion Broadcasting v. FCC*, 395 U.S. 367, 388–89 (1969).

[13]Yochai Benkler and Lawrence Lessig, "Net Gains," *New Republic*, 14 Dec. 1998, p. 12.

or four stations a few decades ago, the advent of cable and satellite options has increased that number to dozens, even hundreds.[14]

## Pervasiveness

Long before there was "Web surfing," we spoke of "channel surfing." The phrase is a handy way of emphasizing that TV viewers often do not have a specific program in mind when they turn on the set. They are settling in to "watch TV" itself. We bring TV sets and radios into our homes and elsewhere and have little control over what kinds of messages might then be transmitted to us. For these reasons and more, broadcast media are often described as pervasive.[15] (Some critics have suggested that "intrusive" would have been a more appropriate word to express the government's real concerns.)

Viewers change channels so often that even well-intentioned disclaimers to the effect that a specific program might be offensive or upsetting may be ineffectual. To be sure, TVs and radios are all equipped with tuners and on–off switches, and the argument is often made that they are the best defense against offensive messages. As Justice Stevens once wrote, however, this argument "is like saying that the remedy for an assault is to run away after the first blow."[16]

Thus, a second reason often offered for an extra dose of regulation applied to the broadcast media is that they intrude on our homes and our psyches more efficiently and insistently than do the print media. (After all, we tend to select a specific book from the shelf; we don't close our eyes and select at random.)

## Protecting the Children

Closely related to the pervasiveness rationale is the concern that the broadcast media are especially accessible (and therefore dangerous) to children. If we think in terms of young, preliterate children, the broadcast media necessarily have an impact on this audience that print cannot. That is one reason why we try to use TV as a way of building prosocial values in youngsters or to help teach them to read. Indeed, from the FCC's perspective, these functions are defining characteristics of "children's programming." Yet we often seek to regulate the electronic media precisely because of the harm we believe they can do to children. When we express concerns about the level of violence or sexual banter on TV, it is this programming's posited effect on children that most irks us. As we shall see, the FCC's definition of "broadcast indecency" includes a reference to the likelihood that there are large numbers of children in the audience. Moreover, the hard-fought compromise over how to regulate broadcast indecency, the creation of a "safe harbor" for such programming late at night and early in the morning, was settled on with children in mind.

---

[14]*FCC v. League of Women Voters of California,* 468 U.S. 364, 376 (1984); *Syracuse Peace Council v. WTVH,* 867 F.2d 654 (D.C. Cir. 1989).

[15]*WUHY-FM,* 24 F.C.C.2d 408, 411 (1970).

[16]*FCC v. Pacifica Foundation,* 438 U.S. 726, 748–49 (1978).

# Things to Remember

## Broadcast Regulations: Licensure and Ownership

Certainly the most fundamental difference between communication law as applied to the print and broadcast media is that one needs to have a federal *license* to engage in broadcasting. The requirements for licensure discussed below may seem commonsense and unremarkable; consider, however, how odd it would seem if the same criteria were applied to the print media. Indeed, application of almost any of these criteria to publishers of books, magazines, and newspapers would seem very reminiscent of the old British system of monopolistic licensing with consent of the Crown.

### Requirements for Licensure

Licensees must be "of good character," which in recent years has generally meant only that they not be convicted felons, nor have a history of lying in previous dealings with the FCC.

Applicants for a broadcast license must also be citizens of the United States. A corporate applicant may qualify if at least 75 percent of its assets are American-owned. This latter rule was waived by the FCC to permit Rupert Murdoch's "News Corporation" (an Australian company) to retain licenses for several TV stations that formed the core of the Fox network.

Broadcast license applicants must have, or be able to hire people who have, the requisite engineering skills to run such a complicated operation. The applicant must also demonstrate sufficient financial resources so as to remain in business for three months even without one penny of advertising revenue coming in. It used to be that applicants had to pledge that they would not try to sell the station for at least three years. This "antitrafficking" rule, designed to discourage speculation on stations and to encourage owners committed to making the stations succeed in the long term, was rescinded by the Commission in the early 1980s.

### How Much Can You Own?

The age of deregulation that began in the early 1980s has all but eliminated limits on the total amount of stations that any one individual or company may own. For several decades, a combination of legislation and FCC regulation set ceilings on the total number of licenses a chain may own at seven AM, seven FM, and seven TV stations; in 1984, the FCC raised the ceiling to twelve stations in each category, and in the early 1990s, the limits were raised once more. The Telecommunications Act of 1996 eliminated all limits on the number of radio stations one chain can own. It provided also that a single entity can own as many TV stations as it likes as long as the totality of those stations' reach does not exceed 35 percent of America's TV households; the 35 percent rule was suspended in April 2001, as part of pending litigation. The same Act also eliminated several cross-media ownership rules. Thus, in the top fifty U.S. media markets, a single company may now own both a TV and a radio station. Broadcast stations may now own cable systems, and vice versa, even within the same service area. Cable TV systems can now provide telephone service, and telephone companies can now go into the cable business. (These latter provisions sometimes have resulted in mergers rather than in head-to-head competition.)

Section 11 of the Telecommunications Act of 1996 instructs the FCC to conduct a biennial review, beginning in 1998 and in every even-numbered year thereafter, of all its regulations restricting station ownership and to propose the elimination of any rule deemed no longer effective or necessary in an era of convergence and increased competition. The Commission need not wait for the biennial report to enact deregulations. In August 1999, for example, the FCC made it much easier for companies to own more than one TV station in a community by liberalizing the "TV duopoly rule." At the same time, the Commission also relaxed cross-ownership rules, thus permitting a company to own not only one or two TV stations, but also up to six radio stations, all in the same market. The Commission's year 2000 report proposed only modest additional changes, such as in relaxing its opposition to having a single company to own both an established major TV network (ABC, CBS, NBC, or Fox) and an emerging network (such as Warner Brothers' WBTN or Universal Studios' UPN); the rule was eliminated in 2001.

In part out of concern that the relaxation of so many of its ownership rules would lead to increased concentration of media holdings—and a decrease in minority voices—the FCC created a plan, in 1999, to create new, low-power FM radio licenses for nonprofit groups. These new stations would be powered by transmitters of no more than 100 watts, with a resulting broadcast radius of about three or four miles. The National Association of Broadcasters and other groups lobbied fiercely against the FCC, and in late 2000 Congress enacted legislation requiring that the process of granting low power licenses be much slower than the Commission had hoped.

In 1995, the FCC rescinded rules governing the major TV networks' freedom to own their own programming. The syndication and financial interest rules ("syn-fin") were adopted in 1970, when ABC, CBS, and NBC collectively commanded well more than 90 percent of the American viewing audience, thus fueling the

FCC's fears that they could effectively prevent independent producers from getting their work on the air. The twenty-five years in which the rules were in force were characterized by a huge diminution of the three networks' dominance, the growth of cable TV, as well as the Fox network's emergence. Although the demise of the syn-fin rules has not necessarily led to dramatic changes in network fare discernible to the average viewer, this particular deregulation was a huge shot in the arm for the networks. Suddenly the networks could continue to derive profits from their most popular programs, even after they went into syndication reruns. The anticipated change in the rules was the major impetus for the Disney company to purchase Capital Cities/ABC, thus enabling one company to derive profits from their products' entire life span.

### Preferences for Minority Ownership

One additional issue related to ownership and licensure is the long and complicated matter of minority hiring and preferences. For many years, one of the criteria the FCC has examined at license renewal time was the management's tangible commitment to equal employment and affirmative action principles. Licensees filled out Form 396, which asks for, among other things, a list of women's and minority organizations contacted when jobs were vacant as well as the ratio of new hires and promotions that had gone to women and to minority group members in the past year. In 1998, however, the D.C. Circuit Court of Appeals found the Commission's equal employment regulations unconstitutional.[17] In response, the commission adopted new rules in January 2000; the FCC would no longer examine stations' tangible progress in achieving a diverse work force. Instead, licensees in their role as employers would be required only to "reach out in recruiting

---

[17]*Lutheran Church, Missouri Synod v. FCC,* 141 F.3d 344, 350 (D.C. Cir. 1998), *request for reh'g en banc denied,* 154 F.3d 494 (D.C. Cir. 1998).

# Things to Remember

## LINCENSURE AND OWNERSHIP ISSUES

- Basic requirements for obtaining a broadcast license include U.S. citizenship, "good character," technical expertise, and financial solvency.

- Limits on the number of TV and radio stations any one person or company can own have been virtually eliminated; moreover, the FCC must make biennial reports to Congress concerning which of the remaining rules can be eliminated.

- The FCC's current affirmative action policy requires only that broadcast licensees widely publicize job openings.

new employees beyond the confines of their business and social contacts."[18] A few months later, even these more modest rules, which stations could have satisfied by such practices as participating in job fairs likely to attract female and minority participants, were struck down by the same court.[19]

Over the years, judicial review of the FCC's affirmative action plans has not always produced consistent results.[20] It is safe to say, however, that the Commission will have a very difficult time justifying affirmative action guidelines requiring specific hiring results, especially if the agency's only rationale is to "enhance diversity" on the air.[21]

## Broadcast Regulations: Consumers and Technology

The FCC, sometimes in direct response to a specific congressional mandate, at other times on its own initiative, has frequently taken steps to improve the technological aspects of broadcasting. Clearly technological considerations are always part of the licensing process. The management of a radio station with a history of engineering glitches that result in extended periods of "dead air" will find that history counted against it at license renewal time. We can also identify times in the history of broadcasting when the FCC has stepped in to bring the entire industry up to a higher standard. For example, over a period of more than twenty years—pursuant to the 1962 All Channel Receiver Act[22]—the Commission promulgated rules requiring that TV sets be able to receive UHF stations as conveniently as they did VHF stations.[23] Two noteworthy ongoing examples of FCC regulations governing technical broadcast standards are digital, high-definition television and signal accessibility for persons with hearing or visual impairments.

### The Switch to HDTV

After many years of internal debates about competing formats, the federal government in 1997 embarked on a long-term commitment to bring the U.S. system of TV transmission into the digital age. Existing TV license holders were granted

---

[18]Report and Order, Review of the Commission's Broadcast and Cable Equal Employment Opportunity Rules and Policies, FCC 00-20, Mass Media Bureau Docket #98-204 (20 Jan. 2000).

[19]*MD/DC/DE Broadcasters Association v. FCC,* 236 F.3d 13 (D.C. Cir. 2001).

[20]*Metro Broadcasting v. FCC,* 497 U.S. 547 (1990); *Lamprecht v. FCC,* 958 F.2d 382 (D.C. 1992); *Adarand v. Pena,* 515 U.S. 200 (1995).

[21]*Hopwood v. State of Texas,* 236 F.3d 256 (5th Cir. 2001).

[22]47 U.S.C. sec. 303 (s).

[23]TV Broadcast Receivers, 47 C.F.R. 15.117; Improvements to UHF Television Reception, 47 C.F.R. Parts 15, 73, and 74 [Gen. Docket No. 78-391; F.C.C. 82-333], 47 F.R. 35975, 18 Aug. 1982.

a second frequency, gratis, with which to start making the transition to high-definition television (HDTV). The plan calls for stations to complete making the switch from analog to digital broadcasting in 2006. Consumers have already purchased a few hundred thousand digital TV receivers—at prices often reaching well over $10,000—and stations in larger and mid-sized markets nationwide have begun doing at least some digital broadcasting.

The analog system of TV broadcasting involves the repeated scanning of 525 horizontal lines of data across the screen; digital systems will scan up to 1,080 lines. Whereas current technology uses about 250,000 pixels (the individual dots that make up the TV screen picture), digital systems will entail as many as 2 million. The picture's height-to-width "aspect ratio" will also change and will become much more similar to that seen in movie theaters. The difference in picture clarity is, by most accounts, quite dramatic. After seeing a digital version of the Disney film *101 Dalmatians,* one critic quipped that "you could see the spots on those dogs in almost as much detail as if you were trying to kidnap them yourself."[24]

The government has come under much criticism for doling out the digital licenses for free, a giveaway worth tens of billions of dollars. It is nonetheless true that TV networks and individual stations will incur major expenses in switching to digital technology. Some estimates range over $10 billion when all the costs of new cameras, antennas, and editing equipment are considered. Converting archival films and videos into digital format can also be quite costly, as much as $100,000 for a feature-length film. Early experiments with this new technology have persuaded TV executives that they also must accept the cost of modernizing their sets so as to adjust to HDTV's unforgiving lens. In the digital age, the cardboard set with a mahogany veneer will "read" as cardboard, not as mahogany.

Many industry insiders have quietly expressed skepticism about the FCC's expectation that the switch to digital transmissions will be complete by 2006. It took longer for color TV to catch on when it was introduced in the 1950s. There is a kind of chicken-and-egg problem in the diffusion of technologies such as HDTV. The average consumer is unlikely to purchase a digital receiver until a high ratio of broadcast programs are transmitted digitally. Yet individual stations are likely to stall on the enormous investment needed to make the switch until they can be assured that there are sufficient viewers out there to justify the expense and to foster optimism about increased advertising rates. Bruce Leichtman, a media analyst for the Yankee Group, offers a sense of perspective. "Don't forget," he says, "we were under government mandate to switch to the metric system in the 1980s."[25]

---

[24]Stephanie McKinnon, "Ready or Not," *Sacramento Bee,* 3 Nov. 1998, p. C1.

[25]Charles Haddad, "Industry Executives Are Crowing over Digital TV, but When Will the Rest of Us Start to Care?" *Atlanta Constitution,* 18 Apr. 1999, p. 1P.

### Accessibility to Audio and Video Signals

Millions of Ame.icans have limited visual or auditory acuity. They may have been born deaf or hard-of-hearing or blind, or they may have lost some of their sense modalities with age. In recent years, Congress has intervened to ensure that television programming be as accessible as practicable to all.

*Closed Captioning.*    Deaf comic Kathy Buckley has a favorite tale about being approached by a hearing fan at a social function. "You know, Ms. Buckley," the fan says, "there is something I have always been curious about. My newspaper's TV section uses the code CC to tell me that a program is 'close captioned for the hearing impaired.' I have always wanted to see what this captioning stuff is all about, so I would start to watch the program, and…nothing. No captioning. I would adjust the fine-tuner as best I can, and still nothing. What gives?" Buckley leans close to the questioner's ear and whispers, "That's easy to explain. Only Deaf people can see captions."

It is an old joke, likely no longer part of Buckley's act. The joke's premise only makes sense in a world predating passage of the Television Decoding Circuitry Act (TDCA) of 1990,[26] which mandated that, as of July 1, 1993, all TV sets with thirteen-inch or larger screens would have to be capable of receiving closed captioning signals. Thus, most Americans now have at least one such TV receiver in their homes, and closed captioning is no longer the exotic commodity that it once was.

Prior to the TDCA's effective date, the only way to receive closed captioning was to hook a TV set up to a separately purchased decoding device. The decoding devices themselves were not always available, of course. For much of broadcasting's history, deaf and hard-of-hearing viewers were often left to guess. For example, on November 22, 1963, deaf viewers would have only seen the words "CBS News Bulletin" on their screens for the better part of a minute, while the rest of America heard the audio portion, telling of JFK's assassination.

The goal of closed captioning is to permit viewers to obtain through visual input information that might otherwise not be available to them. Although the most obvious market for such a service is persons who are deaf and hard of hearing, the technology can also benefit other identifiable groups, such as children learning to read and adults learning English as a second language.[27] The number of persons in the United States who can thus benefit from the increased use of closed captioning numbers in the tens of millions. While the amount of closed captioning has increased dramatically since the technology's emergence in the 1970s, universal service has proven an elusive goal. As of 1997, approximately 75 percent of programming on the three major networks was captioned (including

---

[26] 47 U.S.C.S. sec. 303(v).

[27] Senate Committee on Commerce, Science and Transportation, Hearing on S. 1822, the Communications Act of 1994, p. 614 [Testimony of Mark L. Goldfarb].

100 percent of prime-time programming and 100 percent of "children's" programming). Only 4 percent of all programs aired on the top twenty-five basic cable networks was captioned, however.

It is fair to say that the FCC has not always been an aggressive advocate for captioning. In 1970, the FCC first began to urge broadcast license holders to take the needs of their deaf viewers into account, but this admonition was rather weakly worded, emphasizing that the Commission did not intend to adopt any "definite rules" and that its action was "advisory in nature."[28] Even when broadcast licensees were still required to conduct formal "ascertainment" meetings with community leaders to determine local programming needs, the Commission never required that the deaf community be specifically consulted.[29] The most the Commission had ever explicitly required is that emergency broadcasts be made accessible to the deaf.[30]

A small number of individuals and associations have tried over the years to compel the FCC to require universal closed captioning more explicitly,[31] under two overlapping theories. First, litigants have asserted that a failure to caption constituted violation of the Federal Communication Act's global requirement that licensees function in the "public interest, convenience and necessity." The courts have uniformly rejected this argument, deferring to the FCC's authority.[32]

The second theory was based on the Rehabilitation Act of 1973, as amended in 1978, which provides that "no otherwise qualified individual with handicaps... shall, solely by reason of his handicap, be excluded from participation in, be denied the benefits of, or be subjected to discrimination under any program or activity receiving federal financial assistance."[33] Because broadcast licensees surely are entities that "receive federal financial assistance," litigants argued that the degree to which a licensee has provided closed captioning should be taken into account at license renewal time.

Here, too, the courts have rejected deaf litigants' arguments. "Whatever obligation to caption programs broadcasters may have under Section 504 of the Rehabilitation Act," the D.C. Circuit ruled in 1988, "it is settled that the FCC is not responsible for enforcing it through its licensing procedures."[34] Deaf litigants did

---

[28]*The Use of Telecasts to Inform and Alert Viewers with Impaired Hearing,* 26 F.C.C.2d 917 (1970).

[29]*Amendment of the Primer on Ascertainment of Community Problems by Broadcast Renewal Applicants in Regard to the Community Local Leader Survey,* Docket #78-237, F.C.C. 80-134 (released 4 Apr. 1980).

[30]*Amendment of Part 73 of the Rules to Establish Requirements for Captioning of Emergency Messages on Television,* Docket #20659, 61 F.C.C.2d 18 (1976), *reconsideration denied,* 62 F.C.C.2d 565 (1977).

[31]*Gottfried v. FCC,* 655 F.2d 297 (Cir. 2 1981), *rev'd in part sub nom. Community Television of Southern California v. Gottfried,* 459 U.S. 498 (1983).

[32]*California Association of the Physically Handicapped v. FCC,* 840 F.2d 88 (D.C. Cir. 1988).

[33]29 U.S.C.A. 794 (West Supp. 1987).

[34]*California Association of the Physically Handicapped vs. FCC,* 840 F.2d 88, 92 (D.C. Cir. 1988).

receive some consolation in the form of a ruling by the Department of Education requiring public broadcasting stations to transmit with closed captioning those programs provided in that format by the Department itself.

The situation changed dramatically with passage of the Telecommunications Act of 1996, Section 713 of which instructed the FCC to conduct a study of the current level of closed captioning and to "prescribe such regulations as are necessary" to increase that level dramatically. After following the usual procedure of issuing an NPRM and gathering comments, the Commission, in September 1997 issued an order,[35] amended the next year.[36] The Final Order envisions an eight-year phase-in from 1998 to 2006 toward 100 percent captioning of new programming, whether delivered on broadcast TV, cable systems, or direct broadcast satellite systems. A slightly longer phase-in would be applied to repeat showings of older programs that had not been captioned as well as to programming whose audio track is in Spanish rather than English.

Some categories of programming would be permanently exempted from the captioning requirement. Included among the exemptions are such commonsense categories as primarily textual programs (e.g., community bulletin boards) and programs consisting mostly of instrumental music. Advertisements are also exempted, as are "interstitial announcement" (e.g., "How did the city council vote go? News at 11"). Programs airing only between 2 A.M. and 6 A.M. need not be captioned, nor do locally produced and distributed nonnews programming with limited repeat value (such as local parades, local high school or nonprofessional sports, or community theater productions.)

Exemptions would also apply to TV channels or networks that are very new (no captioning required in the first four years of operation) or very poor (less than $3 million in annual revenue, or where captioning would eat up more than 2 percent of the station's revenues). On an ad hoc basis, programmers would also be free to submit to the Commission evidence that application of the captioning requirement would constitute an "undue" burden or expense for them.

***Video Descriptions.***    It is one of the most famous scenes from contemporary American cinema: Young Elliott Taylor (played by Henry Thomas) befriends the creature we will all soon know as "E.T." The scene lasts for almost five minutes. The audio is limited to some pleasant but mysterious background music, a bit of breathing and chewing, the sound of something crashing to the floor and of a door slamming, and only one word spoken: Elliott's barely whispered "Wow!" In other words, if you were a blind child encountering the Spielberg film for the first time, you would have no idea what was going on.

Enter now the power of video description, the artistically complex method of adding a second audio track, a voice describing the action, to TV programs as

---

[35]*Closed Captioning of Video Programming,* F.C.C. 62 F.R. 48487 (16 Sept. 1997).

[36]*Closed Captioning of Video Programming,* F.C.C. 63 F.R. 55959 (20 Oct. 1998)

well as to films, whether on the big screen or in home video format. WGBH-TV in Boston has been a pioneer in this area, with its trademarked Descriptive Video Service (DVS). Figure 12.1 provides a hint of what blind viewers would learn about Elliott's encounter with E.T. from the DVS version of the film.

Consider another example from the highest grossing film yet, James Cameron's *Titanic*. Jack Dawson (Leonardo DiCaprio) first meets Rose Calvert (Kate Winslet) when the latter is preparing to hurl herself overboard. Visually impaired moviegoers will not know about her plans, however; almost all they will have heard is a minute or so of running accompanied by sobbing and heavy breathing. Figure 12.2 shows how a video description service called TheatreVision fills in the gaps.[37]

As can be appreciated from the video description texts from *E.T.* and *Titanic*, legislation placing on broadcasters the same kinds of demands for the service that the Commission has imposed for closed captioning would likely be subtitled something along the lines of "The English Majors' Full Employment Act."[38] The Telecommunications Act of 1996, however, required only that the FCC "commence an inquiry" as to the extent of available programming with video descriptions. The Act does not prescribe the closing date for any such inquiry, nor

---

[37]The service is the creation of Helen Harris, President of RP International, the leading nonprofit organization in the United States fighting retinitis pigmentosa and other blinding, degenerative eye diseases.

[38]Alderson Reporting Company, Transcript of the 16 Jan. 1998, Meeting of the Advisory Committee on Public Interest Obligations of Digital Television Broadcasters, p. 130 (Peggy Charren of Action for Children's Television).

 **Figure 12.1** *Video Description from* E.T.

Elliott stands at the top of the staircase on the second floor. Holding a bag of candy in one hand, he drops a pile of Reese's Pieces onto the carpeted landing. He backs away to the door of his room, crouches on the floor, and keeps his eyes locked on the candy. The alien's long, pencil-thin fingers reach over the top of the stairs to pick up one of the pieces.... A faint smile spreads across Elliott's mouth.

The alien grabs the rest of the candy, leaving one piece behind. He steps onto the landing to get it. Elliott dumps more Reese's Pieces in the doorway of his room. The alien eagerly reaches for them, and scoops them into his hands....

As the creature stands in the light, we see him clearly for the first time. He has wrinkly, light-brown skin, his stubby torso rests on squat, inch-high legs connected to his webbed feet. Completely bald, he has a broad face, shaped like a squashed heart, with a button nose and great big blue eyes....

**Figure 12.2** *TheatreVision Description from* **Titanic**

Rose leaves the table abruptly and runs wildly down the deck, knocking passengers aside in her distress. Jack lies on a bench on the poop deck, smoking a cigarette and gazing at the stars. He sits up and watches as Rose races past him, only a few yards away.

Nearing the stern of the ship, Rose stops, her face wet with tears, her dark auburn hair falling about her shoulders. She looks behind her, then slowly approaches the railing. She reaches out and places her hands on the stern railing and steps up. Then, using a flagpole for support, she climbs over the rail and stands on the outside of it, facing the sea. In anguish she looks out and stares down into the churning, black water.

*TheatreVision™ © 1998 Helen Harris (creator and producer). Reprinted with permission.*

does it indicate what, if any, regulations should emerge from such an inquiry. In November 1999, the FCC issued an NPRM that would require network-affiliated TV stations in the top markets to broadcast approximately four hours weekly of described programming.

For several reasons, Congress and the FCC treat video descriptions and closed captioning differently. Compared with captioning, creating descriptions is a laborious process. As a general rule, it requires dozens of hours of highly skilled staff time to encode video descriptions on a one-hour television program. It is also a very creative process. To the extent that the goal of closed captioning is production of a verbatim version of spoken dialogue, its creation is a relatively mindless process. Clearly there are some creative elements involved—when and how background music sounds should be characterized, or whether a character's ethnic accent or sarcastic intent should be mentioned—but the bulk of the input is taken directly from the spoken dialogue. By contrast, virtually every word input into a DVS or TheatreVision script requires highly artistic decisions. Should a sunset be described as "beautiful and inspiring" or as "crimson and gold"?

To receive the video description track, home viewers must have a special kind of stereo TV or VCR equipped to receive the secondary audio program (SAP) channel. Interestingly, because the SAP technology was created with second language audio tracks in mind, even most stereo televisions and VCRs do not permit one to listen to both tracks, the "normal" audio output on one speaker and the description audio on the other, simultaneously. This setup makes perfect sense for a second language feature. If you wanted to listen to the Spanish audio track, you would find the English text a distraction. A DVS audio must therefore include both the "normal" dialogue and background noises plus the added descriptive video. The hourly cost of producing video descriptions is therefore much more expensive than that of producing closed captions for the deaf. Then, too, Congress recognized that the diffusion of digital, HDTV technology will increase the number of audio channels on television transmissions from two to four, thus eliminating the need to choose between video descriptions and a Spanish language audio track. It thus made sense to delay rule making until HDTV is the prevalent mode of television reception in the United States.

Retrofitting of broadcast transmission hardware for DVS also is very expensive, typically between $1 million and $2 million per station. (The combined cost of hardware and software for closed captioning transmissions is only a tiny fraction of this amount.) From the station manager's perspective, such an investment would not make much sense, especially given that the hardware would be obsolete after the nationwide transformation to HDTV is complete.

First Amendment considerations constitute yet another reason for an added measure of caution in drafting rules making DVS mandatory. In Chapter 2, we saw that the Supreme Court has interpreted the Free Speech Clause so as to include a corollary right *not* to speak. Suppose that a broadcast licensee, sometime after the 2006 deadline for 100 percent closed captioning, protests an FCC sanction for failure to meet that standard. A constitutional claim would likely not succeed. The station is only forced to "speak" words it already intended to utter via its audio track. By contrast, a licensee sanctioned for failure to offer enough DVS programming might very well succeed in invoking the "right not to speak." The words in a DVS script, after all, are created solely for that script. No character on or off screen has uttered them. Although the government would not be prescribing a specific

 # Things to Remember

**TECHNOLOGY AND ACCESS ISSUES**

■ In 1997, the federal government gave a second frequency to existing TV stations to be used to provide digital, high-definition television service no later than 2006. The multibillion dollar giveaway was much criticized.

■ The Television Decoding Circuitry Act of 1990 mandated that televisions larger than thirteen inches would have to be capable of reading closed captioning.

■ Attempts to litigate in support of universal closed captioning of programming have been unsuccessful, but the Telecommunications Act of 1996 instructs the FCC to create rules that will result in full captioning on broadcast and cable TV. The Commission issued an order in 1999 requiring full captioning (with a few exceptions) by 2006.

■ With respect to video descriptions for the blind, the 1996 Act requires only that the FCC study the issue. The Commission has proposed rules imposing modest requirements on some television stations.

message—a characteristic of most of the Supreme Court's case law establishing the right not to speak[39]—compulsory DVS would seem to force a screenwriter to become a novelist, and this fact alone may carry some weight with the Court.

# Broadcast Regulations: Content

Section 326 of the Federal Communications Act reads: "Nothing in this Act shall be understood or construed to give the [FCC] the power of censorship over the radio communications or signals transmitted by any radio station, and no regulation or condition shall be promulgated or fixed by the Commission which shall interfere with the right of free speech by means of radio communication."

The phrase "no regulation or condition" is very reminiscent of the First Amendment's admonition that Congress shall pass "no law abridging…freedom of speech." Yet if that latter admonition were interpreted literally, this book would have been much shorter. Similarly, both Congress and the FCC frequently legislate and regulate the actual content of media messages. In this section, we look at several categories of restrictions on broadcast media content. Included are regulation of political speech and of sexually oriented speech, children's programming, the V chip as an answer to TV violence, special regulations applied to PBS and NPR stations, and some other miscellaneous content regulations.

### Regulation of Political Speech

Two broad categories of regulations governing broadcasting of political speech can be identified. First are those regulations that apply only when an electoral campaign is under way. Chief among these are the Candidate Access Rule and the Equal Time Rule. There are also regulations concerning political speech in general, although most of these have been rescinded in recent years.

***The Candidate Access Rule.*** Section 312(a) of the Federal Communications Act authorizes the FCC to revoke the license from any TV or radio station that fails to "allow reasonable access to or to permit purchase of reasonable amounts of time…by a legally qualified candidate for Federal elective office on behalf of his candidacy." Section 312 further dictates that, as an election grows near, stations must charge candidates the very lowest rates they make available to their best commercial customers. Although the Act refers only to candidates for *federal* office, station managers understand that an absolute refusal to sell ads to candidates for state and local offices would be seen by the FCC as an abrogation of their overall obligation to broadcast "in the public interest."

---

[39]*Wooley v. Maynard,* 430 U.S. 705 (1977); *West Virginia Board of Education v. Barnette,* 319 U.S. 624 (1943).

The Candidate Access Rule does not indicate its own triggering mechanism; when, exactly, has a campaign begun? In 1981, however, the Supreme Court offered some guidance. The impetus for the decision was the Carter-Mondale campaign's request to purchase a thirty-minute spot on all three major networks in December 1979. None of the networks agreed to the specific request; the campaign complained to the FCC and ultimately obtained a 6–3 victory in the Supreme Court. Chief Justice Warren Burger's majority opinion indicates that the 1980 presidential campaign was in full swing at the time the Carter-Mondale campaign sought airtime. More than a dozen candidates had formally announced their status. Both major parties had already begun the process of convention delegate selection. Moreover, the Iowa caucuses were scheduled for barely a month away.

Look again at the precise wording of Section 312. It requires stations to "allow reasonable access to" airtime *or* "to permit purchase of..." airtime. Does this mean that a willingness to sell airtime precludes any responsibility to cover a candidate's campaign in other ways? Does "reasonable access" mean turning one's studio over to candidates for their own use, unedited by station management, unquestioned by the station's reporters? Or, can such access mean simply covering the candidate's activities during the course of the campaign? That same 1980 presidential race resulted in two separate federal appellate decisions, both flowing from complaints lodged with the FCC by Senator Edward Kennedy, who was then challenging President Carter for the Democratic Party's nomination.[40] In February and March 1980, President Carter's carefully timed press conferences and speeches were carried in their entirety by all three networks. Kennedy, pointing out that one of the press conferences took place on the eve of the New Hampshire primary and was very much in keeping with what pundits called Carter's "Rose Garden" strategy of looking as presidential as possible and not "lowering himself" to campaign for reelection, requested that a similar parcel of time be *given* to his campaign. The networks refused, the FCC upheld the networks' decision, and the D.C. Circuit Court of Appeals supported the FCC. Writing for the three-judge panel, Judge Robinson concluded that Section 312 was never intended to require TV stations to *give* their airtime to candidates. The law is written with the disjunctive "or" so that stations can meet their obligations by selling airtime. Because Kennedy never even asked to buy time, he was not in a position to demand that free time be given him. Although Judge Robinson did *not* suggest that a station could point to its own news coverage of a candidate as a substitute for meeting its Section 312 obligations, he emphasized that Kennedy's campaign was hardly being ignored by the major networks: "CBS had televised Senator Kennedy's response to the press conference on its news programs, PBS had invited him to appear on its McNeil/Lehrer Report, and NBC had proposed an appearance on its *'Today'* program on the morning after the conference."

---

[40]*Kennedy v. F.C.C.,* 636 F.2d 432 (D.C. Cir. 1980); *Kennedy for President Committee v. F.C.C.,* 636 F.2d 417 (D.C. Cir. 1980).

***Equal Time Rule.***    Although Section 312 litigation has been sparse, candidates have frequently challenged FCC rulings concerning a station's obligations under Section 315 of the Federal Communications Act. Often referred to as the Equal Time Rule (even though the statutory language is "equal *opportunities*"), Section 315 has been part of the Federal Communications Act since its passage in 1934. Indeed, it was born as Section 18 of the 1927 Radio Act. The essence of the rule is found at 315(a) of the Act: Anytime a "legally qualified candidate for any public office" is permitted to "use" a broadcasting station, the station's owner must "afford equal opportunities to all other such candidates for that office." The rule also prohibits stations from exercising the "power of censorship over the material broadcast under the provisions of this section."

Note two differences between the Equal Time Rule and the Candidate Access Rule discussed earlier. Unlike Section 312, Section 315 applies to candidates for office at all levels of government, from local dog catcher to president of the United States. Also, candidates earn a right to access under Section 315 only if another candidate for the same office has already been permitted to "use" the station's airwaves. That a political campaign has begun is not sufficient to trigger the rule.

What does it mean to be a "legally qualified candidate"? The FCC employs four guidelines. First, the candidate must have publicly announced his or her intention to run for the office. This rule seems straightforward enough, although candidates are often quite coy about whether they are in fact running for office or reelection. The longer they can avoid making the official announcement, the longer they can continue to appear on camera in various capacities without triggering the Equal Time Rule.

Second, the candidate must be legally qualified to hold the particular office. Winning enough votes is a necessary but not sufficient condition to be elected to public office. For example, the president must be a natural-born citizen and must be no younger than thirty-five when assuming office. Anyone who has already served two terms as president can no longer be a legally qualified candidate for that office. Senators must be at least thirty years old, Representatives at least twenty-five; members of both houses must be residents of the districts or states they represent. Similar age and residency requirements, and in some cases term limits, apply to many state and local offices as well.

Third, the candidate must be qualified for a place on the ballot (or as a write-in candidate). In most circumstances, simply announcing that you are a candidate does not earn you a line on the ballot come Election Day. You must file petitions with the appropriate Board of Elections or similar governmental entity, with sufficient numbers of qualified voters' signatures to meet local rules for ballot placement. If the office for which you are running is permitted to have write-in candidacies, you can be a legally qualified candidate for the purposes of Section 315 by meeting whatever qualifications are prerequisite to that status.

Finally, candidates must have been nominated for the office by a recognized political party, or at least must have made a "substantial showing" of their candidacy. Making a "substantial showing" in this context does not necessarily mean that your polling numbers suggest that you have a good chance of winning the race. Rather, this part of the test for determining a candidate's status should be thought of as more of a "looks like a duck, quacks like a duck" yardstick. What kinds of behaviors do candidates generally engage in, the FCC asks itself. They make speeches about political topics, they establish a campaign headquarters (for low-budget candidates vying for minor offices, this might be their own home or the home of a supporter), they distribute campaign literature, they assemble a committee to help them with their campaigns. These are the kinds of behaviors that count as making a "substantial showing."

The Equal Time Rule is triggered when a broadcast station permits a candidate for elected office to use its airwaves. But what does it mean to *use* a station's airwaves? First, the appearance must be a "positive" one, which does not mean that the candidate has to come off well on camera or say clever things. Rather, the rule is intended to exempt such scenarios as when candidate A, in the course of a media appearance, uses the voice or picture of opposing candidate B while criticizing the opponent.

Uses of the airwaves do not have to be for the purpose of delivering political messages at all. Indeed, TV stations had to be careful about showing old Ronald Reagan movies during his political career, at least at election time. Similarly, when in 1994, NBC broadcast the movie *Necessary Roughness,* which included an appearance by lawyer-turned-actor-turned-politician Fred Thompson, it had to give free air time to Democrat Jim Cooper, Thompson's opponent in the Senate race from Tennessee. Cooper was not owed an amount of time equivalent to the entire running time of the film, but only to the time that Thompson appeared on screen: four minutes and thirteen seconds, in this case. The FCC has so ruled in numerous cases. Only if a candidate is in charge of the TV broadcast does "equal time" mean "equivalent to the entire broadcast's length."

Even a tongue-in-cheek candidate's appearances constitute a use. Comedian Pat Paulsen, who made his own mock candidacy a running gag on the *Smothers Brothers Comedy Hour*, continued the joke in the 1972 campaign and actually filed as a candidate for the Republican nomination. A problem emerged, however. He was also to appear as a guest on a decidedly nonpolitical program called *The Mouse Factory,* owned by the Disney company. The FCC ruled that stations airing that episode would indeed incur the usual Section 315 obligations, and a federal appellate court upheld the Commission. The court also rejected Paulsen's argument that the Commission's ruling applied to entertainers as a class denied them the constitution's promise of equal protection under law in that only they would have to choose between running for office and their usual way of making a living.[41]

---

[41]*Paulsen v. FCC,* 491 F.2d 887 (9th Cir. 1974).

Similar claims of unfair treatment were rejected years later when made by a more serious candidate for lesser office. When William Branch, a general assignment reporter for KOVR-TV in Sacramento, decided to run for a seat on the town council of Loomis, California, a community of about 4,000 residents within his station's viewing area, his employer insisted that he take an unpaid leave of absence for the duration of the campaign, with no guarantee of continued employment thereafter. The station management feared that Section 315 would require it to give many hours of free air time to any other candidates for the Loomis Town Council. The FCC, and later the D.C. Court of Appeals, concluded that Section 315 would indeed apply in such a situation and that none of Branch's constitutional rights had been violated.[42]

Courts have generally interpreted the language in Section 315 warning broadcast licensees not to censor "material broadcast under the provisions of this section" as applicable to more than just one candidate's free use of air time to respond to another candidate's triggering "use." Rather, courts assume that the provision applies to all candidate speech during an election campaign, including political ads candidates place on TV and radio stations.[43]

The "no censorship" rule has frequently caused grief for station managers. In 1972, one of the candidates for the Democratic Party's nomination in Georgia, J. B. Stoner, used a campaign ad with as overtly racist a text as one can imagine. "The main reason why niggers want integration" is that they "want our white women," he charged. Stoner further disparaged all his opponents for office as "race mixers," warning that "you cannot have law and order and niggers too." The NAACP, and the mayor of Atlanta, had sought a declaration from the Commission that stations could not be forced to run such an ad, in part because reactions to it could jeopardize public safety. The Commission rejected this argument and added that "a contrary conclusion here would permit anyone to prevent a candidate from exercising his rights under Section 315 by threatening a violent reaction."[44]

In 1980, the Citizens Party ran a radio ad on behalf of its presidential candidate, Barry Commoner, that began with an exasperated male voice shouting "Bullshit!" A female voice seeks clarification, and the man explains: "Carter, Reagan, and Anderson. It's all bullshit!" At this point, Commoner's voice takes over as he laments that he has to use "such strong language" to get anyone's attention. When NBC initially refused to run the ad, Commoner appealed to the FCC, which ruled in his favor.[45]

---

[42]*In re William H. Branch,* 101 F.C.C.2d 901 (1985), *aff'd, Branch v. FCC,* 824 F.2d 37 (D.C. Cir. 1987).

[43]*Hammond for Governor Committee,* 69 F.C.C.2d 946, 947 (Broadcast Bur. 1978).

[44]*Letter to Lonnie King,* 36 F.C.C.2d 635 (1972).

[45]*In re Complaint of Barry Commoner and LaDonna Harris Against NBC Radio, Memorandum Opinion and Order,* 87 F.C.C.2d 1 (1980).

Three years later, publisher-pornographer Larry Flynt was considering running for president, in large part to tweak the system a bit by submitting excerpts from hardcore sex films as part of his campaign ads. A bill was promptly introduced in Congress that would give broadcasters permission to refuse such advertisements, despite the "no censorship" language in Section 315. The FCC indicated that it would not apply Section 315 against broadcasters confronting such a dilemma, a stance the Commission never had to test because Flynt decided not to run.

In the 1990s, several prolife candidates sought to run ads that included highly graphic images of aborted fetuses. The management of WAGA-TV in Atlanta agreed to run such ads from congressional candidate Daniel Becker, but only at times of day when the number of children in the audience would be small. The FCC sided with the station, but the D.C. Circuit Court of Appeals reversed the Commission's decision and held that even such "channeling" of offensive messages to late night hours was a violation of both Section 312(a) and Section 315.[46]

Given that station managers will have little or no control over the content of political advertisements and other candidate messages filling their airwaves, it would seem logical to assume that stations would be immune from legal liability stemming from those messages. In fact, they are, as the Supreme Court made clear as far back as 1959. A. C. Townley, a U.S. Senatorial candidate in North Dakota, invoked Section 315 so as to obtain airtime on WDAY radio, after two other candidates had used the station's airwaves. Townley used his allotted time to accuse his opponents and a local nonprofit organization of trying to "establish a Communist Farmers Union Soviet right here in North Dakota." When the nonprofit sued not only Townley but also WDAY for libel, the federal district judge excused the latter from the litigation, and the Supreme Court upheld this ruling.[47]

This immunity from libel actions applies only to advertisements placed by the candidates themselves. Ads placed by special interest groups, or even by political parties' congressional campaign committees, do not enjoy such immunity. Thus, for example, when the Democratic Congressional Campaign Committee ran ads in the summer of 2000 that distorted the education voting records of Republican candidates in New Jersey and Kentucky, the general counsel for the House Republicans persuaded TV stations to drop the ads lest they face legal liability.

***Statutory Exemptions to the Equal Time Rule.*** In 1959, largely in response to FCC decisions that it saw as applying Equal Time requirements too strictly to a Chicago station,[48] Congress amended Section 315 so as to exempt certain categories of candidate appearances from triggering stations' obligations to opposing

---

[46]*Becker v. FCC,* 95 F.3d 75 (D.C. Cir. 1996).

[47]*Farmers Educational & Cooperative Union of America v. WDAY,* 360 U.S. 525, 530 (1959).

[48]*In the matter of CBS, Inc. (Lars Daly),* 26 F.C.C. 715 (1959).

candidates. The amendments covered candidate appearances on newscasts, news interview programs, documentaries, and on-the-spot coverage of news events. Let us look at each of these in a bit more detail.

The newscast exemption covers not only such obvious kinds of programs as *NBC Nightly News* or *ABC World News Tonight,* but also news "magazines" such as *20/20,* and *Primetime Live,* and *Dateline* as well as the networks' morning news/ variety programs such as *Today* and *Good Morning America.* As part of its responsibility for the day-to-day administration of Section 315, the FCC has also granted an exemption, on a case-by-case basis, to various syndicated talk shows, such as the old *Donahue* show, *Geraldo,* and *Sally Jesse Raphael.*[49] In 1989, the Commission ruled that some of but not all the weekly *McLaughlin Group* was beyond Section 315's reach. The typical *McLaughlin* program consists of a short news clip, often borrowed from another network, followed by a few minutes of discussion about that event by the show's four panelists. This "news clip, then discussion" format is repeated two or more times during the course of the program. The FCC ruled that a candidate appearance on one of the prerecorded news clips was exempt from the Equal Time Rule, but that the same candidate's appearance in the studio, participating in a panel discussion with the small group of journalists, might not be exempt.[50] The D.C. Circuit Court of Appeals upheld the FCC's decision.[51]

News interview programs are exempt if they are regularly scheduled programs rather than ad hoc "meet the candidates" events. Thus, any of the well-known Sunday morning programs on the various networks, from *Meet the Press* to *This Week* and *Face the Nation,* can invite one candidate for office without having to invite all other announced candidates onto that or later editions of the program. If a network or a local station preempted regular programming to interview one candidate for an hour, however, all other bona fide candidates for the same office would be able to make an Equal Time claim.

To be sure, there have been gray areas in application of this general rule; more often than not in recent years, the FCC has sided with the media. For example, a 1992 appearance by independent presidential candidate Ross Perot on ABC's *Nightline* was ruled exempt, even though the show that night ran much longer than usual (ninety minutes instead of thirty) and was preceded by an hour-long documentary about the Perot candidacy. Upholding the FCC's decision, Judge José Cabranes emphasized that the news value of the Perot appearances was clear from polling data at the time suggesting that he might beat both major party candidates (Bill Clinton and President George H. W. Bush).[52]

In 1976, the FCC pointed to a special interaction between the "newscast" and "news interview" exceptions. A Florida TV station that had interviewed President

---

[49]*Multimedia Entertainment, Inc.,* 56 Rad. Reg. 2d (P & F) 143 (1984).

[50]*In re Oliver Productions, Inc.,* 4 F.C.C.R. 5953 (1989).

[51]*Telecommunications Research and Action Center v. FCC,* 26 F.3d 185 (D.C. Cir. 1994).

[52]*Fulani v. FCC,* 49 F.3d 904 (2d Cir. 1995).

Ford broke the interview footage down into six-minute segments, which it aired on consecutive nights as part of its regular evening newscast. When Ronald Reagan, then challenging Ford for the Republican nomination, demanded equal time, the Commission refused. Even though Ford's use of the airwaves would have triggered the Equal Time Rule had the interview been aired as a single program, the editorial decision to include the footage as part of a regular news program made the use exempt from Section 315's coverage.[53]

Documentary programs are exempt from Section 315's provisions only if the candidate's appearance is "incidental" to the subject matter of the program. The candidate cannot *be* the subject matter. The Commission has offered several criteria to help determine whether a candidate appearance is truly "incidental." The program should not have been designed to aid or advance the candidate's campaign. The decision to have the candidate appear in the documentary should have been made on the basis of "bona fide news judgment." Also, the candidate should not have had any control over the format or the production of the broadcast.

The on-the-spot news exemption covers a wide gamut of situations, most of which tend to favor the interests of incumbents seeking reelection. A public official might show up at the scene of a natural disaster or at a ribbon-cutting ceremony for a new shopping center. Both would be news events. So, too, will press briefings and press conferences (although the FCC maintained to the contrary until 1975). Indeed, in the post-CNN era of twenty-four-hour news cycles, the real difference between the newscast and on-the-spot coverage exemptions is whether the candidate arranges an event deemed sufficiently newsworthy for TV cameras not only to attend, but to cover it *live* instead of waiting for the evening news.

The question of when a staged debate between or among political candidates is exempted as an on-the-spot event has been a long and complicated one for the FCC, Congress, and the courts. In 1960, Congress passed special legislation formally suspending Section 315 insofar as it might have prevented the broadcasting of debates between Senator John F. Kennedy and Vice President Richard Nixon, without having to invite every imaginable minor party candidate on the same stage with them. Partly because of Section 315 fears, and partly because the individual candidates in the interim saw no real advantage to them, there were no head-to-head debates between the two major parties' presidential candidates again until the 1976 campaign.

In the interim, the FCC had decided that debates were exempt from Section 315 as long as they were sponsored by an outside group other than the TV networks or the candidates themselves. Further, the debates would have to be covered live, and it must be clear that media decisions whether to air the debates are based on sound news judgment rather than favoritism for any particular candidate.

---

[53]*Citizens for Reagan v. Station WCKT-TV,* 58 F.C.C.2d 925 (1976).

Thus it was that the League of Women Voters sponsored debates between Ford and Carter in 1976, and Carter and Reagan in 1980. If the philosophy undergirding the Commission's outside sponsorship requirement was that the event should be a news event that would be taking place anyway and that the TV networks independently decided to cover, the notion was exposed as a fiction when, during a Ford–Carter debate in Philadelphia, the audio feed to the networks went dead. The live audience in the auditorium could hear just fine; if the event had not been staged for the cameras' benefit, the debate would have continued uninterrupted. That did not happen, of course. The candidates sat or stood, silently, for twenty-seven minutes!

In any event, the FCC lifted its restriction on network sponsorship in 1983.[54] The 1984 debates between Ronald Reagan and Walter Mondale were still sponsored by the League of Women Voters, which, together with the networks and the candidates themselves, was named as defendant in a suit brought by Citizens Party candidate Sonia Johnson. The D.C. Circuit Court of Appeals denied her request for inclusion in the debates, finding "no basis for disturbing" the FCC's judgment.[55]

More recently, rules governing sponsorship of debates were loosened further as the FCC decided that even the candidates themselves may serve as sponsors. The TV stations involved would have to retain ultimate control as to the amount and type of coverage of the debate, in this case between Michael Dukakis and Richard Gephardt, then vying for the 1988 Democratic Party's presidential nomination.[56]

---

[54]*In re Petitions of Henry Geller et al.*, 95 F.C.C.2d 1236 (1983).

[55]*Johnson v. FCC,* 829 F.2d 157 (D.C. Cir. 1987).

[56]*In re Request for Declaratory Ruling by WCVB-TV,* 2 F.C.C.R. 4778 (1987).

## Things to Remember

### BROADCAST REGULATION AND POLITICAL CAMPAIGNS

- The Candidate Access Rule tells stations that they must make their airwaves available to persons running for federal office and that any advertising time they sell to candidates must be charged at the lowest rates available.

- The Equal Time Rule provides that stations who permit one candidate (for *any* elected office) to "use" their airwaves must provide a comparable time slot to all other candidates for the same office. Not all appearances are "uses," however; among the exemptions are appearances on news and news interview programs and on documentaries whose subject matter is something other than the candidate.

- Stations are not permitted to censor candidates' speech, whether on unpaid news programs or on paid advertisements.

***The Fairness Doctrine: Personal Attack and Political Editorial Rules.***　Since at least 1940, the FCC had required that broadcast licensees use at least part of their airtime to cover politically controversial issues in their communities and to make sure that such coverage be even-handed. Together, these two mandates formed the core of the **Fairness Doctrine.** The past tense is used here because the Commission, as part of its deregulations in the 1980s, indicated it would no longer enforce the doctrine.[57] The Commission's own fact-finding had persuaded it that the Doctrine was producing opposite results from those intended. Instead of encouraging robust dialogue about controversial issues, it made broadcasters fearful of dealing in controversy at all. Organized interest groups, the Commission found, would be more likely to complain over an issue having been covered in a way they perceived as unfair than to even notice that an issue had not been covered. The D.C. Circuit Court of Appeals upheld the FCC's decision.[58] Congress did not agree with the FCC, however, and tried to codify the Doctrine as an amendment to the Federal Communications Act. A bill to accomplish that goal passed both houses in 1987, but President Reagan vetoed it.

Two other doctrines with an equally long, parallel history in FCC rule making are the **Personal Attack Rule** and the **Political Editorial Rule.** Technically, these rules were actually part of the Fairness Doctrine, although not the part which the FCC rescinded in the 1980s. In the late 1990s, the Radio and Television News Directors Association and the National Association of Broadcasters sought repeal of the rules. After several preliminary maneuvers by the FCC and the D.C. Circuit Court of Appeals, the Commission was compelled to rescind both rules a few weeks before Election Day 2000.[59] Despite the court's action, a short explication of the two rules is offered here, in part because they were such an important part of broadcast history, but also because earlier litigation upholding the rules gave the Supreme Court a chance to offer some still-very-relevant insights about the status of broadcast regulation in general.

The Personal Attack Rule made several very explicit demands on any TV or radio station whose airwaves were used to attack "the honesty, character, integrity or like personal qualities of an identified person or group." Here is what the licensee had to do:

- Within one week, notify the person or group.
- Give the person(s) a transcript or video/audiotape of the attack.
- Make an offer of free airtime for the person(s) to reply to the attack.

---

[57]*Memorandum Order and Opinion in Syracuse Peace Council,* 2 F.C.C.R. 5043 (1987), *reconsideration denied,* 3 F.C.C.2d 2035 (1988).

[58]*Syracuse Peace Council v. FCC,* 867 F.2d 654 (D.C. Cir. 1989).

[59]*Radio and Television News Directors Association v. Federal Communications Commission,* 229 F.3d 269 (D.C. Cir. 2000).

Among the several exceptions to the rule are the same ones applying to Section 315—that is, attacks that occured in the context of newscasts, news interviews, and on-the-spot coverage of news events did not trigger the rule. The FCC provided two additional exemptions. First, attacks made by one candidate on another candidate did not trigger the rule, nor did attacks made by a candidate's campaign workers upon opposing candidates or *their* workers. Second, only American individuals and groups could seek relief under the rule. The Political Editorial Rule told licensees their obligations if they chose to use their own station to endorse a candidate for office. Within twenty-four hours of any such on-air endorsement, the station had to notify all other candidates for that office, and provide them with a tape or transcript of the endorsement announcement. The other candidates, or a representative of their choosing, had to be given an opportunity to appear in a similar time segment on the station to make a case for their own election.

In 1969, the Supreme Court upheld both the Personal Attack Rule and the Political Editorial Rule against a charge of unconstitutionality. The *Red Lion* decision was really two consolidated cases. One of these was a frontal attack on both rules by the RTNDA. The other case arose from a specific Personal Attack Rule application to WGCB radio in Pennsylvania, owned by the Red Lion Broadcasting Company. Shortly after the 1964 elections, WGCB carried a fifteen-minute broadcast by the Reverend Billy James Hargis, who used part of his program to criticize Fred J. Cook, author of a book critical of unsuccessful presidential candidate Barry Goldwater. Hargis charged that Cook had been fired by a newspaper for making false charges against city officials, that he then went to work for a Communist-affiliated publication, and that his only purpose in writing his book was to "smear and destroy" Goldwater. Cook demanded free reply time from the station, citing the Personal Attack Rule, and was refused (although the station was willing to sell him time). The FCC sided with Cook, as ultimately did the Supreme Court.[60]

Writing for the Court, Justice White pointed out that there was nothing sacred about the manner in which broadcast licenses are handed out, gratis, in the United States. Licensees would be wise not to think of the frequencies under which they operate as *theirs*. The First Amendment would not have been offended, he suggested, had Congress and the FCC decided from the outset that each available frequency must be shared on a rotating basis among all applicants for that particular license. Surely, then, to require the *sole* possessor of such a license to share his airwaves with others under such highly limited circumstances as the Personal Attack and Political Editorial rules demand is also permissible.

Although the two rules at issue in *Red Lion* are no longer in force, Justice White's words serve as a reminder that broadcast licenses are privileges, and with privileges come responsibilities. It is safe to predict that White's point will continue to be cited by later courts trying to determine the scope of those responsibilities.

---

[60]*Red Lion Broadcasting v. FCC*, 395 U.S. 367 (1969).

# Things to Remember

### Regulation of Sexually Oriented Speech

As seen in Chapter 11, the Supreme Court has long held that *obscene* speech is entirely beyond the First Amendment's protection. There are federal laws against interstate commerce in obscenity, using the mails or public transport to ship obscene materials, and importing such materials. It is no surprise, then, that the United States Code also has a provision (Section 1464) forbidding the use of the airwaves to broadcast obscenity. Such a prohibition has been part of our broadcasting system since adoption of the Federal Radio Act of 1927. The current criminal statute provides for punishments up to two years imprisonment and a $10,000 fine. Imposition of these punishments is virtually unheard of. More typical has been the FCC's imposition of token fines, or even lesser sanctions, such as the insertion of negative comments in the file of a station found in violation of Section 1464.

Just as the government is permitted to impose regulations on the political content of messages sent on the public's airwaves that would be clearly unconstitutional if applied to the print media, so, too, have the courts permitted the FCC to impose an added measure of restraint on the broadcasting of even nonobscene sexual messages. Indeed, by its very own language, Section 1464 permits prosecution of stations that broadcast not only obscene speech, but also indecent or profane speech.

The leading Supreme Court case[61] resulted from an FM radio station in New York broadcasting on a Tuesday afternoon in October 1973 a George Carlin routine called "Filthy Words." The monologue might be described as a popular sociolinguistic treatise on the function of sexual language (see Figure 12.3).

The FCC received one complaint about the broadcast, from a father who was taken by surprise while listening to the radio in the car with his son. After investigating, the Commission determined that the station had violated Section 1464's prohibition of indecent broadcasting. The broadcast was not obscene in

---

[61]*FCC v. Pacifica Foundation,* 438 U.S. 726 (1978).

**Figure 12.3**    *Excerpts from George Carlin's "Filthy Words" Monologue*

I was thinking about the curse words and the swear words, the words that you can't say, that you're not supposed to say, the words you couldn't say on the public airwaves.... The original seven words were *shit, piss, fuck, cunt, cocksucker, motherfucker,* and *tits.... Cocksucker* is a compound word and neither half is really dirty. *Sucker*—that's merely suggestive and the word *cock* is a half-way dirty word, 50% dirty, dirty half the time, depending on what you mean by it....

The big one, the word *fuck,* that's the one that hangs them up the most. In a lot of cases that's the very act that hangs them up the most. So, it's natural that the word would have the same effect.... It leads a double life,

the word *fuck.* First of all, it means, to make love, right? And it also means the beginning of life, it's the act that begins life, so there's the word hanging around with words like *love,* and *life,* and yet on the other hand, it's also a word that we really use to hurt each other with. It's a heavy. It's one that you leave toward the end of the argument, right?...

Now the word *twat* is an interesting word, because it's the only slang word applying to the...sexual anatomy that doesn't have another meaning to it. *Snatch, box,* and *pussy* all have other meanings. Even in a Walt Disney movie, you can say, "We're going to snatch that pussy and put him in a box and bring him on the airplane."

© *1973. Reprinted with permission.*

that it was not designed to appeal to "the prurient interest," and it may very well have had "serious literary, artistic, political, or scientific value." The Commission's definition of broadcast indecency, however, did not include these two features of the *Miller* obscenity test (see Chapter 11 for a review of the test). It was enough that the monologue described sexual or excretory functions in a patently offensive way and that children were likely to be listening, especially given the timing of the broadcast.

The Commission's chosen sanction was not to revoke the station's license, nor to fine it, but only to place in its file a letter describing the incident, which presumably would inform the commissioners' deliberations when license renewal time came around. The station's parent association decided to appeal that ruling, an appeal that produced a Supreme Court decision in 1978. Most of but not all Justice Stevens's opinion carried enough votes to be majority doctrine. Stevens emphasized the propriety of regulating broadcast media more strictly than other modes of communication, emphasizing radio's "pervasiveness" (especially its ability to intrude on one's privacy at home) and its accessibility to children, "even those too young to read."

The *Pacifica* decision tells the FCC that it *may* impose sanctions against licensees who broadcast indecent, nonobscene speech; it does not tell the Commission that it must or should do so. Over the decades, both before and since *Pacifica,* it has been very difficult to predict what kinds of programming would be seen by the Commission as indecent. In the early 1970s, the Commission took action against "topless radio," a genre of talk program typically involving a male emcee enticing female callers to discuss their sex lives with listeners.[62]

After the *Pacifica* decision, the Commission's enforcement of indecency restrictions on licensees was virtually nonexistent for a decade or so. Then, in 1987, the FCC imposed sanctions against a handful of licensees, including a station that had broadcast excerpts from a radio play called *Jerker,* then enjoying a critically acclaimed off-Broadway run. The play's theme was a deadly serious one—gay men redefining the meaning of eroticism in the midst of the AIDS epidemic—but its language was a bit too graphic for the airwaves, the Commission concluded.[63] One of the Commission's other 1987 actions was taken against the highly successful Howard Stern radio program.[64] Actually this was one of several cases the FCC brought against Stern's employers, who eventually settled with the Commission in 1995 for a lump-sum payment of approximately $1.7 million.

The 1990s were characterized by an elongated and sometimes almost comic struggle among the FCC, Congress, and the D.C. Circuit of Appeals to determine what, if any, hours in the program day could serve as a "safe harbor," when stations would be permitted to broadcast admittedly indecent programming without incurring the Commission's wrath (presumably because the number of children in the audience would be small). At different times in the debate, it appeared as if there would be either no such harbor or that the entire broadcast day and night would be sanction-free. At one point, it looked as if PBS and NPR stations that go off the air relatively early at night might be permitted to have a longer harbor than other stations. Then, in 1995, the D.C. Circuit, in upholding some but not all of the relevant federal statute, in essence approved a safe harbor for all stations between 10 P.M. and 6 A.M.[65] The Supreme Court refused to hear the case.

It is not entirely clear to what extent government regulations of indecent speech transmitted on cable systems rather than over-the-air broadcast are constitutionally acceptable. There will be more to say about this point when we review the history of cable regulation in a later section of this chapter. For now, however, suffice it to say that a federal law requiring cable systems to restrict their own retransmissions of nonobscene, sexual programming to the same 10 P.M. to 6 A.M. "safe harbor" used for broadcasters, or to fully scramble such signals shown at other hours, was struck down by the Supreme Court in May 2000. The law's chief defect was that it covered *too little* speech; it applied only to cable channels whose mainstay was sexual speech. A sexually candid movie on the Playboy channel would trigger the rule, but not the same film shown on HBO.[66]

---

[62]*Illinois Citizens Committee for Broadcasting v. FCC,* 515 F.2d 397 (D.C. Cir. 1974).

[63]*In re Pacifica Foundation,* 2 F.C.C.R. 2698 (1987).

[64]*In re Infinity Broadcasting Corporation of Pennsylvania,* 2 F.C.C.R. 2705 (1987).

[65]*A.C.T. v. F.C.C.,* 58 F.3d 654 (D.C. Cir. 1995).

[66]*United States v. Playboy Entertainment Group,* 529 U.S. 803 (2000).

# Things to Remember

---

**SEXUALLY ORIENTED BROADCASTS**

- Section 1464 of the U.S. Code prohibits broadcasting of obscene and indecent programming.
- Even indecent programming may be broadcast between 10 P.M. and 6 A.M.

---

### Regulation of Children's Television

Given that the electronic media's unique ability to reach children has been one of the most frequently raised arguments in favor of government regulation, it is no surprise that the government has long expressed a special interest in children's television. Former FCC Chairman Newton Minow's dismay at the state of children's TV was one of the chief reasons he titled his famous 1961 speech "The Vast Wasteland." Even today, concerns about the effects of the electronic media on children have permeated public discourse about broadcast regulation in general. If consuming electronic media programming were an Adults Only activity, the ongoing debates about sexual and violent imagery would likely have a very different tone, if indeed they would be conducted at all. In this section, we review government regulations of those parts of the commercial broadcast day specifically aimed at children.

For the first several decades of commercial radio and TV, there were virtually no legal requirements concerning children's programming, save for general statements from the FCC to the effect that meeting the needs of children was one of the many items included in broadcasters' overall obligation to function "in the public interest." The FCC also imposed limits on the numbers of commercials that could be aired during, as well as immediately before and after, a children's program. In keeping with the deregulatory mood of the 1980s, the Commission decided it would no longer enforce even these requirements. Commercial stations were in business to make money, after all, so why shouldn't they be able to accept whatever amount of advertising seemed reasonable? Moreover, since most media markets had access to both PBS and to such child-friendly cable networks as Nickelodeon and the Disney Channel, sufficient children's programming was available even in the absence of commercial broadcasters' contributions to the mix.

Increases in the amount of advertising on network programming aimed at children resulted. Public advocacy groups such as Peggy Charren's Action for Children's Television (ACT) pointed to the disturbing phenomenon called the "program-length commercial": children's shows such as *G.I. Joe, Teenage Mutant*

*Ninja Turtles, Super Mario Brothers, Smurfs,* and *Gummi Bears* that were conceived of primarily as vehicles for marketing "action figures" and other toys. ACT won a ruling by the D.C. Circuit Court of Appeals that, while stopping short of demanding any specific new rules, ordered the FCC to provide a more persuasive rationale for its many deregulations of children's TV.[67] In 1992, the Commission decided that there was nothing wrong with program-length commercials as long as no paid advertisements for merchandise associated with the characters on a specific program aired during the program. G.I. Joe action figures could thus still be advertised on *Smurfs* and vice versa.[68]

From the 1950s through the 1980s, the federal government had spent millions of dollars in support of social science research aimed at the relationship between children's viewing of violent programming and their own later antisocial behaviors. Congress first passed legislation requiring TV stations to provide at least some more appropriate programming for children in 1990. The Children's Television Act reimposed limits on the number of commercial minutes that could occur on children's programming; current maximums are ten and a half minutes per hour on weekends and twelve minutes per hour on weekdays. The Act's requirement that broadcasters provide programming designed to further the "development" of children was, however, often criticized for its vagueness. It was not at all unusual for TV stations to petition the FCC to accept as evidence of their having met the law's requirements their airing of such programs as *The Flintstones, The Jetsons,* and *Yogi Bear.* The FCC insisted that licensees take the Act more seriously; in 1996, the Commission adopted rules specifying that all commercial stations must air a minimum of three hours weekly of programming designed to foster the development of children's cognitive and social growth. In 1999, the University of Pennsylvania's Annenberg Public Policy Center gave broadcasters a mixed report card, concluding that the amount and quality of children's programming had improved, but that much of children's fare was still rather uncreative and unnecessarily violent.

One of the most dramatic changes in broadcast regulation in the 1990s was a section of the Telecommunications Act of 1996 requiring that all TV sets with thirteen-inch or larger screens sold in the United States beginning in 1998 would have a microchip, often called the V chip, preinstalled. The chip is designed to read electronic signals embedded in specified TV programs, thus enabling parents to screen out material they think inappropriate for their children. Under much pressure from Congress and the executive branch, the major networks created a rating system that reports on each program's age-appropriateness and that also offers warnings about specific features of a particular episode: V for violence (with FV for fantasy violence in children's shows), S for sexual situations, L for coarse language, and D for suggestive dialogue. Although much praised from many quarters, the

---

[67]*Action for Children's Television v. FCC,* 821 F.2d 741 (D.C. Cir. 1987).

[68]*Children's Television Programming,* 56 F.R. 19611 (1991).

**Figure 12.4**

## TANK M<sup>C</sup>NAMARA®                                  by Jeff Millar and Bill Hinds

Ted Koppel reminds parents that the V chip cannot protect kids from all kinds of TV violence.

*Tank McNamara © 2000. Miller/Hinds. Reprinted with permission of Universal Press Syndicate. All rights reserved.*

V chip has also been criticized from both left and right. Some fear that the technology will embolden TV executives to place ever more violent images on the screen, because they now have a ready answer to any parents who might complain. Conversely, since the rating system cannot distinguish between gratuitous violence and the kinds of violence in such critically acclaimed films as *Schindler's List* or *Saving Private Ryan,* many critics fear that TV fare will grow more and more bland, that networks will self-censor out of fear that the parents will unthinkingly block broad categories of programs.

 **Things to Remember**

### CHILDREN'S TELEVISION

- TV stations must air at least three hours of prosocial programs for children per week.
- The 1996 Telecommunication Act requires that TV sets be equipped with a V chip that, in conjunction with program-by-program coding to be provided by the stations themselves, permit parents to screen out unduly violent or otherwise questionable programming.

### Special Regulations Imposed on PBS and NPR

Questions about how to fund public television and radio in the United States and what their programming day should look like have been matters of ongoing debate ever since passage of the Educational Television Facilities Act of 1962, which first provided federal funding for noncommercial stations, and the Public Broadcasting Act of 1967, creating the Corporation for Public Broadcasting (CPB) as the system's funding mechanism. In the 1960s, the Carnegie Commission suggested that the U.S. should adopt the United Kingdom's practice of funding public broadcasting through a predictable, renewable source, such as a tax on the sale of each TV and radio set. This idea was rejected, however, thus setting up a system of oversight whereby public broadcast representatives must appear before Congress regularly to justify their budget requests. In recent years, Congress has pressed PBS stations to reduce their dependence on government monies by obtaining more favorable merchandising contracts with producers of its most popular programs (See Figure 12.5).

Conservatives charge that too much of the programming on National Public Radio and the Public Broadcasting Service is left-leaning. Liberals also have their gripes with the programming, such as the network's high reliance on government spokespersons. Viewers of all political persuasions complain that, during PBS's periodic fund-raising drives, programs with a proven track record of bringing in the pledge calls are repeated ad nauseam.

 Figure 12.5

Congress has often suggested that the Public Broadcasting System should be able to wean itself from government subsidies by demanding that producers of its more popular programs give PBS a higher percentage of their merchandising profits.

The Public Broadcasting Act of 1967 gives the CPB responsibility for maintaining "strict adherence to objectivity and balance in all programs or series of programs of a controversial nature." No such restrictions are imposed against commercial broadcasters. The law also dictates the manner in which the corporation's board of directors will be appointed.

Some of the legal differences between public and commercial broadcasting in the United States are directly related to program content. Perhaps most obviously, we do not talk about "advertisers" on PBS and NPR, but instead of "underwriters." Messages alerting us as to what individuals, foundations, or corporations have underwritten a program may resemble commercials in some ways, but these are legally mandated to emphasize information rather than persuasion.[69] Companies can say who they are and display their corporate logo. They can say what product they make, which is especially important if the product line and the corporate name are not one and the same. The messages, however, may not tout the quality of the company's products or services the way most commercials do.

There are additional differences between regulations of commercial and noncommercial broadcasters. Recall the earlier discussion of statutory exemptions to the Equal Time Rule. One exemption, for "on-the-spot" coverage of news events, has been applied to candidate debates. In recent years, the FCC has held that this exemption applies even when the TV networks, or the candidates themselves, are the sponsors.

This rule has not applied automatically to debates sponsored by PBS stations. Especially in the case of PBS stations owned by the state, not an unusual circumstance, candidates who are excluded from a candidates' debate can make a frontal First Amendment attack on such editorial decisions. This lesson is apparent from a 1998 Supreme Court decision concerning independent Arkansas congressional candidate Ralph Forbes, who was not invited to join his Republican and Democratic counterparts in a debate sponsored by that state's public broadcasting network in 1992. Writing for a 6–3 Court, Justice Kennedy used public forum analysis and determined that the proposed debate constituted a nonpublic forum. When the government sponsors such a forum, it is permitted to choose who may and may not participate as long as such decisions are not based on favoritism for some speakers' messages over other speakers' messages. The state broadcasting system prevailed, but only by demonstrating that its decision to exclude Forbes had been based on sound journalistic concerns: the shortage of on-air time, and the belief that Forbes was a perennial candidate with little or no chance of winning. The commercial networks would not have to have made such a showing.[70]

Another difference between public and commercial broadcasting stations is the management's freedom to editorialize on the air. For decades, the FCC re-

---

[69]*Commission Policy Concerning the Noncommercial Nature of Educational Broadcasting Stations,* 49 F.R. 13535 (1984).

[70]*Arkansas Educational Television Commission v. Ralph P. Forbes,* 523 U.S. 666 (1998).

quired that commercial broadcasters who choose to speak out for or against particular political candidates had to give free airtime to disfavored candidates to reply with their opposing viewpoints. As was discussed earlier, this Political Editorial Rule was rescinded in 2001.

By contrast, section 399 of the Public Broadcasting Act forbade public broadcast stations from editorializing on the air at all, whether about candidates or about political issues in general. Although the rule against endorsing political candidates still stands, the Supreme Court in 1984 invalidated the more general admonition against editorializing.[71]

Yet another unique feature of public broadcasting regulation became apparent in the 2000 election cycle. The Federal Communications Act prohibits noncommercial stations from receiving money in exchange for running ads from political candidates. Combine this with Section 312's requirement, discussed earlier, that candidates for federal office be provided reasonable amounts of airtime, and it takes little imagination to identify media markets whose public broadcasting outlets could be overrun by political messages. One of the most notable examples of this phenomenon was Maryland congressional candidate Terry Lierman, a Democrat, trying to unseat Republican Connie Morella, a popular, progressive Republican from a majority-Democratic district. Lierman used the relevant federal laws to compel an NPR station in the Washington-Baltimore market to run a thirty-second spot featuring the voice of Representative Patrick J. Kennedy imploring local voters to support Lierman so as to help the Democrats regain control of the House of Representatives. The strategy failed, perhaps in part owing to a backlash from NPR listeners from both political parties, who were unaccustomed to being bombarded by advertising—political or otherwise—on their favorite station.[72]

---

[71]*FCC v. League of Women Voters,* 468 U.S. 364 (1984).

[72]Lori Montgomery and Jo Becker, "Political Ads Shock Public Radio Fans," *Washington Post,* 25 Oct. 2000, p. B1.

 # Things to Remember

### PUBLIC BROADCASTING

Public broadcasting stations are governed by rules not applicable to commercial stations:

- Each program or series is supposed to be objective and balanced.
- Public stations may not have on-air "advertising" per se, although sponsors' names and product or service lines are mentioned in "enhanced underwriting" messages at the beginning or end of each program.
- Station management may not endorse candidates for office.

## Regulation of Cable TV

When the earliest forms of cable television came on the scene in the 1940s, they were viewed by broadcasters as their natural allies. Called community antenna television systems (CATV), their main function was to pick up and retransmit local TV signals to homes in rural communities otherwise too remote to receive high-quality signals with their own roof antennas. Broadcasters became a bit wary of the new industry, however, when cable systems in the 1950s first began using microwave technology to import more distant TV stations. Local stations could thus lose market share.

### The FCC Begins to Regulate Cable

The danger posed by cable system to local broadcast stations' bottom lines was the rationale embraced by the Supreme Court in 1968 in support of the FCC's authority—asserted haltingly and tentatively—to regulate cable. Any industry that could interfere, technically or economically, with local broadcast stations was logically of interest to the Commission.[73] At issue in this particular case were FCC restrictions on CATV systems' importing of distant signals into another market. The Commission was afraid that distant stations would fragment local UHF stations' natural audience base.

Also in the 1960s, when cable companies began to originate their own programming, a phenomenon emerged that is now taken for granted: the home television set being used to receive programs that had never been "broadcast." Suddenly the traditional rationale for regulating electronic media differently from print—the use of the public's airwaves—had to be rethought. This situation is even more true today, when the vast majority of U.S. homes are hooked up to cable systems and do not even have TV roof antennas anymore.

In 1972, a 5–4 Supreme Court majority upheld FCC regulations, soon thereafter abandoned voluntarily by the Commission, requiring that cable systems produce a certain percentage of their own programming rather than serve only as retransmitters of others' signals.[74] But the FCC went too far, a 6–3 majority held in 1979, when it required cable systems to open some of their channel capacity to public, educational, and local government uses and for leased access by independent programmers.[75] The FCC was trying to regulate cable systems as if they were common carriers (like telephone and telegraph companies) that must send messages provided by anyone willing to pay the cost. Congress had decided long ago that over-the-air broadcasters could not themselves be regulated in this manner.

---

[73]*United States v. Southwestern Cable Company,* 392 U.S. 157 (1968).

[74]*United States v. Midwest Video,* 406 U.S. 649 (1972).

[75]*FCC v. Midwest Video,* 440 U.S. 689 (1979).

Since whatever authority the FCC has to regulate stems from the industry's relationship to broadcasting, such authority could not allow common carrier status to be imposed on cable.

Although cable systems do not necessarily use the public's airwaves, they inevitably use the public's telephone poles and streets to lay the miles of coaxial cable needed to connect each subscriber's home to the system's "head-end" (its main switching area). Typically, a cable system will sign a long-term contract with a city or similar local government for the right to lay the cable, and the cities have predictably expected much in return, such as annual franchise fees, promises about quality of customer service, and inclusion of certain kinds of programming or leased network access (e.g., a station for airing city council hearings and other government events).

In 1984, the Supreme Court placed significant restraints on state and local governments' claimed right to regulate cable programming. *Capital Cities Cable v. Crisp*,[76] however, was not as much a victory for the cable industry as for the doctrine of federal preemption, by which valid federal laws trump state or local laws. At issue was an Oklahoma law forbidding advertising for alcoholic beverages. The state's attorney general had determined that this statute was applicable to out-of-state TV signals imported by Oklahoma-based cable systems. Writing for a unanimous Court, Justice Brennan found that the state's law was in conflict with legitimate FCC policies. The Commission's **Must-Carry rule,** which required that cable systems include on their most basic service packages retransmitted signals from all broadcast stations operating within thirty-five miles of the cable company's own studio, was one source of conflict. The likelihood of conflict was especially acute for cable systems based in Oklahoma but close to a bordering state that did not have similar bans on alcohol advertising. (Those same Must-Carry rules were later found unconstitutional by the D.C. Circuit Court of Appeals,[77] and not until 1997 was a similar set of rules upheld by the Supreme Court.)[78] Also, while the FCC did not require cable companies to import more distant signals or to provide such pay services as HBO or CNN, the Commission did encourage cable operators to provide such options to their subscribers. Again, federal law prohibiting cable companies from editing the broadcast signals they retransmit would conflict with the Oklahoma statute. Although no federal law forbade cable systems to edit signals from pay cable networks, Justice Brennan concluded that to require the cable franchisees to do such editing would be an unwarranted encroachment on the franchisees' interests.

---

[76]467 U.S. 691 (1984).

[77]*Century Communications Corporation v. FCC* (II), 835 F.2d 292 (D.C. Cir. 1987); *Quincy Cable TV v. FCC,* 768 F.2d 1434 (D.C. Cir. 1985).

[78]*Turner Broadcasting System v. FCC,* 520 U.S. 180 (1997).

## Congressional Actions

In the 1980s and again in the 1990s, Congress passed major legislation affecting the interests of the cable industry. It is perhaps a commentary on the tentative manner in which the government has approached the whole area of cable regulation that the two pieces of legislation seem to have very different philosophies. Indeed, from the industry's perspective, much of what the Cable Communications Policy Act of 1984 gave, the Cable Television Consumer Protection and Competition Act of 1992 took away. The popular name given to the latter Act suggests something of the intervening history. Congress was concerned that the cable industry was taking advantage of provisions of the 1984 law in monopolistic ways.

Two provisions of the 1984 Act were especially helpful to the cable industry. First, Congress showed an awareness that building cable systems is an enormously expensive endeavor. Companies were unlikely to risk such huge amounts of capital if a few years after winning their initial franchise from a city, the local government finds another company it likes better. Thus, the Act provided cable companies with an expectation of renewal unless the local government could demonstrate that community needs had gone unmet by a franchisee's behavior.

A second key feature of the 1984 Act dealt directly with the financial relationships among the cities, the cable companies, and subscribers. The Act placed a ceiling on the fee that cities could charge cable systems for the ongoing right to use public streets, utility poles, and other resources. Cities would not be permitted to charge more than 5 percent of a cable system's gross revenues as an annual franchising fee.

The 1984 Act also put cities on notice that they could not demand from cable companies any specific cable network offerings. Thus, a local government could insert language into a franchise contract to the effect that the cable system will provide "public affairs programming," but it could not demand, for example, that all the C-SPAN networks be carried twenty-four hours a day. Cities could, however, require cable systems to provide public, educational, and government (PEG) access channels. On most cable systems, these channel spaces are reserved for covering city council and other governmental meetings and for the local university. The "public" in PEG refers to public access channels, which are typically available to any individual or community group, on a first-come, first-served basis. The cable system will provide training and equipment, and sometimes even technicians, to help with production.

Whereas cities *may*, under the 1984 Act, require a certain number of PEG channels, the Act itself requires that cable systems make a number of their channels available at a reasonable fee for "leased access" to profit-making groups. On some systems, these channels are taken up by locally produced shopping networks. Many systems have found, however, that leased access exists in name only in that no group ever stepped forward to rent space on the system.

The most noticeable effect of the 1984 Act was an increase in customer dissatisfaction. Surveys demonstrated that cable rates were increasing at a rate far exceeding that of inflation and that subscribers complained of inattentive service. The Cable Television Consumer Protection and Competition Act of 1992 was designed to address these issues. It reimposed FCC and local governmental authority over rates cable systems could charge their customers. The Act also prohibited cities from signing any new contracts granting any one cable company an exclusive right to offer programming to their residents. For primarily economic reasons, this latter provision has not resulted in many cities having competing cable companies.

Congress also instructed the FCC to create standards for acceptable service. The resulting regulations were quite specific. They required, for example, that cable systems answer their phones within thirty seconds of the first ring and that they maintain some kind of telephone response system twenty-four hours a day, seven days a week. Installation requests would have to be honored within one week, and there must be a system of rebating appropriate portions of monthly fees in response to system outages or similar malfunctions.

The 1992 Act also explicitly empowered the Commission to impose two kinds of ownership limits on cable companies. Horizontal limits placed a cap on the total percent of U.S. households receiving some kind of multichannel programming (whether cable or satellite) that any one cable company could service. Vertical limits instead capped the percent of channels on a cable system that could be owned by the system operator. In early 2001, the D.C. Circuit Court of Appeals vacated the rules, sending them back to the Commission for additional fact-finding and justification.[79] Most observers believe that in the current era of deregulation, it is highly unlikely the Commission will be able to demonstrate to the court's satisfaction the need for such regulations.

The Telecommunications Act of 1996, generally designed to foster competition among communications industries, also had some direct impact on cable. It eliminated some regulation of cable fees immediately and provided for a two-year phaseout of the remaining fees. Perhaps more important is that the law got rid of most barriers that had prevented cable companies, long-distance phone companies, and local phone companies from competing in each other's domains.

A full understanding of this latter provision requires us to conjure in our minds the telecommunications landscape in the United States prior to the breakup of the old American Telephone & Telegraph Company. AT&T, popularly known as "Ma Bell," once had a virtual monopoly on long-distance and local phone service as well as the marketing of telephones themselves. After a quarter century of antitrust litigation brought by the Department of Justice, AT&T signed in 1982 an agreement often referred to in the industry as the Modified Final Judgment (MFJ), the most important provision of which was the selling off of the company's local phone interests into what became the Regional Bell Operating Companies (RBOCs, sometimes called Baby Bells).

---

[79]*Warner Entertainment v. Federal Communications Commission,* 240 F. 3d 1126 (D.C. Cir. 2001).

Under the MFJ, which was subject to ongoing oversight by Judge Harold Greene, RBOCs were not permitted to offer such "information services" as cable TV programming. Several of the regional phone companies litigated further on this point, arguing that their First Amendment rights were abridged by forcing them to serve only as common carriers.[80] That litigation, some of which was ripe for Supreme Court review, was rendered moot when Congress determined, in a portion of the 1996 Act, that local telephone companies could get involved in the information services business in any of a number of ways. They could buy an existing cable system and run it as an independent subsidiary. They could choose to function as a common carrier, creating a service like cable but that would be, in essence, 100 percent leased access, where the phone company would provide no original programming. Phone companies could combine features of these two strategies by instead offering what the Act calls an Open Video System (OVS), which would provide for as much as 33 percent original programming, with the remaining capacity devoted to leased access.

Many critics have concluded that the Telecommunication Act of 1996's main effect has been not the fostering of genuine competition in most markets, but in merger (and acquisition) mania. To be fair, the mania began long before the Act's passage. Westinghouse had purchased the CBS network just prior to the Telecommunication Act's taking effect. General Electric bought RCA (the NBC network's corporate parent) back in 1985, the same year that Capital Cities Cable acquired ABC. The Disney company bought Capital Cities ten years later. Disney later acquired CNN.

It is probably fair to say that passage of the 1996 Act at least accelerated the rate of mergers and acquisitions in the telecommunications industries. Some of the most newsworthy of the dozens of multibillion dollar deals include SBC Communications's merger with Pacific Telesis and with Ameritech, Bell Atlantic's acquisition of both NYNEX and GTE, WorldCom's of MCI, as well as AT&T's purchase of the cable giant TCI. Consider also that, whereas the AT&T breakup had created seven separate RBOCs, there are now only four. In 2000, America Online, weary of fighting for access to cable systems' high-speed home connections, decided to "buy 'em instead of fight 'em" when it announced its intention to purchase Time Warner company, whose cable franchises reach over 20 percent of American cable households. The deal was approved by the various regulatory agencies in 2001.

### Cable TV and the First Amendment

As we have seen, the reasons traditionally offered for regulating broadcast media more strictly than print media are spectrum scarcity (that not everyone who would like could be given a frequency on "the people's airwaves") and the power of TV and radio to intrude on the privacy of the home and to influence young children.

---

[80]*Chesapeake & Potomac Telephone Company v. United States*, 42 F.3d 181 (4th Cir. 1994).

Does cable television manifest these same features of electronic media, and what are the First Amendment implications of the question? The Supreme Court has had a number of occasions to address this issue and has always approached it with caution. The results have not always offered clear guidance, nor have they been completely consistent. In 1986, in the course of ruling that the city of Los Angeles could not sign an exclusive cable contract with one company, the Court majority granted that cable operators perform an "editorial" role like "the traditional enterprises of newspapers and book publishers" when they decide which cable networks to include on their systems.[81] In the very next sentence, however, Chief Justice Rehnquist equated cable's First Amendment rights with those of "wireless broadcasters." Thus, the Court did not say which model of regulation it will use in cable cases: print, broadcast, or some kind of hybrid created especially for the new industry.

A few years later, the Court was asked to rule on the constitutionality of a broad-based sales tax in Arkansas from which the state decided to exempt the sales of subscriptions to magazines and newspapers. A local cable system and a cable subscriber sued on free speech and equal protection grounds in that monthly cable bills were not also exempt from the tax. The Court held that there was no constitutional defect in the tax system, because it did not discriminate on the basis of taxpayers' speech.[82]

In 1994, the Supreme Court took its first look at the Must-Carry rules imposed by the 1992 Cable Act and instructed a lower court on remand to subject the rules to a level of scrutiny somewhere between the strict scrutiny used for print media and the far more lax standards applying to broadcast regulations.[83] The lower court then found the rules constitutional, and the Supreme Court, hearing the case a second time, agreed.[84]

The Must-Carry rules flow in only one direction. Cable companies must carry signals from local broadcasters who wish to be included on the cable system's basic tier of service, but those same local broadcasters cannot be forced to have their signals included on cable systems. A very popular local station whose management knows will be highly desirable to cable subscribers can choose instead to exercise the Act's **retransmission consent** provision through which broadcasters negotiate a fee for the privilege of retransmitting the signal to cable subscribers. In the spring of 2000, when Disney/ABC failed to reach a retransmission agreement with Time Warner, millions of cable subscribers were unable to receive ABC and other Disney-owned programming. Public broadcasting station licensees are treated differently; they may not seek payment from cable systems for retransmission, and their signals will be included on the first tier of service.

---

[81]*City of Los Angeles v. Preferred Communications,* 476 U.S. 488, 194 (1986).

[82]*Leathers v. Medlock,* 499 U.S. 439 (1991).

[83]*Turner Broadcasting System v. FCC* (I), 512 U.S. 622 (1994).

[84]*Turner Broadcasting System v. FCC* (II), 520 U.S. 180 (1997).

In between the first and second *Turner* decisions, the Court had occasion to decide what level of scrutiny should apply to regulations that directly affect cable content.[85] At issue were three related sections of the Cable Television Consumer Protection and Competition Act of 1992. Two sections (10A and 10C) would *permit* cable companies to refuse to transmit sexually indecent material on leased access and public access stations, respectively. A third section of the law (10B) would *require* cable companies to segregate any "patently offensive" material from the leased access stations onto a separate channel and to provide that channel only to subscribers who specifically request it in writing.

The Supreme Court produced a fragmented result, with a majority decision for some points and different plurality opinions for others. In those sections of Justice Breyer's opinion that carried sway with the majority, section 10B (requiring cable operators to "segregate and block" indecent content from leased access stations) was held unconstitutional. A plurality of the justices upheld section 10A, whereas a different plurality found section 10C unconstitutional.

Caution was the defining characteristic of Justice Breyer's majority/plurality opinion in that he refused to commit the Court to any of the competing models—print, broadcast, or common carrier—for adjudicating laws regulating cable content. From Breyer's perspective, that two of the three sections of the Act before the Court dealt with leased access stations was itself a complicating matter. After all, such stations only had a "right" to show up on the cable dial at all because of the earlier 1984 Cable Act. Had that law never been passed, cable companies would have been completely free to decide how to fill their system space.

Even while eschewing the temptation to embrace any one model, Breyer found it helpful to make reference to the broadcast regulation analogy. He called to mind the *Pacifica* decision involving George Carlin's comedy routine. The Court suggested in that case that one of the main reasons for restricting broadcast indecency was to protect children. Many courts and commentators have suggested in the intervening years that the rationale carries diminished force in a cable environment. After all, parents have more control over which cable stations to allow into their homes. They do not have to subscribe to the Playboy network or to similar adult fare. For Breyer, however, the state's interest in protecting children weighs more heavily today than when *Pacifica* was decided. Cable systems boast dozens, often over a hundred, channels compared with the mere handful to which most homes had access in the 1970s. Moreover, because cable subscribers tend to "channel surf" more than do nonsubscribers, children in cable households are more "susceptible to random exposure to unwanted materials."

Justice Breyer also reminded us that the FCC indecency regulations upheld in *Pacifica* amounted to a government ban on a category of speech. At least some of the sections of the 1992 Cable Act, by contrast, merely opened up the *possibility* that this same category of speech would be excluded from a cable system. Al-

---

[85]*Denver Area Educational Telecommunications Consortium v. FCC,* 518 U.S. 727 (1996).

though this line of argument seems to count as a reason for upholding both of the Act's provisions giving cable operators the option of excluding indecent speech, Breyer concluded that the special status of public access stations justified treating them differently from leased access stations. Public access stations have been seen for decades as the price of cutting up the streets, part of the consideration cable companies give municipalities that award them franchises.

Justice Souter's concurring opinion in the *Denver Area* decision is worthy of special mention. Souter established his credentials as a technophile by citing several World Wide Web sites. More important is that he justified the Court's cautious approach to cable by pointing to the reality of media convergence mentioned in this chapter's introductory pages. Media companies are intensely competing "for control over the single wire" that will bring a multitude of services to the home; the justices must thus realize that regulatory standards imposed on one medium may have "immense, but now unknown and unknowable, effects on the others."

In 2000, a Supreme Court majority applied the same kind of strict scrutiny to a cable regulation that it would normally apply to the print media. At issue were sections of the Telecommunications Act of 1996 requiring cable channels the majority of whose fare is "sexually oriented" (and the local cable systems that retransmit their programming to subscribers) to "fully scramble" their signals or to limit their transmissions to between 10 P.M. and 6 A.M. The impetus for the regulation was that existing scrambling technologies are generally imperfect, resulting in "bleeding" of the video and/or audio messages to other channels. Households not subscribing to and not interested in "adult" programming thus receive it anyway.

Most cable franchises carrying signals affected by Section 505 chose the path of least resistance, restricting their hours of transmission to eight overnight hours daily. In striking down the regulation, the majority found that the degree of self-censorship imposed on the cable industry was plainly unacceptable.

Writing for the majority, Justice Kennedy suggested that the Court's decision to employ the most strict level of review in such a case was more a reflection of the regulation's structure than a judicial statement about the overall level of First Amendment protection due the cable industry. The regulation, after all, was triggered not only by the content of messages (sexually oriented ones), but also was limited only to certain speakers (cable channels most of whose fare was sexually oriented). That is, HBO or Showtime, even if they aired an occasional program that might be otherwise covered by the rule, would escape liability, precisely because such programs are not their usual content. Far better, Kennedy said, for cable operators to fully block unwanted channels from a given household upon written request from the subscriber.[86]

When, then, are cable systems exempt from the kinds of regulations that are regularly imposed on the broadcast media, but that would be clearly unconstitutional if applied to print media? While the Court has not yet articulated a clear

---

[86]*United States v. Playboy Entertainment Group,* 529 U.S. 803 (2000).

# Things to Remember

## CABLE REGULATION

- Cable regulation was at first done by a combination of sometimes conflicting FCC policies and rules set forth by local franchising authorities. Congress did not pass the first law governing cable until 1984. The Act was very industry friendly.

- Charges of poor service and inordinately high monthly fees led Congress to create new legislation in 1992, which reimposed pricing controls and established minimal levels of acceptable service.

- The Telecommunications Act of 1996, however, got rid of most cable rate regulations; it also permitted cable companies and local and long-distance phone companies to compete in each other's industries.

- Currently, many of the best-known regulations of broadcast speech apply with equal force to cable programming.

- The Supreme Court has not yet decided what level of scrutiny should be applied to cable content regulations, although in recent decisions a majority is moving more and more toward the print model.

answer to this question, we can intuit a pattern emerging from relevant cases and statutes. In general, regulations aimed at indecent speech—sexual programming that the print media may disseminate freely but that can be highly regulated if appearing on broadcast stations—treat cable more like print. When regulations force broadcast licensees to speak or to otherwise take action—think in terms of speech about political campaigns, or rules demanding accessibility for the disabled—cable is subject to the same controls, even though they too could not be applied to the print media.

As a general rule, Congress has in recent years included the cable industry within the purview of any new statutes governing broadcast content. Thus, for example, those sections of the Telecommunications Act of 1996 mandating closed captioning apply with equal force to broadcast and cable signals. Some of the older broadcast rules were later amended to apply to cable as well, such as the Equal Time Rule, the Reasonable Access rule, and the (now defunct) Personal Attack and Political Editorial Rules.

## Some Other "New Media"

Mark Fowler, who served as chairman of the FCC from 1981 through 1987, once referred to television as "a toaster with pictures." His point was that the federal government does not get very deeply involved in regulating toasters and other appliances (save to make sure they are safe to use) and that the broadcasting industry should be similarly deregulated. His words serve equally well to make the point that, from the viewers' perspective, it hardly matters how the pictures seen on TV got there. Yet, as we have already seen, how those pictures got there determines, in large part, how the message is regulated.

If you use your TV and VCR to view a movie rented from your local video store, government regulation of the content is restricted to that which would be constitutional if applied to the print media. The same movie, if created by a cable TV network and viewed by you on that network, will be subject to additional regulations. For example, the Equal Time Rule could be triggered if it is election time and one of the actors in the movie is running for office. Far more regulation still can apply to the same movie if it is instead aired by a broadcast TV network. Chief among these additional regulations, of course, is the prohibition against broadcasting sexually indecent but nonobscene messages. NBC will thus edit profane language and racy moments that HBO will leave untouched.

VCRs, cable, and broadcast, however, are not the only ways that pictures might come to your TV screen. This final section examines the regulatory framework governing three of the most popular new technologies for providing video programming: satellite master antenna television (SMATV) systems, direct broadcast satellite (DBS) service, and multichannel multipoint distribution service (MMDS).

## SMATV

Satellite master antenna television (SMATV) systems are like minicable companies providing service to residents of a large apartment complex, hotel, or similar venue where a high density of housing units makes it more economical to provide service to all unit dwellers at once than depend on the cable model of having each unit sign up separately. Typically, one or more on-site "earth stations" set up on the rooftop picks up signals directly from satellites and then distributes the signals to each unit via wires or cable. The main difference between SMATVs and traditional cable is that the former do not require digging up or otherwise traversing city streets. The FCC ruled in 1983 that, because SMATV systems usually do not employ public right of ways, local governments have no authority to regulate them. The cable industry appealed the FCC's decision, arguing that exempting SMATV from local government control would give that technology an unfair advantage over cable itself, especially because cable franchise contracts typically prohibit "redlining" (favoring wealthier neighborhoods and failing to hook up poorer areas to the system in a timely fashion), whereas SMATV, by its very nature, gets to pick and choose who will be among its universe of possible customers. The D.C. Circuit Court of Appeals upheld the FCC's decision. Writing for the appellate panel, Judge Edward Tamm conceded that the Commission's actions aimed at encouraging the development of SMATV systems could harm the financial interests of several existing cable franchises, but concluded that "measuring the public interest standard of the Communications Act with sole reference to the impact Commission action would have upon a developed technology ensures a regulatory regime frozen into maintaining the status quo."[87]

The 1984 Cable Act, however, drew a distinction between SMATV systems serving separately owned and managed buildings and those that serve one or more buildings under common ownership or management. Only those systems in the latter "common ownership" category would be exempt from having to obtain a franchise contract with the local government (presuming also that the system did not use public rights of way). In *FCC v. Beach Communications,*[88] the Supreme Court upheld the relevant section of the 1984 Act. But Section 522 of the Telecommunications Act of 1996 effectively eliminates the distinction between "common ownership" and "multiple ownership" SMATVs, instead exempting all SMATVs that serve subscribers without using any public right of way from having to obtain a franchise from their local governments. This does not mean that SMATV operators are entirely beyond FCC or Congressional control, however. The FCC licenses and regulates allotments of space on communications satellites. Then, too, Congress has applied some key provisions of its cable legislation to SMATV systems, most notably the retransmission consent rule. Thus, SMATV companies must obtain local broadcasters' permission to include their signals.

## DBS

As the name suggests, direct broadcast satellite **(DBS)** services send programs directly from studio to home receivers via satellite. The use of satellites in geosynchronous orbit—positioned at the right height and traveling at the right speed and rotation to maintain the same position in the sky—has been a part of the U.S. telecommunications landscape ever since the launching of *Telstar* in the early 1960s. In their first two decades, satellite communication was viewed as a common carrier made available for others to use, whether a TV network sending its "feed" to affiliate stations or a nationally distributed newspaper sending instructions to its regional printing presses. That changed in 1982 when the FCC permitted satellite communications companies to provide their own programming to subscribers.

The DBS business achieved viability in the 1990s, when Hughes Aircraft's DirecTV and Hubbard Broadcasting's United States Satellite Broadcasting (USSB) began offering dozens of channels to customers with specially designed home dishes. These two companies merged in 1999, and DirecTV later that year acquired the competing PrimeStar company, creating a satellite service with over ten million U.S. subscribers and a channel capacity approaching 400. At present,

---

[87]*New York State Commission on Cable Television v. FCC,* 749 F.2d 804, 812 (D.C. Cir. 1984).
[88]508 U.S. 307 (1993).

EchoStar's "Dish" network (with about five million subscribers) is DirecTV's only serious competitor, although more companies will likely enter the business.

In 1983, the FCC determined that DBS companies should not be subject to such broadcasting regulations as the Equal Time Rule and the Candidate Access Rule. DBS did not fit the Communication Act's definition of "broadcasting," the Commission felt, in that the 1934 law always envisioned individual stations situated in and serving local communities, whereas satellite broadcasting by its very nature cannot be so locally attuned. The D.C. Circuit Court of Appeals rejected this view, holding that "when DBS systems transmit signals directly to homes with the intent that those signals be received by the public, such transmissions rather clearly fit the definition of broadcasting." Judge Abner Mikva added that "the fact that Congress did not in 1934 contemplate DBS does not give the Commission a blank check to regulate DBS in any way it deems fit."[89]

The Commission looked at the DBS issue anew in a 1987 statement, concluding that any new media service companies (including DBS) that intend for their signals to be received only by paying subscribers, rather than by the general public, should for this reason be exempted from content rules applying to broadcasters. This time, the federal appellate court upheld the Commission's action.[90] Congress, however, in the 1992 Cable Act, instructed the FCC to create mechanisms through which to apply the Candidate Access Rule and the Equal Time Rule to DBS systems. A few court decisions later,[91] the Commission in February 1999 set forth its final rule, reaffirming that DBS systems must adhere to the same Candidate Access and Equal Time requirements as do broadcasters.[92] Recognizing that many DBS systems do not usually accept advertising, the Commission determined that the rates to be charged candidates for office for advertising time should generally be in sync with those charged by other media to reach a similar audience. Pursuant to a provision of the 1992 Act, the Commission also required that DBS system operators set aside 4 percent of their channel capacity for "noncommercial educational and informational programming," which the Commission purposely defined fairly loosely but which would certainly include PBS or similar educational nonprofit stations. Finally, the Commission expressed its continued belief that DBS systems are generally not equipped to produce *local* public affairs programming, but found that the technology might be growing in such a way as to permit such locally customized transmissions in the future.

Traditionally wired cable companies see DBS services as a serious form of competition. In 1999, a representative of the National Cable Television Association told a Congressional committee that more than twelve million Americans

---

[89]*National Association of Broadcasters v. FCC,* 740 F.2d 1190 (D.C. Cir. 1984).

[90]*National Association for Better Broadcasting v. FCC,* 840 F.2d 665 (D.C. Cir. 1988).

[91]*Daniels Cablevision v. United States,* 835 F. Supp. 1 (D.D.C. 1993); *rev'd sub nom. Time Warner Entertainment v. FCC,* 93 F.3d 957 (D.C. Cir. 1996).

[92]*Direct Broadcast Satellite Public Interest Obligations,* 64 F.R. 5951 (1999).

receive their multichannel services from some kind of business other than their local cable franchisee, that DBS already accounted for 10 percent of the market, and that this percentage was growing.

### MMDS

Sometimes called "wireless cable," a multichannel multipoint distribution service **(MMDS)** uses superhigh microwave frequencies to transmit signals within a limited, line-of-sight range of about twenty-five miles. Channel capacity was originally far more limited than that provided by the larger cable companies, but newer digital compression equipment has expanded that capacity from a few dozen to over 300. The major appeal of MMDSs is that the equipment needed, including a small microwave rooftop antenna, is far less expensive than laying miles of cable.

MMDS systems are licensed by the FCC in the sense that they must be assigned a specific microwave channel for transmission. The systems are not covered by most of the traditional rules governing broadcasting, such as the Equal Time and Candidate Access Rules. Nor are they governed by the Must-Carry rules, although they must obtain local broadcasters' permission to retransmit their signals. Interestingly, MMDS services were originally regulated by the FCC's Common Carrier Bureau because the Commission had always considered the microwave portion of the electromagnetic spectrum as most appropriate for point-to-point transmissions rather than part of a mass medium. In 1994, however, the FCC determined that regulation of this technology could best be accomplished through its Mass Media Bureau.

 # Things to Remember

**OTHER NEW TECHNOLOGIES**

- SMATVs are minicable companies providing service to the residents of a large apartment building, hotel, or similar, high-density dwelling. If such systems do not use streets or other public right of ways, local governments may not impose any restrictions on them. The FCC regulates such companies, however, at least to the extent of granting licenses for use of particular satellites. The retransmission consent rule also applies to SMATV systems.
- DBS systems transmit signals directly from satellites to subscribers' home dishes. Operators are subject to the same kinds of political content regulations as are broadcasters.
- MMDS, or "wireless cable," systems use microwaves to send signals from their studios to subscribers within a narrow, twenty-five mile radius. MMDS systems are regulated by the FCC in that they must be assigned a microwave frequency; the traditional political broadcast speech regulations, however, are not imposed on them.

At first, the more popular cable TV networks refused to market their programming to wireless cable systems. The 1992 Cable Act, however, required cable networks to make their signals available to MMDS systems at prices comparable with those offered to more traditional, wired cable systems.

Industry analysts suggest that MMDS companies are especially likely to exploit two market niches in the next several years. First, owing to an FCC decision in 1998 authorizing the creation of two-way MMDS service, the technology can be used for high-speed Internet access. Second, long-distance phone companies seeking to enter the local telephone market will begin buying up MMDS systems to solve what is often called the "last mile problem," the extraordinary cost of hooking up each and every potential customer in a densely populated area. If that last mile from the switching station to a consumer's home can be done through wireless microwave systems, the cost of laying wires or leasing access to a competing phone company's wires can be saved.

## Chapter Summary

The traditional reliance on distinctions among print, broadcast, cable, and other "new media" is very much in flux as we enter an era of media convergence, wherein communication services will likely be provided to us by a single wire.

The Federal Communications Act of 1934 created the FCC; it still provides the basic framework for regulation of electronic media. A major overhaul of the law was accomplished in the Telecommunications Act of 1996 through which Congress sought to encourage competition among and across communications industries.

The general trend since the early 1980s has been toward deregulating electronic media. Virtually all limits on the number of stations any single person or company may own have been eliminated; so, too, have several regulations governing media content been cut. The FCC is mandated to report to Congress biennially as to the wisdom of even further deregulation.

Some rules do still apply only to electronic media, however; among them are the Reasonable Access Rule, the Equal Time Rule, prohibitions against indecent programming, and a requirement to provide at least three hours of weekly programming designed to aid youngsters' cognitive and social development. TV stations are also mandated to switch to digital broadcasting by 2006.

Special rules apply to NPR and PBS stations, which must strive for balance and objectivity in every single program they broadcast and, unlike their commercial counterparts, may not use their airwaves to endorse candidates for public office.

Cable television, once only a means of retransmitting broadcast signals to rural areas otherwise cut off from television service, has emerged as the primary delivery system for video in the United States. Regulations governing cable have historically been a confusing and sometimes contradictory array of actions by the FCC, Congress, the courts, and local governments. The Supreme Court in 1996 explicitly refused to indicate what standard of review should be used to evaluate regulations aimed at cable content.

Other means of delivering video programming have emerged in recent years, including satellite master antenna television (SMATV), direct broadcast satellite service (DBS), and multichannel multipoint distribution service (MMDS). The FCC, Congress, and the courts have struggled to decide which, if any, regulations normally applied to broadcast stations should apply to these industries as well.

# Communication Law and the Internet

That which is called the Internet is really a Cold War legacy. In 1969, the Department of Defense created the Advanced Research Projects Agency Network (ARPANET), a complex array of computer connections designed to ensure that the military could continue to carry on sensitive communications even in the event of nuclear war. Two features of the system were especially relevant to that goal. The first was a purposefully high degree of redundancy so that messages could be relayed even if some of the network became inoperable. Thus, a message that could not be sent directly from Washington, D.C., to Palo Alto, California, might be sent on a circuitous route beginning in Philadelphia, forwarded to a computer in Pittsburgh, and then to Chicago, Denver, and Salt Lake City before finally reaching Palo Alto. The second feature was a reliance on "packet switching," which breaks down large and complicated messages into manageable chunks (or "packets") that are sent independently to the ultimate destination, where they are finally reassembled into a meaningful whole. If you have ever visited a Web site and noted that the textual elements pop up on the computer screen almost immediately but that you may have to wait for the more colorful graphics to appear, you have seen packet switching at work.

At the same time that the now defunct ARPANET was maturing, other similar computer networks, including BITNET, CSNET, FIDONET, and USENET, developed to link universities, research facilities, businesses, and individuals. The multiple layers of linkages of these and numerous other computer networks to each other formed the basis for the Internet.

The Internet is often thought of as a place. Of course, it is not really a place. It is rather the result of our all having agreed to hook our computers together. Indeed, it is not as much a bunch of computers as it is the way the computers talk to each other. Still, the word "cyberspace" is often used as a synonym for the Internet, a practice that will be adopted here as well.

The whole notion of the Internet as an imaginary place cannot help but call to mind the discussion of the U.S. Supreme Court's public forum analysis (see Chapter 2). There we learned that the Court recognizes that freedom of speech does not translate into a right to say anything we please anywhere and anytime we please. Some times and places are more conducive to communicational activities than others. It is perfectly acceptable to deliver an impassioned and spontaneous political speech on a street corner, but not in a hospital emergency room. That the Court has singled out public streets and parks as the quintessential public fora is something to keep in mind as we explore the still nascent body of Internet law. After all, parks may be fine for speech making, but they are also used for flying kites, jogging, and picnicking. Public street corners are also places we have historically expected to encounter speakers, but that is not their only or even primary function. The Internet may be the first "place" whose *only* function is to facilitate communication. Some commentators have therefore argued that this new medium is the ultimate public forum, purer than pure, and that government should properly permit more freedom of speech in this place than in any other.

Cyberspace attorney Lance Rose argues that a full appreciation of the Internet requires us to recognize that communication events throughout history have been of three kinds: one to one, one to many, and many to many. Prior to the Internet, only the first two levels of communication had been stretched beyond the context of actual participants in one room. One-to-one conversations can take place at a party, but also by telephone between persons thousands of miles apart. One-to-many conversations happen at parties, such as when one person makes a toast to the crowd, yet they are also the essence of radio and TV broadcasts. Prior to the Internet, Rose suggests, many-to-many conversations took place almost exclusively among persons sharing a common time and place, such as the small group at a party that might talk among themselves in the kitchen. Online talk has finally brought this third category of communication within the scope of elec-

 # Things to Remember

### SOME INTERNET BASICS

- Begun by the Department of Defense in the 1960s, the Internet was designed as a means of ensuring that government communications could go on even after a nuclear attack.

- It is the first medium to bring many-to-many communication (akin to a small group of friends having an informal discussion) into the electronic age.

- There is a high degree of redundancy in data transmissions among the computer networks that comprise the Internet; thus, it is impossible to know at any one time how many computer networks are involved or which path any particular message or portion of a message ("packet") has taken.

- The Internet is often thought of as an imaginary place called "cyberspace," leading some theorists to suggest it should be considered the purest of "pure public forums," subject to less government regulation than any other communications medium.

tronic mass media. Unlike television and radio, however, consumers are not restricted to messages sent by huge mass media companies. In cyberspace, "anyone can be heard by many others, either in his or her own town or across the globe," says Rose. The Internet not only "allows groups of all kinds to organize effectively"; it also "enables those who don't fit in where they live to find hundreds or thousands of kindred souls across the world."[1]

The next section of this chapter discusses a handful of unique characteristics of cyberspace communication, always with the goal of at least musing over these features' implications for the structure and application of communication law. Then, we examine the relevant Internet case law to date, including libel, trademark and copyright, invasion of privacy, and the sending of sexual messages. Within each area of the law, we are especially interested in those sections of decisions where judges say exactly what they think this new medium is, and what analogies to more traditional media best describe it.

## What Makes the Internet Different?

Many theorists and jurists who have examined the issue agree that the Internet boasts several unique communication features, each of which has significant implications for the application of communication law to this new technology.

### An Infinite Number of Information Sources

This feature of the Internet is important because it helps us to distinguish cyberspace from the electromagnetic spectrum that governs such more traditional electronic media as radio and television. As seen in Chapter 12, one of the chief arguments used to justify regulations of broadcast media that would be unconstitutional as applied to the print media is "spectrum scarcity." Only so many TV or radio stations can fit onto the spectrum, so not everyone who wishes to obtain a broadcast license can get one. In 1997, the Supreme Court was asked to uphold the Communication Decency Act, which would have made it a criminal offense to transmit indecent sexual messages on the Internet. (A more detailed discussion of the Act appears later in this chapter). One of the government's arguments in favor of the law was that the Federal Communications Commission prohibits the broadcasting of such messages on TV and radio. The Supreme Court, however, rejected the equation of the Internet with the more traditional broadcast media. "Unlike the conditions that prevailed when Congress first authorized regulation of the broadcast spectrum," Justice Stevens wrote for the Court, "the Internet can

---

[1]Lance Rose, *Netlaw: Your Rights in the Online World* (Berkeley, Calif: Osborne McGraw-Hill, 1995), 5–6.

hardly be considered a 'scarce' expressive commodity. It provides relatively unlimited, low-cost capacity for communication of all kinds."[2]

## A Lack of Gatekeepers

Cultural critics and jurists alike have often expressed frustration with the enormous difficulty that ordinary speakers have in trying to reach audiences of meaningful size. Edward Cavazos, vice president and general counsel of Interliant and one of our most prolific writers on Internet law, reminds us how high this "speaker burden" is in the traditional media. If we wish to reach a large audience, we must either have a lot of money or have friends in high places in media industries. Potential book authors, for example, must find someone willing to incur the cost of publishing and distributing their words. Even if they succeed, they face the additional constraint of editorial control. Such control is not limited to books, of course. Only the most established Hollywood movie directors obtain the rights to make the "final cut" on their films. Whatever the medium, rarely do a writer's unfiltered ideas make their way to the audience.

All that changes with the advent of the Internet. No matter what size audience you seek to reach, there is no editor from whom to seek approval. Your message is made instantaneously available to an individual (e-mail), to a select group of like-minded souls of whatever size (via a "listserv"), or to anyone with access to the Internet (through your Web site).[3] Clearly there are significant exceptions to this Internet feature. Many listservs are organized by a human moderator, who may choose not to permit posting of messages deemed irrelevant to the subscribers' common interest. Then, too, online service providers such as America Online (AOL) do enforce a set of rules aimed at preventing subscribers from abusing one another, and AOL will impose sanctions against those who violate the rules. Even these counterexamples do not negate the Internet's extraordinary openness. After all, if a listserv's moderator "censors" some postings, it is only because the list's subscribers have decided for themselves the scope of their discourse. A listserv dedicated to tracking civil rights bills pending in Congress will likely not be much interested in postings expressing adoration for the teen heartthrob of the moment, and vice versa. With respect to rules of discourse imposed by AOL, they tend to be limited to personally abusive or fraudulent conduct. The general rule that any subscriber who wants to write to any other subscriber may do so is still in force.

Although the area of Internet law is still in its infancy, one generalization that seems to fit so far is that the extent to which an Internet Service Provider acts as a gatekeeper often determines whether that provider will be found liable for the transgressions of its subscribers. The more editorial control exercised

---

[2]*Reno v. ACLU,* 521 U.S. 844, 870 (1997).

[3]Edward A. Cavazos, "The Idea Incubator: Why the Internet Poses Unique Problems for the First Amendment," 8 *Seton Hall Constitutional Law Journal* 667 (1998).

by a service provider, the more risk of liability it assumes. Libel plaintiffs do not typically sue only the source of a defamatory remark, but also the media outlet that promulgated it. Contrast this situation with companies that act only as conduits, or "common carriers," of others' messages. The phone company is not prosecuted if some organized crime figures do some of their conspiring by telephone.

The Internet's lack of gatekeepers carries with it another important implication. In Chapter 2, we encountered Elizabeth Noelle-Neumann's "spiral of silence" theory. Noelle-Neumann argued that the political and social perspectives that mass media industries depict are rather middle of the road, that anything too far left, right, or otherwise removed from established norms would not play well, would not garner much of an audience. As a result, she argued, our own interpersonal discourse comes to manifest the same relative blandness, as persons with outlandish ideas will be loath to share them with their neighbors.

The Internet, and especially the phenomenon of the chat room, seems to be pushing things in the opposite direction. One of the defining characteristics of Internet chatter is that companions are chosen on the basis of shared interests rather than on the accident of proximity.[4] As such, chat rooms can serve, for better or worse, as incubators for unpopular ideas, with participants egging each other on to adopt yet more extreme viewpoints. Chat rooms thus can create a new kind of "spiral" of discourse, but it is hardly a spiral of *silence.*

### Parity among Senders and Receivers

Internet discourse forces us to rethink some of our most basic distinctions among broad categories of communication events. Perhaps most fundamentally, it is no longer quite clear what "mass" communication means on the Net. Traditionally, mass communication is thought of as having a fairly large corporation as the source of messages. When we watch a TV network newscast, we realize that the "speaker" is a highly complex organization, that scores of people had a direct hand in deciding what would be included in the broadcast, and that these staff persons were trying in turn to reflect the collective interests of management, stockholders, and advertisers.

In that traditional mass media speakers often have the backing of huge corporate structures, we all know instinctively the difference in "production values" between a network broadcast or a big city newspaper compared with home videos or a neighborhood association newsletter. The Internet changes much of these differences, at least for now. Put plainly, there are only so many things one can do to a Web site to make it slick and professional, and most of these tricks of the trade are equally available to a huge media corporation and to talented, motivated individuals with limited funds. This is why, for example,

---

[4]Andrew L. Shapiro, "The Net That Binds: Using Cyberspace to Create Real Communities," *The Nation,* 21 June 1999, p. 20.

political parodists have had a lark with the World Wide Web; they often set up Web sites that look on the surface to be a presidential candidate's official site, but their purpose is to make fun of the candidate. Several such online comics made quite a name for themselves with their parody Web sites; sometimes, too, the content of the sites seems to cross the line between satire and political dirty tricks, attributing to the candidate outlandish issue stances likely to dissuade potential supporters.[5]

It has often been suggested that the growth of the Internet means that we are *all* publishers now. This admittedly glib assertion may come to have important long-term effects on the structure of U.S. communication law. Consider the many times throughout this book's earlier chapters that we saw the courts treat members of the institutional press differently from the rest of us. In Chapter 9, for example, we saw the difficulty in deciding who is a "reporter" in state reporter shield laws. As more Americans become dependent on the World Wide Web for a good portion of their news, will *all* Internet content providers be considered reporters? There are also times when media industries are more protected from libel suits than other defendants.[6] Again, when will or should an Internet "publisher" be considered a mass media outlet? Consider also that the Privacy Protection Act (see Chapter 9)—the federal law enacted in response to the Supreme Court decision in *Zurcher v. Stanford Daily,* a law requiring in most circumstances that law enforcement officials issue a subpoena rather than search newsrooms—is worded rather broadly. Rather than restricting the Act's provisions to, for example, full-time employees of bona fide media outlets, Congress instead made reference to all persons "reasonably believed to have a purpose to disseminate to the public a newspaper, book, broadcast, or other similar form of public communication." Does not the advent of the Internet mean that virtually *everyone* fits this definition?[7]

## Extraordinarily Low Cost

Chapter 10 included discussion of a Supreme Court's decision involving a ban on residential "For Sale" signs in Willingboro, New Jersey. One of the reasons Justice Marshall gave for overturning the statute was that it precluded homeowners from using the least expensive traditional means of letting people know they are looking for a buyer. To be sure, Marshall allowed, Willingboro residents were still free to

---

[5]Jon Oram, "Will the Real Candidate Please Stand Up? Political Parody on the Internet," 5 *Journal of Intellectual Property Law* 467 (1998); Ben White, "Parody Site Wins at FEC," *Washington Post,* 20 April 2000, p. A4.

[6]*Philadelphia Newspapers v. Hepps,* 475 U.S. 767 (1986).

[7]Mark Eckenwiller, "Constitutional Issues Involving Use of the Internet: Applications of the Privacy Protection Act," 8 *Seton Hall Constitutional Law Journal* 725 (1998).

advertise in the newspaper's real estate section or to hire a professional realtor, but both those options are more expensive than placing a sign on one's lawn.[8]

Although it would be overstating Marshall's point to suggest that the "free" in "free speech" means free from financial cost, his opinion reminds us that the vigor of our First Amendment rights should not depend on the size of our wallets. This logic suggests that speech on the Internet should enjoy a special measure of protection. After all, the "For Sale" signs in Willingboro would reach the eyes only of those walking or driving by a specific home in the course of their daily activities; depending on the home's location, that could mean only a few dozen audience members. By contrast, the Internet permits speakers to reach an audience of thousands, even millions, at little or no cost.

That it is so inexpensive to reach huge audiences online can be a rationale for either furthering Internet speech or for inhibiting it. On the one hand, Internet speakers seem to be the modern-day equivalent of the "lone pamphleteers" whose outrage at the Crown's imposition of the Stamp Tax created at least part of the impetus for the American Revolutionary War. The great ease with which Internet publishers can disseminate their messages, however, often irks their audiences in ways not often seen with other media. Perhaps the best example is the phenomenon called "SPAM," or junk e-mail. This issue is discussed at more length later in this chapter; for now, suffice it to say that online service providers have gone to court to try to eliminate such unwanted commercial messages from their systems.

The dramatic implications of the low cost of Internet transmission are apparent from a scenario that played out in late 2000 and early 2001. A protester of Nike's alleged use of exploited labor in Asia and South America went to the company's Web site, and followed the directions there for ordering a customized pair of athletic shoes. Specifically, the activist requested that the shoes be emblazoned with a single word: *sweatshop*. Nike refused the request, initially claiming that the word fell into the category of "inappropriate slang," later admitting that their basis for refusal was an escape clause they had purposely included in their set of instructions, granting themselves the right to refuse to embroider any slogan it considers "inappropriate."

The activist sent copies of his lengthy e-mail exchange to friends, and that is where the explosion of what he calls the "micromedia" of the Net began. Friends forwarded the mailing to friends of friends, and suddenly the notion of "six degrees of separation" seemed anachronistically quaint, as millions of people worldwide saw the exchange, a phenomenon highly embarrassing to Nike. Eventually more traditional media began to feed on the story as well, resulting in articles in such outlets as *USA Today,* the *Wall Street Journal,* and *Business Week,* as well as a personal appearance on the *Today* program.[9]

---

[8]*Linmark Associates v. Township of Willingboro,* 431 U.S. 85, 93 (1977).

[9]Jonah Peretti, "My Nike Media Adventure," *The Nation,* 9 Apr. 2001, p. 19.

## Jurisdictional Ambiguity

Perhaps you recall, from Chapter 4, the discussion of the lawsuit pursued by Kathy Keeton against *Hustler* magazine. The plaintiff was a New York resident, the magazine's corporate headquarters were in Ohio, and yet her lawsuit was heard by a federal district court in New Hampshire. Keeton chose that forum because of the state's unusually long statute of limitations; the Supreme Court decided that her suit could be brought in New Hampshire, because *Hustler* did distribute some copies of its magazines to that state's residents.

The *Keeton* case was actually a special case of the more general issue of **personal jurisdiction,** of when one state may adjudicate claims involving nonresidents of that state. In 1945, the Supreme Court articulated a general rule to the effect that there must be some kind of "minimal contacts" between a defendant and the "forum state" (the state in which personal jurisdiction is sought). The issue is really one of due process, because it would be fundamentally unfair for citizens of one state to be dragged into the courts of another state with which they had not and never intended to do business.[10] In a 1985 case, the Court allowed that the requisite minimal contacts can be found even if the defendant rarely if ever has set foot in the forum state. "It is an inescapable fact of modern commercial life that a substantial amount of business is transacted solely by mail and wire communications across state lines," Justice Brennan wrote for the Court, "thus obviating the need for physical presence within a State in which business is conducted." Courts can exercise jurisdiction over a resident of another state as long as the potential defendant has engaged in some commercial enterprise "purposely directed towards" residents of the forum state.[11] A plurality decision from 1987 offers several factors that may be used as evidence that a company has done such "purposeful" direction. These criteria include "designing the product for the market in the forum State, advertising in the forum State, establishing channels for providing regular advice to customers in the forum State, or marketing the product through a distributor who has agreed to serve as the sales agent in the forum State."[12]

How should these principles apply on the Internet? The matter is complicated by the fact that Web sites, once uploaded to the Net, are accessible in every state (and indeed, around the world). Internet speech would be unfairly stifled, many commentators have suggested, if the simple posting of a Web site opened one up to nationwide liability.

A few dozen Internet cases have already required courts to determine whether they had jurisdiction over residents of other states. A general rule has emerged that is not at all inconsistent with cases that have involved earlier communication media.[13] The rule is that the creation of a Web site is not in and of

---

[10]*International Shoe v. Washington,* 326 U.S. 310 (1945).

[11]*Burger King Corporation v. Rudzewicz,* 471 U.S. 462, 476 (1985).

[12]*Asahi Metal Industry Company v. Superior Court,* 480 U.S. 102, 112 (1987).

[13]Andrew E. Costa, "Minimum Contacts in Cyberspace: a Taxonomy of the Case Law," 35 *Houston Law Review* 453 (1998).

itself sufficient to create personal jurisdiction, especially if it is a "passive" site that allows visitors to see whatever is posted by the operator but does not function interactively, allowing the visitor to place orders or give other kinds of feedback. Even the existence of a passive site, however, if augmented by some additional manifestations of a purposeful relationship between the defendant and the forum state, can be used as a basis for jurisdiction.

*Cybersell, Inc. v. Cybersell, Inc.*[14] was a case involving a passive Web site. The plaintiff, an Arizona-based company offering Internet advertising and marketing services, and which had registered its name as a service mark, sued the identically named Florida Web site designing business for having violated its trademark by using "cybsell.com" as its Internet domain name. (A later section of this chapter examines more closely the relationship between Internet domain names and traditional trademarks.) The plaintiff argued that the Arizona court should have jurisdiction, "because cyberspace is without borders and a web site which advertises a product or service is necessarily intended for use on a world wide basis." The court rejected this analysis. "While there is no question that anyone, anywhere could access" the Florida corporation's home page, "and thereby learn about the services offered, we cannot see how from that fact alone it can be inferred that [defendant] deliberately directed its merchandising efforts toward Arizona residents."

Another passive Web site case involved the famous Blue Note jazz club in New York City's Greenwich Village. The owner, who had registered his club's name as a federally protected service mark, sued the operator of a club going by the same name in Columbia, Missouri, who had created a Web site. The court in New York refused to accept jurisdiction. U.S. District Judge Sidney Stein emphasized that the Missouri company's Web site was so passive that visitors could not even purchase tickets online, but instead were referred to an old-fashioned phone number to place their orders. Moreover, the site included a disclaimer to the effect that this club was not affiliated with the famous one in New York and even encouraging browsers to attend the better-known club should they ever find themselves in the Big Apple. Interestingly, the Missouri club owner's policy was to have all attendees pick up their tickets at the door; he did not mail tickets. Thus, Judge Stein could confidently declare that "even assuming that the user was confused about the relationship of the Missouri club to the one in New York, such an act of infringement would have occurred in Missouri, not New York."[15]

*Zippo Manufacturing Company v. Zippo Dot Com,*[16] by contrast, involved a more interactive Web site. This trademark infringement suit was brought by the company that manufactures Zippo cigarette lighters against a California company that had used a similar name for its own Web site. At this point in the litigation, the court had only to determine if the defendant's conduct reached the residents of the

---

[14]130 F.3d 414 (9th Cir. 1997).

[15]*Bensusan Restaurant Corporation v. King,* 937 F. Supp. 295, 299 (S.D.N.Y. 1996), *aff'd,* 126 F.3d 25 (2d Cir. 1997).

[16]952 F. Supp. 1119 (W.D. Pa. 1997).

plaintiff's home state of Pennsylvania sufficiently to establish the court's jurisdiction. The court determined that such jurisdiction was justified. The defendant did not merely create an informational Web site, available to all who wished to visit. Rather it was conducting business on the Internet, inviting potential customers to sign online contracts for access to various services. The court also found it relevant that Zippo Dot Com had contracted with a handful of Pennsylvania-based Internet Service Providers and that 3,000 of the defendant's subscribers were from Pennsylvania.

A similar result was reached in *American Network v. Access America/Connect Atlanta, Inc.*,[17] another trademark case, this time involving two similar Internet domain names, the plaintiff's American.com, and the defendant's America.com. In that the plaintiff was a New York corporation and the defendant a Georgia corporation, the issue of jurisdiction again had to be resolved. That the defendant did have a small client base in New York was sufficient to create a link with the forum state, the court ruled.

The Internet is not merely a nationwide but rather a worldwide communications medium, however, which leads to some unusual jurisdictional and enforcement issues. Later in this chapter, we discuss *Reno v. ACLU,* the 1997 case that produced the Supreme Court's very first Internet decision. The issue involved was the constitutionality of the Communication Decency Act, which sought to protect children from unsolicited transmissions of sexual materials online. For now, it is worth noting that one of the problems involved in such legislation is that sexually oriented Web sites can originate halfway around the world just as easily as they can from the next state or the next block. Figure 13.1, a Jimmy Margulies cartoon, neatly encapsulates this particular enforcement issue.

Another jurisdictional issue, thus far unresolved, concerns international Internet sales. Consider, for example, the controversy posed by the purchase by some Americans of J. K. Rowling's popular children's book, *Harry Potter and the Chamber of Secrets.* Some such sales took place at a time when the publisher had granted the rights to distribute the book in the United Kingdom, but the contract for U.S. distribution rights had not yet gone into effect. Because one of the rights granted by copyright law is to determine when and how a work is first sold, such international purchases could be a violation of law. But who would be liable? And would a U.S. court accept jurisdiction? It may be a while before these kinds of issues are resolved, whether by case law, domestic statutory reform, or international treaty.[18]

More generally, that the Internet is such a decentralized and uncontrollable international medium of communication often frustrates government gatekeepers. With varying degrees of success, China tries to block access to sites about Tibet,

---

[17]975 F. Supp. 494, (S.D.N.Y. 1997).

[18]Robert Neuner and David W. Whealan, "Internet Purchasers of Children's Book Create Copyright Stir," *New York Law Journal,* 17 May 1999, p. S6.

Figure 13.1

This Jimmy Margulies cartoon depicts a problem inherent in any Internet content regulation: the U.S. can pass all the laws it wants prohibiting obscenity (or any other categories of content), but that same content will still be available on foreign Web sites.

© *Jimmy Margulies, The Record (N.J.). Reprinted by permission.*

Taiwan, democratic movements and dissident groups, and Saudi Arabia censors sites critical of its royal family. At least twenty countries have some kind of formal Internet censorship policy, although such rules are virtually unenforceable, at least in the sense that information will get through anyway. Some Web sites may be effectively blocked, some high-profile prosecutions may take place, but "Netizens" will still be able to communicate via e-mail, chat rooms, and even new Web sites with code names designed to fool blocking software.[19] The uncontrollable Net can even negate a government's efforts to silence more traditional media. During the Kosovo crisis, the politically and ethnically independent Belgrade radio station, B92, although banned by the government, continued to broadcast intermittently via a Netherlands-based Internet site. It was on the Internet that the Chinese people heard of NATO's apology for having bombed that country's embassy in Belgrade, this part of the story having been initially banned by that country's official media.[20]

Still, international media companies, both traditional and on the Internet, often do act in deference to the sensibilities of nations whose laws are more restrictive than those in the United States. The Paris edition of the *International Herald Tribune,* for example, which is jointly owned by the *New York Times* and the *Washington Post,* is subject to regular legal review to ensure its compliance with libel laws of those nations in which it is distributed.[21] That review no doubt intensified after the paper

---

[19]David L. Marcus, "Nations Strive to Limit Freedom of the Internet," *Boston Globe,* 28 Dec. 1998, p. A1.

[20]Sarah Marriott, "Fighting the Cybercensors," *Irish Times,* 24 May 1999, p. 8

[21]Floyd Abrams, "Cyberspace and the Law," 11 *St. John's Journal of Legal Commentary* 693 (1996).

settled a libel suit with two government officials in Singapore for over $200,000. The piece would surely have been considered protected opinion in U.S. courts.

Perhaps the best-known example of this phenomenon in the online world occurred in December 1995 when a Bavarian prosecutor notified CompuServe that it was under criminal investigation for making available the uncensored Internet, including sexually oriented sites whose content could be banned under German law. CompuServe responded by blocking access—by all its subscribers, children and adults—to several hundred possibly offensive Web sites and online news groups. The move led many Internet enthusiasts to cry "Censorship!" A *Denver Post* editorial warned that the precedent had "horrifying implications: If the provincial government of one part of Germany can force CompuServe to curtail access to the Internet, will it do likewise to suit, say, the attorney general of Utah or partisans of religiously fundamentalist regimes in the Middle East?"[22] A few weeks later, the company backed away from its original stance, restoring the accessibility of all but a handful of discussion groups, while making software available to its subscribers that would effectively block their children's access to offensive portions of the Internet.

---

[22]Pat McGraw, "CompuServe Is a Cyberwimp," *Denver Post,* 18 Jan. 1996, p. B6.

## Things to Remember

### UNIQUE FEATURES OF THE INTERNET

- It is theoretically possible to carry an infinite amount of information on the Internet.
- Its basic structure does not require the use of "gatekeepers"; anyone who wants to post messages can do so.
- Users tend to choose their online "friends" on the basis of shared interests, rather than physical proximity.
- On the Internet, consumers and "publishers" are the same people.
- Even on a humble budget, individuals can make their online presence appear as slick and professional as that of a multibillion dollar corporation.
- This parity among all Internet users challenges traditional legal privileges accorded to the institutionalized press because we no longer can say what it means to be a "reporter."
- Because information posted on the Internet is available to anyone nationwide (and worldwide), courts have had to rethink the matter of personal jurisdiction (i.e., when it is appropriate for one state's courts to accept jurisdiction over a nonresident of that state).
- In general, the more interactive a Web site, the more likely its manager can be sued anywhere, whereas operators of more passive sites do not incur this liability.
- The Internet also poses significant challenges to the flow and control of information across international boundaries.

A more recent international Internet incident involved the U.S.-based Yahoo! as the unsuccessful defendant in a French court stemming from sales of Nazi memorabilia on the company's auction site. Under French law, artifacts from the Third Reich may not be bought and sold. As a result of the verdict, the Internet company prohibited users worldwide from offering such items for sale. In yet another international prosecution, an Australian man was convicted of posting on his Web site materials that could be construed—in violation of German law—as a denial of the Holocaust's having occurred.[23]

## Developments in Communication Law Online

Although the Internet is still in its infancy, a fair amount of relevant communications case law and legislative activity has already accumulated. Indeed, many attorneys around the country make their living in the practice of cyberspace law, which is also the focus of full courses at law schools. In this chapter, we examine four separate areas of communication law as applied to cyberspace: libel, trademark and copyright, privacy, and the transmission of sexually oriented messages.

### Libel Online

If one subscriber to an online service such as Prodigy or CompuServe uses the Net to engage in defamatory speech, should the plaintiff be able to recoup damages from the service provider, or only from the individual speaker? Two relatively early decisions from New York produced opposite results. Soon thereafter, Congress weighed in on the issue and may have effectively settled this specific question.

In *Cubby v. CompuServe, Inc.*,[24] a federal district court ruled that the defendant could not be held liable for defamatory statements made within an electronic newsletter (called "Rumorville") created online for subscribers who participated in a discussion forum focusing on trends in journalism and mass media. The service offered to its subscribers by CompuServe, the court observed, was like "an electronic, for-profit library that carries a vast number of publications." The company cannot possibly have advance knowledge of the contents of all those publications, any more than can "a public library, book store, or newsstand." Imposing liability on CompuServe would be especially inappropriate, the court emphasized, in that the company's relationship with the offending newsletter was rather tenuous, with three layers of contractors and subcontractors.

Contrast this decision with a New York state court's ruling in *Stratton Oakmont v. Prodigy Services.*[25] Here, an anonymous bulletin board (BBS) participant on

---

[23]Leslie Szanto Freidman, "Tips for Avoiding Foreign Hassles on the Internet," *New York Law Journal,* 27 Feb 2001, p. 1.

[24] 776 F. Supp. 135 (S.D.N.Y. 1991).

[25]23 Media Law Rptr. 1794 (N.Y. Sup. Ct. 1995).

Prodigy accused the plaintiff company of fraudulent practices in its handling of its clients' initial public offerings of stocks. The resulting libel suit could proceed against Prodigy, the court held, because unlike CompuServe in the earlier case, the defendant here "held itself out as an online service that exercised editorial control over the content of messages posted on its computer bulletin boards." The company's marketing scheme at the time was predicated on positioning itself as the most "family friendly" of the major online service providers. Prodigy would put its own subscribers on notice that they had an obligation to be civil to each other, not to post insulting messages; the company also used blocking software designed to weed out especially offensive language. In short, the company proudly exercised the kinds of editorial controls that make more traditional publishers liable for their content.

Thus, a rule seemed to be developing that to determine an online company's potential liability in a defamation suit, look to whether the company's relationship with its own online content was more akin to that of a library or bookstore, on one hand, or an actual publisher, on the other.

A portion of the Telecommunications Act of 1996, however, says that "no provider or user of an interactive computer service shall be treated as the publisher or speaker of any information provided by another information content provider."[26] This law has resulted in online service providers escaping liability for their subscribers' transgressions, even when the Internet company clearly intended to benefit from the rhetorical excesses of those subscribers. No case makes this point more clearly than *Blumenthal v. Drudge,* which resulted from online columnist Matt Drudge accusing journalist–*cum*–presidential-advisor Sidney Blumenthal of physically abusing his wife. AOL's motion to be released as a defendant was readily granted by the court, even though the company had signed a contract with the columnist for the rights to include the "Drudge Report" on its system, touted this relationship in some of its marketing materials, and retained the right to edit Drudge's content. The court admitted that the close relationship AOL maintained with Drudge was certainly more akin to that of publisher and journalist than bookstore and author. "Why is this different from AOL advertising and promoting a new purveyor of child pornography or other offensive material? Why should AOL be permitted to tout someone as a gossip columnist or rumor monger who will make such rumors and gossip 'instantly accessible' to AOL subscribers, and then claim immunity when that person, as might be anticipated, defames another?"[27] Federal district Judge Paul Friedman even went so far as to say that he would agree with Blumenthal, if he were "writing on a clean slate." Congress, however, had made it clear that Internet Service Providers were not to be held liable for their customers' postings.

AOL also escaped liability in a disturbing case involving Kenneth Zeran, a young man with an anonymous yet highly persistent enemy. In April 1995, a

---

[26]47 U.S.C.S. sec 230 (c)(1) (1999).

[27]992 F. Supp. 44, 51 (D.D.C. 1998).

prankster posted a notice on an AOL bulletin board, ostensibly offering for sale T-shirts with any of a number of highly offensive slogans ("Visit Oklahoma.... It's a Blast!") making reference to the bombing that month of the Murrah Federal Building in Oklahoma City. The completely fictional posting instructed readers to call "Ken" at Zeran's home phone number in Seattle. Not surprisingly, Zeran received many hateful phone calls, including death threats. When Zeran complained to AOL, the company promised to remove the posting promptly. Similar follow-up notices continued to appear for several days, however; in response to further complaints from Zeran, AOL promised to close the account from which the postings were being generated.

The Court of Appeals for the Fourth Circuit granted summary judgment to AOL. Unlike Judge Friedman in the *Blumenthal* case, here the court expressed its strong support for the relevant portion of the Telecommunications Act. Since ISPs serve millions of users, processing a "staggering" amount of information, they should not "face potential liability each time they receive notice of a potentially defamatory statement." To hold otherwise, the court emphasized, "would create an impossible burden in the Internet context."[28]

By immunizing ISPs from most liability, Congress has thus answered at least one of the Internet's challenges for traditional libel law. Other issues must await future resolution. Consider, for example, the distinctions among categories of libel plaintiffs. In *Gertz v. Welch, Inc.,* covered at length in Chapter 4, the Supreme Court offered two reasons why the First Amendment demands that public officials and public figures have a difficult time obtaining a libel judgment. One of those rationales was that such persons "usually enjoy significantly greater access to the channels of effective communication and hence have a more realistic opportunity to counteract false statements than private individuals normally enjoy."[29]

Does this reasoning apply with full force on the Internet, one of whose defining characteristics is a relative equality of access for all, as both consumers and "publishers"? Persons who are maligned online can and do respond in kind. Flaming begets flaming. Moreover, the aggrieved individuals can reach an audience as large as the one exposed to the original defamation. Some commentators have suggested that the new communication dynamics of the Net will soon require a rethinking of the *Gertz* doctrine. Might it not make more sense, some argue, for all Internet participants to be considered public figures?

Courts have not yet had occasion to rule on this precise point, and sentiment among commentators is by no means unanimous. In a thoughtful essay, Michael Hadley asked readers to consider what might happen if Internet columnist Matt Drudge had hurled false charges of spousal abuse against an obscure

---

[28]*Zeran v. America Online,* 129 F.3d 327, 330, 331, 333 (4th Cir. 1997); see also *Zeran v. Diamond Broadcasting,* 203 F.3d 714 (10th Cir. 2000).

[29]*Gertz v. Welch, Inc.,* 418 U.S. 323, 344 (1974).

# Things to Remember

## LIBEL ONLINE

- A common-law principle seemed to be developing to the effect that Internet Service Providers that exercise editorial control over messages sent by and among subscribers could be liable for damages stemming from a subscriber's defamatory postings.

- A portion of the Telecommunications Act of 1996 negated that presumption by giving ISPs virtually complete immunity from such liability.

- Some commentators have suggested that the traditional distinctions between public figures and private plaintiffs be discarded for Internet libel suits, that all persons who engage in "cyberchatter" should be considered public figures.

private citizen—such as a neighbor against whom he had a grudge—rather than at Sidney Blumenthal, the White House advisor. What would the neighbor do to answer the charges? If he were wealthy, he could take out paid newspaper ads. Were his resources more limited, he might instead set up his own Web page to refute the allegations. Such an obscure site, however, would only languish, sitting passively on a server waiting to be discovered.[30]

## Trademark and Copyright Online

Cyberspace forces us to rethink some of the most basic tenets of intellectual property law. In the online world, we are not certain what it means to make a "copy" of a work, nor is the relationship clear between traditional trademarks and the Internet "addresses" called universal resource locators, or URLs. One of the defining characteristics of the Internet is that it is a computer mediated form of communication where messages are sent digitally. This fact, too, has enormous implications for intellectual property law, for three related reasons. First, the Net makes the mass production of protected works so effortless. Second, unauthorized copies can be distributed worldwide in a matter of seconds. Finally, the enormous volume of copying makes it virtually impossible to track down the original infringer in a chain of Internet piracy;[31] some have even argued that this fact alone will be looked back on as the beginning of the end of copyright law.[32]

---

[30]Michael Hadley, "The *Gertz* Doctrine and Internet Defamation," 84 *Virginia Law Review* 477, 494 (1998).

[31]Jack E. Brown, "New Law for the Internet," 28 *Arizona State Law Journal* 1243 (1996).

[32]John Perry Barlow, "The Economy of Ideas: A Framework for Rethinking Patents and Copyrights in the Digital Age," *Wired,* Mar. 1994, p. 84.

***"Copying" in a Digital World.***   Traditional copyright law does not seem to fit well with the Internet. In the physical world, we recognize the difference between reading something and copying it. You might have seen a funny cartoon or a provocative article in your local newspaper, and perhaps you chose to show it to a friend or to clip it and paste it on your door for any passersby to enjoy. You have not *copied* it. On the Internet, however, to read *is* to copy in that we can access digital expression "only by reproducing it in RAM or on a hard drive, floppy disk, or magnetic tape." Thus, the simple act of reading an online file "violates the copyright holder's exclusive right to reproduce."[33]

In 1995, the Working Group on Intellectual Property Rights, a component of President Clinton's Information Infrastructure Task Force, issued a report on the applicability of copyright law to the digital world. Their report, often referred to in the literature as simply the "White Paper," pointed out that a "copy" is created in all the following instances:

- When a work is placed into a computer, whether on a disk, diskette, ROM, or other storage device or in RAM for more than a very brief period.
- When a printed work is scanned into a digital file.
- When other works—including photographs, motion pictures, and sound recordings—are digitized.
- Whenever a digitized file is uploaded from a user's computer to a bulletin board system or other server.
- Whenever a digitized file is downloaded from a BBS or other server.
- When a file is transferred from one computer network user to another.

The Task Force also said that copyright law protects not only owners' exclusive right to make copies of their work, but also to *display* it. Even here, the digital age and the traditional law do not produce a good fit. To read material from the Internet on your computer screen *is* to display it.

Many commentators have pointed to a fundamental irony here. The Internet is often touted as a revolutionary vehicle for the unlimited exchange of information, yet its infrastructure would seem to give copyright holders a veto over what will be seen and where, power far in excess of that which Congress had ever intended. If you cannot even read a protected work on your computer screen without permission, what will happen to the Fair Use doctrine? After all, in virtually all protected works, some subset of the text consists of the recounting of historical facts, which are themselves not copyrightable.

What does all this mean for the individual Netizen? We may be in violation of copyright law when we incorporate text or graphics created by others on our own

---

[33]Fred Cate, "Law in Cyberspace," 39 *Howard Law Journal* 565, 575 (1996).

Web sites, and perhaps even when we point our site's visitors to others' protected works with hyperlinks. Will copyright holders sue you for these kinds of transgressions or for simply reading their works on your computer screen? Almost certainly not, yet the balance between the rights of copyright holders and users who may wish to read and to comment on others' works seems to have shifted.

More institutional users of the Internet have expressed concern about the poor fit between traditional copyright law and cyberspace as well as a legislative trend toward strengthening the copyright holders' control over Net content. The Digital Millennium Copyright Act (DMCA), enacted in late 1998, has been especially vexing for librarians. That Act contains a provision making it a criminal offense to circumvent any technological locking device that might be used by copyright holders to prevent unauthorized copying.

At one level, such a provision makes sense. If we envision a future in which virtually all intellectual products—books, music, films, and so forth—will be transmitted primarily via the Internet, it is not surprising that movie studios, for example, would want to install devices permitting downloaders to view a film once only. Otherwise, every video rental becomes a video sale. In the summer of 2000, a federal district judge used the DMCA to enjoin a group of computer hackers from posting software that would enable users to circumvent the encryption device used on many DVDs (and thus permitting unauthorized copying).[34]

The encryption device is called CSS (for "content scrambling system"). The hackers, who call themselves MORE (Masters of Reverse Engineering) have achieved a kind of cult status. Computer source coding of their software, aptly enough named DeCSS, has appeared on T-shirts distributed worldwide.

How should the relevant section of the DMCA apply to digitally transmitted books and periodicals? In the physical world, libraries are permitted to make copies of articles from journals in their collections for any number of purposes, such as for interlibrary loans. Individual library users have been similarly accustomed to making photocopies of library materials for their own use, often for research projects. If, however, all knowledge comes to us on the Internet in a "locked" format and librarians are prohibited from unlocking it, we will have entered what a *Washington Post* editorial called a "Pay-Per-View World."[35] Librarians can take some comfort from Congress's having delayed enforcement of criminal penalties for unauthorized circumvention of blocking devices for two years, after which the librarian of Congress will make a report on the implications of the law for such traditional copyright features as the fair use defense and the assumption that some works are "born" into the public domain (usually because they are mostly factual rather than creative).[36]

---

[34]*Universal City Studios v. Reimerdes,* 111 F. Supp. 2d 294 (S.D.N.Y. 2000).

[35]"A Pay-Per-View World," *Washington Post,* 4 Aug. 1998, p. A14.

[36]Pamela Samuelson, "Good News and Bad News on the Intellectual Property Front," *Communications of the Association for Computing Machinery,* 1 Mar. 1999, p. 19.

***MP3 Web Sites and the Music Industry.*** In the "old days," if you owned a phonograph record coveted by a friend of yours, you might make a copy of the record by playing the record with the phonograph linked to a cassette tape deck. Technically, this act would be a violation of copyright law, but none of the record companies would find it worth their while to sue you. It is also worth noting that if your friend wanted to make a copy of that cassette for another person, the resulting second-generation copy would be of audibly inferior quality. Third- and fourth-generation copies would manifest yet further deteriorated sound. In short, there would not be much of an incentive or opportunity for the casual copyright infringer to do much damage.

Enter the digital age, and things change markedly. Many Internet users have installed on their computers software that permits them to make compressed copies of any and all tracks from a CD and to upload this musical data to a Web site, ready for anyone who wishes to download the performances for themselves. Multiple copies and multiple generations of copies using this "MP3" technology lose little if any of the fidelity of the original.

Jay Berman, president of the International Federation of the Phonographic Industry, reported in 1999 that there were over half a million MP3 Web sites and that virtually all boasted pirated works, unauthorized by the copyright holders.[37] The Napster Web site, a clearinghouse for members sharing MP3 music files with each other (in the industry this is called peer-to-peer file sharing), has attracted much attention. Many universities have blocked access to napster.com lest their entire information infrastructures be crippled by heavy student use of the site.

Not surprisingly, a consortium of the largest recording companies sued Napster. In early 2001, the Ninth Circuit Court of Appeals handed down a preliminary ruling to the effect that the plaintiffs would likely succeed in proving Napster guilty of contributing to copyright infringement on the part of its millions of users. The three-judge panel handed the case back to a lower court, which issued an injunction ordering Napster to block access within three days after the plaintiffs assert their copyright ownership. There are many complicating factors in the ruling, not the least of which is that users can evade detection by Napster's filtering software by purposely misspelling the names of songs.[38]

Not all uses of MP3 are illegal or a threat to artists. Often, struggling artists create their own Web sites and give away some of their best work for free in the hopes of being discovered by a recording company's staff surfing the Net or as a way of enticing potential customers to buy their self-produced CDs directly from them.[39]

---

[37]Alice Rawsthorn, "Internet Fast Becoming Copyright Battleground," *Stuart News/Port St. Lucie News* (Stuart, Fla.), 28 Mar. 1999, p. D2.

[38]*A&M Records v. Napster,* 239 F.3d 1004 (9th Cir. 2001), on remand, U.S. Dist. LEXIS 2186 (2001).

[39]Emily A. Vander Veer, "Internet Harmony: Austin Startup Helps Musicians, Fans Unite on The Web," *Austin American-Statesman,* 19 May 1999, p. E12.

Most observers agree that the threat posed by MP3 Web sites to traditional copyright interests will result in the major companies buying rather than fighting the sites. Such predictions reflect the existence of MP3 sites such as Gnutella that are 100 percent peer-to-peer, such that there is no identifiable plaintiff to sue. Indeed, even while litigation against Napster was pending, the German media company, Bertelsmann AG—its portfolio includes BMG Records and CD Now—entered into a financial partnership with Napster, seeking to create a file swapping service for which users will be willing to pay.

***SYSOP/ISP Liability.***     Just as was the case with libel law, the question as to whether ISPs or system operators (SYSOPS) could be held liable for individual subscribers' infringements of copyright has been the focus of both litigation and federal legislation. It is also a source of much confusion among SYSOPS themselves.[40] One of the early cases was *Playboy Enterprises, Inc. v. Frena.*[41] George Frena was the SYSOP of a computer bulletin board called Techs Warehouse, whose content included "adult-oriented" graphics and photos. The impetus for the lawsuit was the plaintiff having discovered that about 170 of those images were photos from *Playboy* magazine and other publications to which it owned the rights.

Frena denied that he himself had ever uploaded any of the photos in question, maintaining that his subscribers were the direct infringers. He testified further that the moment *Playboy* attorneys alerted him about the infringements, he deleted the unauthorized images from his system and began to carefully monitor subscriber uploads. Although that testimony was not directly contested in court, it is apparent that Judge Harvey Schlesinger was unconvinced of Frena's truthfulness in that the defendant had removed the plaintiff's trademarked logo from the photos, substituting his own name and phone number. The plaintiff's motion for summary judgment was granted. Judge Schlesinger emphasized that it really did not matter whether Frena knew of the infringements prior to having been officially notified of them by the plaintiff. "Intent to infringe" is not an element of copyright suits. If Frena were truly an "innocent infringer," that fact may be taken into account later, when damages are assessed.

One of the most litigious copyright plaintiffs in recent years has been the "Religious Technology Center," which owns the copyrights to the writings of L. Ron Hubbard, founder of the Church of Scientology. One of the suits brought by the group was against Netcom, an Internet Service Provider.[42] Judge Ronald White noted that courts in his jurisdiction (the Northern District of California) had never dealt with the issue presented, "whether the operator of a computer bul-

---

[40]Ashley Packard, "Infringement or Impingement: Carving Out an Actual Knowledge Defense for Sysops Facing Strict Liability," *Journalism and Mass Communication Monographs,* Dec. 1998, pp. 1–46.

[41]839 F. Supp. 1552 (M.D. Fla. 1993).

[42]*Religious Technology Center v. Netcom On-Line Services,* 907 F. Supp. 1361 (N.D. Cal. 1995).

letin board service ('BBS'), and the large Internet access provider that allows that BBS to reach the Internet, should be liable for copyright infringement committed by a subscriber of the BBS." The subscriber was Dennis Erlich, once a minister within the church and now one of its harshest critics. Erlich used an Internet discussion group of his design (alt.religion.scientology) to disseminate his views. From the church's perspective, he crossed the line when he began posting to his online group lengthy, nearly verbatim excerpts from some of Hubbard's works.

At first, the church contacted Erlich directly, asking that he cease the online copyright infringement. When he refused, the plaintiff contacted Thomas Klemesrud, the operator of the larger computer bulletin board of which Erlich's was part, and Netcom, which provided the BBS's ultimate access to the Internet. Klemesrud made clear that he would not take any action until the church provided some *evidence* that Erlich had infringed on their copyrights. For its part, Netcom also refused to simply kick Erlich off of the Internet; because of the way the BBS was structured, this could not be accomplished without also denying access to every one of Klemesrud's subscribers.

Judge White determined that Netcom was not responsible for directly infringing on the church's copyrights in that the ISP did not exercise any immediate control over subscribers' postings. He agreed that Netcom itself had made "copies" of the works in question, but only to the extent that "copying" and "posting" data on the Internet are part of the same action, that one cannot read anything online unless it has been "copied." The judge agreed with Netcom's assertion that it should no more be held liable for direct copyright infringement here than should a telephone company "for carrying an infringing facsimile transmission or storing an infringing audio recording on its voice mail" or a highway toll booth operator for whatever criminal activities might take place on the roads.

Judge White cautioned, however, that Netcom might be held accountable for *contributory* infringement of the church's copyrights and for that reason did not fully grant the company's motion for summary judgment. A defendant can incur such liability if, "with knowledge of the infringing activity, [it] induces, causes or materially contributes to the infringing conduct of another." White rejected Netcom's assertion that the notice it had received from the plaintiff lacked sufficient evidence that one of its subscribers had indeed been infringing on a valid copyright. He admitted that copyright infringement cases on the Internet more commonly concern unauthorized copying of computer software, a product category with which online service providers have special expertise and can thus more easily ascertain for themselves if an infringement has taken place. That this case involved old-fashioned text instead would not excuse Netcom from all liability. Although he allowed the lawsuit to go forward on this point, Judge White set up a high barrier for the plaintiffs. Netcom would ultimately prevail even against a claim of contributory infringement, White told the parties, if it could show even a plausible suspicion that Erlich's postings constituted a Fair Use of the church's otherwise protected works.

Sega, the computer gaming software manufacturer, has also had to go to court to protect its copyrighted materials from online infringements. In one case, the company brought suit against Chad Sherman, an online BBS operator whose subscribers uploaded and downloaded dozens of Sega video games. In addition, Sherman marketed a product called "The Super Magic Drive," computer hardware designed to facilitate the copying of video game cartridges onto floppy disks for convenient uploading to the BBS. As in the *Netcom* case, the defendant here also could not be charged with direct infringement, although his conduct did fall squarely within the definition of contributory infringement. That finding was bolstered by Judge Wilken's having concluded that the BBS subscribers' conduct here was so clearly violative of copyright law that the Fair Use defense would never work for them. Their primary motivation for participating in the BBS was to download illegal copies so as to avoid having to buy products directly from Sega.

One fascinating feature of this case is that Sega had itself helped gather evidence in support of getting a search warrant. The company did so by having one of its employees log on to the defendant's BBS to observe firsthand the extent of unauthorized copying. The defendant cried foul—Sega had "unclean hands" and should not benefit from such conduct—but to no avail. Whatever merit the argument would normally have, Judge Wilken concluded, it has none in the context of Internet discourse. The typical computer BBS is, after all, "open to the public, and normally accessed by use of an alias or pseudonym."[43]

A portion of the DMCA, adopted in 1998, addresses the issue of liability for systems operators stemming from their subscribers' content. In effect, the law adopts a stance not too different from that seen in the line of cases reviewed here, although a bit more friendly to online service providers than was the *Frena* court. The federal law exempts service providers and systems operators from liability if they do not know of their subscribers' infringing conduct. The exemption will hold also if the provider, once made aware of the existence on their systems of unauthorized copyrighted material, "acts expeditiously to remove or disable access to the material." The law further protects the service provider from lawsuits that might be brought by subscribers distraught over their noninfringing content having been removed from the system without their consent, as long as the provider believed in good faith that the materials had been posted in violation of copyright law. It is also important that the service provider not gain financially as a direct result of the users's infringing activities.[44] This requirement may serve as a strong incentive for Internet companies to use flat-rate monthly billing, lest they find themselves making more money the more times that pirated copies of materials are downloaded.

---

[43]*Sega Enterprises v. Mapphia,* 948 F. Supp. 923 (N.D. Cal. 1996); see also *Sega Enterprises v. Sabella,* 1995 U.S. Dist. LEXIS 20470 (N.D. Cal. 1995).

[44]P.L. 105-304, sec. 512 (1999).

***Trademark, URL Addresses, and Web Site Interactions.*** One of the most fascinating—and, for those directly involved, perplexing—ways in which cyberspace has affected communication law concerns Internet domain names, which are the heart of a Web site's URL. In the real world, many companies can use the same trademark for very different products or services. Thus, we have Life cereal and also Life the board game, Thrifty car rental and Thrifty drug stores, Universal Van Lines and Universal Pictures. In trademark law, this is called **concurrent registration** of marks. Concurrent registration is the norm as long as two businesses are not in direct competition or marketing complementary products that consumers would presume must come from the same source.[45] In cyberspace, however, there can only be one www.life.com, one www.thrifty.com, and so on.

This restriction on the naming of Internet URLs is actually more a convention than an insurmountable technological barrier. It has been suggested, for example, that "master domain name masks" be created so that there would not be just one McDonalds.com, but rather McDonalds1.com, McDonalds2.com, McDonalds3.com, and so forth; such a system would be akin to finding *the* "John Smith" of interest from among a long list of John Smiths in the phone book.[46] At least for now, though, one and only one entity can be assigned the "space" of a particular URL address.

Since there is no universal Yellow Pages to help consumers associate domain names with company names—and Internet search engines such as Yahoo! and Excite can produce overwhelmingly large numbers of "hits" in response to a request for one specific site—consumers are often left guessing. The wise company seeking an Internet presence needs to predict as best it can whatever addresses consumers will *guess* might be theirs. Such domain names are thus very valuable commodities and have been the impetus for a flurry of litigation.

Internet domain names are actually a series of numbers that computers read in order to "talk" to each other; they are sometimes called Internet protocol, or IP, addresses. But humans do not remember numbers very well, so the IPs are translated into more mnemonic devices. The names consist of two parts, building from right to left. The portion of a name that appears after the "dot" is called the top-level domain (TLD) name. Sometimes they are called gTLDs, the "g" standing for "generic." In the United States, six TLDs have been most commonly used: .com (for profit-making companies), .org (non-profit organizations), .net (computer networks), .edu (educational institutions), .gov (government agencies), and .int (international organizations, such as NATO). Other nations are assigned different TLDs, such as .uk for the United Kingdom and .it for Italy. The International Corporation for Assigned Names and Numbers (ICANN) announced that it plans to

---

[45]*Aunt Jemima Mills Company v. Rigney & Company,* 247 F. 407 (2d Cir. 1917).

[46]Rosanne T. Mitchell, "Resolving Domain Name–Trademark Disputes: A New System of Alternative Dispute Resolution Is Needed in Cyberspace," 14 *Ohio State Journal on Dispute Resolution* 157 (1998).

add seven additional gTLDs: .aero (for aerospace companies), .biz and .info (serving the same function as the current .com, for any profit-making business), .coop (for business cooperatives), .museum (self-evident, no?), .name (for personal Web sites), and .pro (for individual professionals, such as doctors and lawyers). There was much controversy surrounding the closed-door proceedings ICANN used in formulating its decision, and the exorbitant prices it charged companies to simply submit an idea for a new gTLD.

Moving from right to left, we come to the second-level domain name. In "MyBusiness.com," "MyBusiness" is the second-level domain name. Whoever owns the rights to use "MyBusiness.com" as an Internet address might find it helpful to subdivide the second level a bit more. Thus, we might find "Billing_MyBusiness.com" functioning alongside "Jobs_MyBusiness.com," "NewProducts_MyBusiness.com," and so on.

Prior to ICANN's creation in 1999, a Virginia company called Network Solutions, Inc. (NSI) enjoyed a monopoly, granted by the federal government, in the assignment of domain names. If you or your company wanted to obtain the rights to use a specific Internet address, you would make an application to NSI.

When NSI would receive a request to be assigned a specific domain name, it would ask only that the registrant attest to the best of its knowledge that its own use of the name "does not interfere with, or infringe upon, the rights of any third party." NSI would not do an independent search of existing trademarks to see if the proposed domain name might be so similar so as to cause consumer confusion. Later, if a company with a trademark consisting of a word or phrase identical or highly similar to the domain name complained to the NSI, the original registrant was given thirty days in which to contest the challenge. If the two parties could not solve the dispute themselves, they would litigate. NSI can temporarily rescind the original granting of the domain name, pending the ultimate outcome of the dispute, but it does not have the authority to reassign the domain address to the trademark holder. It also does not have the resources to investigate disputes in that it registers hundreds of thousands of new domain addresses every month.

There have been at least three identifiable categories of disputes between trademark holders and URL address holders. First are those situations in which the URL registrant legitimately is doing business under a name that just happens to be the cherished trademark of another company. In this chapter's earlier discussion of jurisdictional problems on the Internet, we encountered a case involving a night club in Columbia, Missouri, whose URL address included the phrase "Blue-Note," which is also the name of a well-known night club in New York City.[47] In that case, the court refused to accept jurisdiction, in that the smaller club's Web site was a "passive" one not set up for such interactions as actually buying tickets

---

[47]*Bensusan Restaurant Corporation v. King,* 937 F. Supp. 295, 299 (S.D.N.Y. 1996), *aff'd,* 126 F.3d 25 (2d Cir. 1997).

online. Had the site been more interactive, and especially if it could be shown that some customers from the New York area had purchased tickets in preparation for a trip to the Midwest college town, the case would have forced the court to address the conflict between the one company's legitimately obtained URL address and the other's federally protected trademark.

A second kind of legal dispute, especially vexing from trademark holders' perspective, has involved the phenomenon of **cybersquatting.** These are folks who never actually intend to do business using the URL addresses for which they apply; rather, they make money by thinking a few steps ahead of large businesses that, for whatever reasons, did not establish an early Internet presence. One particularly well-known squatter has been the Toeppen Company, which has received authorization from NSI for hundreds of domain names with familiar rings, from "aircanada.com" and "neiman-marcus.com" to "camdenyards.com."[48]

---

[48]*Panavision International v. Toeppen,* 945 F. Supp. 1296 (C.D. Cal. 1996).

 Figure 13.2

CLOSE TO HOME    JOHN McPHERSON

"What the ...?! Oh, for cryin' out loud! BIGTONYSALLKAZOOPOLKABAND.COM is already taken as a domain name!"

Do you think the owner of the rights to this particular URL would be considered a cybersquatter?

Even though the legal climate is shifting against the squatter—Congress enacted the Anticybersquatting Consumer Protection Act in 1999, which makes clear that an Internet address can be the basis of a trademark infringement suit[49]—corporations will often settle with them out of court to avoid the expense and delay of litigation.

A third category has involved URL addresses maintained by companies or individuals who intend to prevent consumers from reaching the "natural" owners of the addresses, either because they are business competitors or because they have some more ideological conflict with the trademark holders. For example, Princeton Review Company began using "kaplan.com" as its domain name; site visitors would be treated to a comparison between Princeton's college test prep courses with those offered by the competing Stanley Kaplan Educational Center. An arbitration settlement resulted in Stanley Kaplan being assigned the site name. Or, consider the antics of Steven C. Brodsky, who was personally very opposed to the Jews for Jesus organization. His Web site could be found at "jewsforjesus.org," where visitors would find text highly critical of the group, which eventually obtained an injunction against his further use of the URL address.[50] Also, in June 2000, the owner of "www.peta.org," whose Web site was designed to make fun of the animal-rights group People for the Ethical Treatment of Animals, was told he must relinquish his URL.[51] Prior to the federal district court ruling, visitors to that Web address were introduced to the fictitious "People Eating Tasty Animals."

Many large companies have tried to stay a step ahead of their cyberenemies by themselves buying up URL addresses that might be used to disparage their good names. Thus, for example, United Parcel Service owns the rights to UPSBites.com, UPSstinks.com, IhateUPS.com, and some more X-rated ones as well.[52]

Another mingling of trademark law and the Net has concerned the use of hyperlinks from one Web site to another.[53] When Web site A is linked to Web site B, visitors to A can move to B by clicking on highlighted text or graphics; they need not know B's Internet domain address. Indeed, they might not even know that they have been moved to site B; this is especially true if the link is accomplished through **framing** or "deep linking," as described below.

Linking raises questions of trademark law in a number of ways. To begin with, site A's link to site B might include an unauthorized use of Company B's logo. Without an appropriate disclaimer, visitors may be misled to believe that Company B not only has permitted this use, but also has in some way endorsed Company

---

[49]15 U.S.C.S. sec. 1125 (2000).

[50]*Jews for Jesus v. Brodsky,* 993 F. Supp. 282 (N.J. 1998).

[51]*People for the Ethical Treatment of Animals v. Doughney,* 113 F. Supp. 2d 913 (E.D. Va. 2000).

[52]David Streitfeld, "Making Bad Names for Themselves," *Washington Post,* 8 Sept. 2000, p. E1.

[53]Glenn Mitchell and Craig S. Mende, "Internet Links Raise Issues of Trademark, Other Liability," *New York Law Journal,* 17 May 1999, p. 51.

A's products or services. For example, an injunction issued against the defendant in *Playboy Enterprises v. Universal Tele-Talk, Inc.*,[54] which had made several infringing uses of the Playboy name and its famous bunny logo, included a prohibition against any further linking of its own adult Web site with the plaintiff's site. In another case, Playboy unsuccessfully sought to enjoin a former playmate of the year from mentioning this biographical tidbit on her personal Web site; the court emphasized, however, that its ruling might have been different had the defendant also used the bunny logo.[55] Courts are perhaps more sensitive to the use of logos on Web sites than in other communication fora, because of the very nature of Web "surfing," which is typically done at such a rapid rate (depending on the speed of one's connection to the Internet, of course) that there is no time to sort out mentally the implicit endorsements.[56]

The linking techniques called framing and deep linking can raise special problems. Framing occurs when site B pops up as a window within site A, thus not making clear to visitors that they have indeed moved from one site to another. The practice was at issue in a 1999 case involving the company that owns Hard Rock Cafes and Peter Morton, one of its founders, who had earlier sold most of his interests in the company. Under the sale agreement, Morton retained ownership of the Hard Rock Hotel and Casino in Las Vegas and a right to open additional hotels in specified locations, but he was precluded from using the Hard Rock name or logo in other commercial enterprises. The suit was prompted by Morton's having set up a Web site that he used for, among other things, profiting from a CD marketing contract with a company called Tunes, whose Web site was "framed" within his own. Enjoining Morton from engaging in this practice, Judge Robert Patterson explained that this framing resulted in computer users' not knowing when they have been shifted from one Web site to another in that "the domain name appearing at the top of the computer screen, which indicates the location of the user in the World Wide Web, continues to indicate the domain name of Hard Rock Hotel."[57]

**Deep linking** brings the visitor from site A, upon clicking on the appropriate button, to a page *within* site B rather than to B's home page, thus further increasing the chances that the visitor will not know of the switch and will assume that this new page is simply another part of site A. As the Internet world becomes more and more commercialized, these practices can give the manager of site A and that site's advertisers a "free ride" on site B's content. The practice also effectively bypasses site B's advertisers, thus costing site B's operators revenue (the fewer eyeballs that visit, the less you can charge for ads). In one highly publicized lawsuit,

---

[54]1998 U.S. Dist. LEXIS 17282 (E.D. Pa. 1998).

[55]*Playboy Enterprises Inc. v. Terri Welles,* 7 F. Supp. 2d 1098 (S.D. Cal. 1998).

[56]*Digital Equipment Corporation v. Altavista Technology, Inc.,* 960 F. Supp. 456 (D. Mass. 1997).

[57]*Hard Rock Café International v. Morton,* 1999 U.S. Dist. LEXIS 8340 (S.D.N.Y. 1999).

Ticketmaster sued Microsoft over the latter's deep linking to a page within the former's site. The out-of-court settlement, interestingly, found Microsoft agreeing to link its own visitors directly to Ticketmaster's home page.[58]

Yet another trademark problem posed by the Internet is the matter of **metatags,** the key words that managers embed in their Web sites using hypertext markup language (HTML), invisible to the casual visitor, that help search engines to identify the site. Sometimes companies have been known to use competitors' trademarks among their metatags. For example, suppose that two commercial Web sites are maintained by competing discount travel agencies, the aggressively marketed "cheapestfare.com" and the far more obscure "cheapflights.com." If the Cheapflights company includes "Cheapestfare" among its metatags, Web surfers who use "cheapestfare" as a search engine key word will also "hit" the Cheap Flights company's site. The smaller company will be unfairly riding the coattails of the larger company. In *Brookfield Communications Inc. v. West Coast Entertainment,*[59] a company that marketed online information about the entertainment industry designed both for trivia fans and for Hollywood professionals learned that a competing company had been attracting business to its own Web site by using the word *moviebuff* (the name of a software package marketed by Brookfield) among its metatags. Although the court allowed that the defendant's larger sin was using the word as part of its domain name, the metatag caused additional problems. By fooling search engines to bring unwary customers to westcoastvideo.com instead of to moviebuff.com, the defendant was "improperly benefit[ing] from the goodwill that Brookfield developed in its mark. Using another's trademark in one's metatags is much like posting a sign with another's trademark in front of one's store."

***Databases and Authors' Rights.***    Another novel issue posed by the Internet is whether publishers, having contracted to purchase the rights to distribute authors' work in traditional print media, may, without further payment or permission, redistribute the work in computer databases. A rather elaborate explication of the issue is found in *Tasini v. New York Times.*[60] At issue was whether specific permission must be sought from freelance journalists who had been paid by the *Times* (and other publications) for their work when the paper wished to make those writings available as part of the NEXIS database. When one uses NEXIS's highly sophisticated search engine, the database groups together the articles that meet the searcher's chosen parameters. A *New York Times* article might be on the list alongside a transcript from an *ABC News* broadcast, a *Newsweek* editorial, and perhaps

---

[58]Bob Tedeschi, "Ticketmaster and Microsoft Settle Suit on Internet Linking," *New York Times,* 15 Feb. 1999, p. C6.

[59]174 F.3d 1036 (9th Cir. 1999).

[60]972 F. Supp. 804 (S.D.N.Y. 1997), *motion for reconsideration denied,* 981 F. Supp. 841 (S.D.N.Y. 1997), *rev'd and remanded,* 206 F.3d 161 (2d Cir. 1999).

even some Congressional testimony or other such Washington event covered by any of the exclusively online "magazines" that are part of the database. What you will not see is a mockup of, for example, the full page of the *New York Times* where the article of interest to you had initially appeared.

The litigation focused on Section 201(c) of the Copyright Act, which describes the rights retained by the publisher of a "collective work" (you may recall from Chapter 6 that this is a compilation of smaller works, each one of which is separately copyrightable). A compilation of a few poems each by dozens of poets is a collective work, as is your daily newspaper. Since Section 201(c) gives publishers the right to create without obtaining further permission "any revisions of the collective work"—such as a final edition of a given day's paper—the question became whether inputting the individual articles into the NEXIS databases was consistent with the *Times'* right to publish a "revision."

The courts first had to determine exactly what it is about each day's edition of the *Times* that constituted the creative element added by the paper's editors to that which the individual writers had already provided. Then they had to determine whether that element of creativity was preserved when the authors' writings were transferred into the NEXIS database. With respect to the first point, both federal district Judge Sotomayor and the appellate panel that eventually overruled her agreed that the newspaper's creativity was found in its selection, arrangement, and formatting of reporters' individual contributions.

The district and appellate courts parted ways, however, in their handling of the second inquiry. The district court found that placement of stories into the NEXIS database does not undo the *Times'* own measure of creativity. Even after translated into digital format and coded for Boolean searching, the *Times'* "protected original selection of articles…is preserved electronically." The only reason that the plaintiffs' articles appear in NEXIS is "because the defendant publishers earlier made the editorial determination that those articles would appeal to readers." While the original articles now would appear alongside countless other articles from other publications, that fact alone did not negate the *Times'* initial creative contribution. Indeed, after inclusion into the database, a text's past life as a *New York Times* article enhances its value. Many NEXIS users will, after all, purposely limit the number of "hits" in their search requests by specifying in advance that they are *only* interested in articles that had appeared in such prestigious papers as the *Times*.

Writing for a three-judge panel, Chief Judge Winter of the Second Circuit Court of Appeals found instead that whatever originality the *Times* had added to the freelancers' writing was effectively stripped away by NEXIS. True, one could find out what page of a specific date's *New York Times* originally included a given article, but that is all of the original edition that is retained. NEXIS users do not see the layout of the article; did it run as a slender, single column, or across several columns on the page? They do not see the context of the full page, such as what other articles, photos, or other graphic elements appeared alongside the

# Things to Remember

### TRADEMARK AND COPYRIGHT ONLINE

- The simple act of reading a file on a computer screen cannot help but also involve making a "copy" of the file; this fact alone poses a serious complication for traditional copyright law.

- The Digital Millennium Copyright Act makes it a criminal offense to circumvent any software attached to a work by the copyright holder; librarians fear that it will have the effect of jettisoning the whole idea of Fair Use.

- The Act also immunizes Internet Service Providers and SYSOPS from liability for infringements made by their subscribers of which they were unaware.

- Many suits have been brought in recent years alleging that an Internet domain name is too similar to the plaintiff's trademark. Sometimes the defendant is a cybersquatter, someone who obtained the rights to the domain name only to sell it back to the more legitimate owner.

- Trademark law is also implicated by the unauthorized hyperlinking of one's own Web site to another, especially if the latter company's logo is used as the link.

- Links that do not fully move a visitor from site A to site B, but rather "frame" B within A, cause special problems; the use of inappropriate metatags can also be an infringement.

- Another unsettled question is whether, in the absence of a specific contract clause one way or the other, media outlets may upload their freelancers' work into a database such as NEXIS.

article of interest. They do not see if and where the text jumps to an inside page. Significantly, in the case of front-page articles, users will not know whether the piece had appeared above or below the "fold."

The Second Circuit's having decided that publishers do not have a right to reprint freelancers' work in digital form merely establishes the "default" position, which can always be overridden by language written into individual contracts. Indeed, numerous media companies have already begun to ask their freelancers to sign away their digital rights as a matter of course. As is always the case in such conflicts between writers and publishers, the winner in any specific instance will be the one with the larger measure of clout in negotiating. In any event, the Supreme Court heard oral arguments on the *Tasini* case in March 2001, and was due to issue its ruling a few months later.

### Privacy Online

The Internet's impact on users' privacy dramatically demonstrates the complex and contradictory nature of this new medium. Certainly the Net can be, for better or worse, a privacy-enhancing means of communication. Many pundits have suggested that 1993 will be looked upon as the year the Internet finally "arrived" as a cultural phenomenon. That is when it first became the subject of a *New Yorker* cartoon, which showed two dogs sitting together, interacting intently with a computer screen, the one, winking, advising the other that "on the Internet, no one *knows* you're a dog."

Shielding one's personal identity while online, such as by using a "screen name" when entering a chat room, has become a cyberspace commonplace. Sophisticated software also exists for shielding the identity of the computer and the network from which e-mail is sent. The programs do this by stripping off the identifying information on an e-mail and substituting an anonymous code number or term. Some kinds of software also route messages through many different relay computers around the world, leaving no record of the path a message traveled.[61]

Even to the extent that cyberspace increases our level of privacy, it is both a blessing and a curse. Privacy—perhaps "anonymity" is a better word in this context—is usually seen as a societal good; it permits us to try out new ideas without having to commit prematurely to those ideas. Personal and group privacy have been essential components of the American brand of liberty from the very beginning. Surely Thomas Paine would have been hanged if *Common Sense* had been published under his own name. Yet privacy can be a dangerous thing too, perhaps more so on the Internet than ever before. Cyberspace anonymity enables organized crime and terrorist networks to conspire and can make it far easier for petty crooks to defraud the unwary and abscond with their profits long before their nefarious deeds have been detected.

The digitized world also diminishes our personal privacy in dramatic ways. By its very infrastructure, as a worldwide interlaced network of countless smaller computer networks, the Internet both makes the gathering of personal information much less expensive than ever and facilitates sophisticated cross-referencing of data so as to create highly detailed dossiers on us all.

E-mail is highly susceptible to being intercepted and read while it is being transmitted or while it is sitting on the mail server of either the sender's or recipient's computer networks. To minimize the likelihood of such snooping, privacy experts advise senders to use purposefully bland headings. As one consultant warns, "an E-mail message with a subject like 'CONFIDENTIAL,' 'Don't Let Anyone Else Read This,' or 'Our Secret Rendezvous' is likely to spark the interest of even the most trustworthy system administrator."[62]

In this section, we explore how the Internet affects your privacy interests in your relationship to your job, your government, and the private sector in general.

---

[61]Steve Lohr, "Privacy on Internet Poses Legal Puzzle," *New York Times,* 19 Apr. 1999, p. C4.

[62]Kim Komando, "Ways to Protect Your Privacy on the Internet," *Arizona Republic,* 22 Mar. 1999, p. E2.

***Online Privacy at Work.***   In the workplace, your employer may have installed software that allows him or her to monitor every single key stroke you make at your own office computer terminal. A Florida company called SpectorSoft markets a very inexpensive package to industry that keeps track of every e-mail message employees send and every Web site they visit. The law is clearly on the side of employers; after all, they own the office and the hardware. The Electronic Communications Privacy Act (ECPA) of 1986, which under many circumstances prohibits anyone from eavesdropping on both voice telephone conversations and digitized transmissions such as e-mail, does not apply to your employer. The small handful of cases dealing with employee e-mail privacy, while not argued on the basis of ECPA liability, are consistent with the conclusion that workers have no reasonable expectation of privacy in their office e-mails.

Bonita Bourke, an employee of the Nissan Motor Company, was terminated after her supervisor began to monitor her office e-mail and discovered a number of personal messages, some with sexual content. Bourke's privacy intrusion claim against her boss could not stand, a California appellate court held, in that she was on notice from the beginning of her employment that the e-mail system was for official communications only. That employees had been, as in most offices, given e-mail passwords and told to keep them confidential was not seen to trigger an expectation of privacy. Bourke also claimed that her employer's conduct violated state wiretapping laws, but the court determined that those statutes prohibited only the accessing of messages during transmission, not while the content was stored on the office's e-mail server.[63]

Three years later, another appellate panel in California ruled against an employee who alleged that her termination was a violation of state wiretapping statutes. Alana Shoars's job duties included offering training and user support for users of Epson's e-mail system. She was terminated for refusing to participate in the company's surreptitious monitoring of employee e-mail. She backed up her objections with conduct that many employers would consider insubordination, notably removing e-mail printouts from her supervisor's open office. The court's legal analysis, however, focused on the state statutes themselves, which it again concluded prohibited the reading of others' e-mail only during transmission—as the statute read, while messages are "passing over any wire, line or cable." Clearly the law was better suited for a telegraphic than a digital age, the court allowed, but updating statutes is the legislature's business, not the judiciary's.[64]

Two years later and two thousand plus miles east, a federal district judge in Pennsylvania permitted the firing of a Pillsbury Company employee for writing what might be described as overly candid and highly colorful e-mail messages to his supervisor.[65] Included in these missives were strongly worded criticisms of the

---

[63]*Bourke v. Nissan Motors Company,* No. YC003979, slip op. (Cal. App. Dep't Super. Ct. 1991).

[64]*Shoars v. Epson America,* No. BO73234, slip op. (Cal. Ct. App.), *review denied,* No. SO40065, 1994 Cal. LEXIS 3670 (29 June 1994).

[65]*Smyth v. Pillsbury Company,* 914 F. Supp. 97 (E.D. Pa. 1996).

company's sales management (offering to "kill the backstabbing bastards") and references to a planned holiday party as the "Jim Jones Koolaid affair."

That the employer had repeatedly assured all employees their e-mail transmissions were confidential, would never be monitored, and never be the source of personnel actions against them was seen to be of little consequence. Despite employer misrepresentations, Judge Charles Weiner could not discern "a reasonable expectation of privacy in Email communications voluntarily made by an employee to his supervisor over the company Email system." Weiner distinguished the case before him from an earlier precedent involving a compelled employee urinalysis. Unlike that situation, he concluded, here there was no requirement that the employee "disclose any personal information about himself." Further, the court could not ignore *any* company's interest in "preventing inappropriate and unprofessional comments or even illegal activity over its Email system."

Although even this tiny body of case law seems to be giving employers carte blanche to inspect workers' office e-mail, there is reason to be a bit cautious in drawing such a conclusion. The two California cases are both unpublished ones, at the request of the appellate panels. The judges do not want those opinions to be used as precedents. Then, too, the Pennsylvania case was very narrowly based on that state's "employment at will" doctrine to the effect that, with very few exceptions, employers may fire workers for any reason at all or for no reason at all, regardless of any promises to the contrary. To the extent that states are moving away from that strict doctrine and creating broader "public policy" exceptions, employers would be not only more ethical but also wiser to inform employees truthfully and regularly about the company's policies concerning e-mail privacy.

***Online Privacy and the Government.*** Although the Electronic Communications Privacy Act now prohibits unauthorized interceptions of voice and digital messages by both governmental and private agents, the law was originally conceived of as an antiwiretapping statute limiting the power of law enforcement officials. It is to date the only federal law aimed at protecting Netizens' privacy from government intrusion.

The ECPA protects newer e-mail messages more fully than it does older ones. If a message has been stored on an online system for fewer than 180 days, law enforcement officials must obtain a search warrant to read it. To read messages that have been on a server longer than that, only an "administrative subpoena" is required. Such subpoenas can be issued within a law enforcement agency without having to obtain an independent judge's approval.

Separate portions (or "Titles") of the ECPA prohibit the interception of e-mail messages while they are actually being sent (Title I) and while they are in storage on a server waiting for a subscriber to access them (Title II). Significantly, plaintiffs who are unable to prove actual damages stemming from a law enforcement officer's transgressions are entitled to up to ten times the amount of statutory damages ($10,000 per incident versus $1,000) under Title I. In one case from Austin, Texas, the Secret Service admitted that it had violated Title II when it seized computers operated by a bulletin board operator who was suspected of unauthorized copying of sensitive files about emergency call systems. At the time, the computers' hard drives had on them hundreds of undelivered e-mail messages for many of the system's more than 300 subscribers. No evidence of wrongdoing was found, and the BBS company then sued the government for violation of both Titles I and II of the ECPA. On appeal, the plaintiff renewed its argument that the Secret Service had violated Title I in that e-mail messages in storage on a server, if prevented from being delivered (the trial court found that the Secret Service had read and deleted the private mail), have been "intercepted" within the meaning of the ECPA. Writing for a three-judge appellate panel, Judge Rhesa Hawkins Barksdale disagreed. She emphasized the logic of having two separate bodies of law for interception of live transmissions and reviewing of stored messages, in that the first kind of intervention is far more intrusive. Agents will have no idea when a "real-time" message being sent is relevant to their investigations; the privacy invasion will thus be greater because irrelevant discussions among innocent participants cannot help but be intercepted. With respect to stored e-mail, however, "technology exists [such as 'key word searches'] by which relevant communications can be located without the necessity of reviewing the entire contents of all of the stored communications."[66]

In recent years, in part to allay the fears of persons loath to purchase products online but also in response to Internet users' privacy concerns in general, encryption software has been developed. One popular program is called PGP, short for "pretty good privacy." It works on a "public key" encryption principle. When you install the program on your computer, two sets of coding are created, a public and a private key. You would share your public key with anyone you want to be able to send you encrypted e-mail messages, but only you, using the private key, can decode the encrypted message. A much more sophisticated kind of encryption was developed by University of Illinois Professor Daniel Bernstein while he was a graduate student at the University of California–Berkeley. He calls his software "Snuffle"; it takes input (such as in chat room discourse) and encodes it in such a way, character by character, that persons confronting only the output code may find it impossible to discern what the original input was.

Mind you, your author is neither a computer scientist nor an engineer, and has no idea how Snuffle, which Bernstein describes as a "zero-delay private-key stream encryptor based upon a one-way hash function," accomplishes this task. Apparently, the virtual undecodability of Bernstein's system is not unique. Senator John Kerry of Massachusetts, in a Congressional hearing on the subject conducted in June 1999, reported that there were over 800 encryption devices on the global market and that a significant number of them are "based on encryption algorithms

---

[66]*Steve Jackson Games, Inc. v. United States Secret Service,* 36 F.3d 457, 463 (5th Cir. 1994).

considered too strong to be cracked by even the most powerful computers."[67] In any event, the State Department was sufficiently alarmed by Snuffle to declare it a "munition" prohibited from export under the International Traffic in Arms Regulations. That determination effectively precluded Bernstein from placing on the Internet a computer code version of his software. While Bernstein's lengthy litigation against the government was pending, authority over these kinds of "nonmilitary munitions" [*sic*] was transferred by a presidential executive order to the Department of Commerce. The relevant rules thereafter affecting Bernstein were the Department's Export Administration Regulations (EAR), the constitutionality of which Bernstein amended his initial complaint to challenge. In May 1999, by a 2–1 vote, a panel of the Ninth Circuit Court of Appeals ruled in Bernstein's favor. The "source code" (text readable by sophisticated humans, instructing them how to create lines of text readable by a computer) the plaintiff sought to post to the Net was deemed protected speech. The government had argued that such language was more "functional" than "expressive" in that its ultimate purpose was to make a computer accept commands. Such a distinction would "prove too much," Judge Betty Fletcher reasoned. After all, "computers will soon be able to respond directly to spoken commands," and we would not grant the government "unfettered power to impose prior restraints on speech in an effort to control *its* 'functional' aspects."[68]

If the government cannot defeat encryption software through litigation, perhaps it can do so by enhancing its own ability to decode Internet messages. The FBI created quite a stir in early 2001 when it announced development of software—initially dubbed "Carnivore" but later given the less ghoulish moniker, DCS1000—which would enable the agency to read every single e-mail message flowing in and out of a suspect's Internet Service Provider's network. The bureau also reportedly hopes to develop technology that will permit it to listen in on Internet telephone conversations.[69]

***Online Privacy and the Private Sector.***    Look up the phrase "double whammy" in the dictionary and perhaps you will encounter a photograph of Timothy McVeigh. The highly decorated U.S. Navy Senior Chief Petty Officer no doubt had it hard enough sharing the same name as the infamous Oklahoma City bomber. On top of that, he became a tangible reminder to us all that the privacy we seem to enjoy in our online interactions can be taken from us in an instant. Perhaps you remember the story. Like many AOL subscribers, McVeigh posted a profile of himself on the system using a provocative screen name—in his case, "Boysrch." Gay but relatively closeted, in keeping with the military's "Don't Ask, Don't Tell" policy, McVeigh used only his first name in the profile, which included among his hobbies "driving,

---

[67]Senate Commerce, Science and Transportation Committee, Hearing on Encryption, *Federal Document Clearing House,* June 10, 1999.

[68]*Bernstein v. United States,* 176 F.3d 1132 (9th Cir. 1999); *opinion withdrawn pending en banc review,* 192 F.3d 1308 (9th Cir. 1999).

[69]Duncan Levin, "Big Brother Could Read Your E-Mail," *Baltimore Sun,* 18 Feb. 2001, p. 1C.

boy watching, collecting pictures of other young studs." A naval investigator contacted AOL, one of whose employees—in violation of the company's published policy respecting the privacy interests of subscribers unless actually subpoenaed for information—readily divulged McVeigh's full identity. Predictably, McVeigh was promptly discharged from the Navy. In 1998, McVeigh's lawsuit against AOL was settled out of court. As is usual in such settlements, no public disclosures were made concerning the amount of money paid to McVeigh. It is known that AOL, as part of the agreement, was to provide more rigorous staff training in how to preserve subscribers' privacy interests. It is unlikely, by the way, that AOL's treatment of McVeigh would have been found in violation of federal law. The naval representative who had contacted AOL apparently presented himself as one of McVeigh's regular online correspondents, and the Electronic Communication Privacy Act explicitly excludes ISPs from liability for divulging the contents of or about subscribers' e-mail messages to the intended recipients.[70]

Even ISPs that seek to maintain their subscribers' privacy may be forced to disclose personal data. Obviously that would be the case when an ISP is handed a valid subpoena, but there is more. The late 1990s saw an increase in the incidence of "John Doe" defamation suits, wherein companies that have been criticized by individuals engaged in online chatter seek to compel the intermediary ISP to divulge the true identity of the otherwise anonymous subscribers, who would then presumably be named as defendants. Often what happens instead is that the offended company will immediately drop the defamation suit upon obtaining the names, thus making clear that the real purpose of the litigation was to "out" their online critics. If those critics happen to be disgruntled employees of the company, no one is surprised when they soon become *ex*-employees.[71]

One of the defining characteristics of the Internet is the interconnectedness of the countless computer networks that comprise it. Two important privacy concerns flow from this feature. First, the gathering, compiling, and cross-referencing of users' personal identification has become dramatically more efficient and less expensive than at any time in the past. Second, in some kinds of environments, it is possible to track a user's every keystroke and mouse click; on the Web, this often surreptitious gathering of information is called using "cookies."[72] The two concerns are clearly interdependent in that your online behavior is an important component of your personal marketing profile.

Concerns about how very much personal information about us is shared readily within the corporate world are hardly new. Perhaps you have done your

---

[70]Clifford T. Karafin, "'Don't Ask, Don't Tell': A Discussion of Employee Privacy in Cyberspace in Light of *McVeigh v. Cohen, et al.*" 3 *Virginia Journal of Law and Technology* 7 (1998).

[71]Greg Miller, "'John Doe' Suits Threaten Internet Users' Anonymity," *Los Angeles Times,* 14 June 1999, p. A1.

[72]Katrin Schatz Byford, "Privacy in Cyberspace: Constructing a Model of Privacy for the Electronic Communications Environment," 24 *Rutgers Computer and Technology Law Journal* 1, 47 (1998).

own unscientific test of this phenomenon by purposely misspelling your name on a magazine subscription form and then seeing that same misspelling pop up repeatedly in future "junk mail," thus enabling you to get a sense of who is buying mailing lists from whom. The Internet's contribution to this kind of privacy issue is a difference of both degree and kind. That the compiling of information about us has now become so inexpensive means that mailing list vendors can offer ever more narrowly tailored groupings of names. Thus, a list broker may know not only such basic demographic information about you as name, age, gender, race, zip code, and so forth, but also your political party affiliation, your favorite breakfast cereal, your taste in music and in movie rentals, how often you use an ATM, how much red meat and alcohol you consume, and whether you are taking antidepressant drugs.

The interlacing of computer networks also permits a Netizen of even moderate sophistication, under some circumstances, to learn much more in "real time" about other users than they likely would have chosen to reveal. At the touch of one function key, you can see with whom someone else online is e-mailing or chatting, or even what news group they are reading. A few more clicks and you can gather personal information such as the individual's name, address, occupation, and date of birth.[73]

If ordinary consumers can obtain such details, it is not difficult to imagine how easily corporate users who make it their business to deal in personal information may collect relevant data. Personify, a company in San Francisco, helps businesses not only monitor their customers' visits to their Web sites, but also make personalized "real-time" pricing decisions to avoid losing a sale. Thus, for example, Virtual Vineyards might notice a site visitor clicking here and there, but not quite committing to anything. A message will pop up on the customer's screen: "So, we notice you have been here for 15 minutes but have not bought anything. Suppose we offered you free shipping today. Would that help?" In that such Internet dialogue resembles live behavior at outdoor markets around the world, with sellers trying to size up buyers' interest in their wares by observing relevant nonverbal cues, the phenomenon has been dubbed a "Cyberbazaar."[74] In another development, Internet advertising company Double-Click, in response to innumerable protests and threats of Congressional action, backed off in the spring of 2000 from its plan to merge its huge name and address data to track consumers' online activities. The company had hoped to create a highly detailed and individualized database that could then be marketed to other advertisers.

Much outrage was expressed by citizens' groups in the late 1990s about commercial Web sites that have been used to gather information from children. In response, Congress passed the Children Online Privacy Protection Act, which requires that websites targeted at children gain parental permission before collect-

---

[73] Lawrence Lessig, "The Path of Cyberlaw," 104 *Yale Law Journal* 1743, 1748 (1995).

[74] Elizabeth Weise, "Online 'Cyberbazaars' Practice Fluid Pricing: Web Prices May Depend on Factors That Raise Serious Privacy Issues," *Detroit News,* 17 May 1999, p. S3.

ing personally identifiable information from anyone under thirteen years old.[75] The Federal Trade Commission, charged with enforcing the law, took action against the "Young Investor Web site," which had apparently encouraged users to answer questions about their parents' investment portfolios.[76] There are no federal laws, however, governing commercial Web sites' gathering and use of information provided by adult visitors. Although there had been much talk in the late 1990s about lawmaking in this area, the Clinton administration expressed a strong preference for industry self-regulation. In May 1999, a Georgetown University study reported that approximately two-thirds of Web sites post some kind of privacy policy.[77]

Internet users express concerns not only about how information is gathered about them, but also about the intrusion on their privacy by large numbers of unwanted commercial messages, or "**spam.**" Online mailboxes can quickly fill up with such virtual junk mail, often disguised so as to appear to be a personal message rather than an advertisement, a practice called "**spoofing.**"

In the late 1990s, Congress considered several pieces of legislation aimed at protecting Internet users from unwanted commercial mail. Proposals ranged from requiring that commercial messages be clearly labeled as such (and include the mailer's real identify and return mail address) to the outright banning of all unsolicited commercial e-mail. None of the bills were enacted although several states passed antispam legislation of various kinds. According to the Coalition Against Unsolicited Commercial Email (http://www.cauce.org), California, Colorado, Maryland, Nevada, Virginia, and Washington all have laws on the books. Virginia's statute, enacted in 1999, forbids spoofing and may have an especially significant effect, in that such ISPs as AOL, UUNet, and PSI are all based in the state.

There has also been a modest amount of case law concerning spam. These cases have not involved constitutional privacy claims by the ultimate e-mail recipients; such claims would likely not prevail. Many years ago, a federal court in New York rejected a homeowner's complaint that the Department of Motor Vehicles' policy of making car owners' registration data available to for-profit corporations would violate his personal privacy by increasing the amount of junk mail he would receive. "The mailbox," Judge Frankel remarked, "is hardly the kind of enclave that requires constitutional defense to protect the privacies of life. The short, though regular, journey from mailbox to trash can…is an acceptable burden."[78] Considering that the plaintiff was able to bring his claim into court only because of the state's involvement in the junk mailings, it is clear that individual e-mail recipients would not be able to make constitutional claims against commercial mailers or against the intervening ISPs. Moreover, even if a claim of "state's action" could

---

[75] 15 U.S.C.S. secs. 6501, 6505 (2000).

[76] David Stout, "Agreement Reached on Internet Privacy," *New York Times,* 7 May 1999, p. A24.

[77] Craig Menefee, "Online Privacy Study Draws Mixed Reactions," *Newsbytes PM* [an online news service], 12 May 1999.

[78] *Lamont v. Commissioner of Motor Vehicles,* 269 F. Supp. 880, 883 (S.D.N.Y. 1967).

be made plausibly, perhaps by arguing that Internet access has become a necessity and that ISPs should be considered public utilities,[79] the *Lamont* logic may yet apply. The walk from mailbox to trash can, after all, usually takes longer than a few mouse clicks.

While individuals likely have no constitutional right to be spared the inconvenience of unwanted e-mail, neither do commercial mailers have a First Amendment right to reach an ISP's subscribers.[80] The case law to date, therefore, has mostly involved ISPs suing spam artists, using several different theories of liability. It is important to understand first the nature of the harm that ISPs can experience from large-scale commercial e-mail. Huge mailings—these cases can involve tens of millions of messages over the course of a few months—must sit on the incoming computer network's server until such time as the individual recipients retrieve or delete their mail. Such bulk can incapacitate a network, forcing the ISP to invest in more equipment. Moreover, subscribers will complain repeatedly to their ISPs about such unwanted mailings and may choose to cancel their subscriptions. If a mailer's spoofing entails using the ISP's own trademark as part of its e-mail address, additional bad will may be created among subscribers, who may assume that the spam has been authorized by the ISP.

All these harms were alleged by America Online in the late 1990s against commercial mailers that had used e-mail address "extractor" software to compile a

---

[79]Steven E. Bennett, "Canning SPAM: *CompuServe v. Cyber Promotions, Inc.,*" *32 University of Richmond Law Review* 545 (1998).

[80]*Cyber Promotions, Inc. vs. American Online,* 948 F. Supp. 436 (E.D. Pa. 1996).

 # Things to Remember

**PRIVACY ONLINE**

- The Internet both enhances and diminishes privacy.
- State wiretapping statutes have generally been interpreted so as to protect the privacy of e-mail only at the exact moment of transmission.
- The federal Electronic Communications Privacy Act covers both e-mail in transmission and e-mail in storage, but damages for unauthorized access are potentially much higher when it occurs at the time of transmission.
- The late 1990s saw an increase in the incidence of "John Doe" suits filed by potential libel plaintiffs in an effort to unmask persons who had been maligning them in online discourse.
- The Children Online Privacy Protection Act prevents websites from gathering information from youngsters under thirteen years old without parental permission.
- Congress considered, but did not pass, legislation aimed at curbing spam; several states have passed such laws, and ISPs can sue creators of spam.

list of hundreds of thousands of AOL's subscribers. Some of the defendants specialized in marketing access to sexually oriented Web sites and other pornographic imagery and so focused their extractors on AOL subscribers who participated in "adult talk" chat rooms. A federal district court in Virginia, finding few if any facts in dispute, granted summary judgment to AOL on most of its claims. Liability could be found, the court reasoned, for several reasons. First, for the mailers to continue to use up AOL's network capacity, even after being asked to cease and desist, constituted an actionable trespass. Then, too, the failure to cease these activities was deemed a violation of the federal Computer Fraud and Abuse Act, an anti-"hacking" law that the court felt applicable to any such unauthorized and harmful access to a computer network. Violation of the federal trademark law (the Lanham Act) was also found in the mailers' use of the "aol.com" domain name in their e-mail addresses. Not only was there consumer confusion about the source of the mail; there was also "tarnishment" of AOL's trademark by its involuntary association with large amounts of junk mail. (AOL received over 50,000 subscriber complaints about one defendant and 450,000 complaints about another).[81]

## Sexual Messages Online

Computers have been around for many decades. Univac, the garage-sized monstrosity whose expertise was limited to simple calculations, arrived on the scene in the 1950s. Perhaps the computer age will not *truly* have arrived until the generation young enough not to remember a world *without* PCs grows up and assumes leadership positions in industry and government. At least until then and likely beyond, parents will have a love–hate relationship with the microchip. The computer has opened up possibilities for youngsters never imagined before. Classrooms in U.S. schools are hooked up to Internet pen pals on every other continent, including Antarctica. School children worldwide have traveled "virtually" to archaeological digs in the most far flung places on Earth and have had live interactions with astronauts aboard the *Mir* space station.

Yet the Internet poses serious dangers, too, perhaps unlike any other communication medium. Parents may feel guilty when they let the TV serve as a babysitter, but the worst that will happen is that their kids will see something disturbing or "age inappropriate," as educators are fond of saying. Not so with the interactive, online world. To paraphrase the caption of the famous *New Yorker* cartoon, "On the Internet, they don't know you're a child molester." All too often we hear of children being induced by Internet chatter to meet a new friend, who turns out to be a pederast (see Figure 13.3).

The desire to protect children from inappropriate sexual transmissions was the impetus for Congress to enact the Communications Decency Act (CDA),

---

[81]*America Online v. LCGM, Inc.,* 1998 U.S. Dist. LEXIS 20144 (E.D. Va. 1998); *America Online, Inc. v. IMS,* 24 F. Supp. 2d 548 (E.D. Va. 1998); see also *CompuServe Inc. v. Cyber Promotions,* 962 F. Supp. 1015 (S.D. Ohio 1997) (unauthorized mass e-mail transmission is an actionable trespass).

Figure 13.3

*© 1999* Cincinnati Enquirer. *Reprinted with special permission of King Features Syndicate.*

which was a portion of the Telecommunications Act of 1996. The Supreme Court's 1997 decision overturning key sections of that law is worthy of our attention for several reasons, not the least of which is that it represented the Court's first opportunity to deal with Internet communications.[82]

The Act criminalized the use of a computer network to transmit any obscene or indecent message knowing that the recipient is under eighteen years old. Also prohibited was the posting of any such message in a manner that would be "available" to minors and permitting a minor in one's charge (presumably including one's own child) to have access to such online messages.

Writing for the Court, Justice Stevens emphasized the extraordinary breadth of the CDA's prohibitions on the sending of sexual messages that are merely indecent, rather than obscene. First, he contrasted this statute with the Federal Communications Commission's broadcast indecency policy that had been upheld in its application to the George Carlin monologue, in *FCC v. Pacifica Foundation* (discussed in Chapter 12).[83] The FCC's policy was more narrow. It proscribed the broadcast of indecent texts only at hours when substantial numbers of children were likely to be in the audience. By contrast, the CDA "prohibits a particular

---

[82]*Reno v. ACLU,* 521 U.S. 844 (1997).

[83]438 U.S. 726 (1978).

category of speech from being disseminated every hour of every day." Then, too, the only penalty incurred by the radio station playing the Carlin monologue was the equivalent of a "raised eyebrow" from the Commission, whereas CDA violators could go to jail for up to two years. Equally offensive was the CDA's usurping of parental authority in that the law could reach even parents who sent their seventeen-year-old college freshman e-mail about birth control.

The Court subjected the CDA to its most exacting scrutiny. This adjudicational posture was not a preordained conclusion. Justice Stevens spent much time comparing the Internet with broadcasting, and he determined that there were several significant distinctions. That determination was crucial because, as we saw in Chapter 12, the broadcast media are subjected to many regulations that would be unconstitutional as applied to print media.

Perhaps the most controversial of the distinctions Stevens drew between broadcasting and the Internet was the former's "pervasiveness," especially its accessibility to children. The moment a radio is turned on, all within earshot risk being bombarded by sexual messages best restricted to only adult ears. Web browsing is different, Stevens claimed. A child cannot surf the Web without "some sophistication and some ability to read to retrieve material and thereby to use the Internet unattended." Sexually oriented material is "seldom encounter[ed]" by accident, he argued, in that "receipt of information on the Internet requires a series of affirmative steps more deliberate and directed than merely turning a [radio] dial."

In truth, the contrast between the radio and the Internet is not quite as clear as Stevens posits. If booting up one's computer is the analog for turning on the radio, then he is surely right. Doing the latter, but not the former, can alone result in being subjected to inappropriate sexual content. But Stevens's reference to turning the dial of the radio is telling. The proper computer analogy to that behavior would seem to be clicking a mouse, and that, too, is all one need do to uncover inappropriate materials, at least after a Web search has been conducted.

Obviously Stevens is right about the near impossibility of a preliterate child finding much sexual (or other) content online. The CDA's protections did not stop with literacy, however, but with attaining the age of majority. Older children who input the most innocuous words—"boy," "girl," "teen," "nurse," and so forth—into a search engine will find numerous X-rated sites among their "hits." *Atlanta Journal-Constitution* cartoonist Mike Luckovich pointed this out by depicting an elementary school classroom that was presenting their assigned reports on "pets." The young speaker begins to read his homework to the class: "Sex kittens are hot and horny…," and the teacher, with a facial expression suggesting more resignation than shock, interrupts to inquire whether the pupil had gotten his research material from the Internet.

Stevens's *Reno* opinion also points out, correctly, that on-screen warnings usually appear in huge letters on the home page of a sexually oriented site. Yet often that same home page already includes very sexual imagery. Moreover, as many commentators have pointed out, those warnings may serve to entice rather than dissuade older children.

In the end, Stevens stopped short of concluding that the Internet should *always* enjoy the full amount of First Amendment protection enjoyed by the print media, that *no* law aimed at Internet indecency could possibly be constitutional. Still, after reviewing and distinguishing several relevant precedents, he determined that there is "no basis" for diluting "the level of First Amendment scrutiny that should be applied to this medium."

The CDA soon begat the "son of CDA," as Congress passed the Children Online Protection Act, which would have taken effect in November 1998 had it not been challenged successfully in federal district court.[84] COPA, as it was popularly called, was designed to eliminate some of the flaws the Supreme Court identified in the earlier Communication Decency Act. The law would only be triggered by certain kinds of online sexual materials defined within the statute as "harmful to minors." Companies whose Web sites include such materials could escape liability if they sought to screen out minors by requiring all visitors either to pay by credit card or to cooperate with the company in the creation of some form of adult access code.

Judge Lowell Reed Jr. granted the plaintiff's motion for a preliminary injunction blocking enforcement of the law. (Reed's decision was upheld in June 2000 by the Third Circuit Court of Appeals).[85] Although he agreed with the government that the protection of children from these kinds of sites was a compelling state's interest, COPA was not a narrowly tailored means of accomplishing that end. Many adults, who clearly have a right to view nonobscene sexual materials, would nonetheless shy away from transmitting their credit card number or other identifying code. A far more appropriate strategy, Reed suggested, would be for parents to install some form of blocking software on their home computers.

Many commentators have pointed out the irony of expecting the baby boomer generation to depend on computer software to prevent their far more computer-literate offspring from having free reign on the Internet (see Figure 13.4). Still, blocking software has become very popular in recent years. A 1999 survey conducted by the Annenberg Public Policy Center found 32 percent of respondents with access to the Internet using some kind of blocking software—e.g., Cyber Patrol, Cybersitter, SurfWatch, Web Chaperone—on their home computers.[86] Such software will always be both overbroad (blocking out sites that aren't very "sexy") and underinclusive (failing to block out some very hardcore sites). Still, Judge Reed concluded, the First Amendment demands that parents, not the government, decide how much access to the Internet their children should enjoy.

---

[84]*ACLU v. Reno*, 31 F. Supp. 2d 473 (E.D. Pa. 1999).

[85]217 F. 3d 162 (3rd Cir. 2000).

[86]Joseph Turow, *The Internet and the Family* (Philadelphia: Annenberg Public Policy Center, University of Pennsylvania, 1999).

Figure 13.4

© *1997* Cincinatti Enquirer. *Reprinted with special permission of King Features Syndicate.*

Most of the companies in the cyberspace blocking business depend almost entirely on the software itself identifying key words and phrases on Web sites. The Cyber Patrol company of Massachusetts injects a human element, with several full-time staff who surf the Web and apply company protocols to determine whether or not to block a particular site. The category descriptions are complex. Sites for foot fetishists will likely be classified as "sex talk," but they will not be lumped together with "depictions of sex" unless there is nudity. A site advertising "genital enlargement techniques" gave the screeners pause. The subject had been a plot element in the movie *Austin Powers: International Man of Mystery;* many plastic surgeons advertise that they perform the procedure. But the group decided to block the site, in part because it boasted "a startlingly explicit photograph."[87]

Although parents certainly have a right to block their children's Internet access with blocking software, do public libraries and public schools have a similar right to block their students' and patrons' access? This hotly contested issue came up in the late 1990s and promises to be here for several years to come. In 1997, the Loudoun County, Virginia, public library system adopted a Policy on Internet Sexual Harassment aimed at least as much at protecting one computer station patron from being offended at what pops up on a neighbor's screen as at blocking

[87]John Schwartz, "It's a Dirty Job: Web Childproofers Keep Surfing through Muck," *Washington Post,* 23 June 1999, p. A1.

any individual's Internet access. The board implemented the policy by installing X-Stop software on all its patron computers. Adult patrons were free to "appeal" the software's "decisions" by providing their name and address and their reason for wanting access to a specific site blocked by the software to the librarian on duty, who would then make a case-by-case determination.

Several individuals and organizations, including some whose Web sites were blocked by the library's software, challenged the county's policy. Judge Leonie M. Brinkema determined that the county's conduct was unconstitutional in that it was not the least restrictive means of achieving its laudable goals.[88] She did not offer any opinion as to which, if any, of the less restrictive means proposed by plaintiffs, such as using blocking software only on computer terminals reserved for juveniles or permitting any adult patron to turn off the blocking software without having to go through an appeals mechanism, would themselves be found constitutional.

Brinkema's characterization of the Internet was itself a fascinating feature of the case. The library had claimed that the Internet is akin to a "vast Interlibrary Loan system," arguing that "restricting Internet access to selected materials is merely a decision not to acquire such materials rather than a decision to remove them from a library's collection." The library pressed this point because the Supreme Court had, in *Board of Education v. Pico*[89] (see the discussion of this case in Chapter 2), suggested that library books, once purchased, acquire a kind of "squatter's right" to remain on the shelf, at least insofar as they should not be removed because of their content. Judge Brinkema rejected the library's argument, however, finding instead that the Internet, "unlike a library's collection of individual books," is a "single, integrated system." She analogized the library's use of blocking software to its having decided to buy a set of encyclopedias and then, "laboriously redact[ing] portions deemed unfit for library patrons."[90]

Congress's next foray into the oversexed Internet was the Children's Internet Protection Act (CHIPA), which requires all schools and libraries receiving special earmarked federal monies—a $2.25 billion expenditure aimed at wiring them to the Net—to install blocking software to block sexually oriented websites whenever their juvenile patrons go online.[91] The ACLU and the American Library Association filed suit against the law in the spring of 2001.

Regulation of sexual messages on the Internet raises at least one more novel issue beyond that of how best to protect children from harmful Web sites and

---

[88]*Mainstream Loudoun v. Board of Trustees of the Loudoun County Library,* 2 F. Supp. 2d 783 (E.D. Va. 1998) (rejecting motion to dismiss), 24 F. Supp. 2d 552 (E.D. Va. 1998) (granting summary judgment to plaintiffs).

[89]457 U.S. 853 (1982).

[90]*Mainstream Loudoun v. Board of Trustees of the Loudoun County Library,* 2 F. Supp. 2d 783, 793–94 (E.D. Va. 1998).

[91]20 USCS 7001; 47 USCS 902.

chat rooms. Recall the mechanics of the Supreme Court's *Miller* test for defining obscenity, described in more detail in Chapter 11. The test depends on reference to "contemporary *community* standards," and the Court has made clear that this refers to a statewide or local standard, not a nationwide one. If sexual images are made available on a computer bulletin board, can its operators therefore be prosecuted anywhere, using the standards of a much more conservative community than their home state?

The Sixth Circuit Court of Appeals applied precisely that rule in *United States v. Thomas.*[92] Robert and Carleen Thomas managed an adult-oriented bulletin board out of their home in Milpitas, California. Acting on a citizen's complaint, an investigator in Tennessee assumed an alias to take out a membership in the Thomases' BBS, view sexually explicit materials online, and pay for the UPS delivery of several videotapes advertised on the system. As a result, the Thomases were charged with violating relevant federal statutes prohibiting the interstate transfer of obscenity and were eventually sentenced to over three years in prison. Two of the defendants' arguments in their unsuccessful appeal are especially of interest.

First, the defendants argued that it was inappropriate for a federal court in Tennessee to have assumed jurisdiction of their case and thus for the Memphis jury to have been instructed to use its own community's standards to determine if the images involved were truly obscene. Obscenity prosecutions involving the Internet, they claimed, demand "a new definition of community, i.e., one that is based on the broad-ranging connections among people in cyberspace rather than the geographic locale of the federal judicial district of the criminal trial." In the absence of such a bold new definition, BBS operators "will be forced to censor their materials so as not to run afoul of the standards of the community with the most restrictive standards."

But the Thomases were not the ideal poster children for such creative adjudication, the court found. Theirs was a restricted BBS; visitors had to pay a fee and fill out an application form, including their address, before being granted full access to the system or being allowed to purchase materials. The undercover agent may have lied about his name, but he truthfully indicated that he was from Memphis. The Thomases would have been wise to reject the application. Writing for the appellate panel, Judge Nancy Edmunds chose not to express an opinion about whether a BBS open to all, where the operators would not know who had visited or where they lived, could lead to this same kind of criminal liability.

The Thomases also argued that when a computer in one state downloads an image (in this case, a. gif file) from a computer in another state, nothing obscene, indeed nothing *tangible,* has really crossed state lines. How could they be convicted of interstate transfer of a series of "1"s and "0"s? Very easily, the court replied, in the same way that money laundering schemes can be prosecuted at the federal level, even if only electronic funds transfers are involved.

---

[92]74 F.3d 701 (6th Cir. 1996).

# Things to Remember

### SEXUAL MESSAGES ONLINE

- The Communications Decency Act, Congress's first attempt to protect children from being subjected to inappropriate sexual messages in cyberspace, was struck down by the Supreme Court in 1997.
- Justice Stevens said that he saw no reason to make Internet speech less protected than the print media.
- The Children Online Protection Act was also found unconstitutional; the federal judge suggested parents use some form of Internet blocking device instead.
- Some communites began installing blocking software on public library computers, a practice found unconstitutional by a federal district court in Virginia.

## Chapter Summary

The Internet, begun as a Department of Defense program aimed at ensuring the survival of intragovernmental communications in case of nuclear war, has revolutionized the exchange of information. It boasts a number of unique features—a lack of gatekeepers, the potential for carrying infinite amounts of data, a kind of parity between content provider and consumers, the extraordinarily low cost of data transmission among them—and each poses challenges to traditional legal doctrines.

Cyberspace law is in its infancy. The Supreme Court has only just begun addressing this area of law, although there have been dozens of lower court cases struggling to apply traditional concepts in libel, privacy, intellectual property, and obscenity law to this new medium.

One general rule that has emerged across categories of case law is that Internet Service Providers are least likely to incur liability stemming from their subscribers' online behavior if the ISP acts more like a neutral conduit of data than like an editor. Congress has also attempted to relieve ISPs of some liability for their subscribers' transgressions, via relevant sections of the Telecommunications Act of 1996.

There has also been much legislative activity, both federal and state, specifically aimed at protecting minors from being subjected to inappropriate or harmful messages while online. Thus far, those laws have usually been found unconstitutionally overbroad.

# Glossary

**absolute privilege.** Complete immunity from libel suits provided to elected officials while carrying out their official duties.

**absolutist theory.** Theory of First Amendment jurisprudence emphasizing the absolute prohibition ("Congress shall make no law") on antispeech regulations provided in the First Amendment.

**acquired distinctiveness.** A characteristic attributed to a trademark that was once merely descriptive (e.g., "American" Airlines) but that has become associated in the public's mind with a specific company.

**actual damages.** Monies awarded to plaintiffs who prove that they have been damaged.

**actual malice.** The level of fault required in libel cases governed by *New York Times v. Sullivan:* the defendant published defamatory material either knowing it was false, or "with reckless disregard as to truth or falsity."

**ad hoc balancing.** Method of First Amendment adjudication that balances, on a case-by-case basis, free speech interests against whatever competing interests are involved.

**administrative agency.** Any of the many agencies, such as the Federal Communications Commission and the Federal Trade Commission, created to engage in rule making consistent with established law.

**administrative complaint.** Document filed by federal agency alleging specific wrongdoing to be adjudicated by an administrative law judge.

**administrative law judge.** A judge who hears disputes between individuals and regulatory agencies, a step usually required before proceeding to federal court.

**affirmative disclosure.** Specific facts that the Federal Trade Commission may require advertisers to disclose in future advertising.

**agency rationale.** A justification offered for immunizing reporters from libel suits for reporting on governmental actions; it posits that the media are functioning as the public's agent.

**Alien and Sedition Acts.** Very early laws (1798) criminalizing statements critical of the government

**amicus brief.** An argument filed in an appellate court by parties not directly involved in the litigation.

**amicus curiae.** Person or organization (literally, "friend of the court") filing an amicus brief.

**ancillary powers.** Powers granted to the Federal Communications Commission to regulate entities that do not themselves possess broadcast licenses, but whose practices may affect such licensees.

**answer.** In a civil suit, the initial document filed by the defendant, which may deny the plaintiff's claims, or may offer specific defenses under law.

**appellant.** The party who lost in a lower court and is bringing an appeal to a higher court.

**appellate court.** A court that hears an appeal from adjudication of a case from a lower court.

**appropriation.** The branch of privacy law involving the unauthorized use of someone's name or likeness for commercial purposes.

**arraignment.** A criminal defendant's initial appearance before a judge, at which time formal charges will be made and a plea may be offered.

**block booking.** A scheme, ended by the Supreme Court's 1938 *U.S. v. Paramount* decision, by which theater studios would force movie houses to accept dozens of lesser films in a block so as to have the rights to exhibit a few "name" pictures.

**blurring.** Diminishing the value of a company's trademark by offering for sale many different kinds of wholly unrelated products or services using the same mark.

**brevity.** A provision of the Copyright Act's Classroom Guidelines that limits the length of material (e.g., a book chapter, no more than 10 percent of the book) teachers may copy for distribution to their students.

**brief.** An argument filed in an appellate court, arguing either for the affirmance or reversal of the decision from the lower court.

**cease and desist order.** As its name implies, an order (issued by an agency such as the Federal Trade Commission) demanding that a company stop engaging in an allegedly illegal practice.

**certification mark.** A promise through which a company attests as to a particular quality of its product (e.g., that this frozen pizza uses *Real Cheese*).

**change of venire.** The importation of a jury from a location ostensibly far enough away from the crime site so as to be untainted by any pretrial publicity.

**change of venue.** Moving a trial to a new location so as to avoid the negative effects of pretrial publicity.

**civil (cases).** Court actions prompted by one private party suing another.

**civil contempt citation.** Finding by a judge against a party who fails to perform a particular action (e.g., a reporter refusing to reveal the identity of a source).

**clearly erroneous rule.** A rule of federal civil procedure that states that appellate courts may review not only legal questions but also factual ones if the appellate judges determine that the trial court made a clearly erroneous finding of fact.

**closure order.** A judge's ruling that all or part of a judicial proceeding shall be conducted in private, with no members of the press or public present.

**collateral bar rule ("Dickinson" rule).** Accepted in only some jurisdictions, this rule holds that contempt citations may stand even if the defendant is found by an appellate court to have

had a right to engage in the behavior that resulted in the citation.

**collective mark.** A phrase or logo, protected under trademark law, designed to call to mind an association or organization (e.g., the NAB, National Association of Broadcasters).

**collective work.** A creative work eligible for copyright, consisting of many elements each which of which is also eligible for copyright (e.g., a newspaper edition and its many individual articles).

**common law.** Law as created by judge-made precedent rather than passed into law by a legislature.

**compensatory damages.** Damages designed to make a victim "whole," to undo harm that has been done.

**compilation.** A work formed by the collection and assembly of preexisting materials or of data, eligible for copyright protection to the extent that the selection and arrangement of those materials is itself creative.

**complaint.** Document filed by the plaintiff in a civil case alleging the wrongs done by the defendant.

**concurrent registration.** More than one company using the same brand name for very different products or services (e.g., Life cereal, but also Life the board game).

**concurring opinion.** An opinion written by an appellate judge who agrees with the outcome of the case, but not all the majority's reasoning.

**consent.** A defense in a tort action (including libel and invasion of privacy) claiming that the plaintiff knew of and explicitly indicated approval of, or at least acquiescence to, the defendant's conduct.

**consent decree.** Agreement entered into by two or more parties (e.g., a regulatory agency and a regulated company) and approved by a court.

**consent order.** Ruling by an agency's staff directing a company to behave in prescribed ways.

**conspiracy.** A combination of two or more persons planning to commit a criminal act.

**constitution.**   A government's most basic controlling document, setting forth the structure and powers of the government.

**contempt of court.**   An act or failure to act that either obstructs a court's functioning or otherwise adversely affects the dignity of the court.

**continuance.**   Delaying a trial's beginning.

**contributory infringement.**   Actions that do not directly infringe on the plaintiff's rights, but that enable others to do so (e.g., creating a Web site that enables users to make illegal copies of copyrighted works).

**convergence.**   In media law, the state of affairs when the differences among traditionally separate communications media become less and less identifiable.

**convincing clarity.**   A measure, somewhere between "beyond a reasonable doubt" and "by a preponderance of the evidence," of how satisfactorily a plaintiff has established burden of proof.

**copyright.**   The exclusive right to profit from one's own creative works.

**corrective advertising.**   Advertising including text designed to undo in consumers' minds false impressions created by prior advertising.

**courts of equity.**   Courts empowered to make litigants whole, as best as possible, even in the absence of a clear body of legal precedent (common law).

**criminal [case].**   Legal action taken by a government accusing a defendant of violating a law.

**criminal contempt citation.**   Judicial decree punishing actions (e.g., acting in an unruly fashion in court or violating a gag order) that may interfere with government function.

**criminal libel.**   Defamatory remarks, whether aimed at an individual or a group, prosecuted by the state on the theory that such utterances will tend to lead to violence.

**cumulative effect.**   One of the Classroom Guidelines under the Copyright Act, limiting teachers to copying no more than two works by the same author, no more than three from the same anthology, and no more than nine artifacts total for classroom distribution during any single semester.

**cybersquatting.**   Obtaining the rights to an Internet address bearing the name of a famous person or company with the purpose of later selling it to the "logical" owner.

**DBS.**   Direct broadcast satellite television service.

**decision.**   Court decisions tell us who wins and who loses, not necessarily why.

**deep linking.**   Inserting a hyperlink to one's own Web site, sending visitors to an internal page of another individual's Web site.

**defamation.**   An utterance or printed material asserting the kinds of derogatory facts about another person that may lead to that person's reputation being damaged.

**defendant.**   A person accused by the state of a crime or by a civil plaintiff of a wrongful act.

**deposition.**   A part of the discovery process in which potential witnesses for the opposing side are interviewed with attorneys present and a transcript created.

**derivative work.**   A creative work eligible for copyright protection based in some way on a separate work (e.g., a movie version of a book).

**descriptive mark.**   A trademark that merely describes the product or service (e.g., *lead* pencils or *Korean* restaurant) and is thus not ordinarily eligible for legal protection.

**dicta.**   Portions of a court's decision that are not essential to the disposition of the case (see *holding*).

**direct infringement.**   Infringement on a copyright done by the defendant's own actions.

**discovery.**   The pretrial process of fact finding done by both sides in a civil suit, which may include deposing (formally questioning) prospective witnesses for the opposing side.

**dissenting opinion.**   An opinion written by an appellate judge who disagrees with the outcome of the case (with the majority's decision).

**distinctiveness.**   The main quality that makes a trademark protectible; it sets one product or service apart from competing brands.

**distinguish (a precedent).**   Deciding that an earlier case's facts were sufficiently different from the case at hand so as not to be a useful precedent.

**doctrine of incorporation.** Constitutional doctrine holding that the Fourteenth Amendment's due process clause implies that some of the Bill of Rights' limitations on the federal government also apply to the states.

**documentary materials.** Information and other items gathered by, but not created by, a reporter working on a story.

**due process.** Fundamental fairness; the Fifth Amendment says that life, liberty, and property may not be taken by the state without "due process."

**en banc.** A ruling by an entire federal appellate court (instead of just a three-judge panel).

**Equal Protection Clause.** Provisions in the Fifth and Fourteenth Amendments admonishing the federal government and the individual states, respectively, to treat citizens equitably.

**Espionage Act.** A federal law from the World War I era that criminalized criticizing the government or the war effort.

**Establishment Clause.** Part of the First Amendment, used by the Supreme Court to establish the "separation of church and state."

**executive order.** A change in policy promulgated by the executive branch (e.g., the president or a governor), carrying the effect of law.

**fact, question of.** The kind of "did it happen or didn't it?" question decided by trial courts rather than appellate courts.

**fair comment.** A common-law defense against libel suits, wherein the defendant claims that the alleged libel was an honestly held opinion based on facts reasonably believed to be true.

**Fairness Doctrine.** A body of rules, most of which were rescinded in 1987 and 2000 rulings, which required broadcast licensees to cover controversial political issues and to make such coverage balanced.

**fair report.** A common-law libel defense in which the defendant claims to have offered an accurate report of an utterance made by a public official conducting official duties.

**fair use.** A defense against a copyright infringement suit, based on Section 107 of the copyright law, that tells courts to consider the nature of the original work, the nature of the alleged infringement, the amount taken, and the use's effect on the value of the original copyright.

**false light.** One of the privacy torts, similar to libel, but where the falsity need not be defamatory.

**fault.** In libel law, the element of a defamation suit constitutionalized by the Supreme Court in *New York Times v. Sullivan.*

**federal circuit.** The jurisdiction—generally several states—covered by any of a dozen federal appellate courts.

**Federal Communications Commission.** Federal agency established in 1934; it overseas broadcast, cable, satellite, and telephonic communications systems.

**federal district court.** A federal trial court whose jurisdiction is generally one state or a portion of a state.

**Federal Elections Commission.** Federal agency charged with enforcement of the Federal Elections Campaigns Act, which includes regulations applied to political contributions and expenditures and some content restrictions on political advertising.

**Federal Trade Commission.** Federal agency regulating, among other things, deceptive advertising practices.

**first impression (case of).** A case presenting a novel issue, a controversy never before adjudicated in a specific jurisdiction.

**Food and Drug Administration.** Federal agency that regulates marketing of and advertising for food and drug products.

**for cause (challenge of juror).** The generally unlimited number of options exercised by attorneys for either side in a lawsuit or criminal prosecution, providing the trial judge with a specific reason why a potential juror would not be able to make an unbiased decision in a given case.

**framing.** Surreptitiously sending an online "visitor" from one Web site to another (i.e., site B pops up on screen as if a part of site A).

**Freedom of Information Act.**  Passed by Congress in 1967, the Act provides the mechanism by which citizens can obtain information held in federal government agency files; states also have such laws.

**Free Exercise Clause.**  The First Amendment's prohibition against congressional interference with citizens' right to practice (or "exercise") their religion.

**Free Press Clause.**  The First Amendment's prohibition against congressional interference with freedom of speech.

**Free Speech Clause.**  The First Amendment's prohibition against congressional interference with freedom of the press.

**gag order (restrictive order).**  Judicial order requiring that the target (e.g., attorneys, witnesses, jurors, or the press) refrain from speaking about or publishing specific information associated with a trial.

**Glomar response.**  Federal agency response to a Freedom of Information Act request, refusing to provide the information sought and refusing to confirm or deny the existence of the requested file.

**grand jury.**  A jury empaneled for the purpose of determining whether sufficient cause exists to charge one or more possible defendants with a crime.

**holding.**  The essence of a court's ruling, often in the form of a rule established by the court.

**idea-expression merger.**  Exceptional circumstances in which otherwise uncopyrightable "ideas" can only be expressed in a small number of ways, thus becoming copyrightable.

**identification.**  The element of a libel suit in which the plaintiff establishes that the offensive utterance or publication was "of or about" him.

**indecency.**  Sexually oriented speech that, unlike obscenity, may be regulated despite its manifesting serious value.

**indictment.**  The document by which the government articulates a list of charges against a criminal defendant.

**industry guide.**  Document promulgated by the Federal Trade Commission giving general guidelines concerning acceptable ways to advertise products or services (e.g., when a product can be called "natural," "low fat," or "recyclable").

**informational rationale.**  A justification offered for immunizing reporters from libel suits for reporting the actions of any influential entity, governmental or private; it posits that readers need such information to function as intelligent citizens.

**injunction.**  Judicial action demanding that the target either perform, or cease engaging in, specific conduct.

**intellectual property.**  The conjunction of protections provided by patent, copyright, and trademark law.

**intensity of suspicion test.**  In libel law, the notion that individual plaintiffs may bring suit to the extent that a group to which a defamatory quality is attributed is small or the ratio of the group said to have the quality is large.

**Internet.**  A worldwide systems of communication networks, or the manner in which those networks communicate with each other.

**intrusion.**  One of the four privacy torts; the transgression occurs when another's solitude or seclusion is intruded upon, regardless of whether any information gathered as a result of the intrusion is ever published.

**joint operating agreement.**  Federally approved arrangement in which otherwise competing local newspapers can share the cost of such core functions as printing and distribution.

**judicial review.**  Courts deciding on the constitutionality of legislative or executive branch actions.

**jump cut.**  Continuing a newspaper story on a page other than the one where it started.

**jurisdiction.**  Geographic area governed by a specific court, or subject matters that court is empowered to adjudicate.

**law, question of.**  Question, generally adjudicated by appellate courts, that concerns whether a given factual situation fits the parameters of a legal doctrine or definition.

**libel.**   Factual allegations about another that, if believed, would tend to lower that person's reputation in the eyes of others.

**libel per quod.**   Statements that would only damage another's reputation if other, unreported facts are known by readers.

**libel per se.**   Statements that, if believed, would themselves damage the target's reputation.

**libel-proof plaintiff.**   Plaintiff whose reputation is presumed already so low that no additional criticisms could lower it.

**library building.**   The use of VCRs to make copies of broadcast programs, which the user keeps over time rather than erases with subsequent use.

**likelihood of confusion.**   The mainstay of a traditional trademark infringement suit, alleging that consumers will be confused as to the source of goods or services.

**majority opinion.**   A judicial opinion joined by the majority of the judges on an appellate court.

**memorandum order.**   An appellate court ruling unaccompanied by a formal opinion.

**metatags.**   Language, akin to "key words" in traditional indexing, that lead a computer search engine to include a specific Web site among the "hits" resulting from a search.

**MMDS.**   Multichannel Multipoint Distribution Services, a kind of wireless cable system transmitted directly to special home antennas.

**modify (a precedent).**   A court modifies a precedent when it determines that the general principle espoused in it is relevant to the current case, but that some extrajudicial societal changes dictate that the precedent not be followed closely (e.g., to accuse someone of having a "loathsome" disease might still be libelous, but attitudes toward cancer have changed sufficiently that this particular disease is no longer thought of as loathsome).

**must-carry rules.**   Federal Communications Commission rules requiring that cable systems include local broadcast signals in their most basic tier of service.

**neutral reportage.**   Libel defense, accepted in only a few jurisdictions, positing that an otherwise punishable republication of libelous remarks can be excused if done in a fair and neutral way.

**Newspaper Preservation Act.**   Federal law adopted in 1970 that provided for the creation of joint operating agreements as a way of preserving some degree of competition among daily newspapers.

**obscenity.**   Sexually oriented messages, wholly unprotected by the First Amendment.

**official conduct.**   Part of the *New York Times v. Sullivan* libel rule; public officials can only recover for libels criticizing the way they perform their duties, or that make allegations about personal characteristics likely to affect the performance of those duties.

**opinion.**   A court's indication of its reasons for making its decision.

**oral arguments.**   Arguments made by opposing attorneys, typically for an hour, in front of the judges of an appellate court.

**overturn.**   Ruling by which an appellate court in effect changes its mind, holding that one of its earlier precedents will no longer be honored.

**participant monitoring.**   One party to a telephone conversation taping the conversation without the others' knowledge.

**per curiam opinion.**   An unsigned opinion (literally, "by the Court").

**Petition Clause.**   Section of the First Amendment giving Americans the right to assemble peaceably and to petition their government for redress of grievances.

**petit jury.**   In criminal law, the jury that actually decides the defendant's guilt or innocence.

**peremptory challenge.**   Motion made by one or another opposing attorney, without any reason offered, seeking to remove a potential juror from being empaneled.

**Personal Attack Rule.**   An FCC rule, revoked in 2000, that provided very detailed requirements—including a right to reply—on TV or radio stations that allowed their airwaves to be used to attack the character of any identifiable individual.

**personal jurisdiction.**   A doctrine whereby one state's courts may claim jurisdiction over a citizen from another state.

**plaintiff.**   The party bringing a civil suit against a civil defendant.

**plea.**   A criminal defendant's answer to a charge or indictment, such as a plea of guilty or not guilty.

**plea bargain.**   A criminal defendant's decision to plead guilty to a lesser offense than that for which the government was prepared to try him or her.

**plurality opinion.**   Opinion signed by one or more appellate judges agreeing with the majority's ultimate decision, but not with all its reasoning.

**Political Editorial Rule.**   An FCC rule, revoked in 2000, that required TV and radio stations that chose to air explicit editorial endorsements of candidates to open up their airwaves for free to opposing candidates who wished to reply.

**precedent.**   A court decision made prior to the one being argued at present, which at least one litigant suggests counts as a reason for ruling in a specific way on the current case.

**preferred position balancing.**   First Amendment adjudicating that presumes speech is more important than whatever competing interest is involved in a given case.

**preliminary hearing.**   Any judicial hearing that occurs before the criminal trial itself.

**presentencing report.**   Report given to the judge in a criminal trial, after a defendant has been found guilty, offering arguments for severity or lenience of sentence.

**presumed damages.**   In libel cases, damages due the successful plaintiff even without proof of specific, quantifiable harm.

**Printer's Ink statutes.**   State laws aimed at deceptive advertising.

**prior restraint.**   A law, executive order, or judicial decree prohibiting communicative conduct before it occurs (rather than punishing it after it occurs).

**probable cause.**   The standard of proof required to hold a criminal defendant over for trial; also, the standard used to determine if a search warrant should be granted.

**product disparagement.**   Comments similar to libels, but directed at a company's product line rather than at its management.

**product placement.**   Paying a movie studio to include mentions or depictions of a company's product line in the movie.

**product proximity.**   Thematic or logical relationship between one product line and another; in trademark law, infringement is more likely to be found as proximity increases.

**promissory estoppel.**   A common-law legal doctrine by which, even in the absence of a contract, an agreement may be enforced if failure to do so would result in gross inequity.

**prosecute.**   To bring legal action against a defendant, alleging a violation of criminal law.

**publication.**   In libel law, dissemination of the allegedly libelous remarks to at least one third party.

**public disclosure.**   One of the privacy torts, in which highly private and embarrassing, but true, information about the plaintiff is disseminated.

**public figure.**   In libel law, a plaintiff who is famous or associated with a specific political cause.

**public official.**   In libel law, a government employee perceived to have decision-making authority, who occupies a position that is a frequent topic of public discussion.

**puffery.**   Obviously exaggerated advertising claims (e.g., "we serve the best food in town") that are protected precisely because consumers do not take them literally.

**punitive damages.** Damage awards, above and beyond those granted to compensate the plaintiff for harm, designed to punish the defendant for outrageous conduct.

**recuse.** To remove oneself from participation (as judges will do if they believe their hearing a case would create a conflict of interest).

**reporter shield laws.** State laws providing media representatives some degree of immunity from having to testify in front of judicial bodies.

**republication.** In libel law, publishing a "defamation once removed" (e.g., "Ms. Jones asserted that her ex-husband sexually abused their daughter").

**respondent.** In an appellate hearing, the litigant who won the case at the lower court.

**retraction statutes.** State laws that provide some measure of protection from damages in a libel suit for media outlets that have already published an admission of error.

**retransmission consent.** Permission granted by a broadcaster to a cable or satellite TV company to include its signal among their offerings to subscribers.

**right of reply statutes.** State laws providing persons who feel they have been unfairly criticized by a media outlet a right to air their side of the issue; in 1974, the Supreme Court struck down such laws as they apply to the print media.

**right to publicity.** A hybrid privacy and property right to profit from the commercial exploitation of one's own name or likeness.

**scenes à faire.** In copyright law, the notion that some film genres by their very nature virtually demand that certain stock scenes be included (e.g., a car chase in a crime drama) so that other directors' use of such scenes is not an infringement.

**search warrant.** As provided for by the Fourth Amendment, a document given by a judge to a law enforcement officer permitting the search of a property, where there is reason to believe helpful evidence will be found.

**secondary meaning.** An association in consumers' minds, developed over time, between an otherwise nondistinctive name and a specific product line.

**Securities and Exchange Commission.** Federal agency of relevance to media law in that it can determine eligibility to write financial newsletters.

**self-publication.** In libel law, the unusual situation in which the publication element is established because the defamed person personally will, predictably, have to share the libelous statements with others (e.g., if a person is blind and needs someone to read it aloud).

**service mark.** A word, phrase, or logo designed to conjure up in consumers' minds a specific company's services.

**slander.** A spoken defamation (traditionally, "libel" referred only to printed defamations).

**SLAPP suits.** Libel suits designed to silence public criticism of a powerful individual or group ("Strategic Lawsuit Against Public Participation").

**SMATV.** Satellite Master Antenna Television, like miniature cable systems serving large apartment buildings or office complexes instead of whole towns.

**Smith Act.** Federal law from the 1940s making it a criminal offense to participate in an organization whose mission includes violent overthrow of the government.

**spam.** Unwanted commercial e-mail messages.

**special damages.** Damages awarded for very tangible, demonstrable, out-of-pocket losses.

**Speech and Debate Clause.** Provision of the U.S. Constitution immunizing members of Congress from libel suits flowing from their conduct of their official duties.

**spontaneity.** In the Classroom Guidelines accompanying the federal Copyright Act, a provision immunizing teachers from infringement suits from unauthorized copying for classroom use if there was no time to seek official permission (i.e., the idea to use this material was too spontaneous).

**spoofing.**   Designing a commercial e-mail message so as to appear noncommercial.

**Star Chamber.**   An English court, long ago abolished, that functioned without a jury and could mete out any punishment short of death.

*stare decisis.*   Literally "let the decision stand," an admonition to follow precedent when possible.

**statute.**   A law passed by a legislative body at the state or federal level.

**statute of limitations.**   Time period, usually stemming from the date of an alleged transgression, during which legal action must be commenced for the plaintiff (or, in a criminal prosecution, the state) to prevail.

**statutory construction.**   The process by which a court determines the meaning and effect of ambiguous language in a statute.

**strict liability.**   Doctrine providing that the person whose actions cause a certain result is civilly or criminally liable for such result, even if no degree of negligence can be shown.

**subpoena.**   Judicial document demanding that the recipient appear before the court or produce sought documents.

**summary contempt.**   A judge's power to charge, "convict," and punish a wrongdoer on the spot.

**summary judgment.**   Judicial ruling to the effect that, even if any facts in dispute are presumed in favor of the opposing party, the party seeking the order must prevail; such judgments avoid having to present facts to a jury or even to have a full trial.

**superior court.**   The name usually given to state trial courts.

**supervisory rationale.**   A justification offered for immunizing reporters from libel suits for reporting on governmental actions, emphasizing the public's need to supervise their elected officials.

**Supremacy Clause.**   Federal constitutional provision telling the individual states that their laws may not conflict with established federal law.

**tarnishment.**   Using another's trademark in a way that will tend to bring the company's goods or services into disrepute.

**thematic obscenity.**   Doctrine, long ago rejected by U.S. courts, that permitted works to be found obscene if their theme, or story line, was offensive (e.g., because an adulterer did not get punished).

**third-party monitoring.**   Taping a conversation without the permission of any of the participants.

**time shifting.**   Using a video recorder to tape programs only to view them at a more convenient, later time (not to build a permanent library).

**trade dress.**   Use of the overall look or feel of a product or place of business to conjure up in consumers' minds a specific company.

**trade libel.**   Defamatory remarks aimed at a product line itself rather than on the character of those who produce the products.

**trademark.**   A word, phrase, or logo designed to conjure in consumers' minds associations with a specific company's product line.

**trade regulation rule.**   Federal Trade Commission guidelines governing general advertising practices (e.g., when can a product be called "natural" or "recyclable"), rather than a specific company's advertising practices.

**trial court.**   The first level of a court proceeding from which the losing party may seek review by an appellate court.

**variable obscenity.**   Legal doctrine holding that the definition of obscenity can be somewhat fluid, depending on the target audience (especially if children are exposed to the materials).

**Vaughn index.**   A federal agency's response to a Freedom of Information Act request providing a list of relevant documents in the agency's possession, even while the agency claims that some of or all the documents are not revealable.

**voir dire.** The process of selecting a jury (from the old French, "to say that which one has seen," or to bear truthful witness).

**work for hire doctrine.** In copyright law, an exception to the general rule that the artist/creator owns a copyright; if a work was created as part of an employee's job description, the rights may be enjoyed instead by the employer.

**work product.** Materials actually created by a reporter working on a story.

# Case Index

539

544

#  Subject Index